ICSE Exams 2026

AF819991

All in One®

PHYSICS

Class 10

Authors
Mansi Garg (MSc, BEd.)
Jitendra Kumar (MSc, MEd.)

arihant
SUCCESS AND NOTHING LESS

ARIHANT PRAKASHAN

(School Division Series)

卐 ADMINISTRATIVE & PRODUCTION OFFICES

Regd. Office

'Ramchhaya' 4577/15, Agarwal Road, Darya Ganj, New Delhi -110002
Tele: 011- 47630600, 43518550; Fax: 011- 23280316

卐 *Head Office*

Kalindi, TP Nagar, Meerut (UP) - 250002, Tel: 0121-7156203, 7156204

卐 SALES & SUPPORT OFFICES

Agra, Ahmedabad, Bengaluru, Bareilly, Chennai, Delhi, Guwahati, Hyderabad, Jaipur, Jhansi, Kolkata, Lucknow, Nagpur & Pune.

PO No : TXT-XX-XXXXXXX-X-XX

Published By Arihant Publications (India) Ltd.

For further information about the books published by Arihant, log on to www.arihantbooks.com or e-mail at info@arihantbooks.com

Follow us on

卐 PRICE ₹ 370.00

PRODUCTION TEAM

Publishing Managers	Cover Designer	Inner Designer
Mahendra Singh Rawat & Keshav Mohan	Salman Shaikh	Ankit Tyagi
Project Head	*Page Layouting*	*Proof Readers*
Yojna Sharma	Subhash Chaprana	Ishan, Mansi

Index *cum* Study Planner

One Book- Endless Features

to Help you Succeed

Chapter Outlines

At the start of each chapter, all the topics of the chapter have been listed, so that students may know what they are going to study.

CHAPTER

4

Refraction of Light

SYLLABUS

(i) Refraction of light through a glass block and a triangular prism : qualitative treatment of simple applications such as real and apparent depth of objects in water and apparent bending of sticks in water. Applications of refraction of light.

(ii) Total internal reflection : critical angle; examples in triangular glass prisms; comparison with reflection from a plane mirror (qualitative only). Applications of total internal reflection.

Simplified Theory

It contains the necessary study material well supported by Definitions, Facts, Figures, Flowcharts, etc.

"Change in path of a light ray as it passes from one medium to another medium is called refraction of light."

When light travels from a rarer medium to a denser one, it bends towards the normal ($i > r$) and when travels from a denser medium to a rarer one, it bends away from the normal ($i < r$).

where, i = angle of incidence, r = angle of refraction.

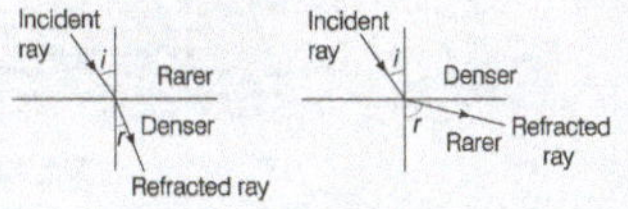

Refraction of light

Check Your Learning

A set of 3-5 Questions given in between the text, helps students to remain connected with the text while studying. They can instantly assess themselves for their understanding.

Second Law

The ratio of sine of angle of incidence to the sine of angle of refraction is constant for a given pair of media. This constant is known as **refractive index** of the second medium w.r.t. first medium. It is expressed as

$$n \text{ or } \mu = \frac{\sin i}{\sin r} = \text{constant}$$

This relation is also known as **Snell's law**.

Check Your LEARNING...

1. Define refraction.
2. Mention the cause of refraction of light, when it passes from one medium to another.
3. What do you mean by optically rarer medium?
4. In which type of incidence, a ray of light does not deviate from its path after refraction?
5. State second law of refraction.

Solved Examples

To explain the application of concept, Solved Examples have been given in between the theory. These examples have been solved in Step-by-step manner, so that students can learn the problem solving process completely.

Example 2. Refractive indices of water and glass are 4/3 and 3/2 respectively. A ray of light travelling in water is incident on the water glass interface at 30°. Calculate the angle of refraction.

Sol. Given, refractive index of water, ${}^a\mu_w = \frac{4}{3}$

Refractive index of glass, ${}^a\mu_g = \frac{3}{2}$

Angle of incidence in water, $i = 30°$

Angle of refraction, $r = ?$

As, $${}^w\mu_g = \frac{{}^a\mu_g}{{}^a\mu_w} = \frac{3/2}{4/3} \Rightarrow {}^w\mu_g = \frac{9}{8}$$

One Book- Endless Features

to Help you Succeed

Quick Revision

At the end of each chapter, QUICK Revision is given. It contains crux of the chapter in pointer form.

QUiCK Revision

- The phenomenon of bending of light entering from one medium to another is called **refraction of light**.
- When a ray of light travels from a rarer medium to a denser medium, it bends towards the normal.
- When a ray of light travels from a denser medium to a rarer medium, it bends away from the normal.
- There are two laws of refraction.

  First Law The incident ray, the refracted ray and the normal at the point of incidence, all lie on the same plane.

  Second Law The ratio of sine of angle of incidence to the sine of angle of refraction is constant for a given pair of media.This is also called **Snell's law**.
- **Refractive index** (n or μ) of a medium is the ratio of speed of light in vacuum (c) to the speed of light in the medium (v) and is given by

$$n \text{ or } \mu = \frac{c}{v}$$

- Refractive index of one medium w.r.t. to another medium is given by, $^1n_2$ or $^1\mu_2 = \frac{\text{Speed of light in medium 1}}{\text{Speed of light in medium 2}}$
- When a light ray, after suffering many reflections and refractions, has its final path reversed and travels back along its initial path then it is called **principle of reversibility of light**.
- The perpendicular distance of separation between the incident ray and the emergent ray is called **lateral displacement**.
- The shift by which an object appears to be raised when it is immersed in water is called the **apparent depth**.

$$\text{Refractive index} = \frac{\text{Real depth}}{\text{Apparent depth}}$$

Chapter Practice

The exercise contains questions in that format in which these are asked in the examinations, Questions have been categorised as 1 mark questions, 2 marks questions, 3 marks questions, and structured questions. All the questions given here are fully solved.

Chapter Assessment

It is the Assessment exercise for the complete chapter. With this exercise, students can access their understanding of the chapter and can prepare for it accordingly.

Chapter Practice

1 Mark Questions

1. When a ray of light travels from rarer medium to denser medium, then it
   (a) bends away from the normal
   (b) bends towards the normal
   (c) goes undeviated
   (d) is reflected back

Sol. (b) When a ray of light travels from rarer medium to denser medium, then due to decrease in its speed, the ray bends towards the normal.

2. In the diagram shown below

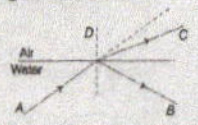

   (a) B is incident ray and C is refracted ray
   (b) A is incident ray and B is refracted ray
   (c) C is incident ray and B is refracted ray
   (d) A is incident ray and C is refracted ray

Sol. (d) When a ray falls obliquely on a surface of air-water interface, then it is partially reflected and partially refracted. Here, A is incident ray, B is reflected ray and C is refracted ray.

3. When a ray of light travels normal to the given surface, then the angle of refraction is [2023]
   (a) 180° (b) 90°
   (c) 0° (d) 45°

Sol. (c) Angle of refraction will zero (0°).

Sol. (a) Given, angle of incidence, $i = 60°$,
angle of refraction, $r = 45°$
Refractive index of the medium B relative to medium A,

$$^A\mu_B = \frac{\sin i}{\sin r} = \frac{\sin 60°}{\sin 45°} = \frac{\left(\frac{\sqrt{3}}{2}\right)}{\left(\frac{1}{\sqrt{2}}\right)} = \frac{\sqrt{3}}{\sqrt{2}}$$

5. Speed of blue light in water is [2023]
   (a) more than green light
   (b) more than orange light
   (c) more than violet light
   (d) more than red light

Sol. (c) Speed of light in water is more than violet light .

6. The refractive index of a diamond is 2.4. It means that, [2021, (Sem-I)]
   (a) the speed of light in vacuum is equal to $\frac{1}{2.4}$ times the speed of light in diamond
   (b) the speed of light in diamond is 2.4 times the speed of light in vacuum
   (c) the speed of light in vacuum is 2.4 times the speed of light in diamond
   (d) the wavelength of light in diamond is 2.4 times the wavelength of light in vacuum

Sol. (c) As, refractive index $= \frac{\text{Speed of light in vacuum}}{\text{Speed of light in medium}}$

So, the refractive index of a diamond equal to 2.4 means that the speed of light in vacuum is 2.4 times the speed of light in diamond.

Chapter Assessment

1 Mark Questions

1. A light ray enters from medium A to medium B as shown in the figure. The refractive index of medium B relative to A will be

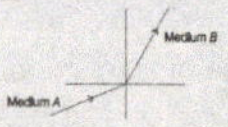

   (a) greater than unity (b) less than unity
   (c) equal to unity (d) zero

2. A ray of light IM is incident on a glass slab $ABCD$ as shown in the figure. The emergent ray for this incident ray is [2021 (Sem-I)]

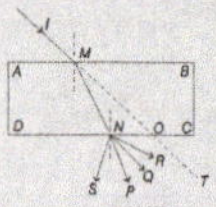

   (a) NQ (b) NR
   (c) NP (d) NS

3. You are given water, mustard oil, glycerine and kerosene. In which of these media, a ray of light incident obliquely at same angle would bend the most?
   (a) Kerosene (b) Water
   (c) Mustard oil (d) Glycerine

   (c) All the colours of the white light move with the same speed
   (d) Yellow light moves with the mean speed as that of the red and the violet light

2 Marks Questions

6. How does the refractive index of a medium depend upon its temperature?
7. "The upper surface of water contained in the beaker and held above the eye level appear silvery". Justify the statement along with a reason.
8. The critical angle for glass-air is 45° for the yellow colour of light.

   Mention whether it will be less than equal to or more than 45° for
   (i) red light and
   (ii) blue light.
9. What will be the change occurred in the angle of minimum deviation produced by a prism, if
   (i) the wavelength of the incident light and
   (ii) the refracting angle of prism increases?
10. A pond appears to be 2.7m deep. If the refractive index of water is 4/3, find the actual depth of the pond. [2020]

    Ans. 3.6 m
11. (i) Name one factor that affects the lateral displacement of light as it passes through a rectangular glass slab. [2015]
    (ii) Does the depth of a tank of water appear to change or remain the same when viewed normally from above? [2012]
12. (i) A ray of light passes from water to air. How does speed of light change?
    (ii) Which colour of light travels fastest in any medium except air? [2014]
13. (i) The refractive index of glass with respect to air is 1.5. What is the value of the refractive index of air with respect to glass?
    (ii) A ray of light is incident as a normal ray on the surface of separation of two different mediums. What is the value of the angle of incidence in this case? [2013]
14. The refractive index of a liquid is $\sqrt{3}$. Determine the speed of light in liquid if the speed of light in vacuum is 3×10^8 m/s.

One Book- Endless Features
to Help you Succeed

Olympiad Section

It includes some special questions based on the pattern of Olympiad and other competitions to give the students a taste of the questions asked in competitions. These are not meant for school examinations.

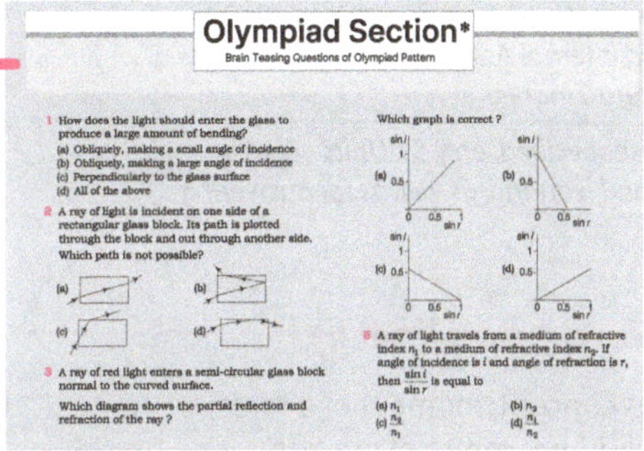
Olympiad Section*

Brain Teasing Questions of Olympiad Pattern

1 How does the light should enter the glass to produce a large amount of bending?
(a) Obliquely, making a small angle of incidence
(b) Obliquely, making a large angle of incidence
(c) Perpendicularly to the glass surface
(d) All of the above

2 A ray of light is incident on one side of a rectangular glass block. Its path is plotted through the block and out through another side. Which path is not possible?

3 A ray of red light enters a semi-circular glass block normal to the curved surface.
Which diagram shows the partial reflection and refraction of the ray ?

Which graph is correct ?

5 A ray of light travels from a medium of refractive index n_1 to a medium of refractive index n_2. If angle of incidence is i and angle of refraction is r, then $\frac{\sin i}{\sin r}$ is equal to
(a) n_1 (b) n_2
(c) $\frac{n_2}{n_1}$ (d) $\frac{n_1}{n_2}$

Sample Question Papers

To make students practice of examination in real sense, there are 3 Sample Question Papers at the end. All these Sample Questions Papers are exactly prepared based on the latest syllabus & pattern of examination.

Internal Assessment of Practical Work

To make this book complete in all aspects, experiments based on latest syllabus have been given.

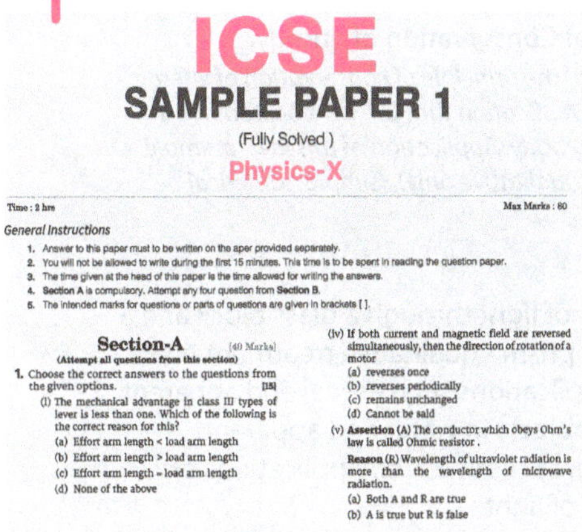
ICSE

SAMPLE PAPER 1

(Fully Solved)

Physics-X

Time : 2 hrs Max Marks : 80

General Instructions

1. Answer to this paper must to be written on the aper provided separately.
2. You will not be allowed to write during the first 15 minutes. This time is to be spent in reading the question paper.
3. The time given at the head of this paper is the time allowed for writing the answers.
4. **Section A** is compulsory. Attempt any four question from **Section B**.
5. The intended marks for questions or parts of questions are given in brackets [ ].

Section-A (40 Marks)

(Attempt all questions from this section)

1. Choose the correct answers to the questions from the given options. [15]
(i) The mechanical advantage in class III types of lever is less than one. Which of the following is the correct reason for this?
(a) Effort arm length < load arm length
(b) Effort arm length > load arm length
(c) Effort arm length = load arm length
(d) None of the above

(iv) If both current and magnetic field are reversed simultaneously, then the direction of rotation of a motor
(a) reverses once
(b) reverses periodically
(c) remains unchanged
(d) Cannot be said

(v) **Assertion** (A) The conductor which obeys Ohm's law is called Ohmic resistor .
Reason (R) Wavelength of ultraviolet radiation is more than the wavelength of microwave radiation.
(a) Both A and R are true
(b) A is true but R is false

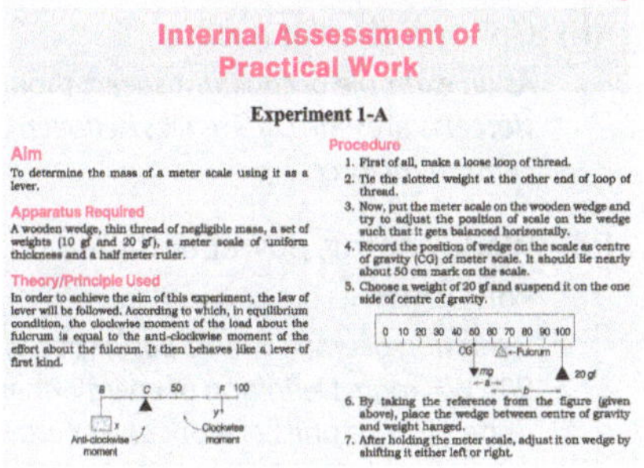
Internal Assessment of Practical Work

Experiment 1-A

Aim

To determine the mass of a meter scale using it as a lever.

Apparatus Required

A wooden wedge, thin thread of negligible mass, a set of weights (10 gf and 20 gf), a meter scale of uniform thickness and a half meter ruler.

Theory/Principle Used

In order to achieve the aim of this experiment, the law of lever will be followed. According to which, in equilibrium condition, the clockwise moment of the load about the fulcrum is equal to the anti-clockwise moment of the effort about the fulcrum. It then behaves like a lever of first kind.

Procedure

1. First of all, make a loose loop of thread.
2. Tie the slotted weight at the other end of loop of thread.
3. Now, put the meter scale on the wooden wedge and try to adjust the position of scale on the wedge such that it gets balanced horizontally.
4. Record the position of wedge on the scale as centre of gravity (CG) of meter scale. It should lie nearly about 50 cm mark on the scale.
5. Choose a weight of 20 gf and suspend it on the one side of centre of gravity.
6. By taking the reference from the figure (given above), place the wedge between centre of gravity and weight hanged.
7. After holding the meter scale, adjust it on wedge by shifting it either left or right.

Latest Course Structure

*There will be **one** paper of **two hours** duration carrying 80 marks and Internal Assessment of practical work carrying 20 marks.*

***Note:** Unless otherwise specified, only S I. Units are to be used while teaching and learning, as well as for answering questions.*

Force, Work, Power and Energy

(i) Turning forces concept; moment of a force; forces in equilibrium; centre of gravity; [discussions using simple examples and simple numerical problems].

Elementary introduction of translational and rotational motions; moment (turning effect) of a force, also called torque and its cgs and SI units; common examples - door, steering wheel, bicycle pedal, etc.; clockwise and anti-clockwise moments; conditions for a body to be in equilibrium (translational and rotational); principle of moment and its verification using a metre rule suspended by two spring balances with slotted weights hanging from it; simple numerical problems; Centre of gravity (qualitative only) with examples of some regular bodies and irregular lamina.

(ii) Uniform circular motion

As an example of constant speed, though acceleration (force) is present. Differences between centrifugal and centripetal force.

(iii) Work, energy, power and their relation with force.

Definition of work. $W = FS\cos\theta$; special cases of $\theta = 0^0$, 90^0. W= mgh. Definition of energy, energy as work done. Various units of work and energy and their relation with SI units.[erg, calorie, kW h and eV]. Definition of Power, $P = W/t$; SI and cgs units; other units; kilowatt (kW), megawatt (MW) and gigawatt (GW); and horse power (1hp=746W) [Simple numerical problems on work, power and energy].

(iv) Different types of energy (e.g. chemical energy, Mechanical energy, heat energy, electrical energy, nuclear energy, sound energy, light energy).

Mechanical energy: potential energy $U = mgh$ (derivation included) gravitational PE, examples; kinetic energy $K= \frac{1}{2} mv^2$ (derivation included); forms of kinetic energy: translational, rotational and vibrational - only simple examples. [Numerical problems on K and U only in case of translational motion]; qualitative discussions of electrical, chemical, heat, nuclear, light and sound energy, conversion from one form to another; common examples.

(v) Machines as force multipliers; load, effort, mechanical advantage, velocity ratio and efficiency; simple treatment of levers, pulley systems showing the utility of each type of machine.

Functions and uses of simple machines: Terms- effort E, load L, mechanical advantage MA = L/E, velocity ratio VR = VE/VL = dE / dL, input (Wi), output (Wo), efficiency (η), relation between η and MA,VR (derivation included); for all practical machines $\eta < 1$; MA < VR.

Lever: principle. First, second and third class of levers; examples: MA and VR in each case. Examples of each of these classes of levers as also found in the human body.

Pulley system: single fixed, single movable, block and tackle; MA, VR and η in each case.

(vi) Principle of Conservation of energy.

Statement of the principle of conservation of energy; theoretical verification that $U + K$ = constant for a freely falling body. Application of this law to simple pendulum (qualitative only); [simple numerical problems].

Light

(i) Refraction of light through a glass block and a triangular prism - qualitative treatment of simple applications such as real and apparent depth of objects in water and apparent bending of sticks in water. Applications of refraction of light.

Partial reflection and refraction due to change in medium. Laws of refraction; the effect on speed (V), wavelength (λ) and frequency (f) due to refraction of light; conditions for a light ray to pass undeviated.

Values of speed of light (c) in vacuum, air, water and glass; refractive index $\mu = c/V$, $V = f\lambda$. Values of μ for common substances such as water, glass and diamond; experimental verification; refraction through glass block; lateral displacement; multiple images in thick glass plate/mirror; refraction through a glass prism simple applications: real and apparent depth of objects in water; apparent bending of a stick under water. (Simple numerical problems and approximate ray diagrams required).

(ii) Total internal reflection: Critical angle; examples in triangular glass prisms; comparison with reflection from a plane mirror (qualitative only). Applications of total internal reflection.

Transmission of light from a denser medium (glass/water) to a rarer medium (air) at different angles of incidence; critical angle (C) $\mu = 1/\sin C$. Essential conditions for total internal reflection. Total internal reflection in a triangular glass prism; ray diagram, different cases - angles of prism (60°60°60°, (60°30°90°, (45°45°90°; use of right angle prism to obtain $\delta = 90°$ and 180°(ray diagram); comparison of total internal reflection from a prism and reflection from a plane mirror.

(iii) Lenses (converging and diverging) including characteristics of the images formed (using ray diagrams only); magnifying glass; location of images using ray diagrams and thereby determining magnification.

Types of lenses (converging and diverging), convex and concave, action of a lens as a set of prisms; technical terms; centre of curvature, radii of curvature, principal axis, foci, focal plane and focal length,; detailed study of refraction of light in spherical lenses through ray diagrams; formation of images - principal rays or construction rays; location of images from ray diagram for various positions of a small linear object on the principal axis; characteristics of images. Sign convention and direct numerical problems using the lens formula are included.(derivation of formula not required).

Scale drawing or graphical representation of ray diagrams not required.

Power of a lens (concave and convex) – [simple direct numerical problems]: magnifying glass or simple microscope: location of image and magnification from ray diagram only [formula and numerical problems not included]. Applications of lenses.

(iv) Using a triangular prism to produce a visible spectrum from white light; Electromagnetic spectrum. Scattering of light.

Deviation produced by a triangular prism; dependence on colour (wavelength) of light; dispersion and spectrum; electromagnetic spectrum: broad classification (names only arranged in order of increasing wavelength); properties common to all electromagnetic radiations; properties and uses of infrared and ultraviolet radiation. Simple application of scattering of light e.g. blue colour of the sky.

Sound

(i) Reflection of Sound Waves; echoes: their use; simple numerical problems on echoes.

Production of echoes, condition for formation of echoes; simple numerical problems; use of echoes by bats, dolphins, fishermen, medical field. SONAR.

(ii) Natural vibrations, Damped vibrations, Forced vibrations and Resonance - a special case of forced vibrations.

Meaning and simple applications of natural, damped, forced vibrations and resonance.

(iii) Loudness, pitch and quality of sound:

Characteristics of sound: loudness and intensity; subjective and objective nature of these properties; sound level in dB (as unit only); noise pollution; interdependence of: pitch and frequency; quality and waveforms (with examples).

Electricity and Magnetism

(i) Ohm's Law; concepts of emf, potential difference, resistance; resistances in series and parallel, internal resistance.

Concepts of pd (V), current (I), resistance (R) and charge (Q). Ohm's law: statement, V=IR; SI units; experimental verification; graph of V vs I and resistance from slope; ohmic and non-ohmic resistors, factors affecting resistance (including specific resistance) and internal resistance; super conductors, electromotive force (emf); combination of resistances in series and parallel and derivation of expressions for equivalent resistance. Simple numerical problems using the above relations. [Simple network of resistors].

(ii) Electrical power and energy.

Electrical energy; examples of heater, motor, lamp,

loudspeaker, etc. Electrical power; measurement of electrical energy, $W = QV = VIt$ from the definition of pd. Combining with Ohm's law $W = VIt = I^2 Rt = (V^2/R)t$ and electrical power $P = (W/t) = VI = I^2R = V^2/R$. Units: SI and commercial; Power rating of common appliances, household consumption of electric energy; calculation of total energy consumed by electrical appliances; $W = Pt$ (kilowatt × hour = kW h), [simple numerical problems].

(iii) Household circuits – main circuit; switches; fuses; earthing; safety precautions; three-pin plugs; colour coding of wires.

House wiring (ring system), power distribution; main circuit (3 wires-live, neutral, earth) with fuse / MCB, main switch and its advantages - circuit diagram; two-way switch, staircase wiring, need for earthing, fuse, 3-pin plug and socket; Conventional location of live, neutral and earth points in 3 pin plugs and sockets. Safety precautions, colour coding of wires.

(iv) Magnetic effect of a current (principles only, laws not required); electromagnetic induction (elementary); transformer.

Oersted's experiment on the magnetic effect of electric current; magnetic field (B) and field lines due to current in a straight wire (qualitative only), right hand thumb rule – magnetic field due to a current in a loop; Electromagnets: their uses; comparisons with a permanent magnet; Fleming's Left Hand Rule, the DC electric motor- simple sketch of main parts (coil, magnet, split ring commutators and brushes); brief description and type of energy transfer(working not required): Simple introduction to electromagnetic induction; frequency of AC in house hold supplies , Fleming's Right Hand Rule, AC Generator - Simple sketch of main parts, brief description and type of energy transfer(working not required). Advantage of AC over DC. Transformer- its types, characteristics of primary and secondary coils in each type (simple labelled diagram and its uses).

Heat

(i) Calorimetry: meaning, specific heat capacity; principle of method of mixtures; Numerical Problems on specific heat capacity using heat loss and gain and the method of mixtures.

Heat and its units (calorie, joule), temperature and its units (°C, K); thermal (heat) capacity $C' = Q/\Delta T$... (SI unit of C): Specific heat Capacity $C = Q/m\Delta T$ (SI unit of C) Mutual relation between Heat Capacity and Specific Heat capacity, values of C for some common substances (ice, water and copper). Principle of method of mixtures including mathematical statement. Natural phenomenon involving specific heat. Consequences of high sp. heat of water. [Simple numerical problem].

(ii) Latent heat; loss and gain of heat involving change of state for fusion only.

Change of phase (state); heating curve for water; latent heat; sp latent heat of fusion (SI unit). Simple numerical problems. Common physical phenomena involving latent heat of fusion.

Modern Physics

(i) Radioactivity and changes in the nucleus; background radiation and safety precautions.

Brief introduction (qualitative only) of the nucleus, nuclear structure, atomic number (Z), mass number (A).Radioactivity as spontaneous disintegration. α, β and γ - their nature and properties; changes within the nucleus. One example each of α and β decay with equations showing changes in Z and A. Uses of radioactivity - radio isotopes. Harmful effects. Safety precautions. Background radiation.

Radiation: X-rays; radioactive fallout from nuclear plants and other sources.

Nuclear Energy: working on safe disposal of waste. Safety measures to be strictly reinforced.

(ii) *Nuclear fission and fusion; basic introduction and equations.*

CHAPTER

01

Force

SYLLABUS

- Turning forces concept : moment of a force; forces in equilibrium; centre of gravity; (discussions using simple example and simple numerical problems). • Uniform circular motion

Force may be defined as an external agency or cause (a push or a pull), which changes or tends to change the state of rest or of uniform motion or the direction of motion of a body.

Its SI unit is **newton (N)** or kilogram-force (kgf), where 1 kgf = gN, if g is the acceleration due to gravity (9.8 ms^{-2}).

Motion of Rigid Body

A rigid body is one whose size and shape remains the same whatever force is applied to different parts of it.

A rigid body, when acted upon by a force can have two types of motion

(i) **Translational Motion or Linear Motion** When a force is applied on a stationary rigid body which is free to move and the body starts moving in a straight path in the direction of applied force, then its motion is called translational motion.

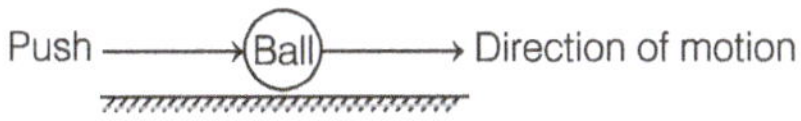

Translational motion of a ball

e.g. On pushing a ball lying on a floor as shown in figure, it starts moving.

(ii) **Rotational Motion** When a force is applied on fixed point of a body which is pivoted at a point, then body starts rotating about that point. Such motion is called rotational motion and the force applied is called **turning force**. e.g.

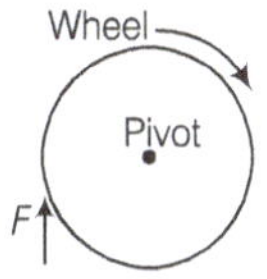

Rotational motion of a wheel

If a wheel is pivoted at its centre and a force (turning) is applied tangentially on its rim as shown in figure, the wheel rotates about its centre.

Torque or Moment of a Force

The turning effect produced by a force on a rigid body fixed about a point (pivot or fulcrum) is called moment of a force or torque.

The turning effect of force or torque on a body depends on two factor given below

(i) The magnitude of force applied and

(ii) The perpendicular distance of line of action of force from the axis of rotation.

Torque is equal to the product of the magnitude of the force and the perpendicular distance of the line of action of force from the axis of rotation. It is represented by τ.

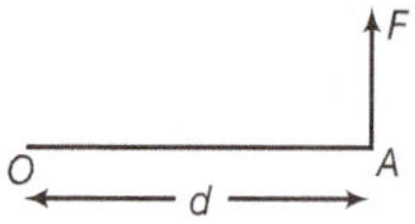

i.e. Torque (moment of force)

= Force × Perpendicular distance of line of action of force from axis of rotation

$$\boxed{\tau = F \times d}$$

where, d is the perpendicular distance (OA) of line of action of force (AF) from the axis of rotation (O).

It is a vector quantity. Its SI unit is newton-metre (N-m) and CGS unit is dyne-cm.

But, if force is measured in gravitational unit, then the unit of moment of force in SI system is kgf × m and in CGS system, the unit is gf × cm.

These units are related as follows

$$1 \text{ N-m} = 10^5 \text{ dyne} \times 10^2 \text{cm} = 10^7 \text{dyne-cm}$$

$$1 \text{ kgf} \times \text{m} = 9.8 \text{N-m}$$

$$\boxed{1 \text{ gf} \times \text{cm} = 980 \text{dyne-cm}}$$

Note • The torque acting on a body is zero, if F = 0 or d = 0. It may be remembered that internal forces acting on the body do not contribute anything to the torque.
• Torque is maximum, when applied force is perpendicular to the axis of rotation.

Clockwise and Anti-clockwise Moments

The direction of turning (sense of rotation) of a body depends on the point of application of force and the direction of force.

If the turning effect on the body is anti-clockwise, then the moment of force is called **anti-clockwise moment** and is taken positive as shown in figure.

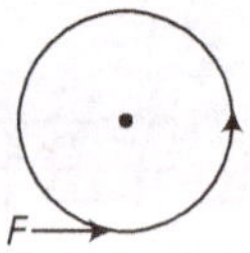

Anti-clockwise (positive)

On the other hand, if the turning effect on the body is clockwise, then the moment of force is called **clockwise moment** and is taken negative as shown in figure.

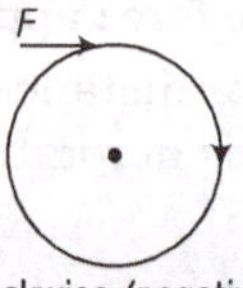

Clockwise (negative)

Common Examples of Moment of Force

Some common examples of moment of force are given as below

(i) It is easier to **open the door** by applying force near the outer edge, away from the hinges or axis of rotation.

(ii) For **turning a steering wheel**, a force is applied tangentially on the rim of the wheel.

(iii) In a bicycle, the toothed wheel is rotated by applying less **force on the foot pedal** which is at a large distance from the axle of rear wheel.

Example 1. The moment of a force of 10 N about a point X is 4 N-m. Find the distance of point of application of the force from the point X.

Sol. Given, moment of force = 4 N-m, $F = 10$ N

Moment of force = Force × Distance

$$\Rightarrow \quad 4 = 10 \times d \Rightarrow d = \frac{4}{10} = \frac{2}{5} = 0.4 \text{ m}$$

Example 2. A wheel of diameter 2 m is shown in figure with axle at O. A force $F = 2$ N is applied at B in the direction shown in figure. Calculate the moment of force about (i) the centre O and (ii) the point A.

Sol. Given, force, $F = 2$ N

Diameter of wheel, $d = 2$ m

Radius of wheel, $r = \frac{d}{2} = 1$ m

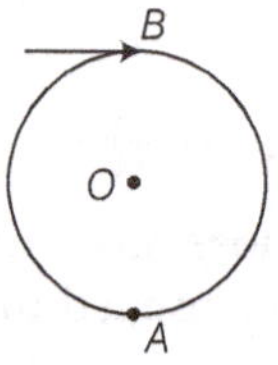

(i) For point O,

Perpendicular distance $OB = \frac{d}{2} = 1$m

$\therefore$ Moment of force, $\tau_O = OB \times F = 1 \times 2 = 2$N-m

(ii) For point A,

Perpendicular distance $AB = 2$ m

$\therefore$ Moment of force, $\tau_A = AB \times F = 2 \times 2 = 4$N-m

Example 3. In figure, a roller of diameter 0.2 m is raised on the pavement AB by the forces F_1 and F_2 each of magnitude 20 N. Compare the torques produced by the two forces.

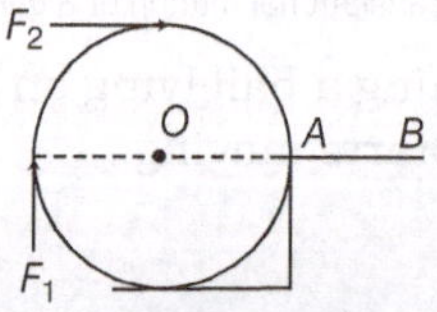

Sol. Given, $F_1 = F_2 = 20$ N

Perpendicular distance of point of rotation A from the force F_1, $d_1 = 0.2$ m

while that of force F_2, $d_2 = \frac{1}{2} \times 0.2 \text{ m} = 0.1 \text{m}$

$$\therefore \frac{\text{Torque produced by force } F_1}{\text{Torque produced by force } F_2} = \frac{F_1 \times d_1}{F_2 \times d_2} = \frac{20 \times 0.2}{20 \times 0.1} = \frac{2}{1}$$

Couple

The pair of equal and opposite forces acting along parallel lines (not on the same line of action) forms a couple.

A couple always produces a rotational motion in a rigid body.

Some common examples of couple are

(i) Opening a tap

(ii) Tightening a screw with a screw driver

(iii) Steering of a four wheeler

Moment of Couple

The moment of couple is defined as the product of force and the perpendicular distance between the lines of action of forces (or couple arm).

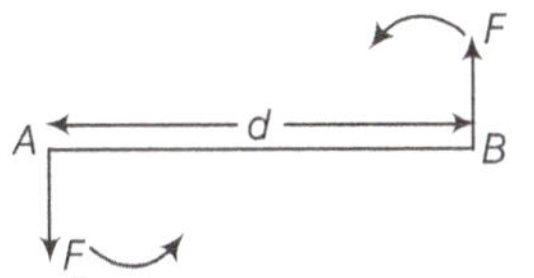

i.e. Moment of couple

= Magnitude of either force × Perpendicular distance between the line of action of forces (or couple arm)

$$\boxed{\text{Moment of couple} = F \times d}$$

Its SI unit is also newton-metre (N-m).

Example 4. A steering wheel of diameter 1 m is rotated anti-clockwise by applying forces each of magnitude 10 N. Draw a diagram to show the application of forces and calculate the moment of the couple applied.

Sol. As the rotation is anti-clockwise, the moments must be anti-clockwise. The direction of the two forces will be as shown in figure. The two forces are forming a couple whose moment is

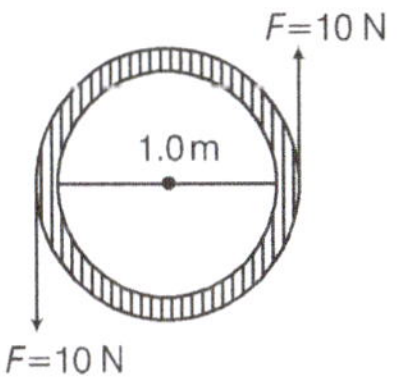

= Magnitude of one of the force × Arm of the couple

$= 10 \times 1.0 = 10$ N-m

Equilibrium of an Object

An object is said to be in equilibrium, if a number of forces acting on it produce no change in its state of rest or of uniform motion. Its motion may be rotational or translational.

Types of Equilibrium

There are three types of equilibrium as given below

(i) **Static Equilibrium** A body is said to be in static (or stable) equilibrium, if a number of forces are acting on it but the body is still at rest. i.e. The vector sum of all forces is zero.
Consider a situation, when a beam is balanced in the horizontal position, then the clockwise moment of right pan is balanced by anti-clockwise moment of left pan and beam has no rotational motion. Hence, beam is said to be in **static** or **stable equilibrium**.

(ii) **Dynamic Equilibrium** A body is said to be in dynamic (unstable) equilibrium, if it remains in its state of motion, even a number of forces are acting on it.
e.g. When a body provided once in motion, then it moves on a smooth surface with a constant velocity and zero acceleration and hence the body is said to be in **dynamic** or **unstable equilibrium**.

(iii) **Neutral Equilibrium** A body is said to be in neutral equilibrium, if on being disturbed from its initial position, it stays in equilibrium in new position also.
e.g. When a cone lying on a horizontal surface moves along a slant height, then it is said that the cone is disturbed from its equilibrium position and it will acquire the equilibrium whenever it is released.

Conditions for Equilibrium

From the above types of equilibrium, we find that the following two conditions must be satisfied for a body to be in equilibrium.

(i) Vector sum of the forces acting on the body should be zero in all directions for translational equilibrium.

i.e. $\boxed{\Sigma F_i = 0}$

(ii) Vector sum of moments of forces acting on the body should be zero for rotational equilibrium.

i.e. $\boxed{\Sigma \tau_i = 0}$

Principle of Moment

According to the principle of moment, if different forces act on a body which is capable to rotate about an axis, but no rotation takes place, then the algebraic sum of moments of all the forces is zero or the body is in equilibrium.

Sum of the anti-clockwise moments
= Sum of the clockwise moments

Note The clockwise moments are taken negative and anti-clockwise moments are taken positive.

Verification of the Principle of Moments

Let us consider a meter ruler suspended horizontally from a rigid support by a strong inextensible thread at O. Now, suspend some slotted weights, says m_1g and m_2g by two spring balances A and B on either side of the thread. So, the meter ruler may tilt to one side.

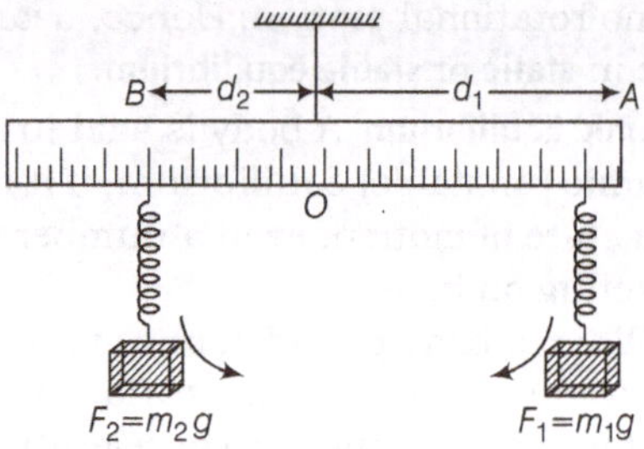

Verification of principle of moments

Now, adjust either the slotted weights on the spring balance or the position of the spring balance on either side of thread in such a way that the meter ruler again becomes horizontal.

Here, first weight tend to turn the meter ruler clockwise, while the second weight tend to turn the meter ruler anti-clockwise.

Let d_1 = distance of weight m_1g on RHS from O,

d_2 = distance of weight m_2g on LHS from O,

$m_1g \times d_1$ = clockwise moment of first weight about the point O

and $m_2g \times d_2$ = anti-clockwise moment of second weight about the point O.

In equilibrium, when the meter ruler is horizontal, it is found that $m_1g \times d_1 = m_2g \times d_2$

or $$F_1d_1 = F_2d_2 \quad \left(\because F_1 = m_1g \text{ and } F_2 = m_2g\right)$$

i.e. Clockwise moment = Anti-clockwise moment

This verifies the principle of moments.

Similarly, **in case of fulcrum** (i.e. lever system)

load × load arm = effort × effort arm

i.e. $$F_1d_1 = F_2d_2$$

This is called principle of moment of a lever.

Example 5. A half meter ruler is suspended by a thread from the mid-point of the ruler as shown in the figure. It balances horizontally when a 50 g and an unknown weight was suspended respectively, from 10 cm and the 45 cm mark.

Calculate the magnitude of weight w.

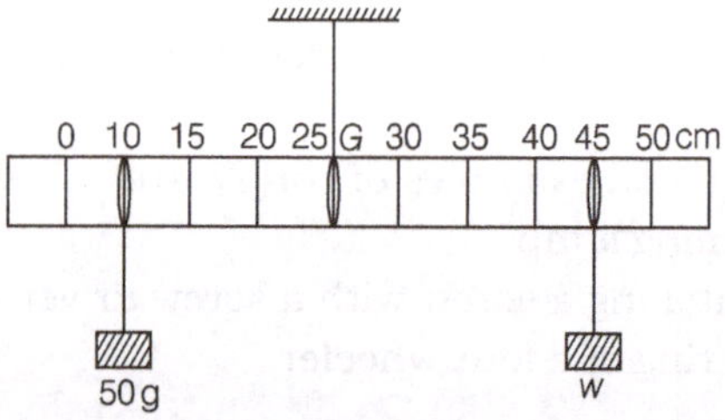

Sol. Since, the ruler is in equilibrium.

∴ According to the principle of moments,

Clockwise moment = Anti-clockwise moment

$\Rightarrow \quad w \times 20 = 50 \times 15$

$\Rightarrow \quad w = \dfrac{50 \times 15}{20} = 37.5$ gf

Example 6. A meter scale is balanced on a knife-edge at its centre. 10 g weight is put one on top of the other at the 12 cm mark and the scale is found to be balanced at 45.0 cm. What is the mass of the meter scale?

Sol. Let total mass of the meter scale is M.

∴ Weight = Mg

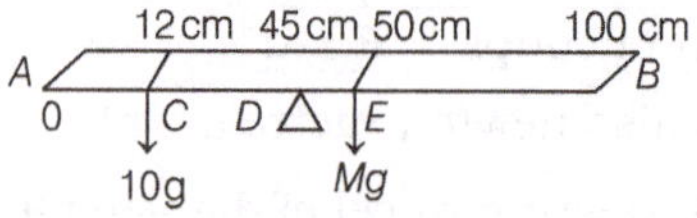

Distance between mid-point E and new centre of gravity (DE)

$= 50 - 45 = 5$ cm

Distance between 12 cm mark and new centre of gravity (CD)

$= 45 - 12 = 33$ cm

From principle of moments in equilibrium,

$Mg \times DE = 10g \times CD$

$M \times 5 = 10 \times 33$

or $M = 66$ g

∴ Mass of the meter scale is 66 g.

Check Your LEARNING...

1 What is the basic difference between pure translational motion and pure rotational motion?

2 A door is hinged at one end and is free to rotate about a vertical axis. Does its weight cause any torque about its axis? Give reason for your answer.

3 The stone of a hand flour grinder is provided with a handle near its rim. Give reason.

4 Can two forces of unequal magnitude produce moment on a body?

5 A faulty balance with unequal arms has its beam horizontal. Are the weights of the two pans equal?

Centre of Gravity

Centre of gravity of a rigid body is the point at which its whole weight can be supposed to act. The centre of gravity of a body has following characteristics

(i) Its position depends upon the distribution of mass of the body.

(ii) It may be inside or outside the body.

e.g. The centre of gravity of a uniform straight wire is at its mid-point. But, if this wire is bent into the form of a circle, then its centre of gravity will be at the centre of circle.

(iii) If the body is of symmetrical shape whose weight is distributed uniformly, then the centre of gravity of the body lies at its geometrical centre.

e.g. In case of a ring, the centre of gravity lies at its centre, where there is no material.

The following table shows the position of centre of gravity of different objects

Object	Figure	Centre of Gravity
Uniform rod	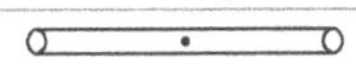	Mid-point of rod
Circular disc	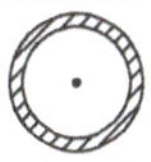	Geometric centre
Sphere (solid or hollow)	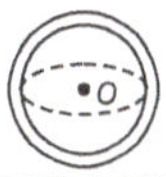	Geometric centre of the sphere
Cylinder	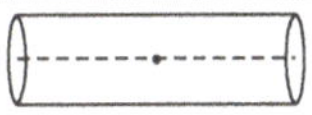	Mid-point on the axis of the cylinder
Circular ring		Centre of the ring
Rectangle or parallelogram	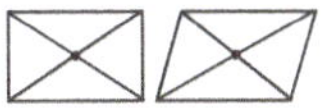	The point of intersection of the diagonals
Triangular lamina	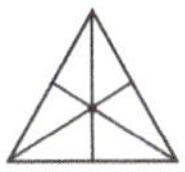	The point of intersection of medians (centroid)
Hollow cone		At a height $\left(\frac{h}{3}\right)$ from the base on its axis
Solid cone		At a height $\left(\frac{h}{4}\right)$ from the base on its axis
Cube/Cuboid	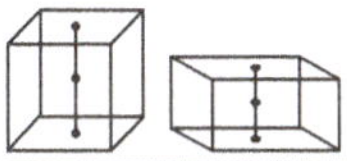	At the point of intersection of diagonals

Note Algebraic sum of moments of weights of constituent particles of the body about centre of gravity is zero.

Centre of Gravity and the Balance Point

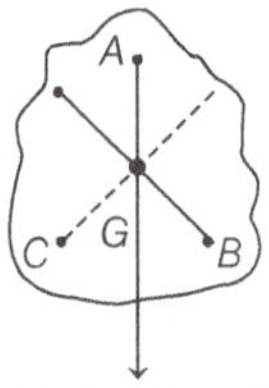

Centre of gravity of irregular lamina

When a body is freely suspended from a point, then it comes to rest or becomes balanced when its centre of gravity lies vertically below the point of suspension. This fact is used to locate the position of centre of gravity of an irregular lamina .

As shown in above figure, the common point (G) of intersection of all lines is the centre of gravity for given lamina.

Note For the stable equilibrium of a body, its centre of gravity must be as low as possible and it must be above the base and near the geometric centre of the body.

Uniform Circular Motion

When a body moves with a constant speed in a circular path, then its motion is known as **uniform circular motion**. However, the direction of motion of the body which is tangential to the circle changes at every point of the circular path as shown below.

Due to this continuous change in direction of motion, the velocity is no longer uniform (only magnitude remains same) i.e. it changes continuously and hence, due to change of its velocity, the motion is said to be an accelerated motion.

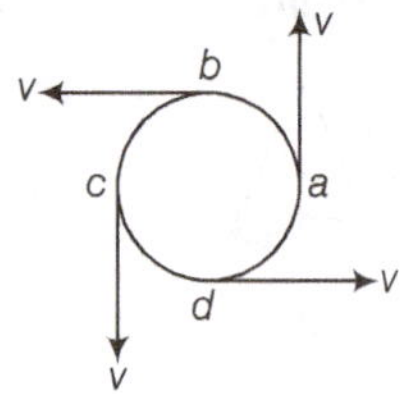

Direction of velocity in a circular path

Note In uniform linear motion, speed and velocity both are constants and acceleration is zero. i.e. It is an unaccelerated motion, while in a uniform circular motion, the speed is uniform but velocity is variable, i.e. it is an accelerated motion.

Centripetal Force

The force which keeps a body moving with a uniform speed along a circular path and directed along the radius towards the centre is called centripetal force.

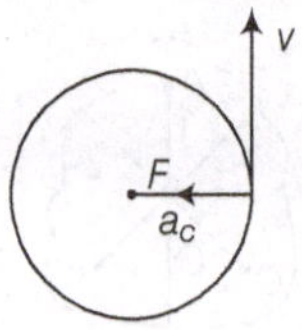

Uniform circular motion

If a body of mass m performing uniform circular motion, then centripetal force,

$$F = \frac{mv^2}{r}$$

where, v = speed of body

and r = radius of circular path.

e.g. When a stone tied at the end of a string is whirled in a circular path by holding it from other end, then the necessary centripetal force is provided by the tension in the string acting towards the centre of circular path.

Centrifugal Force

It is the apparent force that draws a rotating body away from the centre of rotation. It is caused by the inertia of the body as the body's path is continually redirected.

e.g. In whirling a string tied to a stone, the centrifugal force acts opposite to the tension produced in the string.

The centrifugal force is in the opposite direction to the direction of centripetal force, but it is not the force of reaction of centripetal force.

The centrifugal force is not a real force but it is a fictitious force (or virtual force).

Check Your LEARNING...

1. Can it be possible that the centre of gravity be situated outside the material of the body?
2. What is the position of centre of gravity of triangular lamina?
3. Why is the motion of a circulating fan non-uniform?
4. Draw a neat diagram for a particle moving in a circular path with a constant speed and show the direction of velocity at any instant.
5. Is it possible to have an accelerated motion with a constant speed? Explain.
6. Is centrifugal force, the force of reaction of centripetal force?

QUiCK Revision

- A push or pull which changes the state of rest or of uniform motion or the direction of motion of a body is called **force**.
- A **rigid body** is the one whose size and shape remains same whatever force be applied to different parts of it.
- A force that can rotate an object is called **turning force**.
- **Torque** or **moment of force** is given by

  torque (τ) = force (F) × perpendicular distance (d)
- Torque is a vector quantity and its SI unit is newton-metre (N-m).
- A pair of equal and opposite forces acting on an object is called **couple**.

  Moment of couple = Magnitude of either force × Perpendicular distance between the forces
- **Principle of moment** is given by

  sum of anti-clockwise moment = sum of clockwise moment
- **Centre of gravity** of a body is the point at which the algebraic sum of moments of weights of all the particles of the body is zero.
- When a body moves with a constant speed in a circular path, then its motion is known as **uniform circular motion**.
- The force that maintains the uniform circular motion of an object is called **centripetal force** and it is directed towards the centre of the circle.
- The apparent force that draws a rotating body away from the centre of rotation is called **centrifugal force**. It is a pseudo force.

Chapter Practice

1 Mark Questions

1. A body of mass 1 kg moves with a velocity $5\ ms^{-1}$. A force is applied on it for 1ms, such that its velocity is increased to $7\ ms^{-1}$. The force applied on the body is
(a) 2000 N (b) 200 N
(c) 400 N (d) 20 N

Sol. (*a*) Given, mass of body, $m = 1\ kg$

Initial velocity, $u = 5\ ms^{-1}$

Final velocity, $v = 7\ ms^{-1}$

Time taken, $t = 1\ ms = 1 \times 10^{-3} s$

Force, $F = ma = m\left(\frac{v-u}{t}\right)$

$$= 1\frac{(7-5)}{1 \times 10^{-3}} = 2000\ N$$

2. The moment of a force about a given axis depends
(a) on the magnitude of force
(b) on the perpendicular distance of force from the axis
(c) on both the force and its perpendicular distance from the axis
(d) neither on force nor on the perpendicular distance of force from the axis

Sol. (*c*) The moment of force is given by

$$\tau = F \times d$$

So, it depends on both the forces and its perpendicular distance from the axis.

3. Clockwise moment produced by a force about a fulcrum is considered to be **[2023 (Sem-I)]**
(a) positive (b) negative
(c) zero (d) None of these

Sol. (*b*) Clockwise moment produced by a force about a fulcrum is considered to be negative.

4. The relation between CGS and SI unit of moment of moment of force is **[2021 (Sem-I)]**
(a) 1 N-m = 10^5 dyne-cm
(b) 1 N-m = 10^5 dyne
(c) 1 N-m = 10^7 dyne-cm
(d) 1 dyne-cm = 10^7 N-m

Sol. (*c*) We know that,

1 newton = 10^5 dyne

1 N-m = $10^5 \times 10^2$ dyne-cm

1N-m = 10^7 dyne-cm

5. The line joining the centre of gravity of a cuboid and the centre of the earth will fall within the base of the body even after being disturbed by an external force, then the body is said to be in
(a) neutral equilibrium
(b) stable equilibrium
(c) unstable equilibrium
(d) dynamic equilibrium

Sol. (*b*) Since, the line joining the centre of gravity and centre of earth passes through the base of body and the body will regain its position after being disturbed. So, the body is in stable equilibrium.

6. A meter scale is suspended at 50 cm mark to a rigid support with a weight of 150 g attached at 5 cm mark as shown in figure. To balance the scale, a weight of 450 g should be attached at mark

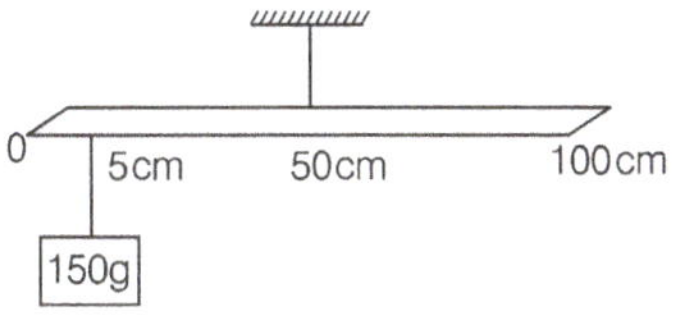

(a) 65 cm (b) 90 cm
(c) 95 cm (d) 100 cm

Sol. (*a*) Let the weight of 450 g be attached at distance *d* as shown below

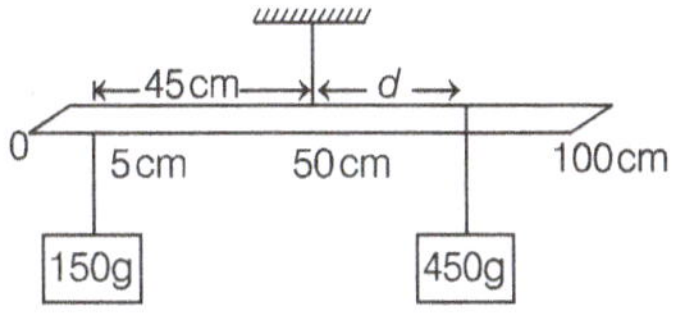

Applying principle of moment,

Sum of anti-clockwise moment = Sum of clockwise moment

$$45 \times 150 = d \times 450$$

$$\Rightarrow \quad d = \frac{45 \times 150}{450}$$

$$= 15\ cm$$

The distance of weight from zero mark

$$= 50 + 15 = 65\ cm$$

7. The centre of gravity at a uniform ball is at
(a) its geometrical centre
(b) its bottom
(c) its topmost point
(d) any point on its surface

Sol. (*a*) Since, the ball is a spherically symmetric body. So, centre of gravity will be at its geometrical centre.

8. The centre of gravity of a bob of a given simple pendulum is at position x on earth. What is its new position on the surface of the moon ?
(a) It remains at the same position x
(b) It is above the position x
(c) It is below the position x
(d) It shifts towards surface of the bob

Sol. (*a*) The centre of gravity of a symmetrical body is independent of its position and the environment. So, the new position of centre of gravity will also be at the same position x on the moon.

9. A particle is acted upon by a force of constant magnitude which is always perpendicular to the velocity of the particle. The motion of the particle takes place in a plane. It means that
(a) its velocity is constant
(b) its kinetic energy is constant
(c) its acceleration is constant
(d) it moves in a straight line

Sol. (*b*) According to given situation, the particle is performing uniform circular motion. The force acting on the particle perpendicular to its velocity is centripetal force. As the speed is constant in uniform circular motion, its kinetic energy is constant.

10. Butter separates from milk, when milk is churned at a high speed. This is because of
(a) centripetal force
(b) centrifugal force
(c) frictional force
(d) adhesive force

Sol. (*b*) When the milk is churned at a high speed, then due to centrifugal force, the lighter particles are pulled outwards. The denser particles, i.e. butter settles at centre.

11. A ball of mass 1 kg is tied to a string of length 2 m and rotated in a circular path with a uniform speed of 10 ms^{-1}. The centripetal force and centrifugal force acting on the body are respectively,
(a) 50 N each, both acting tangentially to the circle
(b) 50 N each, both acting toward the centre of circle
(c) 50 N each, both acting away from the centre of circle
(d) 50 N each, centripetal force is acting toward centre of circle while centrifugal force acting opposite to it

Sol. (*d*) Given, mass, $m = 1$ kg

Radius of circle, $r = l = 2$ m

Speed, $v = 10$ ms^{-1}

Centripetal force,

$$F = \frac{mv^2}{r} = \frac{1 \times 10^2}{2} = 50 \text{ N}$$

The magnitude of centripetal and centrifugal forces are equal but their directions are opposite. i.e. Centripetal force act towards centre of circle while centrifugal force acts away from the centre of circle.

2 Marks Questions

12. (i) What is the position of centre of gravity of a triangular lamina? **[2023]**
(ii) When this triangular lamina is suspended freely from any one vertex, what is the moment of force produced by its own weight in its rest position?

Sol. (i) Refer to table (page 5). **[1]**
(ii) When this triangular lamina is suspended freely from any one vertex, then the moment of force produced by its own weight in its rest position will be zero. **[1]**

13. The diagram shows wheel O pivoted at point A. Three equal forces F_1, F_2 and F_3 act at point B on the wheel.

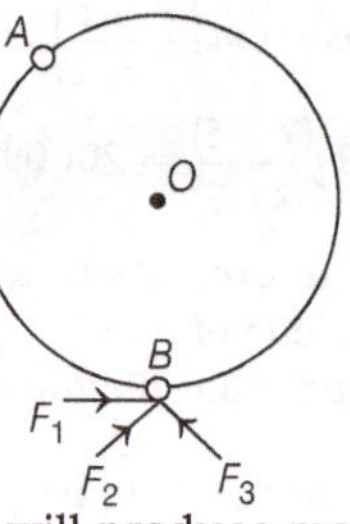

(i) Which force will produce maximum moment about A?
(ii) Give a reason for your answer in (i). **[2023]**

Sol. (i) F_1 **[1]**
(ii) F_1 is at maximum perpendicular distance or force is tangentially applied. **[1]**

14. A metallic ball is hanging by a string from a fixed support. Draw a neat labelled diagram showing the forces acting on the ball and the string. **[2014]**

Sol.

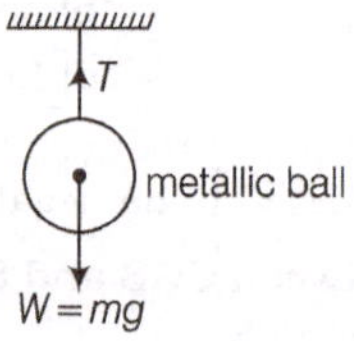

where, T is tension in the string
and W is weight of the ball. Thus

$$T = mg$$

or

$$T = W$$ **[2]**

15. (i) Define 1 kgf.
(ii) How is it related to the SI unit of force?

Sol. (i) 1 kgf is the force with which the earth pulls an object of mass 1kg towards itself. **[1]**
(ii) It is related to force by 1 kgf = mg = 9.8 N
($\because m = 1$ kg, $g = 9.8$ m/s^2) **[1]**

16. A force is applied on
(i) a rigid body and
(ii) a non-rigid body.

How does the effect of the force differ in the above two cases? [2014]

Sol. (i) When a force is applied on a rigid body, it does not change the inter-spacing between its constituent particles and therefore it does not change the dimensions of the object, but causes motion in it. [1]

(ii) On the other hand, when a force is applied on a non-rigid body, it changes the inter-spacing between its constituent particles and therefore causes a change in its dimensions. [1]

17. Give any two effects of a force on a non-rigid body. [2013]

Sol. The two main effects of a force on a non-rigid body are
(i) It can change the state of rest or of motion of the body.
(ii) It can change the size or shape of the body. [1+1]

18. (i) Give one example of pure rotational motion.
(ii) Comment on the movement of particles on the axis of rotation in pure rotational motion.

Sol. (i) Rotation of a potter's wheel. [1]
(ii) The particles on the axis of rotation are stationary in pure rotational motion. [1]

19. (i) What is meant by the term moment of force?
(ii) If the moment of force is assigned a negative sign, then will the turning tendency of the force be clockwise or anti clockwise? [2012]

Sol. (i) The turning effect produced by a force on a rigid body about a point, pivot or fulcrum is called the moment of force. [1]
(ii) If the moment of force is negative, then turning tendency of the force is clockwise. [1]

20. Why is a jack screw provided with a long arm?

Sol. In order to produce maximum turning effect of the screw jack by a force, the force is applied at a point on the body for which the distance from the axis is maximum. So that, the given force provides maximum torque to turn the screw jack.

Numerically, moment of force (torque, which is responsible for turning effect of the body)

= force applied × perpendicular distance of force from axis of rotation

Therefore, the longer arm of the jack screw, the more turning effect on it can apply. [2]

21. (i) Define couple.
(ii) State the SI unit of moment of couple. [ISC 2019]

Sol. (i) A couple is a pair of forces equal in magnitude, oppositely directed and displaced by perpendicular distance. The simplest kind of couple consists of two equal and opposite forces whose lines of action do not coincide and these forces produce turning effect, called a simple couple. [1]
(ii) The SI unit of moment of couple is N-m^2. [1]

22. What do you mean by the terms
(i) static equilibrium and
(ii) dynamic equilibrium?

Sol. Refer to theory (Page 3).

23. Where does the position of centre of gravity lie for
(i) a circular lamina and [2011]
(ii) a triangular lamina?

Sol. (i) The position of centre of gravity for a circular lamina lie at the centre of the circle. [1]
(ii) The position of centre of gravity for a triangular lamina lie at the centroid or the point of intersection of the medians. [1]

24. (i) On what factor does the position of the centre of gravity of a body depend?
(ii) Will a body rotate, if two equal and opposite forces be applied along the same line of action?

Sol. (i) The position of centre of gravity of a body depends upon the shape and size of the body. [1]
(ii) No, because two equal and opposite forces acting on a body in same line of action eliminate the effect of each other. [1]

25. Draw a neat labelled diagram for a particle moving in a circular path with a constant speed. In your diagram, show the direction of velocity at any instant.

Sol. The labelled diagram for a particle moving in a circular path is shown as below

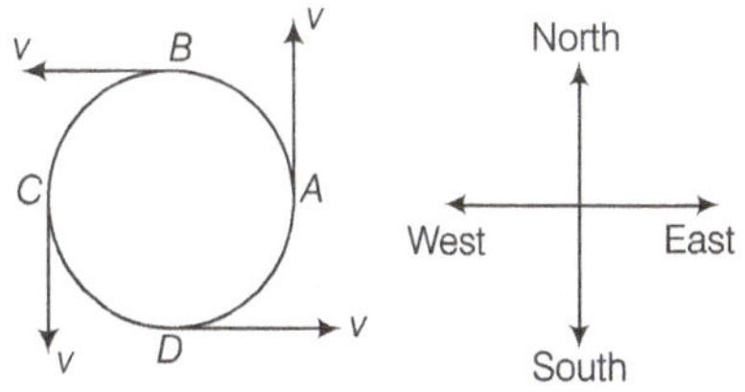

Direction of velocity in circular path

26. Read each statement carefully and state with reasons, if it is true or false.
(i) For a body moving in a circular path with a constant speed, the acceleration is centripetal in nature.
(ii) The net acceleration of a particle in circular motion is always along the radius of the circle towards the centre.

Sol. (i) True, for a body moving in a circular path, the direction of acceleration is perpendicular to the direction of motion at every point. It acts along the radius of the circle and is directed towards the centre, called centripetal acceleration. [1]
(ii) False, because the net acceleration is directed towards the centre only in case of uniform circular motion. [1]

27. (i) For a particle in uniform circular motion, what is the direction of its velocity at any point in its path?
(ii) A stone tied at the end of string is whirled in a circle. If the string breaks, then the stone flies away tangentially. Why?

Sol. (i) Along the tangent to the circle at that point. [1]
(ii) When a stone is going around a circular path, then the instantaneous velocity of stone is along the tangent to the circle.
When the string breaks, then the centripetal force stops to act. Due to inertia, the stone continues to move along the tangent to circular path. So, the stone flies off tangentially to the circular path. [1]

28. (i) Explain the motion of a planet around the sun in a circular path. [2015]
(ii) What is the nature of centripetal force on the planet?

Sol. (i) A planet moves around the sun in a circular path for which the force of attraction on planet by the sun provides the necessary centripetal force. [1]
(ii) The centripetal force on the planet is gravitational force which is attractive in nature. [1]

29. Explain the fictitious force and also explain how does it play an important role in a uniform circular motion?

Sol. A force which is not real is called fictitious force. [1]
Centrifugal force is a fictitious force. It is the apparent force that draws a rotating body away from the centre of rotation. [1]

30. Write the differences between centripetal and centrifugal force.

Sol. Differences between centripetal force and centrifugal force are

Centripetal Force	Centrifugal Force
A force which acts on an object towards the centre of a circle to produce centripetal acceleration, so that the object moves in a circle is known as centripetal force.	A force which does not act on the object moving in the circle but it is equal and opposite force to centripetal force called centrifugal force.
It is a real force.	It is a fictitious force.

3 Marks Questions

31. What do you meant by clockwise and anti-clockwise moments of force ? Explain with the diagram.

Sol. Refer to theory (Page 2).

32. Explain the following.
(i) The screw drivers have long handles? Why?
(ii) It is easier to knock over a person who is standing on one foot than one who is standing on two.
(iii) Why do the wine glasses have a heavy and broad base?

Sol. (i) Torque (τ) = Force (F) $\times$ Perpendicular distance (d)
If the handle is long, the value of d is more, hence more torque (τ) is produced with less effect of force. [1]
(ii) It is easier to knock over a person who is standing on one foot than one who is standing on both because the person standing on one foot has a smaller base area than the person standing on both the feet. Thus, the person standing on one foot is in a less stable equilibrium and can be easily knocked down. [1]
(iii) Wine glass has a broad and heavy base because heavy base lowers its centre of gravity and broad base will adjust the line joining the centre of gravity and centre of the earth fall within the base and keep the glass in stable equilibrium. [1]

33. (i) You always keep your feet wide apart, when receiving the charge from an opponent at football. Explain.
(ii) Why does a rope walker holds a long pole in his hands?
(iii) The passengers in a boat are not allowed to stand while crossing a river. Why?

Sol. (i) While receiving the charge from an opponent at football, we keep our feet wide apart to adjust the centre of gravity, as low as possible to maintain ourselves in stable equilibrium. Thus, on hitting we do not fall. [1]
(ii) The rope walker holds a long pole in his hands to adjust the centre of gravity. When he feels that he is falling towards right, he shifts the pole towards left, so that his centre of gravity is not disturbed and he can balance himself. [1]
(iii) This is because, if the passengers stand, then the centre of gravity of the boat is raised. This may cause the boat to overturn as well as producing imbalance. [1]

34. A stone of mass m is rotated in a circular path with a uniform speed by tying a strong string with the help of your hand. Answer the following questions.
(i) Is the stone moving with a uniform or variable speed?
(ii) Is the stone moving with a uniform acceleration? In which direction does the acceleration act?
(iii) What kind of force acts on the hand and state its direction? [2016]

Sol. (i) The stone is moving with a uniform speed and variable velocity. [1]
(ii) No, the stone is not moving with a uniform acceleration, because the direction of acceleration changes. Acceleration always acts towards the centre of the circular path. [1]
(iii) Reaction force of centripetal force, radially outwards direction from the centre of the circle. [1]

35. (i) With reference to the direction of action, how does a centripetal force differ from a centrifugal force during uniform circular motion?

(ii) Is centrifugal force, the force of reaction of centripetal force?

(iii) Compare the magnitudes of centripetal and centrifugal forces. [2020]

Sol. (i) In uniform circular motion, direction of centripetal force on the body is along the radius of the circular path, from the body towards the centre while the direction of the centrifugal force on the body is along the radius of the circle, from the centre towards the body, i.e. opposite to centripetal force. [1]

(ii) Centrifugal force is caused by the inertia of the body, as the body's path is continually redirected, so it is not the force of reaction of centripetal force. [1]

(iii) Magnitude of centripetal force and centrifugal force are equal. [1]

4 Marks Questions

36. Explain briefly, how can you verify the principle of moment?

Sol. Refer to theory (Page 4).

37. Draw sketch diagram and indicate the position of the centre of gravity of

(i) sphere (solid or hollow (ii) triangular lamina
(iii) parallelogram (iv) cylinder

Sol. Refer to table (Page 5).

38. (i) Centre of gravity of a body on the earth coincides with its centre of mass for a small object and for a large object, it may not. What is qualitative meaning of small and large in this regard ?

For which of the following two of them coincides, a building, a pond, a lake, a mountain ?

(ii) The bottom of a ship is made heavy. Why?

Sol. (i) Centre of mass and centre of gravity are two different concepts. But, if g does not vary from one part of body to other than centre of gravity and centre of mass will coincide.

So, when vertical height of the object is very small compared to radius of earth, we call object small, otherwise we call it extended.

In above context, building and pond are small objects and a deep lake and a mountain are large extended objects. [2]

(ii) The bottom of a ship is made heavy, so that its centre of gravity remains low. This ensures the stability of its equilibrium. [2]

39. (i) Which of the following remains constant in a uniform circular motion, speed or velocity or both?

(ii) Name the force required for a uniform circular motion. State its direction.

(iii) Explain the motion of a planet around the sun in a circular path.

Sol. (i) Speed remains constant in a uniform circular motion. [1]

(ii) Centripetal force is required for a uniform circular motion. Centripetal force is always directed towards the centre. [1]

(iii) For a planet moving around the sun in a circular path, the gravitational force of attraction between the planet and the sun provides the necessary centripetal force. [2]

40. A uniform circular motion is an accelerated motion, explain using diagram.

Sol. A particle is moving in a circular path with uniform speed v in the anti-clockwise direction. The particle travels in each quarter path of the circle AB, BC, CD and DA in same time interval $t = \frac{T}{4}$. Thus, speed of the particle is constant. But the direction of motion of the particle is different at different points on the circular path. [2]

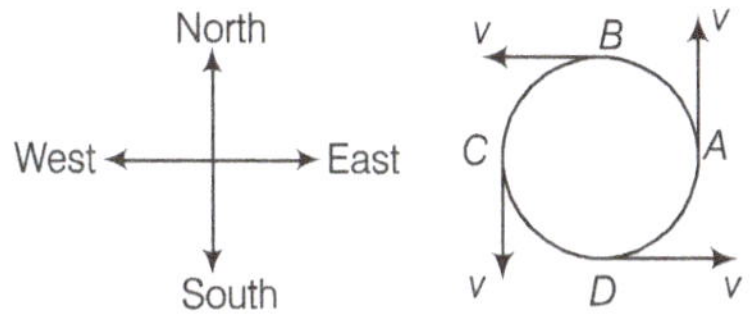

Velocity at point A is in north direction, at point B is in west direction, at point C it is in south direction and at point D it is in east direction. As, velocity is changing at each point, hence the motion is said to be accelerated. [2]

Numerical Type Questions

41. A body of mass 1.5 kg is dropped from second floor of a building which is at a height of 12 m. What is the force acting on it during its fall? (Take, $g = 9.8\ m/s^2$) [2]

Sol. Given, mass, $m = 1.5$ kg, height, $h = 12$ m

$\therefore$ Force acting on the body during its fall

$$= mg = 1.5 \times 9.8$$
$$= 14.7 \text{ N}$$ [2]

42. A metre scale of weight 50 gf can be balanced at 40 cm mark without any weight suspended on it. [2023] [3]

(i) If this ruler is cut at its centre, then state which part [0 to 50 cm or 50 to 100 cm] of the ruler will weigh more than 25 gf.

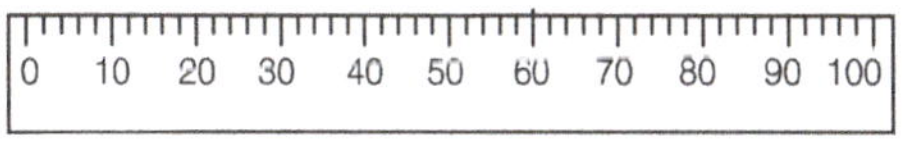

(ii) What minium weight placed on this metre ruler can balance this ruler when it is pivoted at its centre?

Sol. (i) The part of the ruler that is cut from 0 to 50 cm has weight more than 25 gf.

(ii) According to the principle of moment,

$$w(50-0) = 50(50-50)$$
$$w(50) = 50(0)$$
$$w = 0 \text{ gf}$$

43. A uniform metal rod of 5m in length and weight 90 N is suspended horizontally by two vertical wires attached at 50 cm and 3.5 m, respectively from one end of the rod as shown in figure. Find the tension in each wire.

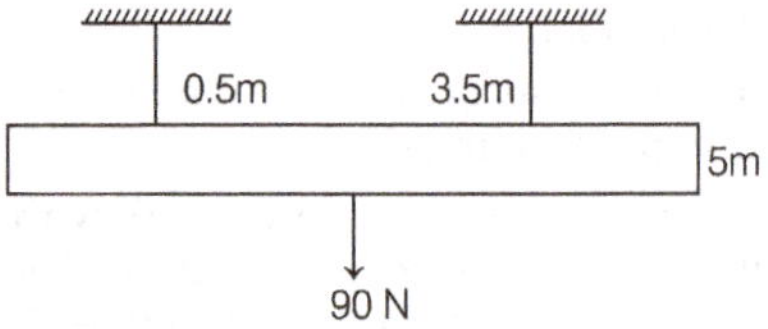

[4]

Sol. Let tension in the wires be T_1 and T_2. As, the rod is uniform its weight act as the centre of gravity of the rod, i.e. at 2.5 m from one end. [1]

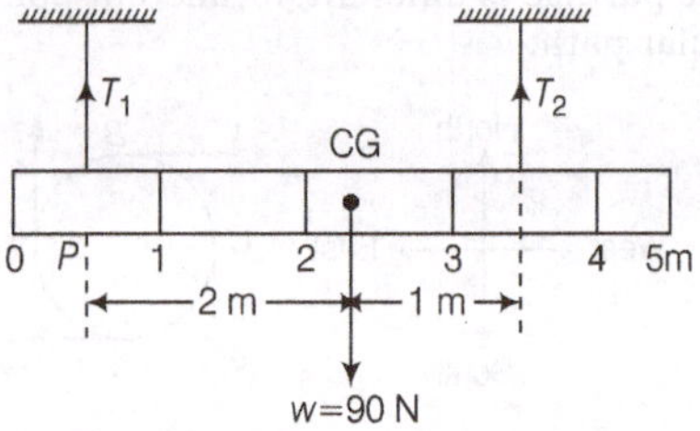

[1]

Now, according to the principle of moment,

sum of upward forces = sum of downward forces

i.e. $T_1 + T_2 = 90 \text{ N}$ ...(i)

Taking moment about CG,

clockwise moment = anti-clockwise moment

$$T_1 \times 2 \text{ m} = T_2 \times 1 \text{ m}$$ [1]

$\Rightarrow$ $T_2 = 2T_1$ ...(ii)

On solving Eqs. (i) and (ii), we get

$$T_1 = 30 \text{ N}$$

and $T_2 = 60 \text{ N}$ [1]

44. A half- metre rod is pivoted at the centre with two weights of 20 gf and 12 gf suspended at a perpendicular distance of 6 cm and 10 cm from the pivot respectively, as shown below.

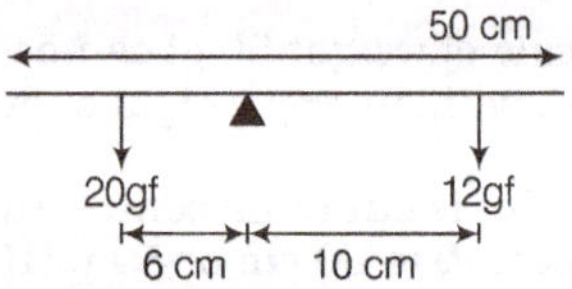

(i) Which of the two forces acting on the rigid rod causes clockwise moment?

(ii) Is the rod in equilibrium?

(iii) The direction of 20 gf force is reversed. What is the magnitude of the resultant moment of the forces on the rod? [3][2018]

Sol. (i) Force due to 12 gf on the rigid rod causes clockwise moment. [1]

(ii) Clockwise moment = 12 gf× 10 cm = 120 gf cm

Anti-clockwise moment = 20 gf× 6 cm = 120 gf cm

∴ Clockwise moment = Anti-clockwise moment

Hence, the rod is in equilibrium. [1]

(iii) According to question, the direction of 20 gf force is reversed. Hence, the total force on rod will move in clockwise direction.

∴ Clockwise moment

= Resultant moment of force

Resultant moment of force

$= (12 \times 10) + (20 \times 6) = 120 + 120 = 240$ gf cm [1]

45. A uniform meter scale of mass 60 g, carrier masses of 20 g, 30 g and 80 g from points 10 cm, 20 cm and 90 cm marks. Where must be the scale hanged with string to balance the scale ? [4]

Sol. Let D is the position of tied hanged string, so that the meter scale and various masses are balanced.

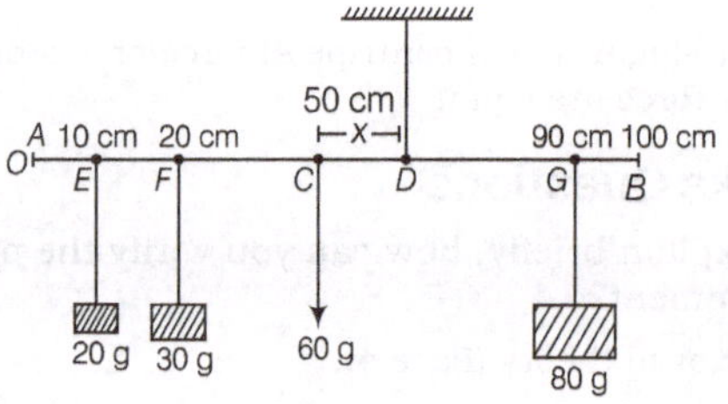

Since, the meter scale is balanced.

∴ Sum of the clockwise moments must be equal to the sum of anti-clockwise moments. [1]

Taking moments about D, we get

$$80 \times GD = 20 \times ED + 30 \times FD + 60 \times CD$$

or $80 \times (40 - x) = 20 \times (40 + x) + 30 \times (30 + x) + 60x$

$\Rightarrow$ $3200 - 80x = 800 + 20x + 900 + 30x + 60x$

$\Rightarrow$ $1500 = 190x$

$\Rightarrow$ $x = \dfrac{1500}{190} = 7.9$ cm [2]

Hence, the string must be tied at 50 + 7.9 = 57.9 cm to maintain balance of meter scale. [1]

46. A meter scale is balanced in horizontal position as shown in figure given below. Find the value of w.

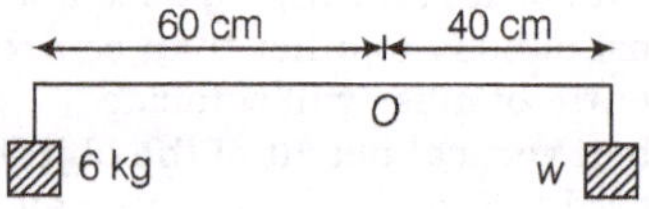

[2]

Sol. Given, $m_1 = 6$ kg

∴ Load, $F_1 = m_1 g = 6g$

Load arm, $d_1 = 60$ cm

Effort, $F_2 = wg$

Effort arm, $d_2 = 40$ cm [1]

According to the principle of moments in equilibrium,

$$F_1 d_1 = F_2 d_2$$

$\Rightarrow$ $6g \times 60 = wg \times 40$

$\Rightarrow$ $w = \dfrac{6 \times 60}{40} = 9$ kg [1]

47. A man can open a nut by applying a force of 150 N by using a lever handle of length 0.4 m. What should be the length of the handle, if he is able to open it by applying a force of 60 N? **[2] [2011]**

Sol. Given, load, $F_1 = 150$ N, load arm, $d_1 = 0.4$ m

Effort, $F_2 = 60$ N, effort arm, $d_2 = ?$

By principle of moments,

$$F_1 \times d_1 = F_2 \times d_2 \quad [1]$$

$$\Rightarrow \quad d_2 = \frac{F_1 \times d_1}{F_2} = \frac{150 \times 0.4}{60} = 1 \text{ m} \quad [1]$$

48. A uniform half-meter rule balances horizontally on a knife-edge at 29 cm mark, when a weight of 20 gf is suspended from one end.

(i) Draw a diagram of the arrangement.

(ii) What is the weight of the half-meter rule? **[3] [2017]**

Sol. (i) Diagram of the arrangement is shown below

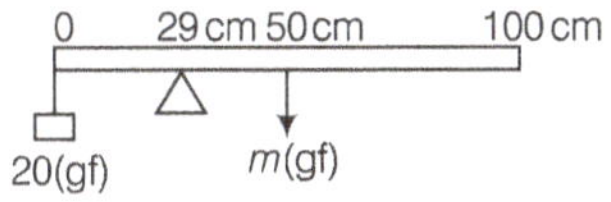

[1½]

(ii) $20(29-0) = m(50-29)$

($\because$ According to principle of moments)

$$\Rightarrow \quad m = 27.6 \text{ gf} \quad [1½]$$

49. A boy of mass 30 kg is sitting at a distance of 2 m from the middle of a see-saw. Where should a boy of mass 40 kg sit, so as to balance the see-saw? **[2] [2012]**

Sol. Let the distance of boy of mass 40 kg from the mean position be x metre.

Using principle of moments,

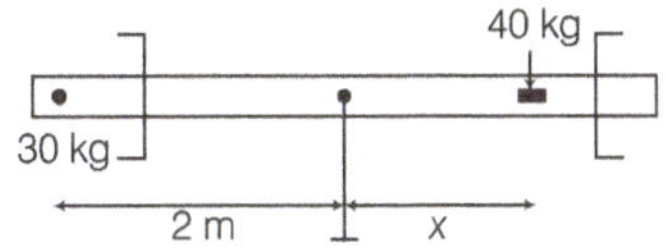

Load × Load arm = Effort × Effort arm **[1]**

$$30g \times 2 = 40g \times x$$

$$\Rightarrow \quad x = 1.5 \text{ m}$$

So, the boy of mass 40 kg should sit at a distance 1.5 m from the middle of see-saw. **[1]**

50. Figure shows a uniform meter rule weighing 100 gf pivoted at its centre O. Two weights 150 gf and 250 gf are hanged from the meter rod as shown in the figure.

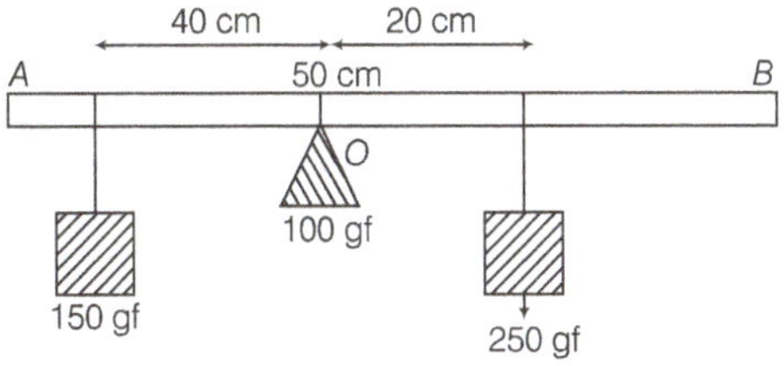

Calculate

(i) the total anti-clockwise moments about O.

(ii) the total clockwise moments about O.

(iii) the difference of anti-clockwise and clockwise moments about O.

(iv) the distance O, where a 100 gf weight should be placed to balanced the meter rule. **[4]**

Sol. According to the figure, given in question, we get

(i) The moments of the weight of 150 gf

$$= 150 \times 40 = 6000 \text{ gfcm} \quad [1]$$

(ii) The moments of the weight of 250 gf

$$= -250 \times 20 = -5000 \text{ gfcm, i.e. clockwise} \quad [1]$$

(iii) The difference of moments

$$= 6000 - 5000$$

$$= 1000 \text{ gfcm} \quad [1]$$

(iv) To balance these 1000 gfcm anti-clockwise moments, 100 gf weight must be at a distance

$$x = \frac{1000}{100} = 10 \text{ cm on the right side of } O. \quad [1]$$

51. A car is of weight 1800 kg. The distance between its front and back axles is 1.8 m. Its centre of gravity is 1.05 m behind the front axle. Determine the force exerted by the level ground on each front wheel and each back wheel. **[4]**

Sol. Total mass of the car = 1800 kg

Let m and $(900 - m)$ kg be the masses of each front wheel and each back wheel, respectively.

Distance of centre of gravity from the front axle

$$= 1.05 \text{ m}$$

$\therefore$ Distance of centre of gravity from the back axle

$$= 1.80 - 1.05 = 0.75 \text{ m} \quad [1]$$

Taking torque about centre of gravity,

$$m \times 1.05 = (900 - m) \times 0.75$$

or $\quad 1.05\,m + 0.75\,m = 900 \times 0.75$

or $\quad 1.80\,m = 900 \times 0.75$

or $\quad m = \dfrac{900 \times 0.75}{1.80} = 375$ kg

$\therefore \quad (900 - m) = 900 - 375 = 525$ kg **[1]**

$\therefore$ Weight of each front wheel, $w_1 = m_1 g$

$$= 375 \times 9.8$$

$$= 3675 \text{ N} \quad [1]$$

Force exerted by the level ground on each front wheel = Force exerted by each front wheel on the level ground $(w_1) = 3675$ N

Weight of each back wheel, $w_2 = m_2 g$

$$w_2 = 525 \times 9.8 = 5145 \text{ N}$$

$\therefore$ Force exerted by the level ground on each back wheel = Force exerted by each back wheel on level ground (w_2)

$$= 5145 \text{ N} \quad [1]$$

52. In a meter rod, half of it is made of copper and rest half of steel as shown in figure. Weights of copper and steel are 9 N and 8 N, respectively.

(i) Is the centre of gravity of the rod at its geometric centre?

(ii) If not, where is it? **[3]**

Sol. (i) Since, the rod is not uniform, half portion of the rod is made up of copper which is heavier.

So, its centre of gravity is not at the geometrical centre. **[1½]**

(ii) Let l be the length of rod XY and C_{copper} and C_{steel} be the centre of gravity of copper and steel part, respectively. If C is the centre of gravity of the combination, then by making moment about C

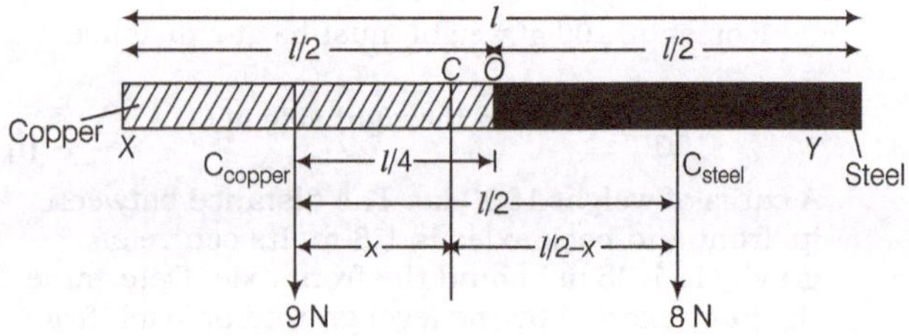

$$9 \times x = 8 \times \left(\frac{l}{2} - x\right)$$

$$\Rightarrow \quad 9x = 8 \times \frac{l}{2} - 8x \Rightarrow 17x = 4l$$

$$\therefore \quad x = \frac{4}{17}l \text{ and } OC = \frac{l}{4} - \frac{4}{17}l = \frac{1}{68}l$$

Hence, the centre of gravity of the combined rod is at point C at a distance of $\frac{1}{68}l$ from the geometrical centre O of the rod towards the copper half. **[1½]**

Structured Questions

53. (i) (a) Where is the centre of gravity of a uniform ring situated?

(b) "The position of the centre of gravity of a body remains unchanged, even when the body is deformed". State whether the statement is true or false. **[3] [2013]**

(ii) Two forces each of 5 N act vertically upwards and downwards, respectively. On the two ends of a uniform meter ruler which is placed at its mid-point as shown in the diagram.

Determine the magnitude of the resultant moment of these forces about the mid-point. **[3]**

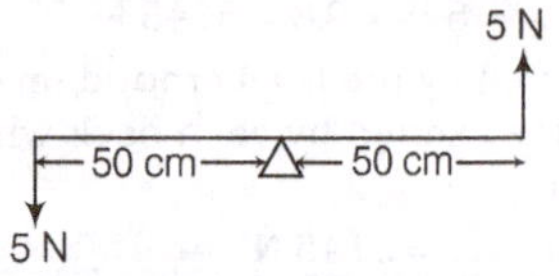

(iii) P, Q and R shows three forces each of magnitude 4N each act in a plane of paper as shown in figure. Point O lies in the same plane.

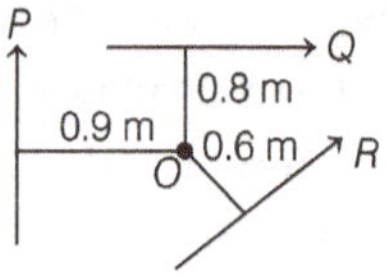

(a) Which force has the least moment about O? Give reason.

(b) Which force has the greatest moment about O? Give reason.

(c) Name the forces producing

I. clockwise

II. anti-clockwise moments

(d) What is the resultant torque about the point O? **[4]**

Sol. (i) (a) The centre of gravity of a uniform ring is situated at the centre of ring which is not part of the body. i.e. It is outside the body. **[1½]**

(b) The statement is false, because it changes its position, when the body is deformed. **[1½]**

(ii) Given, forces, $F_1 = F_2 = 5$ N

Distances, $d_1 = d_2 = 50$ cm $= 0.5$ m **[1]**

Resultant moment = Torque, $\tau = ?$ **[1]**

$\therefore \quad \tau_1 = F_1 \times d_1 = 5 \times 0.5 = 2.5$ N-m

and $\quad \tau_2 = F_2 \times d_2 = 5 \times 0.5 = 2.5$ N-m

$\therefore$ Resultant moment =

$\tau = \tau_1 + \tau_2 = 2.5 + 2.5 = 5$ N-m **[1]**

(iii) (a) Since, moment of force depends on the perpendicular distance of line of action of force from the axis of rotation. Here, distance is smallest for R. So, it has least moment about O.

(b) Similarly, the distance of P is greatest, so it has greatest moment about O.

(c) I. Forces P and Q produce clockwise moment.

II. Force R produce anti-clockwise moment.

(d) Torque due to force P, $\tau_P = F \times d_P = 4 \times 0.9$
$= 3.6$ N-m (clockwise)

Torque due to force Q, $\tau_Q = F \times d_Q$
$= 4 \times 0.8 = 3.2$ N-m (clockwise)

Torque due to force R, $\tau_R = F \times d_R = 4 \times 0.6$
$= 2.4$ N-m (anti-clockwise)

Resultant torque about O, $\tau_O = \tau_P + \tau_Q - \tau_R$ **[1×4]**
$= 3.6 + 3.2 - 2.4 = 4.4$ N-m (clockwise)

54. (i) A very small stone is placed near the periphery of a circular disc which is rotating about an axis passing through its centre.

(a) What will be your observation, when you are standing outside the disc? Explain.

(b) What will be your observation, when you are standing at the centre of the disc? Explain. **[3]**

(ii) A uniform meter scale is in equilibrium as shown in the figure given below.

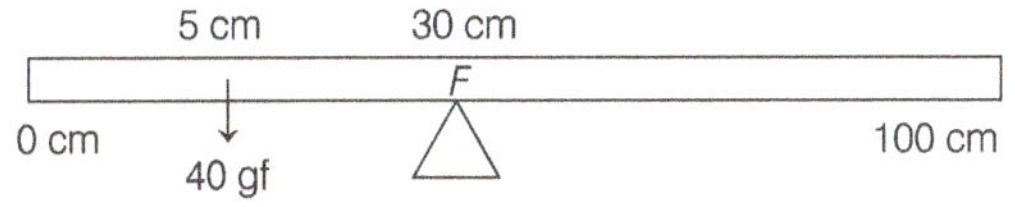

(a) Calculate the weight of the meter scale.

(b) Which of the following option is correct to keep the ruler in equilibrium, when 40 gf-wt is shifted to 0 cm mark; F is shifted towards 0 cm or F is shifted towards 100 cm? **[3] [ISC 2019]**

(iii) Explain the moment of a force with diagram and formula for

(a) the steering wheel of a car,

(b) the pedal and the rear wheel of a bicycle. **[4] [ISC 2019]**

Sol. (i) (a) When we stand outside the circular disc which is rotating on its axis, then the stone seems to move in a circular path. **[1½]**

(b) When we are standing at the centre of disc, then it seems that the stone is moving away from us and falls down. **[1½]**

(ii)

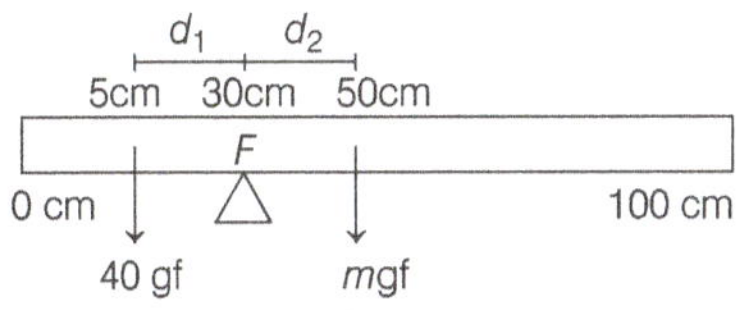

(a) At 50 cm,

Mass of meter scale = mgf

Now, $F_1 d_1 = F_2 d_2$

$$(40)(30-5) = F_2(50-30)$$

$$F_2 = 50 \text{ gf}$$

$$\Rightarrow \quad F_2 = 0.49 \text{ N}$$

$$\therefore \quad F_2 = mg$$

$$0.49 = m \times 9.8$$

$$m = \frac{0.49}{9.8}$$

$$\therefore \quad m = 0.05 \text{ kg}$$ **[1½]**

(b) F is shifted towards 0 cm. **[1½]**

(iii) (a) For turning a steering wheel, a force is applied tangentially on rim of the wheel.

The sense of rotation of wheel is changed by changing the point of application of force without changing the direction of force.

In Fig. (a), when force F is applied at the point A of the wheel, the wheel rotates anti-clockwise; while in Fig. (b), the wheel rotates clockwise when the force F in same direction is applied at the point B of the wheel.

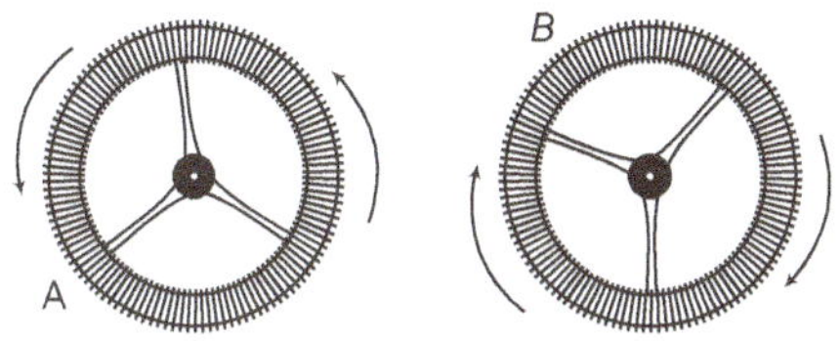

Fig. (a) Anti-clockwise rotation   Fig. (b) Clockwise rotation

[2]

(b) In the case of a bicycle wheel, a small force is applied at the pedal which is at large distance from the axle. Since, in one revolution, the pedal moves through a large distance than the links of the chain. Thus, the applied force gets multiplied and is passed on the rear wheel.

The two pedals provide two such forces and form a torque, i.e. moment of force which rotates the wheel.

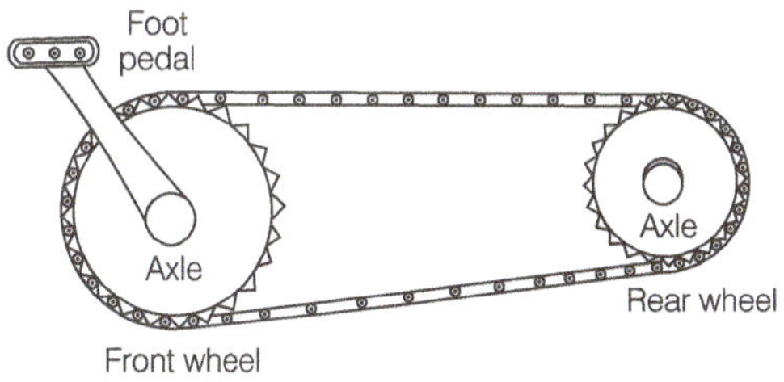

[2]

Chapter Assessment

Section-I

1 Mark Questions

1. The centre of gravity of a hollow cone at height h shown below is at distance x from its vertex. What is the value of x?

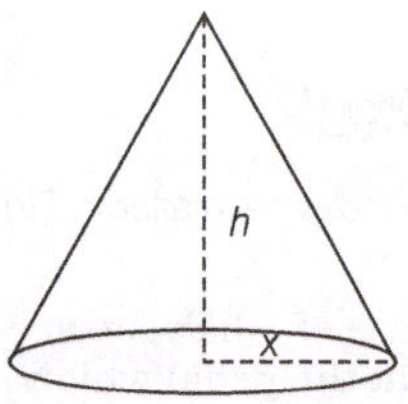

(a) $\frac{h}{3}$ (b) $\frac{h}{4}$ (c) $\frac{2h}{3}$ (d) $\frac{3h}{2}$

2. 1 dyne force can produce an acceleration of ...... cm s^{-2} on an object of mass 100 g.
(a) 1
(b) 0.1
(c) 0.01
(d) 0.001

3. The relation between CGS and unit of moment of force is **[ICSE Sem-I 2022]**
(a) 1 N-m = 10^5 dyne-cm
(b) 1 N-m = 10^5 dyne
(c) 1 N-m = 10^7 dyne-cm
(d) 1 dyne-cm = 10^7 N-m

4. A steering wheel at diameter 0.5 m is rotated anti-clockwise by applying force each of magnitude 5 N as shown in figure. The moment of couple applied is

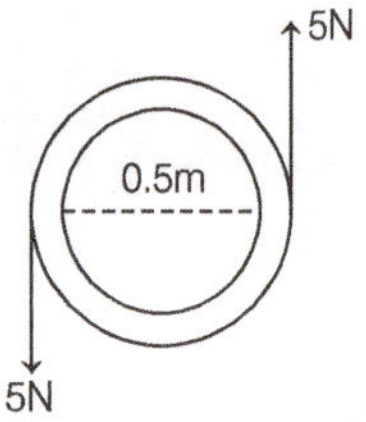

(a) 0.5 N-m
(b) 2.5 N-m
(c) 3.0 N-m
(d) 0.25 N-m

5. A stone tied at the end of a string is whirled by hand in a horizontal circle with uniform speed. Name the force required for this circular motion. **[ICSE Sem-I 2022]**
(a) Centrifugal force
(b) Centripetal force
(c) Force of gravity
(d) Frictional force

6. The bulging of earth at the equator is due to
(a) centripetal force
(b) centrifugal force
(c) gravitational force
(d) electrostatic force

7. Centrifugal force is a
(a) pseudo force acting along the radius and away from the centre
(b) force that keeps the body moving along a circular path with uniform speed
(c) force whose magnitude is less than that of the centripetal force
(d) real force acting along the radius

Section-II

2 Marks Questions

8. Give any two effects of a force on a rigid body.

9. (i) What do you understand by negative and positive moments of a force?
(ii) If the moment of force is assigned a positive sign, then will the turning tendency of the force be clockwise or anti-clockwise?

10. A body is acted upon by two forces each of magnitude F but in opposite directions. State the effect of the force, if
(i) the two forces act at two different points of the body at a separation.
(ii) both forces act at the same point of the body.

11. (i) When a knife is sharpened with the help of a rotating grinding stone, then the spark always travel tangentially to it, why?
(ii) Can a body move on a curved path without having acceleration?

12. (i) Justify that a uniform circular motion is an accelerated motion.
(ii) A women rides in a carnival ferris wheel. What is the direction of her centripetal acceleration at the lowest point?

13. Name the factors affecting the turning effect of a body.

14. (i) Define moment of force.
(ii) Write the relationship between the SI and CGS unit of moment of force.

15. (i) Define equilibrium. **[ICSE 2020]**
(ii) In a beam balance, when the beam is balanced horizontal position, then it is in .... equilibrium.

16. A uniform half meter ruler is suspended from its mid-point. A weight of 50 gf is suspended at one end of it. Where should a weight of 100 gf be suspended to keep the rule horizontal ?

17. In which condition, the following are produced by a force?
(i) Translational motion
(ii) Rotational motion

Structured Questions

18. (i) What is uniform circular motion? Draw a diagram to explain it.
(ii) With reference to their direction of action, how does a centripetal force differ from a centrifugal force? **[2013]**
(iii) In the given diagram, wheel shown has a fixed axle passing through O. The wheel is kept stationary under the action of two forces F_1 and F_2 such that a horizontal force F_1 at P and a vertical force F_2 at Q.
(a) Show the direction of F_2 in the diagram.
(b) Which is the greater force?
(c) Find the ratio between the forces.

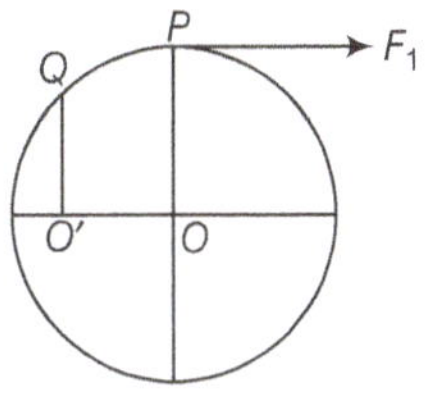

(Given, $PO = 2.5$ cm, $OQ' = 1.5$ cm and $OO' = 2.0$ cm)

19. (i) A uniform meter scale balances horizontally with a string attached at 55 cm mark, when a mass of 25 g is suspended from one end.
(a) Draw a diagram of this arrangement.
(b) Calculate the mass of the scale.
(ii) A one meter scale AB is balanced horizontally across a knife-edge as shown in the figure.

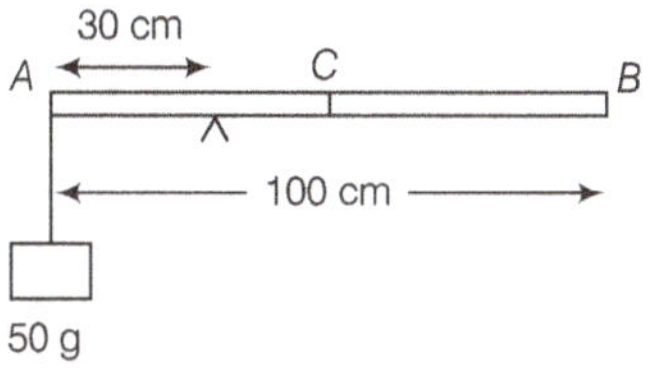

Calculate
(a) the mass of the scale and
(b) the force on the knife-edge.
(iii) How an object is said to be in equilibrium? Explain the types of equilibrium.

20. (i) Two forces each of magnitude 20 N acting at the point A and B at a separation of 100 cm, in opposite directions, calculate the resultant moment of two forces about the point (a) A (b) B and (c) O, situated exactly at the middle of the two forces.
(ii) How does uniform circular motion differ from uniform linear motion ?
(iii) Define couple and prove that
moment of couple = force × couple arm.

21. (i) What do you mean by clockwise and anti-clockwise moment? **[3]**
(ii) State the following terms
(a) Static equilibrium (b) Dynamic equilibrium
(c) Neutral equilibrium **[3]**
(iii) (a) Which types of moment is taken as positive and negative?
(b) Two point objects of mass 1.5 g and 2.5 g, respectively are at a distance of 16 cm apart. The centre of gravity is at a distance x from the object of mass 1.5 g. Find the value of x. **[4]**

For Solutions Scan the Code

Olympiad Section*

Brain Teasing Questions of Olympiad Pattern

1 A particle of mass m is executing a uniform circular motion on a path of radius r. If p is the magnitude of its linear momentum, then what is the radial force acting on the particle?

(a) $\frac{p^2}{mr}$ (b) $\frac{r}{p}$ (c) $\frac{rm}{p^2}$ (d) $\frac{p}{m}$

2 When a car of mass M passes through a convex bridge of radius r with velocity v, then it exerts a force on it. What is the magnitude of the force?

(a) Mg (b) $Mg + \frac{Mv^2}{r}$

(c) $\frac{Mv^2}{r}$ (d) $Mg - \frac{Mv^2}{r}$

3 What type of motions are exhibited by a vehicle and its wheels?

(a) Translatory
(b) Rotatory
(c) Both translatory and rotatory
(d) None of the above

4 A mechanic can open a nut by applying 120 N force while using a lever of 50 cm length. How long should the handle be, if he wishes to open, it by applying a force of only 40N?

(a) 1 m (b) 2 m (c) 1.5 m (d) 2.5m

5 Force in linear motion has its analogue in rotational motion?

(a) Moment of inertia (b) Torque
(c) Angular momentum (d) Weight

6 Essential characteristic of equilibrium is

(a) momentum equals to zero
(b) acceleration equals to zero
(c) KE equals to zero
(d) velocity equals to zero

7 The length of seconds hand of a clock is 10 cm. The angular speed of the tip of the hand is

(a) $\frac{\pi}{3}$ rad s^{-1} (b) $\frac{\pi}{30}$ rad s^{-1}

(c) $\frac{\pi}{300}$ rad s^{-1} (d) $\frac{\pi}{3000}$ rad s^{-1}

8 Two particles of equal masses are revolving in circular paths of radii r_1 and r_2 respectively, with the same speed. Find the ratio of their centripetal forces will be

(a) $\frac{r_2}{r_1}$ (b) $\sqrt{\frac{r_1}{r_2}}$ (c) $\sqrt{\frac{r_2}{r_1}}$ (d) $\frac{r_2^2}{r_1^2}$

9 From the given figure, the moment of force about P and Q and τ_P and τ_Q, then

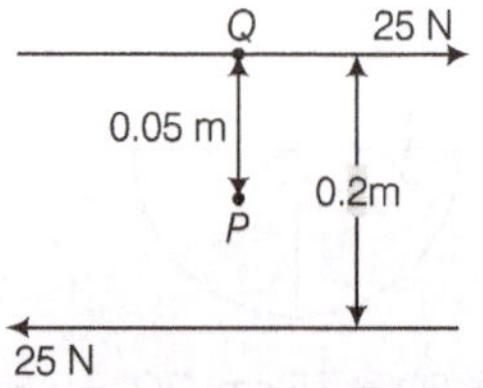

(a) $\tau_P > \tau_Q$ (b) $\tau_P < \tau_Q$
(c) $\tau_P = \tau_Q$ (d) None of these

10 The iron gate of a building is 3 m wide. It can be opened by applying a force of 200 N at its middle. What is the least force required to open this gate?

(a) 50 N (b) 100 N (c) 150 N (d) 200 N

11 A 15 kg mass is pulled along a horizontal frictionless surface with a component of force of 40 N along the east and a component of 30 N along north. What is the magnitude and direction (with respect to the east) of the acceleration of the mass? **[INJSO 2018]**

(a) 4.33 ms^{-2} at an angle of 37°
(b) 3.33 ms^{-2} at an angle of 37°
(c) 3.33 ms^{-2} at an angle of 67°
(d) 8.33 ms^{-2} at an angle of 67°

12 Particles P and Q are undergoing uniform horizontal circular motion along concentric circles of different radii in clockwise sense. P completes each round in 2 minutes while Q does it in 5 minutes. Time required by Q to make one revoluton around P is **[Olympaid 2014]**

(a) 3 min
(b) 10 min
(c) 10/3 min
(d) This is not possible as Q is moving slower than P.

Answers

1. (a)	**2.** (d)	**3.** (c)	**4.** (c)	**5.** (b)	**6.** (b)	**7.** (b)	**8.** (a)	**9.** (c)	**10.** (b)
11. (b)	**12.** (a)								

* *These questions may or may not be asked in the examination, have been given just for additional practice required for olympiads Scholarship Exams etc. For detailed explanations refer Page No. 261.*

CHAPTER

2

Work, Power and Energy

SYLLABUS

(i) Work, energy and power and their relation with force.

(ii) Different types of energy (e.g. chemical energy, Mechanical energy, heat energy, electrical energy, nuclear energy, sound energy, light energy).

(iii) Principle of conservation of energy

In our daily life, we generally use the terms work, energy and power. Work is done by a force to displace an object.

Work and energy both are equivalent to each other. In physics, energy is the **capacity** to do work and power is the rate of work done. The machine or men who does more work in lesser time has more power. The aim of this chapter is to understand the concepts of these three physical quantities, i.e. **work, power** and **energy.**

Work

Work is said to be done, if on applying a force on an object, it is displaced from its position in the direction of force.

After spending lot of time in studies, reading books, drawing diagrams, attending classes, performing experiments, you may get completely exhausted, but have not done any work in terms of science as there is no displacement.

Scientific Conception of Work

From the point of view of science, following two conditions need to be satisfied for work to be done

(i) a force should act on an object

(ii) the object must be displaced.

If any one of the above conditions does not exist, work is not said to be done.

e.g. A girl pulls a trolley and it moves through a distance. In this way, she has exerted a force on the trolley and as a result it is displaced. Hence, work is said to be done.

Work Done by a Constant Force

"Work done by a force on an object is equal to the magnitude of the force multiplied by the displacement moved in the direction of applied force."

Let us assume, if a constant force F acts on an object at point A (shown in the figure), due to which the object gets displaced through a distance s in the direction of the force and reach at point B, then the work done (W) by force (F) on that object will be equal to the product of the force and displacement.

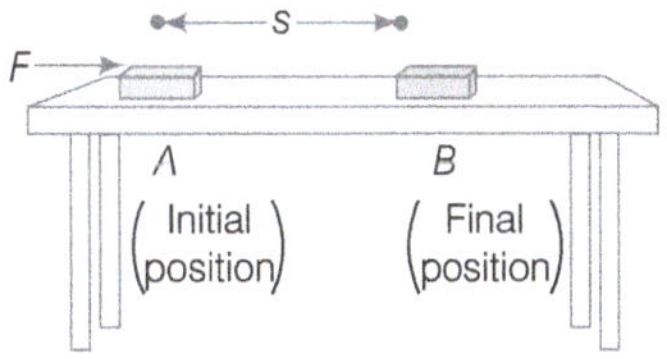

Work done by a force, when the body moves in the direction of force

∴ Work done = force × displacement in the direction of force

or $$W = F \times s \qquad \ldots(i)$$

When force F on an object acts in such a direction that it makes an angle θ with the direction of displacement s, then the work done by the force is

$$\boxed{W = Fs\cos\theta}$$

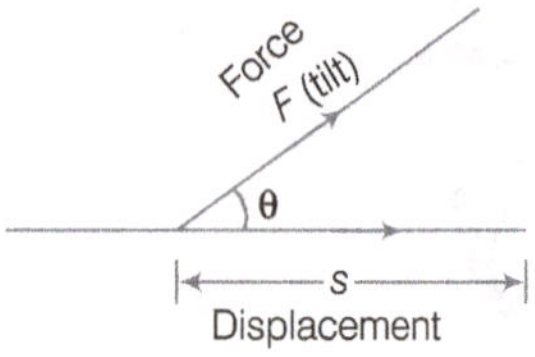

Work done by a force, when the body moves at an angle with the direction of force

In above case, work done depends on

Some important units of work are as follows

(i) magnitude of force and displacement.

(ii) the angle between the force and displacement.

Work is a scalar quantity, it has only magnitude and no direction.

In Eq. (i), if $F = 1$ N and $s = 1$ m, then the work done by the force will be 1 N-m.

The SI unit of work is newton-metre (N-m) or joule (J).

Important Units of Work

Some important units of work are given as

(i) **Joule** It is an absolute unit of work in **SI system**, named after British physicist James Prescott Joule (1811-1869).

One joule of work is said to be done, when a force of one newton displaces a body through a distance of one metre in its own direction.

From work done $(W) = Fs\cos\theta$

$$1\text{ J} = 1\text{ N} \times 1\text{ m} \times \cos 0° = 1\text{ N-m}$$

(ii) The **CGS unit** of work is **Erg**. One erg of work is said to be done, if a force of one dyne displaces a body through a distance of one centimetre in its own direction.

From work done $(W) = Fs\cos\theta$

$$1\text{ erg} = 1\text{ dyne} \times 1\text{ cm} \times \cos 0° = 1\text{ dyne-cm}$$

Relation between Joule and Erg

$$1\text{ J} = 1\text{ N} \times 1\text{ m}$$
$$= 10^5\text{dyne} \times 10^2\text{cm}$$
$$= 10^7\text{ dyne-cm}$$
$$\boxed{1\text{ J} = 10^7\text{ erg}}$$

(iii) **Kilogram-metre** (kg-m) It is the gravitational unit of work in SI system. One kilogram-metre of work is said to be done, when a force of one kilogram weight displaces a body through a distance of one metre in its own direction.

We know, work done $(W) = Fs\cos\theta$

$$1\text{ kg-m} = 1\text{ kg} \times 1\text{ m} \times \cos 0°$$
$$= 9.8\text{ N} \times 1\text{m} \times 1 = 9.8\text{ J}$$

i.e. $\quad 1\text{ kg-m} = 9.8\text{ J}$

(iv) **Gram-centimetre** (g-cm) It is the gravitational unit of work in CGS system. One gram-centimetre of work is said to be done, when a force of one gram weight displaces a body through one centimetre in its own direction.

∴ $1\text{ g-cm} = 1\text{ g-wt} \times 1\text{cm} = 980\text{ dyne} \times 1\text{cm}$

or $1\text{ g-cm} = 980\text{ erg}$

Larger Units of Work

There are some larger units of work, which are very important to be remembered.

They are as follows

1 kilojoule (kJ) $= 10^3$ J ;

1 Megajoule (MJ) $= 10^6$ J ;

1 Gigajoule (GJ) $= 10^9$ J

Example 1. A lawn roller has been pushed by a gardener through a distance of 30 m. What will be the work done by him, if he applies a force of 30 kg-wt in the direction inclined at 60° to the ground? (Take, $g = 10\text{ m/s}^2$).

Sol. Displacement, $s = 30$ m

Force, $F = 30\text{ kg-wt} = 30 \times g = 30 \times 10 = 300$ N

$\theta = 60°$

The work done by the gardener,

$$W = \mathbf{F} \cdot \mathbf{s} = Fs\cos\theta$$
$$= 300 \times 30 \times \cos 60° = 300 \times 30 \times \frac{1}{2}$$
$$= 4500\text{ J} \qquad \left(\because \cos 60° = \frac{1}{2}\right)$$

Example 2. A person is holding a bag by applying a force of 15 N. He moves forward and covers the horizontal distance of 8 m and then he climbs up and covers the vertical distance of 10 m. What will be the work done by him?

Sol. The net work done by the person is the sum of work done to cover the horizontal distance and the work done to climb up in the vertical distance.

$$F = 15\text{ N}, s_1 = 8\text{ m and } s_2 = 10\text{ m}$$

As, person is walking horizontally, therefore the angle between the force applied on the bag and distance covered is 90°.

Thus, $\theta = 90°$

The work done, $W_1 = Fs_1 \cos\theta = 15 \times 8 \cos 90° = 0$ J

Now, the person climbs up and covers the distance of 10 m vertically. Therefore, the angle between the force applied on the bag and the vertical plane is 0°.

Thus, $\theta = 0°$

The work done, $W_2 = Fs_2 \cos\theta = 15 \times 10 \times \cos 0° = 150$ J

The net work done by him, $W = W_1 + W_2 = 0 + 150 = 150$ J

Example 3. A cyclist comes to a skidding stop in 10 m. During this process, the force on the cycle due to the road is 200 N and is directly opposite to the motion.

(i) How much work does the road do on the cycle?

(ii) How much work does the cycle do on the road?

Sol. (i) The stopping force and the displacement make an angle of 180° with each other. Thus, work done by the road or the work done by the stopping force is

$$W_r = Fs\cos\theta = 200 \times 10 \times \cos 180° = -2000 \text{ J}$$

It is, thus negative work that brings the cycle to a halt.

(ii) According to Newton's third law, an equal and opposite force acts on the road due to the cycle. Its magnitude is 200 N. However, the road undergoes no displacement. So, work done by the cycle on the road is zero.

Positive, Negative and Zero Work

- When the force F and displacement s are in the same directions (i.e. angle between direction of force and displacement is 0°), work done is said to be **positive**
  ($\because \cos 0° = 1$).
  e.g. A boy pulls an object towards himself. Here, the direction of force and direction of displacement are same.

$$\boxed{W = +F \times s}$$

Similarly, in free fall of a body of mass m under gravity through a height h from A to B, the force of gravity ($F = mg$) is in the direction of displacement ($s = h$), then the work done by the force of gravity is $W = Fs = mgh$.

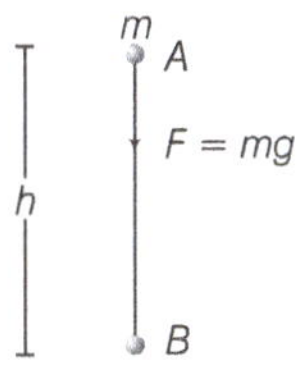

- When the force F and displacement s are in opposite directions (i.e. angle between direction of force and displacement is 180°), work done is said to be **negative** ($\because \cos 180° = -1$).
  e.g. Frictional force acts in the direction opposite to the direction of displacement, so work done by friction will be negative.

$$\boxed{W = -F \times s}$$

- When the force and displacement are in perpendicular directions (i.e. angle between direction of force and displacement is 90°), work done is said to be **zero** ($\because \cos 90° = 0$).
  e.g. A coolie carrying load on his head. In this case, force is acting vertically downward (i.e., weight of load) and displacement is along horizontal direction, i.e. force and displacement are perpendicular to each other.

$$\boxed{W = 0}$$

Check Your LEARNING...

1 State whether the work done by a force applied on a body moving on a horizontal plane with uniform velocity is positive or negative.

2 What should be the angle between force and displacement to get the work (i) maximum (ii) minimum?

3 A coolie carrying a load on his head and moving on a frictionless horizontal platform does no work. Explain the reason, why?

4 What is the work done when you apply a 10 N force on a wall? [*Ans.* zero]

5 If a 5 kg mass is raised to a height of 2 m, calculate the work done against the force of gravity.(Take, $g = 9.8$ ms^{-2}) [*Ans.* 98 J]

Power: Rate of Doing Work

The rate of doing work or the rate at which energy is transferred or used or transformed to other form is called **power**. It is a scalar quantity.

If work W is done in time t, then

$$\text{Power, } P = \frac{\text{Work}}{\text{Time}} \Rightarrow \boxed{P = \frac{W}{t}}$$

The SI unit of power is **Watt** in honour of James Watt having the symbol W. i.e., 1 W = 1 Js^{-1}

In CGS system, 1W = 10^7 erg/s.

Other Important Units of Power

Apart from the units of power in SI and CGS systems, there are some of its major units which are required to be discussed.

1 kilowatt (kW) = 10^3 W

1 Megawatt (MW) = 10^6 W

1 Gigawatt (GW) = 10^9 W

1 Horse Power (HP) = 746 W

Average Power

Average power is the ratio of total work done by force to the total time taken. A power or machine may perform work at different rates at different intervals of time. In such situation, average power is considered by dividing the total energy consumed by the total time taken.

$$\therefore \text{ Average power} = \frac{\text{Total energy consumed}}{\text{Total time taken}}$$

When a force is applied on an object, sets it in motion, then power developed is given by

$$P = \frac{W}{t} = \frac{F \times s}{t} = F \times v \quad \left(\because \frac{s}{t} = v\right)$$

Example 4. Calculate the power of an electric engine which can lift 20 tonne of coal per hour from a mine 180 m depth.

Sol. Given, $m = 20$ tonne

or $m = 20 \times 1000 = 20000$ kg $(\because 1 \text{ tonne} = 1000 \text{ kg})$

$h = 180$ m, $t = 1\text{h} = 3600$ s

$g = 9.8 \text{ m/s}^2$

We know that, power $(P) = \frac{\text{Work }(W)}{\text{Time }(t)} = \frac{mgh}{t}$

$= \frac{20000 \times 9.8 \times 180}{3600}$

$\Rightarrow \quad P = 9800$ W

Example 5. A car of mass 2000 kg is lifted up a distance of 30 m by a crane in 1 min. A second crane does the same job in 2 min. Do the cranes consume the same or different amounts of fuel? What is the power supplied by each crane? Neglect power dissipation against friction.

Sol. Given, $m = 2000$ kg, $s = 30$ m

$t_1 = 1 \text{ min} = 60 \text{ s}, \; t_2 = 2 \text{ min} = 120 \text{ s}$

Work done by each crane,

$W = Fs = mgs \quad (\because F = mg)$

$= 2000 \times 9.8 \times 30 = 5.88 \times 10^5$ J

As, both the cranes do same amount of work, so both consume same amount of fuel.

Power supplied by first crane,

$$P_1 = \frac{W}{t_1} = \frac{5.88 \times 10^5}{60} = 9800 \text{ W}$$

Power supplied by second crane,

$$P_2 = \frac{W}{t_2} = \frac{5.88 \times 10^5}{120} = 4900 \text{ W}$$

Energy

It is the ability to do work. An object having a capability to do work is said to possess **energy**. The object which does the work, losses energy and the object on which work is done, gains energy.

It is a scalar quantity.

Energy has the same units as that of work. The SI unit of energy is joule (J) and in CGS system of units, unit of energy is erg.

Other Important Units of Energy

Some other important units of energy are given as follows

(i) **Units of Electrical Energy** Watt hour (Wh) and kilowatt hour (kWh) are the two bigger units of energy.

(a) The energy consumed by a source of power I W in 1 h, is said to be one **Watt hour.**

1 watt hour (Wh) $= 1\text{W} \times 1\text{h}$

$= 1 \text{ Js}^{-1} \times 3600$ s

$= 3600$ J

$= 3.6$ kJ

(b) The energy consumed by a source of power of 1 kW in 1h, is known as one **kilowatt hour.**

1 kilowatt hour (kWh) $= 1\text{kw} \times 1$ h

$= 1000 \text{ Js}^{-1} \times 3600$ s

$= 3.6 \times 10^6$ J

$= 3.6$ MJ

$[\because 1 \text{ MJ} = 10^6 \text{ J}]$

$\therefore$ 1 kilowatt hour (kWh) = 3.6 MJ

Note 1 kWh is also known as the commercial unit, i.e. board of trade unit.

(ii) **Units of Heat Energy** Calorie and kilocalorie are the two units in which the heat energy is measured.

(a) The quantity of energy which is required to raise the temperature of 1 g of water through 1°C, is known as **1 calorie.**

1 calorie = 4.2 J

(b) The quantity of energy which is required to raise the temperature of 1 kilogram of water through 1°C, is known as **1 kilocalorie.**

1 kilocalorie = 4.2 kJ

(iii) **Unit of Nuclear Energy** (electron volt) 1 electron volt is the energy gained by an electron, when it is accelerated through a potential difference of 1 volt.

i.e. $\quad 1 \text{ eV} = 1.6 \times 10^{-19}$ J

and $\quad 1 \text{ MeV} = 1.6 \times 10^{-13}$ J

Mechanical Energy

It is the form of energy, which is possessed by a body due to its state of rest or motion, position and configuration. Mechanical energy is of two types, i.e. kinetic energy and potential energy.

Kinetic Energy

Energy of a body due to its motion is called **kinetic energy**.

Kinetic energy of a body moving with a certain velocity is equal to the work done on it to make it acquire that velocity. Kinetic energy of an object increases with its speed.

e.g. Due to kinetic energy, a bullet fired from a gun can pierce a target. A moving hammer, drives a nail into the wood. Due to its motion, it has kinetic energy or ability to do work.

- **Calculation of Kinetic Energy** The kinetic energy of an object is measured by the amount of work, it can do before coming to rest. Consider an object of mass m moving with a uniform velocity u. A force F is applied on it which displaces it through a distance s and it attains a velocity v.

Then, work done to increase its velocity from u to v.

$$W = Fs \quad \ldots(i)$$

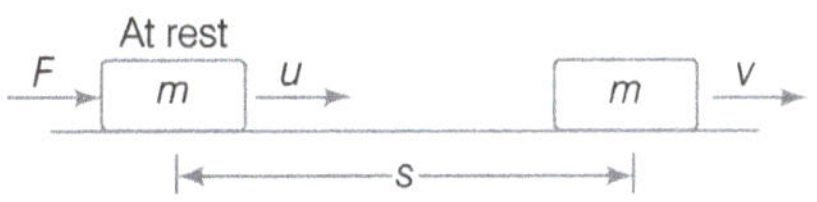

According to the equation of motion,

$$v^2 - u^2 = 2as$$

$$\Rightarrow \quad s = \frac{v^2 - u^2}{2a}$$

where, a is uniform acceleration.

Also, from $F = ma$

Substituting the values of F and s in Eq. (i), we have

$$W = ma \cdot \frac{v^2 - u^2}{2a} \text{ or } W = \frac{1}{2}m(v^2 - u^2)$$

This is known as **work-energy theorem**.

If initial velocity, $u = 0$

Then, $W = \frac{1}{2}mv^2$

It is clear that the work done is equal to the change in the kinetic energy of an object.

Thus, kinetic energy possessed by an object of mass m, moving with a uniform velocity v is

$$\boxed{\text{KE (or } E_K) = \frac{1}{2}mv^2}$$

Some important results can be derived from this formula, which are given below

(i) If the mass of an object is doubled, its kinetic energy also gets doubled.

(ii) If the mass of an object is halved, its kinetic energy also gets halved.

(iii) If the speed of an object is doubled, its kinetic energy becomes four times.

(iv) If the speed of an object is halved, its kinetic energy becomes one-fourth.

(v) Heavy objects moving with high speed have more kinetic energy than small objects moving with less speed.

According to the work-energy theorem, the increase in kinetic energy of a moving body is equal to the work done by a force acting in the direction of the moving body.

Example 6. Determine the kinetic energy of a body of mass 5 kg moving with a velocity 2 ms^{-1}.

Sol. Given, mass of the body, $m = 5$ kg

Velocity of the body, $v = 2\text{ ms}^{-1}$.

Since, kinetic energy is given by,

$$\text{KE} = \frac{1}{2}mv^2$$

$$\therefore \quad = \frac{1}{2} \times 5 \times (2)^2 = \frac{1}{2} \times 5 \times 4 = 10\text{ J}$$

Example 7. A bullet of mass 8 g is fired with a velocity of 80 m/s. Calculate its kinetic energy.

Sol. Given, mass, $m = 8\text{ g} = \frac{8}{1000}$ kg

Velocity, $v = 80$ m/s

$$\text{KE of the bullet} = \frac{1}{2}mv^2 = \frac{1}{2} \times \frac{8}{1000} \times (80)^2$$

$$= \frac{1}{2} \times \frac{8}{1000} \times 80 \times 80 = 25.6\text{ J}$$

Example 8. A van of mass 2000 kg is travelling at 10 ms^{-1}. Calculate its kinetic energy. If its speed increases to 20 ms^{-1}, by how much amount does its kinetic energy increases?

Sol. Given, $m = 2000$ kg, $v_1 = 10\text{ ms}^{-1}$, $v_2 = 20\text{ ms}^{-1}$

Kinetic energy of van at 10 ms^{-1},

$$\text{KE}_1 = \frac{1}{2}mv_1^2 \quad \left(\because \text{KE} = \frac{1}{2}mv^2\right)$$

$$= \frac{1}{2} \times 2000\text{ kg} \times (10\text{ ms}^{-1})^2 = 100000\text{ J} = 100\text{ kJ}$$

Kinetic energy of van at 20 ms^{-1},

$$\text{KE}_2 = \frac{1}{2}mv_2^2 = \frac{1}{2} \times 2000\text{ kg} \times (20\text{ ms}^{-1})^2$$

$$= 400000\text{ J} = 400\text{ kJ}$$

The change in kinetic energy $= KE_2 - KE_1$
$= 400 \text{ kJ} - 100 \text{ kJ} = 300 \text{ kJ}$

So, the kinetic energy of van increases by 300 kJ, when it speeds up from 10 ms^{-1} to 20 ms^{-1}.

Relation between Kinetic Energy (KE) and Momentum (p) of a Body

Kinetic energy (K) and momentum (p) are related as

$$K = \frac{1}{2}mv^2 = \frac{1}{2}(mv)^2\frac{1}{m} = \frac{p^2}{2m} \quad [\because p = mv]$$

$$\boxed{K = \frac{p^2}{2m}}$$

or $\quad p = \sqrt{2mK}$

Case-I If a heavy body of mass m_1 and a light body of mass m_2, both have same momentum, then kinetic energy of heavy body will be less than that of light body.

Since, $\dfrac{K_1}{K_2} = \dfrac{p^2/2m_1}{p^2/2m_2} = \dfrac{m_2}{m_1}$

Since, $m_1 > m_2$

$\therefore \quad \dfrac{K_1}{K_2} < 1 \Rightarrow K_1 < K_2$

Case-II If a heavy body of mass m_1 and light body of mass m_2 both have same kinetic energy, then momentum of heavy body is more than that of light body.

Since, $\dfrac{p_1}{p_2} = \dfrac{\sqrt{2m_1K}}{2m_2K} = \sqrt{\dfrac{m_1}{m_2}}$

Since, $m_1 > m_2$

$\therefore \quad \dfrac{p_1}{p_2} > 1 \Rightarrow p_1 > p_2$

Example 9. A body of mass 50 kg has a momentum of 2000 kg ms^{-1}. Calculate (i) KE of the body (ii) the velocity of the body.

Sol. Given, mass, $m = 50$ kg

Momentum, $p = 2000$ kg-ms^{-1}

(i) $KE = \dfrac{p^2}{2m} = \dfrac{(2000)^2}{2 \times 50} = 40000 \text{ J}$

(ii) Velocity of the body, $v = \dfrac{p}{m} = \dfrac{2000}{50} = 40 \text{ m/s}$

Different Forms of Kinetic Energy

There are three different forms of kinetic energy

(i) **Translational Kinetic Energy** Translational motion is the motion of a body in a straight line path. So, the kinetic energy of the body due to motion in a straight line is known as translational kinetic energy. e.g. A truck moving on a road covering straight path, a freely falling body, etc.

(ii) **Rotational Kinetic Energy** Rotational motion comes into play, when a body rotates about an axis. So, the kinetic energy of body due to rotational motion is known as rotational kinetic energy. e.g. Rotation of earth on its own axis, spinning top, etc.

(iii) **Vibrational Kinetic Energy** Vibrational motion comes into existence, when a body moves to and fro about its mean position. So, the kinetic energy of the body due to its vibrational motion is called vibrational kinetic energy.

e.g. A polyatomic molecule has the vibrational motion in addition to rotational and translational energies.

Check Your LEARNING...

1. How can you define the term 'power'? State its SI unit.
2. What is the necessity of using term 'Average Power' instead of power?
3. Why it is required to use kilowatt hour or board of trade as commercial unit of energy?
4. What amount of energy in kWh is consumed in 10 h by a machine of power 500 W? *Ans.* 5 kWh
5. Compute the speed of 2 kg ball having kinetic energy of 4 J. *Ans.* 2 ms^{-1}
6. Calculate the kinetic energy of a body of mass 0.1 kg and momentum 40 kg ms^{-1}. *Ans.* 8000 J

Potential Energy

The energy possessed by a body due to the change in its position or shape, is called potential energy or we can say that, the potential energy possessed by a body is the energy present in it by virtue of its position or configuration.

e.g. A stretched rubber band, spring, string of the bow, etc. Now, we can say that a body having mass possesses energy, even when it is not in motion.

Examples of potential energy are given below

(i) Water stored in dam has potential energy due to its position at the height.

(ii) A stone lying on the roof of the building has potential energy due to its height.

(iii) A wound spring of a watch has potential energy due to its shape.

Potential Energy of an Object at a Height (Gravitational Potential Energy)

When an object is raised through a certain height above the ground, its energy increases. This is because work is done on it against gravity while it is being raised. The energy present in such an object is the **gravitational potential energy.**

The gravitational potential energy of an object at a point above the ground is defined as the work done in raising it from the ground to that point against gravity.

Expression for (Gravitational) Potential Energy

Consider a body of mass m, lying at a point A on the Earth's surface. Here, its potential energy is zero and its weight mg acts vertically downwards.

To lift the object to another position B at a height h, we have to apply a minimum force which is equal to mg in the upward direction. So, work is done on the body against the force of gravity.

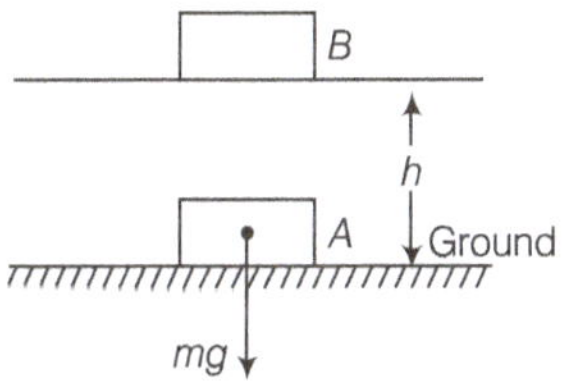

Therefore, work done = force × displacement

$$W = F \times s$$

But, $F = mg$ (weight of the body)

$$s = h,$$

Therefore, $W = mg \times h = mgh$

This work done against gravity is equal to the gain in energy of the body. This is called the gravitational potential energy of the body.

i.e. $\boxed{U \text{ or PE} = mgh}$

The potential energy of an object at a height depends on the ground level or the zero level you choose. An object in a given position can have a certain potential energy with respect to one level and a different value of potential energy with respect to another level.

The work done by gravity depends on the difference in vertical heights of the initial and final positions of the objects and not on the path along which the object is moved.

It is clear from the figure given below.

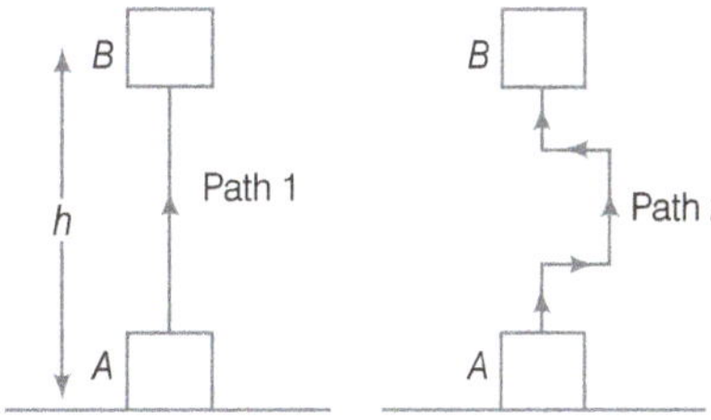

In both the above situations, the work done on the object is mgh.

The another type of potential energy is elastic potential energy which is described below

Elastic Potential Energy

As elasticity is the property by virtue of which a body regains original configuration on the removal of external force. So, elastic potential energy is the energy possessed by the body in the deformed state due to change in its configuration. For example, energy possessed by a compressed or elongated spring is elastic potential energy.

Example 10. Suppose two bodies A and B having equal masses are kept at heights of h and $3\ h$, respectively. Find the ratio of their potential energies.

Sol. Let the mass of each body be m.

$$\text{PE of body} A = mgh$$

$$\text{PE of body } B = mg \times 3h$$

∴ Ratio of potential energies of body A to body B

$$= \frac{mgh}{mg \times 3h} = \frac{1}{3} = 1:3$$

Example 11. A spring is kept compressed by a small trolley of mass 1 kg lying on a smooth horizontal surface as shown in the figure given below:

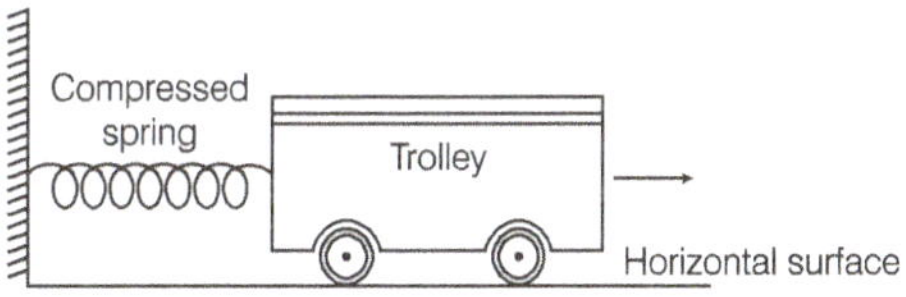

When the trolley is released, it is found to move at a speed of 4 ms^{-1}. What potential energy did the spring possess, when compressed ?

Sol. The potential energy of the spring when compressed

= Kinetic energy of the trolley

$$= \frac{1}{2} \times 1 \times (4)^2$$

$$= \frac{1}{2} \times 4 \times 4 = 8 \text{ J}$$

Various Forms of Energy

There are various forms of energy given below

(i) **Heat Energy** A body possesses heat energy due to the disorderly motion of its molecules. Heat energy is also related to the internal energy of the body. In winter, we generate heat by rubbing our hands against each other.

(ii) **Electrical Energy** Work is said to be done, when electric charge moves from one point to another in an electric field or due to motion of a current carrying conductor inside a magnetic field. This energy is associated with an electric charge, hence called electrical energy. The flow of electric charge causes bulb to glow, motor to run and electric heater to produce heat.

(iii) **Nuclear Energy** When U^{235} nucleus breaks into lighter nuclei on being bombarded by a slow neutron, a tremendous amount of energy is released. Thus, the energy so released is called nuclear energy and this phenomenon is known as nuclear fission. Nuclear reactors and nuclear bombs are the sources of nuclear energy.

(iv) **Light Energy** It is a form of energy due to which we can see the objects around us. We can experience our surroundings, e.g. If we burn a candle, we will notice that this source of heat energy will provide a light energy. The light coming from sun is a natural source of light.

(v) **Sound Energy** It is a form of mechanical energy which causes the sensation of hearing in human or animals. e.g. A vibrating body possesses the sound energy, which is sensed by our ears.

Principle of Conservation of Energy

It states that, the energy can neither be created nor be destroyed but can only be converted from one form to another.

It is one of the fundamental laws and is applied in all the processes taking place in the universe.

Whenever energy in one form disappears, then equivalent amount of energy appears in some other form. Thus, the total energy remains constant.

Conservation of Mechanical Energy in a Freely Falling Body

Consider a body of mass m lying at position A at a height h above the ground. As the body falls, its kinetic energy increases at the expense of potential energy as shown in figure.

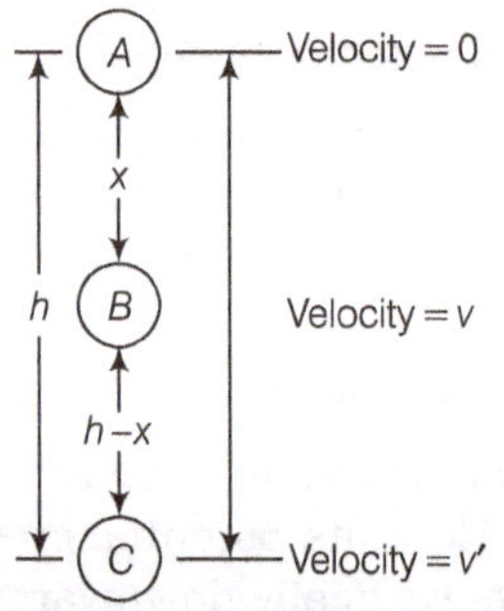

Conservation of energy in a freely falling body

At point A The body is at rest,

KE of the body, $K_A = 0$

PE of the body, $U_A = mgh$

Total mechanical energy, $E_A = K_A + U_A = 0 + mgh$

Mechanical energy at position A, $E_A = mgh$

At point B Suppose the body falls freely through height x and reaches the point B with velocity v. Then,

$$v^2 - 0^2 = 2as \quad \text{(using } v^2 - u^2 = 2as\text{)}$$

$$\Rightarrow \quad v^2 = 2gx$$

$$\therefore \text{ KE, } \quad K_B = \frac{1}{2} m(v')^2 = \frac{1}{2} \times m \times 2gx = mgx$$

$$\text{PE, } \quad U_B = mg(h - x)$$

$$\Rightarrow \quad E_B = K_B + U_B = mgx + mg(h - x) = mgh$$

Mechanical energy at position B, $E_B = mgh$

At point C Suppose the body finally reached at point C on the ground with velocity v'. Then, considering motion from A to C.

$$v'^2 - 0^2 = 2gh \text{ or } v'^2 = 2gh$$

$$K_C = \frac{1}{2} m(v')^2 = \frac{1}{2} \times m \times 2gh = mgh$$

$$U_C = mg \times 0 = 0$$

$$\therefore \quad E_C = U_C + K_C = 0 + mgh = mgh$$

Mechanical energy at position C, $E_C = mgh$

Clearly, as the body falls PE decreases and KE increases by an equal amount. Thus, its total mechanical energy remains constant at all points.

Hence, total mechanical energy is conserved during free fall of the body as shown in figure.

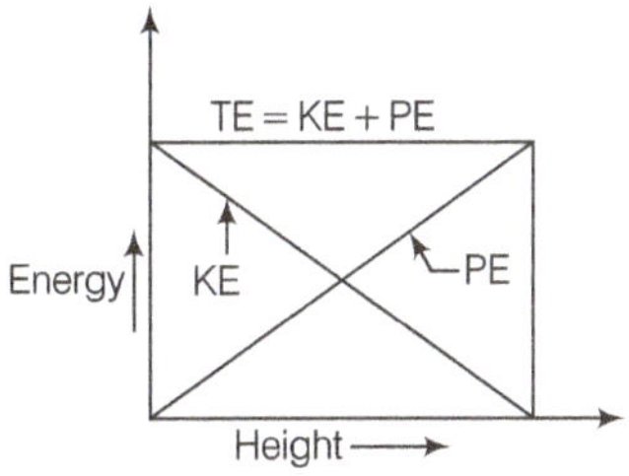

Plot of PE and KE during free fall of a body

Conservation of Mechanical Energy in Simple Pendulum

In an isolated system, the mechanical energy E of the system cannot change which means for isolated system, mechanical energy of the system is conserved.

The oscillatory motion of a simple pendulum is another example of conversion of PE into KE and *vice-versa* and hence conservation of mechanical energy.

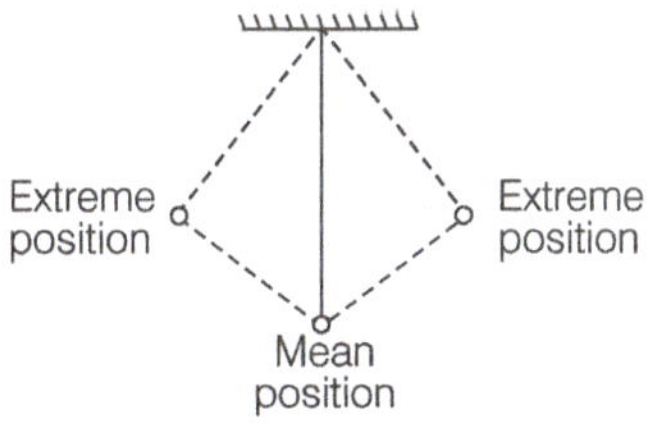

Simple Pendulum

At the mean position, bob of the simple pendulum has maximum KE. The PE at this position is zero.

At the two extreme positions, the bob of the simple pendulum has maximum PE. The KE at these two point is zero.

Example 12. On falling from a height of 20 m, a ball hits the ground. Find out of the velocity with which the ball hits the ground.

Sol. Given, $h = 20$ m, $v = ?$

When the ball hits the ground its kinetic energy is converted into potential energy.

i.e. KE = PE

$$\frac{1}{2}mv^2 = mgh$$

$$\therefore \quad v = \sqrt{2gh} = \sqrt{2 \times 9.8 \times 20}$$

$$= \sqrt{392} = 19.798 \text{ m/s}$$

Example 13. The bob of a pendulum is released from a horizontal position. If the length of the pendulum is 1.5 m, what is the speed with which the bob arrives at the lowermost point?

Sol. On releasing the bob of pendulum from horizontal position, it falls vertically downward by a distance equal to length of pendulum, i.e. $h = l = 1.5$ m.

According to conservation of mechanical energy,

$$\frac{1}{2}mv^2 = mgh$$

$$\Rightarrow \quad v = \sqrt{2 \times gh} = \sqrt{2 \times 9.8 \times 1.5}$$

$$= 5.42 \text{ ms}^{-1}$$

Example 14.

(i) A body of mass 1 kg is allowed to fall freely under gravity. What is the momentum of the body after 5 s?

(ii) What is the height of the freely falling body?

Sol. (i) Given, mass, $m = 1$ kg, $u = 0$, $t = 5$ s, $p = ?$

Velocity of body after 5 s,

$$v = u + at$$

$$= 0 + 10 \times 5 = 50 \text{ m/s}$$

Linear momentum, $p = m \cdot (v) = 1 \times 50 = 50$ kg-m/s

(ii) Kinetic energy of a body

$$= \frac{1}{2}mv^2 = \frac{1}{2} \times 1 \times (50)^2 = 1250 \text{ J}$$

So, for a freely falling body from height h, we get,

$$mgh = \frac{1}{2}mv^2$$

$$\Rightarrow 1 \times 10 \times h = 1250 \Rightarrow h = 125 \text{ m}$$

Example 15. If a body slides on an inclined plane making an angle of 60° from vertical. Find its kinetic energy at the bottom as given in the figure and also find work done (by gravity) on the body.
(Take, initial velocity, $u = 0$, $g = 10 \text{ ms}^{-2}$)

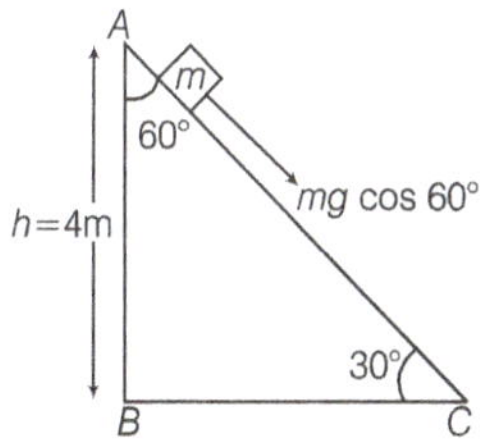

Sol. As, from the figure,

potential energy at the top = mgh

So, according to conservation of energy, kinetic energy at the bottom will be equal to the potential energy at the top.

So, KE at bottom = $mgh = 4mg$

Now, work done, W = force (F) × displacement (s)

$$= mg \cos 60° \times AC$$

$$= mg \times (AC \cos 60°)$$

$$= mg \times (AB) = mg \times (4) = 4mg$$

Transformation of Energy

Energy can be converted from its one form to another. This phenomenon is called transformation of energy. When an object is dropped from a height, its potential energy continuously converts into kinetic energy. When an object is thrown upwards, its kinetic energy continuously converts into potential energy.

e.g.

(i) Green plants prepare their own food (stored in the form of chemical energy) using solar energy through the process of photosynthesis.

(ii) When we throw a ball, the muscular energy which is stored in our body, gets converted into kinetic energy of the ball.

(iii) The wound spring in the toy car possesses potential energy. As the spring is released, its potential energy changes into kinetic energy due to which, toy car moves.

(iv) In a stretched bow, potential energy is stored. As it is released, the potential energy of the stretched bow gets converted into the kinetic energy of arrow which moves in the forward direction with large velocity.

Some Energy Transformations

S.No.	Instrument	Transformation
(i)	Electric motor	Electrical energy into mechanical energy.
(ii)	Electric generator	Mechanical energy into electrical energy.
(iii)	Steam engine	Heat energy into mechanical energy.
(iv)	Electric bulb	Electrical energy into light energy.
(v)	Dry cell	Chemical energy into electrical energy.
(vi)	Solar cell	Solar energy into electrical energy.
(vii)	Atomic bomb	Atomic energy into heat and light energy.

Check Your LEARNING...

1 Does work done by the gravity depends on the path covered by object?

2 If an engine supplies 100 J of energy to a weight of 200 g, how high it can be lifted? *Ans.* 51.02 m

3 How does total energy of the universe remain conserved?

4 How does the total mechanical energy remain constant in a simple pendulum during the oscillations?

5 In dry cell, which type of energy transformation takes place?

QUiCK Revision

- **Work** is said to be done by a force, when a body is displaced through some distance in the direction of the force.
- Work done by a force is the **dot product** of force and displacement.

  $$W = \mathbf{F} \cdot \mathbf{s} = Fs\cos\theta$$

  where θ is the angle between the direction of force (F) and displacement (s).
- Work done is **zero**, if direction of F is **perpendicular to direction of s**.
- Work done is **positive**, if F and s are in the **same direction** and **negative**, if they are in **opposite directions**.
- The capacity to do work is called **energy**.
- The units of work and energy are same. The SI unit of work and energy is **joule** (J).
- The rate at which work is done is called **power**.

  $$\text{Power} = \frac{\text{Work}}{\text{Time}}$$

  The SI unit of power is **watt** (W).
- **Mechanical energy** is the sum of kinetic energy and potential energy.
- The energy possessed by a body by virtue of its motion is called **kinetic energy**.
- The kinetic energy of a body of mass m moving with a velocity v is given by $KE = \frac{1}{2}mv^2$
- The energy possessed by a body due to the change in its position or shape is called its **potential energy**.
- Potential energy possessed by an object of mass m at a height h is given by $PE = mgh$. This is called **gravitational potential energy**.
- Energy can be transformed from one form to another, but the total energy of an isolated system remains constant. Energy can neither be created nor be destroyed. This is called principle of **conservation of energy.**

Chapter Practice

1 Mark Questions

1. Work done on a body depends on
   (a) the magnitude of external force applied on the body only
   (b) the displacement of the body only
   (c) Both the displacement of body and the component of external force acting in the direction of its displacement
   (d) None of the above

Sol. (*c*) The work done on a body is given by

$$W = F \times d$$

So, it depends on both the displacement (d) of the body and the component of force (external) acting in the direction of its displacement.

2. Which of the following statement is incorrect about work?
   (a) Positive work is done by a man lifting a bucket with the help of a rope.
   (b) Work done by friction on a body sliding down an inclined plane is negative.
   (c) Negative work is done by an applied force on a body moving on a rough horizontal plane with uniform velocity.
   (d) Negative work is done by the resistive force of air on a vibrating pendulum in bringing it to rest.

Sol. (*c*) When a force is applied on a body moving on a rough horizontal plane with uniform velocity, then positive work is done on it.

3. When the speed of a moving object is doubled, then its kinetic energy **[2023]**
   (a) remains same (b) decreases
   (c) is doubled (d) becomes four times

Sol. (*d*) Kinetic energy, $K = \frac{1}{2}mv^2$

When speed v becomes double, i.e. $= 2v$,

then $K = \frac{1}{2}m(2v)^2 = 4 \times \frac{1}{2}mv^2 = 4K$

The kinetic energy becomes four times.

4. A coolie raises a load upwards against the force of gravity, then the work done by the load is **[ICSE 2022 Sem-I]**
   (a) zero
   (b) positive work
   (c) negative work
   (d) None of the above

Sol. (*a*) If the displacement of the body is in the direction force the work done is positive.

Hence, work done by coolie rasing a load upwards against gravity is positive.

Whereas work done by the load is zero, as the load itself is not doing any work.

5. 1 J = ... erg **[2021 (Sem-I)]**
   (a) 10^9 (b) 10^7
   (c) 10^5 (d) 10^6

Sol. (*b*) The relation between Joule and erg is

$$1 \text{ J} = 10^7 \text{ erg}$$

6. A man exerts a force of 200 N in pulling a cart at a constant speed of 16 ms^{-1}, the power spent by the man is
   (a) 1600 W (b) 2000 W
   (c) 3200 W (d) 4000 W

Sol. (*c*) Given, force, $F = 200$ N, velocity, $v = 16 \text{ ms}^{-1}$

Power = Force (F) × Velocity (v)

$= 200 \times 16 = 3200$ W

7. Which of the following statement about energy is correct?
   (a) An object having a capability to do work is said to possess energy.
   (b) The object which does the work, loses energy.
   (c) The object on which the work is done, gains energy.
   (d) All of the above

Sol. (*d*) All statements are correct about energy, when an object having a capability to do work is said to possess energy. A body which possesses energy can exert a force on another body. Due to this process, some of the energy is transferred to the another body. So, the object which does the work, loses energy and the object on which the work is done, gains energy.

8. kWh is the unit of
   (a) power (b) force
   (c) energy (d) None of these

Sol. (*c*) Kilowatt hour (kWh) is the unit of electrical energy, used for commercial purpose.

9. One horsepower is equal to **[ICSE Latest Specimen Sem-I]**
   (a) 100 W (b) 735 W (c) 764 W (d) 746 W

Sol. (*d*) 1 hp = 746 W

10. A body at a height possesses
    (a) kinetic energy (b) potential energy
    (c) solar energy (d) heat energy

Sol. (*b*) A body at a height possesses potential energy due to its position above the surface of Earth. It is given by

$$\text{PE} = mgh$$

where, m = mass of body,

g = acceleration due to gravity

and h = height above Earth's surface.

11. The energy conversion in a washing machine is from **[2023]**

(a) magnetic to electrical
(b) electrical to mechanical
(c) electrical to magnetic
(d) magnetic to electrical

Sol. (*b*) In a washing machine, the electrical energy is converted to mechanical energy.

12. A ball of mass m is thrown vertically up with an initial velocity, so as to reach a height h. Which of the following statement(s) is/are correct ?

(a) Potential energy of the ball at the ground is mgh.
(b) Kinetic energy of the ball at the ground is zero.
(c) Kinetic energy of the ball at the highest point is mgh.
(d) Potential energy of the ball at the highest point is mgh.

Sol. (*d*) When a ball is thrown to maximum height of h, its potential energy at highest point, $(\text{PE})_h = mgh$

At this point, its kinetic energy is zero, as velocity becomes zero at highest point.

The potential energy of ball at ground is zero and has maximum kinetic energy equal to potential energy at maximum height, i.e. mgh.

13. A pendulum is oscillating on either side of its rest position. Which of the following statement(s) is/are correct ?

(a) It has only kinetic energy at each position.
(b) It has the maximum kinetic energy at its extreme position.
(c) It has the maximum potential energy at its mean position.
(d) The sum of its kinetic and potential energies remains constant throughout the motion.

Sol. (*d*) When a pendulum is oscillating, about its rest position, then it has maximum kinetic energy at its mean position and maximum potential energy at its extreme position. But the sum of its kinetic and potential energies remains constant throughout the motion.

14. In an electrical cell while in use, the change in energy is from

(a) electrical to mechanical
(b) electrical to chemical
(c) chemical to electrical
(d) chemical to mechanical

Sol. (*c*) In an electrical cell while in use, the chemical energy of electrolytes is converted to an equivalent electrical energy.

15. If A and B of the same mass can climb the third floor of the same building in 3 min and 5 min respectively, then the ratio of their powers of A is to B in an ideal situation is **[ICSE Latest Specimen Sem-I]**

(a) 1:1
(b) 3:5
(c) The information is insufficient to form a conclusion
(d) 5:3

Sol. (*d*) Power $(P) = \dfrac{\text{Energy}}{\text{Time}}$

Both A and B climb the third floor. Therefore energy = mgh

Power $(P) = \dfrac{mgh}{t}$

For A, power $(P_A) = \dfrac{mgh}{3}$ ...(i)

For B, power $(P_B) = \dfrac{mgh}{5}$ ...(ii)

From Eqs. (i) and (ii), we get

$$\frac{P_A}{P_B} = \frac{5}{3}$$

Thus the ratio of their powers of A is to B in ideal situation is 5 : 3.

2 Marks Questions

16. Define work. State its SI unit.

Sol. Work is said to be done, when the force applied on a body displaces it in the direction of force applied on the body. The SI unit of work is joule (J). **[1+1]**

17. Define joule. Give SI unit of work and establish a relationship between the SI and CGS units of work. **[2008]**

Sol. When a force of one newton displaces a body through one metre in its own direction, the work done is said to be 1 joule.

$$1\text{ J} = 1\text{ N} \times 1\text{ m}$$
$$= 10^5 \text{ dyne} \times 100\text{ cm}$$
$$= 10^7 \text{ dyne cm}$$
$$= 10^7 \text{ erg}$$

$\therefore \quad 1\text{ J} = 10^7 \text{ erg}$ **[1]**

This is the required relation between the SI unit and CGS unit of work. **[1]**

18. A man having a box on his head, climbs up a slope and another man having an identical box walks the same distance on a levelled road. Who does more work against the force of gravity and why? **[2014]**

Sol. A man having a box on his head climbs up a slope does more work, because the work done by the man walking on a levelled road is zero, as the angle between displacement and force is 90° and **[1]**

$W = mgs\cos 90° = mgs \times 0 = 0$ **[1]**

19. A man holding bucket of water on his head stands stationary. Is he doing any work? Give reason.

Sol. No, he is not doing any work. It is because, no displacement occurs here.

$\therefore \quad W = F \times s = F \times 0 = 0$ **[1+1]**

20. A satellite revolves around a planet in a circular orbit. What is the work done by the satellite at any instant? Give a reason.

Sol. Force of gravity of the planet provides necessary centripetal force to the satellite to revolve around the planet in circular orbit. When satellite revolves around the planet, then direction of force on the satellite is always perpendicular to its velocity or displacement, hence work done by the satellite at any instant is zero. [2]

21. Is it possible that an object is in the state of accelerated motion due to external force acting on it, but no work is being done by the force? Explain it with an example.

Sol. Yes, when force acts in a direction perpendicular to the direction of displacement.

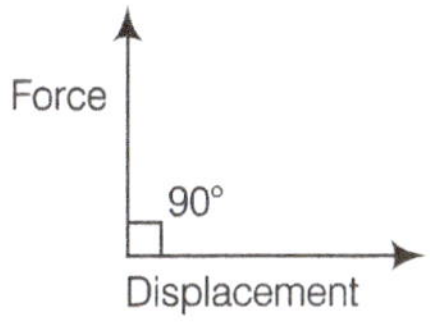

e.g. Earth revolves around the Sun under gravitational force of Sun on Earth, but no work is done by the Sun, though Earth has centripetal acceleration.

22. (i) What should be the angle between the direction of force and the direction of displacement, for work to be negative?
(ii) Name the physical quantity obtained using the formula $\frac{U}{h}$, where U is the potential energy and h is the height. [2023]

Sol. (i) Refer to theory [Page 21]. [1]
(ii) The physical quantity obtained using $\frac{U}{h}$ is force ,

$F = \frac{U}{h}$. [1]

23. Crane A lifts a heavy load in 5 s, whereas another crane B does the same work in 2 s. Compare the power of crane A to that of crane B.

Sol. Time taken to lift load by crane A, $t_1 = 5$ s

Time taken to same work by crane B, $t_2 = 2$ s

$$\therefore \frac{\text{Power of crane } A}{\text{Power of crane } B} = \frac{W_1 / t_1}{W_2 / t_2}$$

$$\frac{P_A}{P_B} = \frac{t_2}{t_1}$$

$$\Rightarrow \frac{P_A}{P_B} = \frac{2}{5} \quad (\because W_1 = W_2)$$

$$\Rightarrow P_A = \frac{2}{5} P_B$$

Thus, power of crane A is two-fifth of crane B.

24. Define a kilowatt hour. How is it related to joule?

Sol. Refer to theory (Page 22).

25. An object of mass m is moving with a constant velocity v. How much work should be done on the object in order to bring the object to rest?

Sol. Change in kinetic energy (KE) = Work done (W).

Given, mass = m, initial velocity, $u = v$

Final velocity, $v = 0$

So, $$W = \frac{1}{2}mv^2 - \frac{1}{2}mu^2$$

$$\Rightarrow W = \frac{1}{2}m(0)^2 - \frac{1}{2}mv^2$$

$$\Rightarrow W = -\frac{1}{2}mv^2$$ [1]

Hence, the work that should be done in order to bring the object to rest is $\frac{1}{2}mv^2$. [1]

26. If the speed of a particle is doubled, what will be the ratio of its new kinetic energy to its new momentum?

Sol. Inititial kinetic energy of particles of mass m moving with velocity v is

$$\text{KE} = \frac{1}{2}mv^2$$

New kinetic energy, $\text{KE}' = \frac{1}{2}m(v')^2 \quad (\because v' = 2v)$

$$= \frac{1}{2}m(2v)^2 = 4\,\text{KE}$$ [1]

and new momentum, $p' = mv'$

$= m(2v) = 2p$

(where, $p = mv$ (initial momentum)

$$\therefore \frac{\text{KE}'}{p'} = \frac{4\,\text{KE}}{2p} = 2 \times \left(\frac{\text{KE}}{p}\right)$$

Hence, ratio gets doubled. [1]

27. Two bodies of masses m_1 and m_2 have equal kinetic energies. What will be the ratio of their linear momentum?

Sol. Given, $K_1 = K_2$

$$\Rightarrow \frac{1}{2}m_1v_1^2 = \frac{1}{2}m_2v_2^2 \Rightarrow \frac{v_1}{v_2} = \sqrt{\frac{m_2}{m_1}}$$

$$\therefore \frac{m_1v_1}{m_2v_2} = \frac{m_1}{m_2}\sqrt{\frac{m_2}{m_1}} \Rightarrow \frac{p_1}{p_2} = \sqrt{\frac{m_1}{m_2}}$$ [2]

28. (i) What is the work done on a body performing uniform circular motion?
(ii) Name the unit of physical quantity obtained by the formula $\frac{2K}{v^2}$, where K is kinetic energy and v is linear velocity. [2018]

Sol. (i) Zero, because centripetal force always acts perpendicular to the displacement of the body. [1]
(ii) We know that,

kinetic energy $(K) = \frac{1}{2}mv^2$ ...(i)

Given, physical quantity $= \frac{2K}{v^2}$

From Eq. (i), we get

$$= \frac{2}{v^2} \times \left(\frac{1}{2}mv^2\right) = m \text{ (mass)}$$

Hence, the unit of physical quantity or mass is kg. [1]

29. (i) Is it possible a body possesses energy without having momentum?
(ii) Is it possible a body possesses momentum without having energy?

Sol. (i) Yes it is possible, it is because a body at rest can possesses the potential energy or energy stored due to position or shape as elastic potential energy, even when there is zero momentum. **[1]**
(ii) No, it is not possible, if a body possesses some momentum, then it must be in motion and so, it must have some kinetic energy. **[1]**

30. Define potential energy. Write an expression for potential energy. Write the SI unit of potential energy.

Sol. The energy possessed by a body due to its configuration is known as potential energy.
The potential energy of a body is given by

$$\text{PE} = mgh$$

The SI unit of potential energy is joule (J).

31. Derive an expression for the gravitational potential energy.

Sol. Let us consider that, m = mass of the object, h = height at which object is placed and F = force required to lift the object against the force of gravity.
Therefore, $F = mg$
Now, work done on lifting the object to height h is **[1]**

$$W = \text{Force} \times \text{Displacement}$$
$$= mg \times h = mgh$$

This work done on the body is stored in it in the form of gravitational potential energy, i.e. U.

$\therefore$ $U = mgh$ **[1]**

32. (i) What is meant by potential energy of a body?
(ii) A body of mass m is raised to a vertical height h through two different paths A and B.

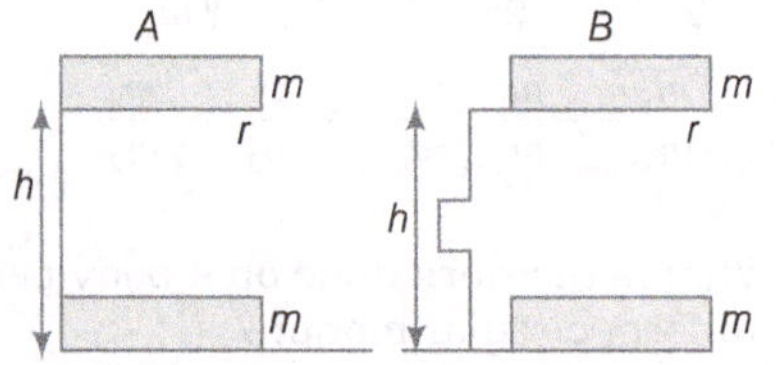

What will be the potential energy of the body in the two cases? Give reason for your answer.

Sol. (i) Energy possessed due to the position of a body is called potential energy. **[1]**
(ii) The work done against gravity in both the cases is mgh. It is independent of the path along which the body is moved and depends only on the initial and final positions of the body. **[1]**

33. A ball is placed on a compressed spring. When the spring is released, the ball is observed to fly away.
(i) What form of energy does the compressed spring possess?
(ii) Why does the ball fly away? **[2012]**

Sol. (i) The compressed spring possesses elastic potential energy. **[1]**
(ii) The ball flies away, because potential energy is converted into kinetic energy and it is also transferred to the ball. **[1]**

34. Write the statement of law of conservation of mechanical energy.

Sol. Refer to theory (Page 26).

35. Mention any two examples in which the mechanical energy of the system remains constant?

Sol. (i) Mechanical energy of the oscillating body of simple pendulum remains constant. **[1]**
(ii) Mechanical energy of a freely falling body remains constant. **[1]**

36. At the bottom of the waterfall, water is warmer than at the top. Give reason.

Sol. When water falls on the ground, its mechanical energy (KE + PE) is converted into heat energy, due to which the temperature of water at the bottom of the waterfall increases. **[2]**

37. The moment, an arrow is shoot from its bow, it has some kinetic energy. From where does it get the kinetic energy?

Sol. On the account of a change in the shape of stretched bow, it possesses potential energy. In order to shoot an arrow, the bow is released. So, the potential energy of the bow changes into kinetic energy. **[2]**

38. What is meant by transformation of energy? Explain with the help of two suitable examples.

Sol. Refer to theory (Page 28).

39. State the energy changes in the following cases while in use
(i) An electric iron. (ii) A ceiling fan. **[2018]**

Sol. (i) An electric iron converts electrical energy into heat energy. **[1]**
(ii) A ceiling fan converts electrical energy into mechanical energy. **[1]**

40. Give one example of each, when
(i) chemical energy changes into electrical energy.
(ii) electrical energy changes into sound energy.

Sol. (i) Dry cell **[1]**
(ii) Loudspeaker **[1]**

3 Marks Questions

41. (i) Derive a relationship between SI and CGS unit of work.
(ii) A force acts on a body and displaces it by a distance s in a direction at an angle θ with the direction of force. What should be the value of θ to get the maximum positive work? **[2018]**

Sol. (i) The SI unit of work is joule

$$1\text{J} = 1\text{N} \times 1\text{m} = 10^5 \text{ dyne} \times 100 \text{ cm}$$
$$= 10^7 \text{ dyne cm} = 10^7 \text{ erg}$$ **[1½]**

(ii) For maximum work done, the angle should be 0°.
i.e. $W_{max} = \mathbf{F} \cdot \mathbf{s} = |F|\,|s| \cos 0° = Fs$ $(\because \cos 0° = 1)$ **[1½]**

42. What is the amount of work done in the following cases? Justify your answer by giving the appropriate reason.

(i) By an electron revolving in a circular orbit of radius r around a nucleus.

(ii) By the force of gravity, when a stone of mass m is dropped from the top of a multi-storeyed building of height h. **[3]**

Sol. (i) Work done is zero as shown in the figure. When electron revolves around the nucleus, a centripetal force F acts along the radius towards the centre O. The displacement s acts tangentially, therefore the angle between the force and the displacement is 90°. Therefore,

$$W = Fs\cos 90° = 0 \quad (\because \cos 90° = 0)$$

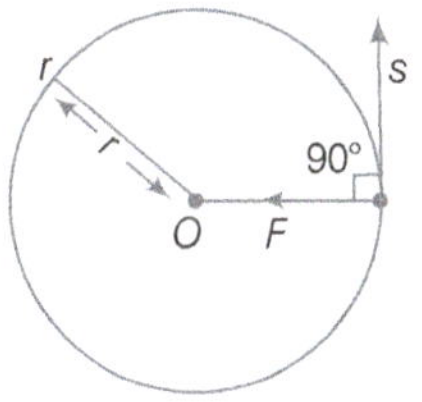

[1½]

(ii) We know that, $W = mgh$

As, the stone is dropped, its PE starts to convert into KE.

Let its speed be v, then from $v^2 = 2gh$

(When stone reaches the ground)

$$\Rightarrow \quad KE = \frac{1}{2}mv^2$$

$$= \frac{1}{2} \times m \times 2gh = mgh$$

$$\Rightarrow \quad W = mgh$$ **[1½]**

43. When a body of mass m moves with a uniform velocity, a force is applied on the body due to which its velocity changes. State, how much work is being done by the force?

Sol. Let us suppose that force acts on the body through a distances, which changes its velocity from u to v.

Let the force acts for a time t.

$\therefore$ Work done by the force $= F \times s$

$$= ma \times s \quad (\because F = ma)$$

$$= m\left(\frac{v-u}{t}\right) \times s$$ **[1½]**

Since, $\frac{s}{t}$ = average velocity $= \frac{u+v}{2}$

Therefore, work done by the force

$$= \frac{m(v-u)(u+v)}{2} = \frac{1}{2}m(v^2 - u^2)$$

$$W = \frac{1}{2}m(v^2 - u^2)$$ **[1½]**

= Change in kinetic energy

It is also called work-energy theorem.

44. Differentiate between the potential energy (U) and the kinetic energy (K).

Sol.

Potential Energy	Kinetic Energy
The energy possessed by a body by virtue of its state of position is known as potential energy.	It is the energy possessed by a body by the virtue of state of motion.
Potential energy of a body is equal to the work done on the body to lift it to a height h.	Kinetic energy of a body is equal to the amount of work done by the body before it comes to rest.
A body possess this energy, even when it is not in motion.	Kinetic energy of the body increases by increasing the motion of the body.

[1 × 3]

45. A car is moving on a levelled road and gets its velocity doubled. In this process,

(i) how would the potential energy of the car change ?

(ii) how would the kinetic energy of the car change ?

(iii) how will its momentum change ? Give reasons for your answer.

Sol. (i) The potential energy of the car remains same, since PE (= mgh) is independent of velocity.

(ii) The kinetic energy of the car becomes four times, since KE$\left(= \frac{1}{2}mv^2\right)$ is proportional to square of velocity.

(iii) The momentum of the car will also get doubled, since momentum ($p = mv$) is proportional to velocity. **[1+1+1]**

46. A girl sits and stands repeatedly for 6 min. Draw a graph to show the variation of potential energy of her body with time.

Sol. The path can be traced as shown below

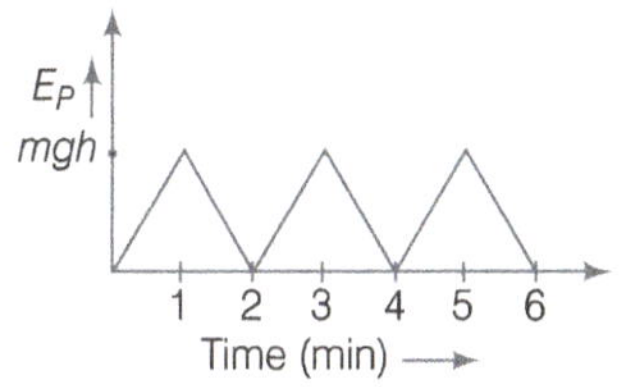

[1]

From the graph shown above, we can take the sitting position of the girl as the position of zero potential energy. Let m be the mass of the girl and h be the position of centre of gravity while standing above the sitting position. **[1]**

The PE while standing is + mgh and while sitting is zero. We can assume that there is no acceleration or deceleration while standing and sitting, this is repeated after every minute. **[1]**

47. The potential energy of a freely falling object decreases progressively.

Does this violate law of conservation of energy? If no/yes, then why?

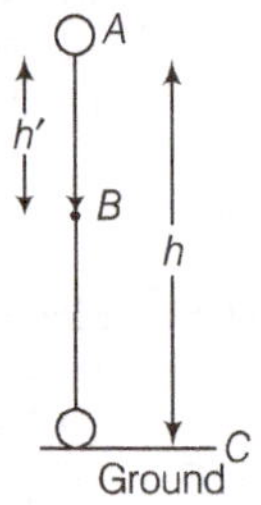

Sol. It is true that the potential energy of freely falling object decreases progressively. But as the object falls down, its speed increases, i.e. the kinetic energy of the object increases progressively (kinetic energy will increase with the increase in speed) and the potential energy of falling object decreases progressively due to decrease in its height. [2]

Thus, we can say that the law of conservation of energy is not violated, because the decrease in potential energy results in the increase of kinetic energy. [1]

48. If a body falls from a height bounces from ground and again goes upwards with loss of a part of its energy.

(i) How will its potential energy change?

(ii) What are the various energy conversions taking place?

(iii) What will be its ultimate energy?

Sol. (i) When it strikes ground, its PE is zero and after bouncing, its potential energy increases gradually. [1]

(ii) At the time it strikes the ground, it has maximum KE and after its bouncing, its KE starts changing into potential energy. [1]

(iii) The ultimate or total energy remains constant at each instant of time during the motion. [1]

49. Write transformation of energy in

(i) solar cell (ii) electric iron

(iii) induction cooker

Sol. (i) Solar energy to electrical energy [1]

(ii) Electrical energy to heat energy [1]

(iii) Electrical energy to heat energy [1]

50. A battery lights a bulb. Describe the energy changes involved in the process.

Sol. A battery contains chemical energy and supplies electrical energy. So, a battery converts chemical energy into electrical energy. In an electric bulb, the electrical energy is first converted into heat energy. This heat energy causes the filament of bulb to become white-hot and produces light energy. [2]

Thus, the energy changes are

Chemical energy ⇒ Electrical energy ⇒ Heat energy ⇒ Light energy [1]

4 Marks Questions

51. Given below are a few situations, study them and state in which of the given cases work is said to be done. Give reason for your answer.

(i) A person pushing a hard huge rock but the rock does not move.

(ii) A bullock pulling a cart up to 1 km on road.

(iii) A girl pulling a trolley for about 2 m distance.

(iv) A person standing with a heavy bag on his head.

Sol. (i) As the displacement is zero in this case, so work done = zero. [1]

(ii) The work done in pulling a cart by the bullock will be positive. As, F and s are in same direction. [1]

(iii) Work done in case of pulling a trolley by the girl will be positive. As, force and displacement are in same direction. [1]

(iv) As there is no displacement, so work done by a person standing with a heavy bag on his head is zero. [1]

52. Explain how do the work is related to direction of force and displacement ?

Sol. When the displacement of the body is not in the direction of the force, then to calculate the amount of work done, we should find the component of the displacement in the direction of force. e.g.

Let us assume that the force F is acting along CD and it displaces the point of application of force from C to E, such that the displacement $CE(= d)$ is at an angle θ to the direction of force. [1]

The component of the displacement in the direction of force is CD.

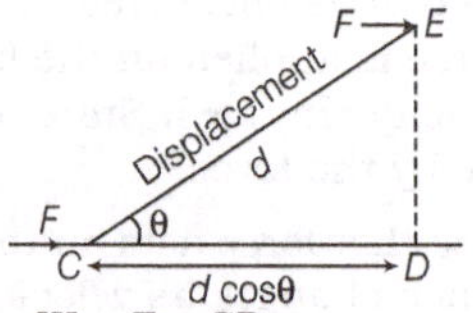

∴ Work done, $W = F \times CD$ ...(i)

In right angled ΔCDE, [2]

$$\cos\theta = \frac{CD}{CE} = \frac{CD}{d}$$

$$\Rightarrow \quad CD = d\cos\theta$$

Substituting this value in Eq. (i), we get

$$W = F \times d\cos\theta$$

which is a required relationship between work, force and the displacement. [1]

53. If a body of mass m is moving with velocity v, then derive an expression for its kinetic energy.

Sol. Consider a body of mass m is moving with velocity v. It is brought to rest by applying an opposing force F. Let it travels a distance s before coming to rest and a be the uniform retardation produced by the force. [1]

Kinetic energy of the body = Work done by the retarding force to stop it.

Kinetic energy = force × displacement ...(i)

Retarding force, $F = ma$ ...(ii)

Initial velocity, $u = v$, final velocity, $v = 0$ [1]

From the relation, $v^2 = u^2 + 2as$

$$0 = v^2 - 2as$$

$\therefore$ Displacement, $s = \dfrac{v^2}{2a}$ ...(iii) [1]

Put the values of F and s from Eqs. (ii) and (iii) in Eq. (i), we get

Kinetic energy, $K = F \times s = ma \times \dfrac{v^2}{2a} = \dfrac{1}{2}mv^2$

$\therefore$ Kinetic energy $= \dfrac{1}{2} \times$ mass $\times$ (velocity)^2 [1]

54. Two protons are brought towards each other. Will the potential energy of the system decrease or increase? What happens, if a proton and an electron are brought nearer?

Sol. The potential energy will increase, because in bringing two protons closer, work has to be done against the force of repulsion. This work done gets stored up in the form of potential energy.

However, the potential energy will decrease, when a proton and an electron are brought nearer to each other.

The work will be done by the force of attraction between them. [2 + 2]

55. Illustrate the law of conservation of energy by discussing the energy changes which occur, when we draw a pendulum bob to one side and allow it to oscillate. Why does the bob eventually come to rest? What happens to its energy eventually? Is it a violation of the law of conservation of energy?

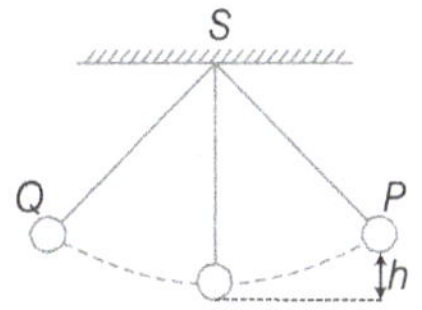

Sol. Let a simple pendulum be suspended from a rigid support S and OS be the equilibrium position of the pendulum. Let the pendulum be displaced to a position P, where it is at rest. At position P, the pendulum has potential energy (mgh). When the pendulum is released from position P, it begins to move towards position O.

The speed of the pendulum increases and its height decreases that means the potential energy is converting into kinetic energy. [1]

At position O, whole of the potential energy of the pendulum is converted into its kinetic energy.

Then, the pendulum swings to other side due to inertia of motion.

As, the pendulum begins to move towards position Q, the speed of pendulum decreases and height increases that means kinetic energy is converting into potential energy. At point Q, whole of the kinetic energy is converted into potential energy. [1]

Thus, we find that the potential energy is converted into kinetic energy and *vice-versa* during the motion of the pendulum. But the total energy remains constant.

When the pendulum oscillates in air, the air friction opposes its motion.

So, some part of kinetic energy of pendulum is used to overcome this friction. [1]

With the passage of time, energy of the pendulum goes on decreasing and finally becomes zero.

The energy of the pendulum is transferred to the atmosphere. So, energy is being transferred, i.e. is converted from one form to another. So, no violation of law of conservation of energy takes place. [1]

56. State the energy changes in each of the following cases given below

(i) Explosion of crackers
(ii) Burning of match stick
(iii) Respiration
(iv) Charging of a battery

Sol. (i) Chemical energy into heat, light and sound energy.
(ii) Chemical energy into light and heat energy.
(iii) Chemical energy into mechanical energy.
(iv) Electrical energy into chemical energy. [1 × 4]

Numerical Based Questions

57. If a force of 10 kg weight is applied on a body and the body gets displaced by 0.5 m. Determine the work done by the force, when the displacement

(i) is in the direction of force.
(ii) at an angle of 60° with the force.
(iii) normal to the force (Take, $g = 10$ Nkg^{-1}). [3]

Sol. Given, force $F = 10$ kg-wt $= 10 \times g = 10 \times 10 = 100$ N.

Displacement, $s = 0.5$ m.

(i) When displacement is in the direction of force, $\theta = 0°$

$\Rightarrow W = Fs \cos 0°$ ($\because \cos 0° = 1$)
$= 100 \times 0.5 = 50$ J [1]

(ii) When displacement is at an angle of 60°,

$\Rightarrow W = Fs \cos 60°$
$= 100 \times 0.5 \times \dfrac{1}{2}$ $\left(\because \cos 60° = \dfrac{1}{2}\right)$
$= 25$ J [1]

(iii) When displacement is normal to the direction of force,

$\Rightarrow W = Fs \cos 90°$
$= 100 \times 0.5 \times 0$ ($\because \cos 90° = 0$)
$= 0$ [1]

58. When a 20 N force acts in two different ways to displace a trolley in the same displacement. Find the ratio of the work done as determined in both the cases. [2]

Sol. In case (i), work done, $W_1 = 20 \times d \cos 0° = 20d$ [1/2]

In case (ii), work done, $W_2 = 20 \times d \cos 60°$

$= 20d \times \frac{1}{2} = 10d$ [1/2]

$\therefore$ The required ratio, $\frac{W_1}{W_2} = \frac{20d}{10d}$

$\Rightarrow \frac{W_1}{W_2} = 2$ [1]

59. A child pulls a toy car through a distance of 20 m on smooth and horizontal floor. The string held in child's hand makes an angle of 60° with horizontal surface. If the force applied by the child be 10N, calculate the work done by the child in pulling the car. [3]

Sol. We know that, work done, when a body moves at an angle to the direction of force is

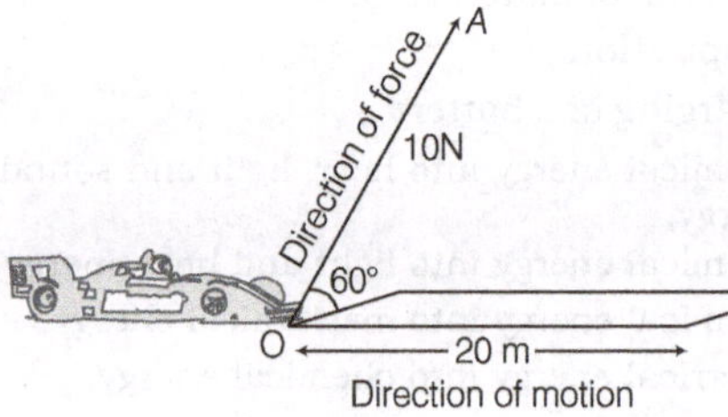

[1]

$W = Fs\cos\theta$ [1]

Here, force, $F = 10$ N

Angle, $\theta = 60°$

and distance, $s = 20$ m

So, on putting values in above formula, we get

Work done, $W = 10 \times 20 \times \cos 60°$

So, $W = 10 \times 20 \times 0.5 = 100$ J [1]

60. An electric motor of power 100 W is used to drive the stirrer in a water bath. If 50% of the energy supplied to the motor is spent in stirring the water, calculate the work done on water in one minute. [2]

Sol. Given, power, $P = 100$ W

Time, $t = 1$ min $= 60$ s

Power used = 50% of power spent

$= \frac{50}{100} \times 100 = 50$ W [1]

Work done on water = Power used × Time

$= 50 \times 60 = 3000$ J [1]

61. Determine the power of the motor in terms of HP of an elevator, which can carry 10 persons of average mass 60 kg through a vertical height of 20 m in 30s [3]

Sol. Given, mass = 60 kg, time = 30 s , h = 20 m

Mass to be lifted $= 10 \times 60 = 600$ kg

Power, $P = \frac{mgh}{t}$ [1]

$= \frac{600 \times 10 \times 20}{30} = \frac{120000}{30}$

$\Rightarrow P = 4000$ W [1]

$= \frac{4000}{746} = 5.36$ HP

($\because$ 1 HP = 746 W) [1]

62. A girl of mass 40 kg runs up stairs and reaches the 8 m high first floor in 5 s. Determine

(i) the force of gravity acting on the body.

(ii) the work done by her against the gravity.

(iii) the power spent by the girl. [3]

Sol. Given, $m = 40$ kg, $h = 8$ m,

$t = 5$ s, $g = 10$ ms^{-2}

(i) Let the force of gravity on the girl be F.

$\therefore F = mg = 40 \times 10 = 400$ N [1]

(ii) Work done by the girl against the gravity,

$W = mgh$

$= 40 \times 10 \times 8 = 3200$ J [1]

(iii) Power spent, $P = \frac{W}{t} = \frac{3200}{5} = 640$ Js^{-1}

$= 640$ W [1]

63. Determine the horse power of an engine, which lifts 4000 m^3 of water from a depth of 50 m in 40 min. [3]

Sol. Mass of water, $m = V \times \rho = 4000 \times 10^3$

$= 4 \times 10^6$ kg

($\because$ density of water, $\rho = 10^3$ kg/m^3) [1]

Time, $t = 40$ min $= 40 \times 60 = 2400$ s

Work done in lifting water $= mgh$

$= 4 \times 10^6 \times 10 \times 50$

$= 2 \times 10^9$ J [1]

Power of engine $= \frac{W}{t} = \frac{2 \times 10^9}{2400} = \frac{10^9}{1200}$ W

$\therefore$ Power in horse power $= \frac{1 \times 10^9}{1200 \times 746}$

[Since, 1 Hp =746 watt]

$= 1117.1$ HP [1]

64. A boy weighing 40 kgf climbs up a stair of 30 steps, each 20 cm high in 4 min and a girl weighing 30 kgf does the same in 3 min. Compare

(i) the work done by them and

(ii) the power developed by them. [3]

Sol. (i) Both of them climbs up the same number of stairs, so work done by them will be equal. [1]

(ii) Power developed by the girl is more, because

power of boy $= \frac{mgh}{t} = \frac{40 \times 10 \times 30 \times 20}{4 \times 100 \times 60} = 10$ W

power of girl $= \frac{30 \times 10 \times 30 \times 20}{3 \times 60 \times 100} = 10$ W

Power developed is same but girl takes lesser time. [2]

65. A pump is used to lift 500 kg of water from a depth of 80 m in 10 s. Calculate

(i) the work done by the pump,

(ii) the power at which the pump works and

(iii) the power rating of the pump, if its efficiency is 40%. (Take, $g = 10\ ms^{-2}$) **[3]**

Sol. Given, $m = 500$ kg, $s = 80$ m, $t = 10$ s

Force, $F = m \times g$

$= 500 \times 10 = 5000$ N

(i) Work done, $W = F \times s$

$= 5000 \times 80$ **[1]**

$= 4 \times 10^5$ J

(ii) Power, $P = \frac{\text{Work } (W)}{\text{Time } (t)} = \frac{4 \times 10^5}{10}$

$= 4 \times 10^4$ W **[1]**

$= 40$ kW

(iii) Power rating $= \frac{\text{Power}}{\text{Efficiency}} = \frac{40 \times 10^3}{0.4}$ **[1]**

$= 100$ kW

66. Calculate the power spent by a crane while lifting a load of mass 2000 kg. at velocity of 1.5 ms^{-1}. (Take, $g = 10\ ms^{-2}$) **[2023] [2]**

Sol. Power, P = Force × Velocity

$P = F \cdot v$

$= m \cdot a \cdot v$ **[1]**

$= 2000 \times 10 \times 1.5$

$= 30000$ W

Therefore, the power spent by crane is 30000 W. **[1]**

67. In an experiment to measure his power, a student records the time taken by him in running up a flight of steps on a staircase.
Use the following data to calculate the power of the student.
(Take, number of steps = 28, height of each step = 20 cm, time taken = 5.4 s, mass of student = 55 kg and acceleration due to gravity = 9.8 ms^{-2}) **[2]**

Sol. Given, $n = 28$, $h = 20$ cm = 0.2 m, t = 5.4 s

$m = 55$ kg, $g = 9.8\ ms^{-2}$

We know that, the power of student is given by

$P = n \times \frac{W}{t} = n \times \frac{mgh}{t}$ $(\because W = mgh)$

$= \frac{28 \times 55 \times 9.8 \times 0.2}{5.4}$

$= 559$ W

68. A boy X can run with a speed of 8 ms^{-1} against the frictional force of 10 N and another boy Y can run with a speed of 3 ms^{-1} against the frictional force of 20 N. Find the ratio of powers of X and Y. **[2]**

Sol. Given, distance travelled by the boy X in 1s = 8 m

Distance travelled by the boy Y in 1s = 3 m

As, we know, work done by the boy X to run against the frictional force of 10 N = 10 N× 8 m= 80 J

So, power of 80 J of work done by $X = \frac{W}{t} = \frac{80\text{ J}}{1\text{ s}}$

$= 80$ W **[1]**

Similarly, work done by the boy Y to run against the frictional force of 20 N = 20 N× 3 m= 60J

Power of $Y = \frac{60\text{ J}}{1\text{ s}} = 60$ W

So, ratio of two values of powers is given by

$\frac{\text{Power of } X}{\text{Power of } Y} = \frac{80}{60} = \frac{4}{3} = 4 : 3$ **[1]**

69. Two bodies A and B have masses in the ratio 5:1 and their kinetic energies are in the ratio 125:9. Find the ratio of their velocities. **[2] [2019]**

Sol. Let mass of body A is m_A and mass of body B is m_B.

Given, $\frac{m_A}{m_B} = \frac{5}{1}$ ...(i)

and $\frac{(KE)_A}{(KE)_B} = \frac{125}{9}$ ...(ii)

We know that, kinetic energy,

$KE = \frac{1}{2} mv^2$

$\therefore \frac{(KE)_A}{(KE)_B} = \frac{\frac{1}{2} m_A v_A^2}{\frac{1}{2} m_B v_B^2}$

From Eqs. (i) and (ii), we get

$\Rightarrow \frac{125}{9} = \frac{5}{1}\left(\frac{v_A}{v_B}\right)^2$

$\Rightarrow \frac{25}{9} = \left(\frac{v_A}{v_B}\right)^2$

$\Rightarrow \frac{v_A}{v_B} = \frac{5}{3}$

Hence, ratio of their velocities is 5 : 3.

70. A force is applied on a body of mass 20 kg moving with a velocity of 40 ms^{-1}. The body attains a velocity of 50 ms^{-1} in 2 s . Determine the work done by the body. **[2] [2013]**

Sol. Given, $m = 20$ kg, $u = 40\ ms^{-1}$, $v = 50\ ms^{-1}$, $t = 2$ s

We know that change in kinetic energy is equal to work done on the body.

Work done $= \frac{1}{2} mv^2 - \frac{1}{2} mu^2$ **[1]**

$= \frac{1}{2} \times 20 \times (50)^2 - \frac{1}{2} \times 20 \times (40)^2$

$= \frac{1}{2} \times 20 \times 2500 - \frac{1}{2} \times 20 \times 1600 = 25000 - 16000$

$\Rightarrow W = 9 \times 10^3$J **[1]**

71. Calculate the work required to be done to stop a car of 1500 kg moving at a velocity to 60 kmh^{-1}. **[2]**

Sol. Change in kinetic energy is equal to the work done W.

Given, initial velocity, $u = 60\ kmh^{-1}$

$= 60 \times \frac{5}{18} = \frac{50}{3}\ ms^{-1}$

$[\because 1\ kmh^{-1} = (5/18)\ ms^{-1}]$

Final velocity, $v = 0$

So, magnitude of change in kinetic energy [1]

$$= \frac{1}{2}mv^2 - \frac{1}{2}mu^2 = W$$

$$\Rightarrow \quad W = \frac{1}{2}m(v^2 - u^2)$$

$$= \frac{1}{2} \times 1500 \times \left(\frac{-50 \times 50}{9}\right)$$

$$= -\frac{1}{2} \times \frac{1500 \times 50 \times 50}{9}$$

$$W = -\frac{625000}{3} = -208333.3 \text{ J}$$ [1]

Hence, the work required to be done to stop a car is 208333.3 J.

72. 6.4 kJ of energy causes a displacement of 64 m in a body in the direction of force in 2.5 s. Calculate
(i) the force applied and
(ii) power in Horse Power (HP). (Take, 1 HP = 746 W) [2] [2009]

Sol. Given, energy, $E = 6.4$ kJ $= 6400$ J, time, $t = 2.5$ s

Displacement, $s = 64$ m, force, $F = ?$,
Power in HP = ?

(i) Energy = Work done = Fs

$$\therefore \quad E = Fs$$

$$\therefore \quad F = \frac{E}{s}$$

$$\Rightarrow \quad F = \frac{6400}{64} = 100 \text{ N}$$ [1]

(ii) Power, $P = \frac{E}{t} = \frac{6400}{2.5} = 2560$ W

$$= \frac{2560}{746} = 3.43 \text{ HP} \quad (\because 1\text{HP} = 746 \text{ W})$$ [1]

73. A child drops a stone of 1 kg from the top of a tower. Find its kinetic energy, 5 s after it starts falling. (Take, $g = 10$ ms^{-2}) [2]

Sol. Given, mass of stone, $m = 1$ kg

Initial velocity, $u = 0$, time, $t = 5$ s

Acceleration due to gravity, $g = 10$ ms^{-2}

As from equation of motion,

$$v = u + gt \quad \text{(for downward motion)}$$

$$\Rightarrow \quad v = 0 + 10 \times 5$$

$$\Rightarrow \quad v = 50 \text{ ms}^{-1}$$ [1]

$\therefore$ Kinetic energy of the stone is given by

$$\text{KE} = \frac{1}{2}mv^2 = \frac{1}{2} \times 1 \times (50)^2 = 1250 \text{ J}$$ [1]

74. A mass of 20 kg is dropped from a height of 0.5 m. Find its
(i) velocity and
(ii) KE, as it just reaches the ground. [2]

Sol. Given, height, $h = 0.5$ m, mass, $m = 20$ kg

(i) $\therefore v^2 = 2gh = 2 \times 10 \times 0.5 = 10 \quad (\because g = 10 \text{ ms}^{-2})$

$$v = \sqrt{10} = 3.16 \text{ ms}^{-1}$$ [1]

(ii) We know that, $\text{KE} = \frac{1}{2}mv^2$

$$= \frac{1}{2} \times 20 \times 10$$

$$= 100 \text{ J}$$ [1]

75. How fast should a man weighing 60 kg run, so that his kinetic energy becomes 750 J ? [2]

Sol. Given, mass, $m = 60$ kg, KE = 750 J [1]

$$\because \quad \text{KE} = \frac{1}{2}mv^2$$

$$\therefore \quad v = \sqrt{\frac{2\text{KE}}{m}} = \sqrt{\frac{2 \times 750}{60}}$$

$$= \sqrt{25} = 5 \text{ ms}^{-1}$$ [1]

76. A moving body weighing 400 N possesses 500 J of KE. Calculate the velocity with which the body is moving. (Take, $g = 10$ m/s^2) [2] [2012]

Sol. Given, weight, $W = 400$ N

Kinetic energy, KE = 500 J

Velocity, $v = ?$ and $g = 10$ m/s^2 [1]

$$\text{KE} = \frac{1}{2}mv^2 = \frac{1}{2}\frac{W}{g}v^2 \quad \left(\because m = \frac{W}{g}\right)$$

$$500 = \frac{1}{2} \times \frac{400}{10} \times v^2$$

$$\Rightarrow \quad v = \sqrt{\frac{500 \times 20}{400}} = 5 \text{ m/s}$$ [1]

77. Determine the decrease in the kinetic energy of a moving body, if its velocity reduces to (1/3) rd of the initial velocity. [2]

Sol. Let us assume that original kinetic energy, $K = \frac{1}{2}mv^2$

When velocity reduces to (1 / 3)rd of the initial velocity.

$$v' = \frac{1}{3}v$$

$$\therefore \text{ New kinetic energy, } K' = \frac{1}{2}m\left(\frac{1}{3}v\right)^2$$

$$= \frac{1}{9}\left(\frac{1}{2}mv^2\right) = \frac{K}{9}$$ [1]

$$\therefore \quad \text{Decrease in KE} = K - K' = K - \frac{K}{9} = \frac{8K}{9}$$ [1]

78. If two bodies have masses in the ratio 1 : 8, have their speed in the ratio 4 : 5, find the ratio of their KE. [2]

Sol. Given, $m_1/m_2 = 1:8$, and $v_1/v_2 = 4:5$

$$\Rightarrow \quad \frac{\text{KE}_1}{\text{KE}_2} = \frac{(1/2)\, m_1 v_1^2}{(1/2)\, m_2 v_2^2}$$

$$= \frac{m_1}{m_2}\left(\frac{v_1}{v_2}\right)^2 = \frac{1}{8} \times \left(\frac{4}{5}\right)^2 = \frac{1}{8} \times \frac{16}{25} = \frac{2}{25}$$

$$\therefore \quad \text{KE}_1 : \text{KE}_2 = 2:25$$

79. A rocket is moving up with a velocity v. If the velocity of this rocket is suddenly tripled, what will be the ratio of two kinetic energies? [2]

Sol. Given, $v_1 = v$ and $v_2 = 3v$

$\therefore$ Kinetic energy of rocket, $K = \frac{1}{2}mv^2$

The ratio of two kinetic energies, $\frac{K_1}{K_2} = \frac{\frac{1}{2}mv_1^2}{\frac{1}{2}mv_2^2}$

$$\frac{K_1}{K_2} = \frac{v_1^2}{v_2^2} = \frac{v^2}{(3v)^2} = \frac{v^2}{9v^2} = \frac{1}{9}$$

Thus, the ratio of two kinetic energies $K_1 : K_2 = 1 : 9$. [2]

80. The kinetic energy of an object of mass m moving with a velocity of 5 ms^{-1} is 25 J. What will be its kinetic energy when its velocity is increased three times? [3]

Sol. Kinetic energy, KE $= \frac{1}{2}mv^2$

where, m = mass of object

and v = velocity of the object.

Here, mass (m) is same in both the cases

$$\therefore \quad \frac{K_1}{K_2} = \left(\frac{v_1}{v_2}\right)^2$$

Initial kinetic energy, $K_1 = 25$ J

Initial velocity, $v_1 = 5$ ms^{-1} [1½]

New kinetic energy, $K_2 = ?$

Final velocity, $v_2 = 3v_1 = 3 \times 5 = 15$ ms^{-1}

$$\therefore \quad \frac{25}{K_2} = \left(\frac{5}{15}\right)^2$$

$$\Rightarrow \quad \frac{25}{K_2} = \frac{1}{9} \Rightarrow K_2 = 225 \text{ J}$$ [1½]

81. A body of mass 50 kg has a momentum of 3000 kg-ms^{-1}. Determine

(i) the kinetic energy of the body.

(ii) the velocity of the body. [2] [2010]

Sol. (i) Kinetic energy, $E_K = \frac{p^2}{2m} = \frac{(3000)^2}{2 \times 50} = 90000$ J [1]

(ii) Velocity of the body, $v = \frac{p}{m} = \frac{3000}{50} = 60$ ms^{-1} [1]

82. A body of mass 0.2 kg falls from a height of 10 m to a height of 6 m above the ground. Find the loss in potential energy taking place in the body. (Take, $g = 10\,ms^{-2}$) [2]

Sol. Given, mass $m = 0.2$ kg,

height, $h_1 = 10$ m, height, $h_2 = 6$ m

$g = 10$ m/s^2

Loss in PE $= mg(h_2 - h_1)$

$= 0.2 \times 10\,(6 - 10) = -8$ J [2]

83. The power of a motor pump is 5 kW. How much water per minute the pump can raise to a height of 20 m? (Take, $g = 10\,ms^{-2}$) [2]

Sol. Given, power, $P = 5$ kW

Time, $t = 60$ s, height, $h = 20$ m

Energy supplied to the pump = Power × Time

$= 5$ kW × 1 min $= 5000$ W × 60 s $= 3 \times 10^5$ J

$\therefore$ Energy, $E = mgh$

$$\Rightarrow \quad m = \frac{E}{gh} = \frac{3 \times 10^5}{10 \times 20} = 1.5 \times 10^3 \text{ kg}$$

So, volume of water lifted per minute $= \frac{\text{mass}}{\text{density}}$

$= \frac{1.5 \times 10^3}{10^3}$ ($\because$ density of water, $\rho = 1000$ kgm^{-3})

$= 1.5$ m^3/min [2]

84. A shotput player throws a shotput of mass 3 kg. If it crosses the top of wall 2 m high at a speed of 4 ms^{-1}. Compute the total mechanical energy gained by the shotput, when it crosses the wall. (Take, $g = 9.8\,ms^{-2}$) [2]

Sol. Given, $m = 3$ kg, $h = 2$ m, $v = 4$ ms^{-1}, $g = 9.8$ ms^{-2}

Total mechanical energy = KE + PE $= \frac{1}{2}mv^2 + mgh$

$= \frac{1}{2} \times 3 \times 16 + 3 \times 9.8 \times 2$

$= 24 + 58.8 = 82.8$ J [2]

85. At a height of 20 m above the ground, an object of mass 4 kg is released from rest. It is travelling at a speed of 20 ms^{-1}, when it hits the ground. The object does not rebound and the gravitational field strength is 10 Nkg^{-1}.

How much energy is converted into heat and sound on impact? [3]

Sol. Given, height above the ground, $h = 20$ m

Mass of the ball, $m = 4$ kg

Speed of the ball while striking the ground,

$v = 20$ ms^{-1}

Acceleration due to gravity, $g = 10$ Nkg^{-1}

According to law of conservation of energy, all the energy of the ball will be converted into sound and heat energy because the ball does not rebound. [1]

$\therefore$ Energy of the ball $= \frac{1}{2}mv^2$

$= \frac{1}{2} \times 4 \times (20)^2 = 800$ J

Hence, 800 J of energy will be converted into heat and sound. [2]

86. A particle is placed at the point x of a frictionless track xyz as shown in figure. It is pushed slightly towards right. Find its speed, when it reaches the point y. (Take, $g = 10$ m/s^2)

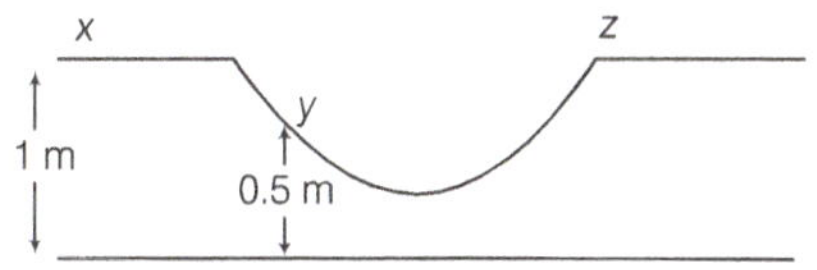

[3]

Sol. Let us take the gravitational potential energy to be zero at the horizontal surface shown in the figure. The potential energies of the particle at x and y are

$$U_x = Mg(1) \text{ and } U_y = Mg(0.5) \quad [1]$$

The kinetic energy at the point x is zero. As the track is frictionless,no energy is lost. The normal force on the particle does no work. Applying the principle of conservation of energy,

$$U_x + K_x = U_y + K_y$$

or, $$Mg(1) + 0 = Mg(0.5) + \frac{1}{2}Mv_y^2$$

or, $$\frac{1}{2}v_y^2 = g(1 - 0.5)$$

$$= 10 \times 0.5 = 5$$

$$v_y = \sqrt{10} \text{ m/s} \quad [2]$$

87. A boy is moving on a straight road against a frictional force of 5 N. After travelling a distance of 1.5 km, he forgot the correct path at a round about of radius 100 m as shown in figure.

However, he moves on the circular path for one and half cycle and then he moves forward up to 2 km. Calculate the work done by him. [2]

Sol. Given, force applied by boy against friction = 5 N

Displacement on the circular path

= one cycle + half cycle = 0 + half cycle

= diameter of circular path

($\because$ displacement depends on initial and final point)

$= 2r = 2 \times 100$ (given, $r = 100$ m)

= 200 m [1/2]

$\therefore$ Total displacement = 1.5 km + 200 m + 2 km

$= 1.5 \times 1000 + 200 + 2 \times 1000$ m ($\because$ 1km = 1000 m)

= 3700 m [1/2]

Work done by boy $= Fs\cos\theta$

$$= 5 \times 3700 \times \cos 0° = 18500 \text{ J} \quad \left(\begin{array}{l}\because \theta = 0° \\ \therefore \cos 0° = 1\end{array}\right) \quad [1]$$

Structured Questions

88. (i) An object thrown at a certain angle to the ground moves in a curved path and falls back to the ground. The initial and final points of the object lie on the same horizontal line.

(a) Draw a figure showing.

(b) What is the work done by the force of gravity on the object? [3]

(ii) A car of mass 120 kg is moving at a speed 18 km/h and it accelerates to attain a speed of 54 km/h in 5 s. Calculate

(a) the work done by the engine.

(b) the power of the engine [4] [2023]

(iii) A body of mass 10 kg is kept at a height of 5 m. It is allowed to fall and reach the ground.

(a) What is the total mechanical energy possessed by the body at the height of 2 m assuming it is a frictionless medium?

(b) What is the kinetic energy possessed by the body just before hitting the ground? (Take, $g = 10$ m/s^2). [3] [2019]

Sol. (i) (a) The path can be traced as shown below

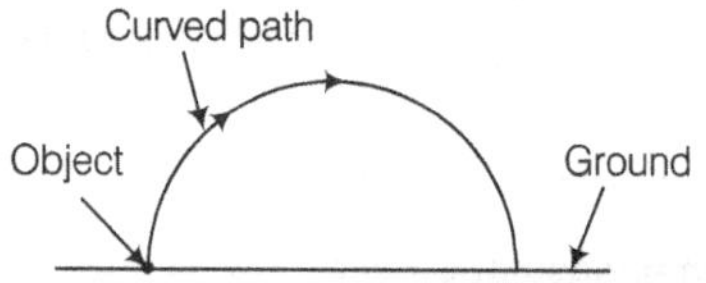

[1½]

(b) The work done by the force of gravity,

$$W = mgh$$

where, h = difference in height of initial and final positions of the object.

According to question, the initial and final positions of the object lie in same horizontal line, so $h = 0$.

$\therefore$ Work done, $W = mg \times 0 = 0$ [1½]

(ii) (a) Work done = Change in kinetic energy

$$= \frac{1}{2}m(v^2 - u^2)$$

Given, $v = 54 \text{ km/h} = 54 \times \frac{5}{18}$ m/s

$$= 15 \text{ m/s}$$

$$u = 18 \text{ km/h} = 18 \times \frac{5}{18} \text{ m/s}$$

$$= 5 \text{ m/s}$$

$$W = \frac{1}{2} \times 120[(15)^2 - (5)^2]$$

$$= \frac{1}{2} \times 120[200]$$

$$W = 12000 \text{ J}$$

(b) power, $P = \frac{W}{t} = \frac{12000}{5} = 2400$ W [1]

(iii) (a) Given, mass of body, $m = 10$ kg

height, $h = 5$ m

So, potential energy at height of 5m

$= mgh = 10 \times 10 \times 5 = 500$ J

If it falls to a height of 2 m, the increase in kinetic energy will be equal to the decrease in potential energy, so the total mechanical energy will equal to potential energy. So, total mechanical energy = 500 J. [1½]

(b) From principle of energy transformation, when body is about to reach the ground, potential energy will be converted to kinetic energy. So, kinetic energy (KE) = 500 J. [1½]

89. (i) In each of the following, a force F is acting on an object of mass m. The direction of displacement is from West to East shown by the longer arrow. Observe the figure carefully and state, whether the work done by the force is negative, positive or zero.

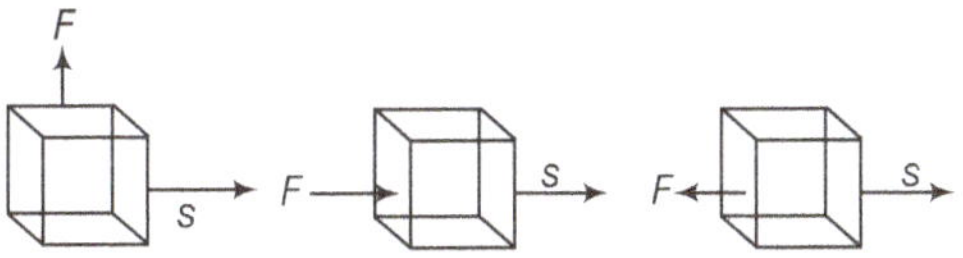

Fig.(I) Fig.(II) Fig.(III)

[3]

(ii) The figure below shows a simple pendulum of mass 200 g. It is displaced from the mean position A to the extreme position B. The potential energy at the position A is zero. At the position B, the pendulum bob is raised by 5 m. **[4]**

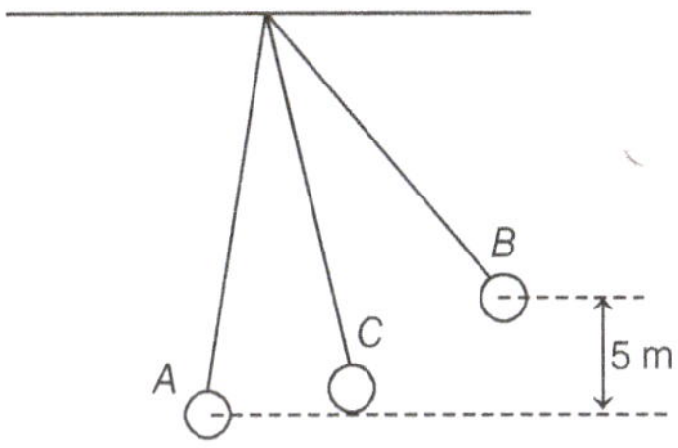

(a) What is the potential energy of the pendulum at the position B?

(b) What is the total mechanical energy at point C?

(c) What is the speed of the bob at the position A, when released from B? **[4]**

(Take, $g = 10\ \text{ms}^{-2}$ and there is no loss of energy)

(d) At which point, potential energy is maximum? Explain.

(iii) A ball of mass 50 g is thrown vertically upwards with an initial velocity of 20 ms^{-1}. Calculate

(a) the initial kinetic energy imparted to the ball,

(b) the maximum height reached if air friction is neglected and

(c) the maximum height reached if 40% of the initial energy is lost against the air friction. (Take, $g = 10\ \text{ms}^{-2}$) **[3]**

Sol. (i) In Fig. (I), angle between F and s is 90°, so work done is zero. **[1]**

In Fig. (II), angle between F and s is 0°, so work done is positive. **[1]**

In Fig. (III), angle between F and s is 180°, so work done is negative. **[1]**

(ii) Simple pendulum is as shown in the figure

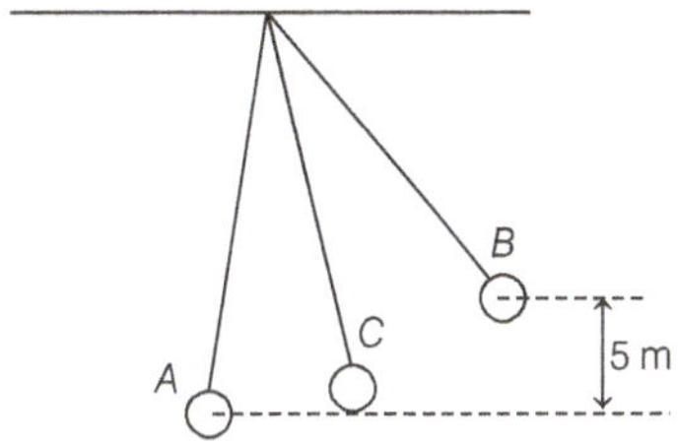

Mass of simple pendulum, $m = 200\ \text{g} = 0.2\ \text{kg}$ **[1]**

(a) Since, B is extreme position, hence total energy at B is present in the form of its potential energy.

$\therefore$ Potential energy, $U = mgh$

$= 0.2 \times 10 \times 5 = 10\ \text{J}$ **[1]**

(b) Since, total mechanical energy (E) remains conserved, hence total mechanical energy at C is

$E = U = 10\ \text{J}$ **[1]**

(c) At point A, whole of the potential energy of the bob is converted into its kinetic energy.

So, $\frac{1}{2} mv^2 = U$

$\Rightarrow \frac{1}{2} \times 0.2 \times v^2 = 10$

$\Rightarrow v^2 = \frac{10}{0.1} = 100$

$\Rightarrow v = \sqrt{100}$

$\Rightarrow v = 10\ \text{m/s}$ **[1]**

(d) Potential energy is maximum at point B because at this point, pendulum reaches at maximum height.

(iii) Given, $m = 50\ \text{g} = 0.05\ \text{kg}$

$u = 20\ \text{ms}^{-1}$, $g = 10\ \text{ms}^{-2}$

(a) Initial kinetic energy, $\text{KE}_i = \frac{1}{2} mu^2$

$= \frac{1}{2} \times 0.05 \times (20)^2 = 10\ \text{J}$ **[1]**

(b) At maximum height,

Potential energy = Initial kinetic energy

$\Rightarrow mgh = \text{KE}_i$

$\Rightarrow h = \frac{\text{KE}_i}{mg}$

$= \frac{10}{(0.05) \times 10} = 20\ \text{m}$ **[1]**

(c) When 40% initial energy is lost, then at maximum height,

Potential energy = 60% of initial kinetic energy

$\Rightarrow mgh = \frac{60}{100} \times \text{KE}_i$

$\Rightarrow h = \frac{6}{10} \times \frac{10}{(0.05) \times 10} = 12\ \text{m}$ **[1]**

90. (i) Read the following statements and state, whether the work done in the following cases is positive or negative.

(a) Work done by friction on a body sliding down an inclined plane. [1]

(b) Work done by a man in lifting a bucket out of the well by means of rope tied to the bucket. [1]

(c) Work done by resistive force of air on a oscillating pendulum in bringing it to rest[1]

(ii) A bullet of mass 5 g travels with a speed of 500 ms^{-1}. If it penetrates a final target which offers a constant resistive force of 1000 N to the motion of the bullet. Find

(a) the initial kinetic energy of the bullet,

(b) the distance through which the bullet has penetrated before coming to rest and

(c) the speed with which the bullet emerges out of the target, if it is of thickness 0.5 m. [3]

(iii) In a dam, water falls at a rate of 1000 kg s^{-1} from a height of 100 m.

(a) Calculate the initial potential energy of the water.

(b) Assuming that 60% of the energy of the falling water is converted to electrical energy, calculate the power generated. (Take, $g = 9.8\ ms^{-2}$) [4]

Sol. (i) (a) In this case, the frictional force acts opposite to the direction of motion of body, so the work done by the friction on a body sliding down an inclined plane will be negative. [1]

(b) In this case, the bucket moves in the direction of the applied force by the man, so the work done will be positive. [1]

(c) The resistive force of air always acts opposite to the direction of motion of the oscillating pendulum due to which the work done will be negative. [1]

(ii) Given, $m = 5\,g = 5 \times 10^{-3}$ kg

$v = 500\ ms^{-1}$

$F = 1000$ N

(a) Initial kinetic energy of bullet,

$KE_i = \frac{1}{2}mv^2$

$= \frac{1}{2} \times 5 \times 10^{-3} \times (500)^2 = 625$ J [1]

(b) If the bullet penetrate through a distance d, then work done against the target material is

W = resistive force $(F) \times$ distance (d)

$= 1000 \times d$

From work-energy theorem, W = KE

$\Rightarrow \quad 1000\,d = 625$

$\Rightarrow \quad d = 0.625$ m [1]

(c) Energy spent in moving through the target material

= Force × Thickness

$= 1000 \times 0.5 = 500$ J

Kinetic energy left $= 625 - 500 = 125$ J

If v' is speed with which the bullet emerges out, then

$\frac{1}{2} \times m \times (v')^2 = 125$

$\Rightarrow \quad v' = \sqrt{\frac{2 \times 125}{5 \times 10^{-3}}} = 223.6\ ms^{-1}$ [1]

(iii) Given, $m = 1000$ kg, $t = 1$ s, $h = 100$ m

(a) Initial potential energy of water, $PE_i = mgh$

$= 1000 \times 9.8 \times 100 = 9.8 \times 10^5$ J [2]

(b) Electrical energy = 60% of PE_i

$= \frac{60}{100} \times 9.8 \times 10^5$

$= 58.8 \times 10^4$ J

Power generated, $P = \frac{\text{Electrical energy}}{\text{Time}}$

$= \frac{58.8 \times 10^4}{1}$

$= 5.88 \times 10^5\ Js^{-1}$ [2]

Chapter Assessment

1 Mark Questions

1. The total work done on a particle is equal to the change in its kinetic energy
   (a) always, if force is conservative
   (b) Only, if gravitational force alone acts on it
   (c) Only, if elastic force alone acts on it
   (d) None of the above
2. If the velocity of a moving car is increased to double, then its kinetic energy is
   (a) increased to double
   (b) increased to four times
   (c) dereased to half
   (d) decreased to one-fourth
3. The usable form of mechanical energy is **[ICSE Latest Specimen Sem-I]**
   (a) elastic potential energy
   (b) kinetic energy
   (c) gravitational potential energy
   (d) None of the above
4. If two bodies one light and other heavy have equal kinetic energies, then which one has a greater momentum?
   (a) Heavy body
   (b) Light body
   (c) Both have equal momentum
   (d) It depends on the actual velocities
5. How fast should a man weighing 600 N run to achieve a kinetic energy of 750 J ?
   (Take, $g = 10\ m/s^2$)
   (a) 5 m/s
   (b) 7 m/s
   (c) 10 m/s
   (d) 7.5 m/s
6. A body has kinetic energy 2500 J. If the mass of the body is 500 g. The velocity of the body is **[ICSE Latest Specimen Sem-I]**
   (a) $\sqrt{10}$ m/s (b) 10 ms^{-1}
   (c) 20 ms^{-1} (d) 100 m/s
7. The energy change during photosynthesis in plants is **[ICSE 2022 Sem-I]**
   (a) heat to chemical
   (b) light to chemical
   (c) chemical to light
   (d) chemical to heat
8. Which of the following graphs shows correct relation of kinetic energy (E), potential energy (U) and height (h) from the ground of a particle ?

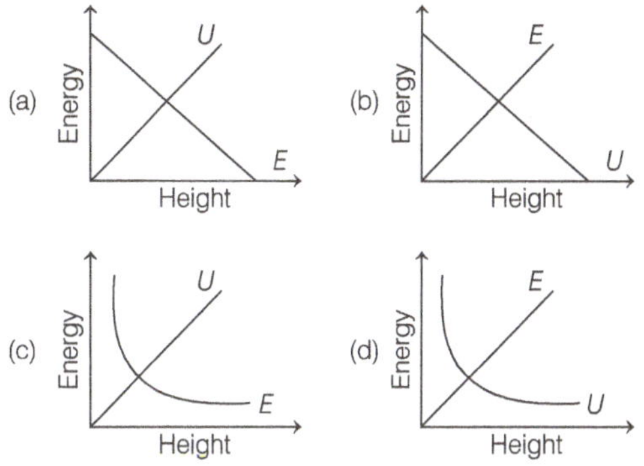

2 Marks Questions

9. If a body of mass m falls through a height h. Establish an expression for the work done by the gravity.
10. Explain any two examples, when the work done is
    (i) positive and (ii) negative.
11. Find the power of an engine required to lift 10^5 kg of coal per hour from a mine 360 m deep.
12. Determine the velocity of a body of mass 100 g having a kinetic energy of 20 J.
13. A rocket of 3×10^6kg mass takes off from a launching pad and acquires a vertical velocity of 1 km s^{-1} at an altitude of 25 km. Calculate (i) PE and (ii) KE.(Take, $g = 10\ ms^{-2}$)
14. A body is acted upon by a force. State two conditions under which the work done could be zero.
15. State the two factors on which the power consumed or produced by a body depends. Explain the answer along with the example.
16. Differentiate between watt and watt hour.
17. State which would have greater effect on kinetic energy of an object doubling the mass or doubling the velocity?
18. A force is applied on a body of mass 10 kg moving with a velocity of 20 ms^{-1}. The body attains a velocity of 30 ms^{-1} in 5 s. Calculate the work done by the body.
19. If an electric heater of power P watt is used for time t hour, so how much energy does it consume? Give your answer for power consumed in expression (i) kWh and (ii) Joule.
20. What do you understand by electron volt and establish its relation with joule?
21. How does rain water possess kinetic energy?
22. How much work is required to be done on a ball of mass 50 g to give it a momentum of 600g cms^{-1}?

23. When a boy of mass 40 kg runs up height of 50 steps each 10 cm high in 5 s. Determine
(i) the work done by the boy and
(ii) the power developed.

24. Rajan exerts a force of 150 N in pulling a cart at a constant speed of 10 m/s. Calculate the power exerted.

25. Calculate the change in the kinetic energy of a moving body, if its velocity is reduced to (1/3)rd of the initial velocity.

26. A girl of mass 35 kg climbs up from the first floor of a building at a height 4 m above the ground to the third floor at a height 12 m above the ground. What will be the increase in her gravitational potential energy? (Take, $g = 10\ ms^{-2}$)

27. State the amount of work done by an object, when it moves in a circular path for one complete rotation. Give your reason to justify your answer.

28. What should the angle between force and displacement be to get the
(i) minimum work and
(ii) maximum work?

29. Explain briefly, why the work done by a fielder, when he takes a catch in a cricket match is negative?

30. How is work done by a force measured, when the force
(i) is in the direction of displacement?
(ii) is at an angle θ to the direction of displacement?

3 Marks Questions

31. (i) When does a force do work?
(ii) What is the work done by the Moon, when it revolves around the Earth?

32. If the power of a motor be 100 kW, at what speed can it raise a load of 50000 N?

33. State the energy changes in the following while in use
(i) burning of a candle and
(ii) a steam engine.

Structured Questions

34. (i) Assume that a boy of mass *m* climbs up a staircase of vertical height *h*. What is the work done by the boy against the force of gravity? What would have been the work done, if he uses a lift in climbing the same vertical height? **[3]**
(ii) Mention the name of three forms of kinetic energy and given one example of each form. **[3]**
(iii) A stone of mass 500 g is thrown vertically upwards with a velocity of $15\ ms^{-1}$. Calculate
(a) the PE at the greatest height,
(b) KE on reaching the ground and
(c) the total energy at its half-way point. **[4]**

35. (i) Define 1 erg of work and establish a relationship between erg and joule. **[3]**
(ii) How much energy is gained by a box of mass 20 kg, when a man
(a) carrying the box waits for 5 min for a bus ?
(b) runs carrying the box with a speed of $3\ ms^{-1}$ to catch the bus ?
(c) raise the box by 0.5 m in order to place it inside the bus ? **[3]**
(iii) Named the energy transformation takes in following instruments.
(a) Steam engine (b) Atomic bomb
(c) Dry cell (d) Electric generator **[4]**

36. (i) What do you mean by gravitational potential energy? Derive an expression for it. **[3]**
(ii) Mention the form of energy that is possessed by a body in the following cases
(a) A shooting arrow
(b) A cocked up spring and an air gun.
(c) A fish moving in water. **[3]**
(iii) Answer the given questions.
(a) Determine the kinetic energy of a body of mass 1 kg moving with uniform velocity of $10\ ms^{-1}$.
(b) If the speed of the car is halved, how does the kinetic energy change? **[4]**

37. (i) A boy pulls a toy car with force 50 N through a string which makes an angle of 30° with the horizontal, so as to move the toy by the distance of 1 m in the horizontal direction. If the string were inclined at an angle of 45° with the horizontal. How much pull would he apply along the string in order to moves it through the same distance of 1 m? **[4]**
(ii) A metal ball of mass 2 kg is allowed to fall freely from rest from a height of 5 m above the ground.
(a) Determine the potential energy possessed by the ball, when initially at rest.
(b) What is the kinetic energy of the ball just before hitting the ground ?
(c) What happens to the mechanical energy after the ball hits the ground and comes to rest? **[3]**
(iii) There is a block *X*, whose weight is 100 N, is pulled up a slope of length 5 m by a constant force *F* =150 N as given in the figure.

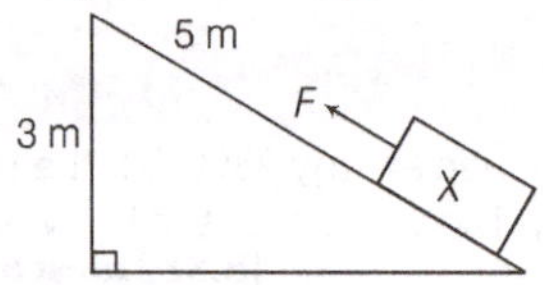

(a) Determine the workdone by the force *F* in moving the block *X*, 5 m along the slope?
(b) By how much amount is the potential energy of block *X* increased?
(c) Point out the difference in work done by the force and the increase in the potential energy of the block. **[3]**

For Solutions Scan the Code

Olympiad Section*

Brain Teasing Questions of Olympiad Pattern

1 A women pushes a trunk on railway platform which has a rough surface. She supplies a force of 100 N over a distance of 10 m. Thereafter, she gets progressively tired and her applied force reduces linearly with distance to 50 N. The total distance by which the trunk has been moved is 20 m. Calculate the net work done by the two forces over 20 m.

(a) 1000 J (b) 500 J (c) 750 J (d) 1500 J

2 A body of mass 0.5 kg travels in a straight line with velocity $v = ax^{3/2}$, where $a = 5\ ms^{-2}$. What is the work done by the net force during its displacement from $x = 0$ to $x = 2$ m?

(a) 150 J (b) 100 J (c) 50 J (d) 200 J

3 A boy P has a mass of 20 kg and is moving with a velocity of 5 ms^{-1}. Another boy Q has a mass of 5 kg and is moving with a velocity of 20 ms^{-1}. Calculate the ratio of the momentum of P and Q.

(a) 2 : 1 (b) 1 : 1 (c) 1 : 2 (d) 3 : 2

4 A boy of mass 40 kg walks up a flight of stairs to a vertical distance of 12 m in a time interval of 40 s. Rate at which the boy is doing work against the force of gravity is

(a) 500 W (b) 400 W (c) 120 W (d) 100 W

5 An electron and proton are detected in a cosmic ray experiment, the first with kinetic energy 10 keV and the second the 100 keV. Obtain the ratio of their speeds. (Take, electron mass = 9.11×10^{-31}kg, proton mass = 1.67×10^{-27}kg, and $1\text{eV} = 1.60 \times 10^{-19}$J)

(a) 12.81 (b) 6.16 V (c) 13.54 (d) 11.62 V

6 A body is moved along a straight road by a machine delivering constant power. The distance moved by the body in time t is proportional to

(a) $t^{1/2}$ (b) $t^{3/4}$ (c) $t^{3/2}$ (d) t^2

7 A pump of 200 W power is lifting 2 kg water per second from an average depth of 10 m. The velocity with which water comes out of the pump. (Take, $g = 9.8\ ms^{-2}$)

(a) 7.5 m/s (b) 10.2 m/s
(c) 12.5 m/s (d) 14.6 m/s

8 A pump motor is used to deliver water at a certain rate from a given pipe. To obtain twice as much water from the same pipe in the same time, the power of the pump has to be increased to

(a) double (b) four times
(c) 8 times (d) None of these

9 A bomb of mass $3m$ kg explodes into two pieces of masses m kg and $2m$ kg. If the velocity of m kg mass is 16 ms^{-1}, then the total kinetic energy released in the explosion is

(a) 200 mJ (b) 150 mJ
(c) 192 mJ (d) 125 mJ

10 If an object is dropped from a height h, then the height from the ground at which the kinetic energy and potential energy are in the ratio 3 : 4 is

(a) $\frac{h}{3}$ (b) $\frac{2h}{3}$ (c) $\frac{2h}{7}$ (d) $\frac{4h}{7}$

11 A load to be moved using a wheelbarrow. The total mass of the load and wheelbarrow is 60 kg. The magnitude of graviational acceleration is 10 ms^{-2}.

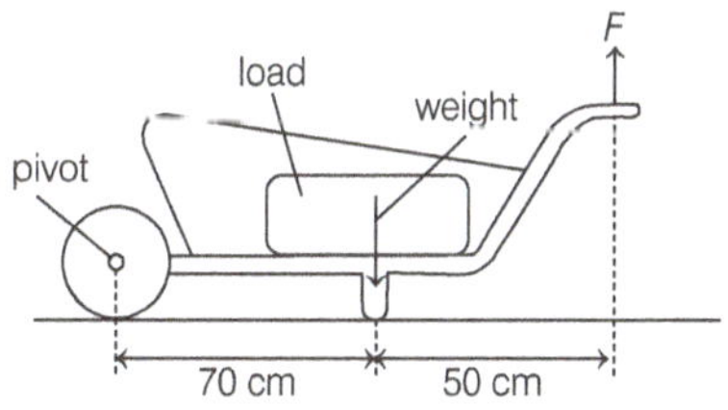

What is the work done, if the handle is raised by 50 cm?

(a) 35.0 J (b) 17.5 J (c) 175 J (d) 350 J

12 During Safari trip in Qatar, a car starts from rest moving eastward. If the net force acting on the car is directly proportional to t^2, where t denotes time. What would the car's kinetic energy be proportional to?

(a) t^2 (b) t^3 (c) t^4 (d) t^6

ANSWERS

1. (c) **2.** (c) **3.** (b) **4.** (c) **5.** (c) **6.** (c) **7.** (b) **8.** (c) **9.** (c) **10.** (d)
11. (c) **12.** (d)

* *These questions may or may not be asked in the examination, have been given just for additional practice required for olympiads Scholarship Exams etc. For detailed explanations refer Page No. 262.*

CHAPTER

3

Machines

SYLLABUS

Machines as force multipliers, load, effort, mechanical advantage, velocity ratio and efficiency; simple treatment of levers, pulley systems showing the utility of each type of machine.

Machine is a device which helps us to do the work at one point and deliver it at another point with a view of accomplishing the work easily.

Basically, machines act as **force multiplier**, i.e. the net effort produced by the machine is much more than the effort applied. e.g. A jack is used to lift a bus or car, pulleys are used to lift heavy loads. In all such examples, the effort is much less than the load. So, we can say that machines act as a force multiplier.

Simple machines can be classified (or categorised) into two major classes, one is lever and other is inclined plane. Further it can be classified as shown below

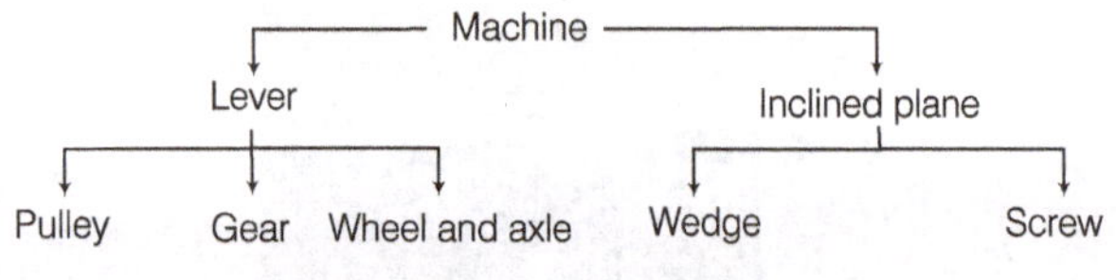

Classification of Machine

In this chapter, we will be exploring all the functions and terms related to machine, there after lever and inclined plane as important types of simple machine will be studied.

Terms Related to Machine

The terms related to machine are as follows

Load It is the resistive or opposing force against which the machine works. It is denoted by L.

Effort It is the force applied on the machine to overcome the load. It is denoted by E.

Mechanical Advantage (MA) It is the ratio of the load to the effort. It is denoted by MA.

It is expressed as, $\boxed{\text{MA} = \dfrac{L}{E}}$

(i) If MA > 1 (i.e. $L > E$), then machine works as force multiplier.

(ii) If MA < 1 (i.e. $L < E$), then machine gains speed, i.e. machine can help us to achieve greater movement of load by smaller movement of effort. e.g. The blades of a scissors are more longer for smaller movement of handles.

(iii) If MA = 1 (i.e. $L = E$), then machine changes the direction of effort, i.e. machine can change the direction of effort to a more convenient direction, e.g. To lift the bucket from well, effort is applied on pulley in downward direction while bucket is pushed in upward direction.

Being a ratio of two like quantities (such as both load and effort are some types of forces) MA has no unit.

Velocity Ratio (VR) It is defined as the ratio of velocity of the effort to the velocity of the load. It is denoted by VR.

It is expressed as,

$$\text{VR} = \frac{\text{Velocity of effort } (v_E)}{\text{Velocity of load } (v_L)}$$

In terms of distance moved by a particular force, velocity ratio is the ratio of the distance moved by the effort to the corresponding distance moved by the load.

$$\therefore \quad \text{VR} = \frac{v_E}{v_L} = \frac{d_E/t}{d_L/t} = \frac{d_E}{d_L}$$

Here, d_L and d_E are the distances moved in same time t by the load and the effort, respectively.

Being a ratio of two like quantities, velocity ratio also has no unit.

Input Work The work done on the machine by the effort is called the work input (W_{input} or W_i). If an effort E causes a displacement d in its own direction, then

$$\text{Input Work} = \text{Effort} \times \text{Displacement} = E \times d$$

Output Work The work done by the machine on the load is called output work.

Output Work = Work done on the load by the machine

Example 1. If a machine is used to lift a load of 50 N, such that resistance due to friction and movable part of machine is 15 N, then the total lifted load is 65 N, i.e. (50 + 15) N. If the displacement is caused through 2 m, then find actual and useful output.

Sol. Actual output = Total load × Distance = 65 N × 2 m = 130 J

and useful output = useful load × distance = 50 N × 2 m = 100 J

Note In some problems or descriptions, only the term output is used. Hence, we will use this output as useful output not as actual output.

Efficiency (η) It is defined as the ratio of work done (W_{output}) by the machine to work done (W_{input}) on the machine. It is denoted by η. It is expressed as

$$\eta = \frac{\text{Work done on the load}}{\text{Work done by the effort}} = \frac{W_{\text{output}}}{W_{\text{input}}}$$

But efficiency is usually expressed in percentage, so we may write

$$\text{Efficiency, } \eta = \frac{W_{\text{output}}}{W_{\text{input}}} \times 100\%$$

Being a ratio of two similar quantities, efficiency also has no unit.

Note Due to friction and weight of the moving parts of a machine of a given design, its velocity ratio does not change but its mechanical advantage decreases and so its efficiency decreases.

Ideal and Actual Machine

Ideal Machine or Perfect Machine

Machine works on the principle of conservation of energy. The machine which converts input work (effort) into output work (load) without any wastage of work is called ideal machine.

Work done (input) = Work done (output)

Thus, an ideal machine can be defined as follows

A machine whose parts are weightless and frictionless, such that whatever the energy given to it, is same as the energy produced by it, is called as an ideal machine. The efficiency of an ideal machine is 100%. An ideal machine cannot be made practically because some part of the input is wasted in moving the parts of the machine and in overcoming the friction between the various parts of a machine.

Actual Machine

In an actual machine, the output energy is always less than the input energy indicating that there is some loss of energy during its operation, reasons of which are listed below

(i) The moving parts of the machine are neither weightless nor smooth or frictionless.

(ii) Different parts of the machine are not perfectly rigid.

(iii) The elastic materials (string) are not perfectly elastic.

Key Points

(i) For all practical or actual machines, efficiency is less than 1 (i.e. $\eta < 1$).

(ii) If mechanical advantage is mentioned in a question, it means only the actual mechanical advantage but not the ideal mechanical advantage.

(iii) A machine of η% efficient means η% of the total energy supplied to the machine and remaining $(100 - \eta)$% of the energy is lost to the surroundings.

(iv) The energy lost in overcoming the frictional force between the moving parts of a machine, is the most common type of loss of energy in it.

Relation between η, MA and VR

Consider a practical machine which overcomes a load L by the application of an effort E in time t. Suppose the displacement of effort be d_E and the displacement of load be d_L.

Now, we can write

Work input (W_{input})

$$= \text{Effort} \times \text{Displacement of effort} = E \times d_E$$

Work output (W_{output})

$$= \text{Load} \times \text{Displacement of load} = L \times d_L$$

$$\text{Efficiency, } \eta = \frac{W_{output}}{W_{input}} = \frac{L \times d_L}{E \times d_E} = \frac{L}{E} \times \frac{d_L}{d_E} = \frac{L}{E} \times \frac{1}{\frac{d_E}{d_L}}$$

As, we know that

$$MA = \frac{L}{E}$$

and

$$VR = \frac{d_E}{d_L}$$

$$\therefore \quad \eta = \frac{MA}{VR} \quad \text{or} \quad \boxed{MA = \eta \times VR}$$

Thus, the mechanical advantage of a machine is equal to the product of its efficiency and velocity ratio. For all practical machines, mechanical advantage is always less than velocity ratio.

i.e. $\quad MA < VR$

Example 2. An effort of 10 kgf is applied on a machine through a distance of 100 cm, when a load of 100 kgf moves through a distance of 5 cm.

Calculate the

(i) velocity ratio,

(ii) mechanical advantage and

(iii) efficiency of the machine.

Sol. Given, effort, $E = 10$ kgf, load, $L = 100$ kgf

Distance moved by effort, $d_E = 100$ cm

and distance moved by load, $d_L = 5$ cm

(i) Velocity Ratio (VR)

$$= \frac{\text{Distance through which the effort moves } (d_E)}{\text{Distance through which the load moves } (d_L)} = \frac{100\text{ cm}}{5\text{ cm}} = 20$$

(ii) Mechanical Advantage (MA)

$$= \frac{\text{Load } (L)}{\text{Effort } (E)} = \frac{100\text{ kgf}}{10\text{ kgf}} = 10$$

(iii) Percentage efficiency,

$$\eta = \frac{MA}{VR} \times 100 = \frac{10}{20} \times 100 = 50\%$$

Example 3. A machine is operated by an effort of 80 N acting downward and moving through a downward displacement of 0.15 m. The load of mass 10 kg, is raised up by 10 cm. Calculate the MA, VR, work input, useful work output and efficiency (Take, $g = 10\text{ ms}^{-2}$).

Sol. $MA = \frac{\text{Load } (L)}{\text{Effort } (E)}$ $\quad$ ($L = 10$ kg-wt $= 10 \times 10 = 100$ N, $E = 80$ N)

$$= \frac{100}{80} = 1.25$$

$$VR = \frac{d_E}{d_L} = \frac{0.15}{0.1} = 1.5$$

$$\text{Work input} = E \times d_E = 80 \times 0.15 = 12\text{ J}$$

$$\text{Useful work output} = L \times d_L = 100 \times \frac{10}{100} = 10\text{ J}$$

$$\text{Efficiency, } \eta = \frac{\text{Output}}{\text{Input}} = \frac{10}{12} = 0.833 = 83.3\%$$

Check Your LEARNING...

1 Name a device that helps us to do the work at one point and deliver it to the another point.

2 What happens, when mechanical advantage (MA) becomes equal to one?

3 Write an expression for calculating the efficiency of a machine.

4 "An ideal machine cannot be made practically." Justify the statement.

5 State whether in actual machines, the output energy is greater or lesser than input energy. Give reason.

6 How are mechanical advantage and velocity ratio related for practical machine?

Lever

A lever is a straight or bent rigid rod which can be turned or rotated about a fixed point called fulcrum. It is one of the most common and simple machine.

Principle of a Lever

Consider a lever (i.e. a straight rod) AB with balanced point at F (fulcrum for the lever). A load L acts at point A of the lever and effort E acts at point B as shown in the diagrams.

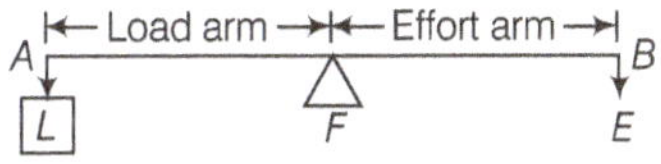

Lever

The perpendicular distance of the effort from the fulcrum is called the **effort arm** i.e. BF. The perpendicular distance of the load from the fulcrum is called the **load arm** i.e. AF. For an ideal lever, it is assumed that the lever is weightless and frictionless. A lever works on the principle of moment. In the equilibrium position of the lever by the principle of moment,

moment of load about the fulcrum

= moment of effort about the fulcrum

The two moments are always in opposite directions.

In figure, the moment of load is anti-clockwise while the moment of effort is clockwise.

Thus, we can write

$$\text{Load} \times \text{Load arm} = \text{Effort} \times \text{Effort arm}$$

This is also called principle of lever.

or $$L \times AF = E \times BF$$

or $$\frac{L}{E} = \frac{BF}{AF}$$

$$\therefore \text{Mechanical Advantage (MA)} = \frac{L}{E} = \frac{\text{Effort arm}}{\text{Load arm}} = \frac{BF}{AF}$$

This relation is known as the **law of levers.**

From the above equation, it is clear that, if

(i) Effort arm = Load arm, MA = 1

(ii) Effort arm < Load arm, MA < 1

(iii) Effort arm > Load arm, MA > 1

Note Mechanical advantage of a lever can be increased either by increasing its effort arm or by decreasing its load arm.

Types of Levers

There are three types of levers

(i) Class I lever

(ii) Class II lever

(iii) Class III lever

Class I Lever

In this type of lever, the effort (E) and the load (L) are situated on either side of the fulcrum (F).

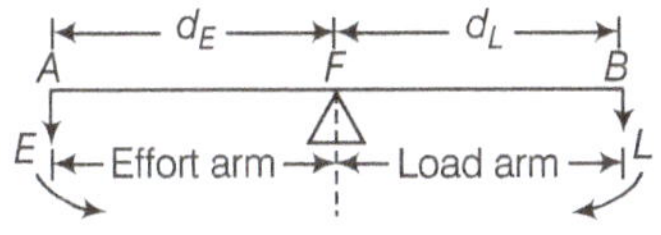

Class I lever

$$\text{MA of class I lever} = \frac{\text{Effort arm}}{\text{Load arm}}$$

$$\text{VR of class I lever} = \frac{d_E}{d_L}$$

Characteristics of a Class I Lever

Some characteristics of class I lever are as follows

(i) Fulcrum lies in between the load and the effort.

(ii) By moving the fulcrum towards the load, i.e. by decreasing load arm, mechanical advantage can be increased.

(iii) For class I lever, the mechanical advantage and velocity ratio can have any value either greater than 1 or equal to 1 or less than 1.

e.g.

- The beam of a common balance (MA = 1)
- A crowbar (MA > 1)
- A pair of scissors (MA < 1)

Examples of Class I Lever

Some examples of class I lever are as follows

(i) **A See-saw** Two boys are playing with a see-saw as shown in the figure. The lighter boy sits far away from the fulcrum as compared to the heavier boy, such that the moments of both of them are same.

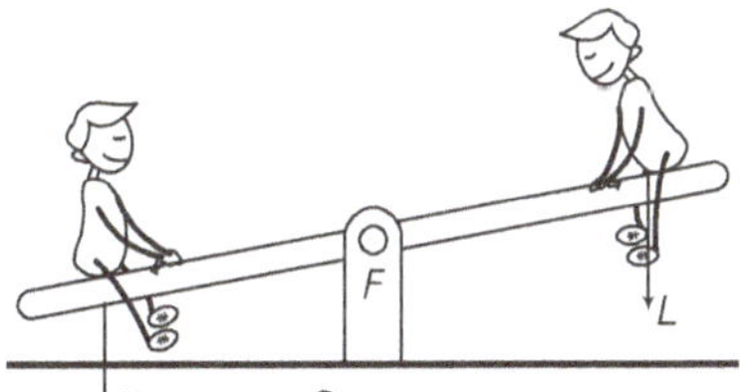

See-saw

(ii) **A Crow-bar** To have the less effort in lifting the load, longer crow-bar with more fulcrum is required. The reason behind the less effort is increasing mechanical advantage with increasing the effort arm.

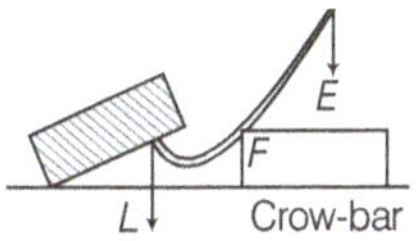

Crow-bar

Another examples of class I lever are a pair of scissors, pliers and a claw hammer.

Example 4. A crow-bar of length 140 cm has its fulcrum situated at a distance of 40 cm from the load. Calculate the mechanical advantage of the crow-bar.

Sol. If fulcrum is situated in the middle of effort arm and load arm, it is a class I lever.

We have length of crow-bar = 140 cm

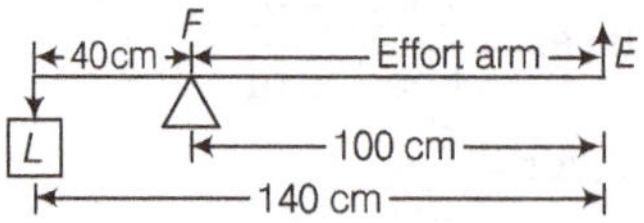

Distance of fulcrum from the load = 40 cm

$\therefore$ Load arm = 40 cm

and effort arm = length of crow-bar − load arm

$= 140 - 40 = 100$ cm

Now, Mechanical Advantage (MA) of crow-bar

$$= \frac{\text{Effort arm}}{\text{Load arm}} = \frac{100}{40} = \frac{5}{2} = 2.5 \text{ cm}$$

Class II Lever

In this type of lever, the load is situated between fulcrum and effort. e.g. A bottle opener, a wheel barrow, a paper cutter, raising the weight of the human body on toes, etc.

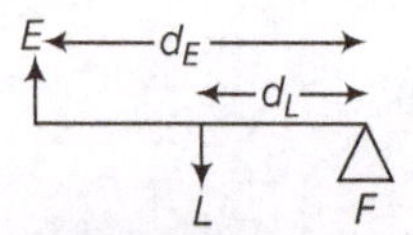

(i) Representation of various force in class II lever

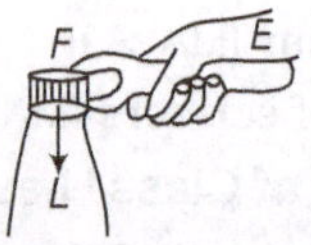

(ii) Bottle opener

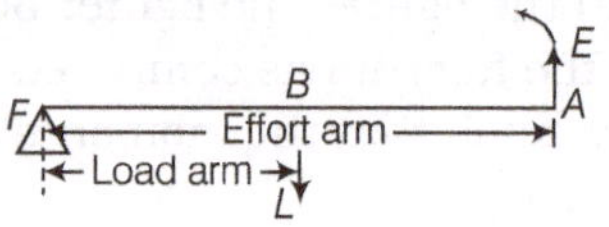

(iii) Class II Lever

Characteristics of a Class II Lever

Some characteristics of class II lever are as follows

(i) Load lies in between the effort and the fulcrum.

(ii) Mechanical advantage and velocity ratio are always more than one because the effort arm is always longer than the load arm.

(iii) If load is moving towards the fulcrum, then load arm decreases and consequently the mechanical advantage increases.

(iv) Class II levers always act as a force multiplier.

Examples of Class II Lever

Some examples of class II lever are

(i) lemon squeezer

(ii) nut cracker

(iii) hinged door

Example 5. The diagram below shows a lever in use.

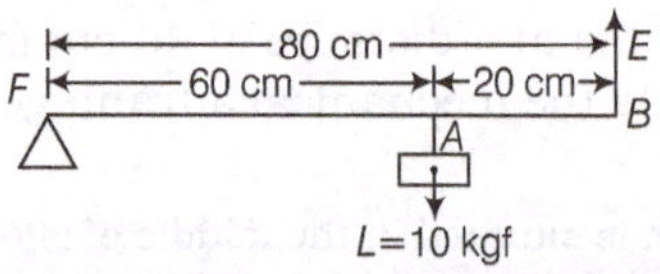

(i) To which class of lever does it belong?

(ii) If FA = 60 cm, AB=20 cm, find its MA.

(iii) Find the value of effort (E).

Sol. (i) From the given figure, it is clear that load lies in between fulcrum (F) and effort (E).

$\therefore$ Lever is of class II.

(ii) From the above figure, MA of lever

$$= \frac{\text{Effort arm } (FE)}{\text{Load arm } (FA)} = \frac{80 \text{ cm}}{60 \text{ cm}}$$

$$= \frac{4}{3} = 1.33 \text{ cm}$$

(iii) On balancing the moments, we can write

$$E \times \text{effort arm } (FE) = L \times \text{load arm } (FA)$$

$$\Rightarrow \quad E \times 80 = L \times 60$$

$$\therefore \quad E = L\left(\frac{60}{80}\right) = 10 \times \frac{3}{4} = \frac{30}{4} \text{ kgf} = 7.5 \text{ kgf}$$

Class III Lever

In this type of lever, effort is situated between the load and the fulcrum. e.g. Sugar tongs, foot treadle, etc.

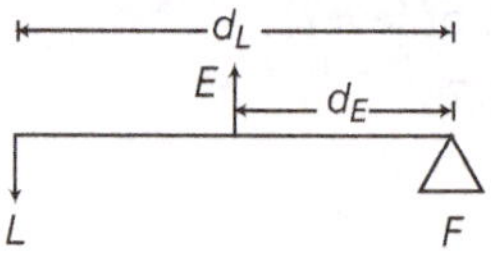

(i) Representation of various force in class III lever

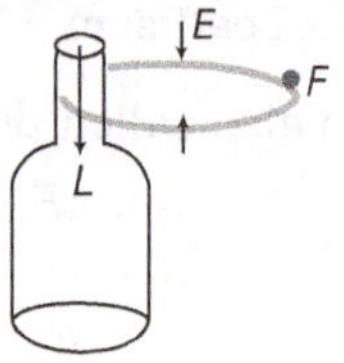

(ii) Sugar tongs

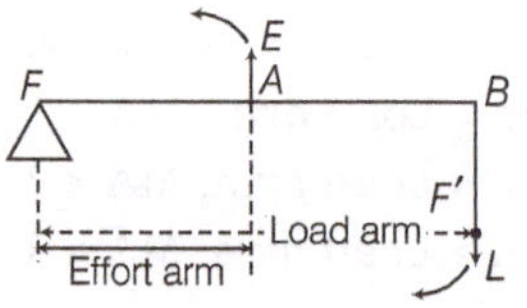

(iii) Class III lever

Characteristics of Class III Lever

Some characteristics of class III lever are as follows

(i) Effort lies in between the fulcrum and the load.

(ii) Mechanical advantage and velocity ratio are always less than one, because the effort arm is always smaller than the load arm.

(iii) These class III levers are also called **speed multiplier** as the load moves through a larger distance as compared to the effort.

Examples of Class III Lever

Some examples of class III levers are

(i) arms used to lift weight

(ii) baseball bat

(iii) broom

(iv) doors

(v) fishing rod
(vi) sling
(vii) tweezers
(viii) stapler

Examples of each Class of levers as Found in human body

In human body, examples of all the three types of levers are found which are given as

1. **Example of Class -1 Lever** Class I lever is found in the action of nodding of the head. In this action, the spine acts as the fulcrum (*F*), load (*L*) at its front part and effort (*E*) is at its rear part as shown in the figure.

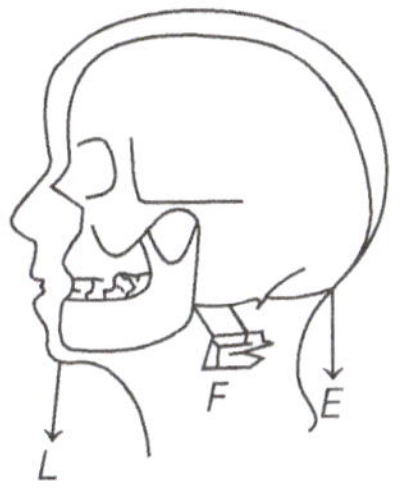

2. **Example of class-II Lever** Class II lever in human body is found in raising the weight of the body on toes. In this action, load (*L*) is in the middle, fulcrum (*F*) is at one end and effort (*E*) by muscles is at the other end as shown in the figure.

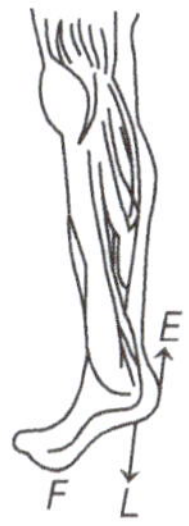

3. **Example of class-III Lever** Class-III lever in human body is found in raising a load by forearm. The elbow joint acts as fulcrum (*F*) at one end, biceps exerts the effort (*E*) in the middle and a load (*L*) on the palm is at the other end as shown in the figure.

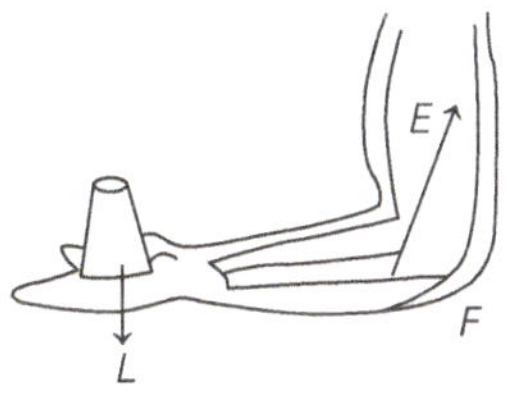

Example 6. The diagram below shows the use of a lever

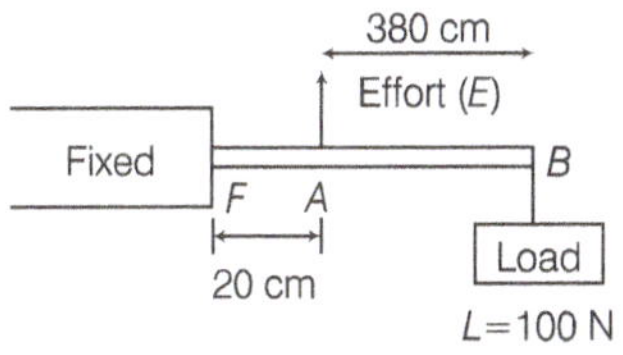

(i) State the principle of moments as applied to the above lever.
(ii) Give an example of this class of lever.
(iii) If $FA = 20$ cm, $AB = 380$ cm, then calculate the mechanical advantage and minimum effort required to lift the load.

Sol. (i) Principle of moment for the given lever can be applied as

$$\text{Effort} \times AF = \text{Load} \times BF$$

or $$E \times (20) = (100)(AB + AF)$$

$\therefore$ $$20\,E = (100)(400) \quad \ldots\text{(i)}$$

(ii) Fire tongs a class III lever has effort in between *F* and *L*.

(iii) From Eq. (i), we can write

$$E = \frac{100 \times 400}{20} = 100 \times 20 = 2000\text{ N}$$

Here, effort arm, $FA = 20$ cm

Load arm, $BF = FA + AB = 20\text{ cm} + 380\text{ cm} = 400\text{ cm}$

$\therefore$ $$\text{MA} = \frac{\text{Effort arm}}{\text{Load arm}} = \frac{20\text{ cm}}{400\text{ cm}} = \frac{1}{20} = 0.05$$

Check Your LEARNING...

1 For a lever, if effort arm becomes equal to load arm, then what effect can be seen in the value of mechanical advantage (MA)?
2 State any two characteristics of lever of class I?
3 Fill up: a scissors is a .... multiplier.
4 Give one example each of class I lever, where the mechanical advantage is
(i) equal to 1 (ii) more than 1.
5 Which class of a lever always act as a force multiplier?
6 Give one example each of a machine which is used to
(i) multiply force
(ii) change direction of application of force.
7 Give an example of lever of third class.
8 Which type of levers have mechanical advantage always less than 1? Give reason. Why such type of levers are used?
9 In which situation, class-II lever is found in human body?

Pulley

Pulley is a wheel on an axle that is designed to support movement and change the direction of a cable or belt along its circumference. A set of pulleys assembled, so that they rotate independently on the same axle to form a block, is called **pulley system**.

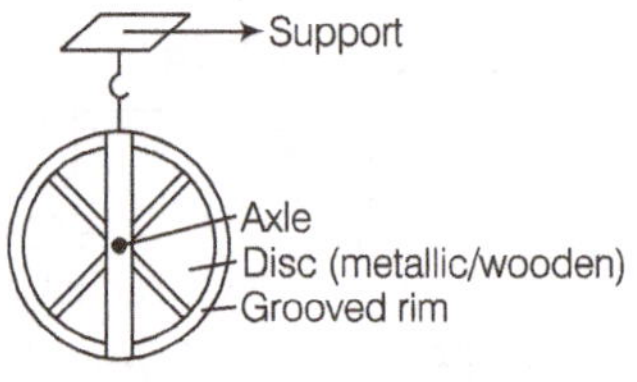

Pulley

A single pulley can be used in two ways as
(i) a fixed pulley (ii) a movable pulley

Single Fixed Pulley

A pulley which has its axis of rotation fixed in position is called single fixed pulley.

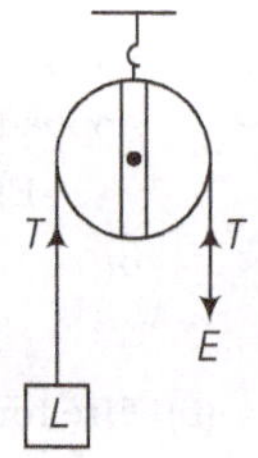

Single fixed pulley

Mechanical Advantage

$$(MA) = \frac{Load}{Effort} = \frac{T}{T} = 1$$

($\because$ load, $L = T$, effort, $E = T$, if pulley is not rotating)

$$\text{Velocity Ratio (VR)} = \frac{d_E}{d_L} = \frac{d}{d} = 1$$

$$(d_E = d \text{ and } d_L = d)$$

$$\text{Efficiency } (\eta) = \frac{MA}{VR} = 1 \text{ or } 100\%$$

A fixed pulley is used only to change the direction of effort to be applied, i.e. with its use, the effort can be applied in a more convenient direction.

Single Movable Pulley

A pulley whose axis of rotation is not fixed in position is called a movable pulley.

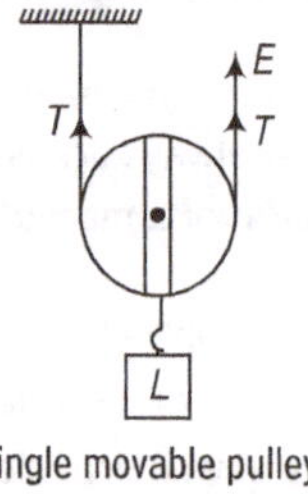

Single movable pulley

Load is balanced by

$$T + T = 2\,T$$

$$\text{Mechanical Advantage (MA)} = \frac{Load}{Effort} = \frac{2T}{T} = 2$$

$$(\because L = 2T \text{ and } E = T)$$

$$\text{Velocity Ratio (VR)} = \frac{d_E}{d_L} = \frac{2d}{d} = 2$$

$$(\because d_E = 2d \text{ and } d_L = d)$$

$$\text{Efficiency } (\eta) = \frac{MA}{VR} \times 100 = \frac{2}{2} \times 100 = 100\% \text{ or } 1$$

Difference between a Single Fixed Pulley and a Single Movable Pulley

Single Fixed Pulley	Single Movable Pulley
It is fixed to a rigid support.	It is not fixed to a rigid support.
Its Ideal Mechanical Advantage (IMA) is 1.	Its Ideal Mechanical Advantage (IMA) is 2.
Its Velocity Ratio (VR) is 1.	Its Velocity Ratio (VR) is 2.
The weight of pulley itself does not affect its mechanical advantage.	The weight of pulley itself reduces its mechanical advantage.
It is used to change the direction of effort from upwards to downwards.	It is used as a force multiplier.
Load moves in a direction opposite to that of effort.	Load moves in the direction of effort.

Example 7. A pulley system has a velocity ratio of 4 and an efficiency 80%. Calculate
(a) the mechanical advantage of the system .
(b) the effort required to raise a load of 500 N by the system.

Sol. Given, velocity ratio of a pulley system (VR) = 4
Efficiency of the pulley system (η) = 80%
We know that,

(a) Efficiency, $\eta = \frac{\text{Mechanical Advantage (MA)}}{\text{Velocity Ratio (VR)}}$

$$\Rightarrow \quad 80\% = \frac{MA}{4}$$

$$\Rightarrow \quad MA = \frac{80}{100} \times 4 = 3.2$$

(b) Load, $L = 500$ N, MA $= 3.2$ and effort, $E = ?$

$$MA = \frac{L}{E} \Rightarrow E = \frac{L}{MA} = \frac{500\text{ N}}{3.2} = 156.25\text{ N}$$

Combination of Pulleys

The combination can be made in two ways
(i) Using one fixed pulley and several movable pulleys.
(ii) Using several fixed pulleys in two blocks known as block and tackle system.

Using One Fixed Pulley and Several Movable Pulleys

According to diagram, we see that one end of each string passing over a movable pulley is fixed, so the other end of string moves up twice the distance moved by the axle of the movable pulley.

If there are n movable pulleys with one fixed pulley, then the mechanical advantage of this system is

$$MA = 2^n$$

So, mechanical advantage of system which has one fixed pulley and three movable pulleys $= 2^3 = 8$

If there are n movable pulleys connected to a fixed pulley, then velocity ratio of this system is

$$VR = 2^n$$

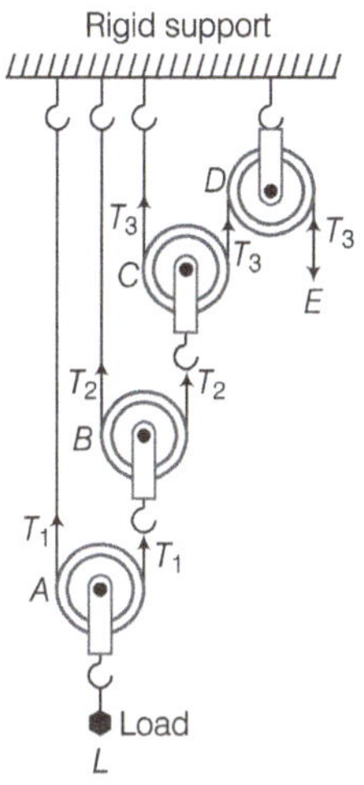

So, velocity ratio of system which has one fixed pulley and three movable pulleys $= 2^3 = 8$

Efficiency of this combination,

$$\eta = \frac{MA}{VR} = \frac{2^n}{2^n} = 1 \text{ or } 100\%$$

Example 8. Diagram given below is representing a pulley system having a velocity ratio 3 and an efficiency of 80%. Calculate the mechanical advantage and effort.

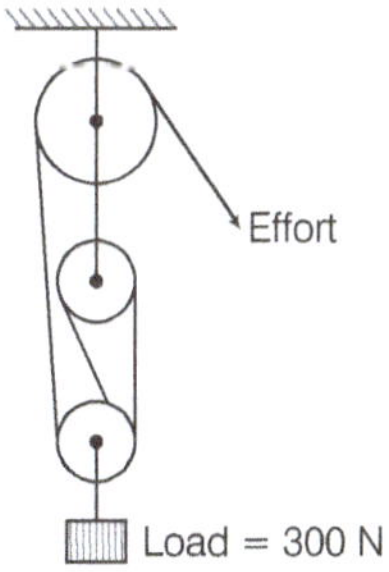

Sol. Since, Mechanical Advantage,

$$MA = \frac{\text{Load}}{\text{Effort}} = VR \times \eta = 3 \times \frac{80}{100} = 2.4$$

$$\therefore \quad \text{Effort} = \frac{\text{Load}}{2.4} = \frac{300}{2.4} = 125 \text{ N}$$

Using Several Fixed Pulleys in Two Blocks (Block and Tackle System)

In this system, two blocks of pulleys are used while usually upper block is fixed and the lower block is movable. If the total number of pulleys used in both the blocks is n and the effort is being applied in the downward direction.

In this case,

$$\text{Load} = nT$$

and $\quad \text{Effort} = T$

Mechanical Advantage (MA)

$$= \frac{\text{Load}}{\text{Effort}} = n$$

In a block and tackle system, if the load moves up through a distance d, the effort end moves through a distance nd because each section of the string supporting the load is loosened by a length d, i.e. if $d_L = d$, then $d_E = nd$

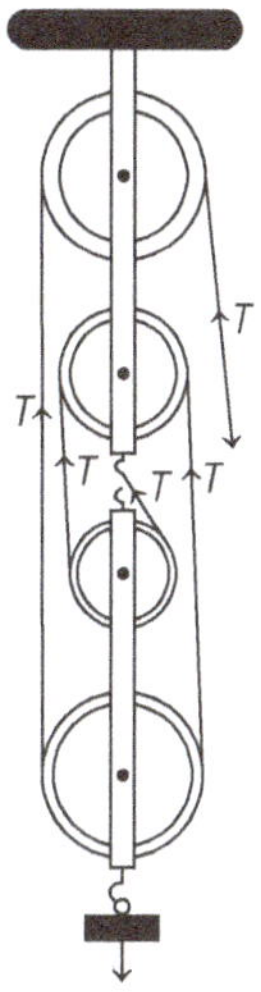

Block and tackle for four pulleys

$$\therefore \quad \text{Velocity Ratio (VR)} = \frac{nd}{d} = n$$

Efficiency of this combination,

$$\eta = \frac{MA}{VR} = \frac{n}{n} = 1 \text{ or } 100\%$$

Effect of Weight of Pulleys on MA, VR and η

But, if total weight of pulleys in the lower block be w, then

$$L + w = nT$$

$$\Rightarrow L = nT - w \text{ and } E = T$$

Mechanical Advantage (MA)

$$= n - \frac{w}{E}, \; VR = n$$

Efficiency, $\boxed{\eta = \frac{MA}{VR} = \frac{(n - w/E)}{n} = 1 - \frac{w}{nE}}$

Example 9. The diagram below shows a system of five pulleys.

(i) Copy the diagram and complete it by drawing strings around the pulleys. Mark the position of load and effort.

(ii) If the load is raised by 2 m, through what distance will the effort move?

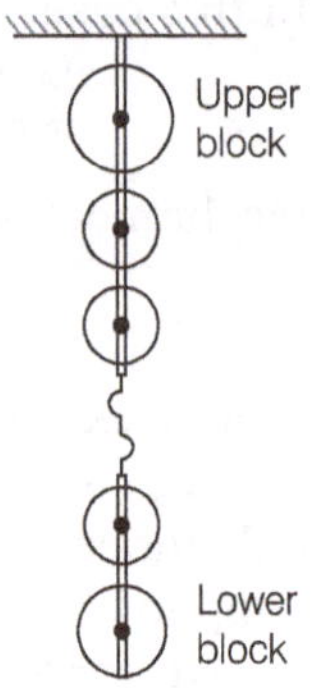

Sol. (i) Complete diagram is shown in the given figure

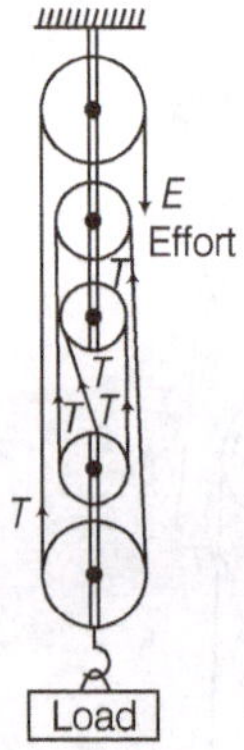

(ii) In block and tackle system, if the load moves through a distance d, the effort moves through a distance nd, where, n is the total number of pulleys in both blocks.

Here, as the load is raised by 2 m, the effort will move through a distance of $5 \times 2 = 10$ m.

Example 10. A pulley system has a velocity ratio 4 and an efficiency of 70%. Draw a labelled diagram of this pulley system. Calculate the mechanical advantage of the system and the value of the effort required to raise a load of 500 N.

Sol. Labelled diagram of the pulley system is shown in figure.

Given, velocity Ratio (VR) = 4, efficiency, η = 70%, load, L = 500 N

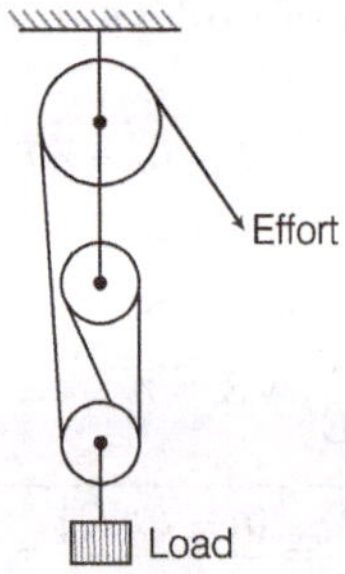

Mechanical Advantage (MA)= ? and effort, E = ?

$$\text{MA} = \frac{\text{Load}}{\text{Effort}} = \text{VR} \times \eta = 4 \times \frac{70}{100} = 2.8$$

and $\quad \text{effort} = \frac{\text{load}}{2.8} = \frac{500}{2.8} = 178.57 \text{ N}$

Example 11. A block and tackle system has the velocity ratio 4, labelled diagram of the system indicating the point of application and the directions of load and effort is given below. A man can exert a pull of 500 N. What is the maximum load he can raise with this pulley system, if its efficiency is 80%?

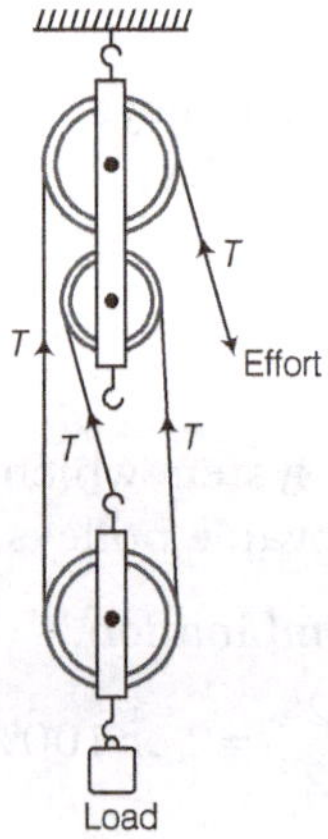

Sol. Given, $\quad$ VR = 4

Efficiency, $\quad \eta = 80\% = \frac{4}{5}$

$$\text{MA} = \text{VR} \times \eta$$

$$\text{MA} = 4 \times \frac{4}{5} = \frac{16}{5} = 3.2$$

But, $\quad \text{MA} = \frac{L}{E}$

$\Rightarrow \quad 3.2 = \frac{L}{500}$

$\Rightarrow \quad L = 500 \times 3.2$

$\Rightarrow \quad L = 1600$ N

The maximum load that can be raised is 1600 N.

Check Your LEARNING...

1 Name a machine which can be used to change the direction of force applied.

2 Define the term "single fixed pulley". State its mechanical advantage and velocity ratio.

3 Name the type of single pulley that has a mechanical advantage greater than one.

4 Why do we use single fixed pulley?

5 What is the value of ideal mechanical advantage of a single fixed pulley?

6 In the case of a single movable pulley, state whether the load moves in the direction of effort or opposite to effort ?

7 How many combination of pulleys are there? Name them.

QUiCK Revision

- **Machine** is a device which helps us to do the work at one point and deliver it at another point with a view of accomplishing the work easily.

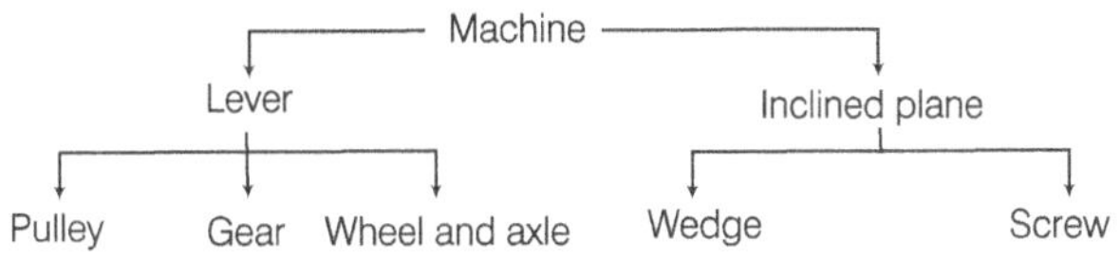

Classification of Machine

- Functions performed by machines are
  (i) as a force multiplies
  (ii) to increase or decrease speed
  (iii) in changing, the direction of effort
  (iv) to change the point of application of effort.
- **Load** It is the resistive or opposing force against which the machine does the work. It is denoted by L.
- **Effort** It is the force applied on the machine to overcome the load. It is denoted by E.
- **Mechanical Advantage** (MA) It is the ratio of the load to the effort. It is denoted by MA.
- **Efficiency** (η) It is the ratio of the work done on the load by the machine to the work put into the machine by the effort.
- **Velocity Ratio** (VR) It is the ratio of the distance moved by the effort d_E to the corresponding distance moved by the load d_L.
- **For an ideal machine**, η is 100%.
- **In actual machine**, the output energy is always less than the input energy.
- **Relation between η, MA and VR** If η is expressed as percentage efficiency, then $\eta = \frac{\text{MA}}{\text{VR}} \times 100$
- A **lever** is a straight or bent rod which can be turned or rotated about a fixed point called fulcrum.
- In **class I lever**, the effort (E) and the resistance (load, L) are situated on either side of the fulcrum (F). e.g. A pair of scissors, handle of water pump, a catapult and the nodding of the human head, etc.
- In **class II lever**, the load is situated between fulcrum and effort. e.g. A bottle opener, a wheel barrow, a paper cutter, raising the weight of the human body on toes, etc.
- In **class III lever**, effort is situated between the load and the fulcrum. e.g. Sugar tongs, foot treadle, etc.
- **Three classes of levers** are found in the human body
  (i) class I lever in the action of nodding of head
  (ii) class II lever in raising the weight of the body on toes
  (iii) class III lever in raising a load by forearm.
- **Pulley** is a wheel on an axle that is designed to support movement and change the direction of a cable or belt along its circumference. A set of pulleys assembled, so that they rotate independently on the same axle to form a block is called **pulley system**.
- A pulley which has its axis of rotation fixed in position is called **single fixed pulley**. For this pulley MA = 1, VR = 1, $\eta = 100\%$.
- A pulley whose axis of rotation is not fixed in position is called a **movable pulley**.
  For this pulley MA = 2, VR = 2, $\eta = 100\%$.
- For combination of pulleys using one fixed pulley and other movable pulley MA $= 2^n$, VR $= 2^n$, $\eta = 100\%$.
- **For block and tackle system** MA $= n$, VR $= n$ with weight of pulley, MA $= n - \frac{w}{E}$, VR $= n$, $\eta = 1 - \frac{w}{nE}$.
- The inclined plane is a sloping surface that behaves like a simple machine whose **mechanical advantage** is always greater than 1.

$$\text{MA} = \frac{1}{\sin\theta}, \text{VR} = \frac{l}{h}$$

Chapter Practice

1 Mark Questions

1. Mechanical Advantage (MA), load (L) and effort (E) are related as
(a) MA $= L \times E$ (b) MA $\times E = L$
(c) $E =$ MA $\times L$ (d) None of these

Sol. (*b*) Mechanical Advantage (MA) $= \frac{\text{Load }(L)}{\text{Effort }(E)}$

$\Rightarrow \quad \text{MA} \times E = L$

2. Select the incorrect statement. **[ICSE Latest Specimen Sem-I]**
(a) A machine always has efficiency less than 100%.
(b) The mechanical advantage of a machine can be less than 1.
(c) A machine can be used as a speed multiplier.
(d) A machine can have mechanical advantage greater than its velocity ratio.

Sol. (*d*) Since, efficiency of a machine,

$$\eta = \frac{\text{MA}}{\text{VR}}$$

As, $\eta \leq 1$

$\Rightarrow \quad \text{MA} \leq \text{VR}$

Thus, the mechanical advantage of a machine cannot be greater than its velocity ratio.

3. A woman draws water from a well using a fixed pulley. The mass of the bucket and the water together is 10 kg. The force applied by the woman is 200 N. The mechanical advantage is (Take, $g = 10 \text{ m/s}^2$) **[ICSE 2022 Sem-I]**
(a) 2 (b) 20
(c) 0.05 (d) 0.5

Sol. (*d*) Given, mass of bucket and water (m) $= 10$ kg

Force applied (F) $= 200$ N

$$\text{Mechanical advantage (MA)} = \frac{\text{Load}}{\text{Effort}} = \frac{10 \times 10}{200} = \frac{1}{2} = 0.5$$

4. The correct relationship between Mechanical Advantage (MA), Velocity Ratio (VR) and efficiency (η) is
(a) MA $= \eta \times$ VR (b) VR $= \eta \times$ MA
(c) $\eta =$ MA $\times$ VR (d) None of these

Sol. (*a*) Efficiency of a machine,

$$\eta = \frac{\text{Output work}}{\text{Input work}} = \frac{L \times d_L}{E \times d_E} = \frac{L}{E} \times \frac{1}{d_E / d_L}$$

Since, $\frac{L}{E} = \text{MA}$ and $\frac{d_E}{d_L} = \text{VR}$

$\Rightarrow \quad \eta = \frac{\text{MA}}{\text{VR}}$

or VR $\times \eta =$ MA

5. Which one of the following statement is correct? **[ICSE Latest Specimen Sem-I]**
(a) A machine is used to have more output energy as compared to input energy.
(b) Mechanical advantage of a machine can never be greater than 1.
(c) If a machine gives convenience of direction, then its mechanical advantage should be greater than 1.
(d) For a given design of a machine, even if the mechanical advantage increases, the velocity ratio remains the same.

Sol. (*d*) For a given design, number of movable component or immovable constraints remain fixed. Therefore, velocity ratio remain the same.

6. A lever for which mechanical advantage is less than 1 has
(a) fulcrum at the mid-point between load and effort
(b) load between effort and fulcrum
(c) effort between fulcrum and load
(d) load and effort acting at the same point

Sol. (*c*) The mechanical advantage of a lever is less than 1, when its effort arm is less than load arm. i.e. The effort is between fulcrum and load.

7. Class II lever are designed to have
(a) MA= VR (b) MA> VR
(c) MA > 1 (d) MA < 1

Sol. (*c*) In class II lever, the effort arm is always longer than the load arm, so its Mechanical Advantage (MA) is always more than 1 i.e. MA > 1.

8. Choose the correct statement.
(a) In a simple machine, the input energy is always equal to output energy.
(b) Actual mechanical advantage is greater than ideal mechanical advantage.
(c) Velocity ratio is the ratio of displacement of the effort to the displacement of the load.
(d) The mechanical advantage of a single fixed pulley is greater than one.

Sol. (*c*) Only statement in option (c) is correct.

$$\text{Velocity ratio} = \frac{\text{Displacement of the effort }(d_E)}{\text{Displacement of the load }(d_L)}$$

In a simple machine, the input energy is always greater than the output energy as some energy is always lost in the process.

Actual mechanical advantage < Ideal mechanical advantage

The mechanical advantage of a single fixed pulley is equal to one.

9. The diagram below shows the balanced position of a meter scale. **[ICSE 2022 Sem-I]**

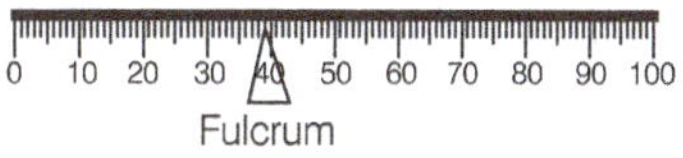

Which one of the following diagrams shows the correct position of the scale, when it is supported at the centre?

(a)
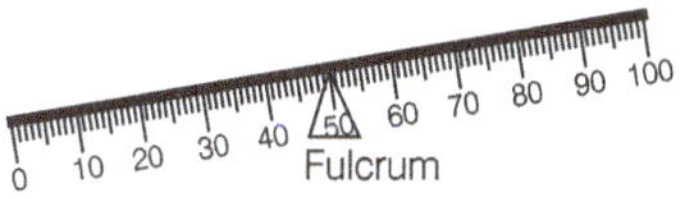

(b)
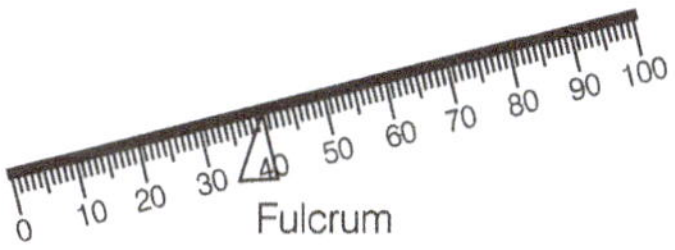

(c)
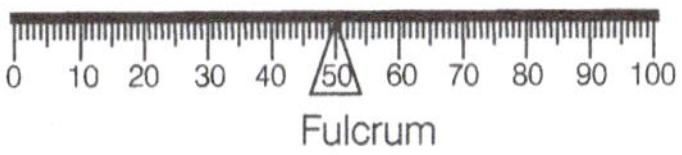

(d)
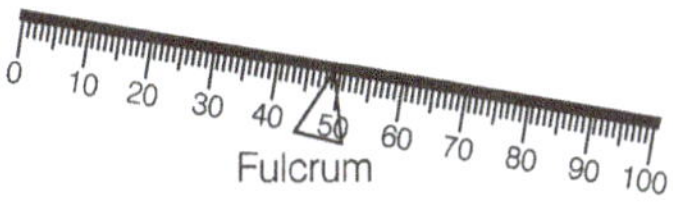

Sol. (*a*) According to principle of moments,

$$40 \times m_1 = 60 \times m_2$$

$$\frac{m_1}{m_2} = \frac{3}{2}$$

Hence, $m_1 > m_2$.

Thus, the meter scale will tilt towards m_1 (left) side when supported at the centre.

Hence, option (a) is correct.

10. If the centre of gravity of a metre scale of mass 80 g lies at the 45 cm mark, then which one of the following diagrams will show the balanced position of the scale? **[ICSE Latest Specimen Sem-I]**

(a)
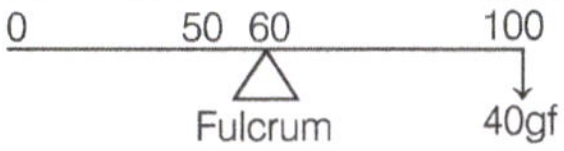

(b)
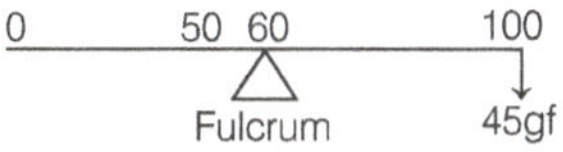

(c)
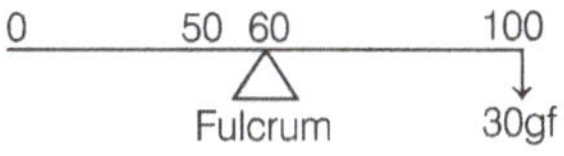

(d)
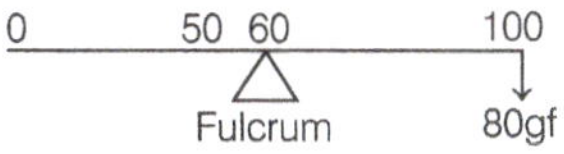

Sol. (*a*) Given, mass (m) = 80 g

Centre of gravity (CG) = 45 cm

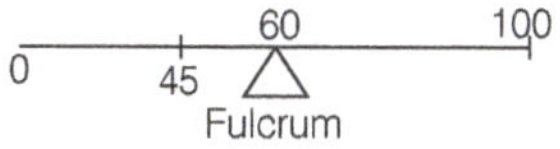

From the principle of moments, we have

$$mg(60 - 50) = mg(100 - 60)$$

$$\Rightarrow \quad mg \times 10 = 10g \times 40$$

$$\Rightarrow \quad m = 40 \text{ gf}$$

Hence, figure (a) represent the balanced position of the scale.

11. A single fixed pulley is used because it
(a) has mechanical advantage greater than 1
(b) has velocity ratio less than 1
(c) gives 100% efficiency
(d) helps to apply the effort in a convenient direction

Sol. (*d*) A single fixed pulley is used because it helps to apply the effort in a convenient direction.

Its mechanical advantage and velocity ratio is 1.

12. A movable pulley is used as
(a) a force multiplier
(b) a speed multiplier
(c) a device to change the direction of effort
(d) an energy multiplier

Sol. (*a*) The movable pulley decreases the force required to pull a load by a multiple of 2 × movable pulleys number. The force will be half of that weight lifted in a movable pulley as the massless pulley forces should be balanced. So, a movable pulley is used as a force multiplier.

13. A pulley system has a single fixed pulley and a single movable pulley. Its mechanical advantage is
(a) 1 (b) 2 (c) 3 (d) 4

Sol. (*b*) A single fixed pulley has mechanical advantage as

$$MA_f = \frac{T}{T} = 1$$

The single movable pulley has mechanical advantage

$$MA_m = \frac{2T}{T} = 2$$

So, the given pulley system has mechanical advantage as, $MA = MA_f \times MA_m = 1 \times 2 = 2$

14. The mechanical advantage of an inclined plane of angle of inclination 60° is equal to
(a) $2/\sqrt{3}$ (b) cosec 30°
(c) Both (a) and (b) (d) None of these

Sol. (*a*) Mechanical advantage of an inclined plane is

$$MA = \frac{l}{h} = \frac{l}{l\sin\theta} = \frac{1}{\sin\theta} = \frac{1}{\sin 60^\circ} = \text{cosec } 60^\circ = \frac{2}{\sqrt{3}}$$

2 Marks Questions

15. Write two functions of a machine.

Sol. Two functions of a machine are given below

(i) A machine can be used to lift a load in one direction by applying effort in convenient direction.

(ii) It can be used to overcome a load at some point by applying an effort at a convenient point. [1+1]

16. With reference to the terms mechanical advantage, velocity ratio and efficiency of a machine, name and define the term that will not change for a machine of a given design. [2016]

Sol. From the given variables, velocity ratio of a machine will not change for a machine of a given design. It is the ratio of the velocity of effort to the velocity of load. [2]

17. When does a machine act as

(i) a force multiplier?

(ii) a speed multiplier?

Sol. (i) A machine having MA > 1 works as force multiplier, e.g. crow-bar. [1]

(ii) A machine having MA < 1 works as speed multiplier, e.g. a pair of scissors. [1]

18. Why cannot a machine be 100% efficient?

Sol. Due to the weights of different parts of machine and friction between its different parts the MA is less than the VR (i.e. MA < VR). Hence, a machine can never be 100% efficient. [2]

19. (i) What is meant by an ideal machine?

(ii) Write a relationship between the mechanical advantage (MA) and velocity ratio (VR) of an ideal machine.

Sol. (i) A machine having 100% efficiency is called an ideal machine. [1]

(ii) The relation between MA and VR is given by

MA = VR $(\because \eta = 100\%)$ [1]

20. What is a lever? State its principle.

Sol. A simple machine that can rotate (capable of turning) freely about a point or axis is called lever.

The principle of lever is [1]

⇒ effort × effort arm length = load × load arm length. [1]

21. (i) Calculate the mechanical advantage of the lever shown in figure.

(ii) How do you define mechanical advantage of a machine?

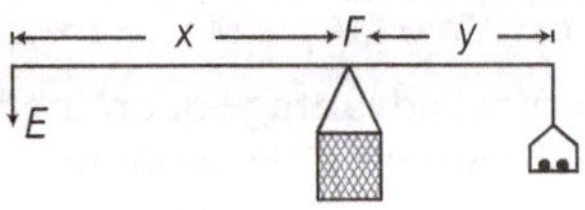

Sol. (i) Clockwise moment = $y \times L$

and anti-clockwise moment = $x \times E$

According to the principle of moment,

clockwise moment = anti-clockwise moment

$\therefore \quad y \times L = x \times E$

or $\quad \dfrac{L}{E} = \dfrac{x}{y}$ [1]

(ii) Mechanical advantage is the ratio of the load lifted to the effort applied.

Hence, in figure, MA $= \dfrac{L}{E} = \dfrac{x}{y}$ [1]

22. The diagram below shows a claw hammer used to remove a nail.

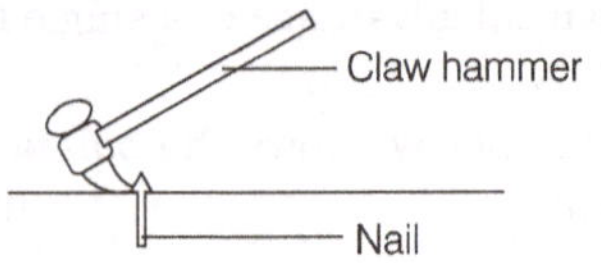

(i) To which class of lever does it belong?

(ii) Give one more example of the same class of lever mentioned by you in part (i) for which the mechanical advantage is greater than one. [2019]

Sol. (i) A claw hammer used to remove a nail is a class 1 lever.

(ii) A longer crow bar is an example of class 1 lever, that have mechanical advantage greater than one.

23. Which class of lever will always have MA > 1 and why? [2017]

Sol. In class II lever, an effort arm is always greater than the load arm and the load is situated between fulcrum and effort. In this lever, the mechanical advantage and velocity ratio are always more than 1. The sketch of such lever is shown below.

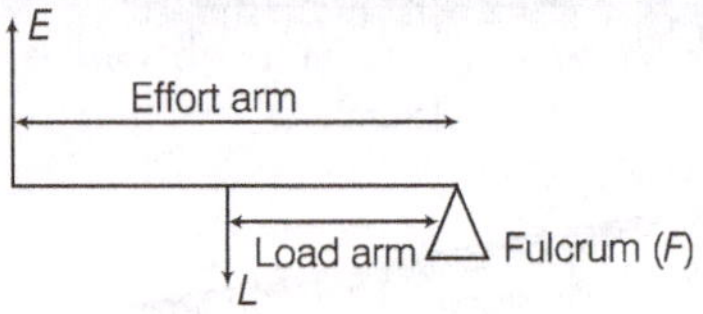

[1+1]

24. The diagram below shows a lever in use

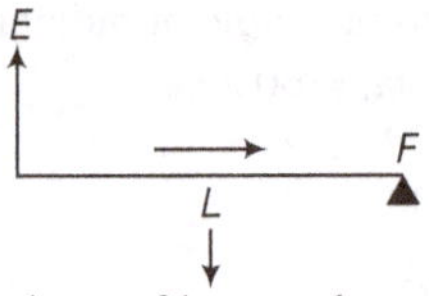

(i) To which class of levers does it belong?

(ii) Without changing the dimensions of the lever, if the load is shifted towards the fulcrum what happens to the mechanical advantage of the lever? [2018]

Sol. (i) It belongs to class II lever because load is situated between fulcrum and effort. [1]

(ii) If load is shifted towards the fulcrum, then mechanical advantages will increase. [1]

25. (i) Identify the class of the lever shown in the diagram below

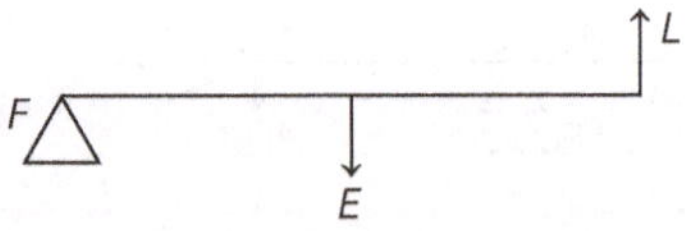

(ii) How is it possible to increase the mechanical advantage of the above lever without increasing its length? [2020]

Sol. (i) The lever given in the diagram is a class 3 lever because effort lies between the load and the fulcrum.

(ii) Mechanical advantage of a lever is the ratio of effort arm to load arm.

i.e. $MA = \frac{\text{Effort arm}}{\text{Load arm}}$

Therefore, MA of lever is increased by shifting the effort (E) towards the load.

26. Copy the diagram of the forearm given below, indicate the positions of load, effort and fulcrum. **[2008]**

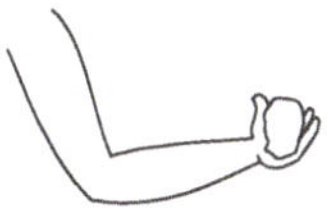

Sol. The below diagram shows the position of load (L), effort (E) and fulcrum (F).

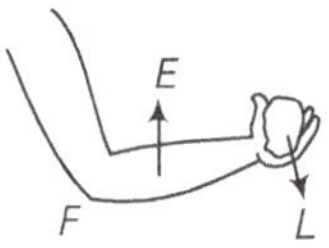

[2]

27. Draw a diagram to show how a single pulley can be used, so as to have its ideal MA = 2. **[2014]**

Sol.

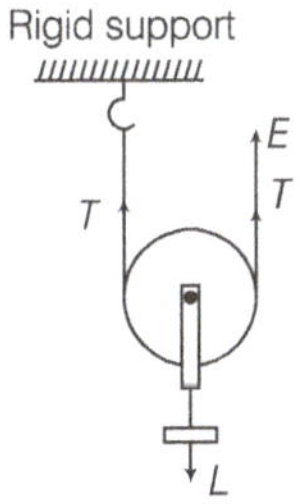

[2]

28. A type of single pulley is very often used as a machine, even though it does not give any gain in mechanical advantage. **[2013]**

(i) Name the type of pulley used.

(ii) For what purpose is such a pulley used?

Sol. (i) The pulley which is used in the arrangement is single fixed pulley. [1]

(ii) Single fixed pulley is used only to change the direction of the force applied. [1]

29. (i) Name a single pulley in which displacement of load and effort is not the same.

(ii) State one advantage of this pulley. **[2023] [2]**

Sol. (i) Single movable pulley [1]

(ii) It can be used as a force multiplier. [1]

30. A block and tackle system of pulleys has a velocity ratio 4. Draw a labelled diagram of the system indicating clearly the points of application and directions of load and effort.

Sol. The labelled diagram of the system is shown as below

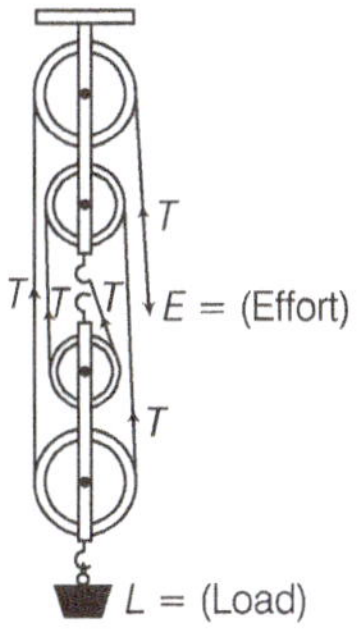

[2]

3 Marks Questions

31. What step could be taken to increase the mechanical advantage of a lever?

Sol. As we know, $MA = \frac{\text{load}}{\text{effort}}$, so to increase MA, length of effort arm should be greater than load arm, because

$$E \times E_d = L \times L_d$$

or $MA = \frac{\text{Effort arm}}{\text{Load arm}}$ [3]

32. Assume that a pair of scissors and a pair of pliers belong to the same class of levers.

(i) Which one has mechanical advantage less than one?

(ii) What is the advantage of a machine whose mechanical advantage is less than one?

Sol. (i) A pair of scissors and a pair of pliers both belong to class I levers.

For class I levers, $MA > 1$ or $MA = 1$ or $MA < 1$

As, we know that

Mechanical advantage $= \frac{\text{Load } (L)}{\text{Effort } (E)} = \frac{\text{Effort arm}}{\text{Load arm}}$ [1]

In a pair of scissors, effort arm is less than the load arm.

$\therefore$ Mechanical advantage of a pair of scissors is less than one. [1]

(ii) The machines with $MA < 1$ can help us to apply the effort at a more convenient point or to gain in speed. [1]

33. With the help of a diagram of a single fixed pulley, obtain expressions for its

(i) mechanical advantage

(ii) velocity ratio

(iii) efficiency in the ideal case.

Sol. The diagram of a single fixed pulley is shown alongside. Suppose, T is the tension in each of the string and in the ideal case string is massless and there is no friction in the pulley bearings, then in equilibrium,

$E = T$ and $L = T$

(i) Mechanical advantage, $MA = \frac{L}{E} = \frac{T}{T} = 1$ **[1]**

(ii) If the effort E moves a distance d downwards, then load L moves the same distance d upwards.

So, Velocity Ratio, $VR = \frac{d_E}{d_L} = \frac{d}{d} = 1$ **[1]**

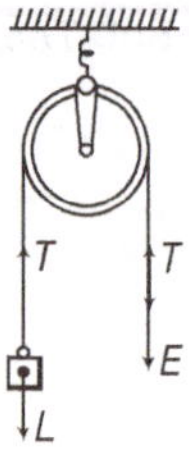

(iii) Efficiency $= \frac{MA}{VR} = \frac{1}{1} = 1$ (or 100%) **[1]**

34. A pulley system comprises two pulleys, one fixed and the other movable.

(i) Draw a labelled diagram of the arrangement and show clearly the directions of all the forces acting on it.

(ii) What change can be made in the movable pulley of this system to increase the mechanical advantage of the system?

Sol. (i) The labelled diagram of the above arrangement is as shown below

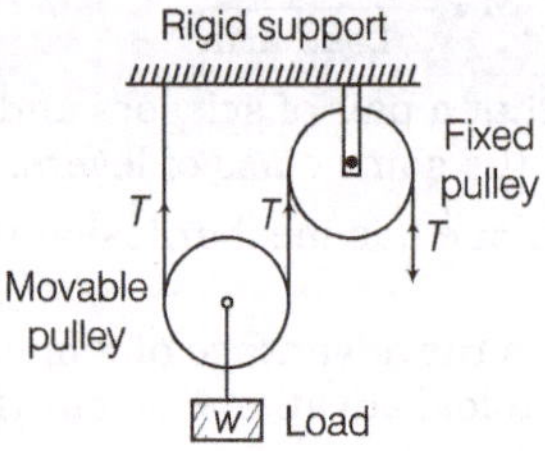

[2]

(ii) To increase the mechanical advantage of the system, we need to reduce the friction between the string and the movable pulley. **[1]**

4 Marks Questions

35. State and explain the working principle of a lever with proper diagram.

Sol. Consider a lever (for a straight rod) AB with balanced point at F (fulcrum for the lever), a load L acts at point A of the lever and effort E acts at point B as shown in the diagrams. **[2]**

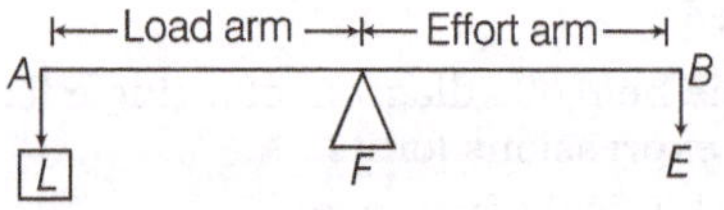

A lever works on the principle of moment. In the equilibrium position of the lever, by the principle of moment,

moment of load about the fulcrum

= moment of effort about the fulcrum **[1]**

The two moments are always equal in magnitude and opposite in directions.

In figure, the moment of load is anti-clockwise while the moment of effort is clockwise. Thus, we can write

load × load arm = effort × effort arm

This is also called principle of lever.

or $L \times AF = E \times BF$ **[1]**

36. Write the class of levers to which following belongs.

(i) A physical balance	(ii) A see-saw
(iii) An oar of a boat	(iv) Human-arm
(v) Pliers	(vi) A claw-hammer
(vii) Rowing of a boat	(viii) A fire tongs
(ix) Sugar tongs	(x) A pair of scissors
(xi) Wheel barrow	(xii) Nut cracker

Sol. Above mentioned levers belong to the following classes

(i) Class I	(ii) Class I
(iii) Class II	(iv) Class III
(v) Class I	(vi) Class I
(vii) Class II	(viii) Class III
(ix) Class III	(x) Class I
(xi) Class II	(xii) Class II

[1/3 ×12]

37. Draw a diagram consisting of four pulleys in block and tackle arrangement.

(i) State how many strands of tackle support the load?

(ii) Draw arrows to represent tension in each strand.

(iii) Find the mechanical advantage of the system stating the assumptions made.

(iv) If load is pulled up by a distance of 1 m, how much does the effort arm move?

Sol. The adjacent diagram shows a block and tackle system of four pulleys.

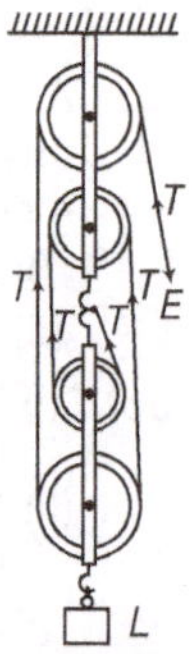

(i) Four strands of tackle support the load.

(ii) The tension in each strand is shown by the arrows marked as T.

(iii) If we neglect the friction of the pulleys and weight of the pulleys in the lower block, then

$L = 4T$ and $E = T$

$\therefore \quad MA = \frac{L}{E} = \frac{4T}{T} = 4$

(iv) If load is pulled up by a distance 1 m, the effort end moves by 4 m. **[1 × 4]**

38. (i) Draw a diagram to show a block and tackle pulley system having a velocity ratio of 3 marking the direction of load (L), effort (E) and tension (T).

(ii) The pulley system drawn lifts a load of 150 N, when an effort of 60 N is applied. Find its mechanical advantage.

(iii) Is the above pulley system an ideal machine or not? **[2018]**

Sol. (i) The labelled diagram of the system is shown below

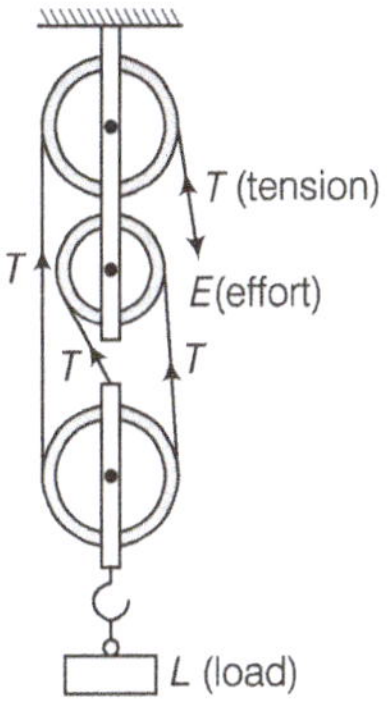

[2]

(ii) Given, load $(L) = 150$ N
Effort $(E) = 60$ N
We know that, Mechanical Advantage

$$(\text{MA}) = \frac{\text{Load}}{\text{Effort}} = \frac{150}{60} = 2.5$$ [1]

(iii) No, the above pulley system is not an ideal machine because velocity ratio (VR = 3) is not equal to mechanical advantage. [1]

39. (i) Write a relation expressing the mechanical advantage of a lever.
(ii) Write an expression for the mechanical advantage of an inclined plane.
(iii) Give two reasons as to why the efficiency of a single movable pulley system is always less than 100%? [2010]

Sol. (i) The relation expressing mechanical advantage of a lever is given by

$$\text{MA} = \frac{\text{Effort arm}}{\text{Load arm}}$$ [1]

(ii) The expression for the mechanical advantage of an inclined plane is given by

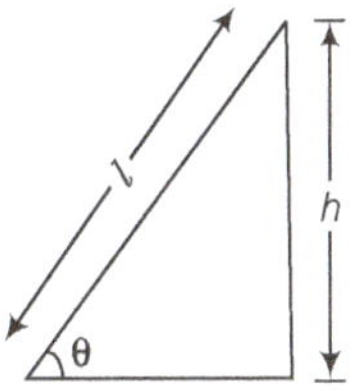

$$\text{MA} = \frac{l}{h}$$

$$= \frac{l}{l\sin\theta} = \frac{1}{\sin\theta} = \text{cosec}\,\theta$$

where, θ is the angle of inclination,
l is the length
and h is the height of inclined plane. [1]

(iii) (a) The weight of movable pulley with its frame is not negligible.
(b) The frictional force between pulley and string is not negligible. [1 × 2]

Numerical Based Questions

40. A crow-bar of length 150 cm has its fulcrum situated at a distance of 50 cm from the load. Calculate the mechanical advantage of crow-bar. [2]

Sol. $$\text{MA} = \frac{\text{Length of effort arm from fulcrum}}{\text{Length of the load arm from fulcrum}}$$ [1]

i.e. $$= \frac{150 - 50}{50} = 2$$ [1]

41. A crow-bar of length 90 cm has its fulcrum situated at a distance of 10 cm from the load. Calculate the mechanical advantage of the crow-bar. [2]

Sol. MA of crowbar,

$$\text{MA} = \frac{\text{Effort arm}}{\text{Load arm}} = \frac{80}{10} = 8$$

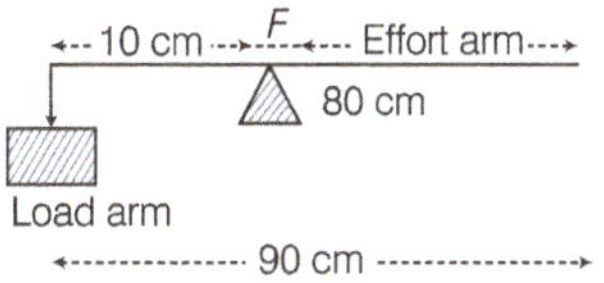

[2]

42. A fire tongs has its arms 30 cm long. It is used to lift a coal of weight 2 kgf by applying an effort at distance 20 cm from the fulcrum. Find
(i) the mechanical advantage of fire tongs and
(ii) the effort needed. [2]

Sol. (i) Effort arm = 20 cm

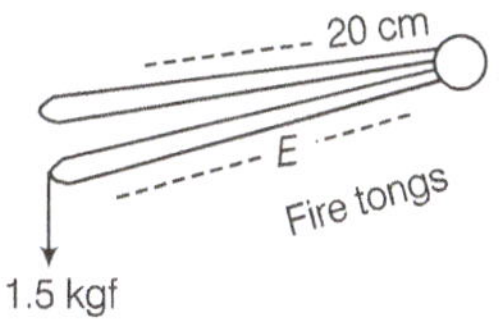

Load arm = 30 cm

$$\text{MA} = \frac{\text{Effort arm}}{\text{Load arm}} = \frac{20}{30} = \frac{2}{3} = 0.66$$ [1]

(ii) $$\text{Effort} = \frac{\text{Load}}{\text{Mechanical Advantage}} = \frac{2\text{ kgf}}{2/3} = 3\text{ kgf}$$ [1]

43. The diagram below shows a lever in use.

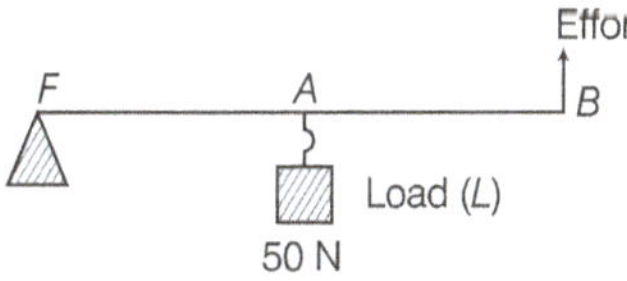

[2]

If $FA = 40$ cm, $AB = 60$ cm, then find the mechanical advantage of the lever. [2011]

Sol. Effort arm = $FA + AB = 40 + 60 = 100$ cm

Load arm = $FA = 40$ cm [1]

$$\therefore \quad \text{MA} = \frac{\text{Effort arm}}{\text{Load arm}} = \frac{FB}{FA} = \frac{100}{40} = 2.5$$ [1]

44. Two forces each of 10 N act vertically upwards and downwards, respectively on the two ends of a uniform meter ruler which is placed at its mid-point as shown in the diagram. Determine the magnitude of the resultant moment of these forces about the mid-point.

Sol.

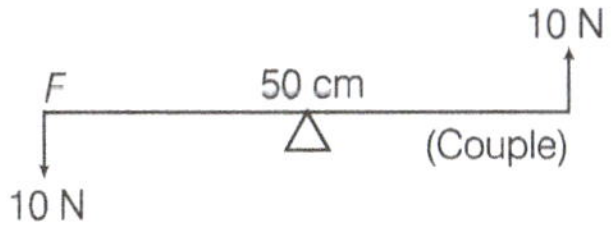

$$M = F \times d \text{ (or) } F \times s$$ [1]

$$\therefore \quad M = 10 \times \frac{50}{100}\text{ m}$$

$$= 10 \times 0.5 = 5\text{ N-m}$$ [1]

45. In the diagram shown below, calculate the resistance (R) offered by the nut, when an effort of 50 N is applied.

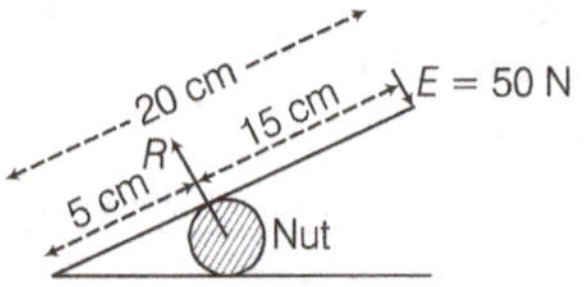

[2]

Sol. Load arm = 5 cm

Effort arm = 15 + 5 = 20 cm [1]

As, we know that,

load × load arm = effort × effort arm

$\Rightarrow \quad R \times 5\text{ cm} = 50\text{ N} \times 20\text{ cm} \Rightarrow R = 200\text{ N}$ [1]

46. A cook uses a fire tong of length 28 cm to lift a piece of burning coal of mass 250 g. If he applies his effort at a distance of 7 cm from the fulcrum, what is the effort in SI unit? (Take, $g = 10\text{ m/s}^2$) [3]

Sol. Given, mass, $m = 250\text{ g} = 0.25\text{ kg}$

Load, $L = mg = 0.25 \times 10\text{ N} = 2.5\text{ N}$ [1]

Distance of load, $L_d = 28\text{ cm} = 0.28\text{ m}$

Distance of effort, $E_d = 7\text{ cm} = 0.07\text{ m}$

Effort, $E = ?$

According to the principle of moment, we have [1]

$E \times E_d = L \times L_d$

$$\Rightarrow \quad E = \frac{L \times L_d}{E_d} = \frac{2.5 \times 0.28}{0.07} = 10\text{ N}$$ [1]

47. In the diagram of a stationary wheel barrow, the centre of gravity is at A. The wheel and the leg are in contact with the ground. The horizontal distance between A and F is 50 cm and that between B and F is 150 cm.

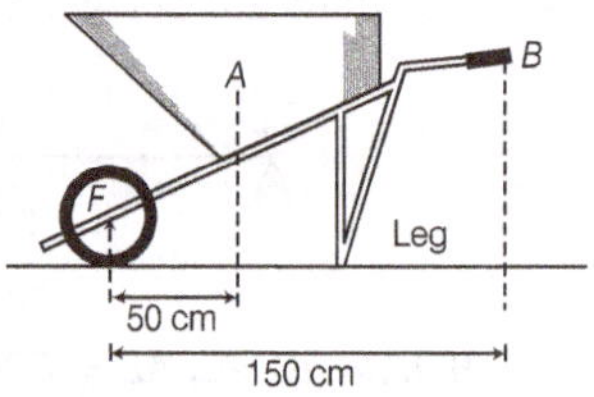

(i) What is the direction of the force acting at A? Name the force.

(ii) What is the direction of the minimum force at B to keep the leg off the ground? What is this force called?

(iii) The weight of the wheel barrow is 15 kgf and it holds sand of weight 60 kgf. Calculate the minimum force required to keep the leg off the ground. [4]

Sol. (i) The direction of the force acting at A is vertically downwards. This force is named as load. [1]

(ii) The direction of the minimum force at B to keep the leg off the ground is acting vertically upwards. This force is called effort. [1]

(iii) Given, weight of wheel, $w_E = 15\text{ kgf}$

Weight of sand, $w_S = 60\text{ kgf}$

Minimum force, $E = ?$

Total load, $L = w_E + w_S$

$= 15 + 60 = 75\text{ kgf}$

Effort arm, $E_a = 50 + 100$ [1]

$= 150\text{ cm} = 1.5\text{ m}$

Load arm, $L_a = 50\text{ cm} = 0.5\text{ m}$

Applying the principle of lever,

load × load arm = effort × effort arm

$\Rightarrow \quad L \times L_a = E \times E_a$

$$\Rightarrow \quad E = \frac{L \times L_a}{E_a} = \frac{75 \times 0.5}{1.5} = 25\text{ kgf}$$ [1]

48. In a single movable pulley system a load of 300 kgf is lifted by an effort of 200 kgf. Find the percentage efficiency of system. [2]

Sol. We know that, VR of single movable pulley = number of supporting segments of string = 2

MA of single movable pulley $= \frac{L}{E} = \frac{300}{200} = \frac{3}{2}$ [1]

Therefore, efficiency is $\eta = \frac{\text{MA}}{\text{VR}} = \frac{3}{2 \times 2} = \frac{3}{4}$

$= 0.75 = 75.00\%$ [1]

49. A pulley system has a velocity ratio of 4 and an efficiency of 90%. Calculate

(i) the mechanical advantage of the system.

(ii) the effort required to raise a load of 300 N by the system. [2]

Sol. Given, velocity ratio, VR = 4

Efficiency, $\eta = 90\%$

(i) Mechanical Advantage,

$$\text{MA} = \text{VR} \times \frac{\eta}{100}$$

$$= 4 \times \frac{90}{100} = 3.6 \quad \left(\because \eta = \frac{\text{MA}}{\text{VR}}\right)$$ [1]

(ii) Effort, $E = ?$, load, $L = 300\text{ N}$

$$E = \frac{L}{\text{MA}} = \frac{300}{3.6} = 83.33\text{ N} \quad \left(\because \text{MA} = \frac{L}{E}\right)$$ [1]

50. A pulley system has four pulleys in all and is 75% efficient. Calculate

(i) MA and

(ii) effort required to lift a load of 1000 N. [3]

Sol. Given, $\eta = 75\%$,

VR = 4 (as the system has 4 pulleys)

(i) Since, $\eta = \frac{\text{MA}}{\text{VR}}$

$\therefore \quad \text{MA} = \eta \times \text{VR} = \frac{75}{100} \times 4 = 3$ [1½]

(ii) Also, $\text{MA} = \frac{\text{Load}}{\text{Effort}}$

$$\text{Effort} = \frac{\text{Load}}{\text{MA}} = \frac{1000}{3} = 333.33\text{ N}$$ [1½]

51. A pulley system has three pulleys. A load of 120 N is overcome by applying an effort of 50 N. Calculate the mechanical advantage and efficiency of this system. [3] [2016]

Sol. According to question, load = 120 N

Effort = 50 N

$\therefore$ Mechanical Advantage $= \frac{\text{Load}}{\text{Effort}} = \frac{120}{50} = 2.4$ [1]

Now, % efficiency $= \frac{\text{MA}}{\text{VR}} \times 100 = \frac{2.4}{3} \times 100 = 80\%$ [2]

52. From the diagram given below, answer the questions that follow [3]

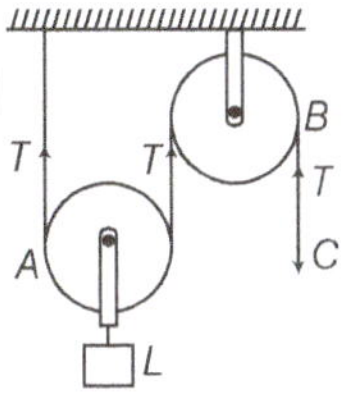

(i) What kind of pulleys are A and B?

(ii) State the purpose of pulley B.

(iii) What effort has to be applied at C to just raise the load $L = 20$ kgf ? (neglect the weight of pulley A and friction) [3] [2016]

Sol. (i) According to questions,

A is a movable pulley while B is a fixed pulley. [1]

(ii) The purpose of pulley B is to change the point of application of effort and load in the same direction. [1]

(iii) Given, load = 20 kgf, MA = 2 and

we know that, $\text{MA} = \frac{\text{Load}}{\text{Effort}}$

$\therefore \quad \text{Effort} = \frac{\text{Load}}{\text{MA}} = \frac{20}{2} = 10 \text{ kgf}$ [1]

53. A block and tackle system of pulleys has a velocity ratio 4. What is the value of the mechanical advantage of the given pulley system, if it is an ideal pulley system? [2]

Sol. Given, velocity ratio,

$\text{VR} = 4$, load $L = 4T$ effort $= T$

$\therefore \quad \text{MA} = \frac{\text{Load}}{\text{Effort}} = \frac{4T}{T} = 4$ [2]

54. The pulley system shown in the figure is used to raise 500 kgf object. What is the mechanical advantage and what force is exerted?

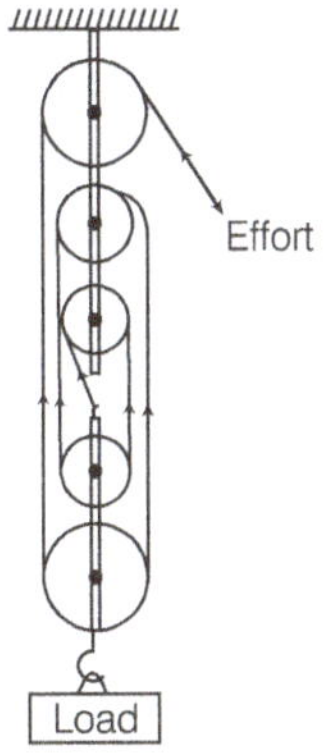

[2]

Sol. Given, MA = number of segments holding the load = 5

Load, $L = 500$ kgf

Effort, $E = ?$

We know that, $\text{MA} = \frac{\text{Load}}{\text{Effort}}$

or $\quad \text{Effort} = \frac{\text{Load}}{\text{MA}} = \frac{500}{5} = 100 \text{ kgf}$ [1+1]

55. A boy uses a single fixed pulley to lift a load of 50 kgf to same height. Another boy uses a single movable pulley to lift the same load to the same height. Compare the effort applied by them. Give a reason to support your answer. [4] [2017]

Sol. In first case, the pulley is single fixed,

$\text{MA} = 1$

But, $\quad \text{MA} = \frac{L_1}{E_1} \Rightarrow 1 = \frac{50}{E_1}$

$\Rightarrow \quad E_1 = 50 \text{ kgf}$ [2]

In second case, the pulley is single movable,

$\therefore \quad \text{MA} = 2 \Rightarrow 2 = \frac{50}{E_2}$

$\Rightarrow \quad E_2 = 25 \text{ kgf}$

$\Rightarrow \quad \frac{E_1}{E_2} = \frac{50}{25} = \frac{2}{1}$ [2]

56. A pulley system with VR = 4 is used to lift a load of 175 kgf through a vertical height of 15 m. The effort required is 50 kgf in the downward direction. (Take, $g = 10$ N/kg).

Calculate

(i) distance moved by the effort

(ii) work done by the effort

(iii) MA of the pulley system

(iv) efficiency of the pulley system [4] [2017]

Sol. (i) We know that, $\text{VR} = \frac{\text{distance moved by effort } (D_E)}{\text{distance moved by load } (E_L)}$ [1]

$4 = \frac{D_E}{15} \Rightarrow D_E = 60 \text{ m}$

(ii) Work done by the effort = Force × displacement

$= 50 \times 10 \times 60 = 30000 \text{ J}$ [1]

(iii) $\text{MA} = \frac{L}{E} = \frac{175}{50} = 3.5$ [1]

(iv) Efficiency, $\eta = \frac{\text{MA}}{\text{VR}} = \frac{3.5}{4} = 0.875 = 87.5\%$ [1]

57. A block and tackle with five pulleys is found to have a MA of 3, when a load of 10 N is raised by it. Calculate

(i) the effort applied

(ii) VR

(iii) efficiency and

(iv) the total resistance R due to friction. [4]

Sol. Number of pulleys in the block and tackle = 5

MA= 3, $L = 10$ N, $E = ?$

Total resistance, $R = ?$, $\eta = ?$

(i) Since, we know that, $E = \frac{L}{\text{MA}} = \frac{10}{3} = 3.33$ N [1]

(ii) Now, we know that velocity ratio of a pulley block and tackle is equal to the total number of pulleys.

$\text{VR} = n = 5$ [1]

(iii) Efficiency $(\eta) = \frac{MA}{VR} \times 100 = \frac{3}{5} \times 100 = 60\%$ **[1]**

(iv) $L + R = VR \times E = 5 \times 3.33 = 16.65$

Resistance due to friction,

$R = 16.65 - L = 16.65 - 10 = 6.65$ N **[1]**

Structured Questions

58. (i) A uniform meter scale can be balanced at the 70.0 cm mark, when a mass of 0.05 kg is hung from the 94.0 cm mark.

(a) Draw a diagram of the arrangement. **[3]**

(b) Find the mass of the meter scale. **[2011]**

(ii) If the weight of wheel barrow is 10 kgf and the weight of sand in it is 50 kgf, with the help of information given in figure. Calculate the minimum effort required to keep the leg just off the ground.

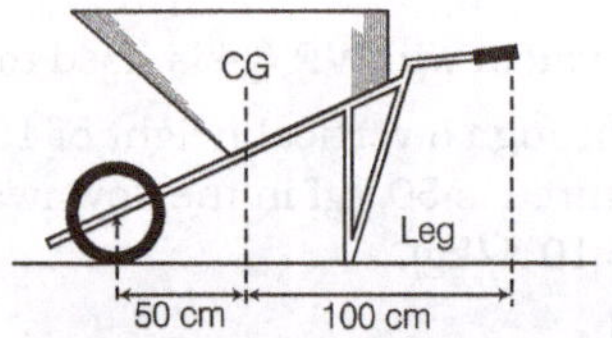

[3]

(iii) A block and tackle system has VR = 5

(a) Draw a neat labelled diagram of a system indicating the direction of its load and effort.

(b) Rohan exerts a pull of 150 kgf. What is the maximum load he can raise with this pulley system, if its efficiency –75%? **[4]**

Sol. (i) (a) The diagram of the above arrangement is shown as below **[1]**

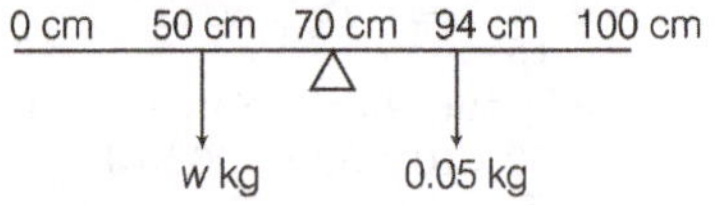

(b) Let w be the weight of the scale. **[1]**

By principle of moments, we get

$w \times (70 - 50) = 0.05(94 - 70)$

$\Rightarrow \quad w \times 20 = 0.05 \times 24$ **[1]**

$\Rightarrow \quad w = \frac{0.05 \times 24}{20} = 0.06$ kg **[1]**

(ii) Total load of wheel barrow = 50 + 10 kgf

Load = 60 kgf

Load arm = 50 cm

Effort = ?

Effort arm = 150 cm **[1]**

Load × Load arm = Effort × Effort arm

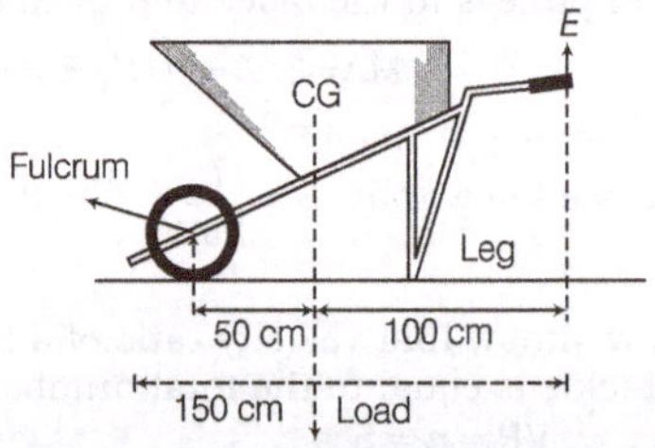

[1]

$\Rightarrow \quad 60 \times 50 = E \times 150$

$\Rightarrow \quad E = \frac{60 \times 50}{150} = 20$ kgf **[1]**

(iii) (a) Velocity ratio is always equal to the number of strands of tackle supporting the load. For velocity ratio 5, there will be 5 strands supporting the load.

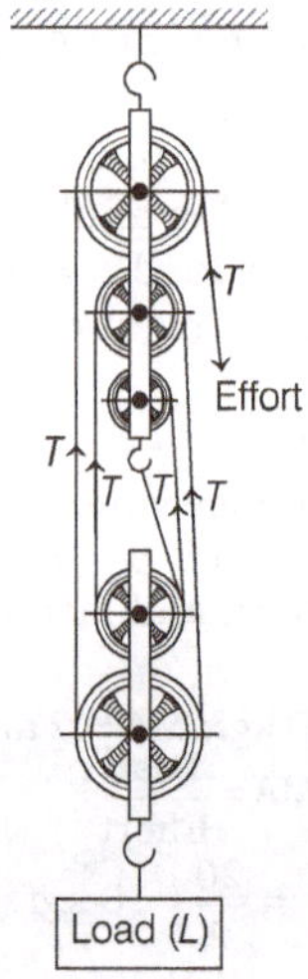

[2]

(b) Given, $E = 150$ kgf, $\eta = 75\% = 0.75$, VR = 5

$\therefore \quad MA = L / E = VR \times \eta = 5 \times 0.75 = 3.75$

$\Rightarrow \quad L / 150 = 3.75$

$\Rightarrow \quad L = 3.75 \times 150 = 562.5$ kgf **[3]**

59. (i) (a) State the class of levers and the relative positions of load (L), effort (E) and fulcrum (F) in each of the following cases:

I. A bottle opener II. Sugar tongs

(b) Why is less effort needed to lift a load over an inclined plane as compared to lifting the load directly? **[2012] [3]**

(ii) A force of 10 kgf is required to cut a metal sheet. A shear used for cutting a metal sheet has its blades 10 cm long, while its handle is 20 cm long. What effort is needed to cut a sheet? **[3]**

(iii) A block and tackle pulley system has a velocity ratio 3. **[2007]**

(a) Draw a labelled diagram of this system. In your diagram, indicate clearly the points of application and the directions of the load and effort.

(b) Why should the lower block of this pulley system be of negligible weight? **[4]**

Sol. (i) (a) I. A bottle opener is a class II lever. In this case, the load is in between the fulcrum and the effort.

II. Sugar tongs are class III lever. In this case, the effort is in between the fulcrum and the load. **[1+1]**

(b) Less effort is needed to lift a load over an inclined plane as compared to lifting the load directly, as the mechanical advantage increases. **[1]**

(ii) Length of blades = Load arm = 10 cm = $\frac{10}{100}$ m

Load, $L = 10$ kgf, effort needed, $E = ?$ **[1]**

Length of handle = Effort arm = 20 cm = $\frac{20}{100}$ m

$\therefore E \times$ effort arm $= L \times$ load arm

$\Rightarrow \quad E \times \frac{20}{100} = 10 \times \frac{10}{100}$ **[1]**

$\Rightarrow \quad E = \frac{100}{20} = 5$ kgf **[1]**

(iii) (a) The labelled diagram of the system is shown below

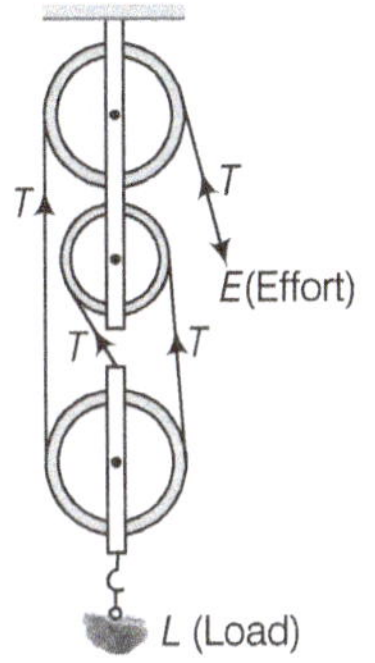

[2]

(b) If the total weight (w) of pulleys in the lower block is in the balanced position.

Then, efficiency, $\eta = \frac{\text{MA}}{\text{VR}} = \frac{n - \frac{w}{E}}{n} = 1 - \frac{w}{nE}$

From the expression, it is clear that for greater efficiency $\frac{w}{nE}$ should be negligible.

Thus, the pulleys in the lower block should be as light as possible. **[2]**

60. (i) A block and tackle system of pulleys has velocity ratio 4. **[3]**

(a) Draw a neat labelled diagram of the system indicating clearly the points of application and direction of load and effort.

(b) What will be its velocity ratio, if the weight of the movable block is doubled? **[2020]**

(ii) A block and tackle system of pulleys has velocity ratio 4 .

(a) Draw a labelled diagram of the system indication clearly, the direction of the load and the effort

(b) What is the value of the mechanical advantage of the given pulley system, if it is an ideal pulley system ? **[2023] [3]**

(iii) The figure below shows a pulley arrangement.

(a) Copy the figure and mark the direction of tension on each strand of the string.

(b) What is the velocity ratio of the arrangement?

(c) If the tension acting on the string is T, then what is the relationship between T and effort E?

(d) If the free end of the string moves through a distance x, then find the distance by which the load is raised. **[4]**

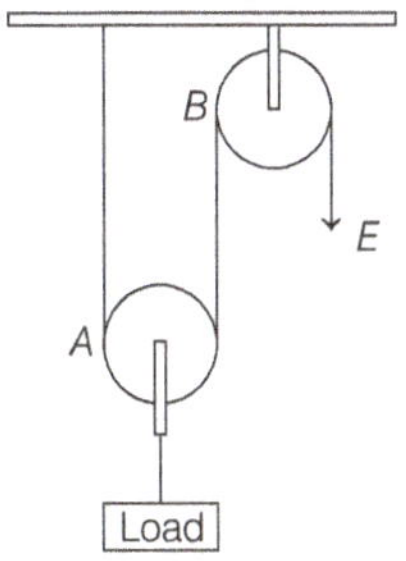

Sol. (i) (a) Refer to Sol. of Q. 30 on page no. 59.

(b) Given, velocity ratio (VR) = 4

$\therefore$ Efficiency, $\eta = \frac{\text{MA}}{\text{VR}} = \frac{\text{MA}}{4} \Rightarrow \eta = \frac{\text{MA}}{4}$ ...(i)

When movable load is doubled, then MA is also increased to double, i.e. 2 MA.

$\therefore$ Efficiency, $\eta = \frac{2\text{MA}}{\text{VR}}$ ...(ii)

From Eqs. (i) and (ii), we have

$\frac{2\text{MA}}{\text{VR}} = \frac{\text{MA}}{4} \Rightarrow \text{VR} = 8$

(ii) (a) **Diagram** Refer to theory [Page 53]

(b) Given, Velocity Ratio (VR) = 4

Load = $4T$

Effort = T

Mechanical advantage (MA) = $\frac{\text{Load}}{\text{Effort}} = \frac{4T}{T} = 4$

Hence, the mechanical advantage of pulley is 4. **[1+1+1]**

(iii) (a)

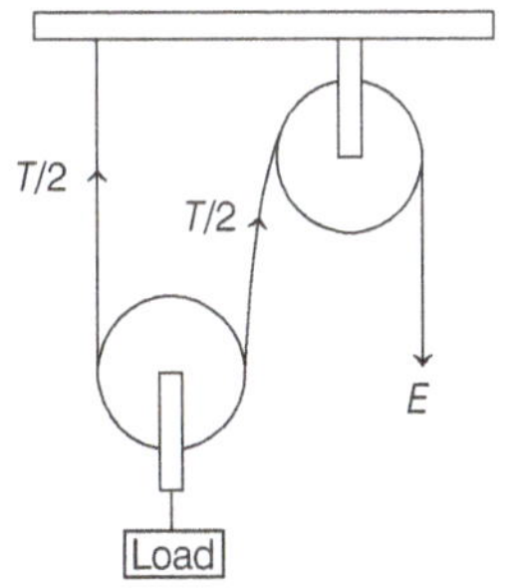

[1]

(b) Velocity ratio of the system, which one fixed pulley and one movable pulley, then velocity ratio = $2^1 = 2$ **[1]**

(c) The relation between T and effort E is given by

$\frac{T}{2} = E$

$T = 2E$ **[1]**

(d) If the free end of the the string moves through a distance x, then the load is raised by $\frac{x}{2}$ distance. **[1]**

Chapter Assessment

1 Mark Questions

1. A fulcrum divides a crow-bar in the ratio of 3 : 1. What weight will be lifted, if an effort of 100 N is applied at the end of its longer arm?
(a) 400 N (b) 100 N
(c) 300 N (d) 500 N

2. The MA of sugar tongs is
(a) < 1 (b) $= 1$
(c) > 1 (d) None of these

3. A machine is driven by a 100 kg mass that falls 8 m on 4 s. It lifts a load of mass 500 kg. What is the power output, input power to the pulley is
[Take, $g = 10 \text{ m/s}^2$]
(a) 2000 W (b) 1000 W
(c) 2500 W (d) 150 W

4. If $FA = 40$ cm, $AB = 60$ cm, find MA of the lever.

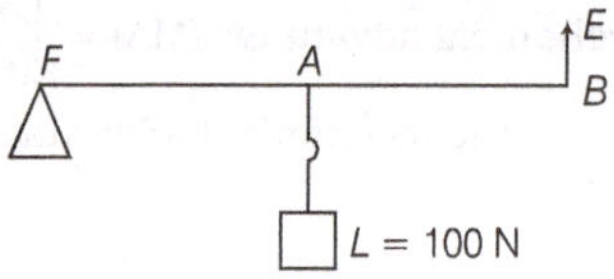

(a) 1 (b) 1.5 (c) 2 (d) 2.5

5. The MA of a machine is 5 and its efficiency is 80%. It is used to lift a load of 200 kgf to a height of 20 m. What is the effort required?
(a) 10 kgf (b) 20 kgf (c) 40 kgf (d) 50 kgf

2 Marks Questions

6. Write an expression to show the relationship between mechanical advantage, velocity ratio and efficiency for a simple machine.

7. Which class of levers has a mechanical advantage always greater than one? What change can be brought about in this lever to increase its mechanical advantage?

8. The diagram below shows a lever in use.

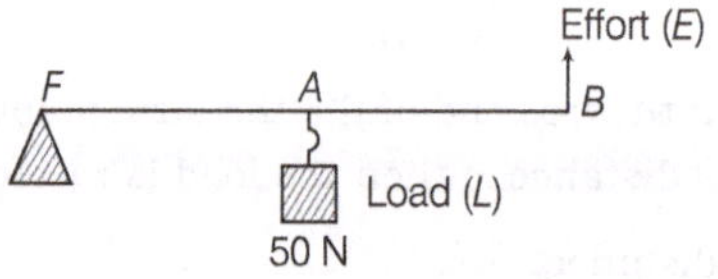

(i) Which class of lever does it belong?
(ii) If $FA = 30$ cm, $AB = 50$ cm, then find the mechanical advantage of the lever.

9. A crow-bar of length 100 cm has its fulcrum situated at a distance of 25 cm from the load. Calculate the mechanical advantage of crow-bar.

10. A pulley system has a velocity ratio of 3 and an efficiency of 80%. Calculate
(i) the mechanical advantage of the system.
(ii) the effort required to raise a load of 480 N by the system.

11. What is the relationship between the mechanical advantage and the velocity ratio for
(i) ideal machine (ii) practical machine ?

12. To use a machine as a force multiplier, what types (class) of lever should preferably be used? Draw a sketch of such a lever.

13. Why is the mechanical advantage of a lever of third order is always less than 1? Give one example of this class of lever.

14. The mechanical advantage of a machine is 4 and its efficiency is 60%. It is used to lift a load of 300 kgf to a height of 15 m. Calculate
(i) the effort required and.
(ii) the work done on the machine.
(Take, $g = 10 \text{ m /s}^2$)

15. Draw a diagram of a class II lever. Give one example of this kind of lever.

16. (i) Why is the mechanical advantage of a lever of the second order always greater than one?
(ii) Name the type of single pulley that has a mechanical advantage greater than one.

17. A cook uses a fire tong of length 30 cm to lift a piece of burning coal of mass 500 g. If he applies his effort at a distance of 10 cm from the fulcrum, what is the effort in SI unit? (Take, $g = 10 \text{ m/s}^2$)

18. A boy draws water from a well using a fixed pulley. The mass of the bucket and water together is 5 kg. The force applied by the boy is 60 N. Calculate the mechanical advantage. (Take, $g = 10 \text{ m/s}^2$)

Structured Questions

19. (i) A pair of scissors and a pair of pliers belong to the same class of levers.
(a) Which one has mechanical advantage less than one?
(b) State the usefullness of such a machine whose mechanical advantage is less than 1. [3]
(ii) (a) Which simple machine is used by the labourers to load heavy barrels, etc. on a truck?
(b) Does a single fixed pulley help us to multiply the force? In what way is it useful? [3]
(iii) The alongside figure shows the combination of a movable pulley P_1 with a fixed pulley P_2 used for lifting up a load w.

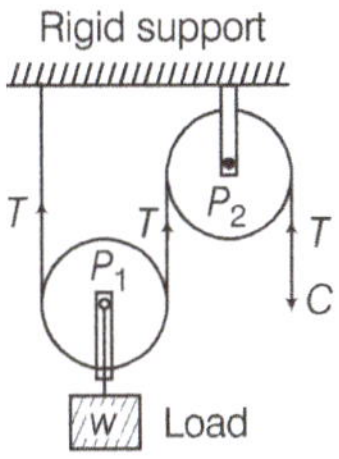

(a) State the function of the fixed pulley P_2.

(b) If the free end of the string moves through a distance x, find the distance by which the load w is raised.

(c) Calculate the force to be applied at C to just raise the load $w = 20$ kgf, neglecting the weight of the pulley P_1 and friction. **[4]**

20. (i) Name the type of single pulley that can act as a force multiplier. Draw a labelled diagram of the above named pulley. **[3]**

(ii) (a) Draw a simplified diagram of lemon crusher, indicating direction of load and effort.

(b) Why is less effort needed to lift a load over an inclined plane as compared to lifting the load directly? **[3]**

(iii) Consider the combination of a movable pulley P_1 with a fixed pulley P_2 used for lifting a load w.

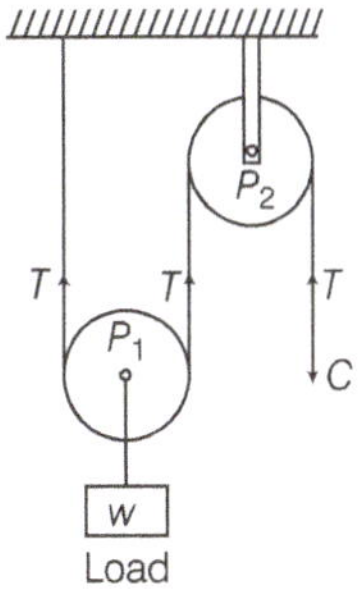

(a) What is the function of the fixed pulley P_2?

(b) If the free end of the string moves through a distance y, find the distance by which the load w is raised.

(c) Calculate the force to be applied at C to just raise the load $w = 30$ kgf, neglecting the weight of the pulley P_1 and friction. **[4]**

21. (i) In which class of lever, see-saw and crow-bar occur. Explain with suitable reason.

(ii) Mention the three important characteristics of class III lever.

(ii) Show that mechanical advantage and velocity ratio are 1 and 1 respectively, for single fixed pulley and that of 2 and 2 respectively, for single movable pulley.

For Solutions Scan the Code

Olympiad Section*

Brain Teasing Questions of Olympiad Pattern

1 A woman draws water from a well using a fixed pulley. The mass of the bucket and water together is 6 kg. The force applied by the woman is 70 N. The mechanical advantage is

(a) 0.96 (b) 0.86
(c) 0.76 (d) 0.66

2 A boy uses a single movable pulley to lift a load of 50 kgf to some height. Another boy uses a single fixed pulley to lift the same load to same height. The ratio of efforts applied by them is

(a) 2 (b) 1
(c) $\frac{1}{2}$ (d) 4

3 A block and tackle system has VR = 5. Rahul exerts a pull of 150 kgf. What is the maximum load he can raise with this pulley system, if its efficiency is 75%?

(a) 500.2 kgf
(b) 562.5 kgf
(c) 661.5 kgf
(d) 332.4 kgf

4 A pulley system has a VR = 5. If the efficiency of the system is 80%, find its MA.

(a) 1 (b) 2
(c) 3 (d) 4

5 A pulley system has MA = 4. If a load of 10 kgf is pulley by a distance of 2 m in 10 s, calculate the power developed by the effort.

(a) 15 W (b) 20 W
(a) 25 W (b) 4.9 W

6 A machine is used to displace a load of 400 N through 50 cm by an effort of 100 N. If the efficiency of machine is 80%, then the resistance due to the movable parts of the machine and friction is

(a) 50 N (b) 100 N (c) 150 N (d) 200 N

7 Calculate the resistance offered by a lemon, when an effort of 0.06 N is applied. The effort arm of the squeezer is 10 cm and the load arm is 3 cm. Assuming that, the effort is applied at the end of effort arm.

(a) 0.1 N (b) 0.5 N
(c) 0.2 N (d) 0.8 N

8 A person draws 10 kg water from a well at depth of 5 m using a single fixed pulley by applying an effort of 120 N. Then, the efficiency of the machine is (Take, $g = 10\ ms^{-2}$)

(a) 83% (b) 87%
(c) 75% (d) 92%

9 A block and tackle system of pulley contains 8 pulleys. A load of 1000 kgf is lifted by effort of 250 kgf. The ratio of mechanical advantage and velocity ratio is

(a) 0.25 (b) 1 (c) 0.75 (d) 0.5

10 A screw jack is used to lift a vehicle of weight 10000 N through a height of 0.25 m from the ground. If the length of the rod is 0.3 m, then the effort used to lift the loads is

(a) 1326 N (b) 1296 N
(c) 1724 N (d) 926 N

ANSWERS	1. (b)	2. (c)	3. (b)	4. (d)	5. (d)	6. (b)	7. (c)	8. (a)	9. (d)	10. (a)

* *These questions may or may not be asked in the examination, have been given just for additional practice required for olympiads Scholarship Exams etc. For detailed explanations refer Page No. 263.*

CHAPTER
4

Refraction of Light

SYLLABUS

(i) Refraction of light through a glass block and a triangular prism : qualitative treatment of simple applications such as real and apparent depth of objects in water and apparent bending of sticks in water. Applications of refraction of light.

(ii) Total internal reflection : critical angle; examples in triangular glass prisms; comparison with reflection from a plane mirror (qualitative only). Applications of total internal reflection.

"Change in path of a light ray as it passes from one medium to another medium is called refraction of light."

When light travels from a rarer medium to a denser one, it bends towards the normal ($i > r$) and when travels from a denser medium to a rarer one, it bends away from the normal ($i < r$).
where, i = angle of incidence, r = angle of refraction.

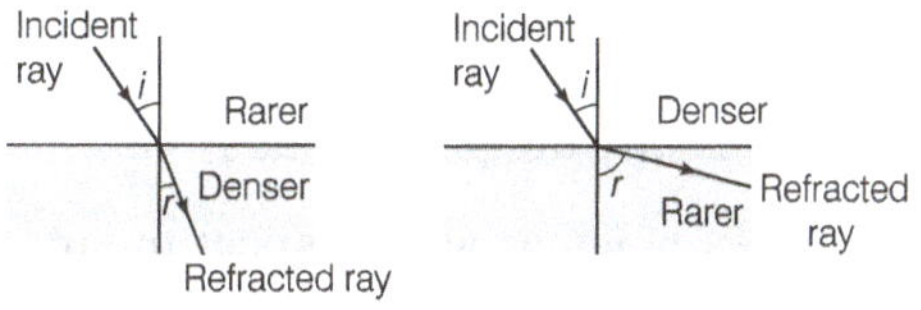

Refraction of light

Some Important Terms Used in Refraction of Light

Some important terms used in refraction of light are as follow

(i) **Incident Ray** It is a ray of light which strikes the plane surface or a ray of light which travels towards the another optical medium.

(ii) **Point of Incidence** It is that point where an incident ray strikes the other optical medium.

(iii) **Normal** It is a straight line always perpendicular to the point of incidence.

(iv) **Angle of Incidence** It is an angle which the incident ray makes with the normal.

(v) **Refracted Ray** It is a ray of light which gets deviated from its path after entering in another optical medium.

(vi) **Angle of Refraction** It is an angle which the refracted ray makes with the normal.

Causes of Refraction

The speed of light is different in different media. It is lesser in denser medium and greater in rarer medium. So, when light enters into a denser medium its speed reduces and it bends towards the normal. Also, when it enters into a rarer medium, its speed increases and it bends away from the normal.

Note When light is incident normally $i = 0°$, the speed of light changes but the direction of light does not change.

Partial Reflection and Refraction due to Change in Medium

Partial reflection and refraction occurs when a light wave is travelling between two mediums. Some of the wave is reflected back and the rest is refracted through the other medium.

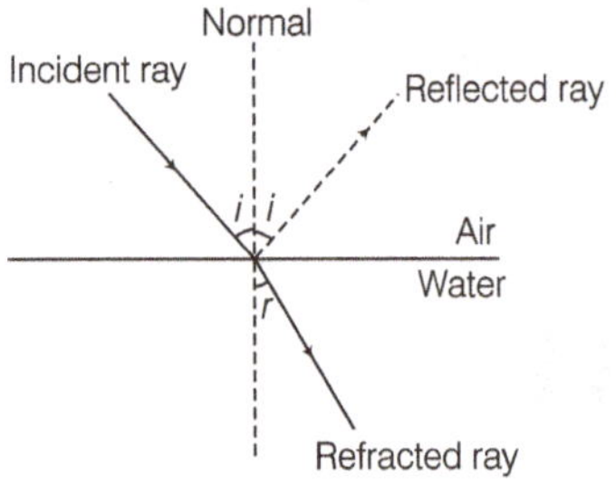

Note Partial reflection and refraction depends on angle of incidence. For 0° angle of incidence-mostly refraction, little or no reflection. For angle θ ($45° < \theta < 90°$) little refraction, mostly reflection.

Laws of Refraction

There are two laws of refraction of light which are stated as below

First Law

The incident ray, the refracted ray and the normal at the point of incidence, all lie in the same plane.

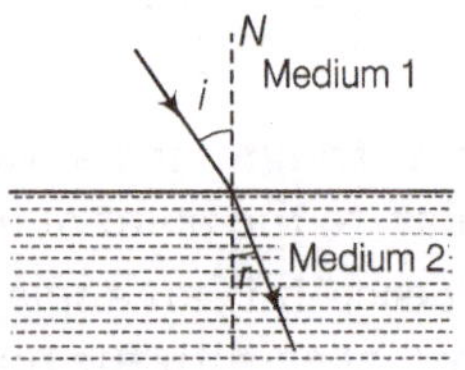

Laws of refraction

Second Law

The ratio of sine of angle of incidence to the sine of angle of refraction is constant for a given pair of media. This constant is known as **refractive index** of the second medium w.r.t. first medium. It is expressed as

$$n \text{ or } \mu = \frac{\sin i}{\sin r} = \text{constant}$$

This relation is also known as **Snell's law**.

Check Your LEARNING...

1. Define refraction.
2. Mention the cause of refraction of light, when it passes from one medium to another.
3. What do you mean by optically rarer medium?
4. In which type of incidence, a ray of light does not deviate from its path after refraction?
5. State second law of refraction.

Refractive Index

The extent of the change in direction that takes place in a given pair of media is expressed in terms of the refractive index.

${}_1\mu_2$ represents refractive index of medium 2 with respect to medium 1, when light is going from medium 1 to medium 2.

$${}_1\mu_2 = \frac{\mu_2}{\mu_1} = \frac{\sin i}{\sin r}$$

The refractive index of a medium with respect to vacuum, is called **absolute refractive index of the medium**. The absolute refractive index of a medium is simply called its refractive index.

For glass/water pair, ${}_w\mu_g = \frac{{}_a\mu_g}{{}_a\mu_w}$

The refractive index has no unit as it is the ratio of two similar quantities.

Note Refractive index of air is minimum and refractive index of diamond is maximum.

Relation between Refractive Index and Speed of Light

If c is the speed of light in air and v is the speed of light in medium, then the refractive index of the medium is

$$\mu = \frac{\text{Speed of light in vacuum/air}}{\text{Speed of light in medium}} = \frac{c}{v}$$

Hence for any two media, the refractive index of second medium with respect to first medium is equal to the ratio of the velocities of lights in the medium.

Refractive index of glass with respect to air,

$${}_a\mu_g = \frac{\text{Velocity of light in air}}{\text{Velocity of light in glass}} = \frac{c}{v_g} \quad \text{...(i)}$$

Refractive index of water with respect to air,

$${}_a\mu_w = \frac{\text{Velocity of light in air}}{\text{Velocity of light in water}} = \frac{c}{v_w} \quad \text{...(ii)}$$

On dividing Eq. (ii) from Eq. (i), we get

$$\frac{{}_a\mu_w}{{}_a\mu_g} = \frac{v_g}{v_w} = {}_g\mu_w$$

Values of μ for common substances

μ of water = 1.33
μ of glass = 1.52
μ of diamond = 2.41

Example 1. If refractive index of water is 1.33, then determine the speed of light in this medium, if the speed of light in vacuum is given by $3\times 10^8\ ms^{-1}$.

Sol. Since, refractive index of water can be given by

$$\mu_w = \frac{\text{Speed of light in vacuum}}{\text{Speed of light in water}}$$

$$\Rightarrow \quad 1.33 = \frac{3\times 10^8}{\text{Speed of light in water}}$$

$$\therefore \text{ Speed of light in water} = \frac{3\times 10^8}{1.33} = 2.25\times 10^8\ ms^{-1}$$

Example 2. Refractive indices of water and glass are 4/3 and 3/2 respectively. A ray of light travelling in water is incident on the water glass interface at 30°. Calculate the angle of refraction.

Sol. Given, refractive index of water, ${}^a\mu_w = \frac{4}{3}$

Refractive index of glass, ${}^a\mu_g = \frac{3}{2}$

Angle of incidence in water, $i = 30°$

Angle of refraction, $r = ?$

As, $${}^w\mu_g = \frac{{}^a\mu_g}{{}^a\mu_w} = \frac{3/2}{4/3} \Rightarrow {}^w\mu_g = \frac{9}{8}$$

According to Snell's law,

$$\frac{\sin i}{\sin r} = {}^w\mu_g \Rightarrow \frac{\sin i}{\sin r} = \frac{9}{8} \Rightarrow \sin r = \frac{8}{9}\sin i$$

$$\Rightarrow \quad \sin r = \frac{8}{9}\sin 30° = \frac{8}{9}\times\frac{1}{2} = 0.444$$

$$\sin r = 0.444 \Rightarrow r = \sin^{-1}(0.444) = 26.38°$$

Factors Affecting the Refractive Index of Medium

There are following factors on which the refractive index of medium depends

(i) **Wavelength of Incident Light** The refractive index of a medium decreases with increase in wavelength of incident light.

Since, the speed of light is different for different colours of light, thus the light travels slower in case of low wavelength which leads to increase in refractive index.

$$\therefore \quad \mu_{red} < \mu_{violet}$$

(ii) **Temperature** The refractive index of a medium decreases with increase in temperature of medium.

($\because$ velocity of light increases with increase in temperature of medium)

$$\therefore \quad \mu_{T_1} > \mu_{T_2} \text{ as } T_1 < T_2$$

(iii) **Optical Density of a Medium** Refractive index of a medium depends on optical density of a medium, more optically denser medium has larger value of refractive index and *vice-versa*.

Conditions for No Refraction

There are following two conditions under which a ray of light passes undeviated from medium 1 to medium 2

(i) When the refractive index of medium 2 is same as that of medium1.

(ii) When the angle of incidence at the boundary surface of the two media is zero ($i = 0°$).

Relation between Speed, Frequency and Wavelength of Light

The equation that relates wavelength and frequency is $$c = f\lambda$$

where, c = speed of light in vacuum,

f = frequency of light and λ = wavelength of light.

Effect on Speed, Wavelength and Frequency Due to Refraction of Light

The effects due to refraction of light on speed, frequency and wavelength are given below as

(i) Speed of light increases when light passes from denser to rarer medium and it decreases when light passes from rarer to denser medium.

(ii) Frequency is a characteristic of light, therefore it remains same as light travels from one medium to another.

(iii) Wavelength of light increases when light passes from denser to rarer medium (as speed also increases) and it decreases when light passes from rarer to denser medium (as speed also decreases) but its frequency remains constant.

Principle of Reversibility of Light

When a light ray after suffering any number of reflections and refractions, has final path reversed and travels back along its entire initial path, then this is called principle of reversibility of light.

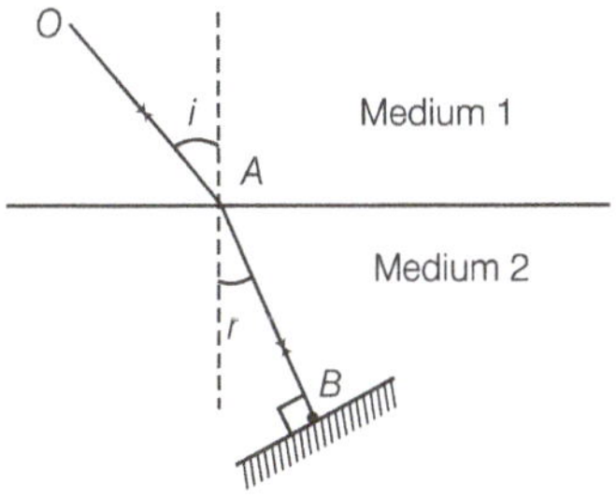

Reversibility of light

In the given figure, OA is an incident ray in medium 1 and AB is the refracted ray in medium 2. By Snell's law, the refractive index of medium 2 relative to medium 1 is given by ${}^1\mu_2 = \dfrac{\sin i}{\sin r}$ ...(i)

where, i and r are the angles of incidence and refraction respectively.

Suppose, the ray AB is reflected back by a plane mirror. Now, BA is the incident ray and AO is the refracted ray.

Correspondingly, r is angle of incidence and i is angle of refraction. Again by Snell's law, the refractive index of medium 1 relative to medium 2 is given by ${}^2\mu_1 = \dfrac{\sin r}{\sin i}$ ...(ii)

Multiplying Eqs. (i) and (ii), we have

$$ {}^1\mu_2 \times {}^2\mu_1 = \frac{\sin i}{\sin r} \times \frac{\sin r}{\sin i} = 1 \text{ or } {}^1\mu_2 = \frac{1}{{}^2\mu_1} $$

Thus, the refractive index of medium 2 relative to medium 1 is equal to the reciprocal of the refractive index of medium 1 relative to medium 2.

Refraction Through a Rectangular Glass Block

When a light ray enters into a glass slab, then the emergent ray is parallel to the incident ray but it is shifted sideward slightly. In this case, refraction takes place twice, first when ray enters into glass slab from air and second when exits from glass slab to air.

Both refractions have been shown in figure (here, glass slab is denser medium and air is rarer medium). The extent of bending of the ray of light at opposite parallel faces AB and CD of rectangular glass slab is equal and opposite. So, the ray emerging from face CD is parallel to incident ray but shifted sideward slightly.

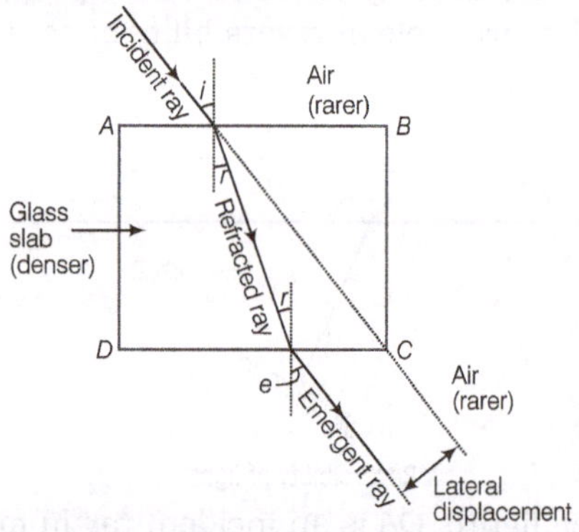

Refraction of light through a glass block

where, i = angle of incidence,
r = angle of refraction
and e = angle of emergence.

Lateral Displacement

The perpendicular distance between the emergent ray and incident ray when the light passes out of a glass slab is called lateral displacement.

It can be calculated by the formula,

$$ \text{lateral displacement} = \frac{t \sin (i - r)}{\cos r} $$

where, t = thickness of the glass block,
i = angle of incidence and r = angle of refraction.

The lateral displacement depends upon the following factors

(i) thickness of the glass block,

(ii) angle of incidence and

(iii) refractive index of glass.

Example 3. A ray of light is incident at angle of 45° on one face of a rectangular glass slab of thickness 10 cm and refractive index 1.5. Calculate the lateral shift produced.

Sol. Here, $i = 45°$, $t = 10$ cm, $\mu = 1.5$

Lateral shift = ?

So, $\mu = \dfrac{\sin i}{\sin r}$

$\Rightarrow \sin r = \dfrac{\sin i}{\mu}$

$\sin r = \dfrac{\sin 45°}{1.5}$

$\Rightarrow \sin r = \dfrac{0.707}{1.5}$

$\Rightarrow \sin r = 0.4713$

$\Rightarrow r = \sin^{-1}(0.4713)$

$\Rightarrow r = 28.14°$

$\therefore$ Lateral shift $= \dfrac{t \sin(i - r)}{\cos r}$

$= \dfrac{10 \sin(45° - 28.14°)}{\cos 28.14°}$

$= \dfrac{10 \sin 16.86°}{\cos 28.14°}$

$= \dfrac{10 \times 0.2900}{0.8818} = 3.3$ cm

Multiple Images in Thick Glass Plate/Mirror

When an object is placed in front of thick glass mirror, then its multiple images are formed. It happens due to multiple reflection from two layers (front and back surfaces). As only the second surface is silvered, therefore, the second image would be brightest.

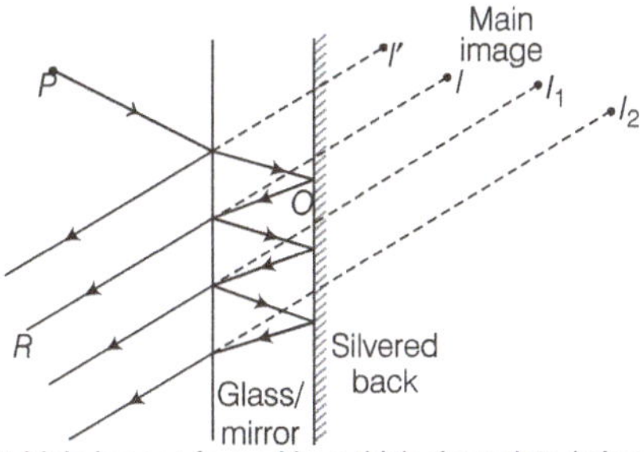

Multiple images formed by a thick glass plate/mirror

Further images would be formed due to multiple reflections. These images would become fainter due to absorption of light by medium.

A thick glass plate also behaves like a thick plane mirror.

Check Your LEARNING...

1. Write the two factors on which the refractive index of a medium depends.
2. If a ray of light falls perpendicularly on a glass slab, what will be its angle of refraction? Give the reason in support of your answer.
3. During the refraction of light, the frequency of light remains constant. Explain the reason.
4. State principle of reversibility.
5. A ray of monochromatic light enters a liquid as shown in diagram.

   Here, $\angle i = 45°$, $\angle r = 30°$

   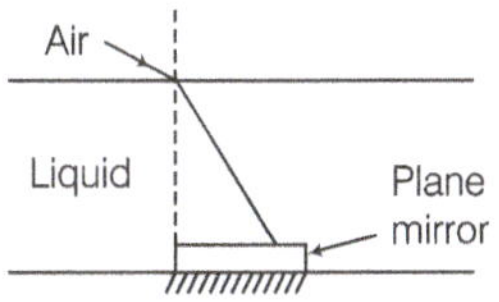

   Show the path of ray after it strikes the mirror and goes into air.
6. Which image formed by the thick glass plate is brightest?

Simple Applications of Refraction of Light

Simple applications of refraction of light are given below

Real and Apparent Depths

An object placed in a denser medium when viewed from a rarer medium, it appears to be at a depth lesser than its real depth. This is because of refraction of light.

Consider an object is placed in water (denser medium) and is being seen from air (rarer medium).

Let O be a point object at an actual depth OA below the free surface of water XY. A ray of light incident normally on XY, along OA passes straight along OAA'.

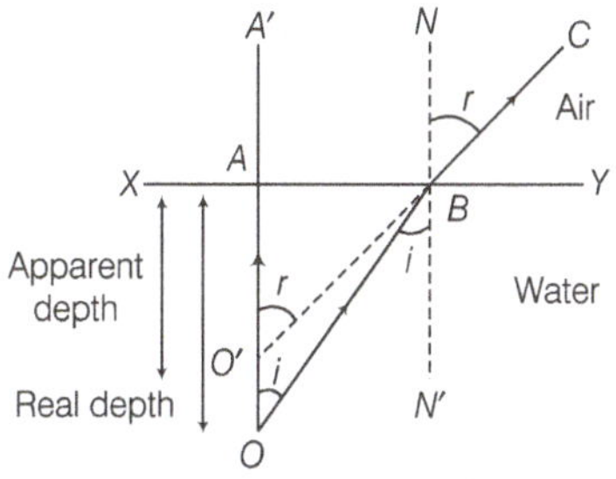

Real and apparent depth

Another ray of light from O incident at $\angle i$ on surface XY along OB deviates away from normal. It is refracted at $\angle r$ along BC. On drawing backwards, CB meets on OA at O'. Therefore, O' is virtual image of O.

Hence, apparent depth = $O'A$

Real depth = OA

$$\therefore \quad {}^a\mu_w = \frac{OA}{O'A} = \frac{\text{Real depth}}{\text{Apparent depth}}$$

If x is the real depth of water surface and ${}^a\mu_w$ is the refractive index of water with respect to air, then the normal shift (d) in position of point object is given by

$$d = \text{Real depth} - \text{Apparent depth}$$

$$\therefore \quad d = x - \frac{x}{{}^a\mu_w}$$

$$\left(\because \text{Apparent depth} = \frac{\text{Real depth}}{{}^a\mu_w} = \frac{x}{{}^a\mu_w} \right)$$

or $$\boxed{d = x\left(1 - \frac{1}{{}^a\mu_w}\right)}$$

The shift by which an object seemed to be raised, depends upon

(i) refractive index of the medium,
(ii) thickness of the denser medium and
(iii) the colour of the incident light.

Note The apparent depth of an object lying in a denser medium is always less than its real depth for all angles of observation in a rarer medium.

Example 4. A mark is made at the bottom of a beaker and a microscope is focused on it. The microscope is then raised through 0.015 m. To what height water must be poured into the beaker to bring the mark again at focus? $\left(\text{Take, } {}^a\mu_w = \frac{4}{3}\right)$

Sol. Given, ${}^a\mu_w = \frac{4}{3}$

Normal shift = 0.015 m

If x is the height upto which water must be poured into the beaker, then

normal shift, $d = x\left(1 - \frac{1}{{}^a\mu_w}\right)$

$$0.015 = x\left(1 - \frac{1}{4/3}\right) \Rightarrow 0.015 = x\left(\frac{1}{4}\right)$$

$\Rightarrow \quad x = 0.060\text{m} = 6\text{ cm}$

Example 5. Velocity of light in glass is 2×10^8 m/s and that in air is 3×10^8 m/s. By how much would an ink dot appear to be raised, when covered by a glass plate 6 cm thick?

Sol. Given, velocity of light in glass, $v = 2 \times 10^8$ m/s

Velocity of light in air, $c = 3 \times 10^8$ m/s

Thickness of glass plate, $x = 6$ cm

Normal shift, $d = ?$

Refractive index of glass with respect to air

$$\mu = \frac{c}{v} = \frac{3 \times 10^8}{2 \times 10^8} = 1.5$$

Normal shift, $d = x\left(1 - \frac{1}{\mu}\right)$

$$\Rightarrow \quad d = 6\left(1 - \frac{1}{1.5}\right) = \frac{6 \times 0.5}{1.5} = 2\text{ cm}$$

Apparent Bending of Stick Under Water

A stick partially immersed in water appears to be bent because of the refraction of light coming from the part of stick that is under water.

If we consider a stick YX immersed obliquely in water, with its part ZX submerged within the water.

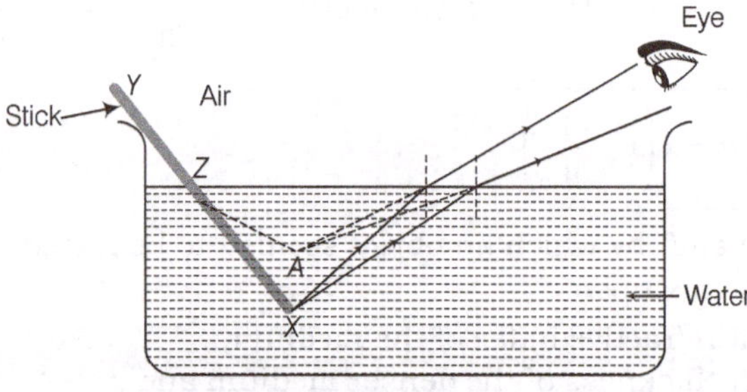

Apparent bending of stick under water

A divergent beam coming from bottom X, after refraction will bend away from the normal. So at this moment, the refracted beam reaches at eye and retraces back a straight line path.

Due to this, the rays appear to originate from point A,which is higher than X. Thus, it is true for any point between X and Y. So, the stick appears to be bent and short within the water. It appears magnified because the image is formed close to the eye.

Some Consequences of Refraction of Light

Some consequences of refraction of light are given below

1. Advanced Sunrise and Delayed Sunset

The density of atmosphere around the earth is not uniform throughout due to which, it has layers of different densities which work as optically rarer and denser medium. The refraction of light due to these atmospheric layers is called **atmospheric refraction.**

The Sun is visible to us about two minutes before the actual sunrise and about two minutes after the actual sunset.

This is because of atmospheric refraction. When the Sun is slightly below the horizon, the sunlight coming from less dense to more dense air, is refracted downwards.

Because of this, the Sun appears to be raised above the horizon and so the rising of Sun can be seen about two minutes before actual sunrise. Similarly, due to atmospheric refraction, the Sun can be seen for about two minutes even after the Sun has set below horizon.

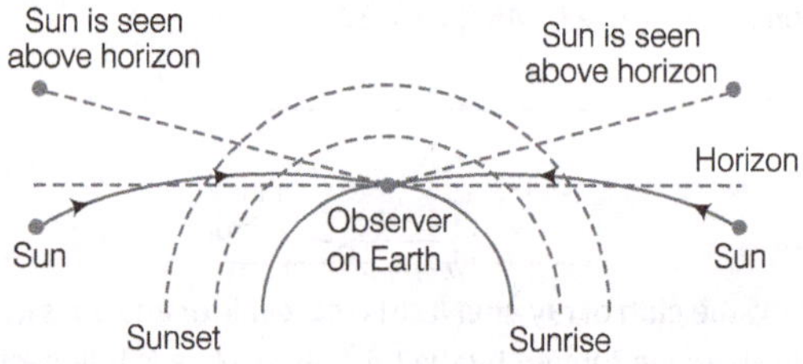

Note At sunrise and sunset, the Sun appears flattened. This apparent flattening of the Sun's disc is also due to atmospheric refraction.

2. Planets do not Twinkle

Planets are much closer to the Earth and hence appear larger in size as compare to stars. So, they can be taken as a collection of large number of point sized sources of light. The total variation in the amount of light entering our eye from all these individual point sized sources will average out to zero which nullify the twinkling effect of each other. So, planets do not twinkle.

3. Shimmering Effect Around a Camp Fire

During camping, when we sit around a camp fire, the face of the person sitting opposite to you, appears to shimmer. This occurs due to the refraction of light. The rays of light reflected from the face of the person sitting opposite to you on passing the hot fire get refracted. As, we know that the hot air is rapidly moving and its optical density is continuously changing, due to which the path of the refracted rays also changes. This gives rise to the shimmering effect.

Prism

A transparent refracting medium bounded by at least two lateral surfaces, inclined to each other at certain angle is called a **prism.** It has two triangular bases and three rectangular lateral surfaces. The angle between two lateral surfaces is called **angle of prism** (A).

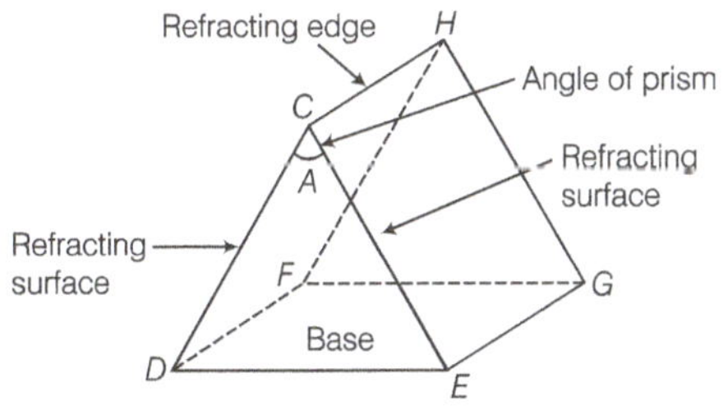

Prism

The two rectangular plane inclined surfaces through which the light passes, are known as **refracting surfaces**. The line along which the two surfaces (refracting) meet is called the **refracting edge**.

Refraction of Light through a Glass Prism

In the diagram given below, a ray of light PQ is entering from air to glass at the first surface AB. The light ray on refraction gets bent toward the normal. At the second surface AC, the light ray enters from glass to air, so it bents away from the normal.

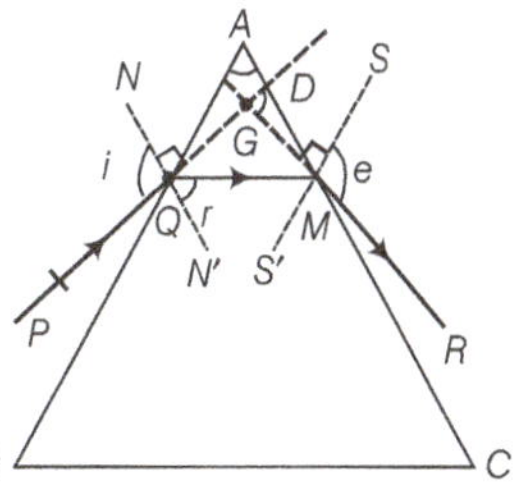

Refraction of light through a triangular glass prism

The above diagram shows refraction through a prism, where,

PQ = incident ray, QM = refracted ray,
MR = emergent ray, $\angle A$ = angle of prism,
$\angle i$ = angle of incidence, $\angle r$ = angle of refraction,
$\angle e$ = angle of emergence and $\angle D$ = angle of deviation.

Note When a ray of light passes through a prism, it bends towards the thicker part of the prism.

Angle of Deviation

It is the angle which the emergent ray (produced backward) makes with the incident ray (produced forward). It is given by $\angle D = \angle i + \angle e - \angle A$.

There are four factors on which the value of angle of deviation produced by the prism depends.

These are as follow

(i) **Dependence of Angle of Deviation on the Angle of Incidence** (i) Experimentally, it has been observed that with the increase in the incident angle, the angle of deviation first decreases, then reach a minimum value and then it also increases. This is depicted in i-D graph shown below.

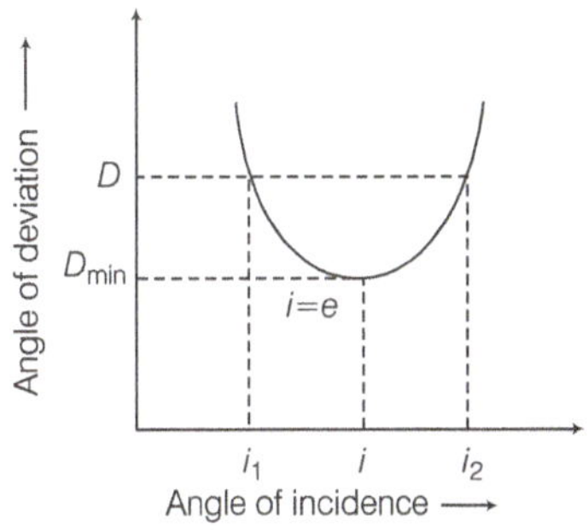

The position of prism with respect to the incident ray at which the incident ray suffers minimum deviation is known as position of minimum deviation.

At this position of minimum deviation,

$$D = D_{min},\ i = e \text{ and } r_1 = r_2 = r$$

Hence, $A = 2r$

$$\Rightarrow \quad r = \frac{A}{2} \quad \text{...(i)}$$

$$\therefore \quad D_{min} + 2r = 2i$$

$$\Rightarrow \quad D_{min} = 2i - 2r$$

$$\Rightarrow \quad D_{min} = 2i - A$$

$$\Rightarrow \quad i = \frac{D_{min} + A}{2} \quad \text{...(ii)}$$

As, refractive index of prism, $\mu = \dfrac{\sin i}{\sin r}$

$$\therefore \quad \boxed{\mu = \frac{\sin\left(\frac{D_{min} + A}{2}\right)}{\sin\left(\frac{A}{2}\right)}}$$

[from Eqs. (i) and (ii)]

(ii) **Dependence of Angle of Deviation on the Refractive Index** (μ) Experimentally, it is found that as the refractive index of the material decreases, the angle of deviation decreases.

(iii) **Dependence of Angle of Deviation on the Colour or Wavelength of Light** (λ) For a given prism, the violet light deviates most whereas the red light deviates least.

(iv) **Dependence of Angle of Deviation on the Angle of Prism** (A) The angle of deviation (D) increases with increase in the angle of prism.

Example 6. What should be the angle of incidence, if a ray of light incident on the refracting surface of a equilateral prism suffers a minimum deviation of 40°?

Sol. We know from the relation, $A + D = i + e$

The minimum deviation can be calculated as

$$D = D_{min} \text{ and } i = e \Rightarrow D_{min} = 2i - A \text{ or } i = \frac{D_{min} + A}{2}$$

Given, $D_{min} = 40°$ and $A = 60°$ (for equilateral prism)

$$\Rightarrow \quad i = \frac{40° + 60°}{2} = 50°$$

Check Your LEARNING...

1. What is the relation between real and apparent depth?
2. Define atmospheric refraction.
3. Why planets do not twinkle?
4. What are the different factors on which the angle of deviation depend?
5. Does refractive index increases with the increase in angle of deviation?

Critical Angle

The angle of incidence in denser medium for which angle of refraction in rarer medium is 90° is called critical angle. Its value depends on the nature of two media in contact.

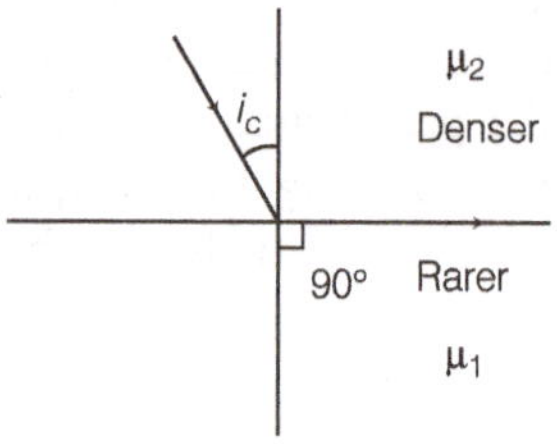

From Snell's law, $\mu_2 \times \sin i_c = \mu_1 \times \sin 90°$

$$\therefore \quad \frac{\mu_1}{\mu_2} = \frac{\sin i_c}{\sin 90°}$$

$$\Rightarrow \quad \frac{\mu_1}{\mu_2} = \sin i_c$$

$$\Rightarrow \quad \frac{\mu_2}{\mu_1} = \frac{1}{\sin i_c}$$

$$\Rightarrow \quad {}^1\mu_2 = \frac{1}{\sin i_c} = \text{cosec}\, i_c$$

The critical angle for a given pair of media depends on their refractive index, which in turn depends on the following two factors.

(i) **Effect of Colour of Light** As violet light has the highest value of refractive index, while red light has the least value of refractive index. So, due to this reason, the critical angle for a pair of media is least for violet light and most for red light. Therefore, the critical angle increases with increase in the wavelength of light.

(ii) **Effect of Temperature** When the temperature of medium is increased, its refractive index decreases, due to which, the critical angle for that pair of media increases. Therefore, the critical angle increases with an increase in temperature.

Example 7. If the refractive index of a glass is 1.5. Determine the critical angle for it.

Sol. Since, we know that

$${}^1\mu_2 = \frac{1}{\sin i_c} \quad \text{or} \quad {}^a\mu_g = \frac{1}{\sin i_c}$$

$$\therefore \quad 1.5 = \frac{1}{\sin i_c}$$

$$\Rightarrow \quad \sin i_c = \frac{1}{1.5} \Rightarrow i_c = \sin^{-1}\left(\frac{1}{1.5}\right)$$

$$\Rightarrow \quad i_c = \sin^{-1}(0.666) \Rightarrow i_c = 41.80° \approx 42°$$

Total Internal Reflection (TIR)

When a ray of light travelling from a denser medium to rarer medium, is incident at the interface of the two media at an angle greater than the critical angle, then the ray is totally reflected back to denser medium.

This phenomenon is called **total internal reflection (TIR).**

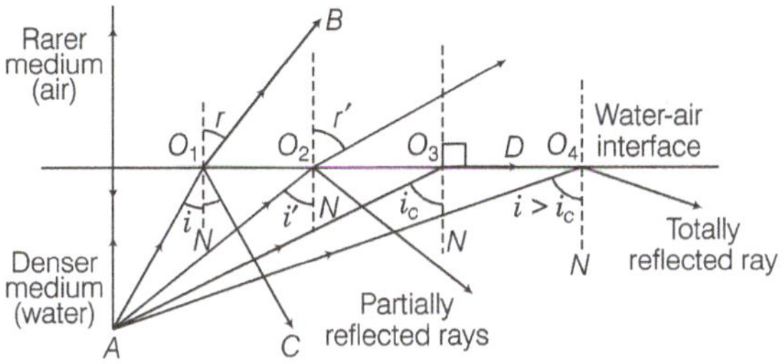

Refraction and internal reflection of rays from a point A in the denser medium (water) incident at different angles at the interface with a rarer medium (air)

Necessary conditions for total internal reflection to takes place are as follow

(i) The ray incident on the interface of two media should travel from denser medium to rarer medium.

(ii) The angle of incidence should be greater than critical angle for the two media.

Total Internal Reflection in a Prism

The phenomenon of total internal reflection has been considered in three different prism which are given below as

1. TIR in Prism of Angles (45°, 45° and 90°) i.e., Right-Angled Isosceles Prism

When a prism has 90° angle between its two refracting surfaces and the two other angles each of 45°, then the prism is called **total reflecting prism.**

As, the light incident normally on any of its face, it then gets total internally reflected. Because of this property, this prism is used for the following three purposes.

(i) **Deviation through 90° Angle** When a parallel beam of light strikes normally on the face DC, it does not suffer any refraction and then strikes the face CE at an angle of 45°.

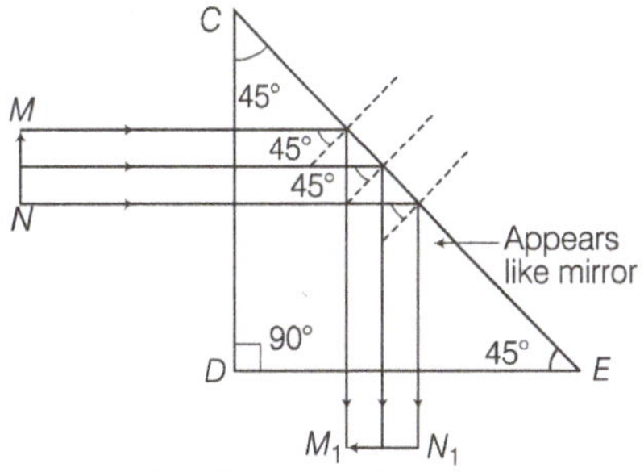

Deviation through 90° angle

As, we know that the critical angle for, the glass is 42°, so total internal reflection takes place. Due to this, the beam makes an angle of reflection of 45° and turns completely through 90°. It strikes the face DE normally and emerges out in the air, thus prism behaves like a mirror.

This action of prism is used in periscope.

(ii) **Deviation through 180° Angle** If a parallel beam of light is incident normally on the face CE of the right angled isosceles prism, the beam passes undeviated till it strikes the face CD at an angle of 45°.

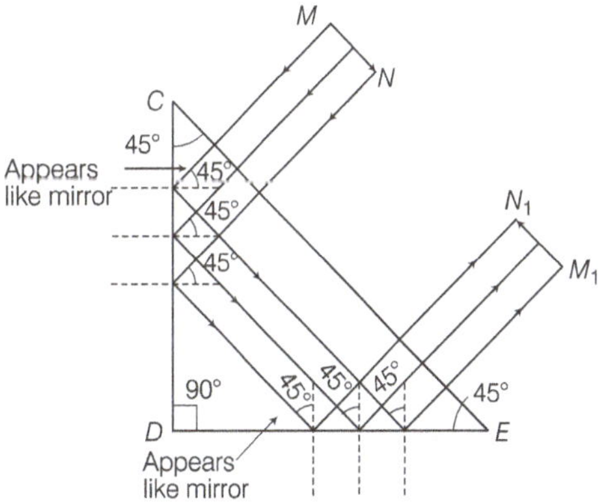

Deviation through 180° angle

Then, total internal reflection takes place and the beam turns completely through an angle of 90° in order to strike the face DE at an angle of 45°.

Then at the face DE, another TIR takes place and again the beam turns through an angle of 90° in order to strike the face CE normally. Finally, the beam comes out of the prism without suffering any refraction.

As a result, the beam turns through 180°.

This action of prism is used in a binocular and camera.

(iii) **No Deviation** The rays of light parallel to the hypotenuse (*CD*) strikes the surface *EC*.

These rays then suffers refraction and strike the face *CD* with an angle greater than 42°. Due to this, total internal reflection takes place. Then, the rays turn and strike the face *ED*.

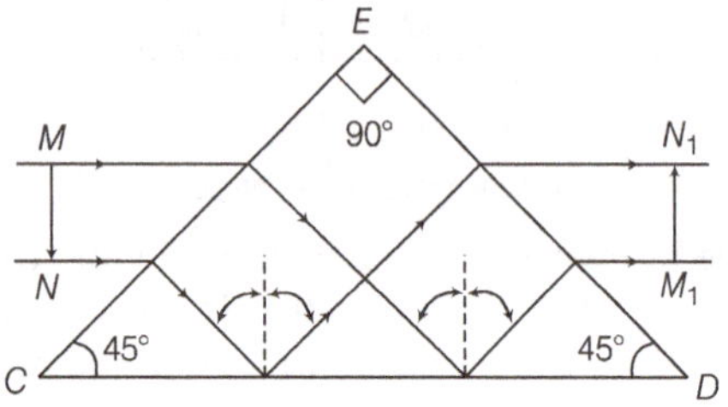

No deviation

On finally coming out from the face *ED*, these refracted rays suffer another refraction. During this, the rays revert themselves, i.e., the inverted image *MN* appears as N_1M_1.

This action of prism is used in a slide projector.

2. TIR through a Prism where Each Angle is 60° i.e., Equilateral Prism

The figure given below shows an equilateral prism i.e., each angle of 60°. If a ray falls normally on the face *PQ*, then without any refraction it falls on the face *QR* at an angle 60° since, this angle is greater than the critical angle of glass. So, total internal reflection takes place. Thus, this prism can be used to deviate a ray of light by 60°.

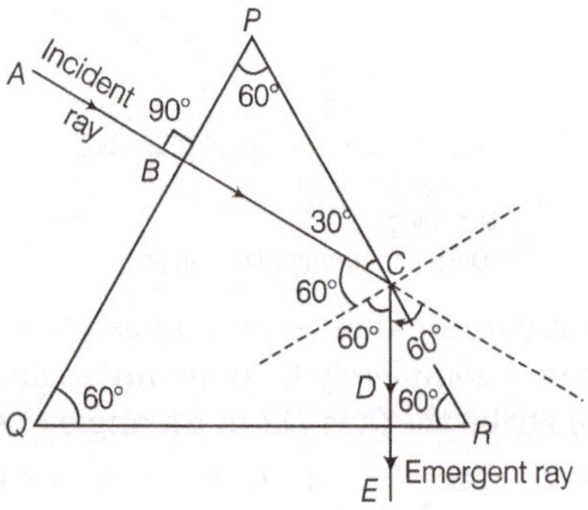

Total internal reflection through an equilateral prism

3. TIR through Prism of Angles (30°, 60° and 90°) i.e., Right-Angled Prism

The figure given below shows a prism with angles, 30°, 60° and 90° i.e., right angled prism. If a ray of light falls normally on the face *QR*, then it falls on the face *PR* without any deviation.

Since, the angle of incidence is 60° which is greater than the critical angle of glass (42°) so TIR takes place. On reflection, the ray falls on the face *PQ*, where it gets refracted with an angle less than 60°. Therefore, this prism can be used to deviate a light ray through an angle less than 60° by TIR.

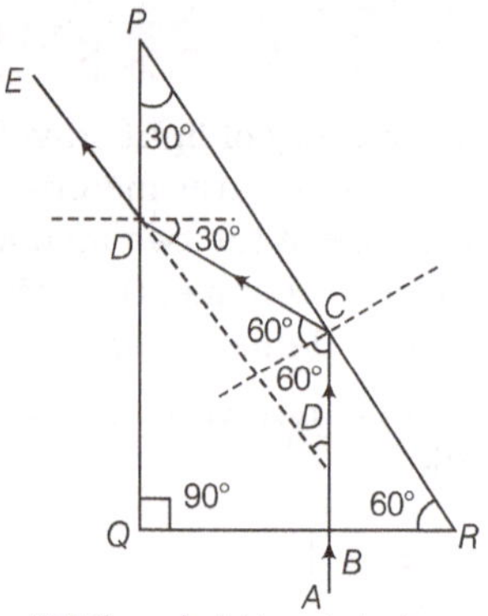

TIR through right angled prism

If the ray of light falls on other two faces i.e., *PR* and *PQ*, then the previous case does not take place i.e., no total internal reflection happens.

This has been depicted in the figures given below

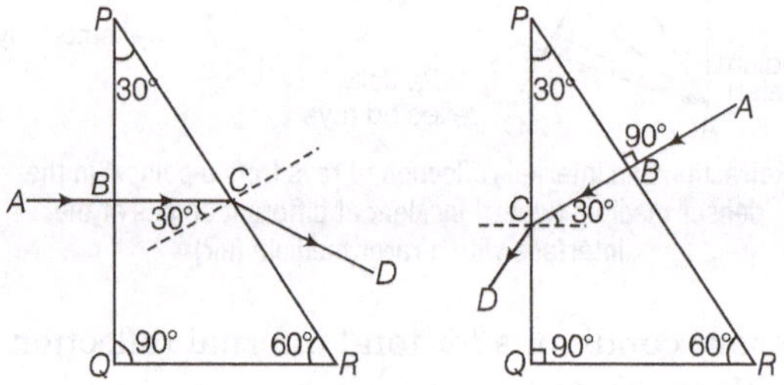

Note There is an exception, when a ray of light incident normally on the hypotenuse of the prism below the foot of perpendicular from opposite corner, then it suffers TIR and gets deviated by an angle greater than 60°.

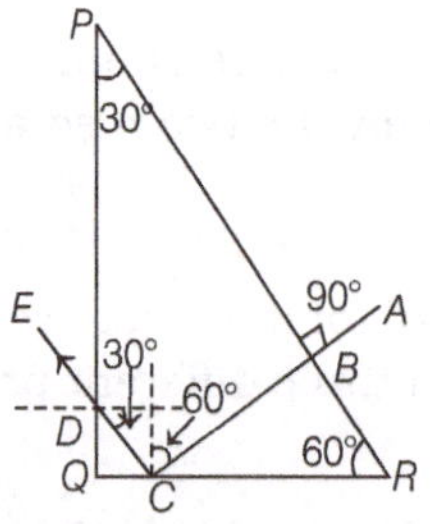

Comparison between Total Internal Reflection and Reflection from a Plane Mirror

Total Internal Reflection	Reflection from a Plane Mirror
This is the phenomenon in which light travels from denser to rarer medium at an angle greater than the critical angle for that pair of media, then the rays are totally reflected back.	In this light falls on plane mirror at any angle of incidence and then a little part of light gets reflected and rest get refracted and absorbed.
The energy of the reflected ray is same as that of incident ray i.e., no loss of energy.	The energy of the reflected rays is less than that of incident ray i.e., there is loss of energy.
The brightness of the image is very good and does not decrease even after a long use of TIR device.	The brightness of the image is not very good and decreases with the increase in time.

Some Consequences of Total Internal Reflection

Total internal reflection is also very prominent in our daily life also.

Some of these consequences are given below

(i) Optical fibre are used to transmit light over large distances without any loss of energy.

(ii) If a glass vessel is cracked, then it often shines like a mirror.

(iii) Brilliance of diamond.

(iv) In deserts, in daytime, a person often see a pool of water at a distance. It is because of the phenomenon of mirage.

Check Your LEARNING...

1 Among the following substances, which one has the highest value of critical angle? Turpentine, glass, water, diamond.

2 How does the critical angle changes with the change in the temperature of surrounding?

3 State total internal reflection.

4 Name any two instruments in which total reflecting prism is used.

5 Mention one difference between refraction of light from a plane mirror and total internal reflection from a prism.

QUiCK Revision

- The phenomenon of bending of light entering from one medium to another is called **refraction of light**.
- When a ray of light travels from a rarer medium to a denser medium, it bends towards the normal.
- When a ray of light travels from a denser medium to a rarer medium, it bends away from the normal.
- There are two laws of refraction.

  First Law The incident ray, the refracted ray and the normal at the point of incidence, all lie on the same plane.

  Second Law The ratio of sine of angle of incidence to the sine of angle of refraction is constant for a given pair of media.This is also called **Snell's law**.
- **Refractive index** (n or μ) of a medium is the ratio of speed of light in vacuum (c) to the speed of light in the medium (v) and is given by

$$n \text{ or } \mu = \frac{c}{v}$$

- Refractive index of one medium w.r.t. to another medium is given by, ${}^1n_2$ or ${}^1\mu_2 = \dfrac{\text{Speed of light in medium 1}}{\text{Speed of light in medium 2}}$
- When a light ray, after suffering many reflections and refractions, has its final path reversed and travels back along its initial path then it is called **principle of reversibility of light**.
- The perpendicular distance of separation between the incident ray and the emergent ray is called **lateral displacement**.
- The shift by which an object appears to be raised when it is immersed in water is called the **apparent depth**.

$$\text{Refractive index} = \frac{\text{Real depth}}{\text{Apparent depth}}$$

- A transparent refracting medium bounded by five plane surfaces inclined at some angles is known as **prism**.
- The angle between two refracting surfaces is called angle of prism (A) or refracting angle and the angle between the incident ray and the emergent ray is called the **angle of deviation (D)**.
- **Critical angle** for a pair of media is defined as the angle of incidence in denser medium for which the angle of refraction becomes 90°.
- When a ray of light is travelling from a denser medium to rarer medium, is incident at the interface of the two media at an angle greater than the critical angle, the ray is totally reflected back to the denser medium. This phenomenon is called **total internal reflection**.

Chapter Practice

1 Mark Questions

1. When a ray of light travels from rarer medium to denser medium, then it
(a) bends away from the normal
(b) bends towards the normal
(c) goes undeviated
(d) is reflected back

Sol. (*b*) When a ray of light travels from rarer medium to denser medium, then due to decrease in its speed, the ray bends towards the normal.

2. In the diagram shown below

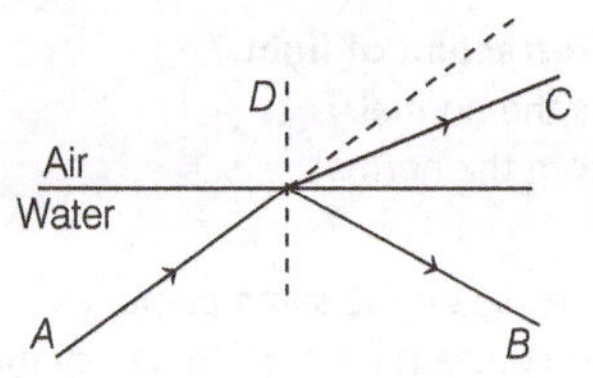

(a) *B* is incident ray and *C* is refracted ray
(b) *A* is incident ray and *B* is refracted ray
(c) *C* is incident ray and *B* is refracted ray
(d) *A* is incident ray and *C* is refracted ray

Sol. (*d*) When a ray falls obliquely on a surface of air-water interface, then it is partially reflected and partially refracted. Here, *A* is incident ray, *B* is reflected ray and *C* is refracted ray.

3. When a ray of light travels normal to the given surface, then the angle of refraction is **[2023]**
(a) 180° (b) 90°
(c) 0° (d) 45°

Sol. (*c*) Angle of refraction will zero (0°).

4. Figure shows a ray of light as it travels from medium *A* to medium *B*. Refractive index of the medium *B* relative to medium *A* is

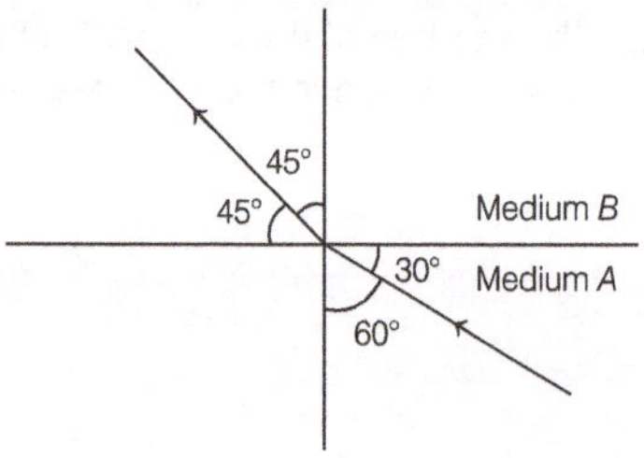

(a) $\frac{\sqrt{3}}{\sqrt{2}}$ (b) $\frac{\sqrt{2}}{\sqrt{3}}$
(c) $\frac{1}{\sqrt{2}}$ (d) $\sqrt{2}$

Sol. (*a*) Given, angle of incidence, $i = 60°$,
angle of refraction, $r = 45°$
Refractive index of the medium *B* relative to medium *A*,

$$^{A}\mu_{B} = \frac{\sin i}{\sin r} = \frac{\sin 60°}{\sin 45°} = \frac{\left(\frac{\sqrt{3}}{2}\right)}{\left(\frac{1}{\sqrt{2}}\right)} = \frac{\sqrt{3}}{\sqrt{2}}$$

5. Speed of blue light in water is **[2023]**
(a) more than green light
(b) more than orange light
(c) more than violet light
(d) more than red light

Sol. (*c*) Speed of light in water is more than violet light .

6. The refractive index of a diamond is 2.4. It means that, **[2021, (Sem-I)]**
(a) the speed of light in vacuum is equal to $\frac{1}{2.4}$ times the speed of light in diamond
(b) the speed of light in diamond is 2.4 times the speed of light in vacuum
(c) the speed of light in vacuum is 2.4 times the speed of light in diamond
(d) the wavelength of light in diamond is 2.4 times the wavelength of light in vacuum

Sol. (*c*) As, refractive index $= \frac{\text{Speed of light in vacuum}}{\text{Speed of light in medium}}$

So, the refractive index of a diamond equal to 2.4 means that the speed of light in vacuum is 2.4 times the speed of light in diamond.

7. A small air bubble in a glass block, when seen from above appears to be raised because of
(a) refraction of light
(b) reflection of light
(c) reflection and refraction of light
(d) None of the above

Sol. (*a*) The apparent shift in the position of an object in a denser medium is due to the refraction of light.
Hence, due to refraction of light, the air bubble in the glass block appears to be raised when viewed from above.

8. An object in a denser medium when viewed from a rarer medium appears to be raised. The shift is maximum for
(a) red light
(b) violet light
(c) yellow light
(d) green light

Sol. (*b*) The shift in the position of an object is given by

$$d = x\left(1 - \frac{1}{\mu}\right)$$

Since, $\mu_{red} < \mu_{violet}$ and the violet light has maximum refractive index. So, the shift will be maximum for violet light.

9. Beams of light are incident through the holes *A* and *B* and emerge out of box through the holes *C* and *D* respectively as shown in the figure.

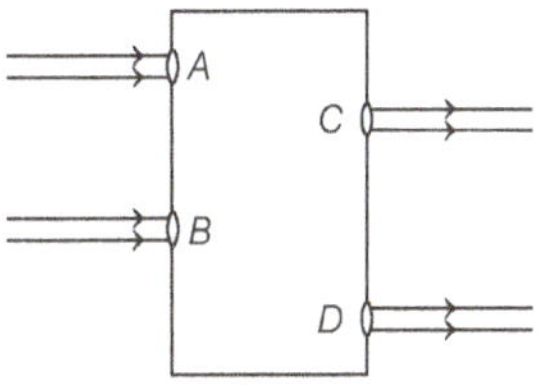

Which of the following could be inside the box?
(a) A rectangular glass slab (b) A convex lens
(c) A concave lens (d) A prism

Sol. (*a*) Here, the emergent rays are parallel to the direction of the incident ray. Therefore, a rectangular glass slab could be inside the box as the extent of bending of light ray at the opposite parallel faces *AB* (air-glass interface) and *CD* (glass-air interface) of the rectangular glass slab are equal and opposite. That is why the ray emerges parallel to the incident ray.

10. In refraction of light through a prism, the light ray
(a) suffers refraction only at one face of the prism
(b) emerges out from the prism in a direction parallel to the incident ray
(c) bends at both the surfaces of the prism towards its base
(d) bends at both the surface of the prism opposite to its base

Sol. (*c*) In refraction of light through a prism, the light ray bends at both the surfaces of prism towards its base as shown below

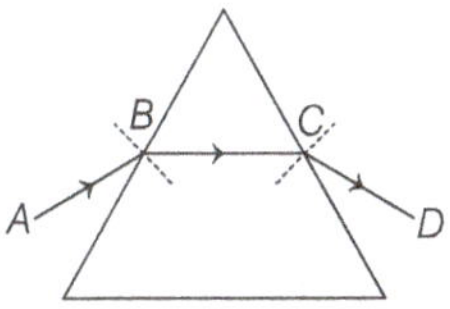

11. Small air bubbles rising up a fish tank appear silvery when viewed from some particular angle is due to the **[2023]**
(a) reflection
(b) refraction
(c) dispersion
(d) total internal reflection

Sol. (*d*) Small air bubbles rising up a fish tank appear silvery when viewed from some particular angle is due to the phenomena of total internal reflection.

12. A totally reflecting right angled isosceles prism can be used to deviate a ray of light through
(a) 30° (b) 60°
(c) 75° (d) 90°

Sol. (*d*) A totally reflecting right angled isosceles prism can deviate a ray of light through 90° or 180°. When a ray of light incident normal on the surface *AB*, it does not undergo refraction but strikes the surface *AC* at an angle 45°, which is greater than critical angle of glass, that is 42°. The ray undergoes total internal reflection and strikes face *BC* normally and emerges out of it. Thus, the ray is rotated though 90°.

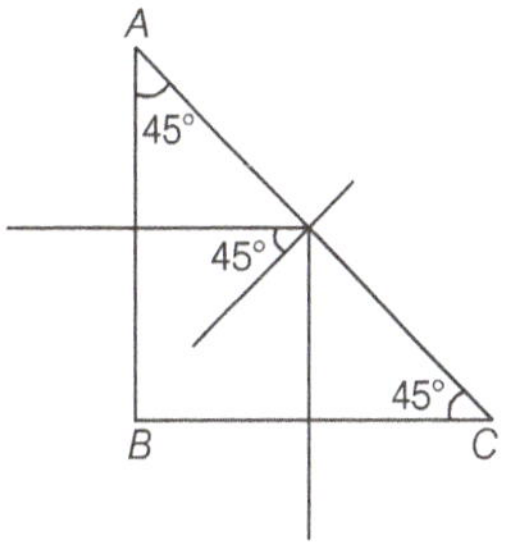

13. Which one of the following diagrams show the correct path of this ray till it emerges out of the prism?

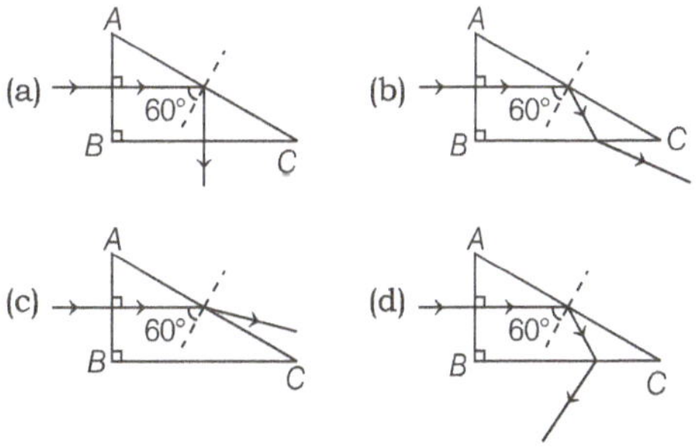

Sol. (*b*) When ray falls normally, then it goes undeviated in second medium. Here, angle of incidence at face *AC* is 60°, which is greater than critical angle of glass, i.e. 42° . Hence, the ray suffers total internal reflection at face *AC* and fall on face *BC* obliquely. Now, it emerges out moving away from the normal as shown in option (b).

14. Diamonds glitter in the dark because
(a) they emit light
(b) they have a very small critical angle due to very high refractive index
(c) due to the fluorescence
(d) chemical reaction in the diamond produces light energy

Sol. (b) As the refractive index of diamonds is very high, so, its critical angle is very small. Due to this the ray entering it suffers total internal reflection multiple times, producing glittering effect.

2 Marks Questions

15. When a ray of light does not change its path during refraction, state what will be the angle of incidence and angle of refraction of this ray?

Sol. When a ray of light is incident perpendicularly to the interface surface of the two medium, then it passes without any deviation. **[1]**

So, due to this reason, the angle of incidence and angle of refraction, both will be zero degree. **[1]**

16. With the help of a suitable diagram, represent the refraction of light rays from

(i) rarer to denser.

(ii) denser to rarer.

Also, label each diagram.

Sol. (i) **Rarer to denser**

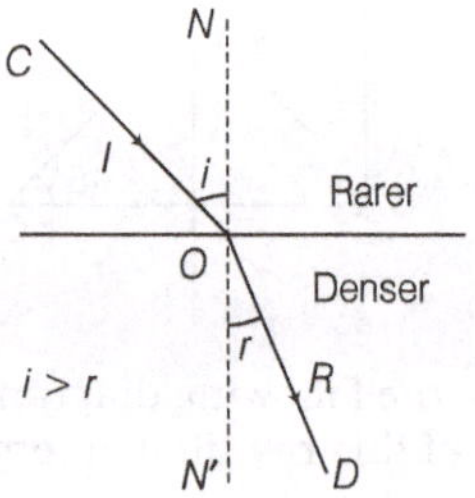

where, CO = incident ray, OD = refracted ray and NN' = normal. **[1]**

(ii) **Denser to rarer**

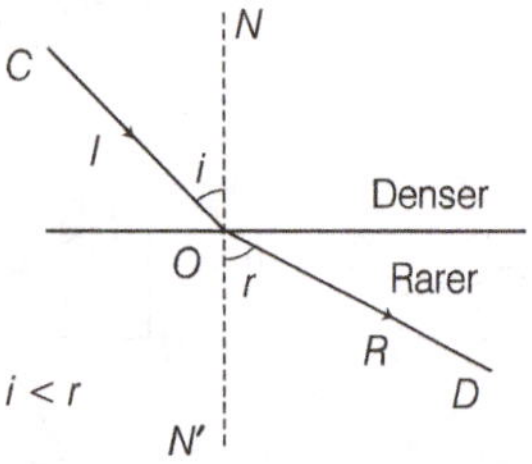

where, CO = incident ray, OD = refracted ray and NN' = normal. **[1]**

17. State the laws of refraction of light.

Sol. Refer to theory (Page 70).

18. How can you define the term "refractive index of a medium"? State whether it can be less than 1 or not?

Sol. The ratio of the velocity of light in vacuum to the velocity of light in a medium is known as the refractive index of that medium.

i.e. Refractive index of a medium

$$= \frac{\text{Velocity of light in vacuum}}{\text{Velocity of light in that medium}}$$ **[1]**

The absolute refractive index of a substance cannot be less than one because it would mean that the speed of light is more in that substance than in free space, which is not possible. **[1]**

19. If ${}^{a}\mu_g$ is refractive index of glass with respect to air and ${}^{g}\mu_a$ is refractive index of air with respect to glass. Express the refractive index of glass with respect to water (${}^{w}\mu_g$) in terms of refractive index of water and glass with respect to air.

Sol. As, we know that according to the definition of refractive index,

$${}^{w}\mu_g = \frac{v_w}{v_g}$$ **[1]**

Now, multiply and divide in numerator and denominator by v_a,

$$\Rightarrow \quad {}^{w}\mu_g = \frac{v_w . v_a}{v_g . v_a}$$

$$\Rightarrow \quad {}^{w}\mu_g = \frac{v_a / v_g}{v_a / v_w} \quad \left(\text{But } \frac{v_a}{v_g} = {}^{a}\mu_g \text{ and } \frac{v_a}{v_w} = {}^{a}\mu_w\right)$$

$$\therefore \quad {}^{w}\mu_g = \frac{{}^{a}\mu_g}{{}^{a}\mu_w}$$ **[1]**

20. "Refractive index of a medium is least for the red colour of light". Justify this statement.

Sol. Since, in prism, the red colour of light is bent the least and it is a fact that the bending of light rays increases on increasing the refractive index of the medium. **[1]**

As, wavelength of red is maximum, refractive index of a medium is least for the red colour of light. **[1]**

21. If a light of a single colour is passed through a liquid having a piece of glass suspended in it, so on changing the temperature of the liquid, at a particular temperature, the glass piece is not seen.

(i) At what situation, the glass piece will not be seen?

(ii) Why is the light of a single colour used?

Sol. (i) The glass piece cannot be seen when the refractive index of the liquid becomes equal to refractive index of the glass. **[1]**

(ii) Since, the refractive index of medium is different for different colour of light.

So due to this, light of a single colour is used. **[1]**

22. A boy uses blue colour of light to find the refractive index of glass. He then repeats the experiment using red colour of light. Will the refractive index be the same or different in the two cases? Give a reason to support your answer. **[2016]**

Sol. Since, the refractive index of the medium is always inversely proportional to the wavelength of light. Moreover, it is known that wavelength of the red colour is more than that of the blue colour. So, the refractive index in case of blue colour of light will be greater than that of red colour of light. **[2]**

23. Draw the diagram given below and clearly show the path taken by the emergent ray. **[2014]**

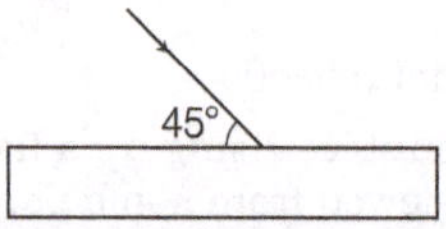

Sol. In refraction through a rectangular glass slab, incident ray and emergent ray are parallel to each other, hence the emergent ray RS is as shown below

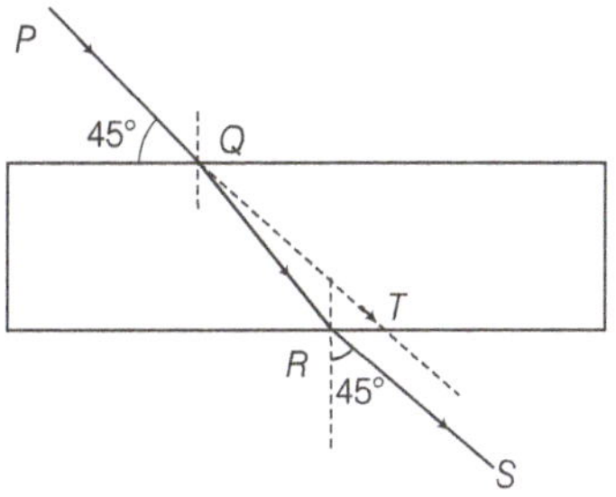

[2]

24. "If a lighted candle is placed in front of thick glass plane mirror, then several images can be observed, but the second image is brightest." Explain, the reason for this statement.

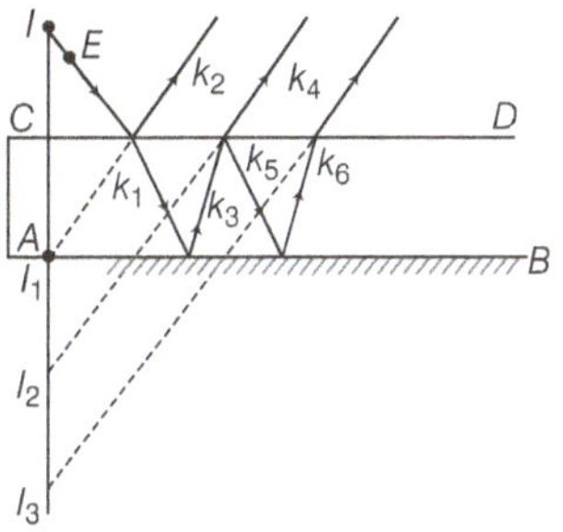

Sol. Since, first image is formed by reflected ray k_2 from the transparent surface *CD*.

The reflection from the transparent surface *CD* is very small due to which I_1 is not so much bright. Image I_2 is formed by the refracted ray k_4. As, most part of the incident ray *E* refract by refracted ray k_1, so a small part of k_1 can be absorbed by the mirror at the same time, the maximum part of k_1 is reflected by reflected ray k_3. **[1]**

Some part of $k_3$is reflected by ray k_5 but its most part is refracted by k_4. Other image is formed by ray k_5, which is less bright than by k_4. So, due to this reason I_2 is brightest. **[1]**

25. How is the refractive index of a material related to
(i) real and apparent depth?
(ii) velocity of light in vacuum or air and the velocity of light in a given medium? **[2017]**

Sol. (i) When an object is placed under water (or any other medium), then observing it from outside the water (or medium) it appears to be raised above. The ratio of real depth and apparent depth is equal to the refractive index of the medium.

$$\text{Refractive index, } \mu = \frac{\text{Real depth}}{\text{Apparent depth}}$$ **[1]**

(ii) The refractive index of the medium is the ratio of the velocity of light in vacuum (or air) to the velocity of light in that medium.

$$\mu = \frac{\text{Velocity of light in vacuum } (c)}{\text{Velocity of light in medium } (v)}$$ **[1]**

26. Does the depth of the tank of a water appear to change or remains the same, when viewed normally from the above? **[2012]**

Sol. No, when the depth of a tank of water is viewed normally, no refraction takes place as the light rays passes through the medium undeviated. Thus, the depth of the tank remains the same because it is a case of normal incidence, where $\angle i = \angle r = 0°$. **[2]**

27. Fish swimming in a pond seems to be nearer than its actual depth. Explain why?

Sol. A fish can be seen by observer when the rays of light coming from the fish enters into observer's eyes.

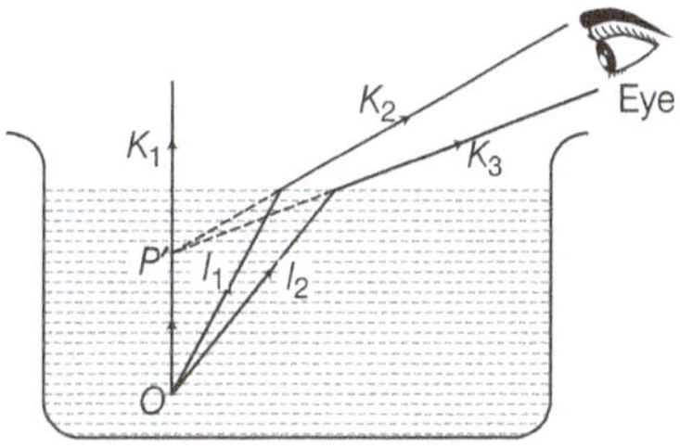

[1]

Consider the above figure, if I_1 and I_2 are the two rays coming from a point on fish *O*.

These rays passes water (denser) to air (rarer) and then deviate from the normal through path K_2, K_3 and form an image at *P'*, which is virtual and above *O*. Due to this reason, fish in the water seems to be very nearer than its actual depth. **[1]**

28. Light passes through a rectangular glass slab and through a glass prism. In what way does the direction of the two emergent beams differ? **[2014]**

Sol. In a rectangular glass slab, the emergent ray is parallel to the incident ray but they are not along the same line, whereas in the prism, the emergent ray is not parallel to the incident ray. **[1]**

This differ because in glass slab, the two surfaces at which refraction occurs is parallel to each other, but in prism they make same angle. **[1]**

29. Draw a ray diagram to show the refraction of a monochromatic ray through a prism when it suffers minimum deviation. **[2017]**

Sol. When a ray of light passes through a prism, it bends towards the thicker part of the prism.

Let the incident ray *PQ* falls on the face *AB* of prism and emerges out from the face *AC* as *RS*.

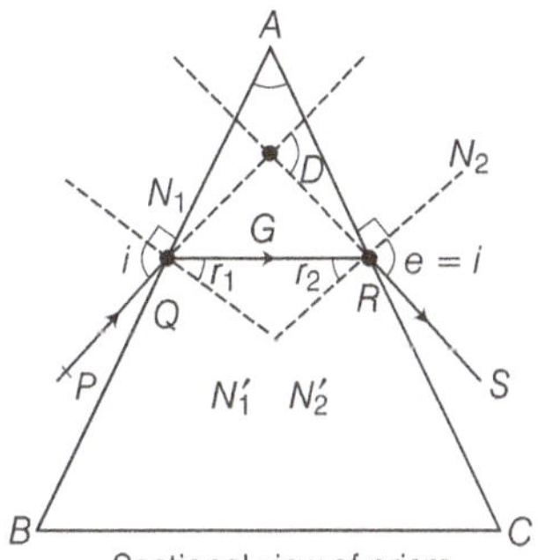

Sectional view of prism

Here, PQ = incident ray, QR = refracted ray
RS = emergent ray, $\angle A$ = angle of prism
$\angle i_1$ = angle of incidence,
$\angle r_1, \angle r_2$ = angles of refraction,
$\angle e$ = angle of emergence and $\angle D$ = angle of deviation.
When the ray suffers minimum deviation, $e = i$. **[2]**

30. State the dependence of angle of deviation.
(i) On the refractive index of the material of the prism.
(ii) On the wavelength of light. **[2016]**

Sol. (i) Since, refractive index of the prism is directly proportional to the angle of deviation.
So, larger the refractive index, larger will be the deviation angle.
(ii) Since, refractive index of material is inversely proportional to the wavelength of light. So, smaller the wavelength of light larger will be the deviation angle. **[2]**

31. Name the factors affecting the critical angle for the pair of media. **[2014]**

Sol. The main factors affecting the critical angle for the pair of media are
(i) the refractive index of a medium. **[1]**
(ii) the temperature of surrounding. **[1]**

32. (i) State the relation between the critical angle and the absolute refractive index of a medium.
(ii) Which colour of light has a higher critical angle? Red light or Green light. **[2018]**

Sol. (i) The relation between the critical angle C and the absolute refractive index (μ) of medium is given by

$$\mu = \frac{1}{\sin C}$$

or $$\sin C = \frac{1}{\mu}$$ **[1]**

(ii) As $\mu_{green} > \mu_{red}$
Therefore, critical angle (C) for red colour is higher than that of green colour light. **[1]**

33. The following diagram shows a 60°, 30°, 90° glass prism of critical angle 42°. Copy the diagram and complete the path of incident ray AB emerging out of the prism marking the angle of incidence on each surface. **[2018]**

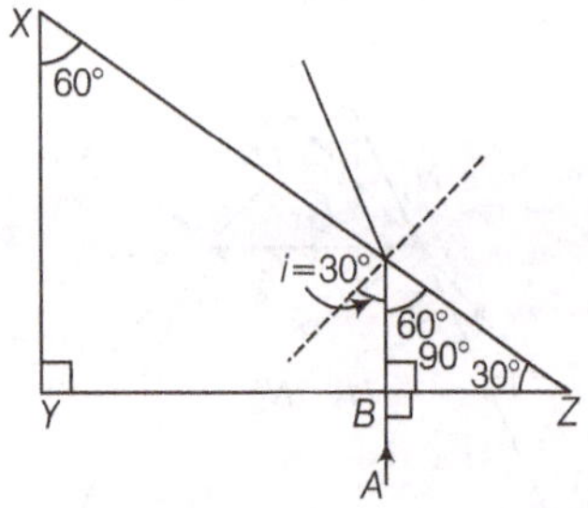

Sol. Given, $i_C = 42°$

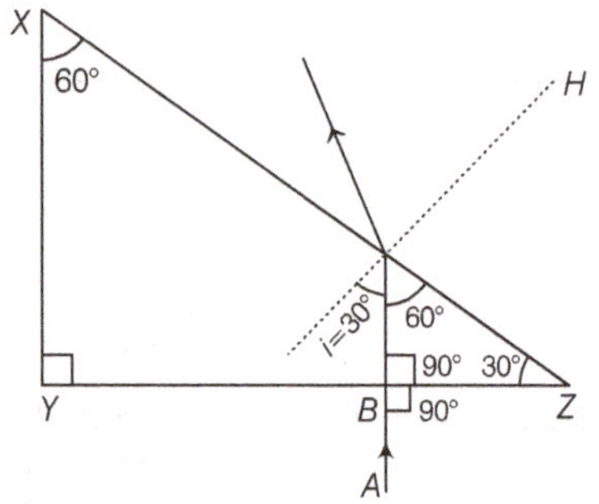

[1]

As angle of incidence on face XZ is less than i_C so, ray is refracted as shown in the above figure. **[1]**

34. State the conditions required for total internal reflection of light to take place. **[2017]**

Sol. The necessary conditions for the total internal reflection are as follows
(i) The light must travel from a denser medium to a rarer medium.
(ii) The angle of incidence must be greater than the critical angle (i_c) for the pair of media. **[2]**

35. Copy the diagram given below and complete the path of light ray till it emerges out of the prism. The critical angle of glass is 42°. In your diagram, mark the angles wherever necessary. **[2016]**

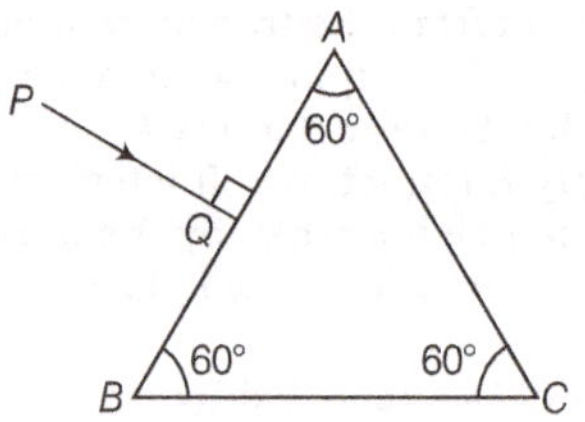

Sol. The ray diagram is given below

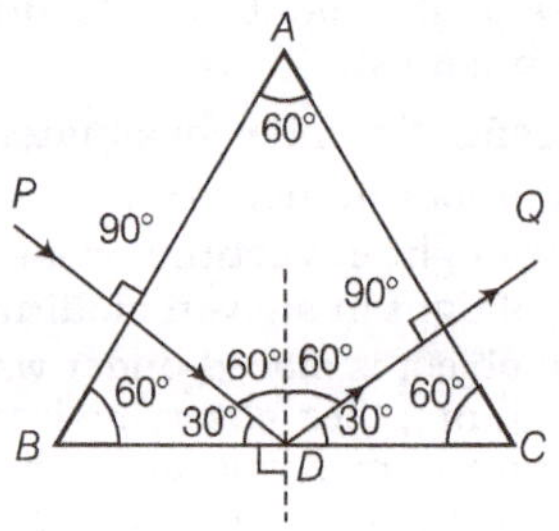

[2]

3 Marks Questions

36. (i) Write a relationship between angle of incidence and angle of refraction for a given pair of media.
(ii) When a ray of light enters from one medium to another having different optical densities it bends. Why does this phenomenon occur?
(iii) Write one condition where it does not bend when entering a medium of different optical density. **[2016]**

Sol. (i) For a given pair of media, the relationship between the angle of incidence and angle of refraction is given by

$$ {}_1\mu_2 = \frac{\sin i}{\sin r} $$

where, i = angle of incidence, r = angle of refraction and ${}_1\mu_2$ = refraction index of the second medium with respect to the first medium. **[1]**

(ii) The phenomenon of refraction occurs because light travels at different speeds in different medium. If a ray of light travels through air and enter into a more denser medium, such as water, they slow down and bend towards the normal. **[1]**

(iii) When a ray of light is incident normally to the surface, then it passes straight from one medium to another medium without any bending. **[1]**

37. When a ray of monochromatic green light enters a liquid from air as shown in the figure given below.

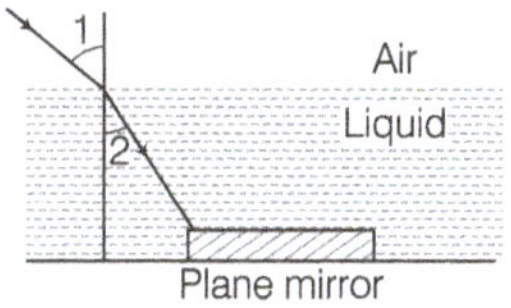

The angle 1 is 45° and angle 2 is 30° .

(i) Determine the refractive index of the liquid.

(ii) Represent in the diagram showing the path of the ray after it strikes the mirror and re-enters air. Mark in the diagram wherever necessary.

(iii) Draw the diagram again if plane mirror becomes normal to the refracted ray inside the liquid. Name the principle used.

Sol. According to Snell's law,

(i) refractive index of liquid $\frac{\sin i}{\sin r} = \frac{\sin \angle 1}{\sin \angle 2}$

$$ = \frac{\sin 45°}{\sin 30°} = \frac{\frac{1}{\sqrt{2}}}{\frac{1}{2}} = 1.4 $$ **[1]**

(ii) The path of the reflected and refracted ray is shown below.

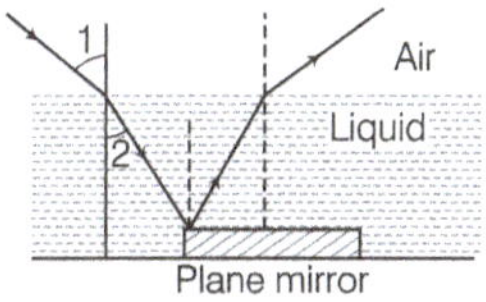

[1]

(iii) The principle used is the principle of reversibility of light.

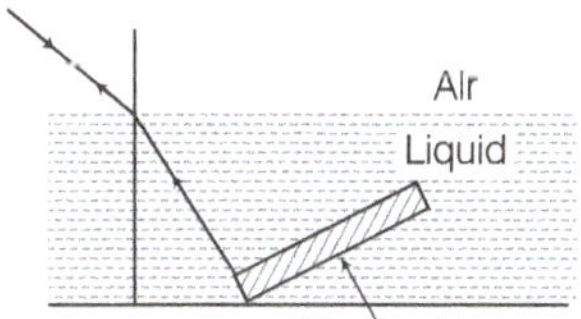

[1]

38. A ray of monochromatic light is incident from air on a glass slab. **[2010]**

(i) Draw a labelled ray diagram showing the change in the path of the ray till it emerges from the glass slab.

(ii) Name the two rays that are parallel to each other.

(iii) Mark the lateral displacement in your diagram.

Sol. (i) **Ray diagram**

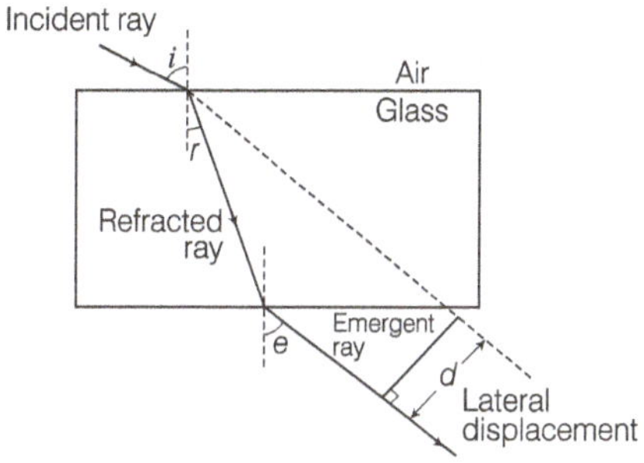

[1]

(ii) Two rays that are parallel to each other are incident ray and emergent ray. **[1]**

(iii) The perpendicular distance between the incident ray and emergent ray is the lateral displacement, which is marked as d in the above diagram. **[1]**

39. How does the value of angle of deviation produced by a prism change with an increase in the **[2009]**

(i) value of angle of incidence and

(ii) wavelength of incident light ?

Sol. (i) If the value of angle of incidence increases, then there is a corresponding decrease in the angle of deviation. For a particular value of angle of incidence, the angle of deviation becomes minimum after which it starts rising with further increase in the value of angle of incidence. **[1½]**

(ii) If the value of the wavelength of incident light increases, then angle of deviation decreases. **[1½]**

40. Explain the meaning of reversibility of light.

Sol. Refer to theory (Pages 71 and 72).

41. (i) Draw a labelled ray diagram to illustrate

(a) critical angle

(b) total internal reflection for a ray of light moving from one medium to another.

(ii) Write a formula to express the relationship between refractive index of the denser medium with respect to rarer medium and its critical angle for that pair of media. **[2008]**

Sol. (i) The labelled diagram of critical angle and total internal reflection is given below **[1]**

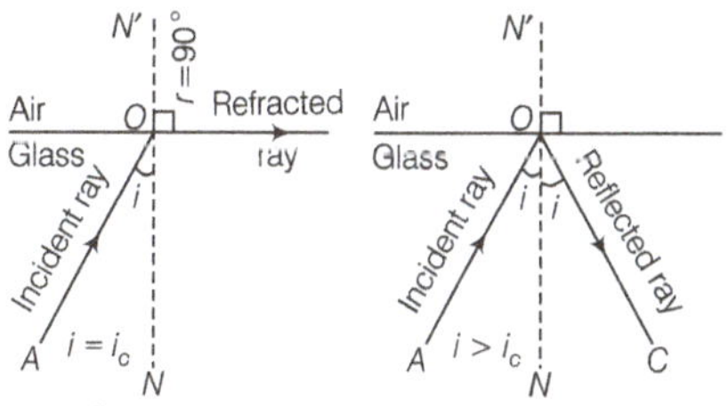

(a) Critical angle (b) Total internal reflection

[1]

(ii) The formula to express the relationship between refractive index of the denser medium with respect to rarer medium and critical angle is given by

$$\mu = \frac{1}{\sin i_c} = \operatorname{cosec} i_c$$

where, i_c is the critical angle. **[1]**

42. Draw the diagram of a right angled isosceles prism which is used to make an inverted image erect. **[2018]**

Sol.

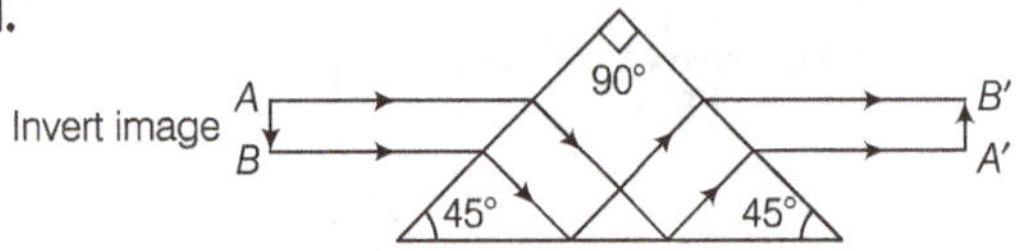

[3]

43. Copy the diagram given below and complete the path of the light ray PQ, as it emerges out of the prism by marking necessary angles. The critical angle of glass is 42°. **[2023]**

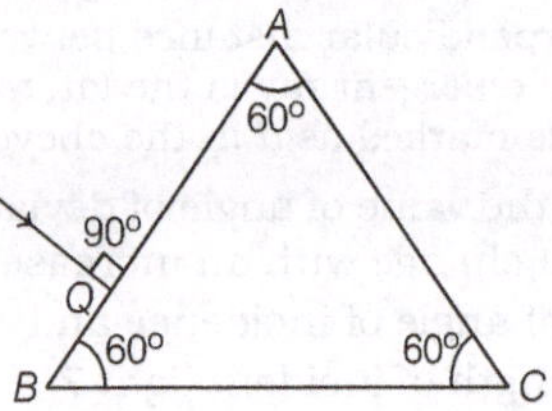

Sol.

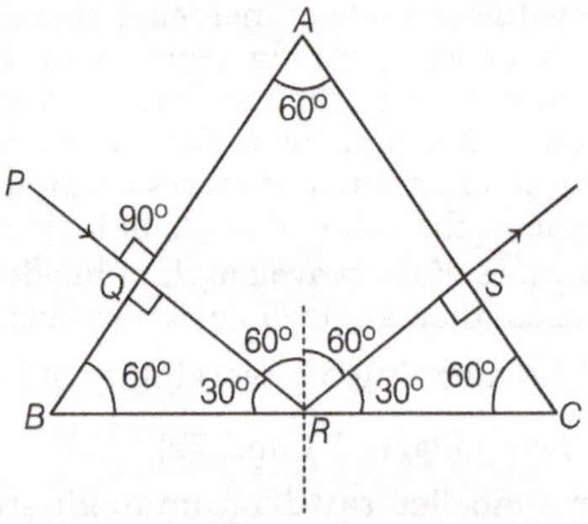

[1]

In the diagram, the ray PQ enters the prism from side AB. Its' angle of incidence is 0°, thus it undergoes any refraction. When this light reaches at BC. its angle of incidence is 60°, which is more than the critical angle 42°. Thus, the incident light (QR) does not enter into next medium instead it undergoes total internal reflection. When this reflected light ray (QS) reached side AC, its angle of incidence is 0°. Again it does not undergo any refraction, which causes the angle of emergence to become 0°. **[2]**

44. The diagram below shows the ray OP travelling through an equilateral prism of a certain material.

(i) Calculate the value of i_2, if the angle of deviation is 43°.

(ii) What is the ray QS called ? **[2023]**

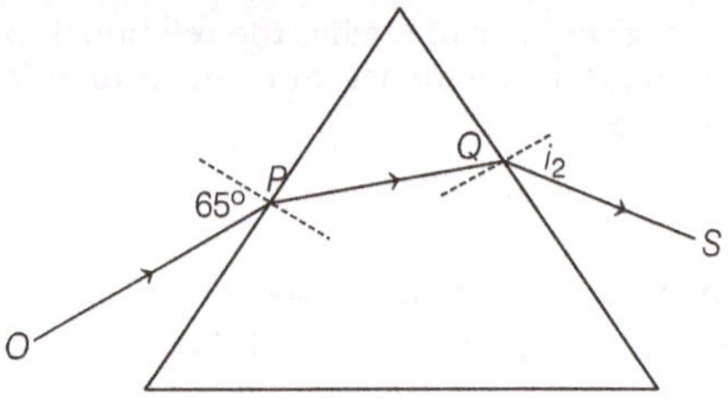

Sol. (i) Given, angle of deviation $\delta = 43°$

Angle of incidence , $i = 65°$

From the relation, $\delta = i - r$

$$i_2 = r = i - \delta$$

$$i_2 = r = 65° - 43° = 22°$$ **[2]**

(ii) The ray QS is the emergent ray . **[1]**

45. A ray of light XY passes through a right angled isosceles prism as shown below.

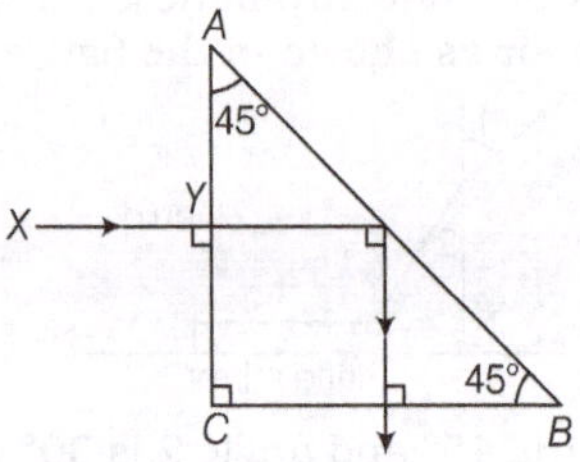

(i) What is the angle through which the incident ray deviates and emerges out of the prism?

(ii) Name the instrument where this action of prism is put into use.

(iii) Which prism surface will behave as a mirror? **[2018]**

Sol. (i) 90°

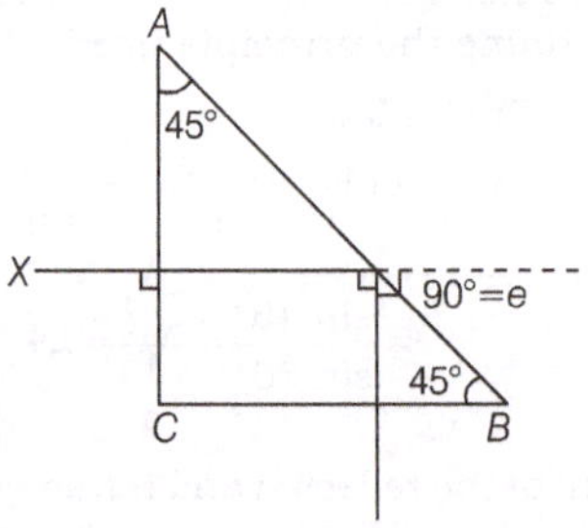

(ii) Periscope

(iii) Surface AB behaves like a mirror. Because on this surface, total internal reflection occurs. **[3]**

46. A ray of light travels from water to air as shown in the diagram given below.

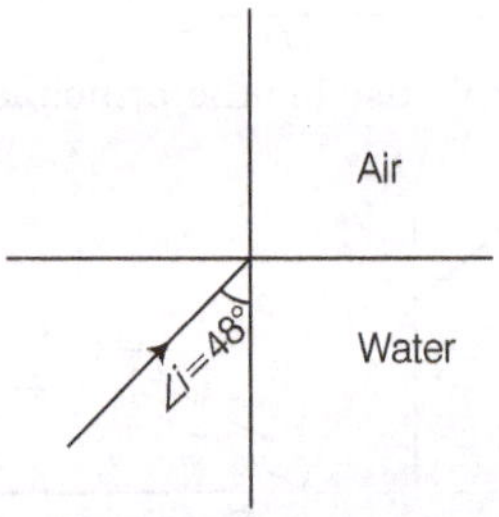

(i) Copy the diagram and complete the path of the ray. Given, the critical angle for water is 48°.

(ii) State the condition, so that total internal reflection occurs in the above diagram. [2017]

Sol. (i) According to given ray diagram, we see that angle of incidence is just equal to critical angle, hence angle of refraction will be equal to 90° which is shown as,

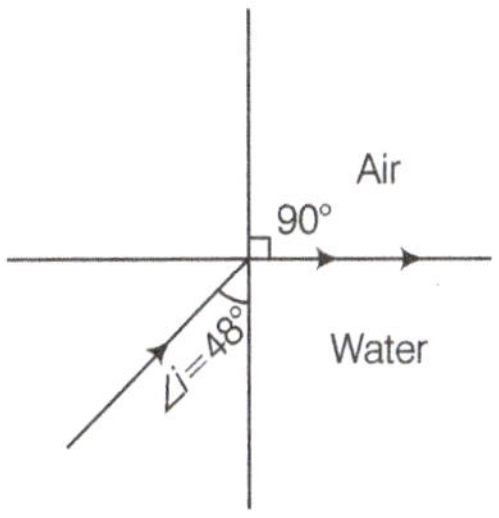

[1½]

(ii) Required condition for TIR in the above diagram is that, the angle of incidence should be greater than the critical angle, i.e., $\angle i > 48°$. [1½]

4 Marks Questions

47. The diagram below shows two parallel rays-*A* (Orange) and *B* (Blue) incident from air, on air-glass boundary.

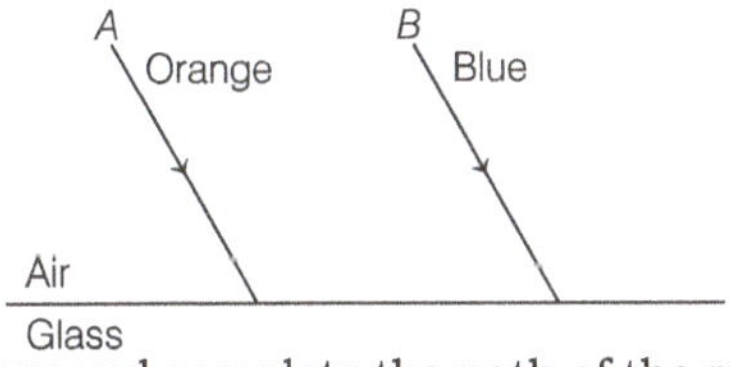

(i) Copy and complete the path of the rays *A* and *B*.

(ii) How do the speeds of these rays differ in glass ?

(iii) Are the two refracted rays in glass parallel ? Give a reason. [2023]

Sol. (i)

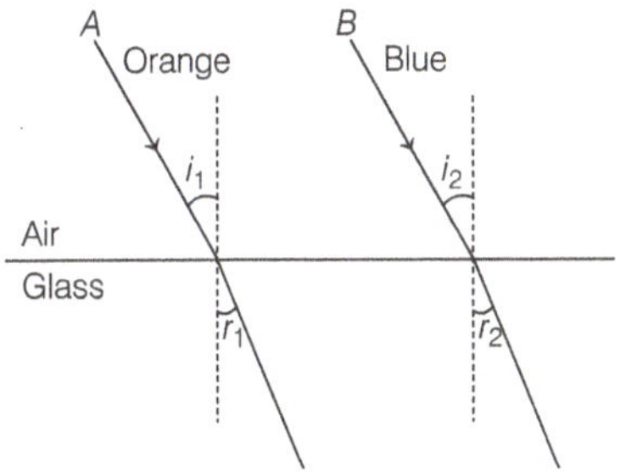

(ii) Speed of orange light is more than speed of blue light in glass medium.

(iii) No, the two refracted rays are not parallel this is due to thc fact that $v_{Orange} > v_{Blue}$ blue i.e. the speed of orange light is more, so the orange light bends less and blue light bends more in glass medium.

48. (i) With the help of a well-labelled diagram, show that the apparent depth of an object such as a coin in water is less than its real depth.

(ii) How is the refractive index of water related to the real depth and the apparent depth of a column of water? [2007]

Sol. (i) A ray from bottom of the tank *A* (coin) is striking normally at *B* goes straight.

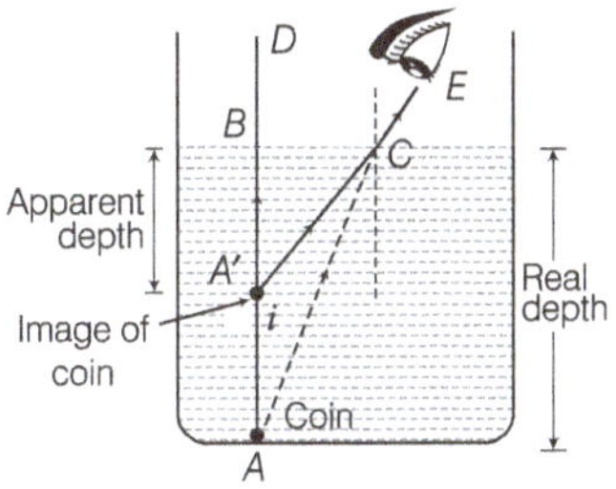

Another ray from *A* striking the interface at *C* is refracted towards *E* and when produced back, it appears to come from *A'*. When *BD* and *CE* enter the eye, these form an image of *A* (coin) at *A'* (coin). Thus, the depth appears to be at *A' B* instead of the actual *AB*. [2]

(ii) The refractive index of water related to the real depth and the apparent depth of a column of water is given by

$$\text{Refractive index, } \mu = \frac{\text{Real depth}}{\text{Apparent depth}}$$ [2]

49. A ray of light is incident at 45° on an equilateral prism in the diagram below.

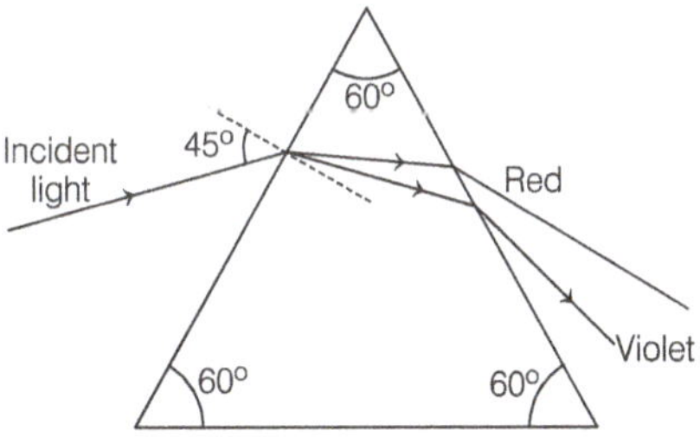

(i) Name the phenomenon exhibited by the ray of light when it enters and emerges out of the prism.

(ii) State the cause a above phenomenon mentioned by you. [2023]

Sol. (i) The phenomena exhibited by the ray of light when it enters and emerges out of the prism is known as refraction. [2]

(ii) Refer to theory (Page - 75). [2]

50. *PQ* and *PR* are two light rays emerging from the object *P* as shown in the figure. [2006]

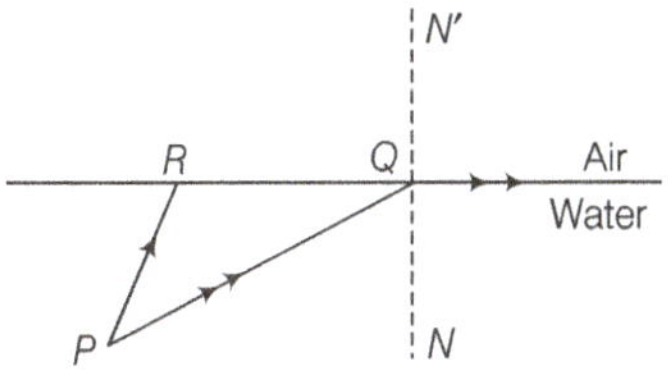

(i) What is the special name given to the angle of incidence ($\angle PQN$) of ray PQ?

(ii) Copy the ray diagram and complete it to show the position of the image of the object P, when seen obliquely from above.

(iii) Name the phenomenon that occurs, if the angle of incidence $\angle PQN$ is increased still further.

Sol. (i) The special name given to the angle of incidence $\angle PQN$ of ray PQ is critical angle. **[1]**

(ii) The complete diagram is shown below

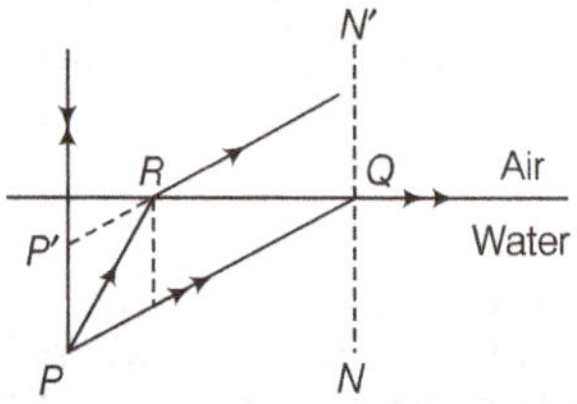

The image of the object P will be formed at P' when seen obliquely from above. **[2]**

(iii) Total internal reflection occurs, if the angle of incidence $\angle PQN$ is increased still further. **[1]**

51. Answer the following questions.

(i) Write a note on "total reflecting prism".

(ii) State three actions that it can produce.

(iii) With the help of a diagram, show one action of total reflecting prism.

Sol. (i) A prism having an angle of 90° between its two refracting surfaces and the other two angles each equal to 45°, is known as total reflecting prism. It is because the light incident normally on any of its faces, suffers total internal reflection inside the prism. **[1]**

(ii) Given below are the three actions produced by it, i.e.

(a) It can deviate a ray of light through 180° i.e., in prism binoculars.

(b) It can erect the image (inverted) without producing deviation in its path.

(c) It can deviate a ray of light through 90°. **[2]**

(iii)

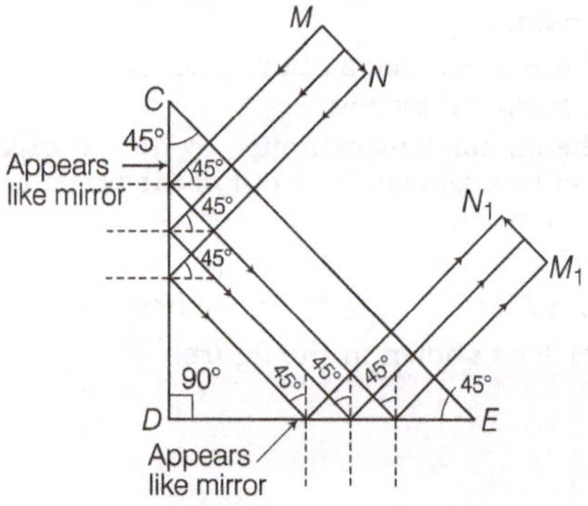

Deviation through 180° angle **[1]**

52. Mention some differences between the reflection of light from a plane mirror and total internal reflection of light from a prism. **[2007]**

Sol. Refer to theory (Page 78).

Numerical Based Questions

53. If the speed of light in air is 3×10^8 ms^{-1}, determine the speed of light in glass. The refractive index of glass is 1.5. **[2]**

Sol. Given, speed of light, $c = 3\times 10^8 \text{ms}^{-1}$

Refractive index, $\mu = 1.5$

$\because \quad \mu = \frac{c}{v} = \frac{\text{Velocity of light in air}}{\text{Velocity of light in a medium}}$ **[1]**

$\Rightarrow \quad 1.5 = \frac{3\times 10^8}{v}$

$\Rightarrow \quad v = \frac{3\times 10^8}{1.5}$

$\Rightarrow \quad v = 2\times 10^8$ m/s. **[1]**

54. The speed of light in diamond is 125000 km/s, if the speed of light in air is 3×10^8 m/s, then determine the refractive index of the diamond. **[2]**

Sol. Velocity of light in air, $v_a = 3\times 10^8 \text{m/s}$

Velocity of light in diamond, $v_d = 125000$ km/s $= 125\times 10^6$ m/s **[1]**

$${}^a\mu_d = \frac{v_a}{v_d} = \frac{3\times 10^8}{125\times 10^6} = \frac{300\times 10^6}{125\times 10^6} = \frac{12}{5} = 2.4$$ **[1]**

55. When a coin is placed at the bottom of a beaker containing water of refractive index $\frac{4}{3}$ to a depth of 12 cm, so by what height, does the coin appear to be raised when seen from vertically above? **[2]**

Sol. Shift of image = Real depth of water $\left(1 - \frac{1}{\mu_w}\right)$

$\because$ Real depth of water = 12 cm (given)

$\mu_w = \frac{4}{3}$ (given) **[1]**

$\therefore$ Shift of image of coin

$$= 12\left(1 - \frac{1}{4/3}\right)$$

$$= 12\left(1 - \frac{3}{4}\right) = 12\left(\frac{1}{4}\right)$$ **[1]**

$= 3$ cm

56. Determine the angle of emergence for a ray of light which suffers minimum deviation for an equilateral prism. Determine the angle of minimum deviation (D_{min}). [Angle of incidence for the ray of light, $i = 48°$] **[2]**

Sol. For an equilateral prism, $\angle A = 60°$

When ray suffers minimum deviation,

then angle of incidence, (i) = angle of emergence (e)

$\Rightarrow \quad i = e = 48°$

$\therefore \quad D_{\text{min}} = 2i - A$ **[1]**

$= 2(48°) - 60° = 96° - 60° = 36°$ **[1]**

57. Determine the time taken by a ray of light when it passes through a glass sheet of thickness 2 mm and ${}^a\mu_g = \frac{3}{2}$. **[2]**

Sol. As we know, ${}^a\mu_g = \dfrac{v_a}{v_g}$

$\Rightarrow \quad v_g = \dfrac{v_a}{{}^a\mu_g} = \dfrac{3\times10^8}{3/2}$

$\Rightarrow \quad v_g = 2\times10^8$ m/s. **[1]**

$$\text{Time} = \frac{\text{Distance}}{\text{Speed}} = \frac{2\text{ mm}}{2\times10^8\text{ m/s}} = \frac{2\times10^{-3}}{2\times10^8} = 10^{-11}\text{ s}$$

$\therefore$ Time to pass in 2 mm glass $= 10^{-11}$s. **[1]**

58. (i) A coin kept inside water ($\mu = 4/3$) when viewed from air in a vertical direction appears to be raised by 3.0 mm, Find the depth of the coin in water.

(ii) How is the critical angle related to the refractive index of a medium? **[2023]**

Sol. (i) Given, $\mu = \dfrac{4}{3}$, Shift = 3mm

Let x be the real depth , then

Apparent depth $= \dfrac{x}{\mu} = \dfrac{3}{4}x$

Shift = Real depth − Apparent depth

$= x - \dfrac{3}{4}x = \dfrac{1}{4}x$

Given, $\dfrac{1}{4}x = 3$ mm

$\therefore x = 12$ mm

Thus, the depth of coin is 12 mm in water.

(ii) Refer to theory [Page 76].

59. If the refractive index of glass is 3 / 2, determine the critical angle for glass-air surface.

(Take, $\sin 42° = 2/3$) **[2]**

Sol. Given, $\mu = \dfrac{3}{2}$

If i_c is the critical angle, then

$\sin i_c = \dfrac{1}{\mu} = \dfrac{1}{3/2} = \dfrac{2}{3}$ **[1]**

$\Rightarrow \quad \sin i_c = \sin 42° \Rightarrow i_c = 42°$. **[1]**

60. Determine the approximate value of critical angle for **[2]**

(i) glass-air surface (ii) water-air surface.

Sol. (i) Since, $\sin i_c = \dfrac{1}{{}^a\mu_g}$

$\because \quad {}^a\mu_g = \dfrac{3}{2}$

$\therefore \quad \sin i_c = \dfrac{2}{3} \Rightarrow \sin i_c = 0.6667$

$\Rightarrow \quad \sin i_c = \sin 42°$

$\Rightarrow \quad i_c = 42°$ **[1½]**

So, critical angle for glass-air surface is 42°.

(ii) As, ${}^a\mu_w = \dfrac{4}{3}$, then critical angle for water-air surface can be calculated by

$\sin i_c = \dfrac{1}{{}^a\mu_w} \Rightarrow \sin i_c = \dfrac{3}{4} \Rightarrow \sin i_c = \sin 48.6.$ **[1½]**

$\Rightarrow i_c = 48.6°$

So, critical angle for water-air surface is 48.6°.

61. A ray of light enters a glass slab $PQRS$, as shown in the diagram. The critical angle of the glass is 42°. Copy the diagram and complete the path of the ray till emerges from the glass slab. Mark the angles in the diagram wherever necessary. **[2011] [2]**

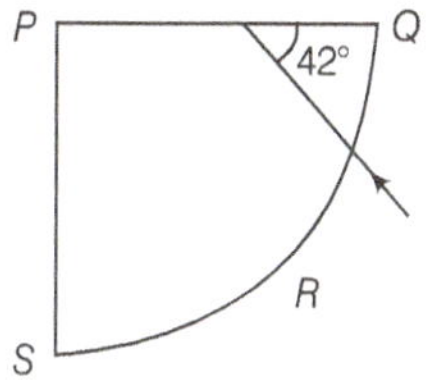

(a)

Sol. At point A in fig. (b), $i = 48°$ and $i_c = 42° \Rightarrow i > i_c$

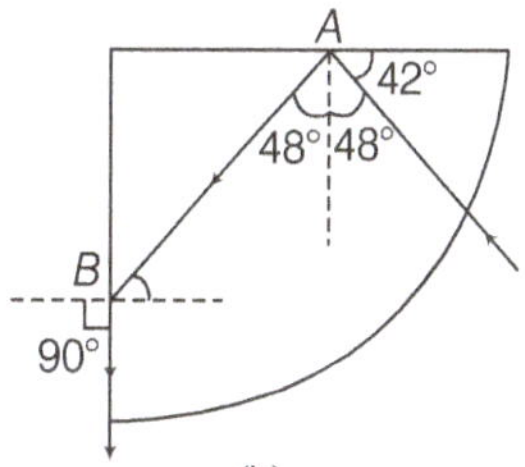

(b) **[1]**

While at point B, $i = 42° \Rightarrow \quad i = i_c$

Therefore, $\quad r = 90°$ **[1]**

Structured Questions

62. (i) A diver in water looks obliquely at an object AB in air.

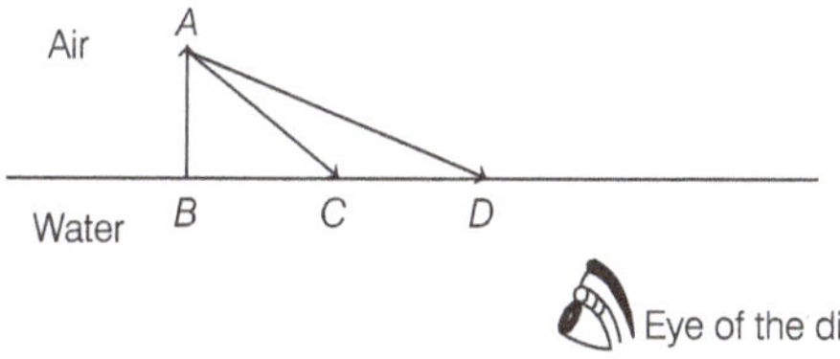

(a) Does the object appear taller, shorter or of the same size to the diver?

(b) Show the path of two rays AC and AD starting from the tip of the object as it travels towards the diver in water and hence obtain the image of the object. **[2020] [4]**

(ii) Complete the path of the ray AB through the glass prism in PQR till it emerges out of the prism. Given the critical angle of the glass as 42°. **[2020] [3]**

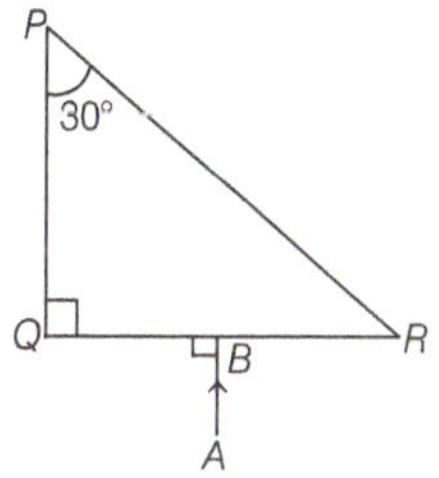

(iii) If a ray of light of wavelength 5400 Å suffers refraction from air to glass, determine the wavelength of light in glass. (Take, ${}^a\mu_g = 3/2$) [3]

Sol. (i) (a) When a diver in water looks obliquely at an object *AB* in air, then object *AB* appears taller than its actual size, because when the ray coming from denser medium to rarer medium then they deviates away from the normal, hence they make larger image.

(b)

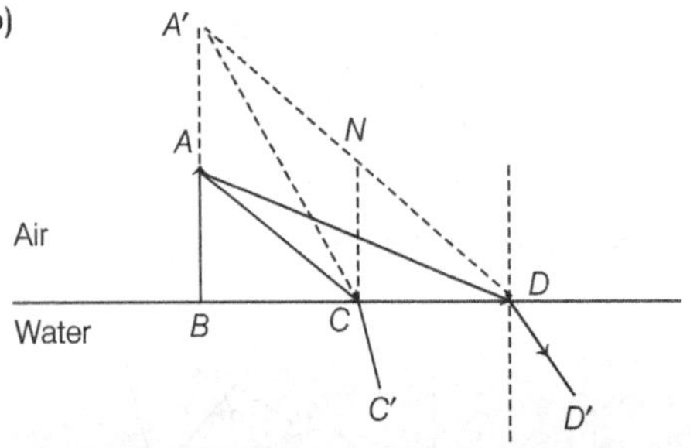

When rays of light coming from rarer medium to denser medium, then it bends towards normal. Hence, path of rays *AC* and *AD* are shown above in figure. [3]

The image of object *AB* is shown in the figure as *A′ B*.

(ii) Refer to text on page no. 78
[TIR through prism angles (30°, 60° and 90°)]

(iii) Given, $\lambda = 5400$, Å $= 5400 \times 10^{-10}$ m, ${}^a\mu_g = 3/2$

As, frequency remains same, $v = f\lambda$ [1]

$\Rightarrow 3 \times 10^8 = f \times 54 \times 10^{-8}$

$\Rightarrow \quad f = \dfrac{3 \times 10^8}{54 \times 10^{-8}} = \dfrac{3}{54} \times 10^{16}$ [1]

$= \dfrac{300}{54} \times 10^{14} = 5.55 \times 10^{14}$

$\because {}^a\mu_g = \dfrac{3}{2} \Rightarrow {}^a\mu_g = \dfrac{\text{Velocity of light in vacuum}}{\text{Velocity of light in glass}}$

$\Rightarrow \quad v = \dfrac{c}{{}^a\mu_g} = \dfrac{3 \times 10^8}{3} \times 2 = 2 \times 10^8 \text{ ms}^{-1}$ [1]

Now, $\quad v = f\lambda \Rightarrow 2 \times 10^8 = 5.55 \times 10^{14} \times \lambda$

$\Rightarrow \quad \lambda = \dfrac{2 \times 10^8}{5.55 \times 10^{14}}$

$\Rightarrow \quad \lambda = 3600$ Å [1]

63. (i) How does the angle of deviation formed by a prism change with the increase in the angle of incidence?

Draw a graph showing the variation in the angle of deviation with the angle of incidence at a prism surface. [3] [2020]

(ii) When a ray of light travelling in air is incident on the glass surface at angle of incidence 60°. Determine the angle of refraction in glass, if refractive index of glass is 3/2. [3]

(iii) The diagram below shows a point source *P* inside a water container. Four rays *A*, *B*, *C* and *D* starting from the source *P* are shown upto the water surface.

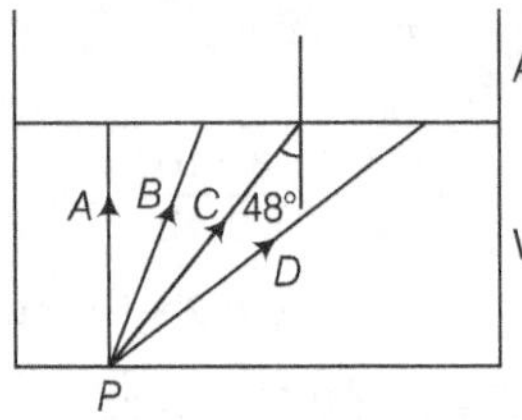

(a) Show in the diagram, the path of these rays after striking the water surface. The critical angle for water-air surface is 48°.

(b) Name the phenomenon which the rays *B* and *D* exhibit. [2017] [4]

Sol. (i) If the angle of incidence is increased gradually, then angle of deviation first decreases, attains a minimum value (δ_m) and then again starts increasing.

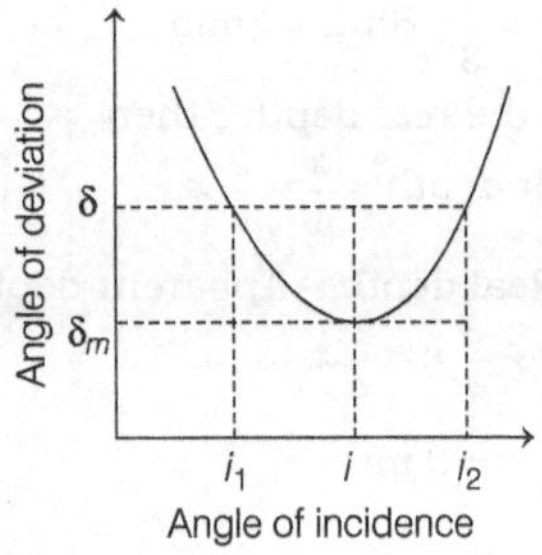

When angle of deviation is minimum, the prism is said to be placed in the minimum deviation position.

(ii) Given, $\angle i = 60° \Rightarrow {}^a\mu_g = \dfrac{3}{2}$

As, $\quad {}^a\mu_g = \dfrac{\sin i}{\sin r}$ [1]

$\Rightarrow \sin r = \dfrac{\sin i}{{}^a\mu_g}$ [1]

$\Rightarrow \quad \sin r = \dfrac{\sin 60°}{\frac{3}{2}} = \dfrac{\sqrt{3} \times 2}{2 \times 3} \Rightarrow \sin r = \dfrac{1}{\sqrt{3}}$ [1]

$\therefore \quad \sin r = \sin 35° \Rightarrow r = 35°$

(iii) (a) **Ray diagram**

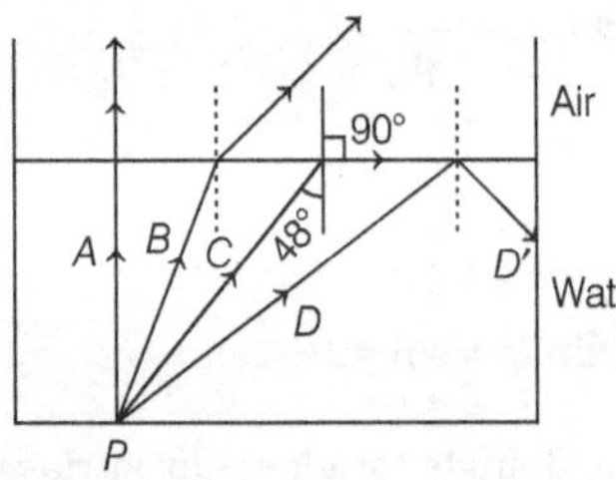

[2]

(b) From the ray diagram, for ray *C*, angle of incidence is 48°, which is equal to the critical angle, hence angle of refraction is 90°.

Ray *B* exhibits refraction. Because angle of incidence is less than the critical angle i.e. $i < i_c(48°)$. The rays *D* exhibits total internal reflection because angle of incidence is more than the critical angle. i.e. $i > i_c(48°)$. [2]

Chapter Assessment

1 Mark Questions

1. A light ray enters from medium *A* to medium *B* as shown in the figure. The refractive index of medium *B* relative to *A* will be

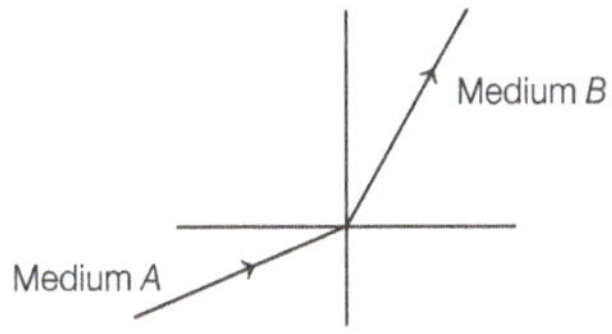

(a) greater than unity (b) less than unity
(c) equal to unity (d) zero

2. A ray of light *IM* is incident on a glass slab *ABCD* as shown in the figure. The emergent ray for this incident ray is **[2021 (Sem-I)]**

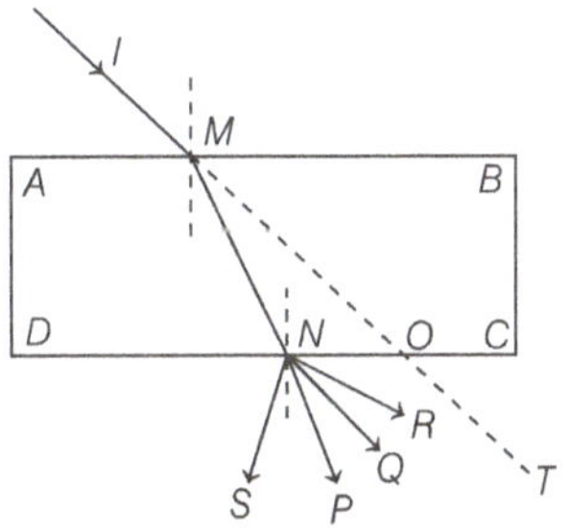

(a) *NQ* (b) *NR*
(c) *NP* (d) *NS*

3. You are given water, mustard oil, glycerine and kerosene. In which of these media, a ray of light incident obliquely at same angle would bend the most?
(a) Kerosene (b) Water
(c) Mustard oil (d) Glycerine

4. Twinkling of stars is due to atmospheric
(a) refraction of light by water droplets
(b) refraction of light by different layers of varying refractive indices
(c) reflection of light by dust particles
(d) internal reflection of light by clouds

5. Which of the following statements is correct regarding the propagation of light of different colours of white light in air?
(a) Red light moves fastest
(b) Blue light moves faster than green light
(c) All the colours of the white light move with the same speed
(d) Yellow light moves with the mean speed as that of the red and the violet light

2 Marks Questions

6. How does the refractive index of a medium depend upon its temperature?

7. "The upper surface of water contained in the beaker and held above the eye level appear silvery". Justify the statement along with a reason.

8. The critical angle for glass-air is 45° for the yellow colour of light.
Mention whether it will be less than equal to or more than 45° for
(i) red light and
(ii) blue light.

9. What will be the change occurred in the angle of minimum deviation produced by a prism, if
(i) the wavelength of the incident light and
(ii) the refracting angle of prism increases?

10. A pond appears to be 2.7m deep. If the refractive index of water is 4/3, find the actual depth of the pond. **[2020]**
Ans. 3.6 m

11. (i) Name one factor that affects the lateral displacement of light as it passes through a rectangular glass slab. **[2015]**
(ii) Does the depth of a tank of water appear to change or remain the same when viewed normally from above? **[2012]**

12. (i) A ray of light passes from water to air. How does speed of light change?
(ii) Which colour of light travels fastest in any medium except air? **[2014]**

13. (i) The refractive index of glass with respect to air is 1.5. What is the value of the refractive index of air with respect to glass?
(ii) A ray of light is incident as a normal ray on the surface of separation of two different mediums. What is the value of the angle of incidence in this case? **[2013]**

14. The refractive index of a liquid is $\sqrt{3}$. Determine the speed of light in liquid if the speed of light in vacuum is 3×10^8 m/s.

15. (i) Define critical angle.
(ii) State one important factor which affects the critical angle of a given medium. **[2019]**

16. (i) What is the relation between the refractive index of water with respect to air $({}_a\mu_w)$ and the refractive index of air with respect to water $({}_w\mu_a)$?
(ii) If the refractive index of water with respect to air $({}_a\mu_w)$ is $\frac{5}{3}$. Calculate the refractive index of air with respect to water $({}_w\mu_a)$. **[2019]**

17. The diagram alongside shows a light source P embedded in a rectangular glass block $ABCD$ of critical angle 42°. Complete the path of the ray PQ till it emerges out of the block. [Write necessary angles].

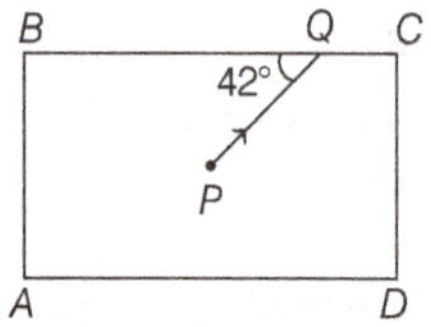

[2019]

18. A ray of light falls normally on a rectangular glass slab. Draw a ray diagram showing the path of the ray till it emerges out of the slab. **[2020]**

19. Complete the path of the monochromatic light ray AB incident on the surface PQ of the equilateral glass prism PQR till it emerges out of the prism due to refraction. **[2020]**

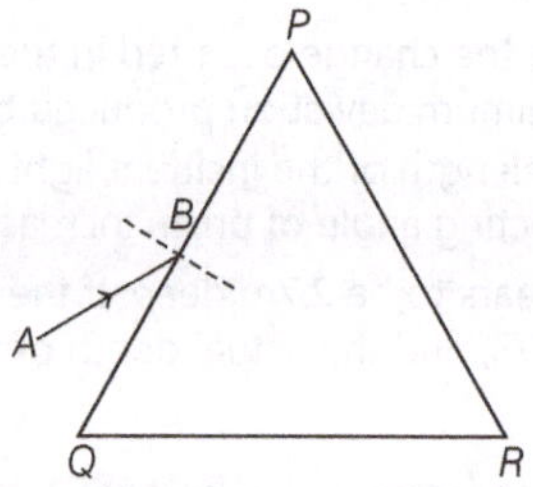

Structured Questions

20. (i) If an object is viewed through a glass prism with its vertex pointing upwards, then it appears to be displaced upwards. Explain why? **[3]**

(ii) (a) A diagram given below is to be completed in order to show the rays coming out of prism D.

(b) Mention the principle used for completing the ray diagram.

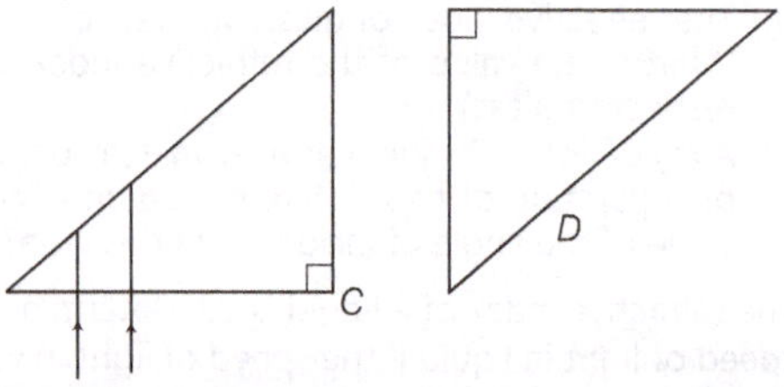

[4]

(iii) Jatin puts a pencil into a glass container having water and is surprised to see the pencil in a different state.

(a) What change is observed in the appearance of the pencil?

(b) Name the phenomenon responsible for the change.

(c) Draw a ray diagram showing how the eye sees the pencil. **[3] [2015]**

21. (i) Given below is a diagram showing the section of a semi-circular glass block having centre at O. D, E, F are the monochromatic rays of light of the same colour.

(a) I. Mark the critical angle by i_c.

II. Draw the path of rays F and D after they strike the edge GH.

(b) Name the phenomenon which the rays F and D exhibit.

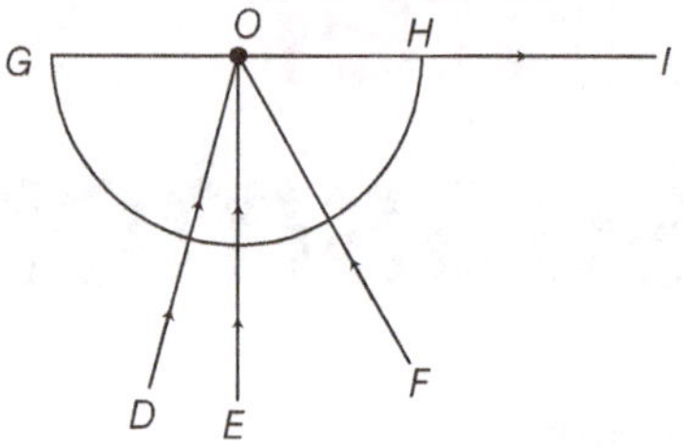

[3]

(ii) (a) Draw the ray diagram showing the refraction of light through a triangular glass prism and write the relation among angle of deviation, angle of incidence, angle of emergence and angle of prism.

(b) Show the variation of angle of deviation with angle of incidence. **[4]**

(iii) If a ray of light OE passes through a right angled prism as shown in the figure.

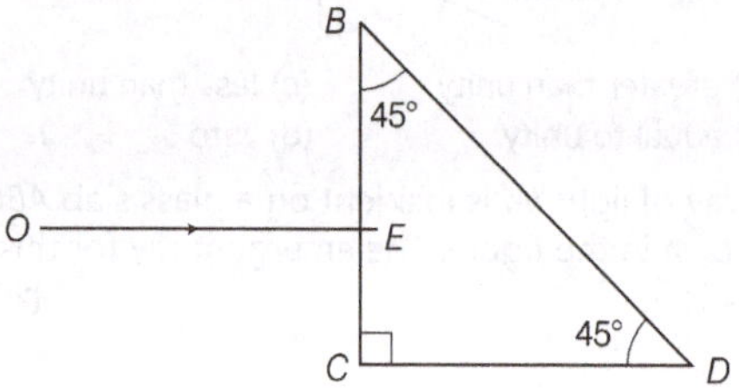

(a) Mention the angle of incidence at the faces BD and CD.

(b) Give the name of phenomenon which the ray suffers at the face BD. **[3]**

22. (i) Explain the factors affecting the critical angle for a given pair of media. **[3]**

(ii) With the help of a suitable diagram, explain refraction and total internal reflection of light rays at different angle of incidences. **[3]**

(iii) If a ray of light is incident normally on one face of the equilateral glass prism, answer the following questions.

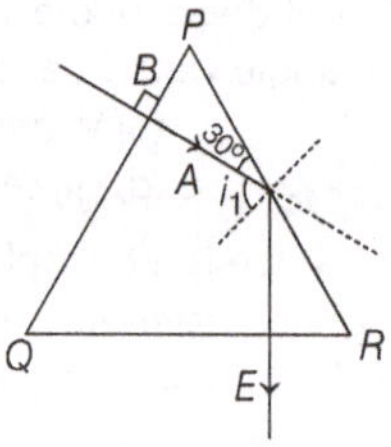

(a) Determine the angle of incidence on first face of prism.

(b) Calculate the angle of refraction from first face of the prism.

(c) Find the angle of incidence (i_1) at the second face of the prism.

(d) Will the ray of light suffers minimum deviation by the prism? **[4]**

For Solutions Scan the Code

Olympiad Section*

Brain Teasing Questions of Olympiad Pattern

1 How does the light should enter the glass to produce a large amount of bending?

(a) Obliquely, making a small angle of incidence
(b) Obliquely, making a large angle of incidence
(c) Perpendicularly to the glass surface
(d) All of the above

2 A ray of light is incident on one side of a rectangular glass block. Its path is plotted through the block and out through another side.

Which path is not possible?

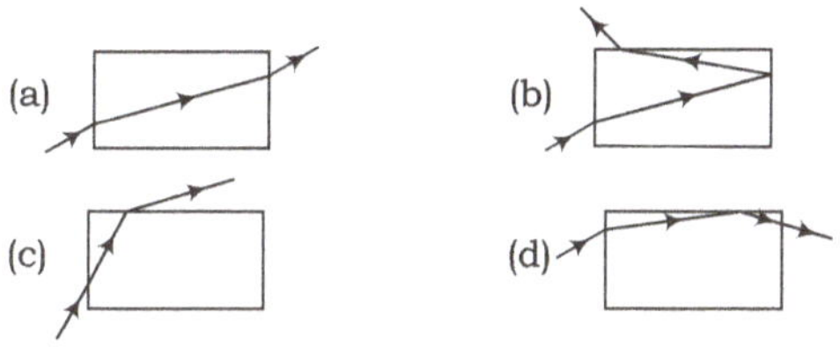

3 A ray of red light enters a semi-circular glass block normal to the curved surface.

Which diagram shows the partial reflection and refraction of the ray ?

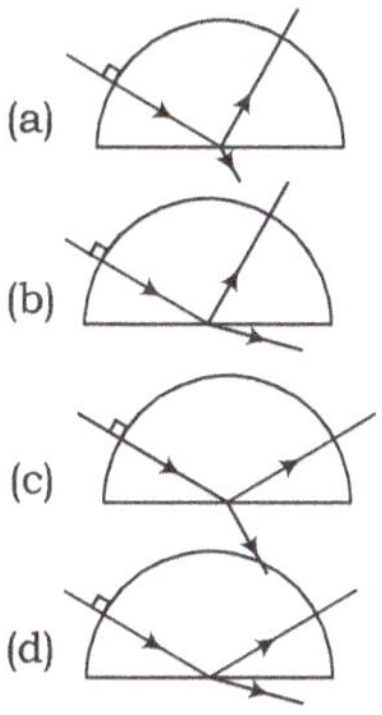

4 A ray of light enters a glass block at an angle of incidence i, producing an angle of refraction r in the glass.

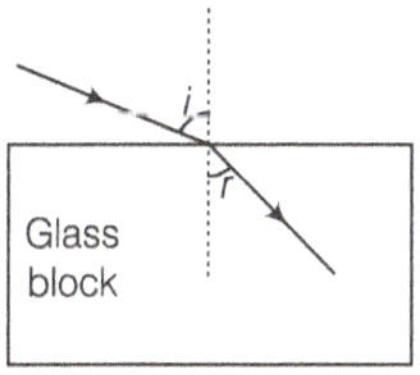

Several different values of i and r are measured and a graph is drawn of $\sin i$ against $\sin r$.

Which graph is correct ?

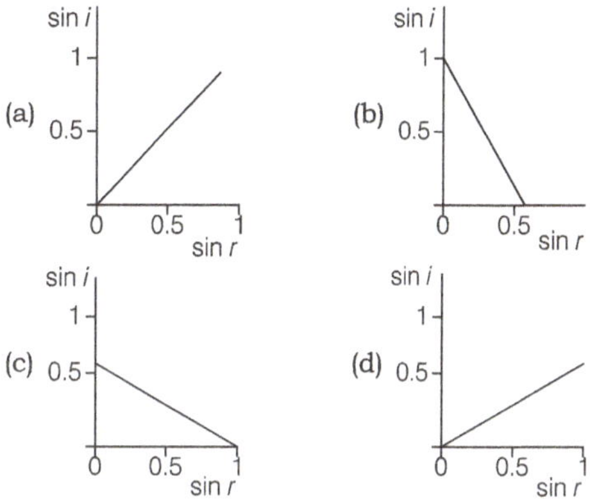

5 A ray of light travels from a medium of refractive index n_1 to a medium of refractive index n_2. If angle of incidence is i and angle of refraction is r, then $\dfrac{\sin i}{\sin r}$ is equal to

(a) n_1
(b) n_2
(c) $\dfrac{n_2}{n_1}$
(d) $\dfrac{n_1}{n_2}$

6 A light ray is travelling in a medium having frequency 2×10^{14} Hz and wavelength 5000 Å. The refractive index of the medium is

(a) 1.5
(b) 1.7
(c) 2.5
(d) 3

7 A ray of light in incident on surface of glass slab at an angle 45°. If the lateral shift produced per unit thickness is $\dfrac{1}{\sqrt{3}}$ m, the angle of refraction produced is

(a) $\tan^{-1}\left(\dfrac{\sqrt{3}}{2}\right)$
(b) $\tan^{-1}\left(1-\sqrt{\dfrac{2}{3}}\right)$
(d) $\sin^{-1}\left(1-\sqrt{\dfrac{2}{3}}\right)$
(d) $\tan^{-1}\left(\sqrt{\dfrac{2}{\sqrt{3}-1}}\right)$

8 A transparent cube of 0.21 m edge contains a small air bubble. Its apparent distance when viewed through one face of the cube is 0.10 m and when viewed from the opposite face is 0.04 m. The actual distance of the bubble from the second face of the cube is

(a) 0.06 m
(b) 0.17 m
(c) 0.05 m
(d) 0.04 m

9 The absolute refractive index of medium P is 1.5. When light is incident on an interface between medium P and medium Q at an angle of incidence of 30° in medium P, the angle of refraction is θ where $\sin\theta = 7/20$. The speed of light in medium Q is given by

(a) 1.4×10^8 m/s
(b) 3.0×10^8 m/s
(c) 2.5×10^8 m/s
(d) 2.1×10^8 m/s

10 White light is incident on one of the refracting faces of a prism. Inside the prism,

I. at normal incidence, the blue light slows down more than the red light

II. at normal incidence, blue light refracts same as red light

III. for oblique incidence, blue light bends more than red light

IV. for oblique incidence, blue light slows down more than the red light

Which of the above statements are correct?

(a) I and IV
(b) I, III and IV
(c) II, III and IV
(d) I, II, III and IV

ANSWERS									
1. (b)	**2.** (c)	**3.** (d)	**4.** (a)	**5.** (c)	**6.** (d)	**7.** (b)	**8.** (a)	**9.** (a)	**10.** (b)

* *These questions may or may not be asked in the examination, have been given just for additional practice required for olympiads Scholarship Exams etc. For detailed explanations refer Page No. 264.*

CHAPTER

05

Lenses

SYLLABUS

• Lens • Refraction Through an Equi-convex Lens and an Equi-concave Lens • Image • Ray Diagram for Principal or Construction Rays • Image Formation of Lenses • Lens Formula • Linear Magnification • Power of a Lens • Magnifying Glass or Simple Microscope • Applications of Lenses

We all are familiar with the use of lenses in our daily life through spectacles and other resources. The shape of lenses is responsible for their applications in a particular area. On the basis of shape mainly, there are two types of lenses: convex and concave. In this chapter, we will explore these two types of lenses with their related aspects.

Lens

It is a transparent refracting medium bounded by two surfaces of which, one or both surfaces are spherical.

Lenses are of two types

(i) Convex or Converging Lens

A lens which is thicker at the centre and thinner at its end is called convex lens. It is also known as converging lens because it converges a parallel beam of light rays passing through it.

Convex lenses are of three types as shown below

(a) Double-convex lens (b) Plano-convex lens (c) Concavo-convex lens

(a) A **double-convex** lens has two outward curving sides and is simply called convex lens.

(b) The **plano-convex** lens is flat on one side and curved outward on the other side.

(c) The **concavo-convex** lens has an inward curved from one side and has a more outward curve on the other side in the same direction.

(ii) Concave or Diverging Lens

A lens which is thinner at the centre and thicker at its ends is called a concave lens. It is also known as diverging lens because it diverges a parallel beam of light rays passing through it.

Concave lenses are of three types as shown below

(a) Double-concave lens (b) Plano-concave lens (c) Convexo-concave lens

(a) A **double-concave** lens has two inward curving sides and is simply called concave lens.

(b) **Plano-concave** lens has a flat surface and one inward curving side.

(c) **Convexo-concave** lens has one outward curving side with one greater inward curving side in the same direction.

Some Definitions Related to Lenses

Some definitions related to lenses are discussed as follow.

Optical Centre

The centre point of a lens is known as its optical centre. It is a point of the lens, directed to which the incident rays refract without any deviation in the path.

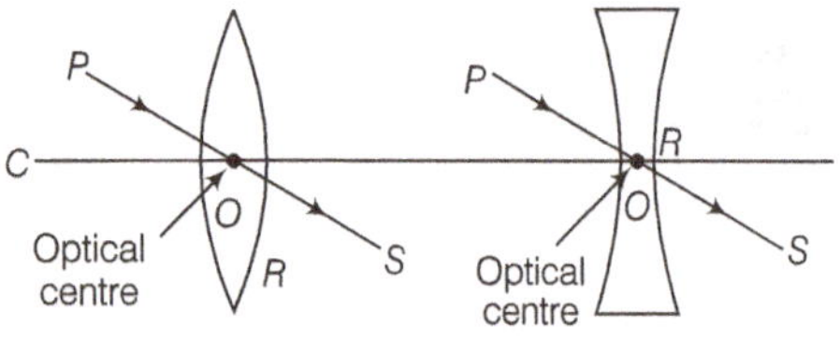

Optical centres of convex lens and concave lens

Centres of Curvature

The centres of the two imaginary spheres of which the lens is a part are called centres of curvature of the lens.

A lens has two centres of curvature with respect to its two curved surfaces.

Radii of Curvature

The radii of the two imaginary spheres of which the lens is a part are called radii of curvature of the lens. A lens has two radii of curvature. These may or may not be equal.

Note A plane surface can be considered as to be a spherical surface of infinite radii of curvature.

Principal Axis

The imaginary line joining the two centre of curvature is called principal axis of lens. It also passes through the optical centre.

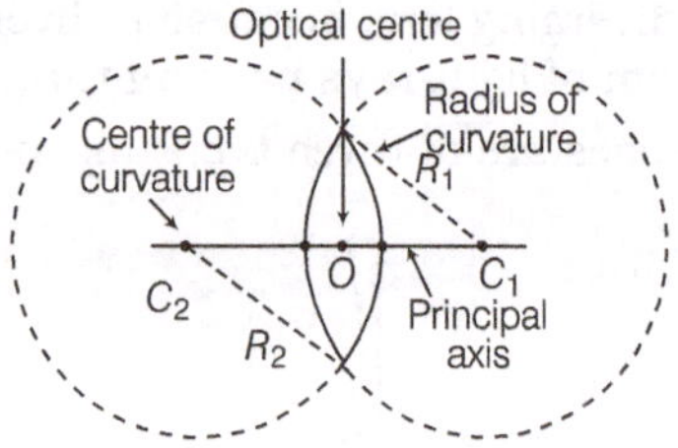

(a) Convex lens

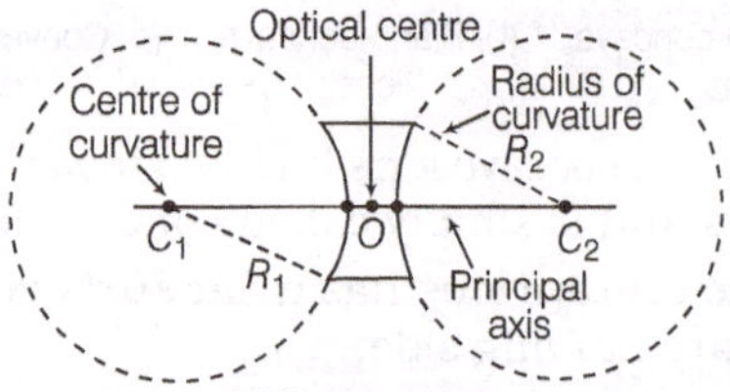

(b) Concave lens

Principal Focus

Rays of light can pass through any side of the lens in any direction. Hence, there will be two principal foci on either side of the lens. They are referred to as the first principal focus and the second principal focus of a lens.

(i) **First Principal Focus** The point on the principal axis such that the rays starting from this point (in convex lens) or appearing to go towards this point (in concave lens), after refraction through the lens become parallel to the principal axis, is called first principal focus.

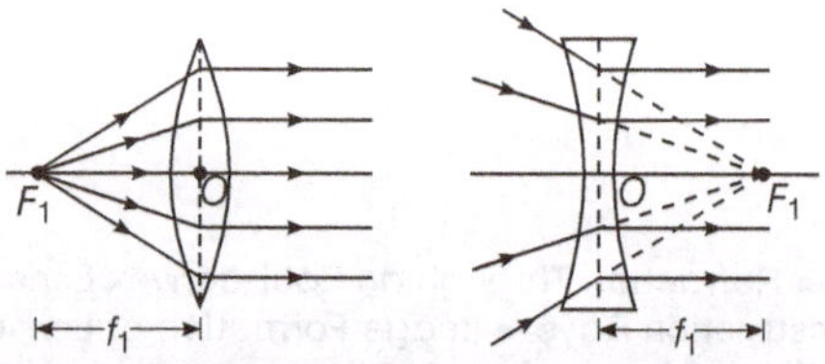

First principal focus of convex and concave lenses

(ii) **Second Principal Focus** It is the point on the principal axis at which the rays coming parallel to the principal axis converge (in convex lens) or passing through it appear to diverge (from concave lens) after refraction from the lens.

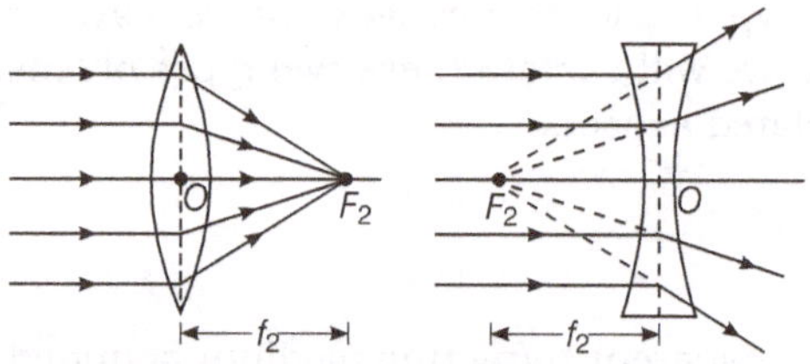

Second principal focus of convex and concave lenses

Both the foci of convex lens are real while that of concave lens are virtual.

Focal Length of Lens

The distance between the focus and optical centre of a lens is called focal length of lens.

Some important points related to focal length are given below

(i) Focal length of a lens implies the second focal length.

(ii) If the medium on both sides of the lens is same, the first and second focal lengths are equal.

(iii) Focal length of a lens depends on the refractive index of material of lens.

(iv) If a lens is placed in water instead of air, its focal length increases.

(v) A thick lens has less focal length than a thin lens of same material.

Focal Plane

The plane passing through the focus and perpendicular to the principal axis is called focal plane.

Aperture

The effective diameter of the circular outline of a spherical lens is called its aperture.

Refractive Axis

It is an imaginary axis, passing through the optical centre and perpendicular to the principal axis of the lens.

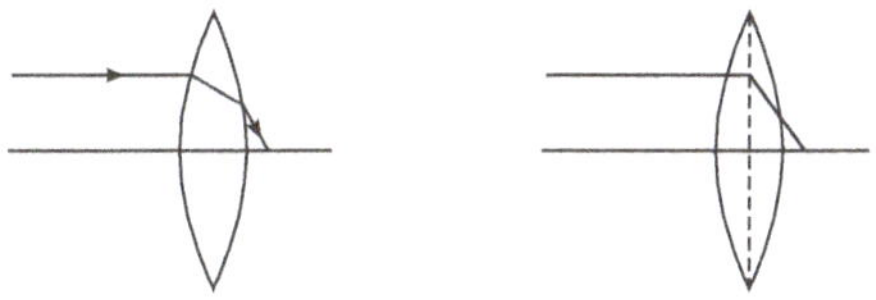

(a) Real path of ray

(b) Path of ray as shown with reference to refraction axis

Check Your LEARNING...

1. What do you mean by concavo-convex lens?
2. Why and which lens is called diverging lens?
3. Define principal focus of convex lens.
4. What type of lens is an air bubble inside the water?
5. Draw a diagram to represent the refractive and principal axis of a concave lens.

Action of a Lens as a Set of Prism Converging and Diverging Action of Lenses

The converging and diverging action of lenses can be explained by considering a lens made up of large number of different small angles prisms.

A converging lens can be supposed to be made up of a number of prisms with the base of each prism **towards** the centre of the lens.

A diverging lens can be supposed to be made up of a number of prisms with the base of each prism **away from** the centre of the lens.

A prism has a tendency to bend a light ray towards its base, on this basis converging and diverging action can be explained.

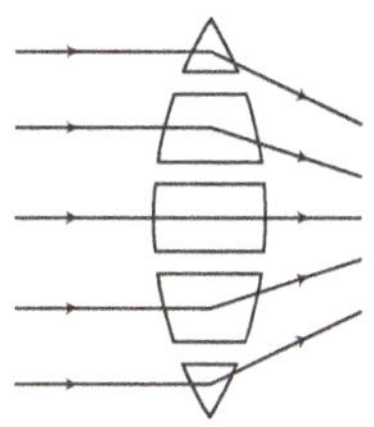

Converging action of convex lens

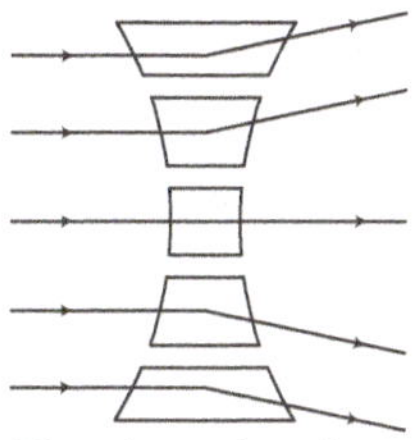

Diverging action of concave lens

Refraction Through an Equi-convex Lens and an Equi-concave Lens

Figure given below, shows the refraction of a ray of light at the two surfaces of an equi-convex lens and an equi-concave lens.

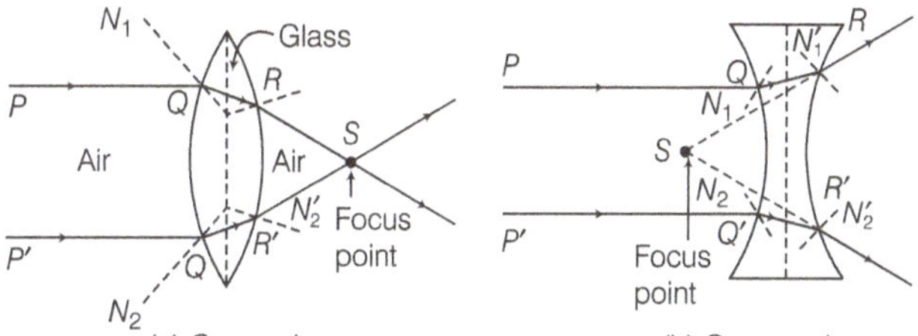

(a) Convex lens

(b) Concave lens

It is clear from the figure that, a convex lens bends the ray of light towards its middle, i.e. it converges the light. While a concave lens bends a ray of light towards its edges(or away from its middle), i.e. it diverges the light.

Image

The point where the rays meet or appear to meet after refraction from the lens is called image of that point of the object.

There are two types of images

Real Image

If the rays from a point of an object after refraction through the lens actually meet at a point, the image formed is called real image.

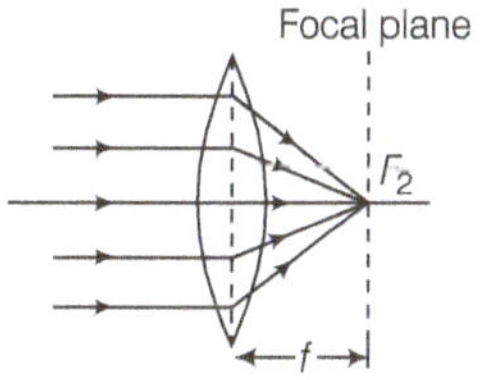

Real image formed by convex lens

Virtual Image

If the rays from a point on an object after refraction through the lens do not actually meet at a point, but they appear to diverge or converge from or to a point, the image formed is called virtual image.

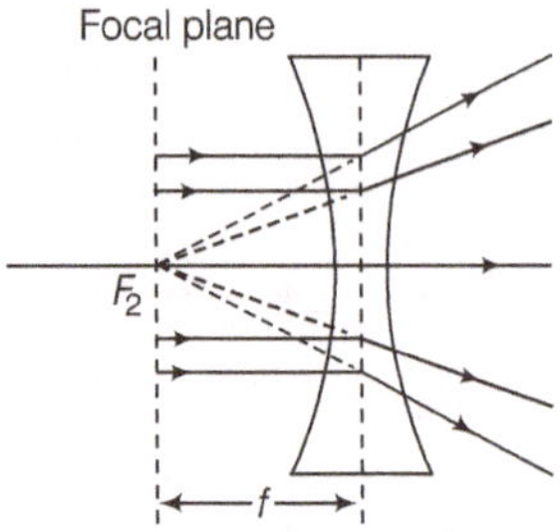

Virtual image formed by concave lens

Ray Diagram for Principal or Construction Rays

We can represent image formations by lenses using ray diagrams. By drawing these diagrams, we can determine the position, size and nature of the image formed by a lens. The figures given shows the path of ray which help in the formation of image through a concave lens and convex lens separately.

Generally three principal rays are used for the construction of the ray diagrams.

(i) Rays which are **parallel to the principal axis** after refraction, will pass through principal focus in case of convex lens and will appear to be coming from principal focus in case of concave lens.

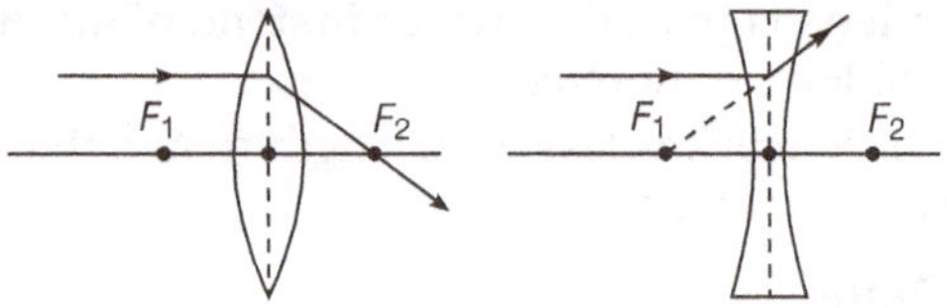

(ii) Ray **passing through or directed to the focus** will emerge parallel to the principal axis.

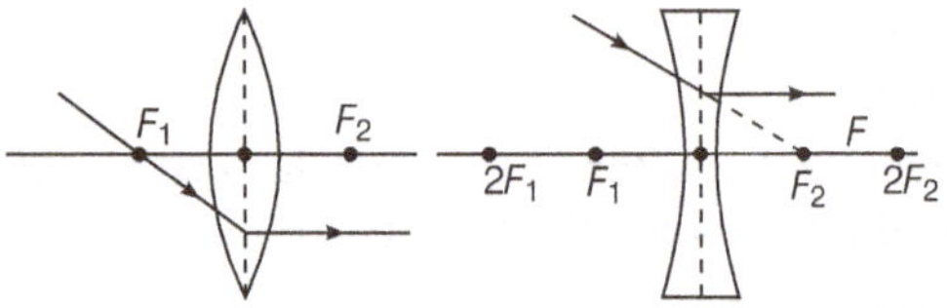

(iii) Ray **directed to optical centre** will emerge out undeviated.

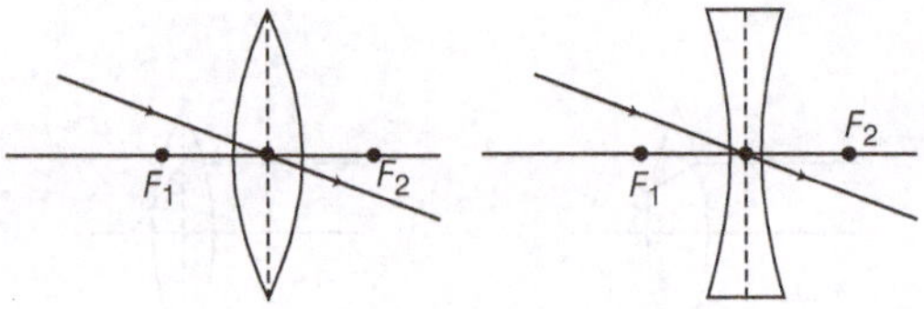

Check Your LEARNING...

1 How many times does a ray incident on a lens gets refracted after being deviated from its path?
2 Write one difference between real and virtual image.
3 Draw a ray diagram to show a ray passing through the focus of convex lens.
4 Give the position from which a ray passes undeviated through optical centre of the lens.
5 Which lens always forms a virtual image of an object?

Image Formation of Lenses

Formation of Image by a Convex Lens

The table given below illustrates the ray diagrams alongwith the position and nature of an image, formed by convex lens for various positions of an object.

Position of Object	Ray Diagram	Position of Image	Nature and Size of Image
At infinity	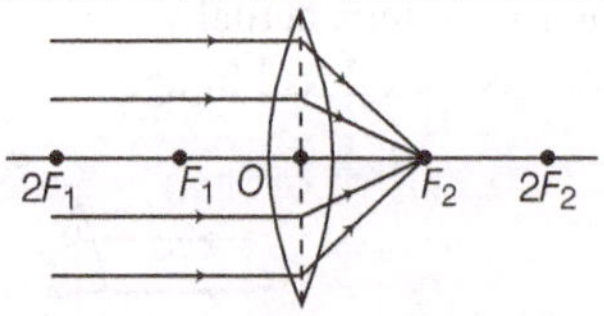	At F_2	Real, inverted and extremely diminished
Beyond $2F_1$ (at finite distance)	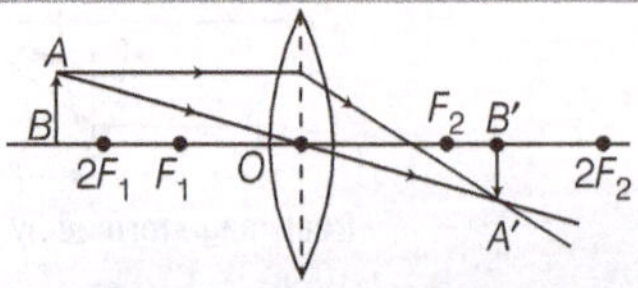	Between F_2 and 2 F_2	Real, inverted and diminished

Position of Object	Ray Diagram	Position of Image	Nature and Size of Image
At $2F_1$	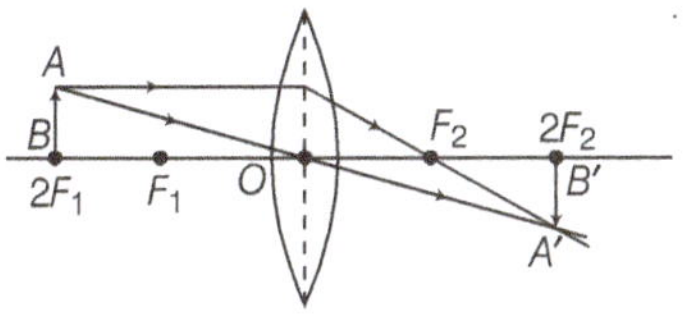	At $2F_2$	Real, inverted and of same size as that of object
Between F_1 and $2F_1$	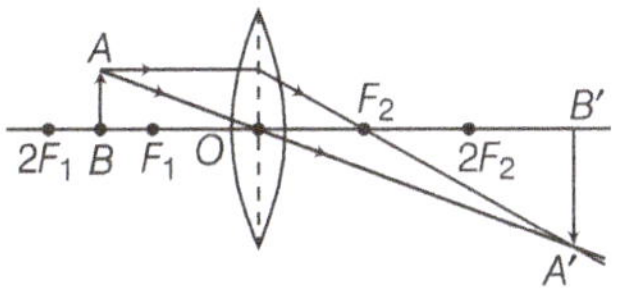	Beyond $2F_2$	Real, inverted and magnified
At F_1	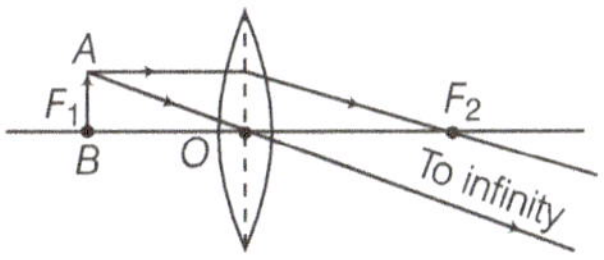	At infinity	Real, inverted and highly magnified
Between lens and F_1	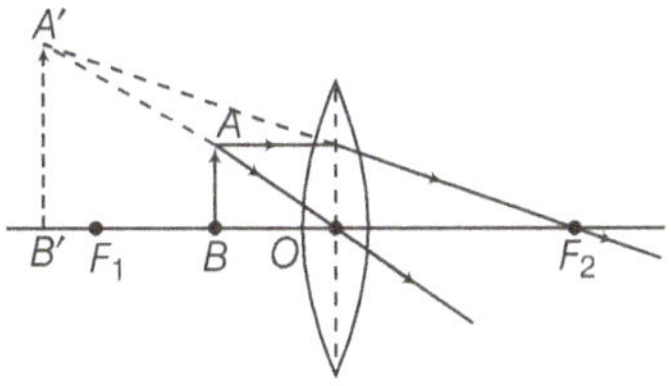	On same side of the lens as the object	Virtual, erect and magnified

Formation of Image by a Concave Lens

For studying the image formation by concave lens, there are only two positions of an object that are considered. Firstly, when the object is at infinity and the second position is when the object is at finite distance from the lens. The table given below illustrates the ray diagrams alongwith the position and nature of image, formed by concave lens for the given two positions of the object.

Position of Object	Ray Diagram	Position of Image	Nature and Size of Image
At infinity	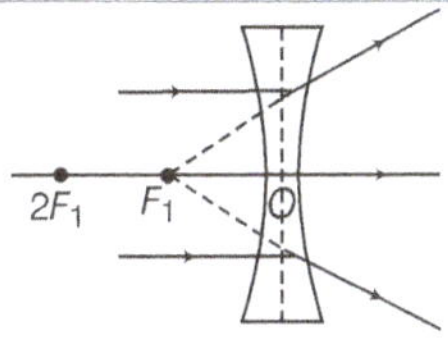	At focus on same side of lens as object	Virtual, erect and highly diminished
At finite distance	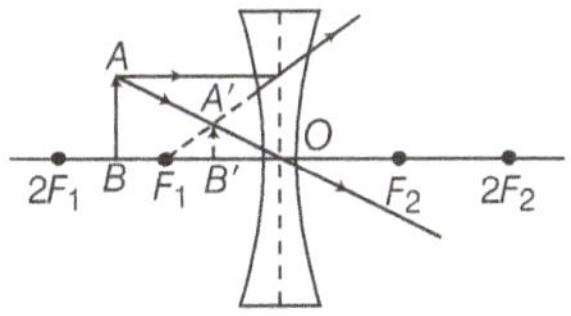	Between focus and optical centre on the same side of lens as object	Virtual, erect and diminished

Differentiate Between a Convex and a Concave Lens

(i) **By Touching** If the lens is thick in the middle and thin at the edges, the lens is convex and if the lens is thin in the middle and thick at the edges, the lens is concave.

(ii) **By Seeing the Image**

(a) On keeping the lens near a printed page, if letters appear magnified, the lens is convex and if the letters appear diminished, the lens is concave.

(b) On seeing a distant object through the lens, if its inverted image is seen, the lens is convex and if the upright image is seen, the lens is concave.

Lens Formula

It is a relation between focal length of a lens and distance of object and image from optical centre of the lens.

If u = object distance, v = image distance and f = focal length, then $\frac{1}{f} = \frac{1}{v} - \frac{1}{u}$.

This is called the lens formula.

Linear Magnification

The ratio of height of image (h_i) to the height of object (h_o) is called linear magnification (m).

Linear magnification, $m = \frac{h_i}{h_o}$ or $m = \frac{v}{u}$

It is **positive,** when image formed is **virtual** and is **negative,** when image formed is **real.**

Sign Convention for Spherical Lenses

To derive the relevant formulae for refraction by spherical lenses, we must first adopt a sign convention for measuring distances.

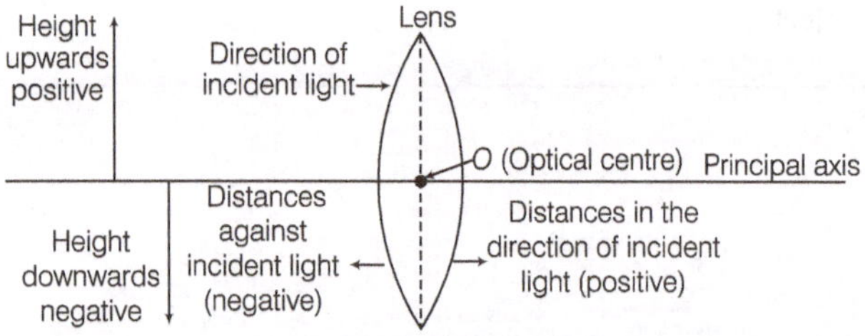

According to the cartesian sign convention,

(i) all the distances are measured from the optical centre (*O*) of the lens.

(ii) the principal axis of the lens is taken as *X*-axis and the optical centre as origin.

(iii) distances measured in the direction of the incident light are taken as positive and opposite to the direction of incident light as negative.

(iv) the heights measured upwards with respect to *X*-axis and normal to the principal axis of the lens are taken as positive and the heights measured downwards are taken as negative.

Example 1. A convergent beam of light passes through the diverging lens of focal length 0.2 m and comes to focus 0.3 m behind the lens. Find the position of the point at which the beam would converge in the absence of the lens.

Sol. Given, focal length, $f = 0.2$ m

Image distance, $v = -0.3$ m

Object distance, $u = ?$

According to lens formula,

$$\frac{1}{v} - \frac{1}{u} = \frac{1}{f}$$

$$\Rightarrow \quad \frac{1}{u} = \frac{1}{v} - \frac{1}{f} = \frac{1}{-0.3} - \frac{1}{0.2} = \frac{-0.5}{0.06}$$

$$u = \frac{-0.06}{0.5}$$

Object distance, $u = -0.12$ m

Example 2. A concave lens has a focal length 15 cm. At what distance should an object be placed from the lens so that it forms an image at 10 cm from the lens? What is the nature of the image?

Sol. Given, focal length, $f = -15$ cm

Image distance, $v = -10$ cm

Object distance, $u = ?$

According to lens formula, $\frac{1}{v} - \frac{1}{u} = \frac{1}{f}$

i.e. $$\frac{1}{-10} - \frac{1}{u} = \frac{1}{-15}$$

$$\therefore \quad \frac{1}{u} = \frac{-1}{10} + \frac{1}{15} = \frac{-1}{30}$$

$$\Rightarrow \quad u = -30 \text{ cm}$$

As, it is a concave lens, the image is virtual, erect and diminished.

Example 3. A 5 cm tall object is placed perpendicular to the principal axis of a convex lens of focal length 20 cm. The distance of the object from lens is 30 cm. Determine the

(i) position, (ii) nature and

(iii) size of image formed.

Sol. Given, object size, $h_o = 5$ cm

Object distance, $u = -30$ cm

Focal length, $f = +20$ cm

Using lens formula, $\frac{1}{v} - \frac{1}{u} = \frac{1}{f} \Rightarrow \frac{1}{v} = \frac{1}{u} + \frac{1}{f}$

$\Rightarrow \quad \frac{1}{v} = -\frac{1}{30} + \frac{1}{20} = \frac{1}{60}$

$\Rightarrow \quad v = 60$ cm

Since, magnification, $m = \frac{h_i}{h_o} = \frac{v}{u}$

$\Rightarrow \quad m = \frac{h_i}{5} = \frac{60}{-30} \Rightarrow h_i = -10$ cm

Therefore, the image is real, inverted and magnified.

Power of a Lens

The ability of a lens to deviate light rays towards or away from its principal axis is called power of lens. It is defined as the reciprocal of the focal length in metres. It is expressed as

$$\text{Power, } P = \frac{1}{f \text{ (in m)}}$$

Its SI unit is dioptre (D). The power of convex lens is **positive** and that of concave lens is **negative**. If many thin lenses are in contact with each other, then the total power is the algebraic sum of powers of individual lenses.

i.e. $\quad P = P_1 + P_2 + P_3 + \dots$

Example 4. A convergent lens of power 8 D is combined with a divergent lens of power – 10D. Calculate

(i) power of combination and

(ii) focal length of combination.

Sol. Given, power of convergent lens, $P_1 = 8$ D

Power of divergent lens, $P_2 = -10$ D

(i) Power of combination, $P = P_1 + P_2 = 8 - 10 = -2$D

(ii) Focal length of combination,

$$f = \frac{1}{P} = \frac{1}{-2} = -0.5 \text{ m} = -50 \text{ cm}$$

Magnifying Glass or Simple Microscope

Principle

It is based on the principle that when an object is placed between the first principal focus and the optical centre of a convex lens, it forms an erect, virtual and enlarged image on the same side of the object.

Construction

Magnifying glass is a kind of convex lens of short focal length mounted in a metallic frame with a holder.

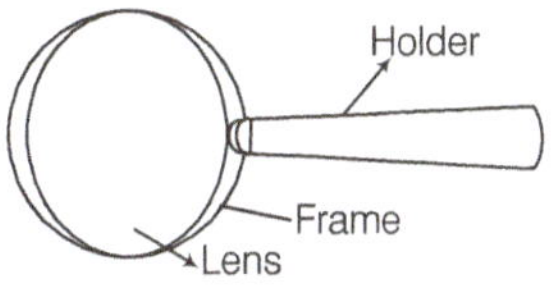

Magnifying glass (or simple microscope)

Way of Using the Microscope

The lens is placed near the eye and the object is at such a distance from the lens such that the image is formed at the least distance of distinct vision (D) = 25 cm from the lens.

Note The minimum distance, at which an object can be seen most distinctly without any strain is called the **least distance of distinct vision (D)**. For a healthy normal eye of an adult, it is 25 cm.

Ray Diagram and Magnification

Consider a ray diagram for location of image ($A'B'$) of an object (AB) due to a simple microscope.

The object AB is placed between focus F_1 and optical centre O of the lens.

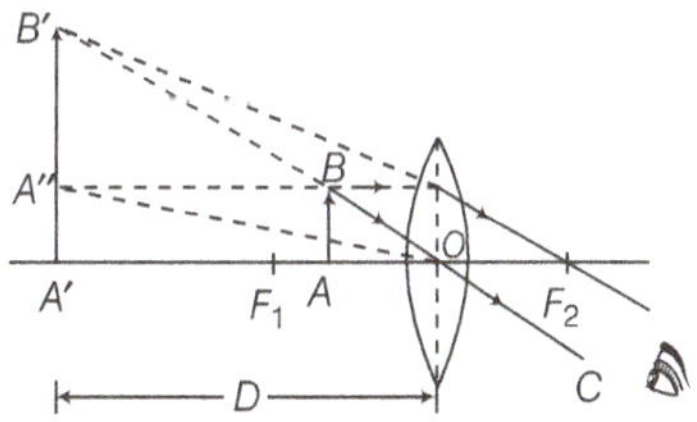

Ray diagram for location of image and magnification

Magnified and erect image $A'B'$ is formed atleast distance of distinct vision (D) from O. The magnifying power of the microscope is defined as the ratio of the $\angle B'OA'$ subtended by the image $A'B'$ at the eye to the $\angle A''OA'$ subtended by object AB at the eye.

It is expressed as $m = \frac{A'B'}{AB}$

Also, magnifying power of microscope, $m = 1 + \frac{D}{f}$

Applications of Lenses

Some applications of lenses are discussed as follows

(i) We usually use spectacles when our eyesight weakens. They either consist of convex lens or concave lens or both.

A person suffering from long sightedness, i.e. hypermetropia, use convex lens while a person suffering from short sightedness, i.e. myopia, uses concave lens.

(ii) They are used in a spectroscope which uses convex lens for obtaining pure spectrum.

(iii) In telescope, camera, slide projector, etc., convex lens is used which forms a real and inverted image of an object.

(iv) In galilean telescope, a concave lens is used as an eyelens to obtain an erect final image of the object.

(v) Convex lens of short focal length fitted in a steel frame with a handle, is used as a magnifying glass.

Note
- In order to photograph a distant object, the lens is moved closer to the film and for near object, the lens is moved away from the film. This adjustment of the lens is called **focusing**.
- The maximum variation in the power of the lens for focussing near or far objects clearly at retina is called **power of accommodation**.
- The time for which impression or sensation of an object continues in the eye is called persistence of vision. It is about (1/16)th of a second.

Check Your LEARNING...

1. Which type of lens produce
   (i) diminished virtual image
   (ii) magnified virtual image?
2. What is the minimum distance between an object and its real image formed by a convex lens?
3. What happens to the image formed by a convex lens if its lower part is blackened?
4. Name the lens which acts as magnifying glass.
5. Two lens of power − 3 D and + 2.5 D are placed in contact. Find the total power of combination of lens. Calculate the focal length of this combination. [*Ans.* −0.5 D, −200 cm]

QUiCK Revision

- **Lens** is a transparent medium bounded by two surfaces in which, one or both surfaces are spherical.
- **Convex lens** is a lens which is thicker at the centre and thinner at its end.
- **Concave lens** is a lens which is thinner at the centre and thicker at its end.
- The centre point of a lens is known as its **optical centre**.
- The centre of the two imaginary spheres of which the lens is a part is known as **centre of curvature** of lens.
- The radii of the two imaginary spheres of which the lens is a part are called **radii of curvature** of lens.
- The imaginary line joining the two centres of curvature is called **principal axis** of lens.
- The distance between focus and optical centre of a lens is known as **focal length** of lens.
- The plane passing through the focus and perpendicular to the principal axis is known as **focal plane**.
- The effective diameter of the circular outline of a spherical lens is known as **aperture** of lens.
- An imaginary axis, passing through the optical centre and perpendicular to the principal axis of the lens is called **refractive axis**.
- The converging and diverging action of lenses can be explained by considering a lens made up of large number of different small angled prisms.
- Image formation by convex lens for different positions of object

Position of Object	Position of Image	Relative Size of Image	Nature of Image
At infinity	At focus F_2	Highly diminished, point-sized	Real and inverted
Beyond $2F_1$	Between F_2 and $2F_2$	Diminished	Real and inverted
At $2F_1$	At $2F_2$	Same size	Real and inverted
Between focus F_1 and $2F_1$	Beyond $2F_2$	Enlarged	Real and inverted
At focus F_1	At infinity	Highly magnified	Real and inverted
Between focus F_1 and optical centre O.	On the same side of the lens as the object	Enlarged	Virtual and erect

- Image formation by concave lens for different positions of object

Position of Object	Position of the Image	Relative Size of Image	Nature of Image
At infinity	At focus F_1	Highly diminished, point-sized	Virtual and erect
At finite distance	Between focus F_1 and optical centre O	Diminished	Virtual and erect

- **Lens Formula**
  It is given by, $\frac{1}{v} - \frac{1}{u} = \frac{1}{f}$

where, v = distance of image from the optical centre of lens,
u = distance of object from the optical centre of lens
and f = focal length of lens.

- **Linear Magnification**

$$m = \frac{\text{Height of image } (h_i)}{\text{Height of object } (h_o)} \quad \text{or} \quad m = \frac{\text{Image distance } (v)}{\text{Object distance } (u)}$$

  If m is positive, image is **virtual** and if m is negative, image is **real**.
- The ability of a lens to converge or diverge light rays is known as **power** of lens. It is denoted by P.
- The SI unit of power is dioptre (D).

$$\text{Power, } P = \frac{100}{\text{Focal length } f \text{ (in cm)}} \text{ D}$$

- For **concave lens**, power and focal length are negative.
  For **convex lens**, power and focal length are positive.
- **Magnifying glass** is a kind of convex lens of short focal length mounted in a metallic frame with a holder.

Chapter Practice

1 Mark Questions

1. A ray of light after refraction through a lens emerges parallel to the principal axis of the lens. The incident ray passes through
(a) its optical centre
(b) its first focus
(c) its second focus
(d) the centre of curvature of the first surface

Sol. (*b*) As the ray after refraction through the lens emerges parallel to the principal axis of the lens, so ray must be passing through its first focus.

2. A ray of light incident on a lens parallel to its principal axis, after refraction passes through or appears to come from
(a) its first focus
(b) its optical centre
(c) its second focus
(d) the centre of curvature of its second surface

Sol. (*c*) When a parallel ray is incident on the lens, then after refraction, it passes through or appears to come from its second focus.

3. For the object placed between the optical centre and focus of a convex lens, the image is
(a) real and enlarged
(b) real and diminished
(c) virtual and enlarged
(d) virtual and diminished

Sol. (*c*) When an object is placed between optical centre and focus of a convex lens, then the image formed is virtual and enlarged. It is formed in the same side of object.

4. A concave lens produces only .... image. **[2023]**
(a) real, enlarged
(b) virtual, enlarged
(c) virtual, diminished
(d) real, diminished

Sol. (*c*) A concave lens produces virtual and diminished image

5. For an object placed at a distance 20 cm infront of a convex lens, the image is at a distance 20 cm behind the lens. The focal length of the convex lens is
(a) 20 cm (b) 10 cm
(c) 15 cm (d) 40 cm

Sol. (*b*) Given, object distance, $u = -20$ cm

Image distance, $v = 20$ cm

Using lens formula, $\frac{1}{v} - \frac{1}{u} = \frac{1}{f}$

$$\Rightarrow \quad \frac{1}{(20)} - \frac{1}{(-20)} = \frac{1}{f}$$

$$\Rightarrow \quad f = \frac{20}{2} = 10 \text{ cm}$$

6. An object of height 10 cm is placed in front of a concave lens of focal length 20 cm, at a distance of 25 cm from the lens. Is it possible to capture this image on a screen? Select a correct option from the following. **[2021 (Sem-I)]**
(a) Yes, as the image formed will be real.
(b) Yes, as the image formed will be erect.
(c) No, as the image formed will be virtual.
(d) No, as the image formed will be inverted.

7. If the magnification produced by a lens is -0.5, the correct statement is
(a) the lens is concave
(b) the image is virtual
(c) the image is magnified
(d) the image is real and diminished formed by a convex lens

Sol. (*d*) Given, $m = -0.5$

Since, the magnification is negative, so the lens used is convex and as $m < 1$. So, the image formed is real and diminished.

8. On reducing the focal length of a lens, its power
(a) decreases
(b) increases
(c) remain same
(d) first increase, then decrease

Sol. (*b*) Since, power $(P) = \frac{1}{\text{focal length } (f)}$

So, as f is reduced, the power of lens P will increase.

9. Two thin lenses of power 3D and − 2D are placed in contact, then power and focal length of the lens combination is
(a) + 2D, + 100 cm
(b) +1D, + 100 cm
(c) + 5D, + 20 cm
(d) + 1D, − 100 cm

Sol. (*b*) Given, power of lenses,

$$P_1 = 3\text{D}, P_2 = -2\text{D}$$

Power of combination of the lens,

$$P = P_1 + P_2 = 3\text{D} - 2\text{D} = +1\text{D}$$

$$\text{Combined focal length} = \left(\frac{1}{P} \times 100\right) \text{cm}$$

$$= \frac{1}{1} \times 100 = 100 \text{ cm}$$

10. A magnifying glass forms a
(a) real and diminished image
(b) real and magnified image
(c) virtual and magnified image
(d) virtual and diminished image

Sol. (c) A magnifying glass or lens forms a virtual and magnified image of an object placed between the first principal focus and optical centre of the convex lens.

11. The maximum magnifying power of a convex lens of focal length 5 cm can be
(a) 25 (b) 10 (c) 1 (d) 6

Sol. (d) Given, focal length, $f = 5$ cm

Since, magnifying power, $m = 1 + \frac{D}{f}$

Here, $D = 25$ cm (least distance of distinct vision)

$\Rightarrow \quad m = 1 + \frac{25}{5} = 6$

2 Marks Questions

12. Define convex lens and give its nature of refraction.

Sol. A lens which is thicker at the centre and thinner at its end is called convex lens. [1]

It is also called converging lens as it converges the light rays passing through it. [1]

13. What is the difference between double convex and a bi-convex lens?

Sol. In double convex lens, the two surfaces may have any values for the two radii of curvature of the two surfaces while the bi-convex lens, the radii of curvature of the two surfaces have the same value. So, all double convex lens may not be bi-convex, but every bi-convex lens is a double convex lens. [2]

14. (i) If the lens is placed in water instead of air, how does its focal length change?
(ii) Which lens, thick or thin has greater focal length? [2] [2019]

Sol. (i) The refractive index of water is more than air.
When lens is placed in water, its focal length increases
(ii) A thin lens has greater focal length.

15. Where should an object be placed infront of a convex lens in order to get [2]
(i) an enlarged real image [2020]
(ii) and enlarged virtual image?

Sol. (i) Object is placed between F and $2F$.
(ii) Object is placed between optical centre and F.

16. (i) An object is placed infront of a converging lens at a distance greater than twice the focal length of the lens. Draw a ray diagram to the formation of the image. [2007]
(ii) An object is placed infront of a convex lens such that the image formed has the same size as that of the object. Draw a ray diagram to illustrate this. [2006]

Sol. (i) The ray diagram to show the formation of the image is shown below [1]

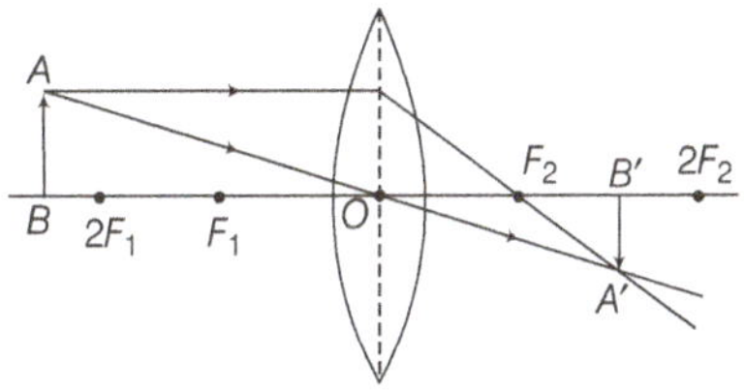

(ii) The ray diagram to show the formation of the image is shown below

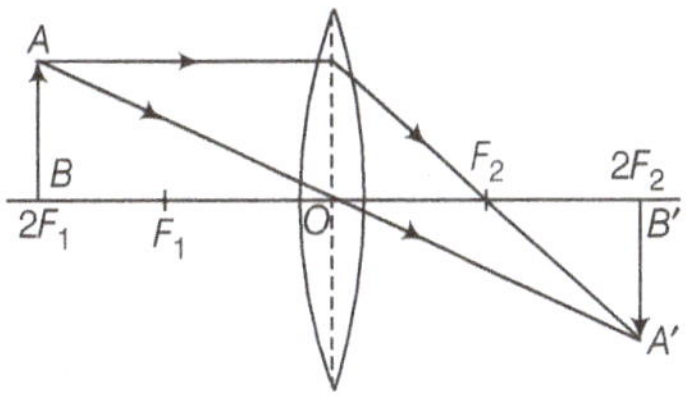

[1]

17. An object AB is placed between $2F_1$ and F_1 on the principal axis of a convex lens as shown in the diagram.

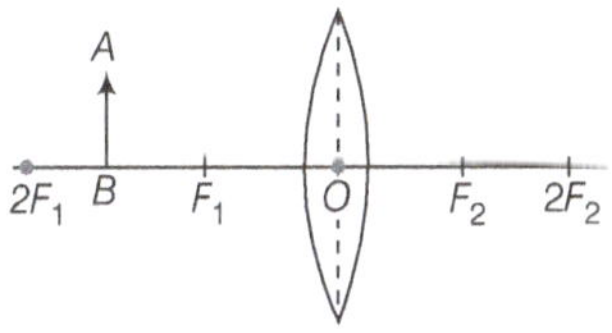

Copy the diagram and using these rays starting from point A, obtain the image of the object formed by the lens. [2013]

Sol. The formation of image is shown below

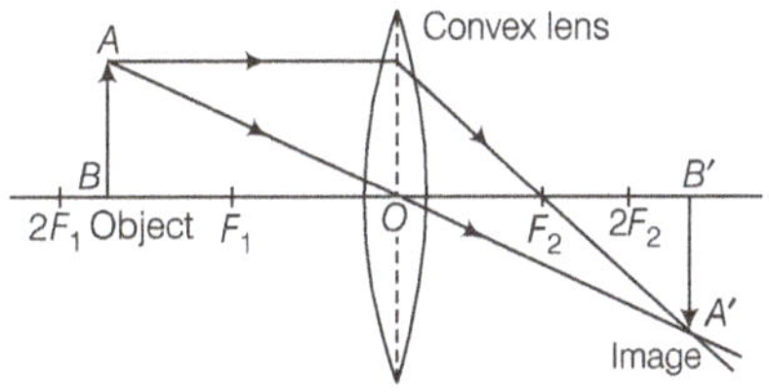

[2]

18. We can burn a piece of paper by focusing the sun rays by using a particular type of lens. [2010]
(i) Name the type of lens used for the above purpose.
(ii) Draw a ray diagram to support your answer.

Sol. (i) To collect all sun's rays to a particular point (called focus) we use a converging lens, i.e. convex lens. [1]

(ii) The ray diagram is shown below

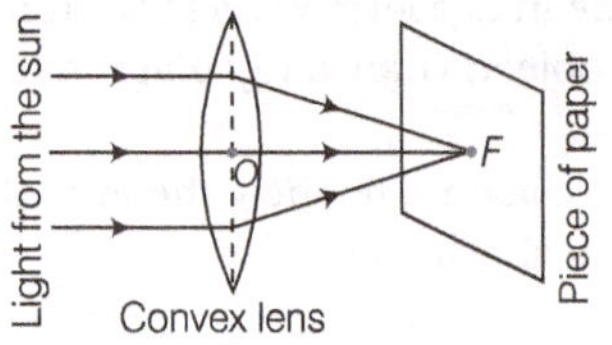

[1]

19. State two characteristics of the image of an extended source, formed by a concave lens.

Sol. The two characteristics of the image of an extended source formed by a concave lens are

(i) virtual and [1]

(ii) highly diminished, if the object is at infinity/ diminished, if the object is between optical centre and infinity. [1]

20. State the position of the object in front of a converging lens if

(i) it produces a real and same size image of the object.

(ii) it is used as a magnifying lens. [2018]

Sol. (i) To get real and same size image, object is placed at $2F$. [1]

(ii) To use a converging lens as magnifying lens object must be placed between lens and first focus. [1]

21. A ray of light, after refraction through a concave lens, emerges parallel to the principal axis. Draw a ray diagram to show the incident ray and its corresponding emergent ray. Can we obtain a real image with the help of a concave lens?

Sol. The ray diagram to show the incident ray and its corresponding emergent ray is shown below

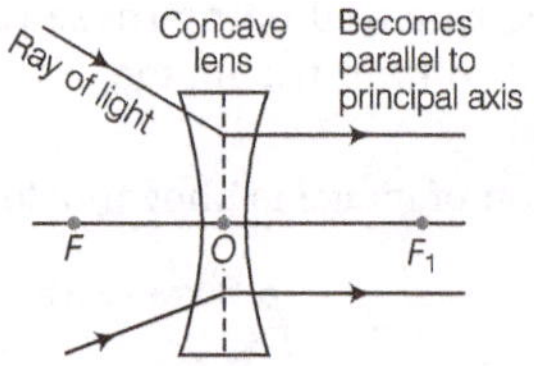

[1]

Yes, When a concave lens is kept in front of a convex lens (additional) it produces real image. [1]

22. (i) Is it possible for a concave lens to form an image of size two times that of the object ? Write Yes or No.

(ii) What will happen to the focal length of the lens, if a part of the lens is covered with an opaque paper? [2023]

Sol. (i) No, a concave lens cannot produce a image two times, that of the size of object . [1]

(ii) If a part of lens is covered, then the focal length will not changed. [1]

23. You are provided with a printed piece of paper. Using this paper, how will you differentiate between a convex lens and concave lens? [2012]

Sol. When the printed piece of paper is moved near to both the lenses and the letters appear as

(i) erect and diminished, then the lens is concave lens. [1]

(ii) erect and magnified, then the lens is convex lens. [1]

24. Figs. (a) and (b) are shown below, the incident and transmitted rays through lens kept in a box in each case. Draw the lens and complete the path of rays through it.

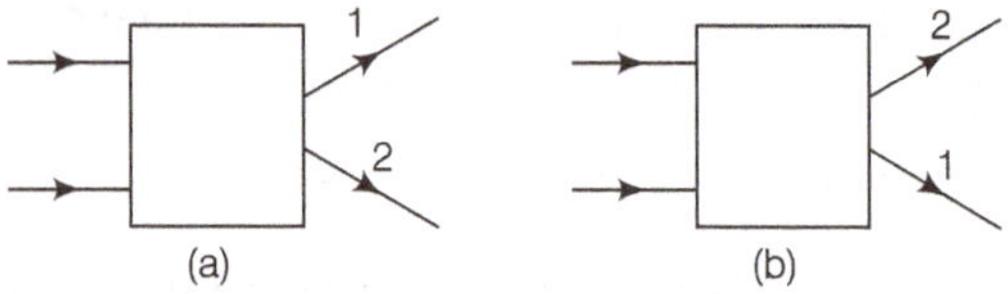

Sol. The ray diagram is as follows

(i) From Fig. (a), we see after passing through a box, rays get diverged, hence a concave lens will be there inside the box.

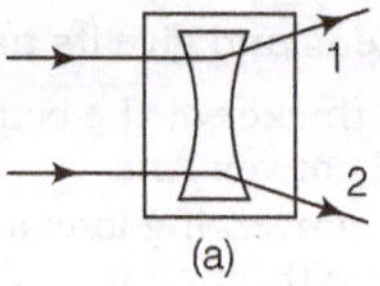

[1]

(ii) From Fig. (b), we see after passing through a box, rays get converged, hence a convex lens will be there inside the box.

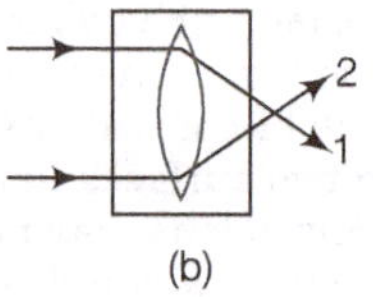

[1]

25. The power of a lens is – 5D.

(i) Find its focal length.

(ii) Name the type of lens. [2018]

Sol. Given, power of lens = – 5 D

(i) We know that,

Power of lens $(P) = \dfrac{1}{f(\text{focal length})}$ or $f = \dfrac{1}{P}$

$\Rightarrow \quad f = \dfrac{1}{-5} = -0.2 \text{ m} = -20 \text{ cm}$ [1]

(ii) The power of lens is negative, therefore lens is concave. [1]

3 Marks Questions

26. State the changes in the position, size and nature of the image of an object when brought from infinity upto a concave lens. Illustrate your answer by drawing diagrams.

Sol. When an object is brought from infinity upto a concave lens, then position of image is shifted from focus toward optical centre of concave lens, size of image increases, while nature of image is same (i.e. virtual). [1]

When object is placed at infinity

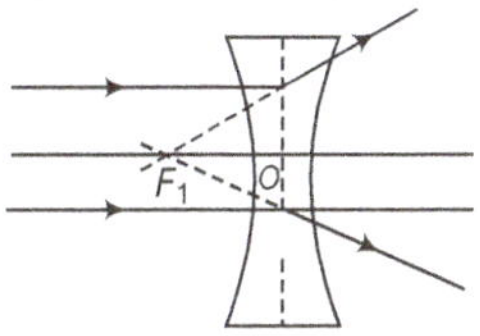

Image is formed at focus **[1]**

When object is placed at finite distance

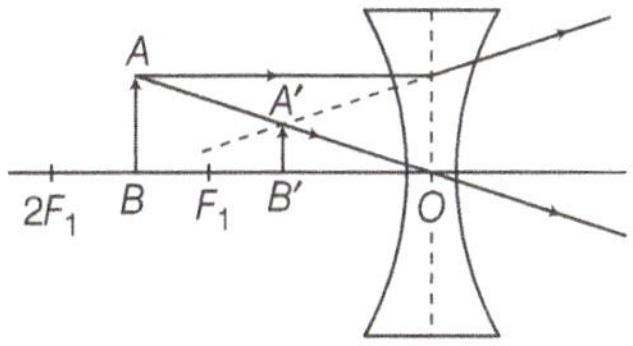

Image is formed between focus and optical centre **[1]**

27. An object AB is placed between O and F_1 on the principal axis of a converging lens as shown in the diagram.

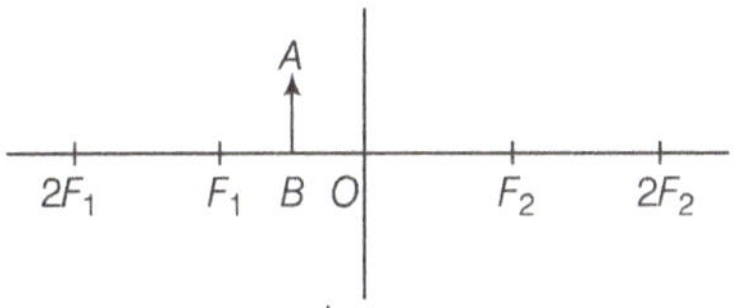

Lens

Copy the diagram and by using three standard rays starting from point A, obtain an image of the object AB. **[2018]**

Sol. Image $A'B'$ formed by object AB by converging lens is shown below using three standard rays starting form point A.

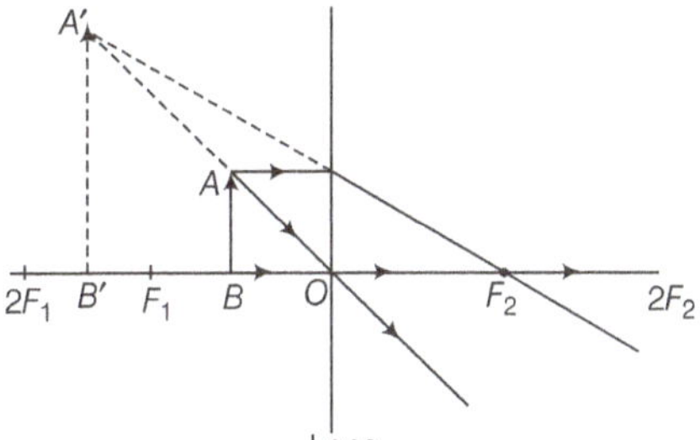

Lens **[3]**

28. Draw a labelled diagram showing how an image of a small object can be projected on large screen. State two characteristics of the image.

Sol. The ray diagram is shown below

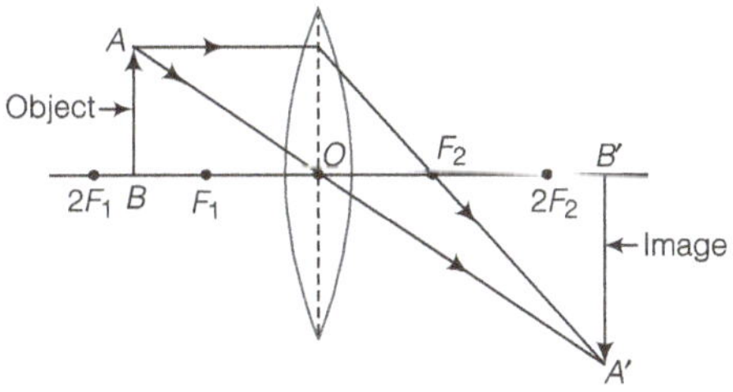

[1]

Characteristics of an image are

(i) image is real and inverted

(ii) image is enlarged. **[1+1]**

29. A lens forms an erect, magnified and virtual image of an object.

(i) Name the lens.

(ii) Draw a labelled ray diagram to show the image formation. **[2014]**

Sol. (i) A convex lens forms an erect, magnified and virtual image of an object when the object is placed between the focus and optical centre. **[1]**

(ii) The ray diagram showing the formation of image is shown below

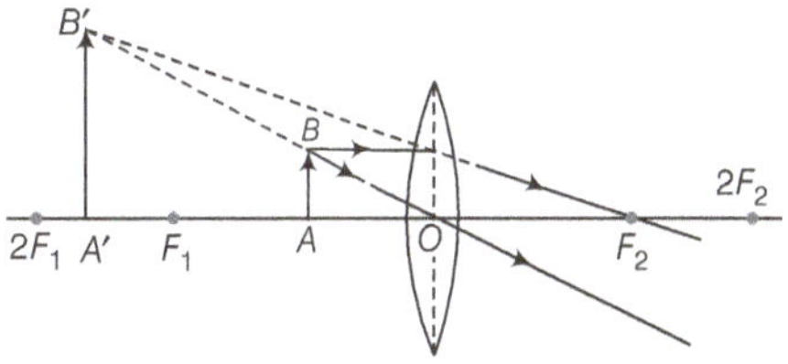

[2]

30. (i) Copy and complete the diagram to show the formation of the image of an object AB.

(ii) What is the name given to X? **[2009]**

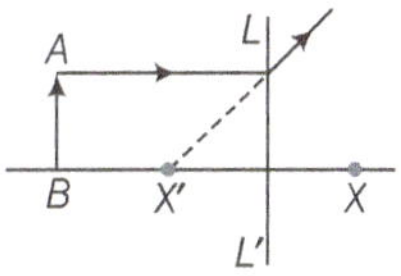

Sol. (i) The ray diagram showing the formation of the image ($A'B'$) of the object AB is shown below

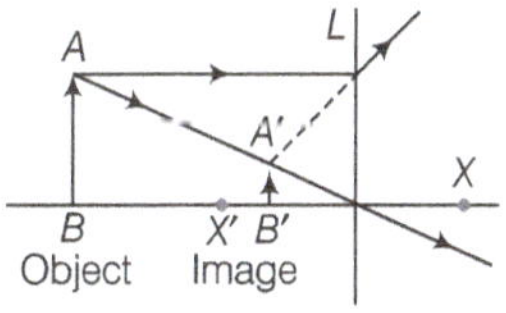

[2]

(ii) X is the first principal focus. **[1]**

31. Figure below shows a lens treated as a combination of two prisms and a glass block.

(i) Name the lens formed by the combination.

(ii) Draw the refraction of two incident rays parallel to its principal axis.

(iii) What is the linear magnification produced by given lens ?

Sol. (i) The lens is formed by the combination is a concave lens. **[1]**

(ii) The ray diagram is shown as below

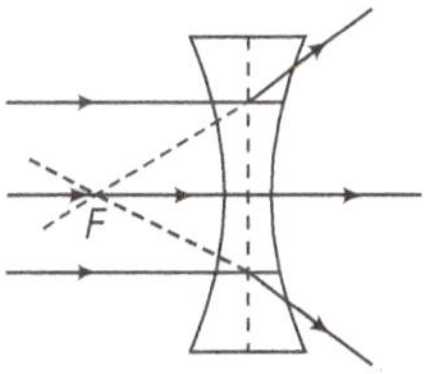

[1]

(iii) Since, concave lens forms always a diminished image, hence its linear magnification is always less than one.

32. A linear object is placed on the axis of a lens. An image is formed by refraction in the lens. For all positions of the object on the axis of the lens, the positions of the image are always between the lens and the object.

(i) Name the lens.

(ii) Draw a ray diagram to show the formation of the image of an object placed in front of the lens at any position of your choice except infinity. **[2008]**

Sol. (i) The lens is concave lens. **[1]**

(ii) The ray diagram showing the formation of image is shown below when the object is placed between focus f and $2f$.

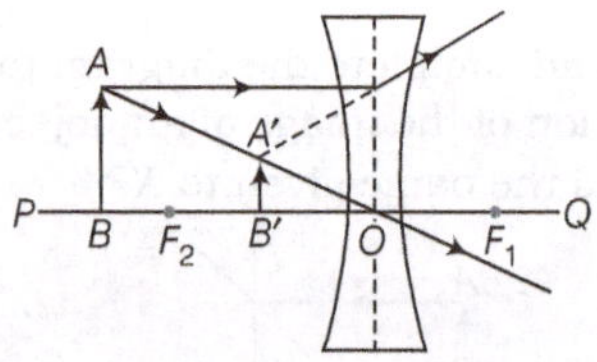

AB = object, $A'B'$ = image **[2]**

33. A lens forms an upright and diminished image of an object when the object is placed at the focal point of the given lens.

(i) Name the lens.

(ii) Draw a ray diagram to show the image formation. **[2017]**

Sol. (i) The lens is concave lens. **[1]**

(ii) The ray diagram is shown below

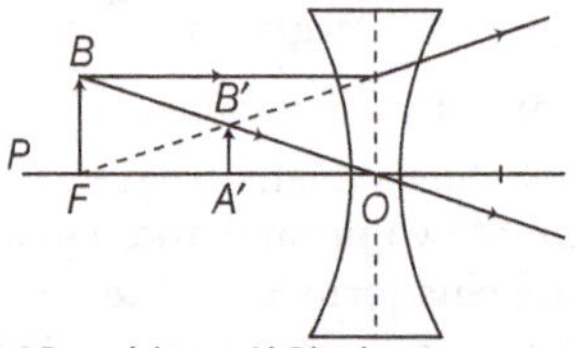

AB = object, $A'B'$ = image **[2]**

34. A lens produces a virtual image between the object and the lens.

(i) Name the lens.

(ii) Draw a ray diagram to show the formation of this image. **(2016)**

Sol. (i) The lens is concave lens. **[1]**

(ii) The ray diagram is given below

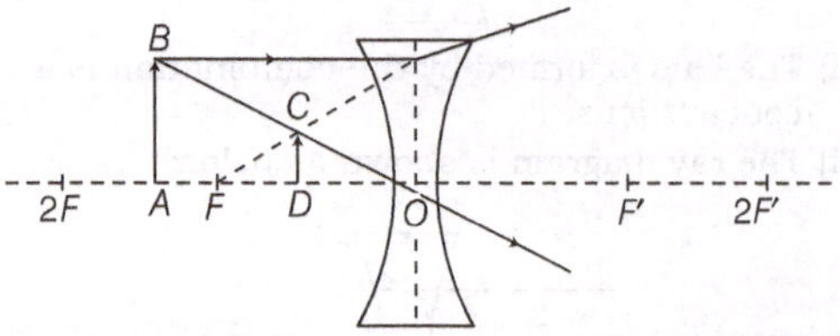

[2]

35. Draw a ray diagram to illustrate the action of a convergent lens as a reading lens or a magnifying glass.

Sol. A convex lens of small focal length can be used as a reading glass or a magnifying glass.

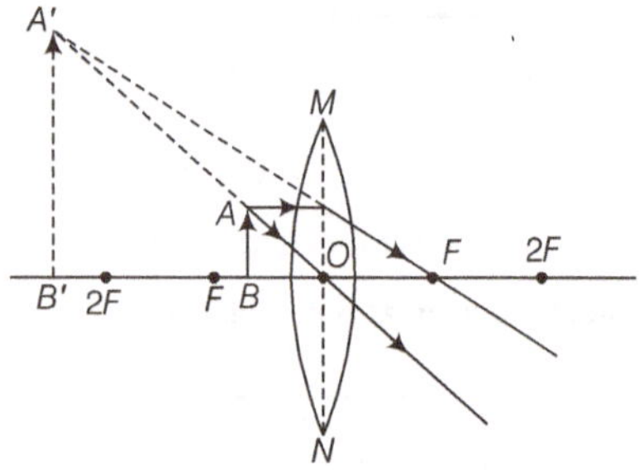

When an object is placed within the focal length of the lens, then a virtual, erect and magnified image is formed. **[3]**

36. A converging lens is used to obtain an image of an object placed in front of it. The inverted image is formed between F_2 and $2F_2$ of the lens.

(i) Where is the object placed?

(ii) Draw a ray diagram to illustrate the formation of the image obtained. **[2012]**

Sol. (i) The object is placed beyond $2F_1$. **[1]**

(ii) The ray diagram to illustrate the formation of the image is shown below

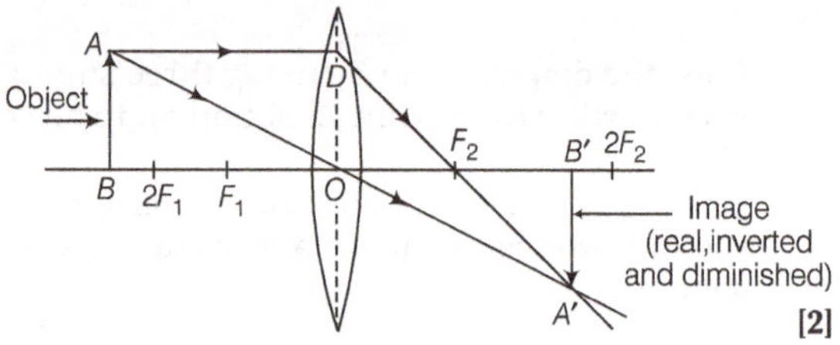

[2]

4 Marks Questions

37. Draw ray diagrams showing the image formation by a convex lens when an object is placed

(i) between optical centre and focus of the lens.

(ii) between focus and twice the focal length of the lens.

(iii) at twice the focal length of the lens.

(iv) at infinity.

Sol. (i) An enlarged, virtual and erect image of an object forms beyond F on the same side as that of object.

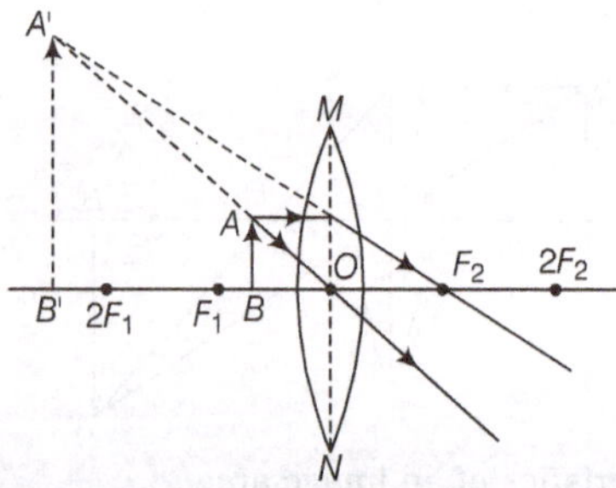

[1]

(ii) An enlarged, real and inverted image of an object forms beyond $2F$ on the other side of the lens.

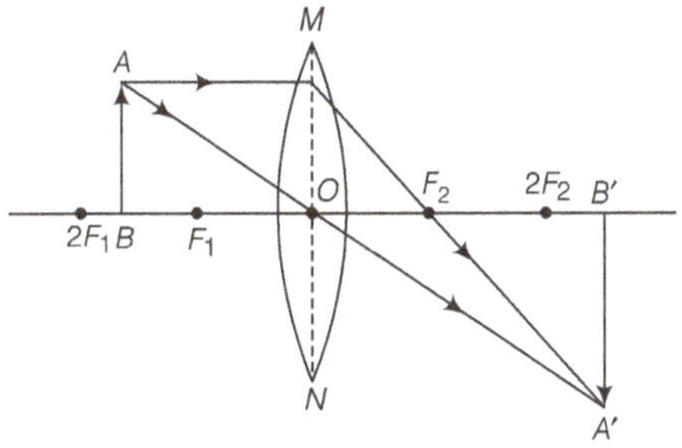

[1]

(iii) An real and inverted image of an object an equal to the size of the object, forms at $2F$ on the other side of the lens.

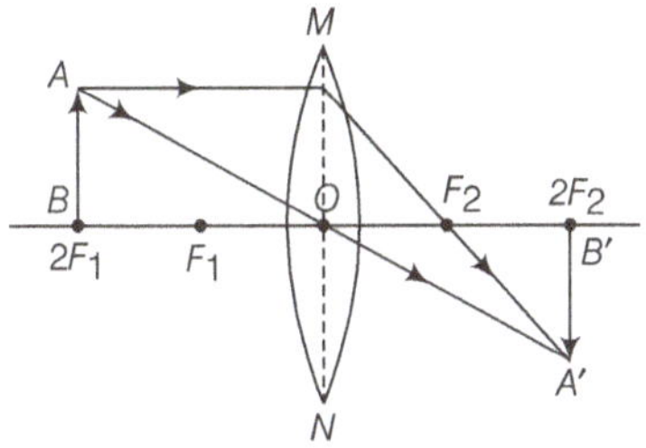

[1]

(iv) The real, inverted and highly diminished image of the object forms at focus F on the other side of the lens.

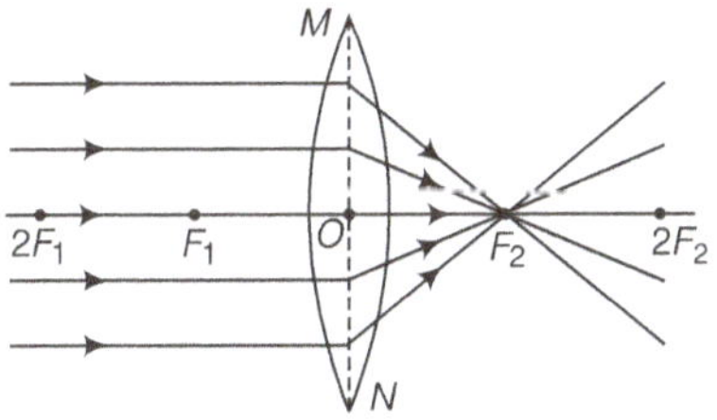

[1]

38. A thin converging lens form a real magnified image and a virtual magnified image of an object in front of it.

(i) Write the positions the objects in each case.

(ii) Draw ray diagrams to show the image formation in each part.

(iii) How will the following be affected on cutting this lens into two halves along the principal axis?

(a) Focal length

(b) Intensity of the image formed by half lens

Sol. (i) (a) Object is placed between F and $2F$.

(b) Object is placed between optical centre and F. [1]

(ii) The ray diagrams are as shown below

(a)

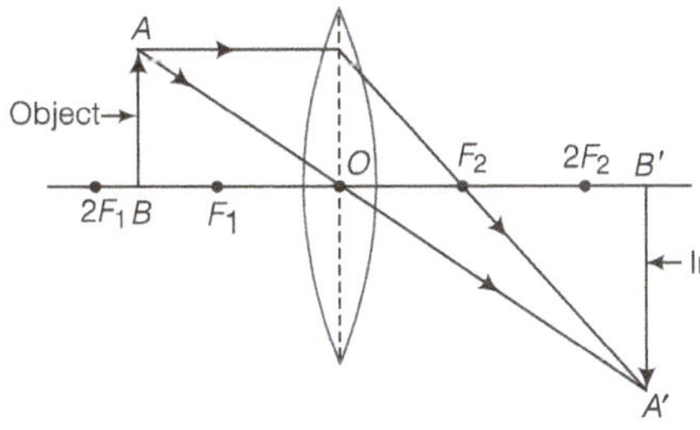

[1]

(b)

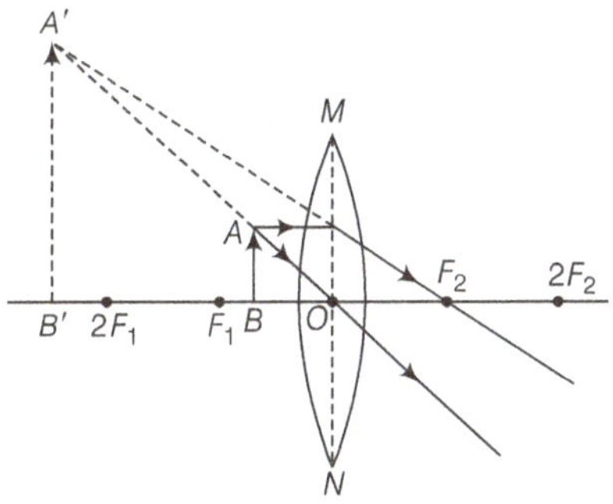

[1]

(iii) (a) There will be no change in focal length.

(b) Intensity will become one-fourth. [1]

39. A student wants to burn a piece of paper using a convex lens in day light, rather than using match stick or any direct flame. Will he be able to, if yes justify your answer with a ray diagram?

Sol. Yes, he will be able to burn a piece of paper using a convex lens in day light without using match sticks or any flame. When the sun rays coming from infinity passes through the convex lens and the paper being kept at the focus of the lens, then rays after passing the lens would converge at the focus as shown in figure below.

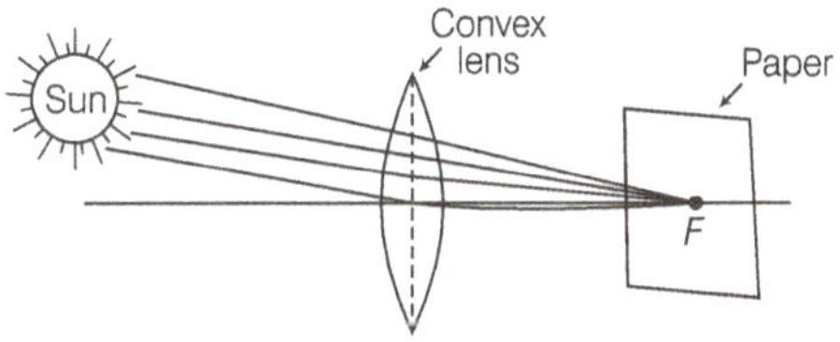

[2]

When the paper and the lens are held in the same position for sometime, then the paper will burn out. This is because of the heat produced by the sun's rays as they are concentrated on the spot, where these rays are bring to focus at lens focal point. [2]

40. A ray is directed towards a lens as shown in the figure below. The lens is being depicted as a combination of a glass slab and two prisms.

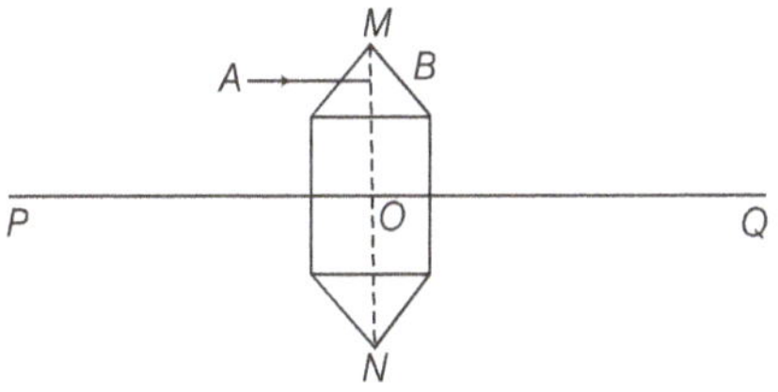

Answer the following questions.

(i) Name the lens which is formed by this combination.

(ii) What is PQ line called?

(iii) Complete the ray diagram.

(iv) The incident ray after refraction actually meet or appears to meet line PQ at a point. What is this point called?

Sol. (i) The lens is convex lens. [1]

(ii) The line PQ is called principal axis. [1]

(iii) **Ray diagram**

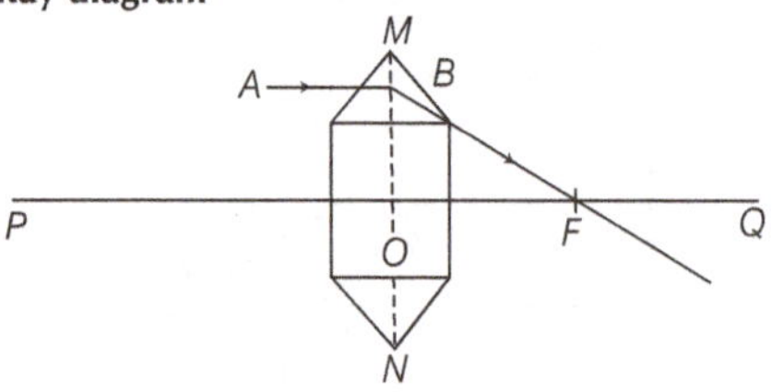

[1]

(iv) When a incident ray parallel to the principal axis falls on a convex lens, then after refraction, the emergent ray actually meet at a point on line PQ. This point is known as focus point of the lens. [1]

41. The figure given below shows a ray directed towards a lens MN.

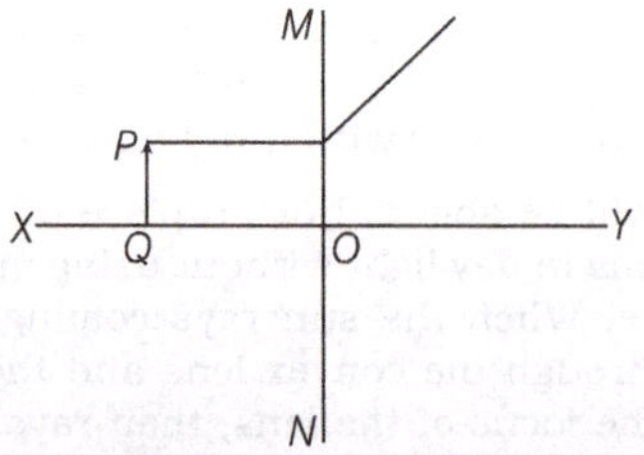

Study the above ray diagram and answer the following questions.

(i) Name the lens.
(ii) What is line XY called?
(iii) The image of the object PQ is formed between which points?
(iv) Write the nature of the image.

Sol. (i) The lens is concave lens. [1]
(ii) The line XY is called principal axis. [1]
(iii) The image of the object PQ is formed between points Q and O. [1]
(iv) The image will be virtual and erect. [1]

Numerical Based Questions

42. The focal length of a convex lens is 25cm. Calculate the power of the lens. [2] [2014]

Sol. Given, focal length, $f = 25$ cm $= 0.25$ m

Power, $P = \frac{1}{f} = \frac{1}{0.25} = 4$ D [2]

43. Express the power of a concave lens of focal length 20 cm with its sign. [2]

Sol. Power, $P = \frac{1}{f}$, where f is focal length.

As, $f = -20$ cm

$\Rightarrow \quad P = -\frac{1}{20} = -\frac{100}{20} = -5$ D

Hence, power of a concave lens is –5 D. [2]

44. Two lenses have power of (i) + 2 D (ii) – 4 D. What is the nature and focal length of each lens? [2]

Sol. (i) Given, $P = +2$ D

Since, power is positive, so the lens is convex lens.

Focal length, $f = \frac{1}{P} = \frac{1}{2} = 0.5$ m

$= 50$ cm [1]

(ii) Given, $P = -4$ D

Since, power is negative, so the lens is concave lens.

Focal length, $f = \frac{1}{P} = \frac{1}{-4} = -0.25\text{ m} = -25$ cm [1]

45. Rohit while playing with an old lens discovers that, if he holds the lens 20 cm away from a wall opposite to a window, he can see sharp but inverted images of outside world on the wall. What is the power of the old lens holded by him? [2]

Sol. Since, the rays from far away objects in outside world get focussed at principal focus, the distance between lens and wall is equal to focal length, i.e. 20 cm. [1]

$\therefore$ Power of lens, $P = \frac{100}{f\text{ (in cm)}} = \frac{100}{20} = 5$ D [1]

46. A convex lens has focal length of 20 cm. At what distance from the lens should the object be placed, so that the image is formed at 40 cm on the other side of the lens? Also, state the nature of the image formed. [2]

Sol. Given, $f = 20$ cm, $v = 40$ cm, $u = ?$

Now by using, $-\frac{1}{u} + \frac{1}{v} = \frac{1}{f}$

We have, $-\frac{1}{u} = \frac{1}{f} - \frac{1}{v} = \frac{1}{20} - \frac{1}{40}$

or $-\frac{1}{u} = \frac{1}{40}$

or $u = -40$ cm [1]

Thus, the object should be placed at a distance of 40 cm in front of the convex lens. Negative sign shows, the image formed is real and inverted. [1]

47. An object is placed at a distance of 12 cm from a convex lens of focal length 8 cm. Find

(i) the position of the image
(ii) nature of the image. [4] [2018]

Sol. Given, distance of object $(u) = -12$ cm

Focal length of lens $(f) = 8$ cm

(i) We know that, $\frac{1}{f} = \frac{1}{v} - \frac{1}{u}$

$\Rightarrow \quad \frac{1}{8} = \frac{1}{v} - \frac{1}{(-12)}$

$\frac{1}{v} = \frac{1}{8} - \frac{1}{12} \Rightarrow \frac{1}{v} = \frac{3-2}{24}$

$\frac{1}{v} = \frac{1}{24} \Rightarrow v = 24$ cm [2]

(ii) Real, inverted and magnified [2]

48. An object is placed perpendicular to the principal axis of a convex lens of focal length 20 cm. If the distances of the object is 30 cm from the lens, find the position, nature and magnification of the image. [3]

Sol. Given, $f = 20$ cm, $u = -30$ cm

$v = ?, m = ?$

Now by using lens formula, $\frac{1}{v} - \frac{1}{u} = \frac{1}{f}$

We have, $\frac{1}{v}-\frac{1}{(-30)}=\frac{1}{20}$

or $\frac{1}{v}=\frac{1}{20}-\frac{1}{30}$ or $\frac{1}{v}=\frac{1}{60}$ or $v = 60$ cm

Thus, the image is formed at 60 cm on the other side (i.e. right side) of the lens. [2]

Magnification, $m=\frac{v}{u}=\frac{60}{-30}=-2$

Thus, magnification is – 2.

Image formed by convex lens is real and inverted. [1]

49. A convex lens of focal length 10 cm is placed at a distance of 60 cm from a screen. How far from the lens should an object be placed, so as to obtain a real image on the screen ? [2023] [3]

Sol. Given focal length , $f = 10$ cm

Image distance from object , $u = -60$ cm

According to lens formula,

$$\frac{1}{v}-\frac{1}{u}=\frac{1}{f}$$ [1½]

$$\Rightarrow \frac{1}{v}=\frac{1}{f}+\frac{1}{u}=\frac{1}{10}-\frac{1}{60}$$

$$\frac{1}{v}=\frac{5}{60}$$

or $v = 12$ cm from the lens [1½]

50. A 6 cm tall object is placed perpendicular to the principal axis of a convex lens of focal length 25 cm. The distance of the object from the lens is 40 cm. [3]

By calculation, determine

(i) the position and

(ii) the size of the image formed.

Sol. Given, height of object, $h_o = 6$ cm

Focal length of lens, $f = 25$ cm

Distance of object, $u = -40$ cm

(i) Using lens formula, $\frac{1}{f}=\frac{1}{v}-\frac{1}{u}$

$$\Rightarrow \frac{1}{v}=\frac{1}{f}+\frac{1}{u}=\frac{1}{25}+\frac{1}{(-40)}$$

$$=\frac{8-5}{200}=\frac{3}{200}$$

$$v=\frac{200}{3}=66.67 \text{ cm}$$ [1½]

(ii) ∴ Magnification, $m=\frac{h_i}{h_o}=\frac{v}{u}$

$$\Rightarrow h_i=\frac{v}{u}\times h_o=\frac{66.67}{-40}\times 6=-10 \text{ cm}$$ [1½]

51. A concave lens of focal length 20 cm forms an image at a distance of 10 cm from the lens. What is the distance of the object from the lens? Also, draw ray diagram. [3]

Sol. Given, $f = -20$ cm (sign convention), $v = -10$ cm

(∵ image formed by concave lens is virtual)

By using lens formula, $\frac{1}{v}-\frac{1}{u}=\frac{1}{f}$

We have, $-\frac{1}{u}-\frac{1}{10}=-\frac{1}{20}$

or $\frac{1}{u}=\frac{1}{20}-\frac{1}{10}=-\frac{1}{20}$ or $u = -20$ cm [1½]

Ray diagram

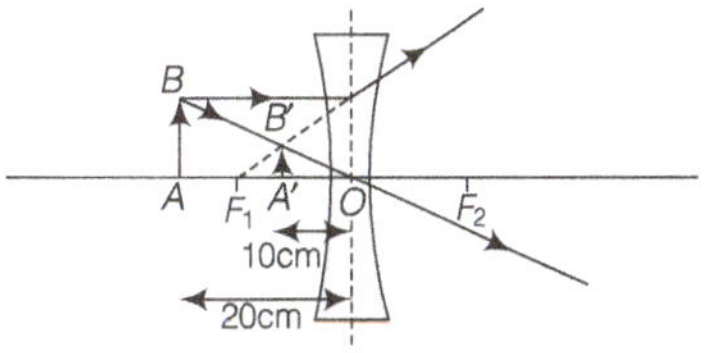

[1½]

Thus, the object is placed at 20 cm from the concave lens.

52. An object of height 5 cm is placed perpendicular to the principal axis of a concave lens of focal length 10 cm. If the distance of the object from the optical centre of the lens is 20 cm, determine the position, nature and size of the image formed using the lens formula. [3]

Sol. Given, height of object, $h_o = 5$ cm,

Focal length, $f = -10$ cm,

Distance of object, $u = -20$ cm, $v = ?$

Using lens formula, $\frac{1}{f}=\frac{1}{v}-\frac{1}{u}$

$$\Rightarrow \frac{1}{v}=\frac{1}{f}+\frac{1}{u}=\frac{1}{(-10)}+\frac{1}{(-20)}=\frac{-1}{10}-\frac{1}{20}$$

$$=\frac{-2-1}{20}=\frac{-3}{20}$$

$$\Rightarrow v=-6.67 \text{ cm}$$

Image is at 6.67 cm from concave lens. [1½]

As, magnification, $m=\frac{h_i}{h_o}=\frac{v}{u}$

$$\Rightarrow h_i=h_o\times\frac{v}{u}=5\times\frac{-6.671}{-20}=\frac{5}{3}=1.67 \text{ cm}$$

The image is virtual, erect and diminished. [1½]

Structured Questions

53. (i) The given ray diagram illustrates the experimental set-up for the determination of the focal length of a converging lens using a plane mirror.

(a) State the magnification of the image formed.

(b) Write two characteristics of the image formed.

(c) What is the name given to the distance between the object and optical centre of the lens in the given diagram? **[2005]**

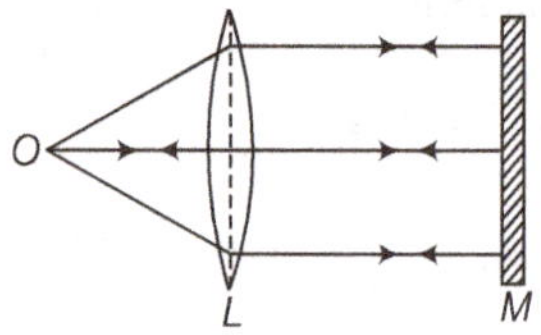

[3]

(ii) Define the power of a lens. Write its expression and its SI unit. **[3]**

(iii) The image of an object formed by a lens is of magnification -1. If the distance between the object and its image is 60 cm, what is the focal length of the lens? If the object is moved 20 cm towards the lens, where would the image be formed? State reason and also draw a ray diagram in support of your answer. **[4]**

Sol. (i) (a) As, the distance of image from lens is same as that of object, therefore its magnification is equal to one because position of image coincides with position of object.

(b) The image formed is real, inverted and of same size as that of object.

(c) The distance between the object and optical centre of the lens is named as focal length of the lens. **[1 × 3]**

(ii) It is defined as the ability of a lens to converge or diverge light rays. It is the reciprocal of focal length in metre. **[1]**

$$P = \frac{1}{f \text{ (in m)}}$$ **[1]**

Its SI unit is dioptre (D). **[1]**

(iii)

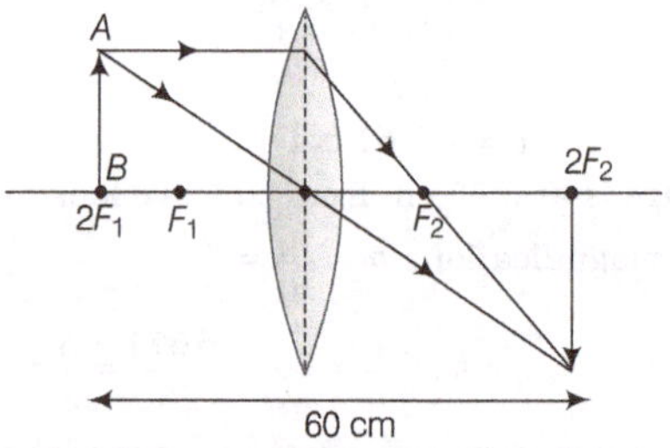

Given, $m = -1$, negative sign shows that image is real and inverted.

$\therefore |m| = 1$, it means that $h_i = h_o$

and this is possible in convex lens.

It implies that object and image both will be at $2F$.

So, $v = u$.

Object distance, $u = -30$ cm

Image distance, $v = +30$ cm

According to lens formula,

$$\frac{1}{f} = \frac{1}{v} - \frac{1}{u}$$

$$\Rightarrow \frac{1}{f} = \frac{1}{30} - \left(\frac{-1}{30}\right)$$

$$\Rightarrow f = 15 \text{ cm}$$

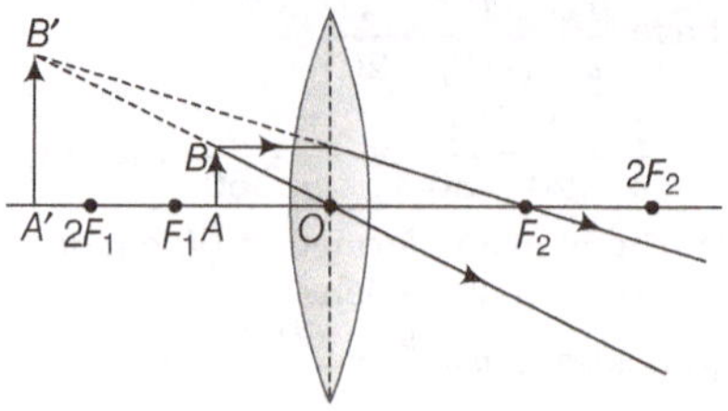

Now, object is moved 20 cm towards the lens.

$\because$ Object distance $u = -10$ cm

Focal length $f = +15$ cm

Again, using lens formula,

$$\frac{1}{v} - \frac{1}{u} = \frac{1}{f}$$

$$\Rightarrow \frac{1}{v} = \frac{1}{15} + \frac{1}{(-10)}$$

$$\Rightarrow \frac{1}{v} = \frac{1}{15} - \frac{1}{10} = \frac{2-3}{30}$$

$$\Rightarrow v = -30 \text{ cm}$$

54. (i) A virtual, diminished image is formed when an object is placed between the optical centre and the principal focus of a lens.

(a) Name the type of lens which forms the above image.

(b) Draw a ray diagram to show the formation of the image with the above stated characteristics. **[3] [2019]**

(ii) An object is placed at a distance 24 cm in front of a convex lens of focal length 8 cm.

(a) What is the nature of the image so formed?

(b) Calculate the distance of the image from the lens.

(c) Calculate the magnification of the image. **[3] [2019]**

(iii) A lens of focal length 20 cm forms an inverted image at a distance of 60 cm from the lens.

(a) Identify the lens.

(b) How far is the lens present in front of the object?

(c) Calculate the magnification of the image. **[4] [2020]**

Sol. (i) (a) When an object is placed between the optical centre and the principal focus of a concave lens, then virtual and diminished image of object is formed. **[1½]**

(b) **Ray diagram**

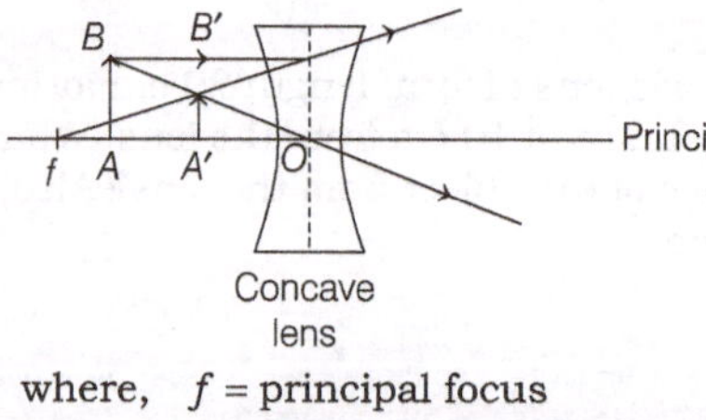

[1½]

where, f = principal focus

and O = optical centre of lens.

(ii) Given,

Object distance, $u = -24$ cm (for convex lens)

Focal length of lens, $f = 8$ cm

(a) As for convex lens, if $|u| > |f|$ then real and inverted image is formed and as $|u| > 2|f|$ then it diminished. **[1]**

(b) As we know that,

$$\frac{1}{f} = \frac{1}{v} - \frac{1}{u}$$

where, v is the image distance from lens.

$$\frac{1}{v} = \frac{1}{f} + \frac{1}{u}$$

$$v = \frac{uf}{f+u} = \frac{(-24)(8)}{(8)+(-24)}$$

$$= \frac{(-24)\times 8}{-16} = 12 \text{ cm}$$ **[1]**

(c) As we know that,

Magnification, $m = \frac{v}{u} = \frac{12}{-24} = -0.5$

Here, negative sign indicates that the image is inverted. **[1]**

(iii) (a) A convex lens forms both erect and inverted images while a concave alwasys forms erect image, hence the lens must be convex type. **[1]**

(b) Given $v = 60$ cm, $f = 20$ cm

By lens formula,

$$\frac{1}{v} - \frac{1}{u} = \frac{1}{f} \Rightarrow \frac{1}{60} - \frac{1}{u} = \frac{1}{20}$$

$$\Rightarrow \frac{1}{u} = \frac{1}{60} - \frac{1}{20} = -\frac{2}{60} = -\frac{1}{30}$$

$$\Rightarrow u = -30 \text{ cm}$$

Hence, lens is at a distance of 30 cm infront of the object. **[2]**

(c) Magnification of the image,

$$m = \frac{v}{u} = \frac{60}{(-30)} = -2$$ **[1]**

55. (i) An erect, diminished and virtual image is formed when an object is placed between the optical centre and principal focus of a lens.

(a) Name the type of lens, which forms the above image.

(b) Draw a ray diagram to show the formation of the image with the above characteristics. **[3]**

(ii) A concave lens of focal length 15 cm forms an image 10 cm from the lens. How far is the object placed from the lens? Draw the ray diagram. **[3]**

(iii) At what distance should an object be placed from a convex lens of focal length 18 cm to obtain an image at 36 cm from it? What will be the magnification produced in this case? **[4]**

Sol. (i) (a) The type of lens used is concave lens. **[1]**

(b) The ray diagram showing the formation of image is shown as

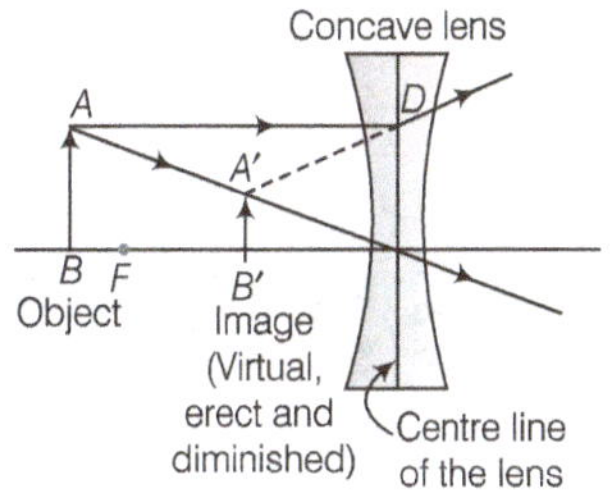

[2]

(ii) Given, focal length, $f = -15$ cm

Image distance, $v = -10$ cm

By lens formula, $\frac{1}{f} = \frac{1}{v} - \frac{1}{u}$

or $$\frac{1}{u} = \frac{1}{v} - \frac{1}{f} = \frac{1}{-10} - \frac{1}{(-15)}$$

$$= \frac{1}{15} - \frac{1}{10} = \frac{-1}{30}$$

$\therefore$ $u = -30$ cm from the lens.

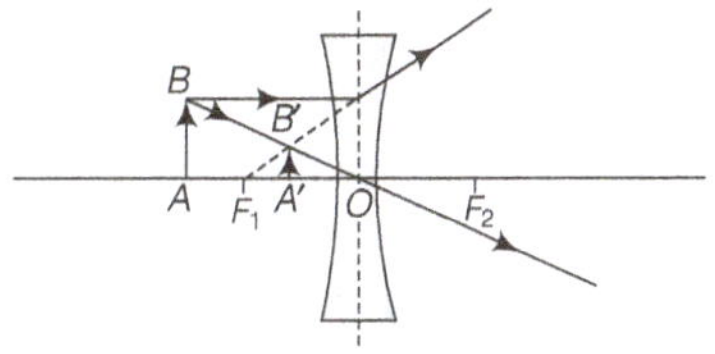

Thus, the object is placed at 30 cm from the concave lens. **[3]**

(iii) Given, focal length of lens, $f = 18$ cm

Distance of image, $v = \pm 36$ cm

($\because \pm$ sign as an image can be on either side of lens)

Distance of object, $u = ?$

Magnification produced, $m = ?$

From lens formula, $\frac{1}{v} - \frac{1}{u} = \frac{1}{f}$

$$\Rightarrow \frac{1}{u} = \frac{1}{v} - \frac{1}{f} = \frac{1}{\pm 36} - \frac{1}{18} = \frac{1}{36} - \frac{1}{18}$$

[Taking + ve sign]

$$= \frac{1}{36} - \frac{1}{18} = \frac{1-2}{36}$$

$$= \frac{-1-2}{36} = \frac{-1}{36}$$

$\therefore$ $u = -36$ cm

Taking – ve sign, $\frac{1}{u} = \frac{1}{-36} - \frac{1}{18} = \frac{-3}{36} = \frac{-1}{12}$

$\therefore$ $u = -12$ cm

If $u = -36$ cm and $v = 36$ cm, then

$$m = \frac{v}{u} = \frac{36}{-36} = -1$$

Image is real and inverted.

If $u = -12$ cm and $v = -36$ cm, then

$$m = \frac{v}{u} = \frac{-36}{-12} = 3$$

Image is virtual and erect. **[4]**

Chapter Assessment

1 Mark Questions

1. Where should an object be placed in front of a convex lens to get a real image of the same size of the object?
   (a) At the principal focus of the lens
   (b) At twice the focal length
   (c) At infinity
   (d) Between the optical centre of the lens and its principal focus

2. Which of the following lenses would you prefer to use while reading small letters found in dictionary?
   (a) A convex lens of focal length 50 cm
   (b) A concave lens of focal length 50 cm
   (c) A convex lens of focal length 5 cm
   (d) A concave lens of focal length 5 cm

3. If a symmetrical convex lens of focal length f is cut into two parts along the principal axis as shown in the figure, the focal length of each part will be

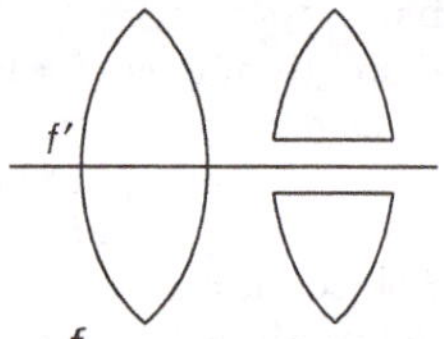

(a) $\frac{f}{2}$ (b) $\frac{f}{4}$ (c) f (d) ∞

4 An object of height 8 cm is placed at a distance of 40 cm in front of a convex lens of focal length 20 cm. The size of image is
   (a) 12 cm (b) 4 cm (c) −8 cm (d) 16 cm

5 From the diagram shown below, identify the characteristics of the image that will be formed.
[Latest Specimen Questions Paper]

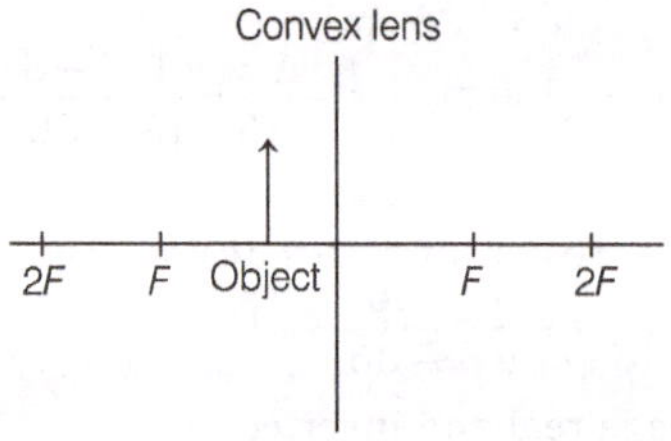

   (a) Real
   (b) Diminished
   (c) Formed within the focal length
   (d) Virtual

6 Assuming all lenses shown are of the same material, state which lens has the maximum power.
[ICSE Examination 2021-22]

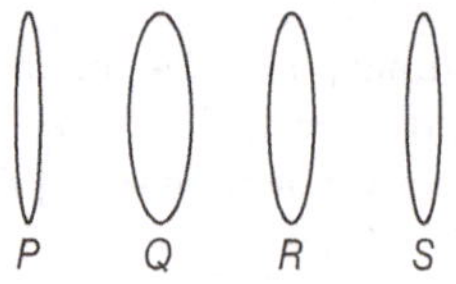

   (a) R (b) P
   (c) Q (d) S

2 Marks Questions

7. The diagram given below shows an object O and its image I. Copy the diagram and draw suitable rays to locate the lens and its focus.

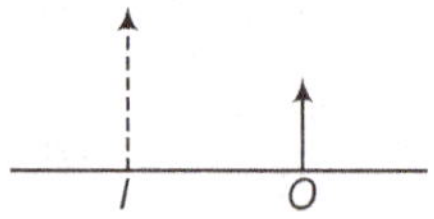

8. In an optical camera,
   (i) state the nature of the lens used.
   (ii) state two characteristics of the image formed by the lens.

9. One-half of a convex lens of focal length 10 cm is covered with a black paper. Can such a lens produce an image of a complete object placed at a distance of 30 cm from the lens? Draw a ray diagram to justify your answer.

10. A 4 cm tall object is placed perpendicular to principal axis of a convex lens of focal length 20 cm. The distance of the object from the lens is 15 cm. Find the nature, position and the size of the image.

11. Copy and complete the following table.

Type of Lens	Position of Object	Nature of Image	Size of Image
Convex	At F		
Concave	At infinity		

12. The diagram shows a point source of light S, a convex lens L and a plane mirror M. These are placed such that rays of light from S return to it after reflection from M.

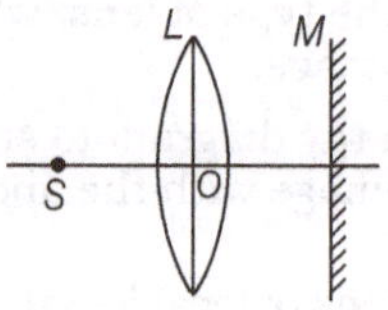

   (i) What is the distance OS called?
   (ii) To which point (left of S or right of S) will the rays return, if M is moved to the left and brought in contact with L?

13. Distinguish between a real and a virtual image.

14. An object is placed in front of a concave lens. Is it possible that the image formed has the same size as that of the object? If yes, then draw the ray diagram.

15. Find the focal length of a lens of power + 4.0 D. What type of lens is this?

Structured Questions

16. (i) Explain the action of a simple microscope as a magnifier. Draw the ray diagram for the image formation. [3]
(ii) State three characteristics of the image of an extended source, formed by a concave lens. [3]
(iii) A convex lens has focal length equal to 25 cm. An object is placed at a distance 12.5 cm from the lens. Draw the diagram to find the position of image. [4]

17. (i) (a) Where should an object be placed so that, a real and inverted image of the same size as the object is obtained using a convex lens?
(b) Draw a ray diagram to show the formation of the image as specified in the part a (i). [2015] [3]
(ii) A lens produce an erect and magnified image of an object when the object is placed at 20 cm from its optical centre.
(a) Identify the nature of lens.
(b) What is the position of the image if the focal length of the lens is 25 cm? [3]
(iii) An object is placed in front of a lens between its optical centre and the focus and forms a virtual, erect and diminished image.
(a) Name the lens which forms this image.
(b) Draw a ray diagram to show the formation of the image with the above stated characteristics. [2011] [3]

18. (i) An object is placed at a distance of 10 cm from a lens of power – 4D. Find the position and nature of image so formed. [3]
(ii) An object is placed perpendicular to the principal axis of a convex lens of focal length 10 cm. The distance of the object from the lens is 15 cm. Find the position of the image. What is the nature of the image formed? [3]
(iii) (a) Where should an object be placed so that, a real and inverted image of double the size of the object is obtained using a convex lens?
(b) Draw a ray diagram to show the formation of the image as specified in the part (i).
(c) Ramesh claims to have obtained an image thrice the size of the object with a concave lens. Is he correct? Give reason for your answer. [4]

19. (i) Draw the different path of principal rays refracted by convex lens and concave lens used for the formation of image. [3]
(ii) Mention any three applications of lenses. [3]
(iii) Write the principle and working of magnifying glass using suitable diagram. [4]

20. (i) How can you differentiate between a convex and a concave lens by (a) touching and by (b) seeing the image? [3]
(ii) A lens of focal length 20 cm forms an inverted image at a distance of 60 cm from the lens.
(a) Identify the lens.
(b) How far is the lens present infront of the object?
(c) Calculate the magnification of the image. [3]
(iii) An object is placed at a distance 24 cm in front of a convex lens of focal length 8 cm. [2019]
(a) What is the nature of the image so formed?
(b) Calculate the distance of the image from the lens.
(c) Calculate the magnification of the image. [4]

For Solutions Scan the Code

Olympiad Section*

Brain Teasing Questions of Olympiad Pattern

1 Which of the following is true for rays coming from infinity?

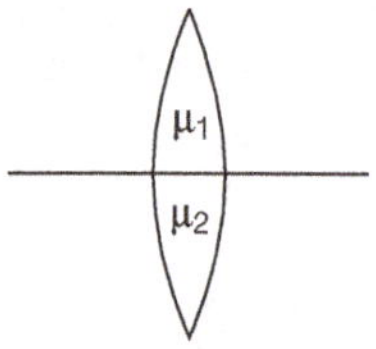

(a) Two images are formed
(b) Continuous image is formed between focal points of upper and lower lens
(c) One image is formed
(d) None of the above

2 The image when obtained from a concave lens of focal length f is magnified up to n times the size of the object. What is the distance of the object from the lens?

(a) $\left(\frac{1-n}{n}\right)f$ (b) $\left(\frac{1+n}{n}\right)f$
(c) $\left(1-\frac{1}{n}\right)f$ (d) $\left(1+\frac{1}{n}\right)f$

3 When the object is at infinity, what is the nature of image formed by concave lens?

(a) Real, inverted, enlarged
(b) Real, inverted, same size
(c) Virtual, erect, enlarged
(d) Virtual, erect, diminished

4 Consider the following statements in context with the sign conventions for spherical lens and choose the incorrect one.

I. All the distances are measured from the pole of the lens.
II. The distances measured against the direction of incident light are taken as negative.
III. The distances measured downward and perpendicular to the principal axis are taken as negative.

(a) Only I
(b) Only II
(c) III only
(d) All are incorrect

5 The diagram shows an image formed at a distance 36 cm from the lens LL' of focal length 12 cm. With respect to this, answer the questions that follow.

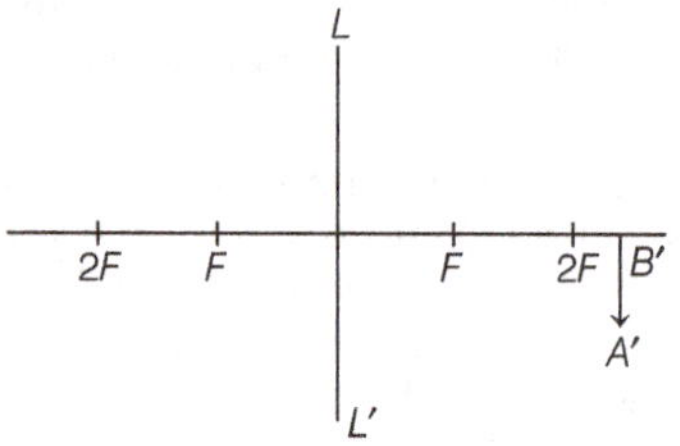

The position of the object on the left hand side should be **[Latest Specimen Questions Paper]**

(a) between 12 cm to 30 cm from the lens
(b) beyond 24 cm from the lens
(c) between 12 cm to 24 cm from the lens
(d) within 12 cm from the lens

6 If two convex lenses are in contact with each other, then

(a) diverging power increases
(b) converging power increases
(c) diverging power decreases
(d) converging power decreases

7 A double convex lens, made of a material of refractive index μ_1, is placed inside two liquids of refractive indices μ_2 and μ_3 as shown $\mu_2 > \mu_1 > \mu_3$. A wide, parallel beam of light is incident on the lens from the left. The lens will give rise to

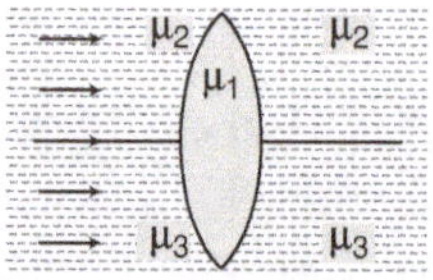

(a) a single convergent beam
(b) two different convergent beams
(c) two different divergent beams
(d) a convergent and a divergent beam

8 An object of height 10 cm is placed in front of a concave lens of focal length 20 cm, at a distance of 25 cm from the lens. Is it possible to capture this image on a screen? Select a correct option from the following. **[ICSE Examination 2021-22]**

(a) Yes, as the image formed will be real
(b) Yes, as the image formed will be erect
(c) No, as the image formed will be virtual
(d) No, as the image formed will be inverted

9 Two lenses of power – 3.5 D and + 1.0 D one placed in contact with each other. What is the focal length of this combination?

(a) 10 cm (b) 20 cm (c) 30 cm (d) 40 cm

10 A convex lens of focal length 40 cm, two concave lenses of focal length 40 cm and 15 cm, respectively are placed in contact. The power of the combination in dioptre is

(a) + 1.5 (b) – 1.5
(c) + 6.67 (d) – 6.67

11 The diagram shows an object *O* placed 3 cm away from a converging lens of focal length 6 cm.

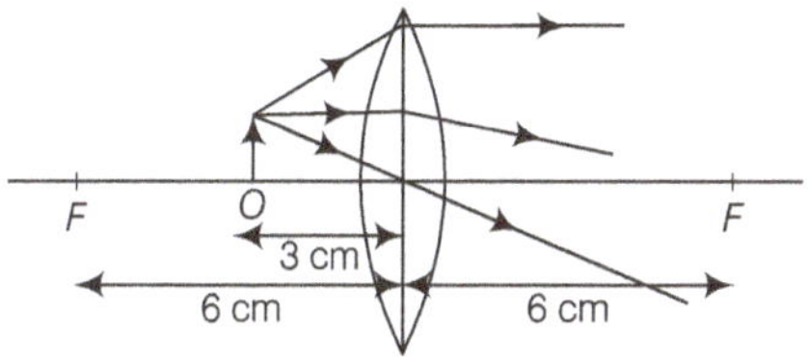

What type of image is produced?

(a) Real, upright and diminished
(b) Real, inverted and magnified
(c) Virtual, upright and magnified
(d) Virtual, inverted and diminished

12 Observe the diagram which shows the path of an incident ray through an optical plane *LL′* of a lens. The focal length of the lens is 20 cm. **[ICSE Examination 2021-22]**

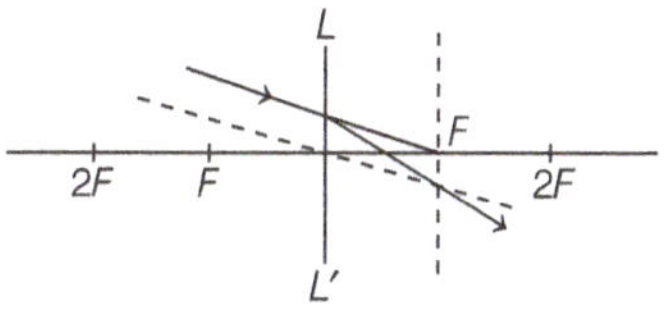

This type of lens can be used

(a) to correct hypermetropia
(b) to correct myopia
(c) to diverge light
(d) in the front door peephole

13 A needle placed 45 cm from a lens forms an image on a screen placed 90 cm on the other side of the lens. What is the power of the lens?

(a) +10 D (b) –10 D (c) +3.33 D (d) –3.33 D

14 White light from a distant extended source is incident on a convex lens. Its image is seen on a screen kept at the focal plane of the lens. The top half of the lens is covered with a green filter and bottom half with a red filter. Choose the correct statement. **[Olympiad 2019]**

(a) The top half of the image will be green and the bottom half will be red.
(b) The top half of the image will be red and bottom half will be green.
(c) The image will be white.
(d) The image will be yellow.

ANSWERS									
1. (a)	**2.** (a)	**3.** (d)	**4.** (a)	**5.** (c)	**6.** (b)	**7.** (d)	**8.** (c)	**9.** (d)	**10.** (d)
11. (c)	**12.** (a)	**13.** (c)	**14.** (d)						

* *These questions may or may not be asked in the examination, have been given just for additional practice required for olympiads Scholarship Exams etc. For detailed explanations refer Page No. 266.*

CHAPTER 06

Spectrum of Light

SYLLABUS

• Prism • Dispersion of White Light by a Glass Prism • Scattering of Light • Electromagnetic Spectrum

In the previous chapters, we have learnt that when a ray of light travels from one medium to another, it gets deviated from its path. It is because of the difference in the speeds of light in two media. This deviation will not occur if the angle of incidence becomes zero.

Since, the deviation always occurs at the boundary of the two media. Therefore, the magnitude of the deviation depends on the angle of incidence at the interface of two media and the refractive index of the second medium with respect to the first medium. In this chapter, we will study about the refraction of light through prism, which constitutes the phenomenon of dispersion.

Prism

Prism is a transparent refracting medium bounded by at least two lateral surfaces, inclined to each other at a certain angle. It has two triangular bases and three rectangular lateral surfaces. The angle between two lateral surfaces is called **angle of prism** (*A*).

Deviation Produced by a Triangular Prism

In the figure given ahead, a ray of light *PQ* is incident on the prism at its first surface *AB*. The light ray on refraction gets bent towards the normal by an angle δ_1. At the second surface *AC*, the light ray enters from glass to air, so it bends away from the normal by an angle δ_2. The diagram shows refraction through a prism

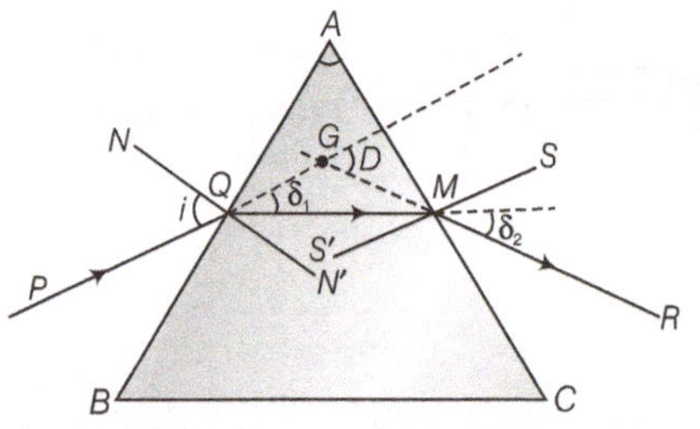

Deviation of light ray through a triangular glass prism

where,

PQ = incident ray, QM = refracted ray,
MR = emergent ray, $\angle A$ = angle of prism,
$\angle i$ = angle of incidence and $\angle D$ = angle of deviation.

This represents the deviation of light rays produced by a prism.

Note When a ray of light passes through a prism, it bends towards the thicker part of the prism.

Therefore, the net deviation produced in the emergent ray *MR* w.r.t. the incident ray *PQ* can be given as, D or $\delta = \delta_1 + \delta_2$

In chapter 4, we have already discussed the dependence of angle of deviation on various factors in details.

Dependence of Angle of Deviation on the Colour (or Wavelength) of Light

As, for light of different colours, the refractive index of a given transparent medium is different, it decreases with increase in the wavelength of the light. Therefore, the refractive index of the material of prism is maximum for the violet colour and least for red light. As a result, a given prism deviates the violet light most and the red light least.

Also, from the definition of refractive index,

i.e. $$\mu = \frac{\text{Speed of light in vacuum}}{\text{Speed of light in medium}}$$

As, speed of violet light is minimum and red is maximum in a medium, so $\mu_{violet} > \mu_{red}$

As, $$\boxed{\mu = \frac{\sin i}{\sin r}}$$

where, r is the angle of refraction.

$$\Rightarrow \quad \sin r = \frac{\sin i}{\mu}$$

So, for a particular value of i, $r_{violet} < r_{red}$.

Hence, $\delta_{violet} > \delta_{red}$, because $\delta = i - r$.

Dispersion of White Light by a Glass Prism

The phenomenon of splitting of white light into its constituent colours, when it passes through a prism is called **dispersion**. This band of seven colours so obtained, the VIBGYOR (V = violet, I = indigo, B = blue, G = green, Y = yellow, O = orange and R = red) is called **spectrum**.

Isaac Newton was the first one to use a glass prism to obtain the spectrum of light.

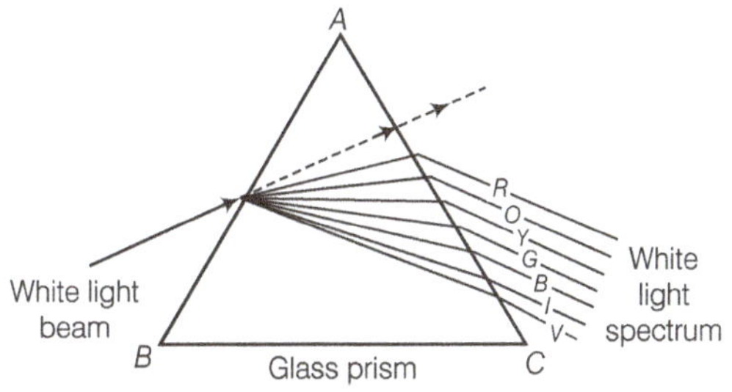

Dispersion of white light by a glass prism

White light gets dispersed only at one surface of prism AB. But the deviation occurs at both the surfaces of prism, i.e. AB and AC. Also, prism never produce any colour, rather it just helps in splitting the components of white light.

Note A similar band of seven colours is produced when a beam of white light from an electric bulb falls on a triangular glass prism.

Cause of Dispersion

Light rays of different colours, travel with the same speed in vacuum and air but in any other medium, they travel with different speeds and bend through different angles, which leads to the dispersion of light.

Red light has the maximum wavelength and **violet light** has the minimum wavelength. So in any medium, red light travels fastest and deviates least, while violet light travels slowest and deviates most.

i.e. $$\text{Wavelength} \propto \text{Velocity} \propto \frac{1}{\text{Deviation}}$$

Note
- If δ_r, δ_y and δ_v are the deviations for red, yellow and violet components of white light, then mean deviation is measured by δ_y as yellow light falls in between red and violet, $\delta_v - \delta_r$ is called **angular dispersion**.
- The dispersive power of a material is defined as the ratio of angular dispersion to the mean deviation when a white beam of light is passed through it. It is given by $\boxed{\omega = \frac{\delta_v - \delta_r}{\delta_y}}$

Recombination of White Light

Newton showed that the reverse of dispersion of light is also possible. He kept two prisms close to each other, one in erect position and the other in an inverted position. The light gets dispersed when passes through the first prism. The second prism receives all the seven coloured rays from first prism and recombines them into original white light. This observation shows that sunlight is made up of seven colours. Any light that gives spectrum similar to that of sunlight is called **white light**.

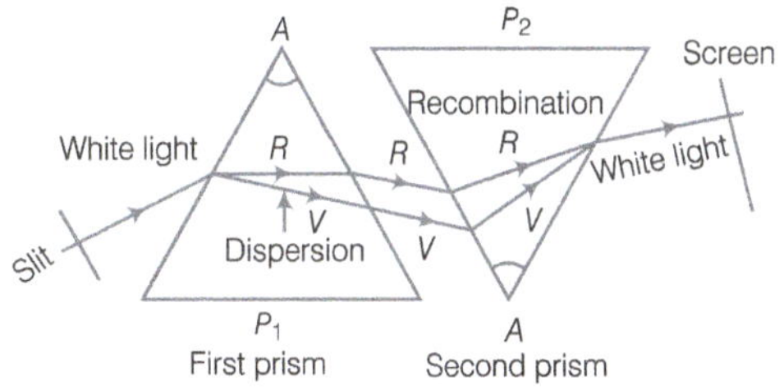

Recombination of the spectrum of white light

Rainbow

A natural spectrum appearing in the sky after a rain shower is called rainbow. It is caused by dispersion of sunlight by tiny water droplets, present in the atmosphere. It is always formed in a direction opposite to that of the sun.

The water droplets act like small prisms. They refract and disperse the incident sunlight, then reflect it internally and finally, refract it again when it comes out of the raindrop. Due to the dispersion of light and total internal reflection, different colours reach the observer's eye. It can also be seen on a sunny day by looking at the sky through a waterfall or through a water fountain, with the sun behind you.

Note Red colour appears on the upper side of the rainbow and violet on the lower side, in case of primary rainbow.

Check Your LEARNING...

1. When a monochromatic beam of light undergoes minimum deviation through equilateral glass prism, state how does the beam pass through the prism with respect to the base?
2. Among seven constituents colours of white light, which colour travels
   (i) fastest and (ii) slowest in glass?
3. What do you understand by the term dispersion of light?
4. Name the subjective property of light related with its wavelength.
5. Name the phenomenon which is responsible for the formation of rainbow.

Scattering of Light

The reflection of light from an object in all directions is called scattering of light. The colour of scattered light depends on the size of scattering particles and wavelength of light. Very fine particles scatter mainly blue light while particles of larger size scatter light of longer wavelength (red light). If the size of the scattering particles is large enough, then the scattered light may even appear white.

Note
- The blue light present in sunlight is scattered 10 times more than the red light.
- Scattering $\propto d^6$, where, d = diameter of particle.
- According to Rayleigh,
  amount of scattering $\propto \frac{1}{\lambda^4}$, where λ = wavelength of light.

Some Phenomena Based on Scattering of Light

Some phenomena based on scattering of light are

Tyndall Effect

The path of a beam of light passing through a true solution is not visible. However, its path becomes visible when it passes through a colloidal solution, where the size of the particles is relatively larger.

This scattering of light when it passes through a colloidal solution is called Tyndall effect. The earth's atmosphere is a heterogeneous mixture of minute particles of smoke, tiny water droplets, suspended particles of dust and molecules of air which becomes visible due to scattering of light.

Blue Colour of Sky

During the day time, sky appears blue. This is because the size of the particles in the atmosphere is comparable to the wavelength of blue light. So, they are more effective in scattering the light of shorter wavelengths (blue end of spectrum). Hence, when sunlight passes through the atmosphere, the fine particles scatter the blue colour more strongly than red. This scattered blue light enters our eye. Hence, during the day time, the sky appears blue. It should be noted that the sky appears black to the passengers flying at higher altitudes because scattering of light is not prominent at such height due to the absence of particles.

Red Colour of Sun at Sunrise and Sunset

Light from the sun near the horizon passes through thicker layers of air and covers larger distance in the atmosphere before reaching our eyes. Due to this, most of the blue light and shorter wavelengths are scattered away by the particles near the horizon. Therefore, the light that reaches our eyes is of longer wavelengths. This gives rise to the reddish appearance of the sun and the sky. However at the noon, the light from the sun overhead would travel relatively shorter distance. So, it appears white as only a little of the blue and violet colours are scattered.

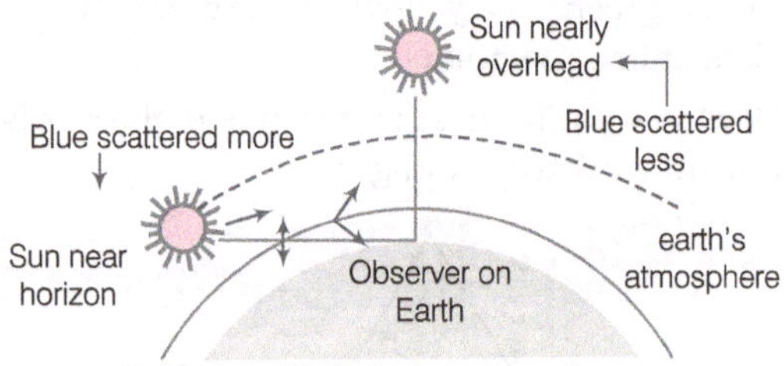

Reddening of the sun at sunrise and sunset

Note
- If the earth had no atmosphere, then sky would have looked dark and black.
- White colour of sky at noon, white colour of clouds, use of red light for danger signal, etc., are all due to scattering of light.

Electromagnetic Spectrum

The orderly arrangement of electromagnetic waves in increasing or decreasing order of wavelength λ or frequency ν is called electromagnetic spectrum. The range of wavelength of electromagnetic spectrum varies from 10^{-12} m to 10^4 m, i.e. from γ-rays to radio waves.

A spectrum which has defined boundaries, i.e. various bands of colours do not overlap with each other is called **pure spectrum** whereas the spectrum which do not have defined boundaries is called **impure spectrum**.

The region in the spectrum beyond red and before violet is called **invisible spectrum**.

Broad Classification of Spectrum in the Increasing Order of Wavelength

The figure shown below shows the various parts of the electromagnetic spectrum with approximate wavelength range.

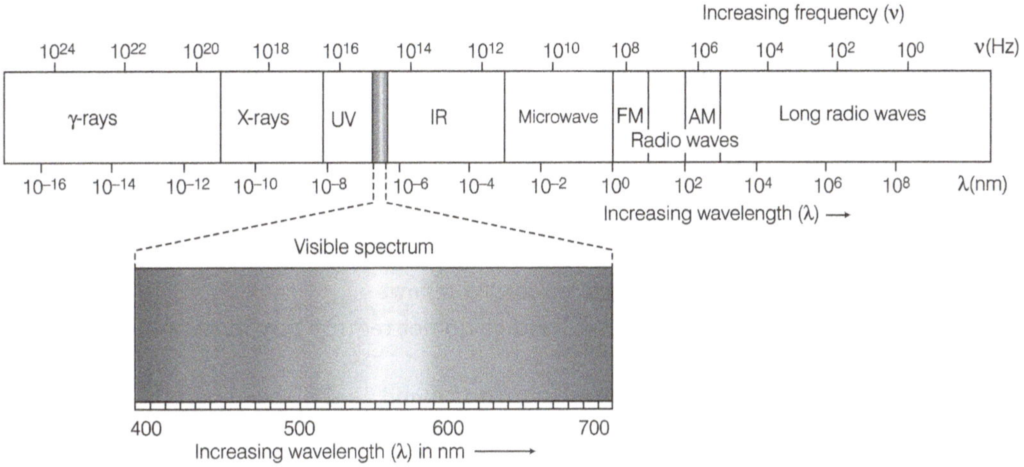

Properties of Different Electromagnetic Waves

Type	Wavelength range	Production	Detection	Effect on photographic plate	Penetrating power	Applications	Discoverer
Radio wave	> 0.1 m	Rapid acceleration and decelerations of electrons in aerials	Receiver's aerials	Do not affects	High	In amplitude modulation, ground wave propagation, TV waves and cellular phones	Marconi
Microwave	0.1 m to 1 mm	Klystron valve or magnetron valve	Point contact diodes	Do not affects	High	In RADAR's, microwave oven, study of atomic and molecular structures	Hertz
Infrared wave	1 mm to 700 nm	Vibration of atoms and molecules	Thermopiles bolometer, infrared photographic film	Do not affects	Passes through rock salt but absorbed by prism	In physical theraphy and weather forecasting	William Herschel
Visible light	700 nm to 400 nm	Electrons in atoms emit visible light when they move from higher energy level to a lower energy level	The eye, photocells, photographic film	Affects	Reflects by human body, but passes through glass prism	To see things	Newton

Type	Wavelength range	Production	Detection	Effect on photographic plate	Penetrating power	Applications	Discoverer
Ultraviolet rays	400 nm to 1 nm	Inner shell electrons in atoms moving from higher energy level to a lower energy level	Photocells, photographic film	Strongly affect	Only passes through quartz	In burglar alarms, sterlise surgical instruments	Prof. J. Ritter
X-rays	1 nm to 10^{-3} nm	X-ray tubes or inner shell electrons	Photographic film, strongly affect Geiger tubes, ionisation chamber	Strongly affect	High	To detect the fracture, diseased organs, stones in body, etc. for scientific research	Roentgen
Gamma rays	$< 10^{-3}$nm	Radioactive decay of the nucleus	Geiger tubes, films	Affects	High	In nuclear reaction, treatment of tumour and cancer, kill pathogenic microorganisms	Becquerel and Curie

General Properties of Electromagnetic Spectrum

Common properties to all electromagnetic spectrum are as follows

(i) The electromagnetic waves of entire wavelength range do not require any material medium for their propagation.

(ii) They all travel with the same speed in vacuum which is same as the speed of light in vacuum, i.e. 3×10^8 m/s.

(iii) They exhibit the properties of reflection and refraction.

(iv) These waves are not deflected by the electric and magnetic fields.

(v) These waves are transverse waves.

Properties and Uses of Infrared Waves

These waves were discovered by **Herschel.** These waves are also called **heat waves**. These waves are produced from the heat radiating bodies and molecules.

They have high penetration power. Their frequency range is from 3×10^{11} Hz to 4×10^{14} Hz.

Uses of infrared waves are given below

(i) These are used in physical therapy.

(ii) These are used in satellite for army purpose.

(iii) These are used in weather forecasting.

(iv) These are used for producing dehydrated fruits.

(v) These are used in solar water heater, solar cells and cooker.

Properties and Uses of Ultraviolet Rays

These rays were discovered by **Ritter** in 1801. These are produced by special lamps and very hot bodies. The sun is an important source of UV-rays but fortunately absorbed by ozone layer. Their frequency range is from 10^{14} Hz to 10^{16} Hz.

Uses of ultraviolet rays are given below

(i) These are used in burglar alarm.

(ii) These are used in checking mineral sample.

(iii) These are used to study molecular structure.

(iv) To kill germs in water.

(v) To sterilise surgical instruments.

Relation between Frequency, Speed and Wavelength of Electromagnetic Waves

All electromagnetic waves move with same speed (c) (3×10^8 m/s) in vacuum but their frequencies (ν) and wavelength (λ) are different.

The relation between frequency (ν), speed (c) and wavelength (λ) of electromagnetic waves is

$$\text{Frequency }(\nu) = \frac{\text{Speed of electromagnetic wave }(c)}{\text{Wavelength }(\lambda)}$$

Example 1. An electromagnetic wave of frequency 40 MHz travel in free space in the x-direction. Determine the wavelength of the wave.

Sol. Given, frequency, $\nu = 40$ MHz $= 40\times 10^6$ Hz

Speed of wave, $v = 3\times 10^8$ m/s

Using the relation,

$$\text{Wavelength of wave, } \lambda = \frac{\text{Speed of wave }(v)}{\text{Frequency }(\nu)}$$

Substituting the given values, we get

$$\lambda = \frac{3\times 10^8}{40\times 10^6} = 7.5 \text{ m}$$

Example 2. What is the wavelength of an electromagnetic wave whose frequency is 10^{15}Hz? Name this electromagnetic wave.

Sol. Given, frequency, $\nu = 10^{15}$ Hz,

Speed of wave, $v = 3\times 10^8 \text{ms}^{-1}$

Using the relation,

$$\text{Wavelength of wave, } \lambda = \frac{\text{Speed of wave }(v)}{\text{Frequency }(\nu)}$$

Substituting the given values, we get

$$\lambda = \frac{3\times 10^8}{10^{15}} = 3\times 10^{-7} \text{ m} = 300 \text{ nm}$$

Such a wave is infrared wave, whose wavelength varies from 10 nm to 400 nm.

Check Your LEARNING...

1. Which characteristic property of light is responsible for the blue colour of the sky?
2. The backlight of a motor is red, why?
3. Arrange the electromagnetic waves in the descending order of their wavelength.
   (a) Microwaves (b) Infrared rays
   (c) Ultraviolet (d) γ-rays
4. Name the region beyond the violet end of the spectrum.
5. Write the equation for the relation between the frequency and wavelength of light in vacuum.
6. Calculate speed of EM wave in a glass slab in which frequency of EM wave is 4×10^{14} Hz and wavelength is 500 nm. ***Ans.*** 2×10^8 m/s

QUiCK Revision

- **Prism** is a portion of a transparent refracting medium bounded by two plane surfaces inclined each other at a certain angle.
- **Angle of Deviation** It is the angle between incident and emergent ray. It depends on angle of prism, angle of incidence and angle of emergence, refractive index of the material of the prism.
- **Deviation of light** caused by a prism is inversely proportional to its wavelength.
- **Dispersion** It is a phenomenon of splitting of white light into its constituents colours. It is caused because of the different velocities of lights of different wavelength in same medium.
- **Red light** deviates the least whereas **violet light** deviates most.
- **Spectrum** It is the band of colours obtained on the screen when a white light splits into component colours by the prism. It is of two types, **pure spectrum** and **impure spectrum**.
- **Rainbow** It is a natural phenomenon due to the dispersion of light formed by the rain drop, when sunlight falls on it. It is formed due to refraction, dispersion and total internal reflection of light.
- **Scattering of Light** It is the reflection of light from an object in all directions. It only takes place when the size of the scattering object is very small as compared to the wavelength of the light.
- Blue colour of the sky, reddish appearence of sun at sunrise and sunset, etc., are due to scattering of light.
- **Electromagnetic Spectrum** It is the orderly distribution of electromagnetic radiations according to their wavelength or frequency.
- All the electromagnetic radiations travel with the same speed in vacuum which is same as the speed of light in vacuum. i.e. 3×10^8 m/s.
- **Ultraviolet radiations** wavelength range varies from 1 nm to 400 nm and **infrared radiations** wavelength range varies from 700 nm to 1 mm.

Chapter Practice

1 Mark Questions

1. The deviation produced by an equilateral prism does not depend on the **[2021 (Sem-I)]**
   (a) angle of incidence
   (b) size of the prism
   (c) material of the prism
   (d) colour of light used

Sol. (*b*) In an equilateral prism, the deviation produced does not depend on the size of the prism.

2. When a white light ray falls on a prism, the ray at its first surface suffers
   (a) no refraction
   (b) only dispersion
   (c) only deviation
   (d) Both deviation and dispersion

Sol. (*d*) When a white light ray falls on a prism, the ray at its first surface suffers both deviation and dispersion. The ray on entering the prism is deviated by an angle towards the base of prism and also splits into its seven component colours causing dispersion of light.

3. In the spectrum of white light by a prism, the colour at the extreme end opposite to the base of prism is
   (a) violet (b) yellow
   (c) red (d) blue

Sol. (*c*) On passing white light through a prism, the band of colours obtained on screen is called spectrum. Starting from the base, the order of colours is violet, indigo, blue, green, yellow, orange and red. So, red is at the extreme end opposite to the base of prism.

4. In the white light of the sun, maximum scattering by the air molecules present in the earth's atmosphere is for
   (a) red colour
   (b) yellow colour
   (c) green colour
   (d) blue colour

Sol. (*d*) The intensity of scattered light is inversely proportional to the fourth power of the wavelength of light. Since violet or blue end has lower wavelength, so they are scattered most by the air molecules. Hence, among given colours, maximum scattering is for blue colour.

5. To an astronaut in a spaceship, the earth appears
   (a) white (b) red
   (c) blue (d) black

Sol. (*c*) Due to scattering of sunlight by the earth's atmosphere, the earth appears blue to an astronaut in a spaceship.

6. The wavelength range of white light is **[ICSE 2022 Sem. I]**
   (a) 4000 nm to 7000 nm (b) 400 nm to 700 nm
   (c) 40 nm to 70 nm (d) 4 nm to 7 nm

Sol. (*b*) The white light or the visible band of spectrum lies in the wavelength range of 400 nm to 700 nm.

7. The most energetic electromagnetic radiation are
   (a) microwaves (b) ultravoilet waves
   (c) X-rays (d) gamma rays

Sol. (*d*) Gamma rays are the most energetic electromagnetic radiation of wavelength less than 0.1 Å or 0.01 nm. They can easily penetrate the thick metallic sheets and can pass through human body also.

8. The wavelength of red light is 800 nm. If speed of light is 3×10^8 ms^{-1}, then its frequency is
   (a) 3×10^{14} Hz (b) 3.75×10^{14} Hz
   (c) 4.25×10^{14} Hz (d) 4.8×10^{14} Hz

Sol. (*b*) Given, $\lambda = 800$ nm $= 800 \times 10^{-9}$ m

$$c = 3 \times 10^8 \text{ ms}^{-1}$$

Since, frequency, $\nu = \dfrac{c}{\lambda} = \dfrac{3 \times 10^8}{800 \times 10^{-9}} = 3.75 \times 10^{14}$ Hz

9. Two waves A and B have wavelengths 0.01 Å and 9000 Å, respectively. The ratio of their speeds, when they travel in vacuum is
   (a) 1 : 2 (b) 1 : 3
   (c) 1 : 9 (d) 1 : 1

Sol. (*d*) According to wavelength of two waves A and B, both waves occur in the category of electromagnetic waves. Since, speed of EM wave in vacuum is constant as 3×10^8 m/s, hence

$$\therefore \quad v_A : v_B = 1 : 1$$

2 Marks Questions

10. Briefly mention, how does the deviation produced by a triangular prism depend on the colours (or wavelengths) of light incident on it?

Sol. Since, the refractive index of glass increases with decrease in wavelength of light. So, the deviation caused by a prism also increases with decrease in the wavelength of light. e.g. As wavelength of violet less than wavelength of red, hence $\delta_{red} < \delta_{violet}$. **[2]**

11. Draw a ray diagram showing the dispersion through a prism when a narrow beam of white light is incident on one of its refracting surfaces. Also, indicate the order of the colours of the spectrum obtained.

Sol. Ray diagram showing the dispersion of white light through a prism is shown below

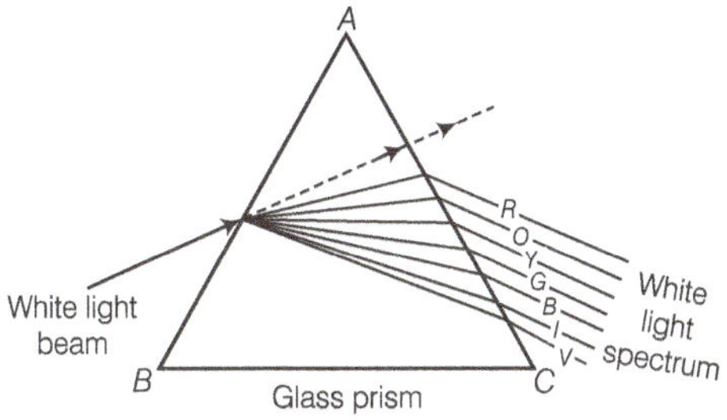

[1]

The order of the colours of the spectrum are given below

V = violet, I = indigo, B = blue,

G = green, Y = yellow, O = orange and R = red. [1]

12. Explain the cause of dispersion of white light through a prism.

Sol. The speed of light for different colours is same in air but it is different for different colours in any other transparent medium. The speed of light in a transparent medium decreases with the decrease in the wavelength of light. [1]

Since, the refractive index of the medium depends on the wavelength of the light. So, different colours of different wavelengths are deviated through different angles of deviation through a glass prism. This causes the dispersion of white light. [1]

13. Is it possible that a glass slab disperse the light? If not, why?

Sol. No, it is not possible that a glass slab disperse the light, because it has parallel rectangular faces. [1]

When a white light is incident on the glass slab, it gets dispersed into different colours but these different colours combine to form white light on emerging from the other parallel face. [1]

14. Name the four colours of the spectrum of white light which have wavelength longer than the blue light. Also, name the light amongst the given, which shows maximum deviation.

Sol. The four colours of the spectrum of white light which have wavelength longer than the blue light are green, yellow, orange, red. [1]

Green shows the maximum deviation amongst the given lights. [1]

15. How will you use two identical prisms so that a narrow beam of white light incident on one prism emerges out of the second prism as white light? Draw the diagram.

Sol. A narrow beam of white light incident on one of the prisms emerges out of the identical prism placed in an inverted position with respect to the first prims, as shown in the figure given below. [1]

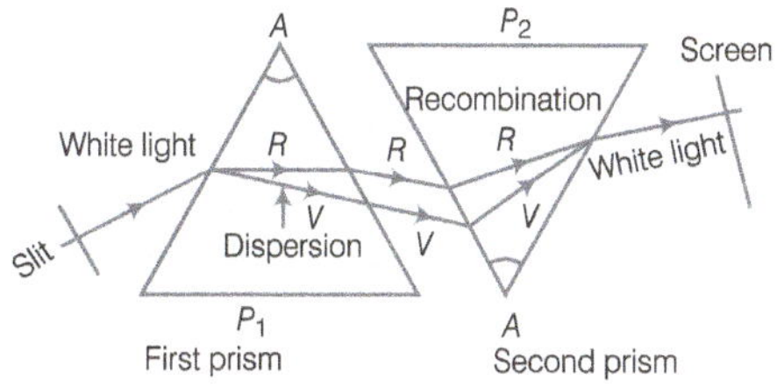

[1]

16. What do you understand by term spectrum of light? Name one natural spectrum formed by sunlight after rain.

Sol. The band of seven colours formed on the screen when a white light passes through a glass prism, is known as spectrum of light. [1]

Rainbow is a natural spectrum formed by the sunlight after rain. [1]

17. (i) What is meant by dispersion of light?

(ii) In the atmosphere, which colour of light gets scattered the least? [2012]

Sol. (i) The phenomenon of splitting of white light by a prism into its constituent colours is known as dispersion of light. [1]

(ii) In the atmosphere, red colour of light gets scattered the least due to its highest value of wavelength. [1]

18. (i) Define scattering.

(ii) The smoke from a fire looks white. Which of the following statements is true?

I. Molecules of the smoke are bigger than the wavelength of light.

II. Molecules of the smoke are smaller than the wavelength of light. [2018]

Sol. (i) The process of absorption and then re-emission of light energy is called scattering of light. When sunlight passes through the earth's atmosphere, much of the light gets scattered (i.e. the light spreads in all directions) by the fine dust particles and air molecule in it. [1]

(ii) As molecules of the smoke are bigger than the wavelength of light, as a result they scatter all wavelengths which overlaps to give white colour. [1]

19. Why is it difficult to drive on a foggy day?

Sol. On a foggy day, most of the light gets scattered by the particles in the fog. Due to this, visibility reduces. Hence, it becomes difficult to see and is difficult to drive also on a foggy day. [2]

20. Briefly mention, why does the sky at noon appear white?

Sol. During the time of noon, the sun is directly above our head. Due to which, the sunlight travels relatively shorter distance as compare to the time when sun is at the horizon. So, we get light rays directly from the sun without much scattering. Therefore, the sky at noon appears white. [2]

21. Why is the red colour used as a sign of danger? [2014]

Sol. The scattering of light is found to be inversely proportional to the fourth power of the wavelength of light. Thus, the scattering of red light is very much less than that of yellow light. Therefore, red colour signals can be seen upto a longer distance, so it is used as a sign of danger.

22. An electromagnetic radiation is used for photography in fog.
(i) Identify the radiation.
(ii) Why is this radiation mentioned by you, ideal for this purpose? [2019]

Sol. (i) Infrared radiation are used in photography in fog and mist and also at night. [1]
(ii) Because infrared radiation have long wavelength. As they are having low frequency, hence the energy associated with them is also low. So, they do not scatter much and can penetrate appreciably through it. [1]

23. Explain the following statement.
"The photographic dark rooms are provided with infrared lamps".
Write any other use of infrared radiations.

Sol. Since, infrared lamps do not affect the photographic film. Due to this reason, the dark rooms are provided with infrared lamps. [1]
Infrared radiations are used for producing dehydrated fruits. [1]

24. (i) Why is white light considered to be polychromatic in nature?
(ii) Give the range of wavelength of these electromagnetic waves which are visible to us. [2009]

Sol. (i) Since, polychromatic light consists of many colours each having its characteristic wavelength. Therefore, white light is also a polychromatic light because it is made up of seven colours, containing different wavelengths. [1]
(ii) 400 nm to 700 nm is the range of visible spectrum. [1]

25. Mention two properties of infrared radiations that are not true for visible light.

Sol. Two properties are
(i) they are absorbed by glass. [1]
(ii) they do not affect the ordinary photographic film. [1]

26. (i) Name the radiations which are absorbed by greenhouse gases in earth's atmosphere.
(ii) A radiation *X* is focused by a particular device on the bulb of a thermometer and mercury in it shows a rapid increase. Name the radiation.

Sol. (i) Infrared radiations are low energy radiations, which are absorbed by CO_2, present in earth's atmosphere. [1]
(ii) Infrared radiations trapped by the bulb of the thermometer increases the mercury level. [1]

27. (i) Name the high energetic invisible electromagnetic waves, which help in the study of the structure of crystals.
(ii) State an additional use of the waves mentioned in part (i). [2015]

Sol. (i) X-rays are used to study the structure of a crystal.
(ii) Uses of X-rays are
I. In surgery for the detection of fractures foreign bodies like bullets, stones in human body, etc.
II. For detecting faults, cracks, flaws and holes in the final products of metals.
III. To cure untrackable skin diseases and malignant growths.

28. If the wavelengths for the light of red and blue colours are nearly 7.8×10^{-7} m and 4.8×10^{-7} m respectively,
(i) which colour has a greater speed in vacuum?
(ii) which colour has a greater speed in glass? [2020]

Sol. (i) In vacuum, both the colours (i.e. red and blue) will have the same speed. [1]
(ii) In glass, red light has a greater speed because its deviation is least due to its higher wavelength. [1]

3 Marks Questions

29. It is seen that the white light splits into bands of seven colours when passed through the glass prism. With reference to this observation, answer the following questions.
(i) State the conclusion that you draw about the white light.
(ii) Name the sequence of colours from the base of the prism.
(iii) Do all the bands are of same width? If not, then why?

Sol. (i) After reading the given observation, we can conclude that white light is polychromatic due to which refraction and dispersion of white light takes place.
(ii) The sequence of colours from the base of prism is violet, indigo, blue, green, yellow, orange and red.
(iii) Bands of colours will be of different width, as their widths depend on the range of frequency or wavelength of a colour.
As, the wavelength of colour increases, its bandwidth also increases. So, red colour has maximum and violet has minimum bandwidth. [1 + 1 + 1]

30. The figure given below shows a thin beam of white light from a source *S* striking on one face of prism.

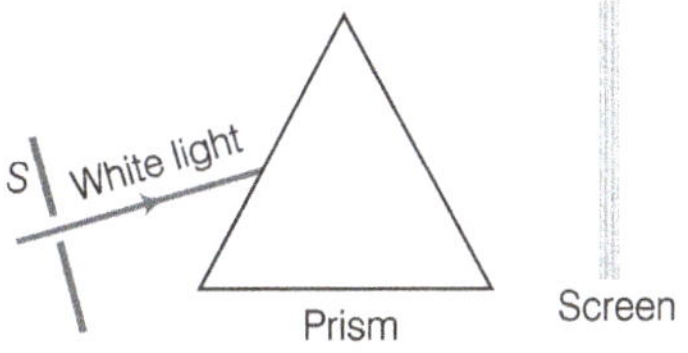

(i) In order to show the effect of the prism on the beam, complete the diagram, so that it can represent what is seen on the screen.

(ii) Assume if a slit is placed between the prism and the screen to pass only the light of green colour, then what observation will you get on the screen?

(iii) State the conclusion that you draw from the observation in part (ii) above.

Sol. (i) As we can see in the figure, a pattern of seven colours is formed on the screen with red on the top and violet at the bottom. [1]

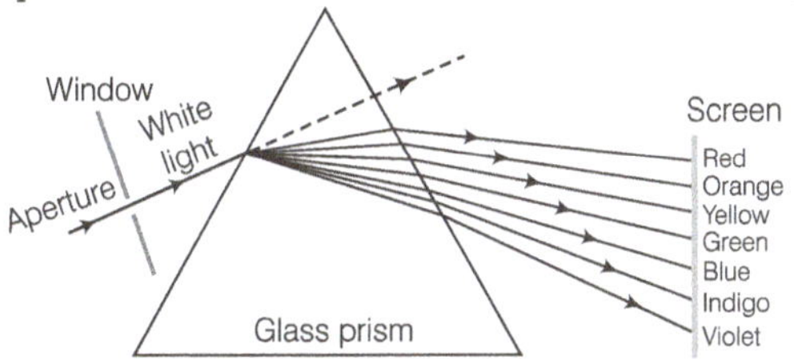

(ii) Since, a green filter transmits only green light. Therefore, it is placed between the prism and the screen, the spectrum on the screen will appear dark except for the region near the green part in the original spectrum. [1]

(iii) It proves that the prism by itself produces no colour. [1]

31. (i) A glass slab is placed over a page on which the word VIBGYOR is printed with each letter in its corresponding colour.

(a) Will the image of all the letters be in the same place?

(b) If not, state which letter will be raised to the maximum. Give a reason for your answer.

(ii) What will be the colour of an object which appears green in white light and black in red light?

Sol. (i) (a) No; The image of all the letters are not in the same place, because the letter of each colour have different frequency or wavelength. [1]

(b) The letter V for violet is raised more because wavelength is least for violet colour, hence deviation is most. [1]

(ii) The colour of an object which appears green in white light and black in red light will be green. [1]

32. Why do we see a rainbow in the sky only after rainfall?

Sol. We see a rainbow in the sky only after rainfall due to dispersion of sunlight by tiny water droplets, present in the atmosphere. These droplets act like small prism. They refract and disperse the incident sunlight, then reflect it internally and finally refract it again when it comes out of the raindrop. Hence, due to dispersion of light and total internal reflection, different colours are seen by the observer's eye. [3]

33. Explain how scattering of light depends upon particle size?

Sol. Since, scattering of the light is proportional to diameter of particle and inversely proportional to the fourth power of wavelength of light. So, very fine particles scatter mainly blue light while particles of larger size scatter light of longer wavelength. If the size of the scattering particles is very large, the scattered light may appear white. [3]

34. State three common properties to all type of electromagnetic radiations.

Sol. Three common properties to all electromagnetic radiations are

(i) They do not require any material medium for their propagation. [1]

(ii) They all travel with the same speed in vacuum, which is same as the speed of light in vacuum. i.e., $3 \times 10^8 ms^{-1}$. [1]

(iii) They exihibit the properties of reflection and refraction. [1]

35. Which type of rays exist beyond visible red end of the electromagnetic spectrum? State one property and one use of these rays.

Sol. Beyond visible red end of electromagnetic spectrum, infrared rays exist. They have frequency less than and wavelength greater than that of red light. [1]

Property They are detected by their heating property. [1]

Use They are used in photography at night and also in mist and fog. [1]

36. (i) Suggest one way in each case by which we can detect the presence of

(a) infrared radiations and

(b) ultraviolet radiations.

(ii) Give one use of infrared radiations. [2011]

Sol. (i) (a) We can detect infrared radiation by using a thermopile or a blackened bulb thermometer. [1]

(b) We can detect the presence of ultraviolet radiation by using silver chloride solution. [1]

(ii) Infrared radiations are used in muscular therapy and for taking photographs in fog. [1]

4 Marks Questions

37. A narrow beam of white light is passing through a glass prism *ABC* as shown in the diagram.

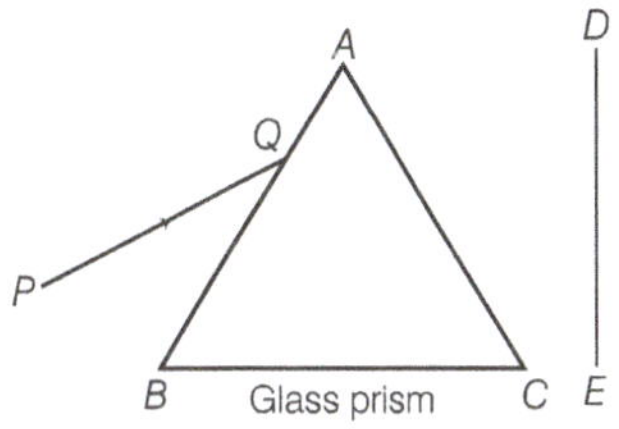

Trace it on your answer sheet and show the path of the emergent beam as observed on the screen *DE*.

(i) Write the name and cause of the phenomenon observed.
(ii) Where else in nature is this phenomenon observed?
(iii) Based on this observation, state the conclusion which can be drawn about the constituents of white light.

Sol. The path of the light incident on the prism is shown below

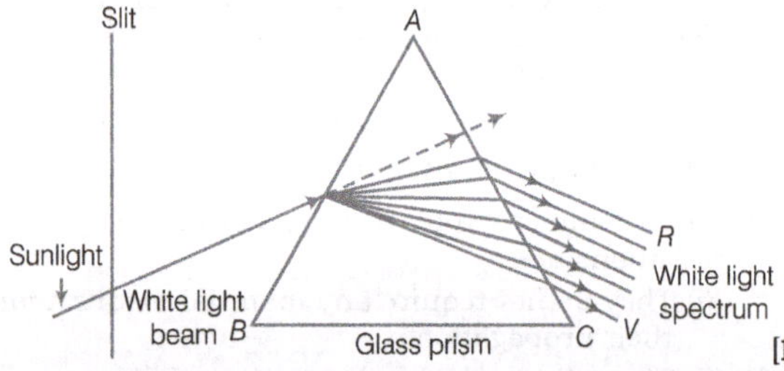

[1]

(i) The phenomenon of splitting of white light into its constituent colours is called dispersion of light. It is caused because different constituent colours of light travel with different speeds in the medium other than air/vacuum and bend through different angles. [1]
(ii) This phenomenon is observed in formation of rainbow. [1]
(iii) Based on phenomenon of dispersion, we can conclude that
(a) white light consists of seven colour and [½]
(b) violet light suffers maximum deviation and red light suffers minimum deviation. [½]

38. Explain, how can you nullify the deviation effect with dispersion?

Sol. First of all, take two prisms *XYZ* and *ABC* of same material and same refracting angles (here, we can also take different material and different refracting angles prisms).

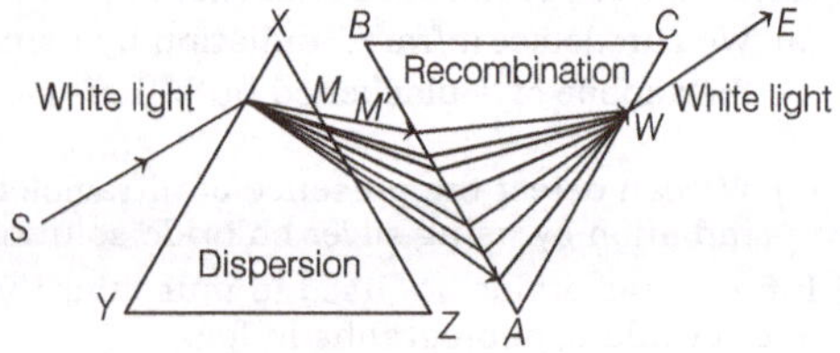

[1½]

Both prisms are placed inverted as shown in the figure above. When a ray of white light passes through prism *XYZ*, the emergent rays *MM'* and *NN'* bends towards the base *YZ* of prism *XYZ* with colour red or violet respectively and form the band of seven colours between red and violet rays. The seven colours enter into prism *ABC* and bends towards base *BC* of prism. [1½]

Since, $\mu_V > \mu_R$, so violet $N'W$ ray bends the most and $M'W$ (red) bends the least and overall colours meet at *W* and emerges out as a white light *WE* as shown in the figure. [1]

39. What is meant by scattering of light? Mention the factor on which it depends. Explain why
(i) the colour of the clear sky is blue and
(ii) for astronauts sky appears darker?

Sol. The reflection of light from an object in all directions is called scattering of light.

The colour of scattered light depends on the size of scattering articles and wavelength of light.

i.e. Scattering $\propto d^6$ (where, d = diameter of particle)

and scattering $\propto \frac{1}{\lambda^4}$ (where, λ = wavelength of particle) [2]

(i) During the day time sky appears blue. This is because the size of particles in the atmosphere is smaller than the wavelength of visible light. So, they are more effective in scattering the light of shorter wavelengths i.e., blue light. [1]
(ii) Since, at such a height there is no atmosphere i.e. no particles. Therefore, no scattering of light takes places. Hence, for astronauts, the sky appears dark. [1]

40. Infrared radiations are used in warfare. Explain with reason, why. [2023]

Sol. Infrared radiations are used in warfare because they are not visible and they are not absorbed much in medium. They have high penetration power, so it can penetrate through haze without being scattered.

Numerical Based Questions

41. An electromagnetic wave has a frequency of 500MHz and a wavelength of 60 cm. Calculate velocity. [2]

Sol. Given, frequency, $\nu = 500\text{ MHz} = 500 \times 10^6\text{Hz}$,

Wavelength, $\lambda = 60$ cm

$$\text{Velocity, } v = \nu\lambda = 500 \times 10^6 \times \frac{60}{100}$$
$$= 3 \times 10^8 \text{ ms}^{-1}$$

42. The wavelength of electromagnetic radiation is 900 nm. Find its frequency. (Take, speed of radiation = $3 \times 10^8 \text{ms}^{-1}$) [2]

Sol. Given, wavelength, $\lambda = 900$nm

$$= 900 \times 10^{-9}\text{m}$$
$$= 9 \times 10^{-7}\text{m}$$

Speed of radiation, $v = 3 \times 10^8 \text{ms}^{-1}$

As we know,

$$\text{Frequency, } \nu = \frac{\text{Speed of electromagnetic radiation}}{\text{Wavelength}}$$

Substituting the given values, we get

$$\nu = \frac{3 \times 10^8}{9 \times 10^{-7}}$$
$$= 0.34 \times 10^{15}$$
$$= 3.4 \times 10^{14}\text{ Hz}$$

43. A radio can tune into any station in 7.5 MHz to 12 MHz band, what is the corresponding wavelength band? [2]

Sol. Given, frequency range = 7.5 MHz to 12 MHz

$= 7.5 \times 10^6$ Hz to 12×10^6 Hz

Speed of radio waves, $v = 3 \times 10^8 \text{ms}^{-1}$

From the relation,

Speed of wave (v) = Wavelength (λ) × Frequency (ν)

$$\Rightarrow \quad \lambda = \frac{v}{\nu}$$

$$\therefore \quad \lambda_1 = \frac{3 \times 10^8}{7.5 \times 10^6} = 40 \text{ m}$$

and $$\lambda_2 = \frac{3 \times 10^8}{12 \times 10^6} = 25 \text{ m}$$

$\therefore$ The corresponding wavelength band is 40 m-25 m.

Structured Questions

44. (i) A type of electromagnetic wave has wavelength 50 Å.
(a) Name the wave.
(b) What is the speed of the wave in vacuum?
(c) State one use of this type of wave. [3] [2014]

(ii) Name the radiations
(a) that are used for photography at night.
(b) used for detection of fracture in bones.
(c) whose wavelength range is from 10 nm to 400 nm. [3] [2013]

(iii) What do you understand by the term scattering of light? Which colour of white light is scattered the least and why? [4] [2016]

Sol. (i) (a) The wave is X-rays as its range is 0.1 Å to 100 Å. [1]
(b) The speed of light in vacuum is 3×10^8 m/s. [1]
(c) They are used for detection of fractures in bone, teeth, etc. [1]

(ii) (a) Infrared radiations [1]
(b) X-rays are [1]
(c) Ultraviolet rays [1]

(iii) The process, in which light rays get diffused or deflected by collision with particles of the medium that it traverses is called scattering of light. Red colour of white light is scattered the least and violet colour is scattered the most. It is because violet colour has shorter wavelength than red colour. [4]

45. (i) Name any four regions of electromagnetic spectrum (other than visible light) in increasing order of their wavelength.

(ii) Two parallel rays of red and violet light travelling through air, meet the air glass boundary as shown in the given figure.

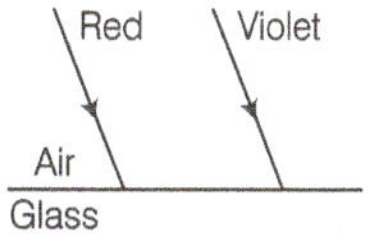

(a) Will their paths inside the glass be parallel? Give a reason for your answer.
(b) Compare the speeds of the two rays inside the glass. [2010]

(iii) Give reasons for the following. [3]
During the day,
(a) clouds appears white and
(b) sky appears blue. [2020]

Sol. (i) The four regions of electromagnetic spectrum in increasing order of wavelengths are γ-rays, X-rays, ultraviolet rays and infrared rays. [3]

(ii) The given situation is shown below.

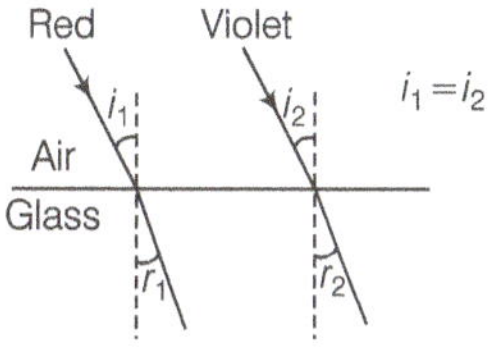

(a) No, the paths of two parallel rays of red and violet colours travelling through glass will not be parallel, because on entering the glass both the rays deviate to different extents, i.e. $r_1 > r_2$.
(b) The red colour deviates less while violet colour deviates more. Therefore, the speed of red colour in glass is more than the speed of violet colour in glass. i.e. $v_{violet} < v_{red}$. [3]

(iii) (a) As light passes through a cloud, it interacts with the water droplets, which are much bigger than the atmospheric particles that exist in the sky. Sunlight is scattered by much larger water droplets. These scatter all colours almost equally, so the sunlight appears to white, hence clouds appears white.
(b) Refer to theory (page 120) [4]

Chapter Assessment

1 Mark Questions

1. The colour of white light which is deviated least by a prism is **[ICSE 2022 Sem. I]**
(a) green (b) yellow (c) red (d) violet

2. The source of ultraviolet light is
(a) electric bulb (b) red hot iron ball
(c) sodium vapour lamp (d) carbon arc-lamp

3. A radiation *X* is focused by a proper device on the bulb of a thermometer. Mercury in the thermometer shows a rapid increase. The radiation *X* is
(a) infrared radiation (b) visible light
(c) ultraviolet radiation (d) X-rays

4. The wavelength of X-rays is 0.01 Å. Its frequency will be (Take, speed of X-rays $= 3 \times 10^8\ ms^{-1}$)
(a) 3×10^{10} Hz (b) 3×10^{20} Hz
(c) 3×10^{18} Hz (d) 3×10^{6} Hz

5. A beam of monochromatic light undergoes minimum deviation through an equilateral prism. With respect to its base, the beam will pass through the prism
(a) parallel to the base
(b) perpendicular to the base
(c) at 45° with the base
(d) at 60° with the base

2 Marks Questions

6. What are the necessary conditions that are to be followed to obtain a pure spectrum on a screen?

7. Explain the reason for the given statement. "Light of different colours is deviated through different angles by a prism".

8. Write a note on the following terms.
(i) Monochromatic light
(ii) Polychromatic light

9. When a ray of light is passed through a hollow glass prism, it does not give spectrum. Explain why?

10. "Do the ratio of speed of red and blue radiations in glass is smaller than one, greater than one or equal to one"? Give reason.

11. State one harmful effect each of ultraviolet and infrared radiations.

12. Give reasons for the following.
(i) Smoke out of a chimney sometimes appears blue.
(ii) Infrared radiations are used to detect diseases in crops.

13. Briefly tell, how do the sky appear when seen from the moon (or outer space)? Give reason in support of your answer.

14. An electromagnetic wave travels in vacuum along *z*-direction. If the frequency of the wave is 30 MHz, what is its wavelength? **[Ans. 10 m]**

15. (i) Name a material of prism required for obtaining a spectrum of ultraviolet light.
(ii) Name the radiations which can be detected by a thermopile. **[2014]**

Structured Questions

16. (i) Explain any three factors on which the deviation produced by a prism depends. **[3]**
(ii) If a player is wearing a uniform consisting of a red shirt and a white short as seen in a white light, so state what will be the appearance of shirt and the short in
(a) red light and (b) blue light? **[3]**
(iii) (a) "The sunlight appears yellow". Justify this statement along with a reason.
(b) Name the extreme colours in pure spectrum of light.
(c) Which colour of the light in the spectrum of white light through prism is deviated most and why? **[4]**

17. (i) Briefly mention the name and wavelength of electromagnetic wave whose frequency is 10^{12}Hz. Can you produce and use it in the kitchen? **[3]**
(ii) A certain electromagnetic wave has a wavelength of 625 nm.
(a) What is the frequency of the wave ?
(b) What region of the electromagnetic spectrum is it found? **[3]**
(iii) What do you mean by electromagnetic spectrum and its types ?
Arrange the electromagnetic spectrum in increasing order of wavelength. **[4]**

18. (i) In day-light, an object appears red when seen through a red glass and black when seen through a blue glass. Give reason. **[3]**
(ii) The wavelengths for the light of red and blue colours are nearly 7.8×10^{-7}m and 4.8×10^{-7}m, respectively.
(a) Which colour has the greater speed in a vacuum?
(b) Which colour has a greater speed in glass? **[3]**
(iii) Mention the four general properties of electromagnetic spectrum. **[4]**

For Solutions Scan the Code

Olympiad Section*

Brain Teasing Questions of Olympiad Pattern

1 A passenger in an aeroplane
(a) will never see a rainbow
(b) may see a rainbow as concentric circles
(c) may see a rainbow as concentric arcs
(d) may see a rainbow as straight bands

2 When white light is dispersed by a prism, compared with blue light, the red light is
(a) slowed down less and refracted less
(b) slowed down less and refracted more
(c) slowed down more and refracted less
(d) slowed down more and refracted more

3 Which amongst the given figures below correctly depicts the dispersion of white light by a glass prism?

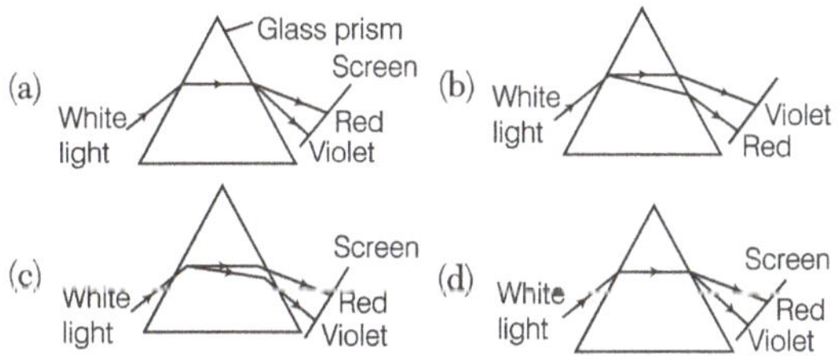

4 Consider the following statement and choose the incorrect one (s).
I. The blue colour of clear sky is due to the presence of atmosphere on the earth.
II. The greyish appearance of sky is due to the presence of smoke and dust particles in the atmosphere.
III. Emergency signals and danger signals are red because red light can travel long distance without being scattered.
IV. When electromagnetic waves strike a matter, then scattering takes place.

(a) I, IV (b) I, II, IV
(c) II, IV (d) None of these

5 State T for true and F for false.
I. To recombine the spectrum to obtain white light, the dispersive prism and recombination prism should be in same position.
II. If a glass prism is dipped in water, its dispersive power decreases.
III. When sunlight comes down through the clouds, tyndall effect is observed.
IV. Headlights are made of yellow colour because of its long wavelength and low scattering.

	I	II	III	IV		I	II	III	IV
(a)	T	T	T	T	(b)	F	T	T	T
(c)	F	F	T	T	(d)	F	T	F	T

6 Violet has the smallest wavelength, but colour of sky is blue. Why?
(a) Most of the violet rays are absorbed by the atmosphere
(b) Our eyes are less sensitive to violet colour
(c) Both (a) and (b)
(d) Neither (a) nor (b)

7 If a ray of light enters glass prism (as shown in figure) of refractive index 1.5, then the speed of light inside the prism will be

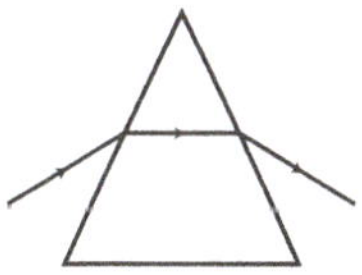

(a) $0.2 \times 10^8 \, ms^{-1}$ (b) $2 \times 10^9 \, ms^{-1}$
(c) $2 \times 10^7 \, ms^{-1}$ (d) $2 \times 10^8 \, ms^{-1}$

8 In a science project, a student tried to show rainbow formation using artificial rain and strong source of white light as shown in figure below. What should be the position of observer to observe the rainbow?

(a) Looking towards the source
(b) Looking towards the raindrops with the source behind him
(c) Looking anywhere in the room
(d) Looking towards the raindrop such that he is equally inclined towards the source of raindrops

ANSWERS

1.	2.	3.	4.	5.	6.	7.	8.
(b)	(a)	(c)	(d)	(b)	(c)	(d)	(b)

* *These questions may or may not be asked in the examination, have been given just for additional practice required for olympiads Scholarship Exams etc. For detailed explanations refer Page No. 267.*

CHAPTER

7

Sound

SYLLABUS

• Range of Hearing • Free (or Natural), Forced and Damped Vibrations • Reflection of Sound Waves • Echo • Characteristics of Sound • Resonance

Sound is a form of energy which produces a sensation of hearing in our ears. It is produced by vibrating objects. Vibration means a kind of rapid to and fro motion of an object. We can produce sound by striking the tuning fork, by plucking, scratching, rubbing, blowing or shaking different objects. They all produce sound due to vibrations.

Basically sound require a material medium (solid, liquid or gas) for their propagation, so they are called mechanical waves.

Propagation of Sound in Air

When a vibrating object moves forward in air (or any medium), it pushes and compresses the particles of air around it, creating a compression which starts to move away from the vibrating object. When the vibrating object moves backwards, then it creates rarefaction. **Compression** is the part of a longitudinal wave in which the particles of the medium are closer to one another than they normally are and it is the region of high pressure. It is denoted by *C*.

Rarefaction is the part of a longitudinal wave in which the particles of the medium are farther apart than they normally are and it is the region of low pressure. It is denoted by *R*.

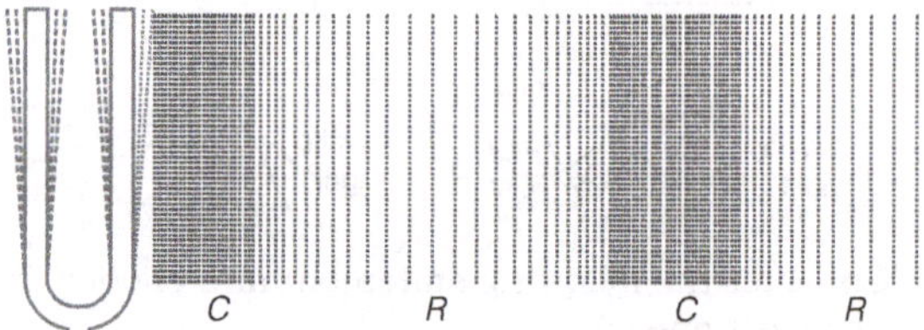

A vibrating object creating a series of compressions (*C*) and rarefactions (*R*) in the medium

As the object moves back and forth rapidly, a series of compressions and rarefactions is created in air. These make the sound wave that propagates through the medium.

Terms Related with Sound Waves

Sound waves can be described by following terms

Wavelength

The distance between the two consecutive compressions or two consecutive rarefactions, is called the **wavelength**. It can also be described by distance between two consecutive crest or two consecutive trough as shown below.

Wavelength is the minimum distance in which sound wave repeats itself. It is represented by a Greek letter lambda (λ). Its SI unit is metre (m).

The sound wave can also be represented graphically by the following curve.

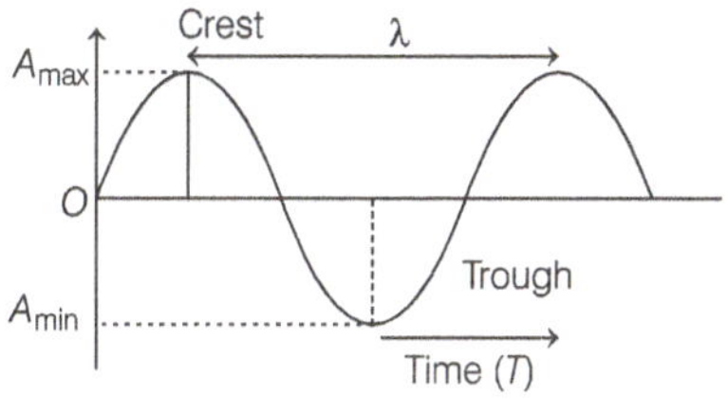

where, λ = wavelength,

T = time period,

A_{max} = maximum amplitude in positive direction

and A_{min} = maximum amplitude in negative direction.

Frequency

It tells us how frequently an event occurs. The number of complete waves (or oscillations) produced in one second is called frequency of the wave/sound. It is the number of vibrations or the number of crest/trough that occur per second.

If we can count the number of the compressions or rarefactions that crosses per unit time, we will get the frequency of sound wave.

It is denoted by ν (Greek letter, nu). Its SI unit is hertz (Hz). 1 hertz is equal to 1 vibration per second.

1 kHz = 1000 Hz

Note The frequency of a wave is fixed and does not change even when it passes through different substances but wavelength and amplitude changes.

Time Period

The time taken by two consecutive compressions (crest) or rarefactions (trough) to cross a fixed point is called the time period of the sound wave. It is denoted by symbol T. Its SI unit is second (s). The time period of a wave is the reciprocal of its frequency i.e.,

$$\text{Time period } (T) = \frac{1}{\text{Frequency } (\nu)}$$

or

$$\text{Frequency } (\nu) = \frac{1}{\text{Time period } (T)}$$

Amplitude

The maximum displacement of the particles present in the medium from their original mean positions on passing a wave through the medium, is called amplitude of the wave. It is usually denoted by the letter A. Its SI unit is metre (m).

Speed

The distance travelled by a wave in one second is called speed of the wave or velocity of the wave. Under the same physical conditions, the speed of sound remains the same for all frequencies. It is represented by letter v.

$$\text{Speed} = \frac{\text{Distance travelled}}{\text{Time taken}}$$

Its SI unit is metre per second (m/s or ms^{-1}).

Relationship between Speed, Frequency and Wavelength of a Sound Wave

Suppose distance travelled by a wave is λ (wavelength), in time T, then the speed is given by

$$v = \frac{\lambda}{T}$$

We know that, $f = \nu = \frac{1}{T}$

Therefore, $v = \lambda \times \nu$

or $\boxed{v = \nu\lambda}$

or Speed (Velocity) = Frequency × Wavelength

It should be noted that the frequency is dependent on the vibrating source whereas speed of the wave (or wavelength) is dependent on the medium in which the sound waves travel.

Example 1. A sound travels at a speed of 330 ms^{-1}. If its wavelength is 1.5 cm, then calculate the frequency of sound wave.

Sol. Given, speed of sound, $v = 330$ m/s

Wavelength, $\lambda = 1.5$ cm $= 0.015$ m

Frequency, $\nu = ?$

We know that, $v = \nu\lambda$

So, $\nu = \frac{v}{\lambda} = \frac{330}{0.015} = 22000$ Hz or 22 kHz

Also, for the reflection of sound wave, it is necessary that the size of the reflecting surface must be bigger than the wavelength of the sound wave

Speed of Sound in Different Media

It has already been stated that sound waves are mechanical (or elastic) waves. Mechanical waves are of two types

(i) **Longitudinal waves** If the displacement of the particle is along the direction of the propagation of wave, the wave is said to be longitudinal.

The velocity of sound (or longitudinal) wave in a gas (or any fluid) at constant temperature (T) and pressure (p) having density (ρ) is given by

$$v = \sqrt{\frac{\gamma p}{\rho}}$$

where, γ is the ratio of specific heat capacities $\left(\frac{C_p}{C_V}\right)$. Its value is 1.4 for air.

(ii) **Transverse waves** If the displacement of the particle is perpendicular to the direction of the propagation of wave, the wave is said to be transverse.

The velocity of transverse wave in an inextensible stretched string (or a rigid body) having tension T and mass per unit length m is given by

$$v = \sqrt{\frac{T}{m}}$$

Example 2. A string of 4 m length having 2 kg mass is stretched by 10 N force. Find the speed of the wave, when it is struck by a gentle stroke.

Sol. Given, mass = 2 kg

Length = 4 m

Mass per unit length, $\mu = \frac{2}{4} = \frac{1}{2}$

Tension, T = Force = 10 N

Speed of the wave, $v = \sqrt{\frac{T}{\mu}} = \sqrt{\frac{10}{\frac{1}{2}}}$

$= \sqrt{20} = 4.472 \text{ ms}^{-1}$

Range of Hearing

The average frequency range over which the human ear is sensitive is called **audible range.** The audible range of sound for human beings is from 20 Hz to 20000 Hz.

Infrasonic Sound

The sound of frequencies lower than 20 Hz are known as infrasonic sounds or infrasound, which cannot be heard by human beings.

Ultrasonic Sound

The sounds of frequencies higher than 20000 Hz are called as ultrasonic sounds or ultrasound which cannot be heard by human beings. Bats can hear ultrasonic sounds having frequencies upto 120000 Hz. Bats, dolphins, tortoise and rats can also produce ultrasonic sounds as well as hear ultrasonic sound.

Reflection of Sound Waves

Like light, sound can also be made to change its direction and bounce back when it falls on a hard surface. This bouncing back of sound in same medium, when it strikes a hard surface is known as reflection of sound.

It does not require a smooth and shining surface like that of mirror, it can be reflected from any surface whether it is smooth or rough. Sound is reflected in the same way as light and follows the same laws of reflection.

Also, for the reflection of sound wave, it is necessary that the size of the reflecting surface must be larger than the wavelength of the sound wave.

Echo

When a person shouts in a big empty hall or near a hillside, we first hear his original sound, after that we hear the reflected sound of that shout. This reflected sound is called echo. So, **the phenomena of repetition of sound caused by reflection of sound waves is called an echo.**

As the sensation of sound persists in our brain for about 0.1 s. So, to hear a distinct echo, the time interval between the original sound and the reflected sound must be atleast 0.1 s.

The speed of sound in air is 344 m/s, so the distance travelled by the sound in 0.1 s

= speed × time = 344 × 0.1

= 34.4 m

Since, sound has to travel twice the distance from source to reflecting surface and from reflecting surface to listener. So, echo will be heard, if the minimum distance between the source of sound and the obstacle

$= \frac{34.4}{2} \text{ m} = 17.2 \text{ m}$

This distance will change with the change in temperature. Echoes may be heard more than once due to successive multiple reflections.

The rolling of thunder is due to successive reflections of sound from a number of reflecting surfaces, such as clouds and the land.

Note The persistance of sound in a big hall due to repeated reflections from the walls, ceiling and floor of the wall is known as reverberation.

Conditions for Formation of Echoes

The conditions for formation of echoes are as follows

(i) The size of the obstacle/reflector must be large as compared to the wavelength of the incident sound (for reflection of sound to take place).

(ii) The minimum distance between the source of sound and the reflector should be atleast 17 m (so that the echo is heard distinctly after the original sound is over).

(iii) The intensity or loudness of the sound should be sufficient enough, so that the reflected sound can be heard clearly. The original sound should be of short duration.

Determination of Speed of Sound by the Method of Echo

The phenomenon of echo can be used to determine the speed of sound in air.

Let d be the distance between the observer and the obstacle and v be the speed of sound. Then, the total distance travelled by the sound to reach the obstacle and then to come back is $2d$ and the time taken is given by

$$\text{Time taken} = \frac{\text{Total distance travelled by the sound}}{\text{Speed of sound}}$$

$$= \frac{2d}{v} \quad \text{or} \quad d = \frac{vt}{2}$$

$$\Rightarrow \quad \boxed{v = \frac{2d}{t}\ \text{ms}^{-1}}$$

Example 3. A boy is standing in the middle of a big square field. There is a tall building on one side of the field. He explodes a cracker and hears its echo 0.4 s later. What is the size of the square field? (Given, speed of sound in air is 330 m/s)

Sol. Given, speed of sound in air, $v = 330\ \text{ms}^{-1}$

Time taken for hearing the echo, $t = 0.4$ s

As we know, distance travelled by the sound,

$$2d = v \times t = 330\ \text{ms}^{-1} \times 0.4\ \text{s} = 132\ \text{m}$$

As in 0.4 s, sound has to travel twice the distance between the boy and the building.

Hence, the distance between the boy and the building is

$$= \frac{d}{2} = \frac{132}{2} = 66\ \text{m}$$

Side of the square field

= Twice the distance between the boy and the building

$= 2 \times 66\ \text{m} = 132\ \text{m}$

So, size of the square field = (side of the square field)^2

$= (132\ \text{m})^2 = 132\ \text{m} \times 132\ \text{m} = 17424\ \text{m}^2$

Example 4. A boy fires a gun and heared its echo after 5s. The boy then moves 310 m towards the hill and fires the gun again. This time, he heared the echo after 3s. Calculate the speed of the sound.

Sol. Given, time, $t = 5$ s

Let d be the distance of the hill from the boy and v be the velocity of sound which is to be determined.

Using the formula, $t = \frac{2d}{v}$.

Substitute the given values, we get

$$\Rightarrow \quad 5 = \frac{2d}{v} \Rightarrow d = \frac{5v}{2} \quad \text{...(i)}$$

When the boy moves through a distance 310 m towards the wall, then $d' = d - 310$ and $t' = 3$ s.

$$\Rightarrow \quad 3 = \frac{2(d-310)}{v}$$

$$\Rightarrow \quad d - 310 = \frac{3v}{2} \quad \text{...(ii)}$$

From Eqs. (i) and (ii), we get

$$v = 310\ \text{ms}^{-1}$$

Uses of Echoes

The method used by some animals like bats, tortoises and dolphins to locate the objects by hearing the echoes of their ultrasonic squeaks is known as **echolocation**. They search out prey and fly in dark night by **emitting** and **detecting reflections** of **ultrasonic waves.**

Uses of echoes by bats, dolphins, fishermen, medical field and in SONAR are given below.

Bats

Bats emit high frequency or high pitched ultrasonic squeaks while flying and listen to the echoes produced by reflection of their squeaks from the obstacles or prey in their path.

From the time taken by the echo to be heard, bats can determine the distance of the obstacle or prey and can avoid the obstacle by changing the direction or catch the prey.

However, certain prey's can hear the high frequency ultrasonic squeaks of a bat and can know, where the bat is flying nearby and are able to escape.

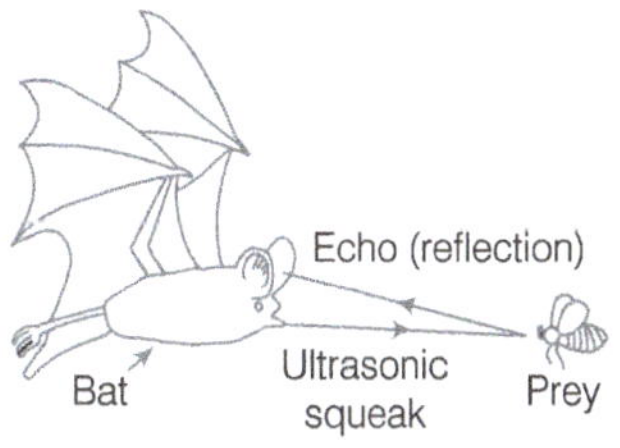

Bats can search their prey in the darkness of night by the method of echolocation

Dolphins

Dolphins uses the same method as used by bats, in order to locate the obstacles or prey. They also emit the ultrasonic waves and hear their echoes to detect their enemy and obstacles or for hunting their prey.

Fishermen or Trawlermen

Initially, they send ultrasonic waves from a source. These waves are received and reflected by the fish.

After that, the receiver of the fisherman receive the echo and the total time t of the to and fro journey of the wave is recorded. The distance of fish is calculated by using the relation $\boxed{d = \frac{vt}{2}}$.

where, v is speed of ultrasonic waves (near about 1400 m/s in water). This helps them to catch the fishes easily.

Medical Field

In the medical field, echoes of the ultrasound is used to investigate the internal organs of human body such as liver, gall bladder, pancreas, kidneys, uterus, heart, etc.

These waves can penetrate through the human body and different type of tissues and get reflected in different ways from a region, where there is a change of tissue density.

In this way, ultrasound helps us to investigate internal organs of human body and to give pictures of these organs by converting the reflected waves into electrical signals. These pictures or images are then displayed on a monitor or printed on a film. This technique is called ultrasonography. Similarly, ultrasound is also used for diagnosing heart diseases by scanning the heart from inside. This technique is **echocardiography.**

SONAR

The word **SONAR** stands for **Sound Navigation And Ranging**. It is an apparatus used to find the depth of a sea or to locate the under water things like shoals of fish, shipwrecks, hills, ice bergs, sunken ships, enemy submarines, etc. It uses ultrasonic waves to measure the distance, direction and speed of underwater objects.

SONAR consists of two parts

(i) A transmitter (for emitting ultrasonic waves)

(ii) A receiver (for detecting ultrasonic waves), as shown in figure.

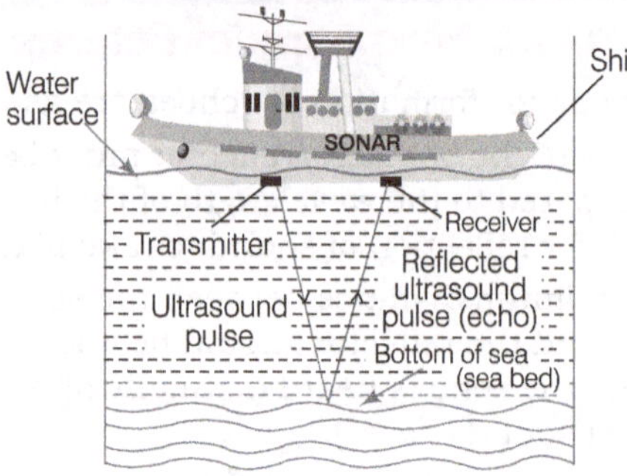

To measure the depth of a sea by using SONAR

The **transmitter** produces and transmits ultrasonic waves. These waves travel down the sea-water towards the bottom of the sea. When these sound pulse strikes the bottom of the sea, then it is reflected back in the form of echo and are sensed by the detector.

The **detector** converts the ultrasonic waves into electrical signals which are appropriately interpreted. The distance of the object that reflects the sound wave can be calculated by knowing the speed of sound wave in water and the time interval between transmission and reception of the ultrasound.

This will give us the depth of the sea.

Let the time interval between transmission and reception of ultrasound signal be t and the speed of sound through sea-water be v.

The total distance $2d$ travelled by the ultrasound is, then $\boxed{2d = v \times t}$

This method is called **echo-ranging**.

Ultrasonic sound waves are used in SONAR, because these waves have very high frequency and very short wavelength, due to which they can penetrate into sea-water to a large extent to locate the underwater objects or to determine the depth of the sea. These waves cannot be confused with engine noises or other sounds made by the ship as they cannot be heard by human beings.

Example 5. Using the SONAR, sound waves are emitted at the surface of water, which after being reflected from bottom of water, are detected. If the time interval from the emission to the detection of the sound waves is 4 s. Calculate the depth of the water. (Take, speed of sound in water is 1450 m/s)

Sol. Time taken by sound waves to travel from surface to bottom, $t = \frac{4}{2} = 2$ s

and speed of sound waves, $v = 1450$ m/s

$\therefore$ Depth of water $= vt = 1450 \times 2 = 2900$ m

Example 6. A submarine produces an ultrasonic waves of velocity 1500 m/s in water. The officer receives signal after 50s of emission of ultrasonic waves. Find the distance of object which is present in the bottom of sea.

Sol. Given, velocity of ultrasonic waves in water,

$$v = 1500 \text{ m/s}$$

Time taken, $t = 50\text{ s}$

Distance between object and submarine, $s = ?$

Using the formula, $d = v \times t$

Substituting the given values, we get

$$= 1500 \times 50 = 75000 \text{ m}$$

As, ultrasonic wave travels twice the distance between object and submarine, so $d = 2s$

As, $2s = 75000$ m, $s = \dfrac{75000}{2} = 37500$ m

$$= 37.5 \text{ km}$$

Check Your LEARNING...

1. Reflection of sound can also takes place at rough surface. Explain, why?
2. Calculate the minimum distance in air required between the source of sound and obstacle to hear echo. (Take, speed of sound in air = 350 ms^{-1}.) *Ans.* 17.5 m
3. How do bats use echo to detect prey?
4. How ultrasound is used to investigate the internal organs of human body?
5. Which type of apparatus is used to find the objects in the sea?
6. What is the significance of transmitter and receiver in SONAR?

Characteristics of Sound

A sound has four characteristics such as **loudness, pitch, quality (or timbre)** and **intensity** by which two sound waves can be distinguished from one another. They are as follows

1. Loudness

It is the measure of the sound energy reaching the ear per second. Greater the sound energy reaching our ear per second, louder the sound will appear to be.

If the sound waves have a small amplitude, then sound will be faint or soft but, if waves have a large amplitude, then the sound will be loud. Also, the amplitude of the sound waves depends upon the force with which an object is made to vibrate.

Sound Level in Decibel (dB)

The unit of loudness is phon and the level of sound is expressed in decibel (dB). Thus, the loudness of a sound in phon is equivalent the loudness in decibel of an equally loud pure sound of frequency 1 kHz. This means, 60 phons is as loud as a 60 dB.

The loudness of the sound wave is proportional

(i) directly to the square of its amplitude $(A)^2$.

(ii) inversely to the square of the distance from the source.

Factors Affecting the Loudness of Sound

Following are the factors affecting the loudness of the sound

(i) Larger is the surface area of the vibrating object, greater would be the amount of energy transferred. Hence, louder will be the sound heard.

(ii) More the density of the medium, louder will be the sound heard.

(iii) In the presence of resonating body near the vibrating object, a louder sound is heard.

2. Intensity

The amount of sound energy passing each second through unit area is known as the **intensity of sound.**

Subjective Nature of Loudness and the Objective Nature of Intensity

Loudness and intensity are not the same terms. **Loudness** is a measure of the response of the ear to the sound. Even when two sounds are of equal intensity, we may hear one as louder than the other, simply because our ear detects it in better way. The SI unit of intensity is **watt per square metre** (W/m^2).

The intensity of sound wave in air is proportional to

(i) the square of the amplitude of vibration $(A)^2$.

(ii) the square of the frequency of vibration $(\nu)^2$.

(iii) the density of air.

Hence, it can be said that for a sound wave loudness has a subjective nature as it depends on the listener, whereas intensity has an objective nature as it a measurable quantity.

3. Pitch (or Shrillness) and Frequency

Pitch is that characteristic of sound by which we can distinguish between different sounds of the same loudness. Due to this characteristic, we can distinguish between a man's voice and woman's voice of the same loudness without seeing them.

Pitch of a sound depends on the frequency of vibration. Greater the frequency of a sound, the higher will be its pitch.

In other words, the faster the vibration of the source, the higher is the frequency and hence higher is the pitch.

Objects of different sizes and conditions vibrates at different frequencies to produce sounds of different pitches.

Figure given below shows the shape of wave for low and high pitched sound

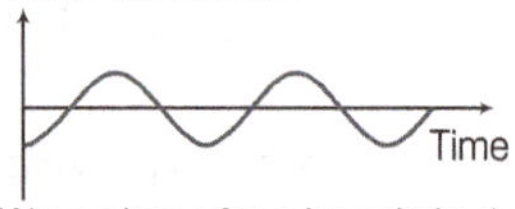

Wave shape for a low pitched sound

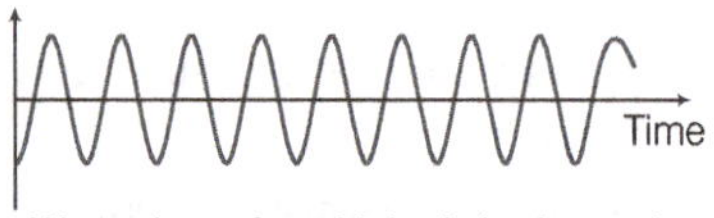

Wave shape for a high pitched sound

Example 7. Two waves of the same pitch have their amplitude in the ratio 2 : 3.

(i) What will be the ratio of their loudness?

(ii) What will be the ratio of their frequencies?

Sol. (i) As, loudness $\propto$ (amplitude)^2

$\therefore$ Its ratio $\left(\frac{2}{3}\right)^2$ becomes $\frac{4}{9}$.

(ii) The ratio of frequencies is 1 : 1, as pitch depends upon the frequency.

4. Quality and Waveforms

The quality (or timbre) of sound is that characteristic of sound which enables us to distinguish one sound from another having the same pitch and loudness.

The pleasant sound is said to be of a rich quality. A sound of single frequency is called **a tone.**

The sound produced due to a mixture of several frequencies is called **a note** and is pleasant in listening too.

The sound produced by different musical instruments like flute, violin, sitar, tanpura, etc., and similarly, sound produced by different singers, can be distinguished from one another on the basis of their quality.

The quality of musical instrument depends on

(i) the shape of the sound wave produced as shown in figure.

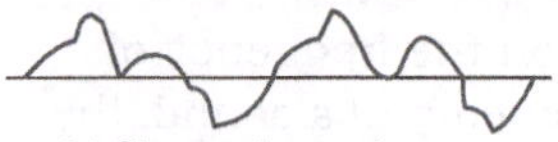
(a) Shape of sound waves produced by a note played on flute

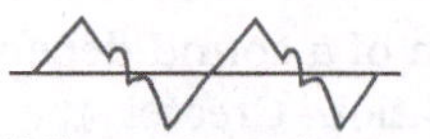
(b) Shape of sound waves when the same note is played on violin

(ii) mixture of frequencies present.

5. Noise and Music

All types of sounds which produces sensation of hearing are of two types basically

(i) music (ii) noise

Differences between Musical Sound and Noise

Musical Sound	Noise
It is a sound which produces a pleasing effect on the listener.	It is a sound which produces an unpleasing effect on the listener.
Its waveform is periodic and regular with no abrupt change in amplitude.	Its waveform is irregular or haphazard with sudden change in its amplitude.
e.g., Any musical instrument.	e.g., Traffic on the road.

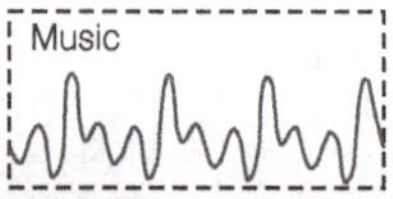

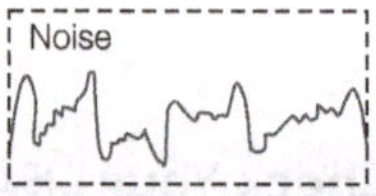

Noise Pollution

The disturbance caused in the environment due to undesirable loud and harsh sound of level above 120 dB from different sources such as loudspeaker, siren, moving vehicles, etc., is known as noise pollution. It causes headache and permanent damage to the ears of listener.

Free (or Natural), Forced and Damped Vibrations

Free Vibrations

If a body vibrates with its natural frequency without the help of any external periodic forces, then it is said to be natural (or free) vibrations.

The amplitude and frequency of a freely vibrating body remains constant with respect to time. In ideal condition, once a body starts vibrating, it continues its vibrations with the same amplitude and frequency forever.

Some examples of natural vibrations are given below

(i) If a tuning fork is struck against a hard rubber pad, then it vibrates with its natural frequency.

(ii) A free suspended pendulum vibrating about its mean position.

(iii) A metal blade clamped at one end is gently disturbed. The blade then vibrates with its natural frequency about the mean position.

(iv) Strings of various musical instruments on being plucked vibrates about the mean position with its natural frequency.

Forced Vibrations

When a body vibrates under the influence of an external periodic force with a frequency equal to that of the external periodic force, then its vibrations are called forced vibrations.

Some examples of forced vibrations are given below

(i) The vibrations produced in the diaphragm of a sound box with frequencies corresponding to the speech of the speaker are the forced vibrations.

(ii) While playing a guitar, the artist forces the strings of the guitar to execute forced vibrations.

(iii) Swing pushed at regular intervals.

Differences between the Free and Forced Vibrations

Free Vibrations	Forced Vibrations
The vibrations of a body in the absence of any resistive forces are called free vibrations.	The vibrations of a body in the presence of external periodic forces are called forced vibrations.
The frequency of the vibrations depends on the shape and size of the body.	The frequency of the forced vibration is equal to the frequency of the applied external force.
The frequency of vibrations is always a constant quantity.	The frequency of forced vibration changes with the change in frequency of applied force.
The amplitude of vibrations does not change with respect to time.	The amplitude of forced vibration is very small, if the frequency of applied force differs widely from the natural frequency of the body.

Damped Vibrations

The periodic vibrations of a body of decreasing amplitude in presence of some resistive force are called the damped vibrations.

The displacement-time graph for the damped vibrations is shown in the figure given below.

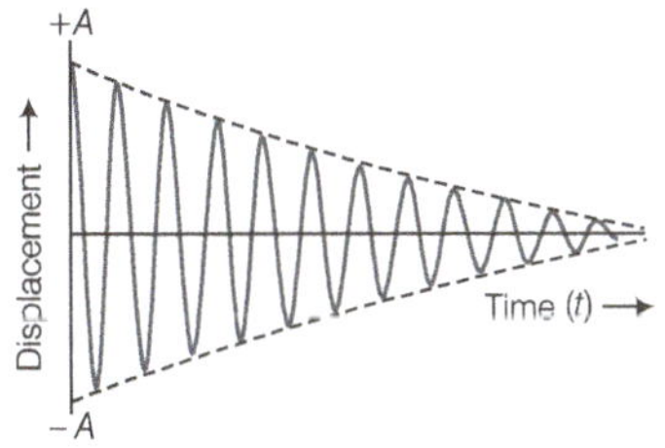

Displacement-time graph for damped vibrations

The amplitude/displacement decreases exponentially with time.

Some examples of a damped vibrations are given below

(i) Vibrations of a tuning fork in air.

(ii) Vibrations of stringed instrument in air.

(iii) Vibrations of a simple pendulum in air.

Differences between the Free and Damped Vibrations

Free Vibrations	Damped Vibrations
The amplitude of free vibrations is constant and theoretically the vibrations continues forever.	The amplitude of damped vibrations gradually decreases with respect to time and in the end, the vibrations ceases.
There is no loss of energy.	In each vibrations, there is some loss of energy.
The vibrations are only under the restoring force and hence no external force acts on the vibrating body.	The opposing force e.g., Friction, etc., acts in the direction opposite to the direction of vibrations.
The frequency of vibrations remains constant and is unaltered and is equal to the natural frequency.	The frequency of vibrations becomes less than the natural frequency.

Resonance

It is a special case of forced vibrations. When the frequency of an externally applied periodic force on a body is equal to its natural frequency, then the body readily begins to vibrate with an increased amplitude.

This phenomenon is known as resonance. The vibrations of large amplitude are called the **resonant vibrations** e.g.,

Some examples of resonant vibrations are

(i) Sympathetic vibrations of pendulum.

(ii) Resonance in radio and TV receiver.

(iii) Resonance in bridge.

(iv) Frequency heard by tuning fork due to resonance with air.

Check Your LEARNING...

1 Is the loudness of sound depends on the amplitude of vibrations of the source? Explain, why?

2 Define decibel and on what factor does it depend?

3 If the amplitude of a wave is doubled, then what will be the effect on its loudness?

4 Low pitch sound has low frequency and high pitch of sound has high frequency. Explain, why?

5 What is range of sound above which noise pollution take place?

6 What is the difference between free vibration and damped vibration on the basis of amplitude?

7 How does the free vibration depend on the frequency?

8 Name one factor which affects the frequency of sound emitted due to vibrations in an air column.

QUiCK Revision

- **Sound** is produced by vibrating objects.
- The bouncing back of sound when it strikes a hard surface is known as **reflection of sound**.
- The repitition of sound caused by reflection of sound waves is called an **echo**.
- The minimum distance between the source of sound and the reflector should be atleast 17 m (so that the echo is heard distinctly after the original sound is over).
- Some animals like bats, dolphins, etc., locate their prey by hearing the echoes of their **ultrasonic squeaks**.
- In the medical field, echoes of the ultrasound is used to investigate the internal organs of human body such as liver, gall bladder, heart, etc.
- **SONAR** stands for sound navigation and ranging.
- SONAR is an apparatus used to find the depth of a sea or to locate the under water things like shoals of fish, shipwrecks, hills, ice bergs, sunken ships and enemy submarines, etc.
- SONAR consists of two parts (i) a transmitter and (ii) a receiver.
- The **transmitter** produces and transmits ultrasonic waves.
- The **detector** converts the ultrasonic waves into electrical signals.
- The measure of a sound energy reaching the ear per second is known as **loudness.**
- The loudness of a sound is measured in **decibel (dB)**. It depends on the sensitivity or the response of our ears.
- The amount of sound energy passing each second through unit area is known as the **intensity of sound**.
- The SI unit of intensity is **watt per square metre** (W/m^2).
- **Pitch** is that characteristic of sound by which we can distinguish between the different sounds of the same loudness.
- The **quality (or timbre)** of sound is that characteristic of sound which enables us to distinguish one sound from another having the same pitch and loudness.
- **Vibration** means a kind of rapid to and fro motion of an object. When an object vibrates, it sets the particles of medium around it in vibration.
- If a body vibrates with its natural frequency without the help of any external periodic forces, then it is said to be natural (or free) **vibrations.**
- The amplitude and frequency of a freely vibrating body remains constant with respect to time.
- When a body vibrates under the influence of an external periodic force with a frequency equal to that of the external periodic force, then its vibrations are called **forced vibrations**.
- The periodic vibrations of a body of decreasing amplitude in presence of some resistive force are called the **damped vibrations**.
- When the frequency of an externally applied periodic force on a body is equal to its natural frequency, then the body readily begins to vibrate with an increased amplitude, this is known as **resonance**.

Chapter Practice

1 Mark Questions

1. The minimum distance between an object and source in air to hear an echo should be
(a) 10 m (b) 17 m (c) 19 m (d) 28 m

Sol. (*b*) The speed of sound in air, $v = 340 \text{ ms}^{-1}$

As the sensation of sound persists in our brain for about 0.1s. So to hear distinct echo the time interval between the original sound and reflected sound must be at least 0.1s. i.e., $t = 0.1$ s

Thus, total distance $= 2d = v \times t = 340 \times 0.1 = 34$ m

Therefore, distance between source object in air should be $d = 17$ m.

2. To detect and locate the prey, bats produce
(a) infrasonic sound
(b) electromagnetic waves
(c) radiowaves
(d) ultrasonic waves

Sol. (*d*) To detect and locate the prey, bats produce ultrasonic waves.

3. By reducing the amplitude of sound, we can
(a) increase loudness (b) decrease loudness
(c) increase pitch (d) decrease pitch

Sol. (*b*) The loudness depends on the amplitude of the sound wave, therefore by reducing the amplitude,the loudness of the wave decreases.

4. Which one of the following diagnostic methods use reflection of sound? **[2021 (Sem-I)]**
(a) CT scan (b) Electrocardiogram
(c) Echocardiogram (d) MRI

Sol. (*c*) Echo cardiogram is the diagnostic method which is based on reflection of sound using ultrasound.

5. Two sounds of same loudness and same pitch produced by two different instruments differ in
(a) quality (b) intensity
(c) amplitude (d) frequency

Sol. (*a*) Quality (or timbre) is a characteristic of waves having different waveforms, hence different instruments can produce sound of same pitch and loudness but of different quality.

6. Two notes are produced from two different musical instruments, such that they have same loudness and same pitch. The produced notes differ in their **[2023]**
(a) waveform (b) frequency
(c) wavelength (d) speed

Sol. (*a*) waveform

7. A wire stretched between two fixed supports, is plucked exactly in the middle then released. It executes
(a) natural vibrations
(b) resonant vibrations
(c) damped vibrations
(d) forced vibrations

Sol. (*a*) When a wire is stretched between two fixed supports is plucked exactly in the middle,then released, it will produce natural vibrations.

8. When a body vibrates under a periodic force, the vibrations of the body are always **[2023]**
(a) natural vibrations
(b) damped vibrations
(c) forced vibrations
(d) resonant vibrations

Sol. (*c*) Forced vibrations occurs when a body vibrates under a periodic force.

9. Free vibrations are **[2022 (Sem-II)]**
(a) the vibrations under the influence of a periodic force
(b) the vibrations with larger amplitude
(c) the vibrations when the frequency continuously decreases
(d) the vibrations with a constant frequency and constant amplitude

Sol. (*d*) Free vibrations are the vibrations with a constant frequency and constant amplitude. It occurs when no external force acts on the body which causes the motion.

10. Resonance is a forced vibration in which **[Latest Specimen (Sem-II)]**
(a) amplitude remains constant
(b) frequency of forced vibration is greater than the free vibration of the body
(c) frequency of forced vibration is equal to the free vibrations of the body
(d) frequency of forced vibration is less than the free vibrations of the body

Sol. (*c*) Resonance is defined as forced vibration in which frequency of forced vibration is equal to the free vibrations of the body.

11. Pendulums *A*, *B*, *C* and *D* are tied to a flexible string *PQ* and are at rest. Pendulum *C* is disturbed. Which of the following statements is true? **[Latest Specimen (Sem-II)]**

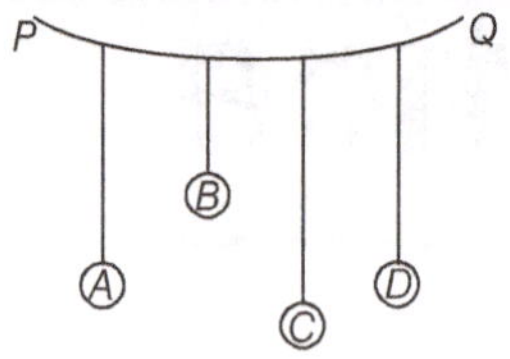

(a) Only pendulum C will start vibrating.
(b) Pendulums A, B and D will also start vibrating but A and D will vibrate with the maximum amplitude.
(c) Pendulums A, B and D will also start vibrating.
(d) Vibrations of pendulum C are forced vibrations.

Sol. (*b*) When pendulum C is disturbed from its position, all pendulums start vibrating. But as the length of A and D are same, so both remain in same phase and resonance takes place. Hence, A and D will vibrate with maximum amplitude.

2 Marks Questions

12. Draw a graph between displacement from mean position and time for a body executing free vibration in a vacuum. **[2020]**

Sol. The amplitude and frequency of a freely vibrating body in vacuum remains constant with respect to time. The displacement-time graph of a body executing free vibration in vacuum is given as **[1]**

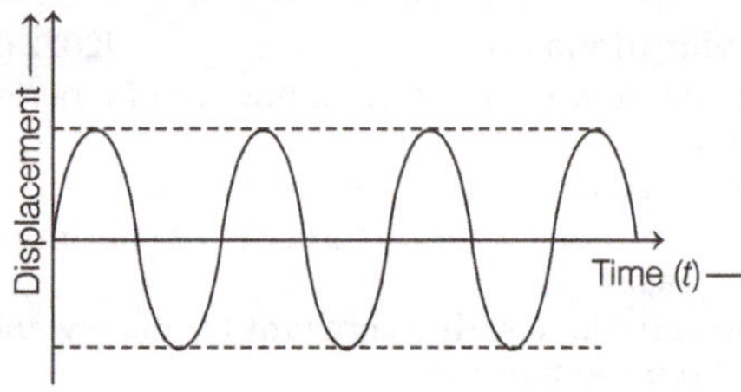

13. Explain why, echoes cannot be heard in a small room?

Sol. For hearing echo, there should be atleast a distance of 17 m between source of sound and body from where sound is reflected. In small rooms, distance is usually less than 17 m, hence echoes cannot be heard. **[2]**

14. A student went to a hill station early in the morning, he could hear the echo of his clap after 0.1 s.

When he went to the same place in the afternoon he could not hear the echo at all, then explain the reason for his changed observation.

Sol. There is a rise in temperature in the afternoon, so the speed of sound increases with increase in temperature. As speed increases, time taken by reflected sound will be less, may be less than 0.1 s in afternoon. That is why the student could not hear the echo at all in the afternoon. **[2]**

15. State the conditions required to hear an echo.

Sol. The conditions for hearing an echo are
(i) The time interval between source sound and reflected sound must be atleast 0.1 s. **[1]**
(ii) The minimum distance between the obstacle and source of sound should be atleast 17.2 m. **[1]**

16. When can we distinctly hear the echo of a sharp sound? Why cannot we hear an echo in a small hall?

Sol. As we know that, to listen echo for a sound wave whose speed in air is 344 ms^{-1} and persistance of sound is 0.1 s, a minimum distance of 17.2 m between observer and reflecting surface is required. As the condition of minimum distance between the source and reflecting surface is not satisfied, so in a small hall we do not hear echoes. **[2]**

17. A girl is sitting in the middle of a park of dimension 12 m$\times$ 12 m. On the left side of it there is a building adjoining the park and on right side of the park, there is a road adjoining the park. A sound is produced on the road by a cracker. Is it possible for the girl to hear the echo of this sound? Explain your answer.

Sol. No, it is not possible for the girl to hear the echo of this sound, because the distance between girl and obstacle (building) is only 6 m approx but echo is heard only, if the minimum distance between the observer at the source of sound and the obstacle is 11.3 m.

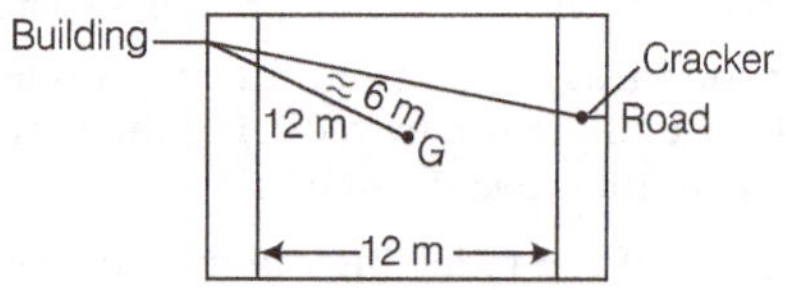

[2]

18. Mention two practical uses of echo.

Sol. Two practical uses of echo are
(i) The method of echolocation, in which some animals like bats, tortoises and dolphins to locate the object by hearing the echoes of their ultrasonic squeaks. **[1]**
(ii) In the medical field, echoes of the ultrasound is used to investigate the internal organs of human body such as liver, gall bladder, pancreas, kidneys, etc. **[1]**

19. What is a SONAR? For what it is used?

Sol. Full form of SONAR is Sound Navigation And Ranging. It is used to measure depth of sea and ocean or to locate under water things, i.e. shoals of fish shipwrecks and enemy submarines.

It uses ultrasonic waves to measure the distance, direction and speed of under water objects. **[1+1]**

20. Can SONAR be used to determine the depth of a sea? Draw a well labelled diagram showing the procedure.

Sol. Yes, SONAR technique can be used to determine the depth of the sea. [1]

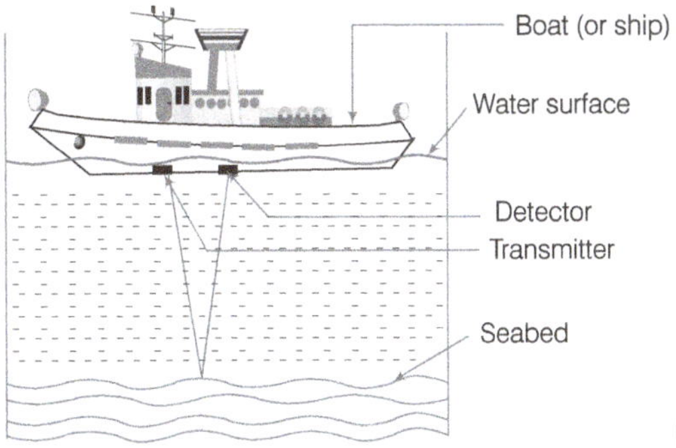

[1]

21. Distinguish between loudness and intensity of sound.

Sol. Difference between loudness and intensity

Loudness	Intensity
It is a subjective quantity. A sound may be loud for one person but may be feeble for another person.	It is an objective physical quantity which does not change for person to person.
It cannot be measured as it is just a sensation which can be felt only.	It can be measured as a physical quantity. [1]
Loudness of sound is measured in the unit of decibel (dB).	Intensity of sound is measured in the unit of watt per square metre (W/m^2).
It depends on the sensitivity of ears.	It does not depend on the sensitivity of ears. [1]

22. What do you understand by intensity of sound? How is it different from loudness?

Sol. Intensity of Sound It is the amount of sound energy passing each second through unit area. [1]
Loudness is a measure of the response of the ear to the sound. Even when two sounds are of equal intensity, we may hear one as louder than the other, as our ear detects it better. Therefore, loudness depends both on the intensity of sound and the response of the ear to that sound. [1]

23. Compare the following in Fig. (a) and Fig. (b) and name them.

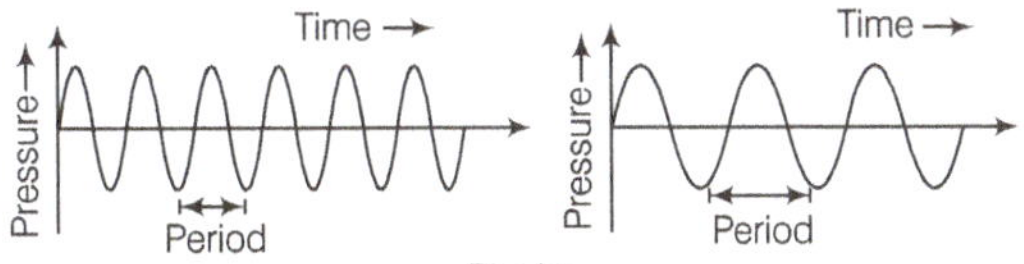

Fig.(a)

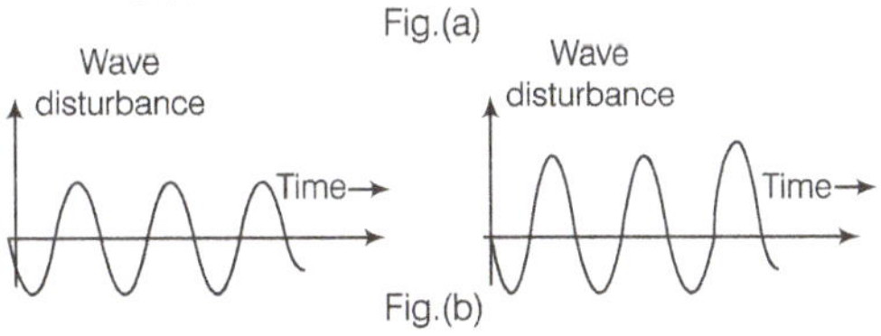

Fig.(b)

Sol. In the Fig. (a), there is a sound wave with same amplitude but different frequencies. First one high pitched, second graph low pitched. [1]
In the Fig. (b), there is a soft sound wave and a loud sound wave of same frequencies, because number of waves are same in both graphs but has different amplitude. [1]

24. Which wave property determines
(i) loudness and
(ii) pitch?

Sol. (i) Loudness of wave is determined by its amplitude. [1]
(ii) Pitch of the wave is determined by its frequency. [1]

25. Figure shows a trace of a sound wave which is produced by a particular tuning fork.

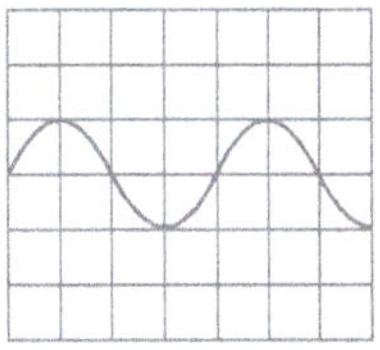

(i) Draw a trace of the sound wave which, has a higher pitch than that shown in figure.
(ii) Draw a trace of the sound wave which is louder than that shown in figure.

Sol. (i)

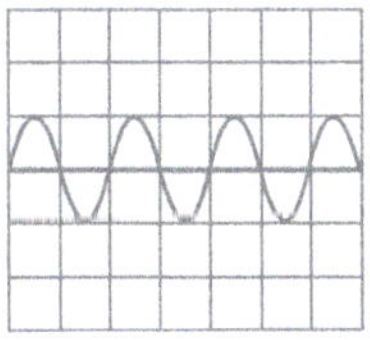

(ii)

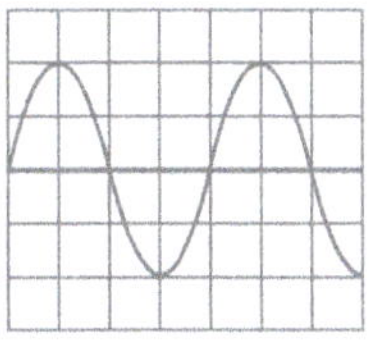

[2]

26. A man playing a flute is able to produce notes of different frequencies. If he closes the holes near his mouth, will the pitch of the note produced, increase or decrease? Give a reason for your answer. [2019]

Sol. If we close the near hole, the wavelength of the sound wave will decrease. As we know that, frequency of the sound wave is inversely proportional to wavelength, so frequency will increase. Greater the frequency of a sound, the higher will be its pitch. Hence, pitch will increase. [2]

27. Two waves of the same pitch have amplitudes in the ratio 1: 3. Calculate the ratio of their
(i) intensities?
(ii) frequencies ? [2019]

Sol. (i) Given, amplitude of two waves, $\frac{a_1}{a_2} = \frac{1}{3}$ ...(i)

We know that, intensity is proportional to amplitude square, i.e. $I \propto a^2$

Ratio of intensity, $\frac{I_1}{I_2} = \left(\frac{1}{3}\right)^2 = \frac{1}{9}$ [1]

(ii) Frequency of the sound wave has no effect on amplitude, so ratio of frequency remains same, i.e. 1 : 3. [1]

28. How does the change in frequency and amplitude affect a musical sound?

Sol. For a musical sound
(i) increase in frequency means increase in its pitch.
(ii) increase in its amplitude means increase in intensity or loudness. **[2]**

29. The ratio of amplitude of two waves is 3 : 4. Calculate the ratio of their
(i) loudness (ii) frequencies?

Sol. (i) Ratio of loudness will be 9 : 16 as loudness depends upon intensity which is directly proportional to the square of amplitude. **[1]**
(ii) Ratio of frequencies will be 1 : 1 as frequency remains same for the two waves. **[1]**

30. Name the subjective property of sound related to its frequency and of light related to its wavelength.

Sol. Property of sound related to frequency, is pitch and property of light related to its wavelength is colour. **[2]**

31. What do you understand by noise pollution? Name one source of sound causing noise pollution. **[2016]**

Sol. Noise pollution is the disturbance or unpleasant sound that may harm the activity or balance of human or animal life. **[1]**
The noise pollution is mainly caused by machines, transportation system, etc. **[1]**

32. Will the sound be audible, if the string is set into vibration on the surface of the moon? Give reason.

Sol. No, we will not hear any audible sound on the surface because sound needs a medium to propagate. Moon has no atmosphere, so sound will not be heard. **[2]**

33. Displacement-distance graph of two sound waves *A* and *B*, travelling in a medium are as shown in the diagram below.

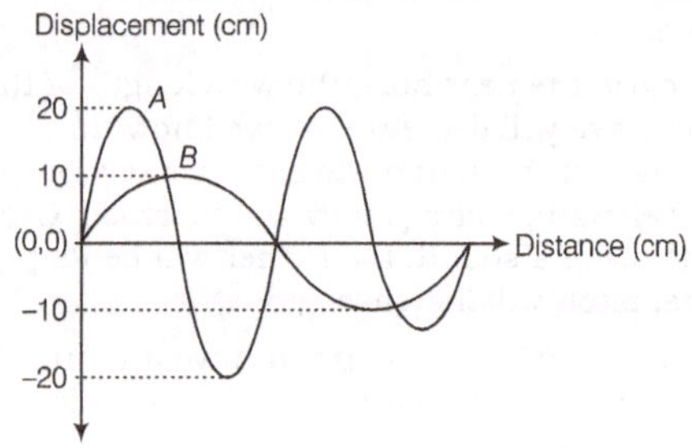

Study the two sound waves and compare their
(i) Amplitudes (ii) Wavelengths **[2018]**

Sol. (i) Amplitude of sound wave, $A = 20$ cm
Amplitude of sound wave, $B = 10$ cm
$\therefore$ Amplitude of sound wave *A* is twice than that of sound wave *B*. **[1]**
(ii) From the graph, it can be seen that wavelength of sound wave *A* is half of the wavelength of sound wave *B*. **[1]**

34. (i) What do you understand by the free vibrations of a body?
(ii) Why does the amplitude of a vibrating body continuously decrease during damped vibrations? **[2018]**

Sol. (i) Free vibrations are the periodic vibrations of a body in the absence of any external force on it. **[1]**
(ii) A body continuously losses its energy due to the presence of frictional force by the surrounding medium in damped oscillations, therefore amplitude of body continuously decreases. **[1]**

35. A metal foot ruler is held at the edge of a table. It is pressed at its free end and then released, it vibrates.
(i) Name the vibrations produced.
(ii) State one way to increase the frequency of these vibrations. **[2023]**

Sol. (i) Damped vibrations will be produced when it is pressed at its free end and then released. **[1]**
(ii) In the presence of resonating body or reducing length of the scale outside table , we can increase the frequency of these vibrations. **[1]**

36. Why stringed musical instruments like the guitar, are provided with a hollow box? Explain.

Sol. The musical instrument like guitar is provide with a hollow box attached to it because vibrating strings of the instrument produce a very weak sound which cannot be heard. Hence, they are provided with a sound box. This box is a hollow chamber and is so constructed that the column of air inside it has a natural frequency which is same as that of the string stretched on it. Hence, due to resonance, helps in producing a loud sound. **[2]**

37. (i) Define the term resonant vibrations.
(ii) Which characteristic of sound, makes it possible to recognise a person by his voice without seeing him? **[2019]**

Sol. (i) The increase in amplitude of oscillation of an electric or mechanical system exposed to a periodic force whose frequency is equal or very close to the natural undamped frequency of the system, called resonant vibrations. **[1]**
(ii) The quality (timbre) of sound **[1]**

3 Marks Questions

38. Does sound follow the same laws of reflection as light does? Explain.

Sol. Yes, sound wave follows the same laws as in case of laws of reflection of light.

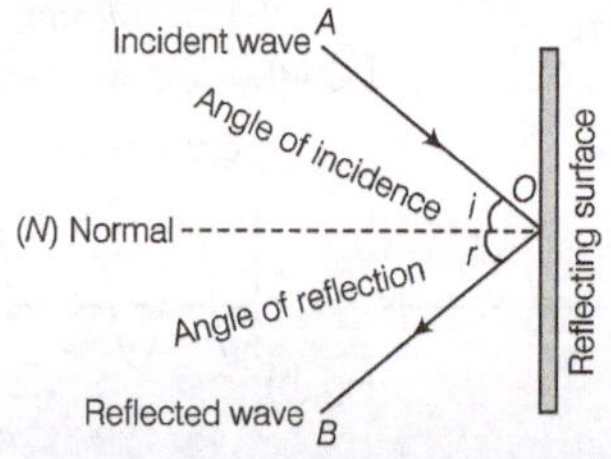

[1]

The laws of reflection of sound are as follows

(i) The incident sound wave (AO), the reflected sound wave (OB) and the normal (ON) at the point of incidence, all lie in the same plane. [1]

(ii) The angle of incidence ($\angle AON$) of sound is equal to the angle of reflection ($\angle NOB$) of sound. [1]

39. (i) What do you understand by the term echo?

(ii) Write two conditions for an echo to take place. [2016]

Sol. (i) Echo is the sound heard after it gets reflected from a rigid surface. [1]

(ii) Two conditions for an echo to take place are given below

(a) There should be a minimum distance of 17.2 m between the listener and the reflecting body. [1]

(b) Reflecting body should be as big as compared to the wavelength of sound. [1]

40. (i) What is meant by an echo? Mention one important condition, i.e. necessary for an echo to be heard distinctly.

(ii) Mention one important use of echo. [2008]

Sol. (i) **Echo** The sound heard after reflection from a distant obstacle after the original sound is ceased is known as echo. To hear echo distinctly, the reflecting surface in air should be at a minimum distance of 17 m from the listener. [2]

(ii) In the medical field, echoes of the ultrasound is used to investigate the internal organs of human body such as liver, gall bladder, pancreas, kidneys, uterus, heart, etc. [1]

41. When a sound is reflected from a distant object, an echo is produced. Assume the distance between the reflecting surface and the source of sound production remains the same. Will you be able to hear echo sound on a hotter day?

Sol. The time taken by echo to be heard,

$$t = \frac{2d}{v}$$ [1]

where, d = distance between the reflecting surface and source of sound and v = speed of sound in air. [1]

As we know that, speed of sound increases with increase in temperature, so on a hotter day, speed of sound will be higher, so the time after which echo is heard will decrease.

If time taken by the reflected sound is less than 0.1 s after the production of original sound, then echo is not heard. [1]

42. Name the factor that determines

(i) loudness of the sound heard

(ii) quality of the note

(iii) pitch of the note [2017]

Sol. (i) **Loudness** Amplitude [1]

(ii) **Quality (or timbre)** Nature of waveform [1]

(iii) **Pitch of note** Frequency [1]

43. (i) Name the characteristic of sound which enables a person to differentiate between two sounds with equal loudness but having different frequencies.

(ii) Define the characteristic named by you in part (i).

(iii) Name the characteristic of sound which enables a person to differentiate between two sounds of the same loudness and frequency but produced by different instruments.

Sol. (i) Pitch or shrillness is that characteristic of sound which enables a person to differentiate between two sounds with equal loudness but having different frequencies. [1]

(ii) Pitch is that characteristic of sound by which an acute (or shrill) note can be distinguished from a grave or flat note. [1]

(iii) Quality is that characteristic of sound which enables a person to differentiate between two sounds of the same loudness and frequency but produced by different instruments. [1]

44. (i) Define pitch.

(ii) Two wires AB and CD of same length are stretched by same amount, which wire will produce sound of greater pitch on plucking?

(iii) Give a reason for your answer.

Sol. (i) Pitch is that characteristic of sound by which we can distinguish between different sounds of the same loudness. [1]

(ii) Wire AB will have sound of greater pitch. [1]

(iii) Since, the diameter of wire AB is less than that of wire CD. So on plucking by same force, the vibrations produced in AB moves faster and have higher frequency. Hence, wire AB will produce sound of greater pitch. [1]

45. What is meant by loudness of sound? State the factor on which it depends. Draw figures to illustrate

(i) soft sound and (ii) loud sound.

Sol. **Loudness** Refer to theory (Page 137). [1]

(i)

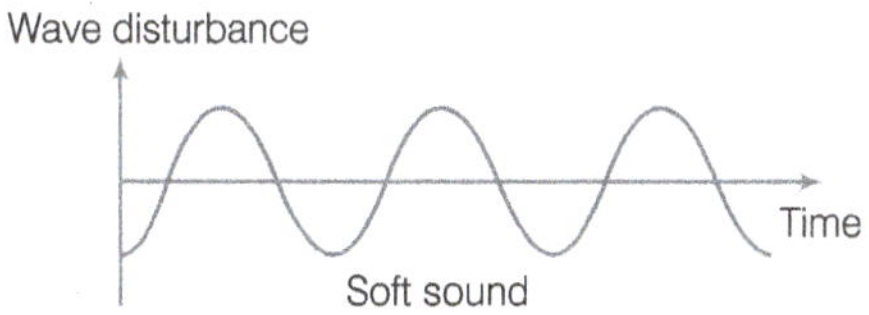

Soft sound [1]

(ii)

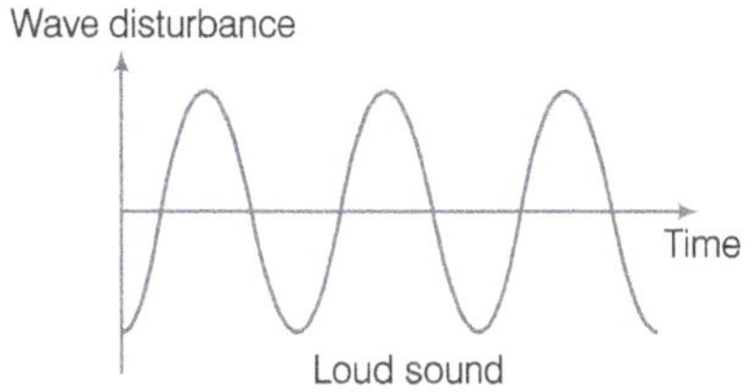

Loud sound [1]

46. A nail was gently touched by the hammer and then was hit harder.

(i) When will be the sound created louder?

(ii) Name the characteristic of sound responsible for change in sound.

(iii) Write the SI unit of loudness.

Sol. (i) Sound will be produced when we beat hammer hard on the nails. [1]

(ii) Amplitude of vibrating body is responsible for change in sound. [1]

(iii) The SI unit of loudness is decibel (dB). [1]

47. (i) What are the factors on which the following characteristics of a musical note depend?

(a) Intensity

(b) Timbre

(ii) How does a trawlerman catch fish in deep water?

Sol. (i) Factors on which the given characteristics of musical note depends are

(a) Intensity depends upon

I. frequency

II. amplitude. [1]

(b) Timbre depends upon

I. waveform of sound

II. frequency

III. resonance and sound pressure. [1]

(ii) A trawlerman sends ultrasonic waves in deep water, which on striking the shoal of fish, return back to him. He notes the time t taken by the waves in going and coming back, then he calculates the depth of water d by using the relation

$$d = \frac{vt}{2}$$

where, v is the velocity of ultrasonic waves in water.

This helps them to catch the fishes easily. [2]

48. Differentiate between the terms

(i) music and noise

(ii) tone and note.

Sol. (i) **Music** The sound which is pleasant to the ears, is called music. It is produced by regular periodic vibrations. There is no sudden change in its amplitude.

e.g. Sound produced from a tabla. [1]

Noise The sound which is unpleasant to the ears, is called noise. It is produced at an irregular intervals. There is sudden change in its amplitude.

e.g. Sound produced in a market and the sound produced by an explosion. [1]

(ii) **Tone** The sound of single frequency is called a tone. [1/2]

Note The sound which is a mixture of several frequencies is called a note. [1/2]

49. (i) What are damped vibrations?

(ii) Mention one example of damped vibration.

(iii) Name the phenomenon that causes a loud sound when the stem of a vibrating tuning fork is kept pressed on the surface of a table.

[2017]

Sol. (i) The periodic vibrations of body of decreasing amplitude in presence of resistive force are called the damped vibrations. The displacement-time graph for the damped vibrations shown in the diagram below.

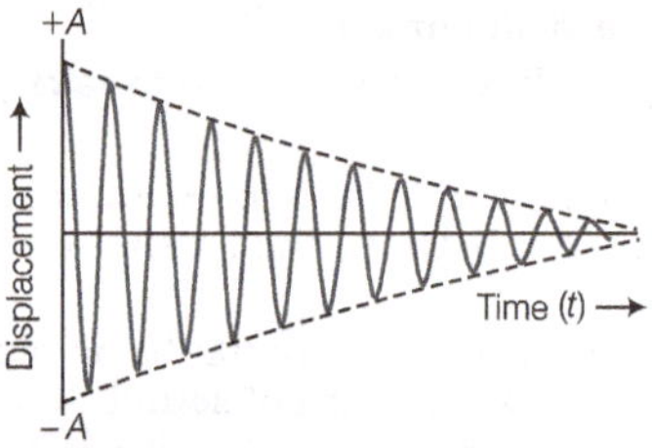

The amplitude, displacement decreases exponentially with time [1]

(ii) Simple pendulum's oscillation. [1]

(iii) **Resonance** Refer to theory (Page 139). [1]

50. (i) Which one of the following graphs A or B shows free vibrations in vacuum and which one shows free vibrations in a medium?

[Latest Specimen Sem-II]

(ii) How did you come to this conclusion?

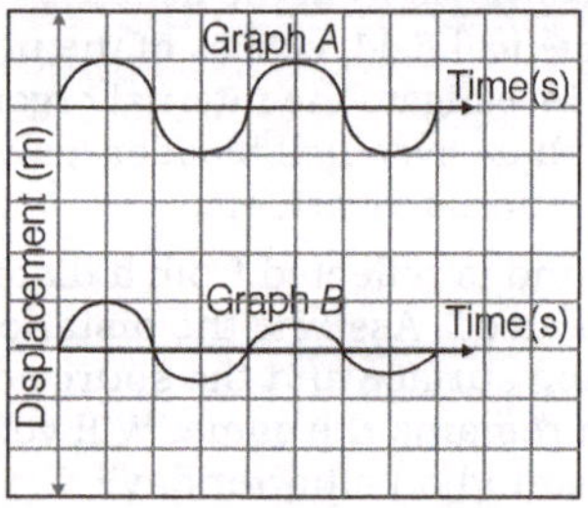

Sol. (i) Graph A shows free vibrations in vacuum and graph B shows free vibrations in a medium. [1]

(ii) In graph A, the amplitude or displacement of the vibration is constant for all time intervals. i.e. No resisting force is present here. So, it shows that the vibrations are in vacuum. In graph B, the amplitude of the vibration is decreasing with time i.e. Resistive forces are present here. So, it shows that the vibrations are in a medium. [2]

51. (i) What is meant by resonance?

(ii) State two ways in which resonance differs from forced vibrations.

Sol. (i) The phenomenon in which body vibrates under the influence of periodic force, where frequency of the applied periodic force is equal to the natural frequency of the vibrating body. Then, the body begins to vibrate with increased amplitude. [1]

(ii) The two ways in which resonance differs from forced vibrations are as

Resonance	Forced Vibrations
This is the phenomenon of setting a body (*A*) into vibrations with the help of another body (*B*), where frequency of (*B*) is equal to the natural frequency of (*A*).	In this, a body (*A*) is set into vibrations under the influence of periodic force of body (*B*). Frequency of vibrations of body (*B*) is different from the natural frequency of the body (*A*).
Vibrations are of larger amplitude.	Vibrations are of smaller amplitude.

[1 × 2]

52. (i) Sound made in front of a tall building 18 m away, is repeated. Name the phenomenon and briefly explain it.

(ii) A tuning fork, held over an air column of a given length, produces a distinct audible sound. What do you call this phenomenon? How does it occur?

Sol. (i) As, we know the minimum distance between source and reflector is 17 m and here the distance is 18 m, so the phenomenon due to which sound is repeated is echo.

Basically, the phenomenon of repetition of sound caused by reflection of sound waves is called an echo. [1½]

(ii) We call the phenomenon as resonance. This occurs when the frequency of forced vibrations produced by the tuning fork becomes equal to the natural frequency of the air column. [1½]

53.

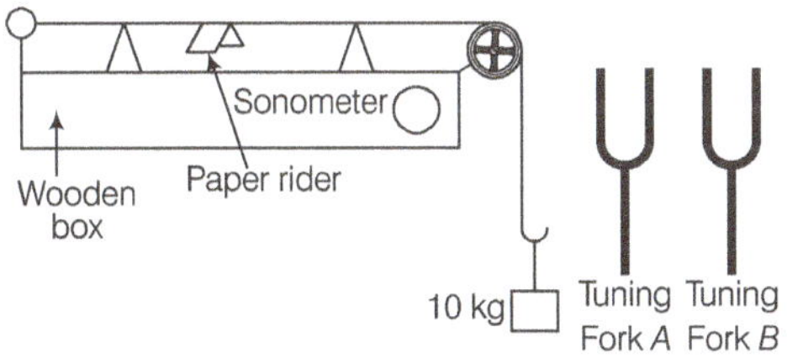

The diagram above shows a wire stretched over a sonometer. Stems of two vibrating tuning forks *A* and *B* are touched to the wooden box of the sonometer.

It is observed that the paper rider (a small piece of paper folded at the centre) present on the wire flies off when the stem of vibrating tuning fork *B* is touched to the wooden box but the paper just vibrates when the stem of vibrating tuning fork *A* is touched to the wooden box.

(i) Name the phenomenon when the paper rider just vibrates.

(ii) Write the phenomenon when the paper rider flies off.

(iii) Why does the paper rider fly off when the stem of tuning fork *B* is touched to the box? [2018]

Sol. (i) Forced vibration [1]

(ii) Resonance [1]

(iii) The paper rider flies off because the natural frequency of vibration of wire matches the frequency of the tuning fork. This results in increase in magnitude of amplitude of vibrations. [1]

4 Marks Questions

54. The adjacent diagram shows three different modes of vibrations *P*, *Q* and *R* of the same string.

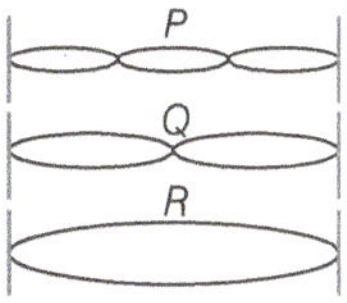

(i) Which of the following vibrations will produce a louder sound and why?

(ii) The sound of which string will have maximum shrillness?

(iii) Calculate the ratio of wavelengths of *P* and *R*. [2014]

Sol. (i) The mode of vibration *R* will produce a louder sound, because its amplitude is more than that of *P* and *Q*. [1]

(ii) The sound of *P* string will have maximum shrillness because its frequency is more than that of *R* and *Q*. [1]

(iii) Frequency, $f_P = 3f$, frequency, $f_R = f$

As, $\lambda = \dfrac{v}{f}$ [1]

∴ The ratio of wavelengths of *P* and *R* is given by

$$\frac{\lambda_P}{\lambda_R} = \frac{v/f_P}{v/f_R} = \frac{f_R}{f_P} = \frac{f}{3f} = \frac{1}{3}$$ [1]

55. The diagram below shows the displacement-time graph for a vibrating body.

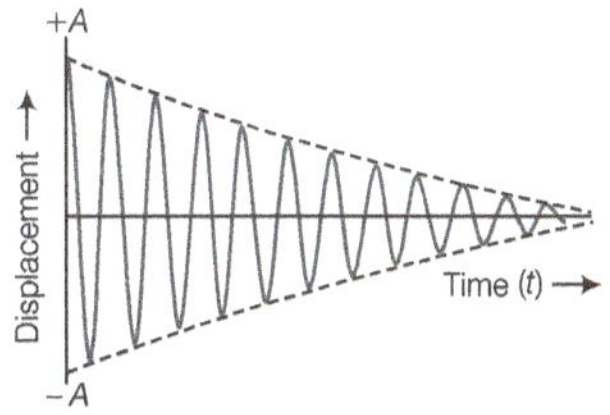

(i) Name the type of vibrations produced by the vibrating body.

(ii) Mention one example of a body producing such vibrations.

(iii) Why is the amplitude of the wave gradually decreasing?

(iv) What will happen to the vibrations of the body after sometime?

Sol. (i) Damped vibrations are produced by the vibrating body. [1]

(ii) A simple pendulum oscillating in air, tuning fork vibrating in air are examples of a body producing such vibrations. [1]

(iii) The amplitude of the wave gradually decreasing, because of friction due to which energy is decreased continuously. [1]

(iv) As its amplitude decreases, so the vibrations of the body finally stops. [1]

56. (i) Give one example each of natural vibration, forced vibration and resonance.
(ii) Mention one practical use of echoes.

Sol. (i) **For Natural Vibration** A tuning fork struck against a hard rubber pad. [1]
For Forced Vibration Vibration produced in the board of a guitar when its string is made to vibrate. [1]
For Resonance While tuning a wireless receiver, we adjust its natural frequency equal to that of the incoming wireless carries waves, so that a loud sound of incoming signal is heard. [1]
(ii) In medical field, echoes of the ultrasound is used to investigate the internal organs of human body such as liver, gall bladder, uterus, etc. [1]

57. (i) Name the phenomenon involved in tuning a radio set to a particular station.
(ii) Define the phenomenon named by you in part (i) above.
(iii) What do you understand by loudness of sound?
(iv) In which units is the loudness of sound measured? **[2016]**

Sol. (i) Resonance is the phenomenon involved in tuning a radio set to a particular station. [1]
(ii) Resonance is the phenomenon in which vibration takes place under the influence of periodic force, where frequency of the applied force is equal to the natural frequency of the vibrating body. [1]
(iii) Loudness is the sensation produced in the ear which enables to distinguish between a loud and a faint sound. [1]
(iv) Loudness of sound is measured in units called decibels (dB). [1]

Numerical Based Questions

58. A sound wave travelling in water has wavelength 0.4 m. Is this wave audible in air? (The speed of sound in water = 1400 ms^{-1}) **[2020]**

Sol. Given, speed of sound in water, $v = 1400\ ms^{-1}$
Wavelength of sound wave in water, $\lambda = 0.4$ m
If f be the frequency of sound wave, then $v = f\lambda$

$$\Rightarrow \quad f = \frac{v}{\lambda} = \frac{1400}{0.4} = 3500 \text{ Hz}$$ [1]

Since, frequency of sound wave remains same in water and air. Hence, $f_{water} = f_{air} = 3500$ Hz.
Since, 20 Hz $< f_{air} <$ 20 kHz, hence given sound wave is audible in air. [1]

59. For hearing the loudest ticking sound heard by the ear, find the angle x in the given figure. [2]

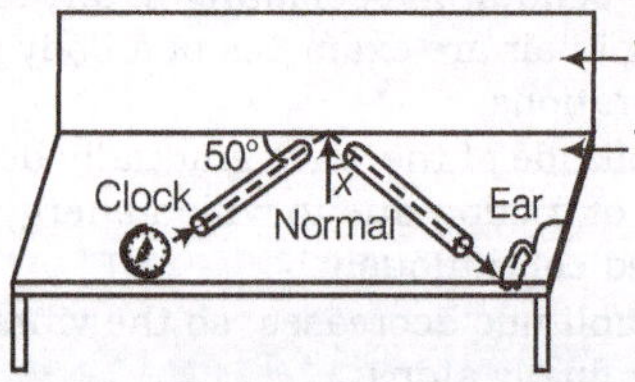

Sol. We know that in laws of reflection, the angle of incidence (x) is always equal to the angle of reflection (x).
Since, AOB is a straight line.

$\therefore \quad \angle AOB = 180°$

$\therefore \quad 50° + x + x + 50° = 180°$

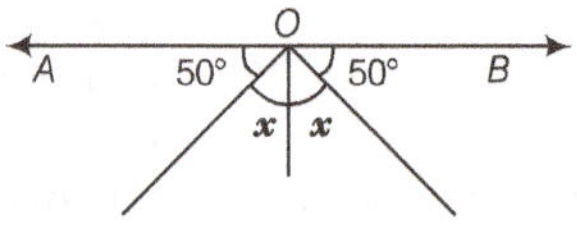

[1]

($\because$ sum of all angles lies on the same side of a line is 180°)

$2x + 100° = 180°$

$\Rightarrow \quad 2x = 180° - 100° \Rightarrow 2x = 80°$

$$\Rightarrow \quad x = \frac{80°}{2} \Rightarrow x = 40°$$

Hence, the value of x is 40°. [1]

60. An observer stands at a distance of 850 m from a cliff and fires a gun. After what time gap will he hear the echo, if sound travels at a speed of 350 ms^{-1} in air? [2]

Sol. Given, distance between sound source and cliff, $d = 850$ m
Total distance travelled by the sound = $2d$ [1]
Speed, $v = 350$ m/s
Time, $t = ?$

$$\therefore \quad v = \frac{2d}{t} \Rightarrow t = \frac{2d}{v} = \frac{2 \times 850}{350} = 4.86\text{s}$$ [1]

61. A ship on the surface of water sends a signal and receives it back after 4 s from a submarine inside the water. Calculate the distance of the submarine from the ship. (Take, the speed of sound in water is 1450 ms^{-1}) [2]

Sol. Given, time, $t = 4$ s, $v = 1450$ m/s
For an echo, total distance = $2d$ [1]

$$\therefore \quad 2d = v \times t \Rightarrow d = \frac{v \times t}{2} = \frac{1450 \times 4}{2} = 2900 \text{ m}$$ [1]

62. Aditi clapped her hands near a cliff and heard the echo after 4 s. What is the distance of the cliff from her, if the speed of sound is taken as 346 ms^{-1}? [2]

Sol. Given, speed of sound, $v = 346\ ms^{-1}$
Time taken for hearing the echo, $t = 4$ s
$\therefore$ Distance travelled by the sound = $v \times t$
$= 346 \times 4 = 1384$ m [1]
In 4 s, sound has to travel twice the distance between the cliff and Aditi. Therefore, the distance between the cliff and Aditi is $\frac{1384}{2} = 692$ m. [1]

63. On a cloudy day, a thunder sound was heard 14s after the flash of lightning. How far was the cloud? (Take, the speed of sound is 340 ms^{-1}) [2]

Sol. Given, speed of sound, $v = 340\ ms^{-1}$
Time taken by thunder to be heard,

$$t = \frac{2d}{v} = 14 \text{ s}$$

$$2d = v \times t = 340 \times 14 = 4760 \text{ m}$$

$$\therefore \quad d = \frac{4760}{2} = 2380 \text{ m}$$

Therefore, the distance of the cloud is 2380m. [2]

64. An ultrasonic wave is sent from a ship towards the bottom of the sea. It is found that the time interval between the sending and the receiving of the wave is 1.5 s. Calculate the depth of the sea, if the velocity of sound in sea water is 1400 ms^{-1}. [2]

Sol. Given, time interval, $t = 1.5$ s, velocity, $v = 1400$ m/s

Distance travelled by the ultrasonic waves during $t = 1.5$ s,

$$2d = v \times t$$
$$= 1400 \times 1.5 = 2100 \text{ m}$$ [1]

$\therefore$ The depth of the sea will be

$$= \frac{d}{2} = \frac{2100}{2} = 1050 \text{ m}$$ [1]

65. A boy stands 60 m in front of a tall wall and claps. The body continues to clap every time an echo is heard. Another boy finds that the time taken between the first and forty-first clap is 16 s. Calculate the speed of sound.

Sol. Distance of boy from the wall, $d = 60$ m

Total distance travelled by the sound

$$= 2d = 2 \times 60 = 120 \text{ m}$$

Time interval between first and forty-first clap = 16 s

Time interval between two successive claps = $\frac{16}{40}$ s.

$\therefore$ Speed of sound, $v = \frac{2d}{t} = \frac{120}{(16/40)} = 300$ m/s [2]

66. A man standing 25 m away from a wall produces a sound and receives the reflected sound.

(i) Calculate the time after which he receives the reflected sound, if the speed of sound in air is 350 ms^{-1}.

(ii) Will the man be able to hear a distinct echo? Give a reason for your answer. [2] [2011]

Sol. Given, distance between man and wall, $d = 25$ m

(i) Velocity of sound, $v = 350$ m/s, $t = ?$

$$\therefore \quad v = \frac{2d}{t}$$

$$\Rightarrow \quad t = \frac{2d}{v} = \frac{2 \times 25}{350} = 0.14 \text{ s}$$ [1]

(ii) Yes, the man will be able to hear a distinct echo, because the least time for distinct echo to be heard is 0.1 s as

$$0.14 \text{ s} > 0.1 \text{ s}$$ [1]

67. The human ear can detect continuous sounds in the frequency range from 20 Hz to 20000 Hz. Assuming that the speed of sound in air is 330 ms^{-1} for all frequencies, calculate the wavelengths corresponding to the given extreme frequencies of the audible range. [2] [2017]

Sol. Applying the formula, $v = \lambda \times \nu$

where, v = speed of sound = 330 ms^{-1},

ν = frequency and λ = wavelength of sound.

We have range of frequencies from 20 Hz-20000 Hz.

Hence, for frequency, $\nu = 20$ Hz, we have

$$330 = \lambda \times 20$$

$$\Rightarrow \quad \lambda = \frac{330}{20} = 16.5 \text{ m}$$ [1]

For frequency, $\nu = 20000$ Hz, we have

$$330 = \lambda \times 20000$$

$$\Rightarrow \quad \lambda = \frac{330}{20000} = 16.5 \times 10^{-3} \text{m}$$ [1]

68. A man standing between two cliffs produces a sound and hears two successive echoes at intervals of 3 s and 4 s, respectively. Calculate the distance between the two cliffs. The speed of sound in the air is 330 ms^{-1}. [3] [2012]

Sol. Given, time taken from nearer cliff, $t_1 = 3$ s

Time taken from farther cliff, $t_2 = 4$ s

Speed of sound in air, $v_a = 330$ m/s

Total distance, $d = ?$ [1]

Distance of man from nearer cliff,

$$d_1 = \frac{v_a \times t_1}{2} = \frac{330 \times 3}{2} = 495 \text{ m}$$

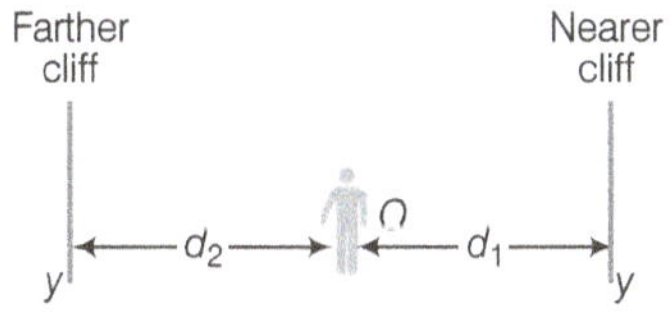

[1]

Distance of man from farther cliff,

$$d_2 = \frac{v_a \times t_2}{2}$$
$$= \frac{330 \times 4}{2} = 660 \text{ m}$$

Total distance between two cliffs,

$$d = d_1 + d_2$$
$$= 495 + 660 = 1155 \text{ m}$$ [1]

69. (i) A man stands at a distance of 68 m from a cliff and fires a gun. After what time interval will he hear the echo, if the speed of sound in air is 340 ms^{-1}?

(ii) If the man had been standing at a distance of 12 m from the cliff, then would he have heard a clear echo? [3] [2010]

Sol. (i) Given, distance between man and cliff, $d = 68$ m

Total distance travelled by the sound = $2d$

Velocity of sound, $v = 340$ m/s and time, $t = ?$

$$\therefore \quad t = \frac{2d}{v} = \frac{2 \times 68}{340} = 0.4 \text{ s}$$ [1½]

(ii) No, he has not heard a clear echo, because to hear a clear echo distinctly, the reflecting surface in air should be at a minimum distance of 17 m from the listener. [1½]

70. A boy standing in front of a wall at a distance of 85 m produces 2 claps per second. He notices that the sound of his clapping coincides with the echo. The echo is heard only once when clapping is stopped. Calculate the speed of sound.

Sol. Let d be the distance of wall from the boy. [3]

Given, $d = 85$ m

To hear the echo, sound has to travel a total distance

$= 2d = 2 \times 85 = 170$ m [1]

Since, 2 claps are produced in one second, therefore each clap is produced after $\frac{1}{2}$ s which is equal to the time taken for the echo to be heard [1]

i.e., $t = \frac{1}{2}$ s $= 0.5$ s

Now, the speed of sound,

$$v = \frac{\text{total distance travelled}}{\text{time taken}}$$

$$= \frac{170}{0.5} = 340 \text{ ms}^{-1}$$ [1]

71. A person is standing at the sea shore. An observer on the ship which is anchored in between a vertical cliff and the person on the shore fires a gun. The person on the shore hears two sounds, 2 s and 3 s after seeing the smoke of the fired gun. If the speed of sound in the air is 320 ms^{-1}, then calculate

(i) the distance between the observer on the ship and the person on the shore.

(ii) the distance between the cliff and the observer on the ship. [4]

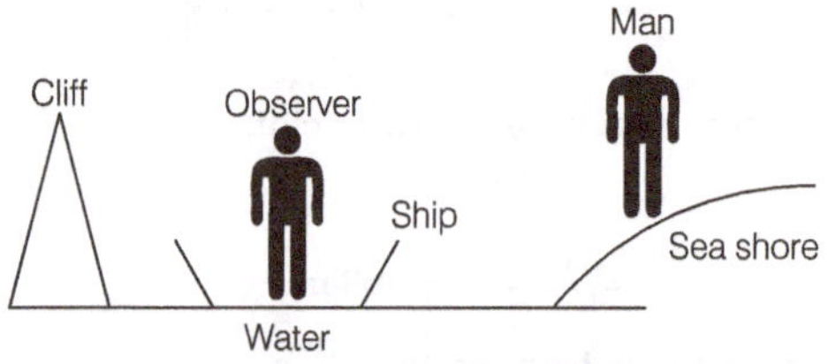

[2018]

Sol.

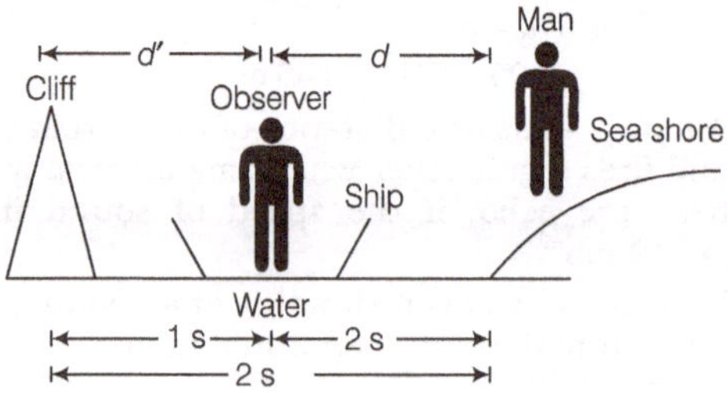

(i) Observer hears direct sound in 2s.

As, velocity $= \frac{\text{distance}}{\text{time}}$

$$320 = \frac{d}{2} \Rightarrow d = 320 \times 2 = 640 \text{ m}$$

∴ Distance between person and observer is 640 m. [2]

(ii) Observer hears reflected sound in 3 s. This means sound goes to cliff and reflect back in remaining one second.

i.e. $t = 1$ s

$$\Rightarrow v = \frac{2d'}{t}$$

$$\Rightarrow 320 = \frac{2d'}{1}$$

$$\Rightarrow \frac{320}{2} = d'$$

$$\Rightarrow d' = 160 \text{ m}$$ [2]

72. (i) The ratio of the amplitudes of two waves is 9 : 16. What is the ratio of their intensities?

(ii) A pendulum has a frequency of 4 vibrations per second. An observer starts the pendulum and fires a gun simultaneously. He hears the echo from a cliff after 8 vibrations of the pendulum. If the velocity of sound in air is 340 ms^{-1}, then what is the distance between the cliff and the observer?

Sol. As intensity is directly proportional to the square of amplitude, so putting the value of amplitude you get the ratio of intensities.

(i) Ratio of amplitudes of two waves $\frac{A_1}{A_2} = \frac{9}{16}$

As, intensity $(I) \propto$ amplitude $(A)^2$.

So, ratio of intensities,

$$\frac{I_1}{I_2} = \frac{A_1^2}{A_2^2}\left(\frac{9}{16}\right)^2 = \frac{81}{256}$$ [1]

(ii) Given, $f = 4 \frac{\text{vibration}}{\text{second}} = 4$ Hz

Velocity of sound, $v = 340$ m/s

Distance between observer and cliff, $d = ?$

4 vibrations take 1 s.

∴ 8 vibrations will require

$$= \frac{1}{4} \times 8 = 2 \text{ s}$$ [1]

Now, $d = \frac{v \times t}{2} = \frac{340 \times 2}{2} = 340$ m

(∵ sound waves have to travel twice the distance between the observer and cliff) [1]

Structured Questions

73. (i) It is observed that during march pasts we hear a base drums distinctly from a distance compared to the side drums.

(a) Name the characteristic of sound associated with the above observation. [2019]

(b) Give a reason for the above observation. [3]

(ii) (a) Which characteristic of sound is affected due to the larger surface of a school bell ?

(b) Calculate the distance covered by the ultrasonic wave having a velocity of 1.5 kms^{-1} in 14 s. when it is received after reflection by the receiver of the SONAR. [2023] [3]

(iii) Two pendulums C and D are suspended from a wire as shown in the figure given below. Pendulum C is made to oscillate by displacing it from its mean position. It is seen that D also starts oscillating.

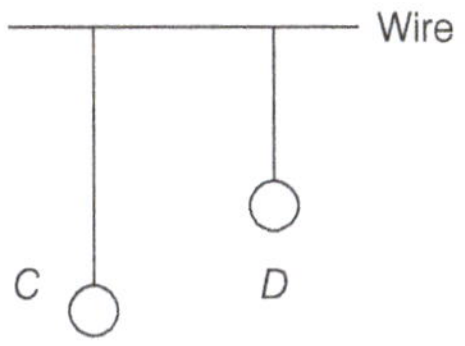

(a) Name the type of oscillation, *C* will execute.

(b) Name the type of oscillation, *D* will execute.

(c) If the length of *D* is made equal to *C*, then what difference will you notice in the oscillations of *D*?

(d) What is the name of the phenomenon when the length of *D* is made equal to *C*? [4]

Sol. (i) (a) Pitch and timbre [1]

(b) Side drums and base drums are made up of different material, so they have different frequency, hence the pitch. The quality (timbre) of sound enables us to distinguish between two sounds. Base drums and side drums have different quality due to different material. [2]

(ii) (a) Loudness is affected due to the larger surface of school bell .

(b) Given, velocity of ultrasonic wave

$= 1.5$ km/s

$= 1500$ m/s

Time taken t=14 s

Using the formula, distance, $2d = v \times t$

$= 1500 \times 14 / 2$

$- 1500 \times 17$

$= 10500$ m

$= 10.5$ km [3]

(iii) (a) *C* will execute damped oscillation. [1]

(b) *D* will execute forced oscillation. [1]

(c) *D* will start executing with very large amplitude. [1]

(d) Resonance [1]

74. (i) (a) Name the waves used for echo depth sounding.

(b) Give one reason for their use for the above purpose.

(c) Why are the waves mentioned by you not audible to us? [3] [2016]

(ii) How is it that, bats are able to fly at night without colliding with other objects? [3]

(iii) (a) A sound made on the surface of a lake takes 3s to reach a boatman. How much time will it take to reach a diver inside the water at the same depth?

(Take, velocity of sound in air = 300 ms^{-1} and velocity of sound in water = 1440 ms^{-1}) [2]

(b) A certain sound has a frequency of 256 Hz and a wavelength of 1.3 m. [4]

(I) Calculate the speed with which this sound travels.

(II) What difference would be felt by a listener between the above sound and another sound travelling at the same speed, but of wavelength 2.6 m? [2017]

Sol. (i) (a) Ultrasonic waves are used for echo depth sounding. [1]

(b) These waves can be confined into a narrow beam and are not easily absorbed in the medium and can travel a long distance. [1]

(c) The frequency of ultrasonic waves is above 20 kHz which is beyond the audibility range of human. [1]

(ii) Bats search out prey and fly at night by emitting and detecting reflections of ultrasonic waves. They emit high frequency ultrasonic squeaks while flying and listen to the echoes produced by reflection of their squeaks from the obstacle, prey or object in their path. From the time taken by the echo to be heard, bats can determine the distance of the object and can avoid the object by changing the direction without colliding with it. [3]

(iii) (a) First calculate the distance between boatman and source, then by using this, calculate the time taken to reach the sound to the diver.

Given, time of sound to reach at boatman, $t = 3$ s

Velocity of sound in air, $v_a = 300$ m/s

Velocity of sound in water, $v_w = 1440$ m/s

Time taken by diver, $t_d = ?$

Depth of lake, $d_l = v_a \times t$ (as given in question)

$= 300 \times 3 = 900$ m

Time taken by sound in water to reach a diver,

$$t_d = \frac{d_l}{v_w} = \frac{900}{1440} = 0.625 \text{ s}$$ [2]

(b) Given, $\nu = 256$ Hz, $\lambda = 1.3$ m

(I) Using the formula,

$v = \nu\lambda = 256 \times 1.3 = 332.8$ m/s ≈ 333 m/s

(II) Now, new wavelength = 2.6 m

$v = \nu \times \lambda \Rightarrow 333 = \nu \times 2.6$

$$\Rightarrow \quad \nu = \frac{333}{2.6} = 128.07 \text{ Hz}$$

Frequency of above sound is 256 Hz, whereas frequency of this calculated sound is 12.8 Hz, because speed of sound is same. [2]

75. (i) (a) Name the system which enables us to locate underwater objects by transmitting ultrasonic waves and detecting the reflecting impulse.

(b) What are acoustically measurable quantities related to pitch and loudness? [3]

(ii) (a) When a tuning fork (vibrating) is held close to ear, one hears a faint hum. The same (vibrating tuning fork) is held such that its stem is in contact with the table surface, then one hears a loud sound. Explain.

(b) A man standing infront of a vertical cliff fires a gun. He hears the echo after 3.5 s. On moving closer to the cliff by 84 m, he hears the echo after 3 s. Calculate the distance of the cliff from the initial position of the man. [4]

(iii) A rear view mirror of motorbike starts vibrating violently at some particular speed of motorbike.

(a) Why does this happen?

(b) What is the name of the phenomenon taking place?

(c) What could be done to stop the violent vibrations? [3]

Sol. (i) (a) **SONAR** The word **SONAR** stands for **Sound Navigation And Ranging**. It is an apparatus used to find the depth of a sea or to locate the under water things like shoals of fish, shipwrecks, hills, ice bergs, sunken ships, enemy submarines, etc. It uses ultrasonic waves to measure the distance, direction and speed of underwater objects. [1]

(b) Acoustically measurable quantity related to pitch is frequency. Pitch of a sound depends on the frequency of vibration. Greater the frequency of a sound, the higher will be its pitch.

In other words, the faster the vibration of the source, the higher is the frequency and hence higher is the pitch.

Objects of different sizes and conditions vibrates at different frequencies to produce sounds of different pitches. Acoustically measurable quantity related to loudness is amplitude.

If the sound waves have a small amplitude, then sound will be faint or soft but, if waves have a large amplitude, then the sound will be loud. Also, the amplitude of the sound waves depends upon the force with which an object is made to vibrate. [2]

(ii) (a) When a tuning fork is held close to ear, then one hears a faint hum because it produce damped vibration. When the stem of vibrating tuning fork is in contact with the table surface, then table surface starts vibrating with same frequency of tuning force. Hence, loud sound is produced due to resonance. [2]

(b) If v be the speed of sound and x be the distance of cliff from initial position of man, then according to first condition of man

$$\frac{2x}{v} = 3.5 \Rightarrow v = \frac{2x}{3.5} \quad \ldots \text{(i)}$$

When man is moved closer to the cliff by 84 m, then

$$\frac{2(x-84)}{v} = 3$$

$$\Rightarrow \quad v = \frac{2(x-84)}{3} \quad \ldots \text{(ii)}$$

From Eqs. (i) and (ii), we have

$$\frac{2x}{3.5} = \frac{2(x-84)}{3}$$

$$6x = 7x - 588$$

$$\Rightarrow \quad x = 588 \text{ m}$$ [2]

(iii) (a) This happens when the frequency with which piston of the engine is vibrating becomes equal to the natural frequency with which the body of the motorbike is vibrating. [1]

(b) The phenomenon is resonance. [1]

(c) The speed of the vehicle should be changed in order to control this types of violent vibrations. [1]

Chapter Assessment

1 Mark Questions

1. Which of the following does not produce a sound wave?
   (a) A bell ringing under water
   (b) A gun fired in a room with no echoes
   (c) A hammer hitting a block of rubber
   (d) An explosion in outer space

2. The frequency of a source is 20 kHz. The frequency of sound wave produced by it in water and air will be
   (a) same as that of source
   (b) > 20 kHz
   (c) < 20 kHz
   (d) depend upon velocity

3. During night, distant sounds such as that of the traffic and the loudspeakers become louder than during day. This is due to
   (a) reflection of sound waves
   (b) refraction of sound waves
   (c) absence of other sounds
   (d) clear perception of hearing

4. A sound wave is reflected from a brick wall. Compared with the incident wave, the reflected wave has

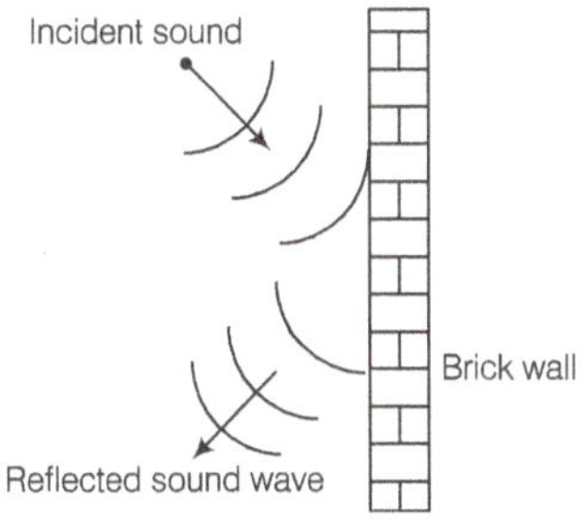

   (a) a greater amplitude
   (b) a shorter wavelength
   (c) the same speed
   (d) the same velocity

5. Pendulums *A*, *B*, *C* and *D* are tied to a flexible string *PQ* and are at rest. Pendulum *C* is disturbed. Which of the following statements is true?

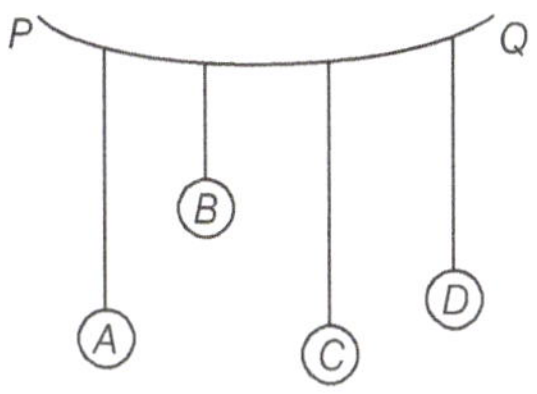

   (a) Only pendulum *C* will start vibrating.
   (b) Pendulums *A*, *B* and *D* will also start vibrating but *A* and *D* will vibrate with the maximum amplitudes.
   (c) Pendulum *A*, *B* and *D* will also start vibrating
   (d) Vibrations of pendulum *C* are forced vibrations.

2 Marks Questions

6. Draw waves of different pitch (low and high).
7. Write two characteristics of noise.
8. Write two uses of SONAR technique.
9. Write a short note on noise pollution.
10. State any two characteristics of a musical sound.

Structured Questions

11. (i) (a) On what factors does the natural frequency of a body depend?
    (b) State condition for a body to execute free vibrations. **[4]**

    (ii) Two musical notes of same pitch and loudness are played on a violin and a piano. The waveforms are as shown in figures below.

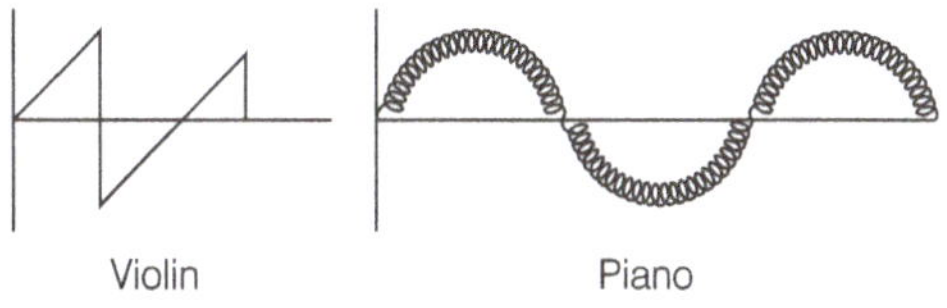

    Explain, why the wave patterns are different? **[4]**

    (iii) (a) Explain natural and forced vibrations with example.
    (b) Explain how do the phenomena of resonance play an important role in machine parts? **[4]**

12. (i) A RADAR is able to detect the reflected waves from an enemy aeroplane, after a time interval of 0.02 ms. If the velocity of the waves is $3 \times 10^8 ms^{-1}$, then calculate the distance of the plane from the RADAR. **[3]**

    (ii) Two waves of the same pitch have their amplitudes in the ratio 3 : 4. What will be the ratio of their
    (a) loudness,
    (b) intensities and
    (c) frequencies **[Ans.** (a) 9: 16 (b) 9 : 16, (c) 1 :1**]**

    (iii) (a) Sometimes when a vehicle is driven at a particular speed, a rattling sound is heard. Explain briefly, why this happens and give the name of the phenomenon taking place?
    (b) Suggest one way be which the rattling sound could be stopped. **[4]**

13. (i) Two men 1.02 km apart stand at the same distance from a vertical hillock. One of them fires a shot and other hears the echo 2s after hearing the direct sound. Find the distance of the man from the hillock, assuming the velocity of sound to be 340 m/s. **[3]**

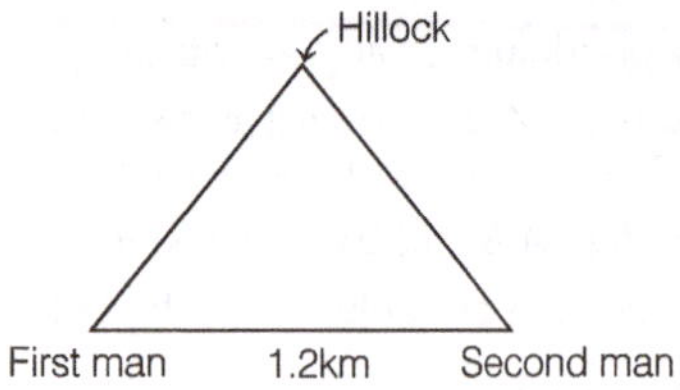

(ii) (a) Write the range of frequency used in echocardiography.

(b) A boy has wooden blocks in his both hands. He claps block together with a regular gap between the claps, so that each clap coincides with the echo of the last clap returning from the wall. Distance between boy and wall is 100m. Time noted for 50 claps is 29s. Calculate the speed of sound. **[3]**

(iii) (a) Two friends were playing on their identical guitars whose string were adjusted to give notes of the same pitch. Will the quality of the two notes be the same? Give a reason for your answer.

(b) Give the relation among wavelength, time period and wave velocity of a wave motion. **[4]**

14. (i) Mention the three conditions for the formation of echo. **[3]**

(ii) Write short note on sympathetic vibrations of pendulums with proper diagram. **[4]**

(iii)

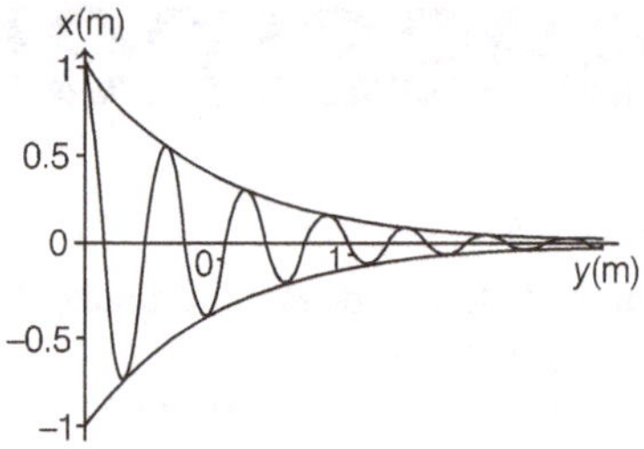

Study the above figure and answer the following

(a) What type of vibration does the above figure represent?

(b) State one reason for which the amplitude of the vibration decreases with time.

(c) Write an example of natural vibrations.

[2022 (Sem-II)] [3]

For Solutions Scan the Code

Olympiad Section*

Brain Teasing Questions of Olympiad Pattern

1 The sound level at a point is increased by 30 dB. By what factor is the pressure amplitude increased?

(a) 16 times (b) 10 times
(c) 8 times (d) 32 times

2 The frequency of a note with high pitch is greater than the frequency of a note with low pitch. Which statement about the note with the high pitch is not correct?

I. It has larger wavelength.
II. It has smaller wavelength.
III. It has greater speed in air.
IV. It has lower speed in air.

(a) Both I and II
(b) Both III and IV
(c) I, II and IV
(d) I, III and IV

3 Given below is a diagram showing a set of percussion instruments (i.e., producing sound on being struck).

Which of the following statements is not true about the percussion instrument?

(a) The surface of the instrument vibrates when struck, thus producing sound.
(b) Louder sound can be produced, if hit with greater force.
(c) When the vibrating surface is touched, then sound will stop.
(d) These instruments can produce only loud sounds.

4 Sound waves of wavelength λ travelling in a medium with a speed of v m/s enter another medium, where its speed is $2v$ m/s. What will be the wavelength sound waves in the second medium?

(a) λ (b) 4λ (c) 2λ (d) 3λ

5 State 'T' for true or 'F' for false.

I. Wave creates disturbance and transmits matter from one place to another.
II. Progressive waves are waves originating from a source such that they never return to the source.
III. In a longitudinal wave, the density of particles is more at a compression.
IV. During a tsunami, the shock waves originating in the ocean bed propagates as both transverse and longitudinal waves.
V. The ripples in water waves are created by the oscillatory movement of water particles.

Codes

	I	II	III	IV	V		I	II	III	IV	V
(a)	F	F	F	T	T	(b)	F	T	T	F	T
(c)	T	F	T	F	T	(d)	F	T	F	T	F

6 The pressure amplitude in sound wave from a radio receiver is 2.0×10^{-2} N/m^2 and the intensity at a point is 5.0×10^{-7} N/m^2. If by turning the volume knob, then the pressure amplitude increased to 2.5×10^{-2} N/m^2. Evaluate the intensity.

(a) 7.8×10^{-6} W/m^2
(b) 7.8×10^{-7} W/m^2
(c) 7.8×10^{-8} W/m^2
(d) 7.8 W/m^2

7. A child hears an echo from a cliff, 4s after the sound from a powerful cracker is produced. How far away is the cliff from the child? (Take, velocity of the sound in air = 330 m/s)

(a) 330 m (b) 660 m
(c) 990 m (d) 165 m

8. A student standing at one end of a closed corridor 86 m long blows a short blast on a whistle and notes a series of echoes. If the time from the blast to the fifth echo is 2.5 s, then the speed of sound is.

(a) 256 m/s (b) 312 m/s
(c) 344 m/s (d) 332 m/s

9. A pendulum has a frequency of 5 vibrations per second. An observer starts the pendulum and fires a gun simultaneously. He hears the echo from a cliff after 8 vibrations of the pendulum. If the velocity of sound in air is 340ms^{-1}, then what is the distance between the cliff and the observer?

(a) 256 m (b) 544 m
(c) 336 m (d) 272 m

10. The natural voices of men, women and children are different and can be distinguished. A student makes three hypotheses
   I. The amplitudes of sound emitted by then are different.
   II. The vocal cords are of different sizes.
   III. The vocal cords vibrate with different frequencies.

   The correct option is

   (a) I only (b) II only
   (c) III only (d) I and II only

11. On a hot, dry summer day of boy is standing between plane parallel vertical cliffs separated by 75m. He is 30 m away from one of the cliffs. Consider speed of sound in air on that hot day to be 360 m/s. The boy claps loudly and hears its successive echoes. The time in seconds at which he hears the first four echoes are respectively :

   (a) $\frac{1}{6}, \frac{1}{4}, \frac{5}{12}, \frac{5}{12}$ (b) $\frac{1}{6}, \frac{1}{4}, \frac{7}{12}, \frac{2}{3}$
   (c) $\frac{1}{4}, \frac{1}{3}, \frac{5}{12}, \frac{7}{12}$ (d) $\frac{1}{6}, \frac{1}{4}, \frac{1}{3}, \frac{5}{12}$

ANSWERS									
1. (d)	**2.** (d)	**3.** (d)	**4.** (c)	**5.** (b)	**6.** (b)	**7.** (b)	**8.** (c)	**9.** (d)	**10.** (b)
11. (a)									

* *These questions may or may not be asked in the examination, have been given just for additional practice required for olympiads Scholarship Exams etc. For detailed explanations refer Page No. 267.*

CHAPTER 08

Electricity

SYLLABUS

- Electric Charge and Electric Current
- Electric Potential and Potential Difference
- Ohm's Law
- Resistance
- Specific Resistance (Resistivity)
- Electromotive Force (emf) of a Cell (ε)
- Combination of Resistors
- Electrical Energy
- Heating Effect of Electric Current
- Electric Power
- House Wiring (Ring System)

Electricity is an essential part of life in today's world. It is a controllable and convenient form of energy. It is being used in almost every sector of modern society like households, commercial, transport and industry, etc., to make life faster and easier.

Electric Charge and Electric Current

Electric Charge

Charge is an intrinsic property of matter which is associated with the sub-atomic particles of the matter, which is defined by excess or deficiency of electrons on a body. A body is said to be **negatively charged**, if it **gains** electrons. e.g. An ebonite rod rubbed with fur acquires negative charge. A body is said to be **positively charged**, if it **loses** electrons.e.g. A glass rod rubbed with a silk cloth acquires positive charge.

The SI unit of electric charge is **coulomb** (C).

The total charge acquired by a body is an integral multiple of magnitude of charge on a single electron. This principle is called **quantisation of charge**.

The possible value of charge on a body can be $q = \pm ne$.

where, q = total charge,

n = number of electrons lost or gained by the body

and e = charge on one electron $(-1.6 \times 10^{-19}\ \text{C})$.

Electric Current

It is defined as the rate of flow of electric charge through any cross-section of a conductor in unit time.

If q amount of charges flows through a conductor in t time, then

$$\text{Electric current, } I = \frac{\text{Charge } (q)}{\text{Time } (t)} = \frac{ne}{t} \qquad (\because q = ne)$$

where, n = number of electrons flowing through the conductor.

The SI unit of electric current is **ampere** (A). It is a scalar quantity. When 1 coulomb of charge flows through any cross-section of a conductor in 1 second, then the electric current flowing through it is said to be 1 ampere.

i.e. $$1 \text{ ampere} = \frac{1 \text{ coulomb}}{1 \text{ second}} \Rightarrow 1\text{ A} = \frac{1\text{C}}{1\text{s}}$$

Smaller units of current are **milliampere** $(1\text{ mA} = 10^{-3}\text{A})$ and **microampere** $(1\mu\text{A} = 10^{-6}\text{A})$.

Note 6.25×10^{18} number of electrons flowing per second through a conductor constitutes a current of 1 A.

Direction of Electric Current

The conventional direction of electric current is taken as opposite to the direction of the flow of electrons (negative charges). In an electric circuit, the current flows from positive terminal of the cell to the negative terminal.

Electric current is a scalar quantity which direction is only conventional.

Example 1. A current of 150 mA flows through a circuit for 2 min. Find the number of electrons that flows through the circuit.

Sol. Given, current, $I = 150$ mA

$$= 150 \times 10^{-3} \text{ A}$$

Time, $t = 2$ min $= 2 \times 60 = 120$ s

Amount of charge, $q = ?$

We know that, $q = I \times t$

$$\Rightarrow \quad q = 150 \times 10^{-3} \times 120$$

$$\Rightarrow \quad q = 18 \text{ C}$$

If n be the number of electrons flowing through the circuit, then $q = ne$

$$\Rightarrow \quad n = \frac{q}{e} = \frac{18}{1.6 \times 10^{-19}} = 11.25 \times 10^{20} \text{ electrons.}$$

Example 2. A total of 6×10^{46} electrons flow through a current carrying conductor when connected through an external power supply for 20 s. Find the value of current in the conductor.

Sol. Given, total number of electrons, $n = 6 \times 10^{46}$

time, $t = 20$ s, current, $I = ?$

We know that, $q = ne$ ...(i)

(from the principle of quantisation of electric charge)

and $I = \frac{q}{t}$ ...(ii)

From Eqs. (i) and (ii), we get

$$I = \frac{ne}{t} = \frac{6 \times 10^{46} \times 1.6 \times 10^{-19}}{20}$$

$$(\because e = 1.6 \times 10^{-19} \text{C})$$

$$= 0.48 \times 10^{27} \text{A}$$

$$= 4.8 \times 10^{26} \text{A}$$

Thus, the current through the conductor is 4.8×10^{26} A.

Electric Potential and Potential Difference

Electric Potential

Electric potential at a point in region of some charge or charges is defined as the amount of work done when a unit positive charge is moved from infinity to that point.

If work done in moving a positive charge q from infinity to the point is W, then electric potential V of that point is

$$V = \frac{W}{q}$$

The SI unit of electric potential is volt (V).
It is a scalar quantity.

Electric Potential Difference (ΔV)

It is defined as work done in moving a unit positive charge from one point to another in region of charges.

Let W be the work done in moving a charge q from point B to point A, then the potential difference $(V_B - V_A)$ between these two points is given by

$$\Delta V = V_B - V_A = \frac{W}{q}$$

The electric potential difference between two points is said to be 1 volt, if 1 joule of work is done in moving 1 coulomb of electric charge from one point to other point.

Thus, $1 \text{ volt} = \frac{1 \text{ joule}}{1 \text{ coulomb}}$

$$\Rightarrow \quad 1\text{V} = \frac{1\text{J}}{1\text{C}} \Rightarrow 1\text{V} = 1\text{J/C} = 1\text{JC}^{-1}$$

Smaller units of electric potential,

$$1 \text{ mV} = 10^{-3}\text{V}, \quad 1\,\mu\text{V} = 10^{-6} \text{ V}$$

Larger units of electric potential,

$$1 \text{ kV} = 10^3 \text{ V}, \quad 1 \text{ MV} = 10^6 \text{ V}$$

Example 3. Calculate the potential difference between two terminals of a battery, if 100 J of work is required to maintain 20 A current for 3 s?

Sol. Given, work done, $W = 100$ J, current $I = 20$ A, time, $t = 3$ s, potential difference, $\Delta V = ?$

We know that, current, $I = \frac{\text{charge}}{\text{time}}$

$\Rightarrow$ Charge, $q = I \times t = 20 \times 3 = 60$ C

The potential difference is given by

$$\Delta V = \frac{W}{q} = \frac{100}{60} = 1.66 \text{ V}$$

Example 4. How much work is done in moving a charge of 2 C from a point of 118 V to a point at 128 V?

Sol. Given, charge, $q = 2$ C

Potential at point A, $V_A = 118$V

Potential at point B, $V_B = 128$ V

Work done, $W = ?$

We know that, potential difference, $\Delta V = V_B - V_A$

$$= 128 - 118 = 10 \text{ V}$$

∴ Work done, $W = \Delta V \times q = 10 \times 2 = 20$ J

So, the work done in moving the charge is 20 J.

Check Your LEARNING...

1 If a body has positive charge, then what does it mean?

2 What is the nature of charged acquired by an ebonite rod when rubbed with a fur?

3 In which direction does current flow in an electric circuit?

4 Is current scalar or vector?

5 The charge on an electron is 1.6×10^{-19}C. Find the number of electrons that will flow per second to constitute a current of 2 A. **Ans.** 1.25×10^{19} electrons

6 If work done in moving a charge of 20 mC from infinity to a point in an electric field is 15 J, then what is the electric potential at this point? **Ans.** 7.5×10^{2} V

Ohm's Law

According to this law, the electric current flowing through a conductor is directly proportional to the potential difference applied across its ends, providing the physical conditions (such as temperature, dimensions, etc.) remain unchanged.

If V is the potential difference applied across the ends of a conductor through which current I flows, then according to Ohm's law,

$$V \propto I \quad \text{(at constant temperature)}$$

or $$V = IR \text{ or } I = \frac{V}{R}$$

where, R is the constant of proportionality called **resistance of the conductor** at a given temperature. From the above formula, it is clear that current is inversely proportional to resistance.

V-I Graph

The graph between the potential difference V and the corresponding current I is found to be a straight line passing through the origin for metallic conductors.

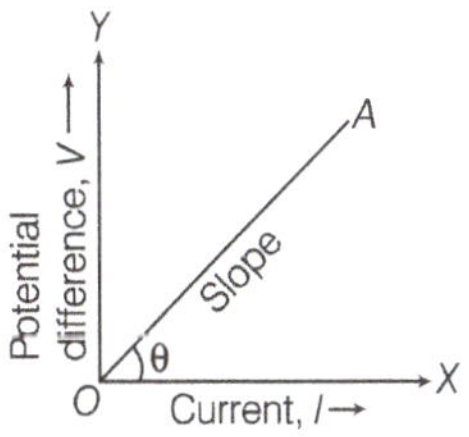

V-I graph for metal conductor

Slope of *V-I* graph, gives resistance,

i.e. $$\text{Slope} = \tan\theta = \frac{\Delta V}{\Delta I} = \frac{V}{I} = \text{Resistance}$$

Ohm's law is obeyed only when the temperature of the conductor remains constant.

Resistance

It is that property of a conductor by virtue of which it opposes/resists the flow of charges through it. Its SI unit is **ohm**, it is represented by the Greek letter Ω.

Resistance of a conductor is given by $R = \frac{V}{I}$.

It is said to be 1 ohm, if a potential difference of 1 volt across the ends of the conductor makes a current of 1 ampere to flow through it.

i.e. $$1 \text{ ohm} = \frac{1 \text{ volt}}{1 \text{ ampere}} \Rightarrow 1\,\Omega = \frac{1\text{ V}}{1\text{ A}} = 1\text{ VA}^{-1}$$

Reciprocal of resistance is known as **conductance (G)**. Its SI unit is siemen (S).

$$\Rightarrow \text{Conductance} = \frac{1}{\text{Resistance}}$$

Example 5. The potential difference between the terminals of an electric heater is 75 V when it draws a current of 5 A from the source. What current will the heater draw, if the potential difference is increased to 150 V?

Sol. Given, potential difference, $V = 75$ V

Current, $I = 5$ A

We know that, $R = \frac{V}{I}$

$$\Rightarrow R = \frac{75}{5} = 15\,\Omega$$

When potential difference is increased to 150 V, then current,

$$I' = \frac{V'}{R} = \frac{150}{15} = 10\text{ A}$$

So, the current through the heater becomes 10 A.

Some Important Terms Related to Resistance

Some important terms related to resistance are as follow

(i) **Resistor** A component in an electric circuit which offers resistance to the flow of electrons constituting electric current is known as resistor. These are used to make those electrical devices, where high resistance is required. It reduces current in a circuit. e.g. Alloys like nichrome, manganin and constantan.

(ii) **Rheostat/Variable Resistance** It is a variable resistor, which is used to control the flow of electric current by manually increasing or decreasing the resistance.

(iii) **Good Conductor** A material which offers low resistance to the flow of electrons or electric current in an electric circuit is known as a good conductor. e.g. Silver, copper, aluminium are good conductors and among these, silver is the best conductor of electricity.

(iv) **Poor Conductor** A material which offers high resistance to the flow of electrons or electric current in an electric circuit is known as poor conductor. e.g. Mercury, lead, stainless steel, alloys of iron and chromium.

(v) **Insulator** A material which offers very high resistance to the flow of electrons or electric current in an electric circuit is known as insulator. e.g. Rubber, dry wood and plastic. Electric current does not flow through it.

(vi) **Semiconductor** A material which offers intermediate resistance (more than conductor and less than insulator) to the flow of electrons or electric current in an electric circuit is known as semiconductor. e.g. Germanium, silicon, etc.

Factors on which the Resistance of a Conductor Depends

The electrical resistance of a conductor depends on the following factors

(i) **Length of the Conductor** The resistance of a conductor R is directly proportional to its length l.

i.e. $$R \propto l \quad \ldots(i)$$

Due to this, when the length of a wire is doubled/halved, then its resistance also gets doubled/halved.

(ii) **Area of Cross-section of the Conductor** The resistance of a conductor R is inversely proportional to its area of cross-section A.

i.e. $$R \propto \frac{1}{A} \quad \ldots(ii)$$

Due to this, when the area of cross-section of wire is doubled, then its resistance gets halved and if area of cross-section of wire is halved, then its resistance will get doubled.

Note When a conductor is stretched (increased its length), then its area of cross-section decreases accordingly but the volume (i.e., area × length) of the conductor remains the same.

(iii) **Nature of the Material of the Conductor** The resistance of a conductor depends on the nature of the material of which it is made. Some materials have low resistance, whereas others have high resistance.

Hence, from Eqs. (i) and (ii), we can write

$$R \propto \frac{l}{A}$$

or $$R = \rho \frac{l}{A}$$

where, ρ is the constant of proportionality called **resistivity** or **specific resistance** (discussed in later section) of the conductor.

(iv) **Effects of Temperature** With the increase in the temperature of a conductor, the random motion of the electrons also increases. Due to this, the collisions between the electrons and the positive ions also increases which opposes the movement of electrons. Therefore, the resistance of a conductor also increases with the increase in its temperature.

Note With rise in temperature, resistance of semiconductors and electrolytes decreases and for alloys, it increases.

Example 6. A wire of given material having length l and area of cross-section A has a resistance of $10\,\Omega$. What would be the resistance of another wire of the same material having length $l/4$ and area of cross-section $2.5A$?

Sol. For first wire, length = l, area of cross-section = A and resistance, $R_1 = 10\,\Omega$

i.e. $$R_1 = \frac{\rho l}{A} = 10\,\Omega$$

$$\Rightarrow \quad \rho = \frac{10A}{l} \quad \ldots(i)$$

For second wire, length = $l/4$, area of cross-section = $2.5\,A$ and resistance,

$$R_2 = \rho \frac{l/4}{2.5A} = \frac{10A}{l} \cdot \frac{l}{4 \times 2.5A} = 1\,\Omega \quad \text{[from Eq. (i)]}$$

So, the resistance of that wire is $1\,\Omega$.

Ohmic and Non-Ohmic Resistors

The conductor which obeys Ohm's law is called **ohmic resistor** (or **linear resistance**). e.g. Silver, nichrome, copper, iron, etc. The V-I graph for these resistor is a straight line passing through the origin.

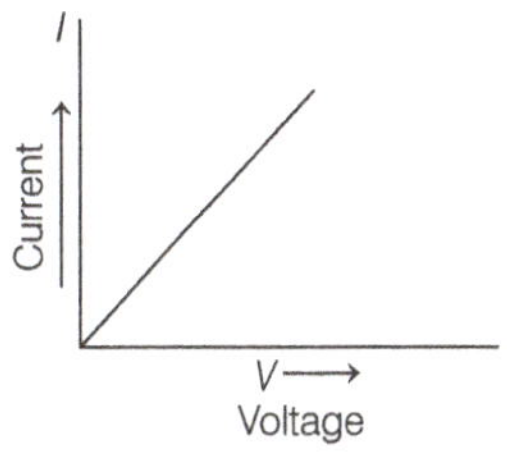

V-I graph of ohmic resistors

Whereas those conductor which does not obey Ohm's law is known as **non-ohmic resistor** (or **non-linear resistance**). e.g. Triode valve, junction diode, transistor, etc. The *V-I* graph for these resistors is a curve line.

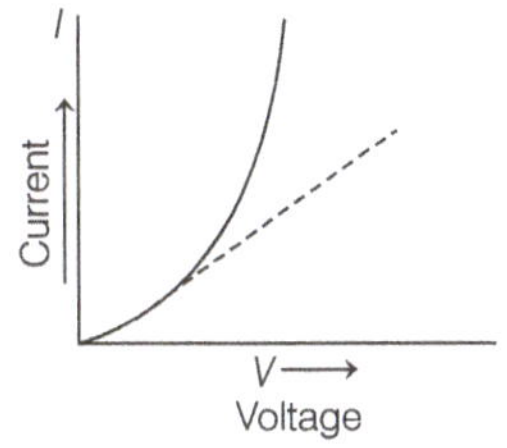

V-I Graph of non-ohmic resistor

Also, it is not necessary for the graph of non-ohmic resistors to pass through the origin.

Specific Resistance (Resistivity)

It is defined as the resistance of a conductor of unit length and unit area of cross-section. Its SI unit is ohm-metre (Ω-m).

The resistivity of a material does not depend on its length or thickness but depends on the nature of the substance and temperature. It is a characteristic property of the material of the conductor and varies only, if its temperature changes. Insulators such as glass, rubber, ebonite, etc., have very high resistivity (10^{12} to $10^{17}\,\Omega$-m), while conductors have very low resistivity (10^{-8} to $10^{-6}\,\Omega$-m).

Alloys have higher resistivity than that of their constituent metals. They are used to make heating elements of devices such as electric iron, heaters, etc. This is because they do not oxidise easily at high temperatures. The high resistivity of alloys also allow dissipation of electrical energy in the form of heat. Tungsten is used almost exclusively for filaments of electric bulbs, whereas copper and aluminium are generally used for electrical transmission lines.

Conductivity

It is defined as the reciprocal of resistivity of a conductor. Its SI unit is mho per metre ($\Omega^{-1}m^{-1}$) or siemen per metre (S/m). It is expressed as

$$\sigma = \frac{1}{\rho}$$

Example 7. Resistance of a metal wire of length 2 m is 30 Ω at temperature 25°C. If the diameter of the wire is 0.6 mm, then what will be the resistivity of the metal at that temperature?

Sol. Given, length of wire, $l = 2$ m

Resistance, $R = 30\,\Omega$

Temperature, $T = 25°$ C

Diameter of wire, $d = 0.6$ mm $= 6 \times 10^{-4}$ m

Resistivity of the wire, $\rho = ?$

We know that, $\rho = \frac{RA}{l} = \frac{R\pi d^2}{4l}$ $\left(\because A = \frac{\pi d^2}{4}\right)$

$$= \frac{30 \times \pi \times (6 \times 10^{-4})^2}{4 \times 2} = 4.24 \times 10^{-6}\,\Omega\text{-m}$$

The resistivity of the metal at 25°C is $4.24 \times 10^{-6}\,\Omega$-m.

Superconductors

The resistance of certain metal or alloy, e.g. mercury, lead, niobium, etc., drop to zero, when they are cooled below a certain temperature (called **critical temperature**). These conductors are known as **superconductors**. In these types of conductors, once a current starts flowing through them, they persist it even when there is no potential difference across them.

Check Your LEARNING...

1. Keeping the potential difference constant, the resistance of a circuit is halved. By how much, does the current change?
2. The potential difference across a wire is 75 V and its electric resistance is 30 Ω. Find out the electric current through the wire. [*Ans.* 2.5 A]
3. Does resistance of a conducting wire depend on temperature?
4. What is the difference between a good conductor and a poor conductor? Give two examples of each.
5. If the length of a wire is halved and its cross-sectional area is doubled, then what would be the resistance of the wire? (Given, initially the resistance of the wire is *R*) [*Ans.* *R*/4]
6. What is the difference between ohmic and non-ohmic resistors?
7. How does resistivity of a conductor change if its length is increased to double?
8. Name the temperature below which mercury behaves as superconductor.

Electromotive Force (emf) of a Cell (ε)

Electric cell has to do some work in maintaining the current through a circuit. The work done by the cell in moving unit positive charge through the whole circuit (including the cell) is called the electromotive force (emf) of the cell. If during the flow of q coulomb of charge in an electric circuit, the work done by the cell is W, then

$$\text{emf of the cell, } \varepsilon = \frac{W}{q}$$

Its unit is joule/coulomb or volt.
If $W = 1$ joule and $q = 1$ coulomb, then $\varepsilon = 1$ volt, i.e. if in the flow of 1 coulomb of charge, the work done by the cell is 1 joule, then the emf of the cell is 1 volt.

Internal Resistance (r)

It is defined as the resistance offered by the electrolyte of the cell to the flow of current through it. It is denoted by r. Its unit is also ohm.
Internal resistance of a cell depends on the following factors

(i) It is directly proportional to the separation between the two plates of the cell.
(ii) It is inversely proportional to the plate area dipped into the electrolyte.
(iii) It depends on the nature, concentration and temperature of the electrolyte and increases with increase in concentration and decreases with increase in temperature of electrolyte.

Terminal Potential Difference (V)

Terminal potential difference of a cell is defined as the potential difference between the two terminals of the cell in a closed circuit (i.e. when current I is drawn from the cell). It is represented by V and its unit is volt. It is always less than the emf of the cell.

i.e. $$V = \varepsilon - Ir$$

Combination of Resistors

Two or more resistors can be connected with each other by different combination methods in order to achieve the desired equivalent resistance in a particular circuit.
There are two methods of joining the resistors together which are as follows

Series Combination of Resistors

When two or more resistors are connected end-to -end, then they are said to be connected in series. The following figure shows the connection of resistors in series

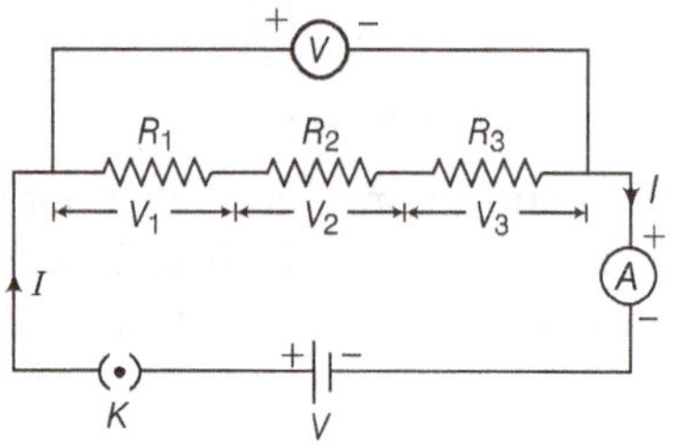

Series combination of resistors

In the given figure, the potential drop across R_1, R_2 and R_3 is V_1, V_2 and V_3. An ammeter is connected in the series.

The symbol —(V)—is of the voltmeter, which is signifying the potential drop in the circuit. An applied potential V produces current I in the resistors and R_1, R_2 and R_3 causing a potential drop V_1, V_2 and V_3 respectively, through each resistor.

Total potential, $V = V_1 + V_2 + V_3$

By Ohm's law, $V_1 = IR_1$, $V_2 = IR_2$ and $V_3 = IR_3$

Thus, $$V = V_1 + V_2 + V_3 = IR_1 + IR_2 + IR_3$$

$$\Rightarrow \quad V = I(R_1 + R_2 + R_3)$$

If R is the equivalent resistance and $V = IR$, hence

$$IR = I(R_1 + R_2 + R_3)$$

$$\Rightarrow \quad R = R_1 + R_2 + R_3$$

Some important points regarding series combination of resistors are as follow

(i) The equivalent resistance is equal to the sum of the individual resistances.
(ii) The equivalent resistance is thus greater than the resistance of either resistor. This is also known as **maximum effective resistance.**
(iii) The current through each resistor is same.
(iv) The potential difference across each resistor is different.

Example 8. Study the following electric circuit. Find the readings of (i) the ammeter and (ii) the voltmeter.

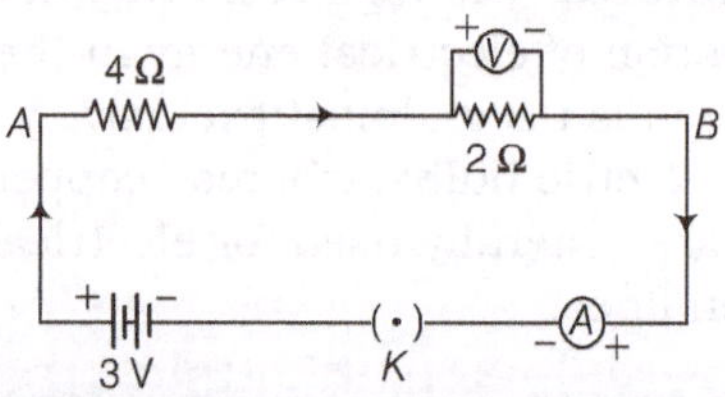

Sol. In the given circuit, the resistance of 4 Ω and 2 Ω are connected in series, so equivalent resistance of the circuit,

$$R = R_1 + R_2 = 4\ \Omega + 2\ \Omega = 6\ \Omega$$

(i) Total current flowing in the circuit

$$(I) = \frac{\text{Potential difference } (V)}{\text{Total resistance } (R)} = \frac{3}{6} = 0.5\text{ A}$$

In series combination, current flowing through each component of the circuit is same and is equal to the total current flowing in the circuit. So, 0.5 A current will flow through the ammeter, therefore its reading will be 0.5 A.

(ii) Reading of voltmeter = Potential difference across 2 Ω bulb

$$\therefore \quad V = IR = 0.5 \times 2 = 1\text{ V}$$

($\because$ current flowing through the 2 Ω resistor is 0.5 A)

Example 9. Three resistors of 5 Ω, 10 Ω and 15 Ω are connected in series with a 12 V power supply. Calculate their combined resistance, the current that flows in the circuit and in each resistor and the potential difference across each resistor.

Sol. Given, $R_1 = 5\ \Omega$, $R_2 = 10\ \Omega$, $R_3 = 15\ \Omega$, $V = 12\text{ V}$, $R = ?$, $I = ?$ and $V_1, V_2, V_3 = ?$

According to question, the three resistors are connected in series combination, then equivalent resistance,

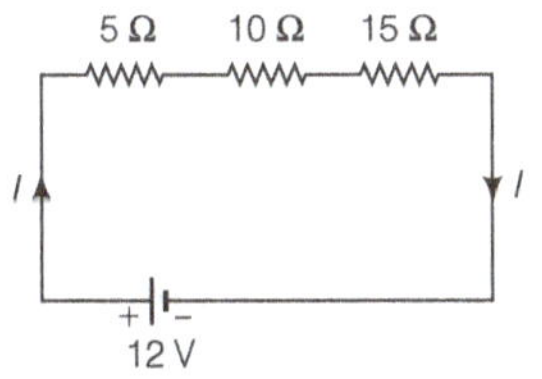

$$R = R_1 + R_2 + R_3$$
$$= 5 + 10 + 15 = 30\ \Omega$$

$\therefore$ The current flowing through the circuit

$$(I) = \frac{\text{Potential of power supply } (V)}{\text{Total resistance of the circuit } (R)}$$
$$= \frac{12}{30} = \frac{2}{5} = 0.4\text{ A}$$

In series combination, the current flowing through each resistor is equal to total current flowing through the circuit. Therefore, current flowing through each resistor is 0.4 A.

$\therefore$ Potential difference across first resistor,

$$V_1 = IR_1$$
$$= 0.4 \times 5 = 2\text{ V}$$

Potential difference across second resistor,

$$V_2 = IR_2$$
$$= 0.4 \times 10 = 4\text{ V}$$

and potential difference across third resistor,

$$V_3 = 0.4 \times 15 = 6\text{ V}$$

Disadvantages of Series Combination

(i) In series combination, if any of the components fails to work, the circuit will break and then none of the components will be able to operate.

(ii) It is not possible to connect a bulb and a heater in series because they need different values of current to operate properly. Due to this, we do not use series circuit.

Parallel Combination of Resistors

When two or more resistors are connected simultaneously between two points, then they form a parallel combination.

The following figure shows the connection of resistors in parallel

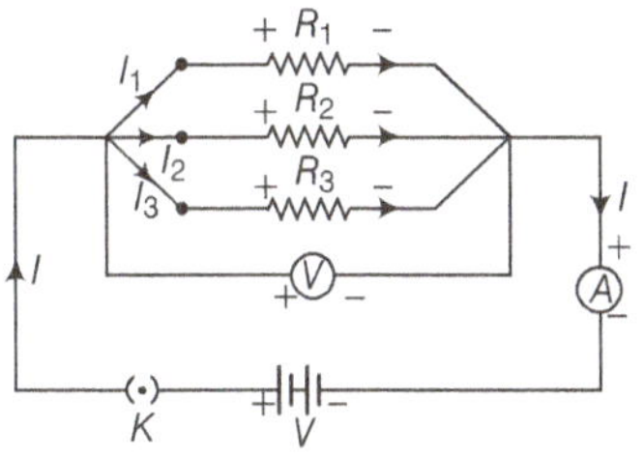

Parallel combination of resistors

An applied potential V produces current I_1 in R_1, I_2 in R_2 and I_3 in R_3.

Total current, $I = I_1 + I_2 + I_3$ ...(i)

By Ohm's law, $I_1 = \dfrac{V}{R_1}$, $I_2 = \dfrac{V}{R_2}$

and $I_3 = \dfrac{V}{R_3}$

If R is the equivalent resistance, then $I = \dfrac{V}{R}$

Thus, $$\frac{V}{R} = \frac{V}{R_1} + \frac{V}{R_2} + \frac{V}{R_3} \qquad \text{[from Eq. (i)]}$$

$$\Rightarrow \quad \frac{V}{R} = V\left(\frac{1}{R_1} + \frac{1}{R_2} + \frac{1}{R_3}\right)$$

$$\Rightarrow \quad \frac{1}{R} = \frac{1}{R_1} + \frac{1}{R_2} + \frac{1}{R_3}$$

Some important points regarding parallel combination of resistors are as follow

(i) The reciprocal of equivalent resistance is equal to the sum of the reciprocal of individual resistances.

(ii) The equivalent resistance is less than the resistance of either resistor. This is also known as **minimum effective resistance.**

(iii) The current from the source is greater than the current through either resistor.

(iv) The potential difference across each resistor is same.

Note For n equal resistances combined in series (equivalent resistance R_s) and in parallel (equivalent resistance R_p), then

$$\frac{R_s}{R_p} = n^2$$

Example 10. Two 40 Ω resistors and a 20 Ω resistor are all connected in parallel with a 12 V power supply. Calculate their effective resistance and the current through each resistor. What is the current flowing through the supply?

Sol. Given, $R_1 = 40\ \Omega$, $R_2 = 40\ \Omega$, $R_3 = 20\ \Omega$, $V = 12\text{V}$, $R = ?$, $I, I_1, I_2, I_3 = ?$

According to circuit, the three resistors are connected in parallel combination, then effective resistance,

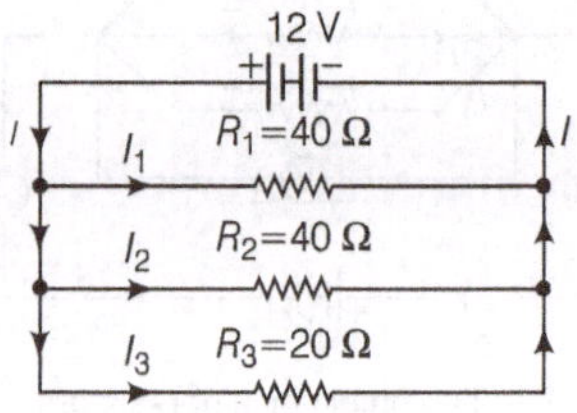

$$\frac{1}{R} = \frac{1}{R_1} + \frac{1}{R_2} + \frac{1}{R_3}$$

$$= \frac{1}{40} + \frac{1}{40} + \frac{1}{20}$$

$$= \frac{1+1+2}{40} = \frac{4}{40} = \frac{1}{10}$$

$$\Rightarrow \quad R = 10\ \Omega$$

So, the three resistors together have an effective resistance of 10 Ω.

Each resistor has a potential difference of 12 V across it.

As in parallel combination, the potential difference across each resistance is equal to the total potential difference applied on the combination.

Also, current, $I = \frac{\text{potential difference } (V)}{\text{resistance}(R)}$

Current through 40 Ω resistor, $I_1 = \frac{12}{40} = 0.3\text{ A}$

Also, $I_2 = 0.3\text{ A}$

Current through 20 Ω resistor, $I_3 = \frac{12}{20} = 0.6\text{ A}$

∴ Current throught the supply,

$$I = I_1 + I_2 + I_3 = 0.3\text{ A} + 0.3\text{ A} + 0.6\text{ A} = 1.2\text{ A}$$

Applications of Parallel Combination in Daily Life

Parallel combination of resistances is very useful in circuits used in daily life. This is because, these circuits have components of different resistances which requires different amounts of current.

Parallel circuit divides the current among the components (electrical gadgets), so that they can have necessary amount of current to operate properly. This is the reason of connecting electrical appliances in parallel combination in household circuit.

Mixed Combination of Resistors

In this type of combination, circuit has some resistances connected in series combination and some in parallel combination. This type of combination is also called **complex circuit.**

While solving problems of mixed combination of resistances, there are many points to be considered which are given as below

(i) Mixed combination circuit can always be reduced to a simple circuit containing only one resistor. For this, examine the given circuit and replace the resistors that are connected in parallel or in series with their equivalent resistances.

(ii) Draw the new circuit after making the changes and repeat the same procedure again as discussed above, till a simple circuit is obtained.

(iii) If the current through or potential difference across a resistor in the complex circuit is to be found, then start with the simple circuit reduced from the complex circuit and gradually work your way back through the circuits, using $V = IR$.

(iv) While calculating the equivalent resistance, do not consider the battery, if its resistance is not given but, if its resistance is given, then consider it and treat it as an individual resistor.

Example 11. Consider the circuit diagram as given below:

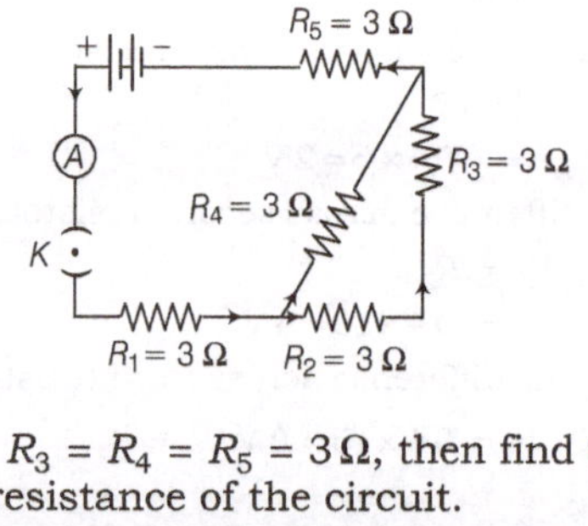

If $R_1 = R_2 = R_3 = R_4 = R_5 = 3\ \Omega$, then find the equivalent resistance of the circuit.

Sol. From the given combination, it can be observed that R_2 and R_3 are in series order. As current through R_2 and R_3 is same, so their equivalent resistance is $R' = R_2 + R_3 = 3\,\Omega + 3\,\Omega = 6\,\Omega$. Now, the given circuit can be redrawn as shown below

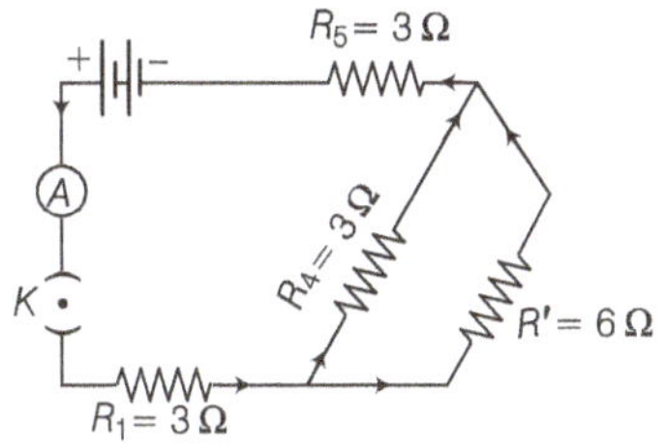

Now, it can be seen that R_4 and R' are in parallel combination. As, currents through R_4 and R' are different. So, their equivalent resistance can be calculated as below

$$\frac{1}{R''} = \frac{1}{R'} + \frac{1}{R_4}$$

$$= \frac{1}{6} + \frac{1}{3} = \frac{1+2}{6} = \frac{3}{6} = \frac{1}{2}$$

$\therefore \quad R'' = 2\,\Omega$

Now, the given circuit can be redrawn as shown below

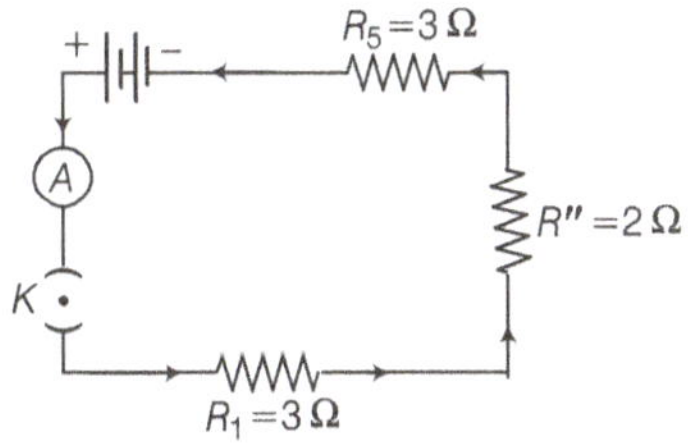

Now, it is clear from the diagram that all the resistances R_5, R'' and R_1 are in series combination. As, current through R_1, R'' and R_5 is same.

$\therefore$ Equivalent resistance of the circuit,

$$R = R_5 + R'' + R_1$$

$$= 3\,\Omega + 2\,\Omega + 3\,\Omega = 8\,\Omega$$

Example 12. Find the equivalent resistance of the following circuit. Also, find the current and potential at each resistor.

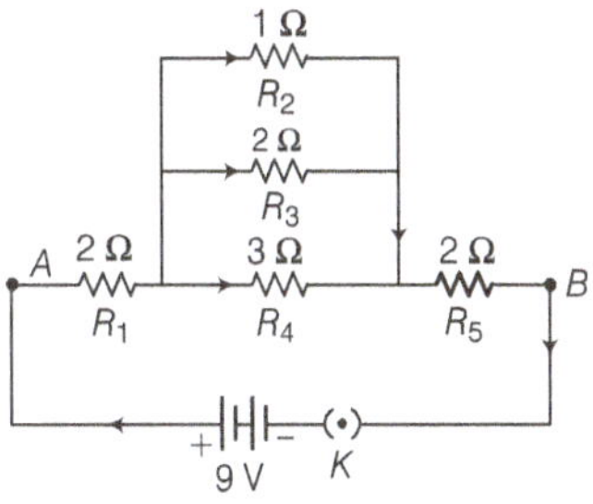

Sol. In the given circuit, R_2, R_3 and R_4 are in parallel combination. As, currents through R_2, R_3 and R_4 are different. Let equivalent resistance of R_2, R_3 and R_4 be R'.

$$\frac{1}{R'} = \frac{1}{R_2} + \frac{1}{R_3} + \frac{1}{R_4}$$

$$= \frac{1}{1} + \frac{1}{2} + \frac{1}{3}$$

$$= \frac{6+3+2}{6} = \frac{11}{6}$$

$\Rightarrow \quad R' = \frac{6}{11}\,\Omega$

Now, the given circuit can be redrawn as shown below

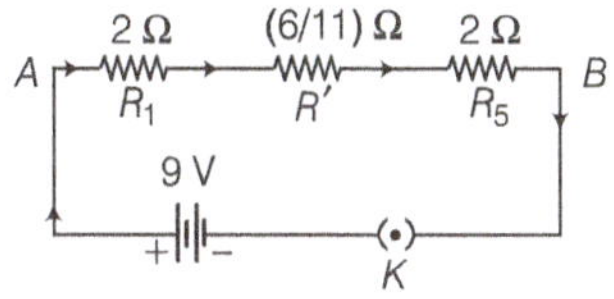

Now, R_1, R' and R_5 are in series combination.
As, current through R_1, R' and R_5 is same.
So, equivalent resistance of the whole circuit,

$$R = R_1 + R' + R_5 = 2 + \frac{6}{11} + 2$$

$$= \frac{22+6+22}{11} = \frac{50}{11}\,\Omega$$

Now, total current flowing through the circuit,

$$I = \frac{V}{R} = \frac{9}{\frac{50}{11}} = \frac{99}{50} \approx 2\text{ A}$$

Current through R_1 and R_5 will be same as these are in series combination and will be equal to the total current flowing through the circuit.

$\therefore \quad I = I_1 = I_5 = 2\text{ A}$

Potential drop at R_1, $V_1 = I_1 R_1 = 2 \times 2 = 4\text{ V}$

Potential drop at R_5, $V_5 = I_5 R_5 = 2 \times 2 = 4\text{ V}$

Now, potential drop at R', V' can be calculated as

$$V = V_1 + V_5 + V'$$

$\Rightarrow \quad 9 = 4 + 4 + V'$

$\Rightarrow \quad V' = 1\text{ V}$

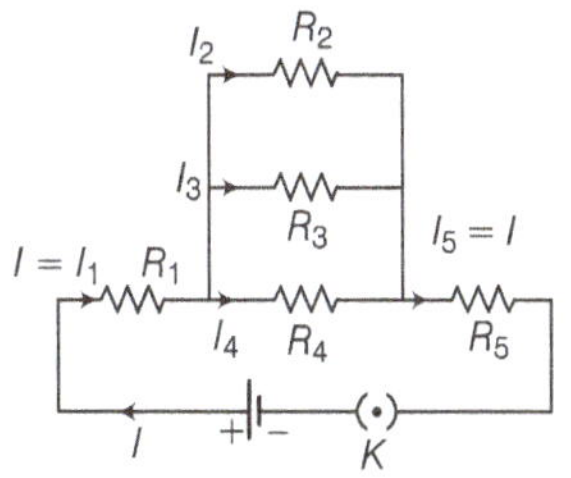

As R_2, R_3 and R_4 are in parallel combination, so potential drop at all resistances will be same as 1 V.

$$V_2 = V_3 = V_4 = V' = 1\text{ V}$$

Current through R_2, $I_2 = \frac{V_2}{R_2} = \frac{V'}{R_2} = \frac{1}{1} = 1$ A

Similarly, $I_3 = \frac{V_3}{R_3} = \frac{V'}{R_3} = \frac{1}{2} = 0.5$ A

and $I_4 = \frac{V_4}{R_4} = \frac{V'}{R_4} = \frac{1}{3} = 0.33$ A

Check Your LEARNING...

1 In which type of combination of different resistors, it will have an equal value of electric current through each resistor?

2 Which type of combination of resistors, will have equivalent resistance less than the least resistance?

3 If different resistors have same value of electric potential across them, then in which way they are connected to each other?

4 Four resistors of equal resistance *R* are connected in parellel, find the equivalent resistance. *Ans.* $R/4$

5 What do you understand by mixed combination of resistance?

6 Three resistances are connected as shown in the figure. Determine the total resistance between *A* and *B*.

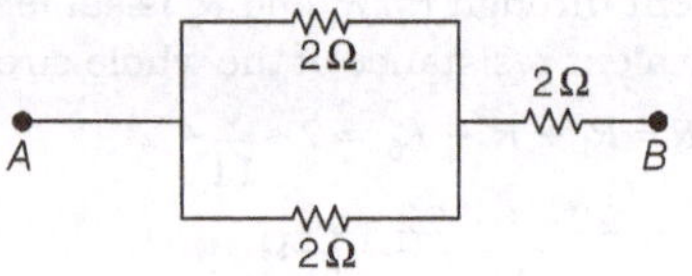

Ans. 3 Ω

Electrical Energy

Now-a-days electricity is used in doing many works through different instruments. Thus, electric energy can be defined as the ability of electric current to do some work through different instrument.

Some examples of electric energy are given below

(i) When an electric current is passed through a heating element of a heater, oven, etc., it gets heated up due to its resistance. Thus, electrical energy is converted into heat energy.

(ii) When an electric current is passed through an electrical motor, its coil begin to rotate and simultaneously the coil gets heated up slightly. The electrical energy is converted into mechanical energy and sometimes into heat energy.

(iii) When an electric current is passed through an electric lamp, the filament of the bulb gets heated and it glows. Thus, electrical energy is converted into heat and light energy.

(iv) When the output of a microphone which is in the form of electric pulses is passed to a loud speaker, thus the electrical energy is converted into sound energy.

Measurement of Electrical Energy

Assuming a conductor as a resistance wire which resists the flow of current through it. So, work must be done by the current source for continuous flow of the current. Now, we calculate the work done by the source when the current *I* flows through a wire of resistance *R*. This work done will be equal to the electric energy.

When an electric charge *q* moves against a potential difference *V*, then amount of work done,

$$W = q \times V \quad \ldots\text{(i)}$$

From definition of current, we know that

$$I = \frac{q}{t} \text{ or } q = I \times t \quad \ldots\text{(ii)}$$

$$\text{From Ohm's law, } \frac{V}{I} = R \text{ or } V = IR \quad \ldots\text{(iii)}$$

Substituting the values of *q* and *V* in Eq. (i), we get

$$W = (I \times t) \times IR = I^2Rt = VIt = \frac{V^2t}{R}$$

$$\therefore \quad \text{Electric energy, } E = W = I^2Rt = VIt = \frac{V^2t}{R}$$

SI unit of electrical energy is joule (J),
where, 1 joule = 1 volt × 1 ampere × 1 second

Commercial Unit of Electrical Energy

To measure the electrical energy consumed commercially, joule is not sufficient. So, to express electrical energy consumed commercially a special unit **kilowatt hour** is used in place of joule. It is also called 1 unit of electrical energy. 1 kilowatt hour or 1 unit of electrical energy is the amount of energy dissipated in 1 hour in a circuit, when the electric power in the circuit is 1 kilowatt.

1 kilowatt hour (kWh)

$$= 3.6 \times 10^6 \text{ joule (J)} = 3.6 \times 10^{13} \text{ erg}$$

Heating Effect of Electric Current

When an electric current is passed through a high resistance wire like nichrome wire, then the wire becomes very hot and produces heat. This is called the heating effect of current.

This effect is obtained by the transformation of electrical energy into heat energy.

e.g. An electric fan becomes warm, if it is used continuously for longer time, etc.

Assuming that all electrical work done or electrical energy consumed is converted into heat energy, i.e. heat produced. So, heat produced is given by

$$H = I^2 \times R \times t$$

Thus, it is known as **Joule's law of heating.**

This law implies that heat produced in a resistor is

(i) directly proportional to the square of current for a given resistance.

(ii) directly proportional to the resistance for a given current.

(iii) directly proportional to the time for which the current flows through the resistor.

Electric Power

It is defined as the amount of electric energy consumed in a circuit per unit time.

If W be the amount of electric energy consumed in a circuit in t seconds, then the electric power is given by

$$P = \frac{W}{t}$$

But W = electric energy = $Vq = VIt$ $\quad (\because q = It)$

$$\therefore \quad P = \frac{VIt}{t}$$

$$\Rightarrow \quad P = VI$$

According to Ohm's law, $V = IR$

$$\therefore \quad P = IR \times I = I^2R$$

$$\Rightarrow \quad = \frac{V^2}{R} \qquad \left(\because I = \frac{V}{R}\right)$$

Thus, $P = VI = I^2R = \dfrac{V^2}{R}$

The SI unit of electric power is watt (W).

Electric power is said to be 1 watt, if 1 ampere current flows through a circuit having 1 volt potential difference.

i.e. 1 watt = 1 volt × 1 ampere = 1 VA

Note
- Bigger units of power are as given below:
  1 kilowatt (kW) = 10^3 W
  1 megawatt (MW) = 10^6 W
  1 gigawatt (GW) = 10^9 W
- Practical unit of power is horse power.
  1 HP = 746 W
- Number of units consumed by electric appliances is
  $= \dfrac{\text{watt} \times \text{hours}}{1000}$

Power Rating of Common Appliances

The electrical appliances such as electric bulb, geyser bulb, heater, etc., are rated with power and voltage. e.g., An electric bulb is rated as 100W-220V, etc.

With the help of the rating of the appliances, we calculate the following two quantities such as

(i) The resistance of the filament of the bulb (coil),

$$R = \frac{V^2}{P} = \frac{(\text{Voltage rating of appliance})^2}{\text{Power rating of appliance}}$$

This is the resistance of the element (filament) of an appliance (bulb) while in use.

(ii) Safe limit of current through the filament of the bulb (coil).

$$I = \frac{P}{V} = \frac{\text{Power rating of appliance}}{\text{Voltage rating of appliance}}$$

If the current exceeds this value, the power supplied at the rated voltage V exceeds the rated power and the appliance gets damaged.

Household Consumption of Electrical Energy

An electric meter measures the electrical energy consumed by the different appliances at home. It always calculate the energy in kWh.

∴ The electrical energy consumed by a household appliance in a certain time (t) is given as

Energy (in kWh) = Power (in kW) × Time (in h)

$$= \frac{\text{Power (in W)} \times \text{Time (in h)}}{1000}$$

$$= \frac{V(\text{volt}) \times I(\text{ampere}) \times t(\text{hour})}{1000}$$

Now, cost of the electricity will be given as,

Cost of electricity = Energy consumed (in kWh) × Rate in rupees per unit

Example 13. An electric fan runs from the 220 V mains. The current flowing through it is 0.5 A. At what rate is the electrical energy transformed by the fan? How much energy is transformed in 2 min?

Sol. Given, potential difference, $V = 220$ V, current, $I = 0.5$ A, time, $t = 2 \text{ min} = 120$ s, power, $P = ?$

We know that,

Power, $P = VI = 220 \times 0.5 = 110$ W

and $E = Pt = 110 \times 120 = 13200$ J

So, the power of fan is 110 W and it transforms 13200 J of energy.

Example 14. An electric iron of resistance 20 Ω takes a current of 5 A. Calculate the heat developed in 0.5 min.

Sol. Given, resistance, $R = 20\,\Omega$, Current, $I = 5$ A

Time, $t = 0.5$ min $= 0.5 \times 60 = 30$ s

Heat, $H = ?$

We know that, heat, $H = I^2Rt$

$$H = (5)^2 \times 20 \times 30$$
$$= 25 \times 20 \times 30 = 15000\text{ J}$$
$$= 1.5 \times 10^4\text{ J}$$

So, the heat developed is 1.5×10^4 J.

Example 15. 200 J of heat is produced in 10 s in a 5 Ω resistance. Find the potential difference across the resistor.

Sol. Given, heat, $H = 200$ J, resistance, $R = 5\,\Omega$,

time, $t = 10$ s, potential difference, $V = ?$

We know that,

heat, $H = I^2Rt \Rightarrow I = \sqrt{\dfrac{H}{Rt}} = \sqrt{\dfrac{200}{5 \times 10}} = 2\text{ A}$

So, the potential difference across the resistor is

$$V = IR \quad \text{(by Ohm's law)}$$
$$= 2 \times 5 = 10\text{ V}$$

Example 16. An electric refrigerator rated 500 W operates 6 hours/day. What is the cost of the energy to operate it for 30 days at ₹4.5 per kWh?

Sol. Energy consumed by refrigerator in 30 days

$$= 500\text{W} \times 6\frac{\text{hour}}{\text{day}} \times 30\text{ days}$$
$$= 90000\text{ Wh} = 90\text{ kWh}$$

∴ Cost of energy to operate the refrigerator for 30 days

$$= 90\text{ kWh} \times ₹\,4.5\text{ per kWh} = ₹\,405$$

Check Your LEARNING...

1. Explain, why the current that makes the heater element very hot, only slightly warms the connecting wires leading to the heater?
2. An electric heater of resistance 500 Ω is connected to a mains supply for 30 min. If 15 A current flows through the filament of the heater, then calculate the heat energy produced in the heater. *Ans.* 20.25×10^7 J
3. What is the maximum power in kilowatts of the appliance that can be connected safely to a 13A, 230V mains socket? *Ans.* 2.99 kW
4. Power of a lamp is 60W. Find the energy in joules consumed by it in 1 s. *Ans.* 60 J
5. What is the heating effect of electric current?
6. What is the safe limit of current through the filament of the bulb?

House Wiring (Ring System)

In a house, the wiring is commonly done by the ring system. A ring system of wiring connecting a lamp, a socket with switch and a fan with regulator is shown in the figure given below.

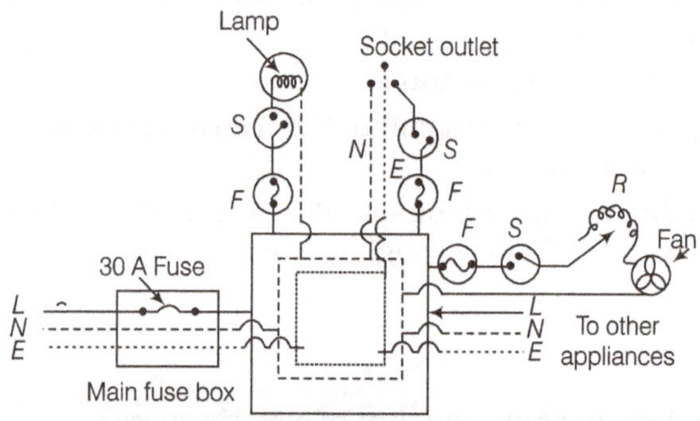

A schematic diagram of main circuit

In this system, the wires starting from the main fuse box run around all the rooms of the house and then come back to the fuse box again forming the ring. The fuse box contains a fuse of rating about 30 A for each ring circuit.

Advantages of the Ring System

The advantages of the ring system are given as

(i) Each appliance can operate independently, without affecting the other appliances connected in the system.

(ii) If a new appliance has been installed in a room, a new line up to the distribution box is not required but it can be directly connected to the ring circuit of the room.

Power Distribution

The electric power is generated at the power generating stations. The power from these stations is transmitted over long distances at a high voltage to minimise the loss of energy in form of heat in the line wires used for transmission.

This is because at high voltages the value of current is very less. Therefore, from the relation of the heating effect produced, i.e. $H = I^2RT$, will also be less at low current. Hence, the energy loss will be least.

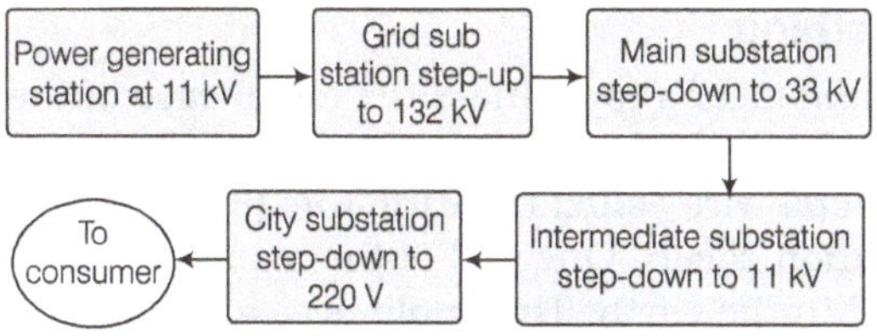

Block diagram representing the power distribution

Components of Household Electric Circuit

1. Main Circuit

Electricity generated at power stations is brought to our homes by two thick copper or aluminium wires. One of these is called **live wire** (in red insulation cover), which is at a potential of 220 V with a frequency of 50 Hz and the other is called **neutral wire** (in black insulation cover), which is at zero potential. There is also a third wire, i.e. earth wire.

The neutral and the earth wires are connected together at the local substation, so that both the wire are at the same potential.

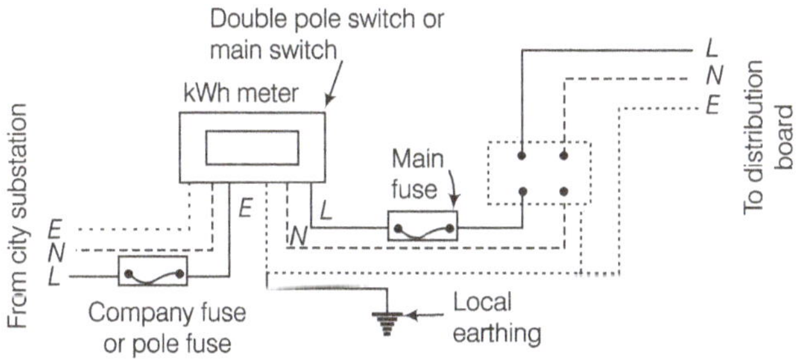

A schematic diagram of main circuit

The live wire carries current from the source to the distribution board while the neutral wire is for the return path of current. The connections are made to the distribution board through a main fuse and a main switch.

The main fuse is connected in the live wire while the main switch is connected in the live and neutral wires. The main switch is a double pole switch. It has an iron covering.

The covering is earthed. This switch is used to cut the connections of the live as well as the neutral wires. Usually, there are two separate circuits in a house, the lighting circuit with a 5 A fuse (bulbs, fans, etc) and the power circuit with a 15 A fuse (geysers, air coolers, etc.).

2. Switch

In an electrical circuit, switch is used to start or stop the flow of current.

Depending upon work, construction and current rating, switches are classified as given below

(i) **Main Switch** It is a two poles or three poles single way switch. Normally, it is DPIC or TPIC type switch. They are used to switch ON/OFF the main line current.

It is basically of two types

(a) **Double Poles Iron Clad or DPIC Switch**
It works as a main switch for single phase AC or DC. A fuse is connected in series with each line. It is used for controlling single phase 2-wire circuits. The switch switches ON/OFF the phase line and neutral line simultaneously. These switches are constructed for 15 A to 200 A and 250 V to 660 V. The metal covering of switch should be compulsorily grounded.

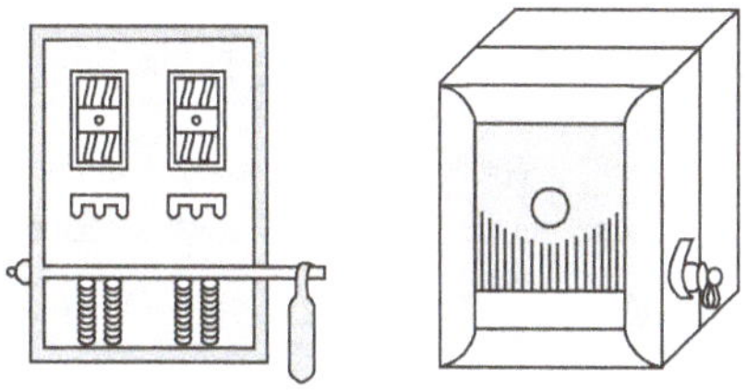
Double poles iron clad switch

(b) **Three Poles Iron Clad or TPIC Switch** It works as a main switch for 3-phase AC line. It is used for controlling a 3-phase power with 4-wire system. A fuse and a neutral link is connected in series with each line. The switch switches ON/OFF all the three phase lines simultaneously. These switches are constructed for 30 A to 400 A and 400 V to 1100 V.

The metal covering of switch should be compulsorily grounded.

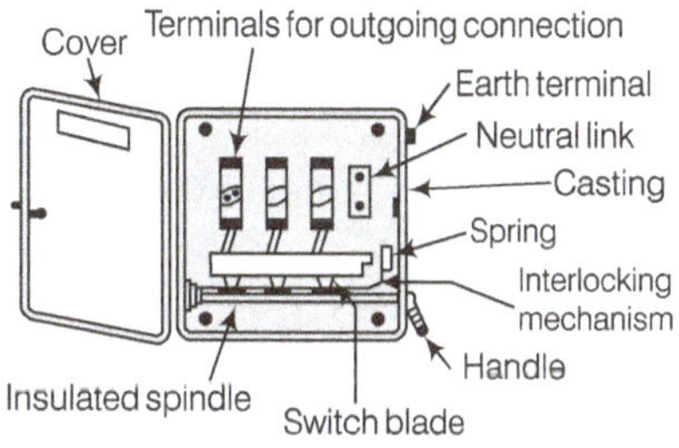

Three poles iron clad or TPIC switch

Note DPIC and TPIC are Different from Other Switches DPIC and TPIC switches are switched ON in upward direction and OFF in downward direction but rest other switches are ON in downward direction and OFF in upward direction. This property makes them different from others.

(c) **Two-way Switch** It means two or more switches in different locations to control one lamp. They all are wired in such a way, so that operation of either switch will control the lights.

This figure illustrates how lights is controlled from two different locations

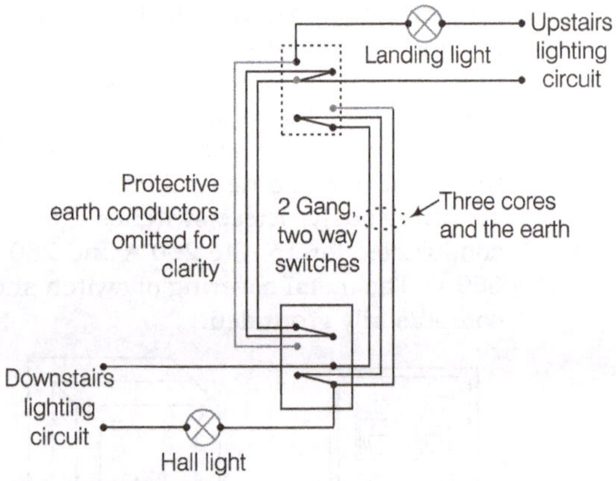

A schematic diagram of two-way switch circuit

3. Staircase Wiring

It is a dual control switch system in which the double pole type switches are used at the top and bottom of a staircase. Let a switch S_1 be fitted at the bottom and a switch S_2 at the top of the staircase. While going up a person puts on the light by operating the switch S_1, so that the connection '*pq*' changes to '*qr*' and makes the current to flow in the circuit. On reaching at the top, he operates the switch S_2 to put off the light so that the connection '*rq*' changes to '*qp*' and the flow of current stops.

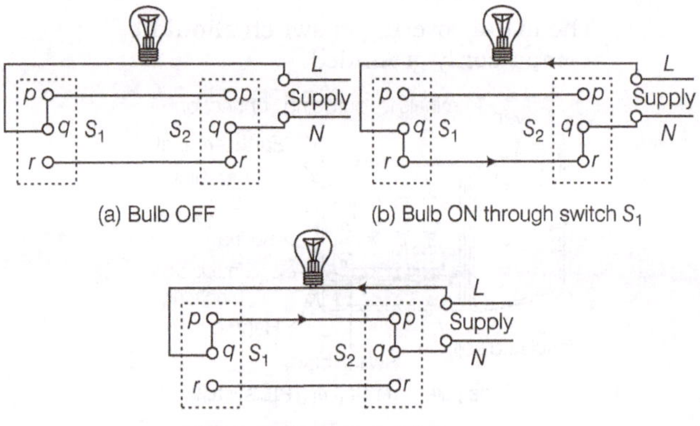

(a) Bulb OFF (b) Bulb ON through switch S_1

(c) Bulb ON through switch S_2

4. Earthing

Earthing means to connect the metal case of the appliance to the earth (i.e. zero potential) by means of a metal wire called the **earth wire** (in green insulation cover). One end of the metal wire is buried in the earth. The appliances are connected to the earth by using the top pin of a 3-pin plug.

Earthing saves us from electrical shocks.

The symbol ⏚ is used for earthing appliances.

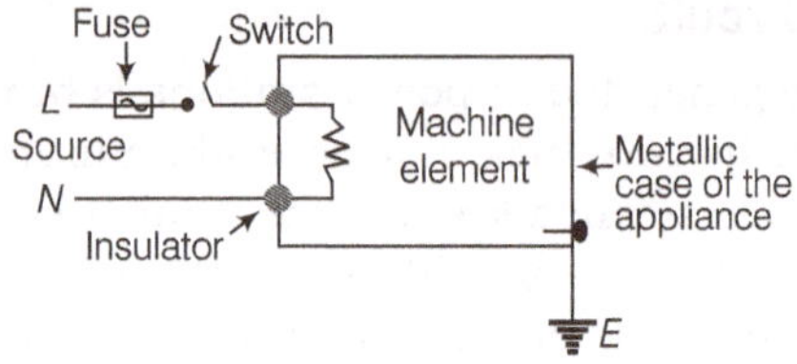

Earthing of an appliance

5. Electric Fuse

Fuse is used as a safety device in household circuits and is based on heating effect of current. It is connected in series with the mains supply.

A fuse consists of an alloy of **lead** and **tin** which has appropriate melting point.

It is required to rate the fuses for different current values such as 1 A, 2 A, 5 A, 10 A, 15 A, etc.

When the current flowing through the circuit exceeds the safe limit, the temperature of the fuse wire increases and due to heating effect, it gets melts and breaks the circuit. This helps to protect the other circuit elements from hazards caused by heavy current.

6. 3-Pin Plug and Socket with Conventional Location of Wires

According to electricity rules, 3-pin socket should be used where third pin is used as the earth pin, it is thick pin and is at the top between the other two pins as left and right pins. Right pin is used as phase and the left pin as neutral.

There is no pin for the earth available in 2-pin socket and it is used in low voltage applications. The pins are splitted at the ends to provide a spring action, so that it gets fit in the socket holes tightly. The earth pin is thicker and longer than the other two. Whereas socket is used to supply the current to the electrical equipment from the switch board. They are of 2-pin with rating 5 A, 250 V and 3-pin of rating 5 A/15 A, 250 V. Similar to switches, sockets are of two types, i.e. one type is fixed above the surface of switch board and second type below the surface of switch board.

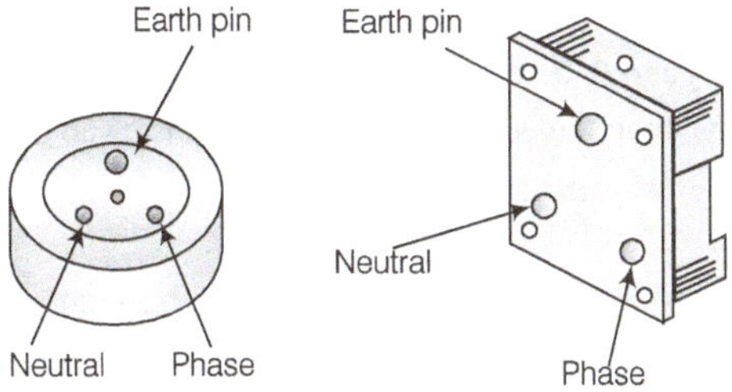

3-Pin socket

Safety Precautions

The safety precautions are as

(i) a switch should not be touched with wet hands.

(ii) the switch should always be connected in the live wire.

(iii) electrical appliances should be properly earthed.

(iv) always use appropriate fuse rating in the live wire of the circuit.

Conventional Colour Coding of Wires

The colour coding of wires in a cable are as

Wires	Colour	
	Old Convention	New Convention
Live	Red	Brown
Neutral	Black	Light blue
Earth	Green	Green or Yellow

Check Your LEARNING...

1 Write an advantage of using ring system in house wiring.
2 What is a two-way switch?
3 Why electrical appliances are earthed?
4 What is a fuse?
5 Write colour codes of live and neutral wires.
6 Name the wire, in which switch is connected.

QUiCK Revision

- An **electric charge** is a physical entity which is defined by excess or deficiency of electrons on a body. The SI unit of electric charge is coulomb (C).
- The total charge acquired by a body is an integral multiple of magnitude of charge on a single electron. This principle is called **quantisation of charge**.
- **Electric current** is defined as the rate of flow of electric charge through any cross-section of a conductor in unit time. Electric current $(I) = \dfrac{\text{Charge }(q)}{\text{Time }(t)}$. The SI unit of electric current is ampere (A).
- **Electric potential** is defined as the amount of work done when a unit positive charge is moved from infinity to a point. Electric potential $(V) = \dfrac{\text{Work done }(W)}{\text{Charge moved }(q)}$. The SI unit of electric potential is volt (V).
- **Electric potential difference** is defined as the work done per unit charge in moving a unit positive charge from one point to other point.
- A closed and continuous path through which electric current flows is known as **electric circuit**.
- According to **Ohm's law**, the electric current flowing through a conductor is directly proportional to the potential difference applied across its ends, providing the physical conditions (such as temperature, dimensions etc.) remains unchanged.
$$V \propto I \quad \text{or } V = IR$$
where, R is the constant of proportionality called **resistance of the conductor** at a given temperature.
- **Resistance** is the property of a conductor due to which it opposes the flow of electric current through it. Mathematically,
$$\text{Resistance }(R) = \frac{\text{Potential difference }(V)}{\text{Electric current }(I)}$$
The SI unit of resistance is ohm (Ω).
- At a given temperature, resistance of a conductor depends on its (i) length l, (ii) cross-section area A and (iii) nature of the material of the conductor.
It is found that $R \propto l$ and $R \propto \dfrac{1}{A}$. Mathematically, $R = \rho\dfrac{l}{A}$
where, ρ is the constant of proportionality called **resistivity** or **specific resistance of the conductor**.
- **Resistivity** of a conductor is defined as the resistance of a conductor of unit length and unit area of cross-section. The SI unit of resistivity is ohm-metre (Ω-m).
- Resistivity of a conductor remains constant on increasing or decreasing its dimensions.
- If R_1, R_2 and R_3 be the individual **resistances** joined in series, then the equivalent resistance R_S is given by
$$R_S = R_1 + R_2 + R_3$$
- If R_1, R_2 and R_3 be the individual resistances joined in parallel, then the equivalent resistance R_P is given by
$$\frac{1}{R_P} = \frac{1}{R_1} + \frac{1}{R_2} + \frac{1}{R_3}$$
- When an electric current is passed through a high resistance wire like nichrome wire, then the wire becomes very hot and produces heat. This is called the **heating effect of current**.
- As per **Joule's law of heating,** the electric energy consumed is given by
$$W = qV = VIt = I^2Rt = \frac{V^2t}{R}$$
- **Electric power (*P*)** is defined as the amount of electric energy consumed in a circuit per unit time $(P) = \dfrac{W}{t}$.
- The SI unit of electric power is watt (W).
- One horse power is equal to 746 watt.
- In the ring system, the wires starting from the main fuse box run around all the rooms of the house and then come back to the fuse box again forming the ring.
- The electric power is generated at the power generating stations. The power from the generating station is transmitted over long distances at a still high voltage to minimise the loss of energy in form of heat in the live wires used for transmission.
- In an electrical circuit, switch is used to start or stop the flow of current.
- **Main Switch** It is a two poles or three poles single way switch.
- Two-way switch means two or more switches in different locations to control one lamp.
- Staircase wiring is a dual control switch system in which the double pole type switches are used at the top and bottom of a staircase.
- To avoid from the risk of electrical shock, the metal body of appliances is earthed. Earthing means to connect the metal case of the appliance to the earth (i.e. zero potential) by means of a metal wire called the **earth wire**.
- **Fuse** is a safety device which protects the electrical circuit from short-circuiting and overload.
- In a 3-pin plug, the top pin is for earthing, the left pin is for live and the right pin is for neutral. The pins are splitted at the ends to provide a spring action, so that the fit in the socket holes tightly. The earth pin is thicker and longer than the other two.
- Conventional colour codes of wires are live-brown, neutral-light blue and earth-green or yellow.

Chapter Practice

1 Mark Questions

1. Choose the correct relation for emf (ε) and terminal voltage V. **[2023]**
   (a) $\varepsilon = V$ (always)
   (b) $V > \varepsilon$ (always)
   (c) $V < \varepsilon$ (when the cell is in use)
   (d) All of the above

Sol. (*a*) $V < \varepsilon$ (when the cell is in use)

2. Which of the following quantity must remain constant for measurement of resistance?
   (a) Temperature
   (b) Area
   (c) Length
   (d) All of the above

Sol. (*d*) For measurement of resistance, all physical conditions (such as temperature, area and length) of the material must remain constant.

3. To determine the equivalent resistance of two resistors when connected in series, a student arranged the circuit components as shown in the figure. But he did not succeed to achieve the objective.

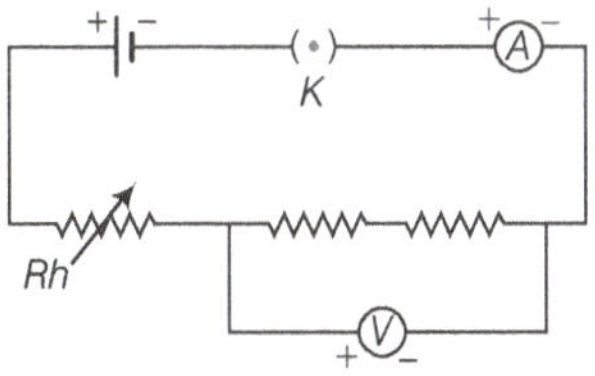

Which of the following mistakes has been committed by him in setting up the circuit?
   (a) Position of ammeter is incorrect
   (b) Position of voltmeter is incorrect
   (c) Terminals of ammeter are wrongly connected
   (d) Terminals of voltmeter are wrongly connected

Sol. (*c*) According to the figure, student has connected the apparatus, but terminals of the ammeter are wrongly connected because ammeter is in series. Hence, positive terminal of ammeters should be connected with positive terminal of cell.

4. Two unequal resistances are connected in parallel by a student. Which of the following is true?
   (a) Current is same in both
   (b) Current is larger in higher resistance
   (c) Voltage drop is same across both
   (d) Voltage drop is lower in lower resistance

Sol. (*c*) In parallel combination of resistors, voltage drop across each resistor is same whereas current through each resistor is different.

5. I. The resistors R_1 and R_2 have not been correctly connected in parallel.
   II. The voltmeter has not been correctly connected in the circuit.
   III. The ammeter and the key have not been correctly connected in the circuit.

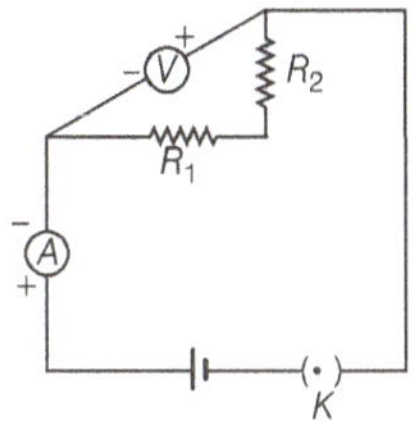

Out of these three, the actual fault in this circuit is/are
   (a) Both I and II (b) Both II and III
   (c) Only I (d) Only II

Sol. (*c*) Only statement I because resistances are connected in series not in parallel.

6. In series combination of resistance,
   (a) potential difference is same across each resistance
   (b) total resistance is reduced
   (c) current is same in each resistance
   (d) All of the above

Sol. (*c*) In series combination, current in all of the resistors in same branch is constant or same. However, the potential difference across each resistor is different.

7. When a current I flows through a wire of resistance R for time t, then the electrical energy produced is given by **[2023]**
   (a) I^2Rt (b) IR^2t
   (c) IRt (d) IRt^2

Sol. (*a*) Electrical energy, $H = I^2Rt$

This is equal to the heat produced, $H = I^2Rt$ and also called Joule's law of heating.

8. Which one of the following statements is correct? **[ICSE Latest Specimen Sem-II]**
   (a) Live wire has zero potential.
   (b) Fuse is connected in a neutral wire.
   (c) Potential of live and earth wires is always same.
   (d) Earth wire is used to prevent electric shock.

Sol. (*d*) Only statement given in option (d) is correct while all other are incorrect, which can be corrected as
   (a) Live wire of a circuit is maintained at a potential of 220 V, while the neutral wire is at zero potential.

(b) Fuse is used as a safety device, so it should be connected to the live wire.

(c) Neutral and earth wires are connected together at the local sub-station. So, both wires will be at same potential.

2 Marks Questions

9. (i) State Ohm's law.

(ii) Diagrammatically illustrate how you would connect a key, a battery, a voltmeter, an ammeter, an unknown resistance R and a rheostat so that it can be used to verify the above law?

Sol. (i) According to Ohm's law, the electric current flowing through a conductor is directly proportional to the potential difference applied across its ends, providing the physical conditions (such as temperature, dimensions etc.) remain unchanged. **[1]**

(ii) To illustrate the Ohm's law, we draw the following circuit as

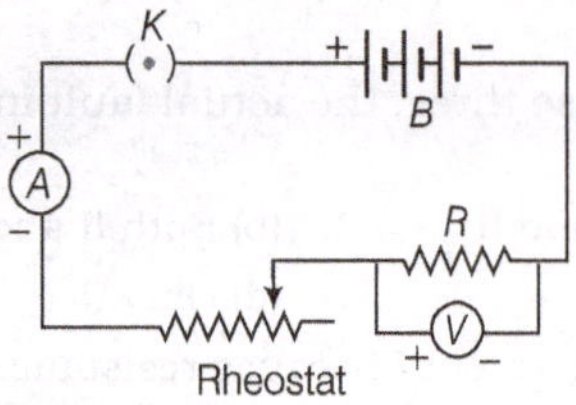

where, B is battery, V is voltmeter and A is ammeter. **[1]**

10. (i) Sketch a graph to show the change in potential difference across the ends of an ohmic resistor and the current flowing in it. Label the axes of your graph.

(ii) What does the slope of the graph represent? **[2008]**

Sol. (i)

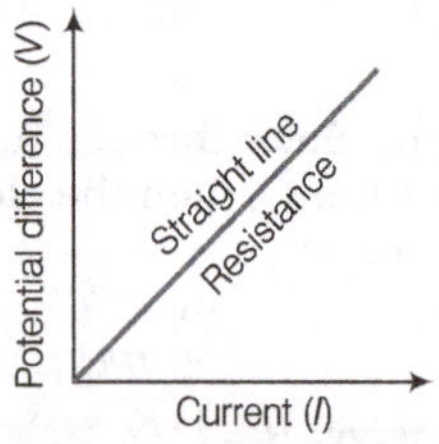

[1]

(ii) The slope of the graph represents resistance of the resistor. **[1]**

11. Define specific resistance and state its SI unit. **[2017]**

Sol. Specific resistance or **resistivity** (ρ) of a conductor is defined as the resistance of a conductor of unit length and unit area of cross-section.

Specific resistance or resistivity is the characteristic property of the material of the conductor and depends only on the nature of the material and temperature. **[1]**

As we know, the resistance is given by

$$R = \rho \frac{l}{A}$$

$$\Rightarrow \quad \rho = \frac{RA}{l} = \frac{\Omega m^2}{m} = \Omega\text{-m}$$

Its SI unit is ohm-m (Ω-m). **[1]**

12. (i) What is an ohmic resistor?

(ii) Two copper wires are of the same length, but one is thicker than the other.

(a) Which wire will have more resistance?

(b) Which wire will have more specific resistance? **[2014]**

Sol. (i) The conductor which obeys Ohm's law is called ohmic resistor or linear resistance. e.g. Silver, aluminium, copper, nichrome, etc. **[1]**

(ii) (a) Thin wires will have more resistance, because the resistance of the wire varies inversely to the area of the wire. i.e. $R \propto \frac{1}{A}$. **[1/2]**

(b) Specific resistance (resistivity) does not depend on the dimensions of wire, hence thick and thin wires, both have same value of specific resistance. **[1/2]**

13. Should the resistance of an ammeter be low or high? Give reason.

Sol. The resistance of an ammeter should be low. An ammeter has to be connected in series with the circuit to measure current. In case, if its resistance is not very low, then its inclusion in the circuit will reduce the current to be measured. In fact, an ideal ammeter is one which has zero resistance. **[2]**

14. The V-I graph for a series combination and for a parallel combination of two resistors is shown in the figure below. Which of the two graphs A or B, represents the parallel combination? Give a reason for your answer. **[2016]**

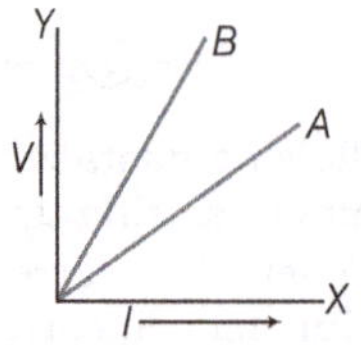

Sol. In parallel combination, resultant resistance becomes less than the resultant resistance in series combination. From the given graph, the slope represents the resistance. According to graph, slope of line A is less than the slope of line B. So, line A represents the parallel combination. **[2]**

15. How does an increase in the temperature affect the specific resistance of a

(i) metal and

(ii) semiconductor? **[2019]**

Sol. (i) If the temperature of the metal is raised, the atom vibrate more strongly and the electrons make more violent collisions with them, so the resistance of the metal increase. Hence, resistivity will increase.

Hence, specific resistance of the metal increase.

(ii) In case of semiconductor as the temperature increases, the electrons in the valence band get excited and jump into the conduction band and hence the conductance increases, which results in the decrease of resistance. As, resistance is directly proportional to resistivity.

Hence, resistivity of semiconductor decreases rapidly with rise in temperature.

16. n resistors, each of resistance R are first connected in series and then in parallel. What is the ratio of the total effective resistance of the circuit in series to parallel combination?

Sol. In series combination,

$$R_S = R + R + R + \ldots n \text{ times}$$

$$\Rightarrow \quad R_S = nR \quad [1/2]$$

In parallel combination,

$$\frac{1}{R_P} = \frac{1}{R} + \frac{1}{R} + \frac{1}{R} + \ldots \; n \text{ times}$$

$$\Rightarrow \quad \frac{1}{R_P} = \frac{n}{R}$$

$$\Rightarrow \quad R_P = \frac{R}{n} \quad [1/2]$$

$$\because \quad \frac{R_S}{R_P} = \frac{nR}{R/n} = n^2 \quad [1]$$

17. Derive an expression for equivalent resistance in the following case

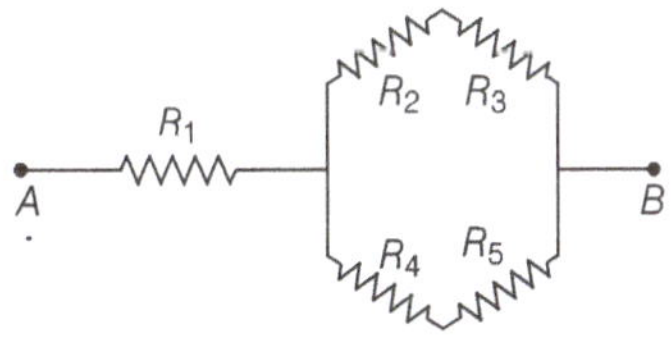

Decide which resistances are in series and parallel. Solve for series and then for parallel. Combine both the results to get the equivalent resistance.

Sol. R_2 and R_3 are in series.

Thus, for this combination,

$$R' = R_2 + R_3$$

Similarly, R_4 and R_5 are in series.

So, $\quad R'' = R_4 + R_5 \quad [1]$

R' and R'' are in parallel.

$$\therefore \quad R''' = \frac{R'R''}{R' + R''} = \frac{(R_2 + R_3)(R_4 + R_5)}{R_2 + R_3 + R_4 + R_5}$$

R_1 and R''' are in series.

$$\therefore \quad R_{eq} = R_1 + \frac{(R_2 + R_3)(R_4 + R_5)}{R_2 + R_3 + R_4 + R_5} \quad [1]$$

18. In an electrical circuit, three incandescent bulbs A, B and C of ratings 40 W, 60 W and 100 W respectively, are connected in parallel to an electric source. Write the order of brightness.

Sol. Bulbs are rated presuming that they all are to be connected with the same supply voltage (say 220 V in India). In parallel combination, voltage remains same, so greater the power (watt), greater the brightness. Therefore, brightness B of three bulbs are as $\quad B_{100} > B_{60} > B_{40}$ [2]

19. (i) What is the colour code for the insulation on the earth wire?

(ii) Write an expression for calculating electrical power in terms of current and resistance.

Sol. (i) The colour code for the insulation on the earth wire is green or yellow. [1]

(ii) The expression for calculating electrical power (P) in terms of current (I) and resistance (R) is given by $P = I^2R$. [1]

20. Why is it not advisable to use a piece of copper wire as fuse wire in an electric circuit? [2020]

Sol. Resistance of copper wire is very low and its melting point is very high but fuse wire must have high resistance (or resistivity) and low melting point. Therefore, fuse wire is not made of copper. [2]

21. (i) Which part of an electrical appliance is earthed?

(ii) State a relation between electrical power, resistance and potential difference in an electrical circuit.

Sol. (i) Metallic body of an electrical appliance is earthed. [1]

(ii) The relation between electrical power, resistance and potential difference in a circuit is given by

$$P = \frac{V^2}{R} \quad [1]$$

22. (i) Which electrical component protects the electric circuit in case of excess current and which can also be used as a switch?

(ii) Name the wire to which this electrical component is connected in an electric circuit. [2023]

Sol. (i) Fuse [1]

(ii) Copper wires connected to fuse in an electrical circuit. [1]

23. Identify the following wires used in a household circuit.

(i) The wire is also called as the phase wire.

(ii) The wire is connected to the top terminal of a three pin socket. [2018]

Sol. (i) Live wire is also called as the phase wire. [1]

(ii) Earth wire is connected to the top terminal of three pin socket. [1]

24. (i) Name the device used to protect the electric circuits from overloading and short circuit.

(ii) On what effect of electricity does the above device work? [2013]

Sol. (i) Electric fuse is used to protect the electric circuit from overloading and short circuits. [1]

(ii) Heating effect of electric current [1]

25. (i) Give two characteristic properties of copper wire which make it suitable for use as fuse wire.

(ii) Name the material which is used as a fuse wire.

Sol. (i) The two characteristic properties of copper wire which make it suitable for use as fuse wire, are given as

(a) it should be of low melting point and high resistivity. [1]

(b) it should be a good conductor of electricity.

(ii) The alloy of tin and lead is used as fuse wire. [1]

26. State the characteristics required in a material to be used as an effective fuse wire. [2016]

Sol. Characteristics required in a material to be used as an effective fuse wire are given below

(i) High resistance and [1]

(ii) Low melting point. [1]

27. 'A geyser is rated 240W-220V'. Explain the meaning of this statement. [2023]

Sol. It means 240 joules of energy is consumed by geyser in one second. [2]

3 Marks Questions

28. (i) Define specific resistance.

(ii) What happens to the specific resistance of a conductor, if its length is doubled ?

(iii) Name a substance whose specific resistance remains almost unchanged with the increase in its temperature. [2023]

Sol. (i) Refer to theory [Page 161]. [1]

(ii) Unchanged [1]

(iii) The specific resistance of manganin remains almost unchanged with the increase in its temperature. [1]

29. (i) A substance has nearly zero resistance at a temperature of 1K. What is such a substance called?

(ii) State any two factors which affect the resistance of a metallic wire. [2010]

Sol. (i) The substance which has nearly zero resistance at a temperature of 1K is called as superconductor. [1]

(ii) The two factors which affect the resistance of a metallic wire are

(a) length of the wire (l), i.e. $R \propto l$

(b) area of cross-section (A), i.e. $R \propto \frac{l}{A}$ [2]

30. Read the following informations :

(i) Resistivity of copper is lower than that of aluminium which in turn is lower than that of constantan.

(ii) Six wires labelled as A, B, C, D, E and F have been designed as per the following parameters :

Wire	Length	Diameter	Material	Resistance
A	l	$2d$	Aluminium	R_1
B	$2l$	$d/2$	Constantan	R_2
C	$3l$	$d/2$	Constantan	R_3
D	$l/2$	$3d$	Copper	R_4
E	$2l$	$2d$	Aluminium	R_5
F	$l/2$	$4d$	Copper	R_6

Answer the following questions using the above data.

(a) Which of the wires has maximum resistance and why?

(b) Which of the wires has minimum resistance and why?

(c) Arrange R_1, R_3 and R_5 in ascending order of their values. Justify your answer.

Sol. (a) Wire C has maximum resistance because it has maximum length, least thickness and highest resistivity. [1]

(b) Wire F has the minimum resistance, since it has least length, maximum thickness and least resistivity. [1]

(using, $R = \rho\frac{l}{A}$)

(c) $R_3 > R_5 > R_1$

(using relation, $R = \rho\frac{l}{A}$ and comparison) [1]

31. (i) Observe the diagram given below and state whether the bulb will glow or not, when we switch ON.

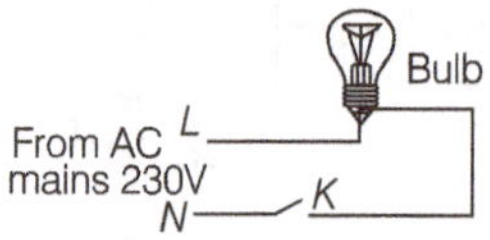

(ii) Is it safe to handle the bulb, when the switch is OFF?

(iii) Give a reason for your answer in (ii). [Latest Specimen Paper Sem-II]

Sol. (i) When the key is closed or the switch is ON, then the circuit is closed and a current start flowing and hence the bulb will glow.

(ii) No

(iii) If we handle the bulb keeping switch OFF, the live wire is still attached to the bulb and by touching it with barefoot or without using proper precautions, the circuit become closed and we can get electric shock.

32. (i) Two sets A and B of three bulbs each, are glowing in two separate rooms. When one of the bulbs in set A is fused, the other two bulbs also cease to glow. But in set B, when one bulb fuses, the other two bulbs continue to glow. Explain why this phenomenon occurs?

(ii) Why do we prefer arrangements of set B for house circuiting? [2014]

Sol. (i) The bulbs of set *A* are connected in series. Therefore, when one bulb is fused, then the current stops flowing. Whereas, the bulbs of set *B* are connected in parallel. Therefore, when one bulb is fused, then current flows through the other bulbs. [2]

(ii) We prefer arrangement of set *B* for house circuiting, because the potential difference in it is same. [1]

33. (i) Which particles are responsible for current in conductors?

(ii) Two which wire of a cable in a power circuit, should the metal case of a geyser be connected?

(iii) To which wire, should the fuse be connected? [2016, 2017]

Sol. (i) Electrons are responsible for the conduction of current in conductors. [1]

(ii) Earth wire of a cable in a power circuit should be connected to the metal case of geyser. [1]

(iii) Fuse should be connected to live wire. [1]

34. (i) A cell is sending current in an external circuit. How does the terminal voltage compare with the emf of the cell?

(ii) What is the purpose of using a fuse in an electrical circuit?

(iii) What are the characteristic properties of fuse wire? [2012]

Sol. (i) Terminal voltage is less than that of emf of the cell because some voltage is lost inside the electrolyte of the cell due to its internal resistance. [1]

(ii) The purpose of using a fuse in an electrical circuit is to limit the electric current in an electric circuit when there is overheating or overloading in the circuit. A fuse is used as safety device. [1]

(iii) The characteristic properties of fuse wire are low melting point and high resistance. [1]

35. (i) An electrical gadget can give an electric shock to its user under certain circumstance. Mention any two of these circumstances.

(ii) What preventive measure provided in a gadget can protect a person from an electric shock? [2013]

Sol. (i) The two circumstances, which give electric shock are as

(a) an electric shock may be caused due to poor insulation of wires.

(b) when wires of electric appliances are touched with wet hands. [2]

(ii) To prevent from electric shocks, the insulation of wires must be of good quality and it should be checked from time to time particularly when they become old. [1]

36. (i) Name the electrical appliance shown in the diagram below.

(ii) Name the material of the wire used in this device.

(iii) Name two important characteristics of this wire. [3] [Latest Specimen Paper Sem-II]

Sol. (i) Electric fuse [1]

(ii) A fuse wire consists of an alloy of lead and tin. [1]

(iii) I. It should have low melting point.

II. It should have high resistivity. [1]

37. (i) Name the colour code of the wire which is connected to the metallic body of an appliance.

(ii) Draw the diagram of a dual control switch when the appliance is switched ON. [2017]

Sol. (i) The colour coding of wires in a cable are as follow

Wires	Colour	
	Old Convention	New Convention
Live	Red	Brown
Neutral	Black	Light blue
Earth	Green	Green or Yellow

[1]

(ii) **Two-Way or Dual Way Switch** It means two or more switches in different locations to control one lamp. This figure illustrates that lights to be controlled from both locations.

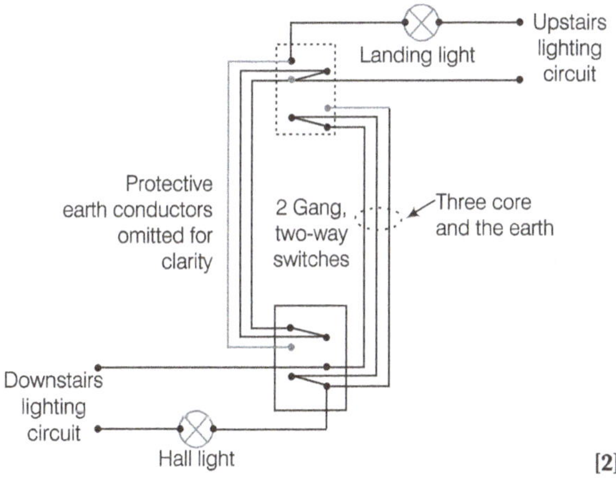

[2]

4 Marks Questions

38. How will you conclude that the same potential difference (voltage) exists across three resistors connected in a parallel arrangement to a battery?

Sol. The experimental set-up comprises of three resistors R_1, R_2 and R_3 which are joined in parallel combination and connecting them with a battery, an ammeter (*A*), a voltmeter (*V*) and a plug key *K*, as shown in Fig. (a). The key *K* is closed and the voltmeter and ammeter readings are recorded.

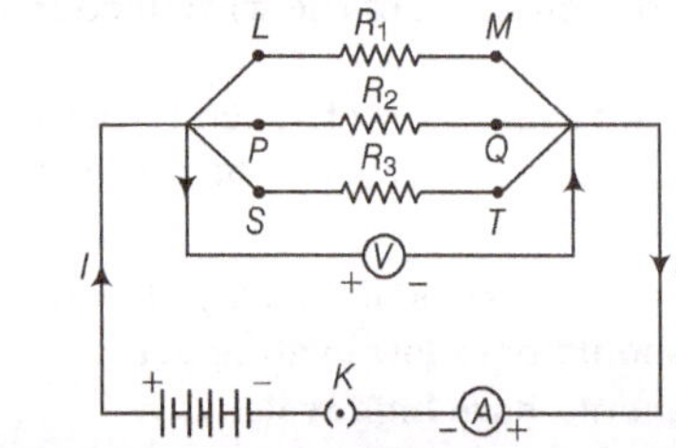

(a)

[1½]

The key *K* is open and removing the ammeter and voltmeter from the circuit and insert the voltmeter *V* in parallel with R_1 and ammeter in series with the resistor R_1, as shown in Fig. (b). Again, the voltmeter and ammeter readings are recorded.

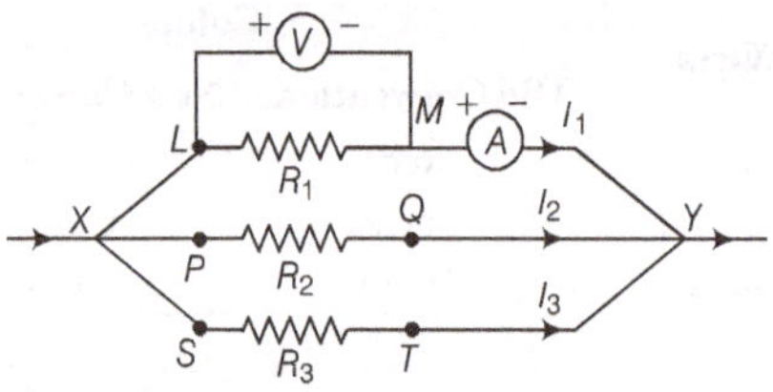

(b)

[1½]

Similarly, measuring the potential differences across resistances R_2 and R_3. It is found that voltmeter gives identical reading which leads to conclude that the voltage or potential difference across each resistor is same and equal to the potential difference across the combination. [1]

39. (i) The potential difference between two points in an electric circuit is 1 V. What does it mean? Name a device that helps to measure the potential difference across a conductor.

(ii) Why does the connecting cord of an electric heater not glow while the heating element does?

(iii) Electrical resistivities of some substances at 20 °C are given as below

Silver	: 1.60×10^{-8} Ω-m
Copper	: 1.62×10^{-8} Ω-m
Tungsten	: 5.2×10^{-8} Ω-m
Iron	: 10.0×10^{-8} Ω-m
Mercury	: 94.0×10^{-8} Ω-m
Nichrome	: 100×10^{-8} Ω-m

Answer the following questions using above data.

(a) Among silver and copper, which one is a better conductor and why?

(b) Which material would you advise to be used in electrical heating devices and why?

Sol. (i) The potential difference between two points is 1 V, means that, if a charge of 1 C is moved from one point to the other, then 1 J of work is required. The potential difference across a conductor is measured by means of an instrument called the voltmeter. [1]

(ii) The electric power *P* is given by

$$P = I^2R$$

The resistance of the heating element is very high. Large amount of heat generates in the heating element and it glows due to over heat. The resistance of connecting cord is very low. Thus, negligible heat generates in the connecting cord and it does not glow. [1]

(iii) (a) Silver is a better conductor due to its lower resistivity.

(b) Nichrome should be used in electrical heating devices due to very high resistivity. [2]

40. Obtain an expression for the heat produced in a conductor when a voltage *V* is applied across it. Heating effect of electric current is desirable as well as undesirable. Explain this statement.

Sol. When an electric charge *Q* moves against a potential difference *V*, then the amount of work done is given by $W = Q \times V$ ...(i)

We also know that, $I = Q/t$

So, $Q = I \times t$ ...(ii)

and from Ohm's law, $V = IR$ ...(iii)

Putting the values of Eqs. (ii) and (iii) in Eq. (i), we get

$$W = I \times t \times I \times R$$

∴ Work done, $W = I^2 Rt$ [1½]

Assuming that all the electrical work done or all the electrical energy consumed is converted into heat energy.

∴ $W = H = I^2Rt$ [1]

Heating effect of electric current is desirable because it as useful for the functioning of electrical bulbs, fans, etc., and undesirable because it leads to unnecessary loss of energy in the form of heat. [1½]

41. (i) Which is the better way to connect lights and other appliances in domestic circuit : series connection or parallel connection? Justify your answer.

(ii) An electrician has made electric circuit of a house in such a way that, if a lamp gets fused in a room of the house, then all the lamps in other rooms of the house stop working. What is the defect in this type of circuit wiring? Give reason.

Sol. (i) Parallel connection is a better way to connect lights and other appliances in domestic circuit. [1]

It is because

(a) when we connect a number of devices in parallel combination, each device gets the same potential as provided by the battery and it keeps on working even, if other devices stop working.

(b) parallel connection is helpful when each device has different resistances and requires different current for its operation as in this case, the current divides itself through different devices unlike series connection. [1]

(ii) Electrician has made series connection of all the lamps in electric circuit of house because of which, if one lamp gets fused, all the other lamps stop working. [1]

This is due to the fact that when devices are connected in series, then if one device fails, the circuit gets broken and all the devices in that circuit stop working. [1]

42. (i) Explain the meaning of the statement "current rating of a fuse is 5A".

(ii) In the transmission of power, the voltage of power generated at the generating stations is stepped up from 11 kV to 132 kV before it is transmitted. Why? [2017]

Sol. (i) Current rating of fuse is 5A means, it is a safety device having short length of thin wire having low melting point of a particular amount of current 5A. Whenever current through this fuse exceeds the 5A limit, it will melt and break the circuit and save main circuit components from damage. [2]

(ii) Step-up transformer increases the amplitude of alternating voltage from 11 kV to 132 kV before it is transmitted to get better efficiency with less loss of energy. [2]

Numerical Based Questions

43. Calculate the amount of charge that flows through a conductor when a current of 5A flows through it for 2 min. [2]

Sol. Given, $I = 5\text{A}$, $t = 2 \text{ min} = 2 \times 60 \text{ s} = 120 \text{ s}$, $q = ?$

We know that, charge, $q = I \times t$

$$= 5 \times 120 = 600 \text{ C}$$

Thus, the amount of charge flowing through conductor is 600 C. [2]

44. A current of 1 A is drawn by a filament of an electric bulb. What would be the number of electrons passing through a cross-section of the filament in 16 s? [2]

Sol. Given, $I = 1 \text{ A}$, $t = 16 \text{ s}$

We know that, current,

$$I = \frac{q}{t} = \frac{ne}{t} \quad (\because q = ne)$$

$$\Rightarrow \quad n = \frac{I \times t}{e} = \frac{1 \times 16}{1.6 \times 10^{-19}} \quad (\because e = 1.6 \times 10^{-19} \text{C})$$

$$= 10^{20} \text{ electrons}$$ [2]

45. Calculate the work done in moving a charge of 4 C from a point at 220 V to a point at 230 V. [2]

Sol. Given, charge, $q = 4$ C

Potential at point A, $V_A = 220$ V

Potential at point B, $V_B = 230$ V

Work done, $W = ?$

$\therefore$ Potential difference, $\Delta V = V_B - V_A$

$$= 230 - 220 = 10 \text{ V}$$

We know that, work done,

$$W = \Delta V \times q = 10 \times 4 = 40 \text{ J}$$ [2]

46. A metal wire of resistance 6 Ω is stretched, so that its length is increased to twice its original length. Calculate its new resistance. [2] [2013]

Sol. Given, $R_1 = 6\,\Omega$, $l_1 = l$

$$l_2 = 2l_1 = 2l, \; R_2 = ?$$

$$R_1 = \rho \frac{l_1}{A_1} \text{ and } R_2 = \rho \frac{l_2}{A_2}$$ [1]

The volume of metal wire remains same.

$$\therefore \quad A_1 l_1 = A_2 l_2 \Rightarrow \frac{l_2}{l_1} = \frac{A_1}{A_2}$$

Now, $$\frac{R_2}{R_1} = \frac{l_2}{A_2} \times \frac{A_1}{l_1} = \frac{l_2}{l_1} \times \frac{l_2}{l_1}$$

$$\Rightarrow \quad R_2 = R_1 \left(\frac{l_2}{l_1}\right)^2 = 6\left(\frac{2l}{l}\right)^2 = 24\,\Omega$$ [1]

47. A copper wire of resistivity 1.63×10^{-8} Ω-m has cross-section area of 10.3×10^{-4} cm^2. Calculate the length of the wire required to make a 20 Ω coil. [2]

Sol. Given, $\rho = 1.63 \times 10^{-8}\,\Omega\text{-m}$

$$A = 10.3 \times 10^{-4} \text{ cm}^2$$

$$= 10.3 \times 10^{-4} \times 10^{-4} \text{m}^2$$

$$R = 20\,\Omega, \; l = ?$$

We know that, $R = \dfrac{\rho l}{A}$

$$\Rightarrow \quad l = \frac{RA}{\rho} = \frac{20 \times 10.3 \times 10^{-4} \times 10^{-4}}{1.63 \times 10^{-8}}$$

$$= \frac{20 \times 10.3 \times 10^{-8}}{1.63 \times 10^{-8}} = 126.38 \text{ m}$$ [2]

48. How is the resistance of a wire affected, if (i) its length is doubled and (ii) its radius is doubled? [3]

Sol. (i) $\therefore \quad R = \dfrac{\rho l}{A}$ $\left(\begin{array}{l}\text{where, } l = \text{length of wire and} \\ A = \text{area of cross - section of wire.}\end{array}\right)$

$$R' = \frac{\rho \cdot l'}{A} = \frac{\rho l \times 2}{A} \quad [\because l' = 2l]$$

$$\because \quad R' = 2R$$

i.e. Resistance will be doubled, if length of the wire is doubled. [1½]

(ii) $\therefore \quad R = \dfrac{\rho l}{A} \Rightarrow R = \dfrac{\rho l}{\pi r^2} \quad (\because A = \pi r^2)$

$$R' = \frac{\rho l}{\pi r'^2} = \frac{\rho l}{\pi (2r)^2} = \frac{\rho l}{\pi r^2} \times \frac{1}{4} = \frac{R}{4}$$

Thus, resistance will decrease by four times, if radius of wire is doubled. [1½]

49. A metal wire has diameter of 0.25 mm and electrical resistivity of $0.8 \times 10^{-8} \Omega$-m.

(i) What will be the length of this wire to make a resistance 5 Ω? [1]

(ii) How much will the resistance change, if the diameter of the wire is doubled? [2]

Sol. Given, diameter = 0.25 mm

$\therefore$ Radius, $r = \frac{0.25}{2} \times 10^{-3}$ m

Resistivity, $\rho = 0.8 \times 10^{-8} \Omega$-m

Resistance, $R = 5\Omega$

(i) We know that, $R = \frac{\rho l}{A}$

$$\Rightarrow \quad l = \frac{RA}{\rho} = \frac{R \times \pi r^2}{\rho} = \frac{5 \times \pi \times \left(\frac{0.25}{2} \times 10^{-3}\right)^2}{0.8 \times 10^{-8}}$$

$$\left(\because A = \pi r^2 \text{ and } r = \frac{D}{2}\right)$$

$$= \frac{5 \times \pi \times 1.56 \times 10^{-8}}{0.8 \times 10^{-8}} = 30.6 \text{ m}$$ [1]

(ii) Resistance,

$$R = \frac{\rho l}{A} = \frac{\rho l}{\pi \left(\frac{D}{2}\right)^2} \quad \left(\because A = \pi r^2 \text{ and } r = \frac{D}{2}\right)$$

$$= \frac{\rho l}{\pi} \times \frac{4}{D^2}$$

New resistance,

$$R' = \frac{\rho l}{A'} = \frac{\rho l}{\pi \left(\frac{2D}{2}\right)^2} \quad (\because D \text{ has become } 2D)$$

$$= \frac{\rho l}{\pi D^2}$$

Now, $\frac{R'}{R} = \frac{\rho l}{\pi D^2} \div \frac{\rho l \times 4}{\pi D^2} = \frac{\rho l}{\pi D^2} \times \frac{\pi D^2}{\rho l \times 4} = \frac{1}{4}$

$\therefore \quad R' = \frac{R}{4}$

Thus, resistance will decrease by 4 times. [2]

50. You have three resistors of values 2 Ω, 3 Ω and 5 Ω. How will you join them so that the total resistance is more than 7 Ω? [2]

(i) Draw a diagram for the arrangement.

(ii) Calculate the equivalent resistance. [2018]

Sol. To get total resistance more than 7Ω. We can connect 2Ω, 3Ω and 5Ω in series.

(i)

[1]

(ii) $R_{eq} = R_1 + R_2 + R_3$ (for series combination)

$R_{eq} = 2 + 3 + 5$

$R_{eq} = 10\Omega$ [1]

51. (i) Calculate the total resistance across AB.

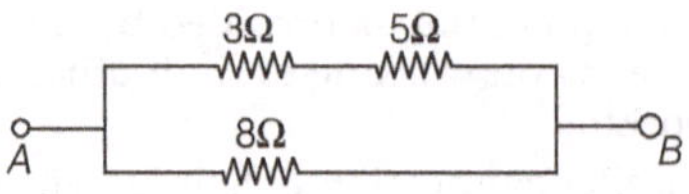

(ii) If a cell of emf 2.4 V with negligible internal resistance is connected across AB, then calculate the current drawn from the cell. [3]

[Latest Specimen Paper Sem-II]

Sol. (i) From figure, 3Ω and 5Ω resistances are in series. So, their equivalent resistance becomes

$R' = 3 + 5 = 8\Omega$

The circuit is now reduced to

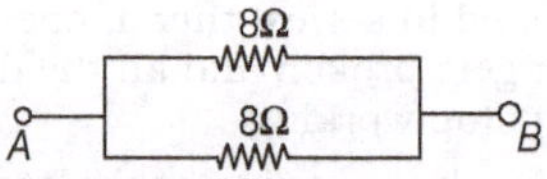

The two 8Ω resistances are in parallel, so equivalent or total resistance between A and B,

$$R'' = \frac{R' \times 8}{R' + 8} = \frac{8 \times 8}{8 + 8} = \frac{64}{16} = 4\Omega$$ [2]

(ii) Given, emf, $E = 2.4$ V

$\therefore$ Current, $I = \frac{E}{R''} = \frac{2.4}{4} = 0.6$ A [1]

52. Calculate the total resistance across AB.

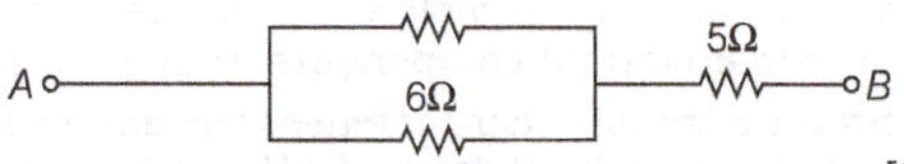

[2] [2020]

Sol. From the figure given in question,

Total resistance between A and B,

$$R_{AB} = (3||6) + 5 = \frac{3 \times 6}{3 + 6} + 5$$

$$= 2 + 5 = 7\,\Omega$$ [2]

53. (i) Find the equivalent resistance between A and B.

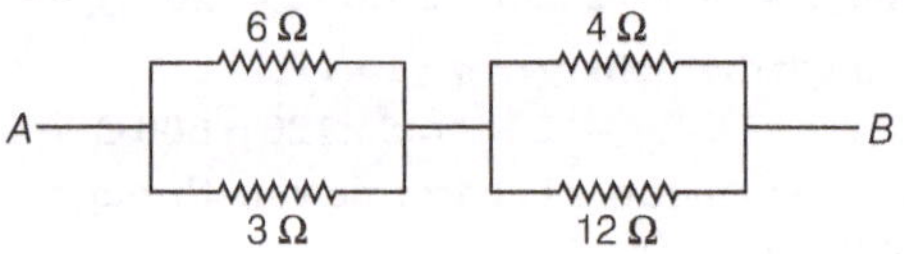

(ii) State whether the resistivity of a wire changes with the change in the thickness of the wire. [3] [2018]

Sol. (i) In the circuit, resistances 6Ω and 3Ω are in parallel combination.

$$\therefore \quad \frac{1}{R_{P_1}} = \frac{1}{R_1} + \frac{1}{R_2}$$

$$R_{P_1} = \frac{R_1 \times R_2}{R_1 + R_2}$$

$$= \frac{6 \times 3}{6 + 3} = \frac{18}{9} = 2\Omega$$

Similarly, 4Ω and 12Ω resistances are in parallel combination.

$$R_{P_2}=\frac{R_3\times R_4}{R_3+R_4}=\frac{4\times 12}{4+12}=\frac{48}{16}=3\Omega$$

Total resistance of circuit,

$$R_T=R_{P_1}+R_{P_2}=2+3=5\Omega$$ [2]

(ii) Resistivity is a material property it does not changes with change in thickness of wire. [1]

54. Calculate the effective resistance across *AB*.

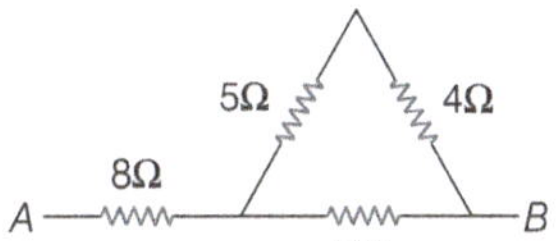

[3] [2019]

Sol.

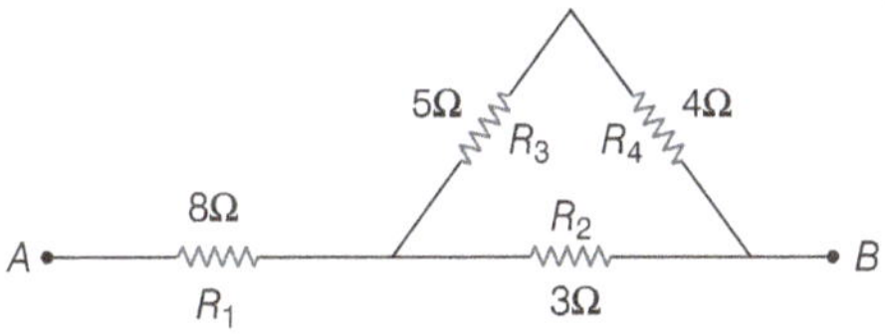

Here, R_3 and R_4 are in series combination, so total resistance $R_5=R_3+R_4=5+4=9\Omega$

So, [1]

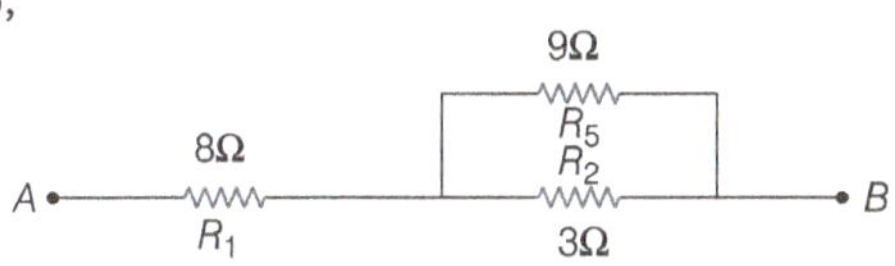

Here, R_5 and R_2 are in parallel combination, so total resistance

$$\frac{1}{R_6}=\frac{1}{R_2}+\frac{1}{R_5}=\frac{1}{3}+\frac{1}{9}$$

$$\frac{1}{R_6}=\frac{4}{9}$$

$$\therefore \quad R_6=\frac{9}{4}\Omega$$ [1]

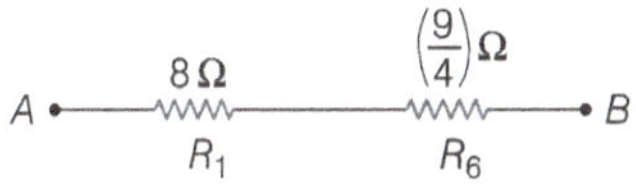

Here, R_1 and R_6 are in series combination, so resultant resistance across *AB*.

Now, equivalent resistance,

$$R_{eq}=R_1+R_6$$

$$=8+\frac{9}{4}=\frac{41}{4}\Omega$$ [1]

55. A music system draws a current of 400 mA, when connected to a 12 V battery.

(i) What is the resistance of the music system?

(ii) The music system is left playing for several hours and finally the battery voltage drops and the music system stops playing when the current drops to 320 mA. At what battery voltage does the music system stop playing? [3]

Sol. Given, current,

$$I=400\text{ mA}$$
$$=400\times10^{-3}\text{A}=0.4\text{ A}$$

Voltage, $V=12\text{ V}$

(i) Resistance of the music system,

$$R=\frac{V}{I}=\frac{12}{0.4}=\frac{120}{4}=30\,\Omega$$ [1]

(ii) Resistance of music system, $R=30\,\Omega$,

Current, $I=320\text{ mA}=0.32\text{ A}$

By Ohm's law, $R=\dfrac{V}{I}$

$\Rightarrow \quad V=IR$

$\Rightarrow \quad V=0.32\times 30$

$\Rightarrow \quad V=\dfrac{32}{100}\times30=\dfrac{960}{100}$

$\Rightarrow \quad V=9.60\text{ V}$ [2]

56. Find the equivalent resistance between points *A* and *B*. [2]

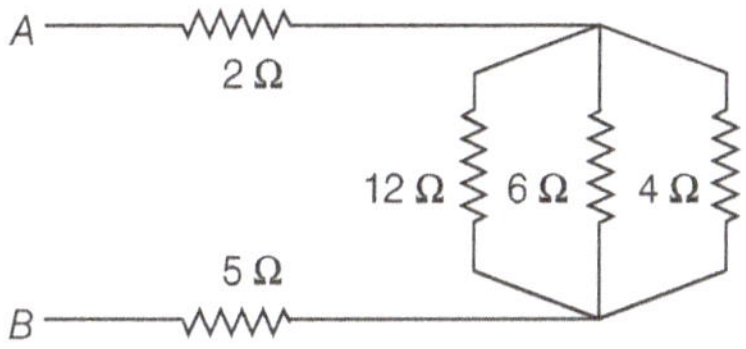

Sol.

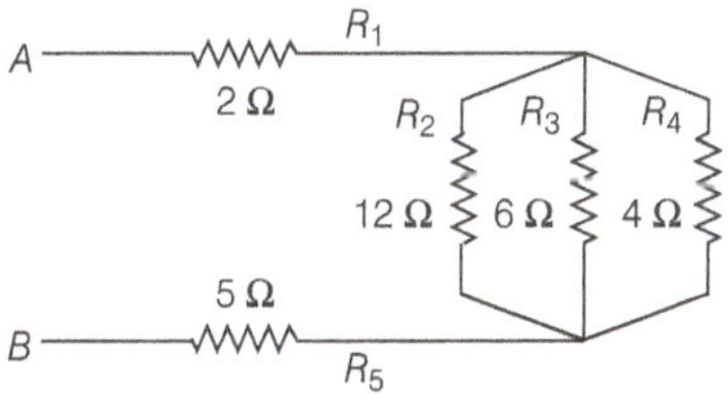

R_2, R_3 and R_4 are in parallel.

So, equivalent resistance corresponding to them

$$\frac{1}{R_P}=\frac{1}{R_2}+\frac{1}{R_3}+\frac{1}{R_4}=\frac{1}{12}+\frac{1}{6}+\frac{1}{4}$$

$$\Rightarrow \quad \frac{1}{R_P}=\frac{1+2+3}{12}=\frac{1}{2}$$

$$\Rightarrow \quad R_P=2\,\Omega$$

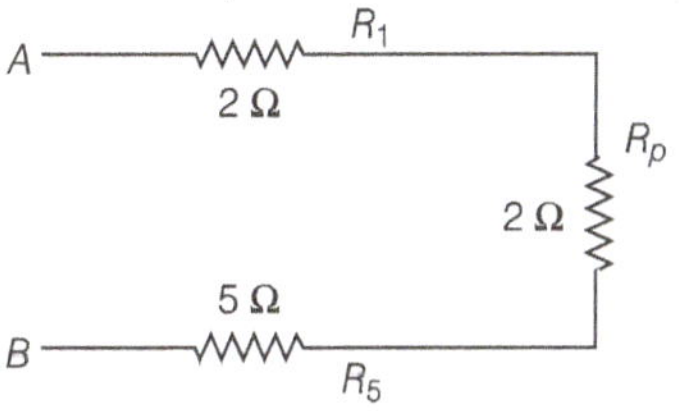

[1]

R_1, R_p and R_5 are in series.

Now, equivalent resistance will be given by

$$R=R_1+R_p+R_5=2+2+5$$

$$R=9\,\Omega$$ [1]

57. Five resistors are connected in a circuit as shown in figure. Find the ammeter reading when the circuit is closed. [3]

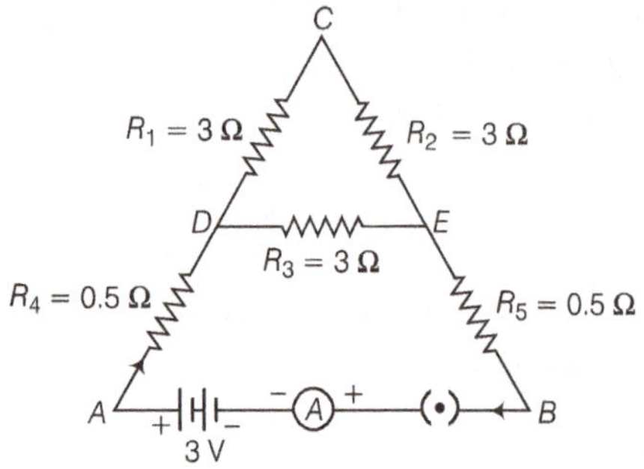

Sol. R_1 and R_2 are in series.

$$R_{S1} = R_1 + R_2 = 3 + 3 = 6\,\Omega$$

R_{S1} and R_3 are in parallel.

$$\therefore \quad \frac{1}{R_P} = \frac{1}{R_{S1}} + \frac{1}{R_3} = \frac{1}{6} + \frac{1}{3} = \frac{1}{2}$$

$$\Rightarrow \quad R_P = 2\,\Omega \quad [1]$$

R_4, R_P and R_5 are in series.

$$\therefore \quad R_S = R_4 + R_P + R_5 \quad [1]$$

$$= 0.5 + 2 + 0.5 = 3\,\Omega$$

Then, current, $I = \frac{V}{R_S} = \frac{3}{3} = 1\,\text{A}$ [1]

58. A circuit diagram is given as shown below

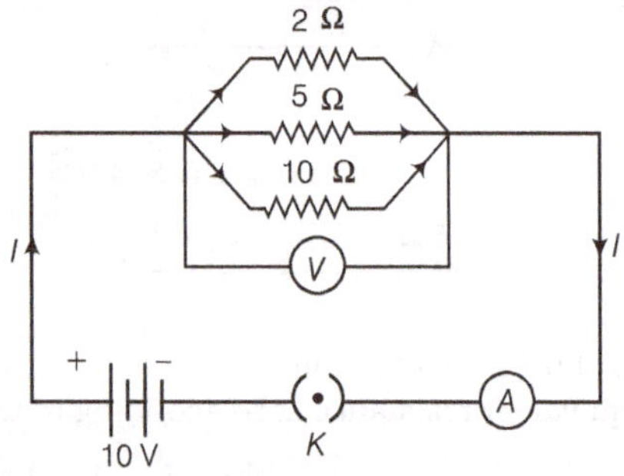

[3]

Calculate

(i) the total effective resistance of the circuit,

(ii) the current through each resistor.

(iii) the total current in the circuit and

Sol. Given, $R_1 = 2\,\Omega$, $R_2 = 5\,\Omega$, $R_3 = 10\,\Omega$, $V = 10\,\text{V}$

(i) Total effective resistance as the combination is in parallel,

$$\frac{1}{R_{\text{eff}}} = \frac{1}{R_1} + \frac{1}{R_2} + \frac{1}{R_3} = \frac{1}{2} + \frac{1}{5} + \frac{1}{10}$$

$$= \frac{5 + 2 + 1}{10} = \frac{8}{10}$$

$$\Rightarrow \quad R_{\text{eff}} = \frac{10}{8} = 1.25\,\Omega \quad [1]$$

(ii) Current through each resistor, $I_1 = \frac{V}{R_1} = \frac{10}{2} = 5\,\text{A}$,

$I_2 = \frac{V}{R_2} = \frac{10}{5} = 2\,\text{A}$ and $I_3 = \frac{V}{R_3} = \frac{10}{10} = 1\,\text{A}$ [1]

(iii) Total current, $I = I_1 + I_2 + I_3 = 5 + 2 + 1 = 8\,\text{A}$ [1]

59. A wire of a uniform thickness with a resistance of 27 Ω is cut into three equal pieces and they are joined in parallel. Find the resistance of the parallel combination. [2] [2006]

Sol. Given, resistance of given wire, $R = 27\,\Omega$

∴ Resistance of small wire

$$= \frac{\text{Resistance of wire } (R)}{\text{Number of pieces of wire}} = \frac{27}{3} = 9\,\Omega$$

Now, the each wire of resistance 9 Ω are connected in parallel.

$$\therefore \quad \frac{1}{R_{\text{eq}}} = \frac{1}{9} + \frac{1}{9} + \frac{1}{9} = \frac{3}{9} = \frac{1}{3} \quad [2]$$

$$R_{\text{eq}} = 3\,\Omega$$

60. Four resistances of 2.0 Ω each are joined end to end, to form a square *ABCD*. Calculate the equivalent resistance of the combination between any two adjacent corners. [2015]

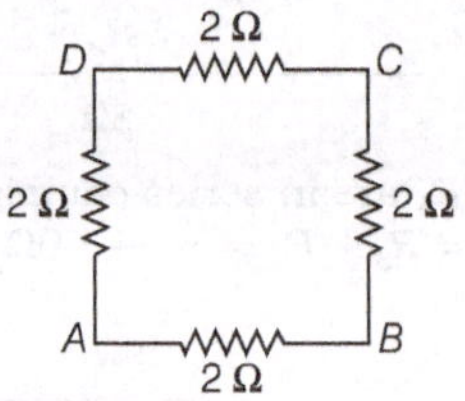

[2]

Sol. Resistance between two adjacent corners *A* and *B* is

$$\frac{1}{R} = \frac{1}{R_{AB}} + \frac{1}{R_{BC} + R_{CD} + R_{AD}}$$

$$= \frac{1}{2} + \frac{1}{2 + 2 + 2} = \frac{1}{2} + \frac{1}{6} = \frac{3 + 1}{6} = \frac{4}{6} = \frac{2}{3}$$

$$\Rightarrow \quad R = \frac{3}{2} = 1.5\,\Omega$$

61. Find the equivalent resistance between points *A* and *B*. [3]

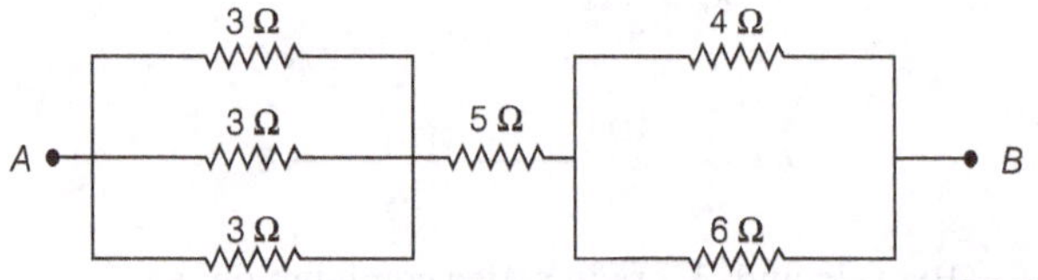

[2014]

Sol. The three resistances, 3 Ω are in parallel,

$$\frac{1}{R_1} = \frac{1}{3} + \frac{1}{3} + \frac{1}{3} = \frac{3}{3} = 1\,\Omega \Rightarrow R_1 = 1\,\Omega$$

and the resistance 4 Ω and 6 Ω are in parallel, [1]

$$\frac{1}{R_3} = \frac{1}{4} + \frac{1}{6} = \frac{3 + 2}{12} = \frac{5}{12}\,\Omega$$

$$\Rightarrow \quad R_3 = \frac{12}{5} = 2.4\,\Omega \quad [1]$$

The resistances R_1, 5 Ω and R_3 are in series, so total resistance,

$$R = R_1 + 5 + R_3 = 1 + 5 + 2.4 = 8.4\,\Omega \quad [1]$$

62. Calculate the equivalent resistance between the points *A* and *B* for the following combination of resistors.

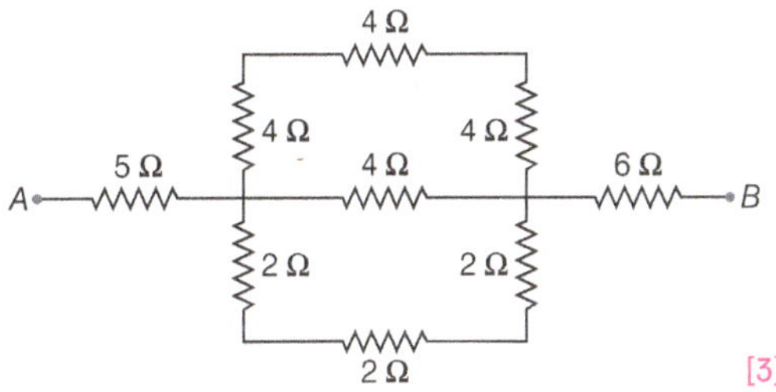

[3] [2013]

Sol. The three resistance each of 4 Ω are in series.

∴ $R_1 = 4 + 4 + 4 = 12\ \Omega$

The three resistance 2 Ω are in series.

∴ $R_2 = 2 + 2 + 2 = 6\ \Omega$

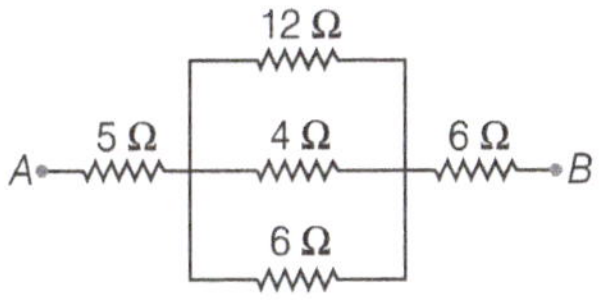

[1]

The resistances 4 Ω, 12 Ω and 6 Ω are in parallel.

∴ $\frac{1}{R_3} = \frac{1}{4} + \frac{1}{12} + \frac{1}{6} = \frac{3+1+2}{12} = \frac{6}{12} = \frac{1}{2}\ \Omega$

⇒ $R_3 = 2\ \Omega$ [1]

The resistors R_3, R_4 and R_5 are in series.

∴ $R_{eq} = R_4 + R_3 + R_5$

⇒ $R_{eq} = 5 + 2 + 6 = 13\ \Omega$ [1]

63. Calculate the equivalent resistance between P and Q from the following diagram.

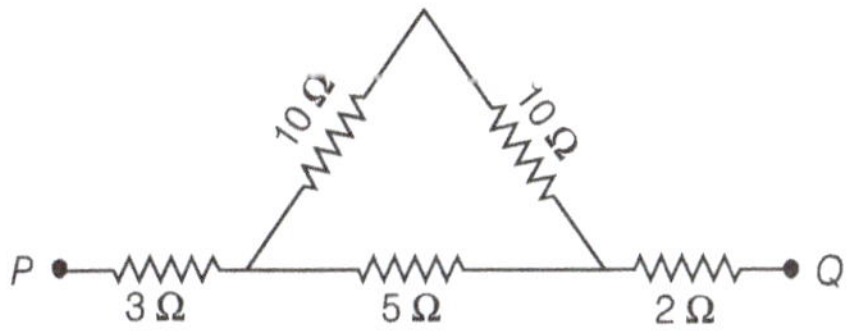

[3] [2012]

Sol. The two resistances 10 Ω are in series.

∴ $R = 10 + 10 = 20\ \Omega$

The resistances 5 Ω and R are in parallel. [1]

∴ $\frac{1}{R_1} = \frac{1}{5} + \frac{1}{20}$

$= \frac{4+1}{20} = \frac{5}{20} = \frac{1}{4}$

⇒ $R_1 = 4\ \Omega$

The resistors R_1, 3 Ω and 2 Ω are in series. [1]

∴ Equivalent resistance,

$R_{eq} = 3 + 4 + 2 = 9\ \Omega$ [1]

64. Calculate the equivalent resistance between A and B from the following diagram.

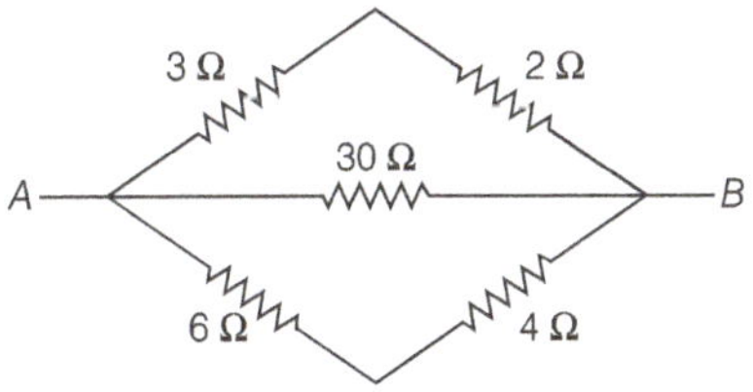

[2] [2011]

Sol. Resistances 3 Ω and 2 Ω are in series.

∴ $R_1 = 3 + 2 = 5\ \Omega$

Also, resistances 6 Ω and 4 Ω are in series.

∴ $R_2 = 6 + 4 = 10\ \Omega$

Equivalent resistance between A and B is

$$\frac{1}{R_{eq}} = \frac{1}{5} + \frac{1}{30} + \frac{1}{10} = \frac{6+1+3}{30} = \frac{10}{30} = \frac{1}{3}$$

$R_{eq} = 3\ \Omega$ [2]

65. Six resistances are connected together as shown in the figure. Calculate the equivalent resistance between the points A and B.

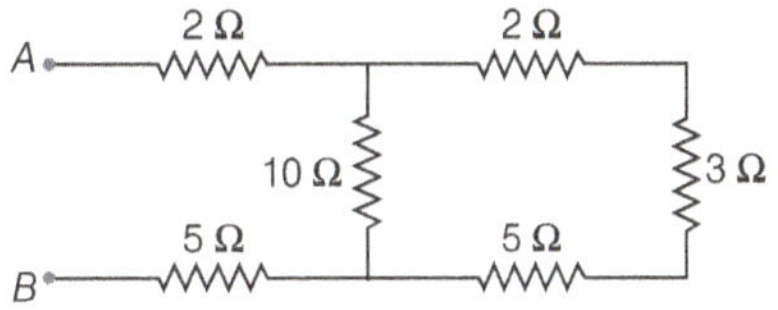

[3] [2010]

Sol. Resistance between the point C and D,

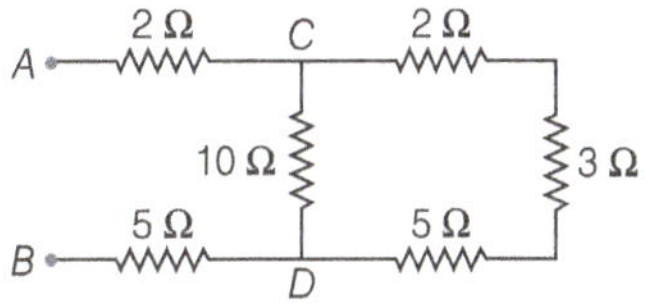

[1]

$$\frac{1}{R_{CD}} = \frac{1}{10} + \frac{1}{2+3+5} = \frac{1}{10} + \frac{1}{10} = \frac{2}{10} = \frac{1}{5}$$ [1]

∴ $R_{CD} = 5\ \Omega$

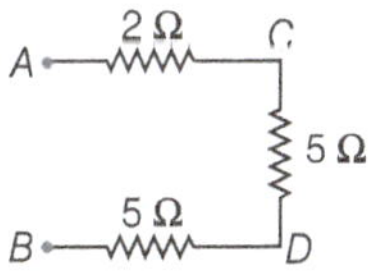

Now, equivalent resistance between the points A and B,

$R_{AB} = R_{AC} + R_{CD} + R_{BD}$

$= 2 + 5 + 5 = 12\ \Omega$ [1]

66. The equivalent resistance of the following circuit diagram is 4 Ω. Calculate the value of x. [2] [2009]

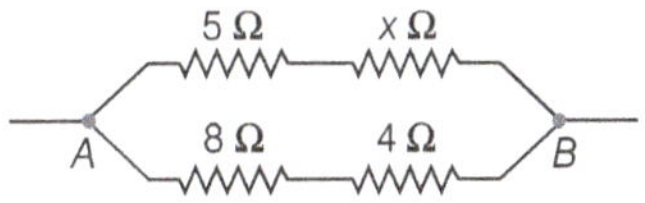

Sol. $\frac{1}{R_{AB}} = \frac{1}{R_1} + \frac{1}{R_2}$

⇒ $\frac{1}{4} = \frac{1}{5+x} + \frac{1}{8+4}$

⇒ $\frac{1}{4} = \frac{1}{5+x} + \frac{1}{12}$

⇒ $\frac{1}{5+x} = \frac{1}{4} - \frac{1}{12} = \frac{3-1}{12} = \frac{2}{12} = \frac{1}{6}$

⇒ $5 + x = 6 \Rightarrow x = 6 - 5 \Rightarrow x = 1\ \Omega$ [2]

67. (i) Find the value of current I drawn from the cell. **[2023]**

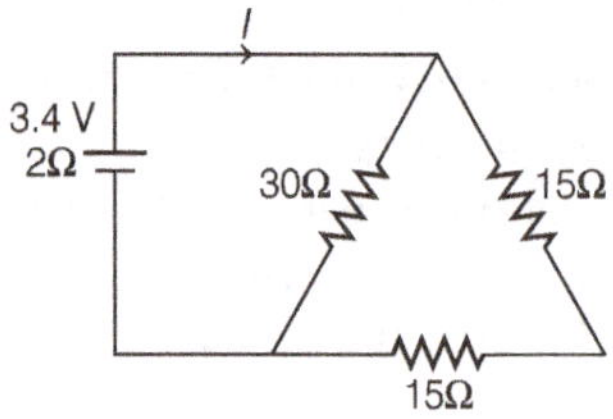

(ii) Calculate the terminal voltage. **[4]**

Sol. (i) In the circuit, the two 15Ω resistances are in series with each other, hence

$$R = 15\Omega + 15\Omega$$
$$= 30\Omega$$

Further R and 30Ω are connected parallel, so

$$R_{eq} = \frac{30 \times 30}{30 + 30} = \frac{900}{60} = 15$$

and internal resistance, $r = 2\Omega$

Net resistance , $R_{eq} + r = 17\Omega$

Current $I = \frac{V}{R} = \frac{3.4}{17} = 0.2$ A **[3]**

(ii) Terminal voltage, $V = I \cdot R_{eq}$

$$= 0.2 \times 15 = 3V$$ **[1]**

68. Five resistors of different resistance are connected together as shown in the figure. A 12 V battery is connected to the arrangement. Calculate **[2010]**

(i) the total resistance in the circuit.

(ii) the total current flowing in the circuit.

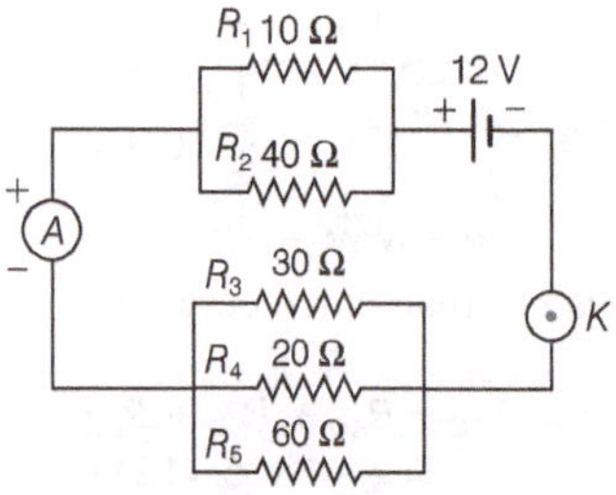

[4]

Sol. (i) $\frac{1}{R_{12}} = \frac{1}{10} + \frac{1}{40} = \frac{4+1}{40} = \frac{5}{40} = \frac{1}{8}$

$\Rightarrow$ $R_{12} = 8\,\Omega$ **[2]**

$$\frac{1}{R_{345}} = \frac{1}{30} + \frac{1}{20} + \frac{1}{60} = \frac{2+3+1}{60}$$

$$\frac{1}{R_{345}} = \frac{6}{60} = \frac{1}{10} \Rightarrow R_{345} = 10\,\Omega$$

Total resistance, $R = R_{12} + R_{345} = 8 + 10 = 18\,\Omega$

(ii) Total current, $I = \frac{V}{R} = \frac{12}{18} = \frac{2}{3} = 0.67$ A **[2]**

69. Three resistors are connected to a 6 V battery as shown in the figure.

Calculate

(i) the equivalent resistance of the circuit.

(ii) total current in the circuit.

(iii) potential difference across the 7.2 Ω resistor. **[2012]**

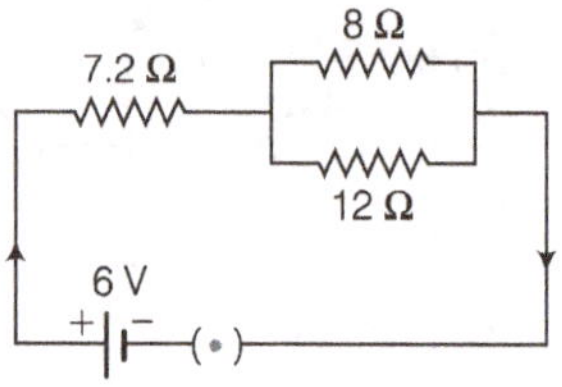

[3]

Sol. (i) Resistances 8 Ω and 12 Ω are in parallel.

$$\therefore \frac{1}{R_1} = \frac{1}{8} + \frac{1}{12} = \frac{3+2}{24} = \frac{5}{24} \Rightarrow R_1 = \frac{24}{5} = 4.8\,\Omega$$ **[1]**

Now, resistances R_1 and 7.2 are in series.

$\therefore$ $R_{eq} = 4.8 + 7.2 = 12\,\Omega$

(ii) $I = ?$

$$I = \frac{V}{R_{eq}} = \frac{6}{12} = \frac{1}{2} = 0.5\text{ A}$$ **[1]**

(iii) Potential difference across 7.2 Ω resistor

$= 0.5 \times 7.2 = 3.6$ V **[1]**

70. Three resistors are connected to a 12 V battery as shown in the figure given below.

(i) What is the current through the 8 Ω resistors?

(ii) What is the potential difference across the parallel combination of 6 Ω and 12 Ω resistors?

(iii) What is the current through the 6 Ω resistor? **[2011]**

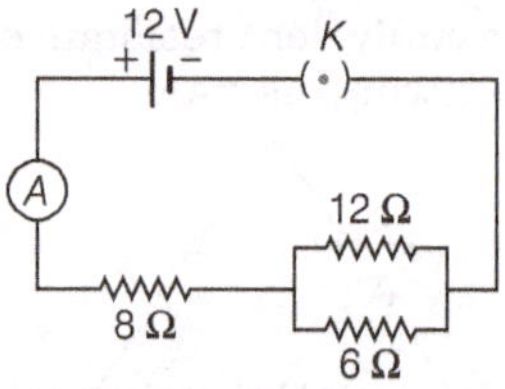

[3]

Sol. (i) Resistances 12 Ω and 6 Ω are parallel.

So, $\frac{1}{R_1} = \frac{1}{12} + \frac{1}{6} = \frac{3}{12} = \frac{1}{4} \Rightarrow R_1 = 4\,\Omega$

Equivalent resistance,

$$R_{eq} = 4 + 8 = 12\,\Omega \Rightarrow I = \frac{V}{R_{eq}} = \frac{12}{12} = 1\text{A}$$ **[1]**

(ii) Potential Difference (PD) across parallel combination of resistances 6 Ω and 12 Ω, **[1]**

$$V = I \times R_1 = 1 \times 4 = 4\text{ V} \quad \left(\because R_{eq} = \frac{6 \times 12}{6 + 12} = 4\,\Omega\right)$$

(iii) Current through 6 Ω resistor $= \frac{4\text{V}}{6\Omega} = 0.67$A **[1]**

71. Three resistors of 6.0 Ω, 2.0 Ω and 4.0 Ω respectively are joined together as shown in the figure. The resistors are connected to an ammeter and to a cell of emf 6.0 V. **[2008]**

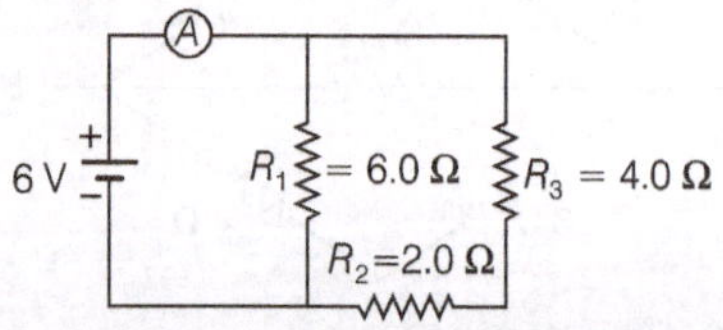

Calculate [2]

(i) the effective resistance of the circuit and

(ii) the current drawn from the cell.

Sol. (i) $R_S = R_2 + R_3 = 2 + 4 = 6\,\Omega$

$$\frac{1}{R_{eq}} = \frac{1}{R_1} + \frac{1}{R_S} = \frac{1}{6} + \frac{1}{6} = \frac{1}{3}$$

$\Rightarrow \quad R_{eq} = 3\,\Omega$ [1]

(ii) $I = \frac{E}{R} = \frac{6}{3} = 2\text{ A}$ [1]

72. (i) Two resistors with resistances 5 Ω and 10 Ω respectively, are to be connected to a battery of emf 6 V, so as to obtain

(a) minimum current and

(b) maximum current. [3]

How will you connect the resistances in each case?

(ii) Calculate the strength of the total current in the circuit in the two cases.

Sol. (i) (a) For obtaining minimum current, the two resistors should be connected in parallel.

(b) For obtaining maximum current, the two resistors should be connected in series. [1]

(ii) Given, $R_1 = 5\,\Omega$, $R_2 = 10\,\Omega$, $V = 6\text{ V}$

For parallel combination, $\frac{1}{R} = \frac{1}{R_1} + \frac{1}{R_2}$

$$= \frac{1}{5} + \frac{1}{10} = \frac{2+1}{10} = \frac{3}{10}$$

$\Rightarrow \quad R = \frac{10}{3}\,\Omega$

∴ Total current in the circuit,

$$I = \frac{V}{R} = \frac{6 \times 3}{10} = 1.8\text{ A}$$ [1]

For series combination,

$$R = 5 + 10 = 15\,\Omega$$

∴ Total current in the circuit,

$$I = \frac{V}{R} = \frac{6}{15} = 0.4\text{ A}$$ [1]

73. (i) Find the value of current I in the circuit given as below

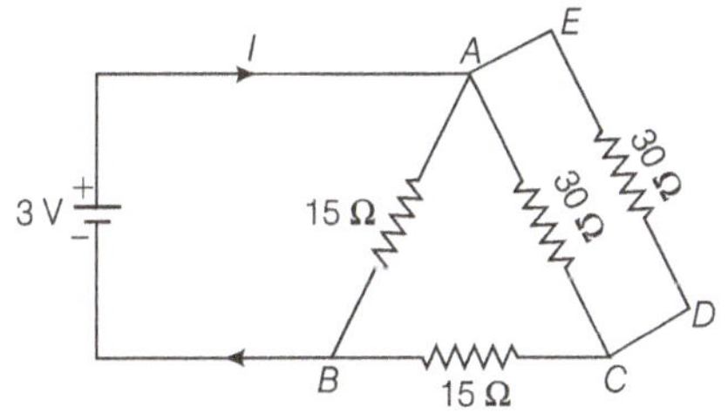

[4]

(ii) You have four resistors of 8 Ω each. Show how would you connect these resistors to have effective resistance of 8 Ω?

Sol. (i) R_{AC} and R_{ED} are in parallel, so

$$\frac{1}{R'_P} = \frac{1}{R_{AC}} + \frac{1}{R_{ED}} = \frac{1}{30} + \frac{1}{30} = \frac{1}{15}$$

$\Rightarrow \quad R'_P = 15\,\Omega$

Now, R'_P and R_{BC} are in series, so

$$R'_S = R'_P + R_{BC} = 15 + 15 = 30\,\Omega$$

Again, R_{AB} and R'_S are in parallel, so

$$\frac{1}{R''_P} = \frac{1}{R_{AB}} + \frac{1}{R'_S}$$

$$= \frac{1}{15} + \frac{1}{30} = \frac{1}{10}$$

∴ $\quad R''_P = 10\,\Omega$

So, current flowing through the circuit is

$$I = \frac{V}{R''_P} = \frac{3}{10} = 0.3\text{ A}$$ [2]

(ii) Two 8 Ω resistors are connected in parallel. Two such parallel combination must be connected in series to get effective resistance of 8 Ω.

Such combination is shown as below

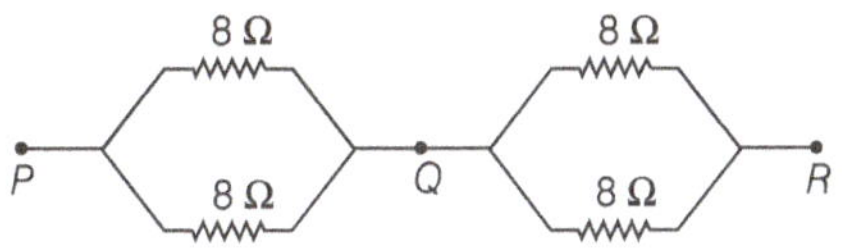

[2]

74. Two resistances when connected in parallel give resultant value of 2 Ω and when connected in series, the value becomes 9 Ω. Calculate the value of each resistance. [4]

Sol. We know that, two resistances are in parallel and hence

$$\frac{1}{R_P} = \frac{1}{R_1} + \frac{1}{R_2}$$

$\Rightarrow \quad R_P = \frac{R_1 R_2}{R_1 + R_2}$

Given, $\quad R_P = 2\,\Omega$

$\Rightarrow \quad 2 = \frac{R_1 R_2}{R_1 + R_2}$ [1]

∴ $\quad 2(R_1 + R_2) = R_1 R_2$ ...(i)

Now, same resistances are in series, $R_S = R_1 + R_2$

Given, $\quad R_S = 9\,\Omega$ and $9 = R_1 + R_2$ ...(ii)

From Eqs. (i) and (ii), we get

$R_1 R_2 = 18$ [1]

Again, using Eq. (ii), we get

$R_2 = 9 - R_1$

∴ $\quad R_1(9 - R_1) = 18$

$\Rightarrow \quad R_1^2 - 9R_1 + 18 = 0$

$\Rightarrow \quad R_1^2 - 6R_1 - 3R_1 + 18 = 0$ [1]

(by splitting the middle term)

$\Rightarrow \quad (R_1 - 6)(R_1 - 3) = 0$

Either, $R_1 = 6$ or $R_1 = 3$ and $R_2 = 3\,\Omega$ or $R_2 = 6\,\Omega$

Thus, two resistances are 3 Ω and 6 Ω. [1]

75. A cell of emf 2V and internal resistance 1.2 Ω is connected with an ammeter of resistance 0.8 Ω and two resistors of 4.5 Ω and 9 Ω as shown in the diagram

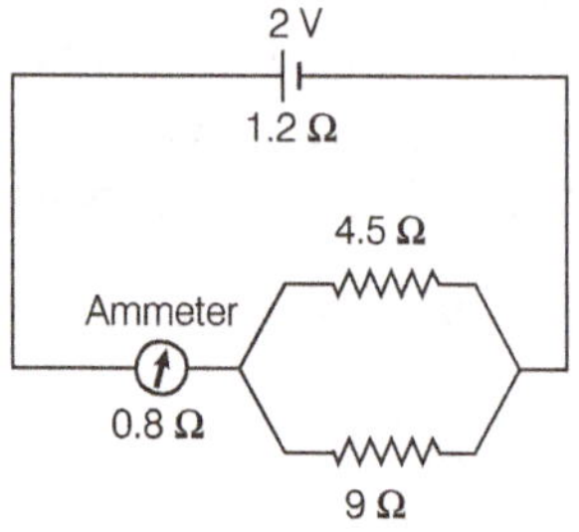

[4]

(i) What would be the reading on the ammeter?
(ii) What is the potential difference across the terminals of the cell? [2015]

Sol. (i) Given, emf of a cell, $E = 2\text{V}$

Internal resistance, $r = 1.2\,\Omega$

Resistance of ammeter $= 0.8\,\Omega$

Two resistances connected in parallel are 4.5 Ω and 9 Ω.

$$\therefore \quad R = \frac{4.5\times 9}{(4.5+9)}$$

We know that,

$$E = I(R + r)$$
$$= I \times \left[\left(\frac{4.5\times 9}{4.5+9}\right) + 0.8 + 1.2\right]$$
$$2 = I(3 + 0.8 + 1.2)$$
$$\Rightarrow \quad 2 = 5I$$

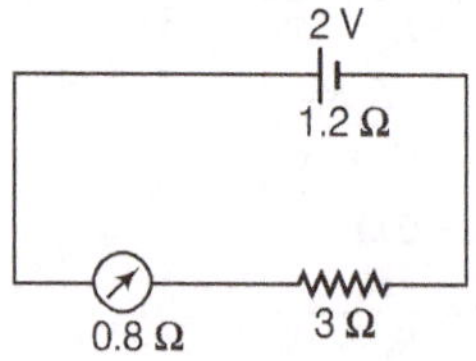

$$\Rightarrow \quad I = \frac{2}{5} \Rightarrow I = 0.4\text{ A}$$ [3]

(ii) Potential difference across the terminals of the cell is given by

$$V = I R_{\text{external}} = 0.4 \times (3 + 0.8)$$
$$= 0.4 \times 3.8 = 1.52\text{ V}$$ [1]

76. A cell of emf 1.5 V and internal resistance 1.0 Ω are connected to two resistors of 4.0 Ω and 20.0 Ω in series as shown in the figure.

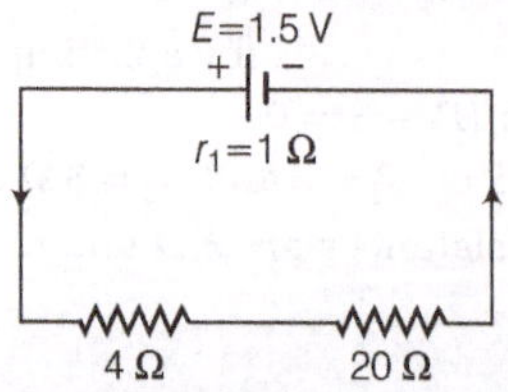

[4]

Calculate the
(i) current in the circuit.
(ii) potential difference across the 4.0 Ω resistor.
(iii) voltage drop across internal resistance when the current is flowing. [2007]
(iv) potential difference across the cell. [4]

Sol. Given, $E = 1.5\text{ V}$, $r = 1\,\Omega$,

$$R_1 = 4\,\Omega,\ R_2 = 20\,\Omega$$

The net external resistance of the circuit,

$$R = R_1 + R_2 = 4 + 20 = 24\,\Omega$$

(i) Current in the circuit,

$$I = \frac{E}{R+r} = \frac{1.5}{24+1} = \frac{1.5}{25} = 0.06\text{ A}$$ [1]

(ii) Potential difference across the 4 Ω resistor,

$$V = IR_1 = 0.06 \times 4 = 0.24\text{ V}$$ [1]

(iii) Voltage drop across internal resistance,

$$V_r = Ir = 0.06 \times 1 = 0.06\text{ V}$$ [1]

(iv) Terminal voltage,

$V =$ Potential difference across the cell

$$= E - Ir = 1.5 - 0.06 = 1.44\text{ V}$$ [1]

77. Four cells, each of emf 1.5 V and internal resistance 2.0 Ω are connected in a parallel. The battery of the cells is connected to an external resistance of 2.5 Ω. Calculate
(i) the total resistance of the circuit.
(ii) the current flowing in the external circuit.
(iii) the drop in potential across the terminals of the cells. [3]

Sol. Given, number of cells, $n = 4$, emf of each cell, $E = 1.5\text{ V}$, $r = 2.0\,\Omega$, $R = 2.5\,\Omega$

(i) Total internal resistance of cells

$$\frac{1}{r'} = \frac{1}{2} + \frac{1}{2} + \frac{1}{2} + \frac{1}{2} = \frac{4}{2}$$
$$r' = 0.5\,\Omega$$

Total resistance of the circuit $= r' + R$ [1]

$$= 0.5 + 2.5 = 3.0\,\Omega$$

(ii) $I = \dfrac{E}{r' + R} = \dfrac{1.5}{3} = 0.5\text{ A}$ [1]

(iii) Potential drop $= E - \dfrac{I}{4} r$

$$= 1.5 - \frac{0.5}{4} \times 2$$
$$= 1.5 - 0.25 = 1.25\text{ A}$$ [1]

78. An electric bulb of resistance 500 Ω, draws a current of 0.4 A. Calculate the power of the bulb and the potential difference at its end. [2] [2017]

Sol. Given, resistance of bulb, $R = 500\,\Omega$, current, $I = 0.4\text{ A}$,

power, $P = ?$, potential difference, $V = ?$

As we know, power, $P = I^2R = (0.4)^2 \times 500$

$\therefore$ Power, $P = 80\text{ W}$

Potential difference,

$$V = IR = 0.4 \times 500 = 200\text{ V}$$ [2]

79. The figure shows a circuit, when the circuit is switched ON, the ammeter reads 0.5 A.
(i) Calculate the value of the unknown resistor R.
(ii) Calculate the charge passing through the 3 Ω resistor in 120 s.
(iii) Calculate the power dissipated in the 3 Ω resistor.
[3] [2013]

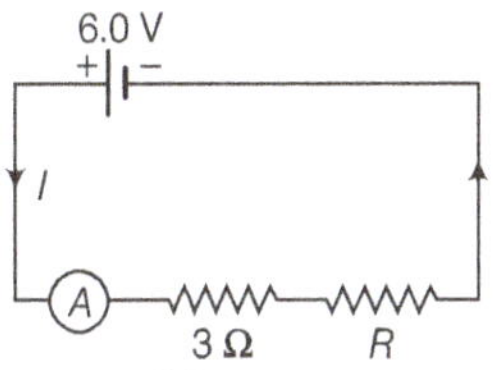

Sol. (i) $I = \frac{V}{R} \Rightarrow 0.5 = \frac{6.0}{3+R}$ **[1]**

$\Rightarrow 3 + R = \frac{6}{0.5} \Rightarrow R = \frac{60}{5} - 3 = 9\ \Omega$

(ii) $Q = I \times t = 0.5 \times 120 = 60\ C$ **[1]**

(iii) $P = VI = I^2R = (0.5)^2 \times 3$
$= 0.25 \times 3 = 0.75\ W$ **[1]**

80. Calculate the quantity of heat produced in a 20 Ω resistor carrying 2.5 A current in 5 min. **[2] [2016]**

Sol. Given, resistance, $R = 20\ \Omega$
Current, $I = 2.5\ A$
Time, $t = 5\ min = 5 \times 60 = 300\ s$ **[1]**
According to Joule's law of heating,

$$H = I^2Rt = (2.5)^2 \times 20 \times 300$$
$$= \frac{625}{100} \times 20 \times 300 = 625 \times 20 \times 3$$
$$H = 37500\ J$$ **[1]**

81. An electrical heater is rated 4 kW, 220 V. Find the cost of using this heater for 12 h, if one kWh of electrical energy costs 3.25. **[2]**

Sol. Given, $P = 4\ kW$, $V = 220\ V$, $t = 12\ h$

$$E = P \times t = 4 \times 12 = 48\ kWh$$

Cost of energy consumed = 48 × 3.25 = ₹156 **[2]**

82. An electric iron is rated 220 V, 2 kW.
(i) If the iron is used for 2 h daily, find the cost of running it for one week if it costs ₹ 4.25 per kWh.
(ii) Why is the fuse absolutely necessary in a power circuit? **[4] [2018]**

Sol. (i) Given, power, $P = 2 \times 10^3\ W = 2\ kW$
Voltage, $V = 220\ V$
Time, t = 2h daily for 1 week = 2 × 7 = 14 h
Electrical energy (in kWh)
$= P \times t = 2 \times 14 = 28\ kWh$
Running cost = 28 × 4.25 = ₹119 **[2]**

(ii) The purpose of using a fuse in an electrical circuit is to limit the electric current in a electric circuit. It prevents overheating or overloading in the circuit when a short circuit occurs. **[2]**

83. An electrical appliance is rated at 1000 kVA, 220 V. If the appliance is operated for 2h, calculate the energy consumed by the appliance in
(i) kWh (ii) joule **[2]**

Sol. Given, $P = 1000\ kVA = 1000\ kW$, $t = 2h$
(i) Energy consumed in kWh,
$E = P \times t = 1000 \times 2 = 2000\ kWh$ **[1]**
(ii) Energy consumed in joule,
$E = 2000 \times 3.6 \times 10^6 J = 7.2 \times 10^9\ J$ **[1]**

84. Two bulbs are marked 100 W, 220 V and 60 W, 110 V. Calculate the ratio of their resistance. **[3] [2011]**

Sol. Given, $P_1 = 100\ W$, $P_2 = 60\ W$, $V_1 = 220\ V$,
$V_2 = 110\ V$, $\frac{R_1}{R_2} = ?$

We know that, power is given by **[1]**

$$P = \frac{V^2}{R}$$

$\therefore$ $R_1 = \frac{V_1^2}{P_1}$ and $R_2 = \frac{V_2^2}{P_2}$

$\Rightarrow$ $R_1 = \frac{(220)^2}{100}$ and $R_2 = \frac{(110)^2}{60}$

$$\frac{R_1}{R_2} = \frac{\frac{(220)^2}{100}}{\frac{(110)^2}{60}} = \frac{(220)^2 \times 60}{(110)^2 \times 100} = \frac{12}{5}$$ **[2]**

85. An electric heater is rated 1000 W-200 V. Calculate **[2]**
(i) the resistance of the heating element and
(ii) the current flowing through it. **[2009]**

Sol. Given, $P = 1000\ W$, $V = 200\ V$ **[1]**

(i) $R = \frac{V^2}{P} = \frac{200 \times 200}{1000} = 40\ \Omega$

(ii) $I = \frac{P}{V} = \frac{1000}{200} = 5A$ **[1]**

86. If the current I through a resistor is increased by 100% (assume that temperature remains unchanged), then find the increase in power dissipated. **[3]**

Sol. Since, $P = I^2R$
Current after increased by 100%

$$= I + \frac{100I}{100} = 2I$$
$$P' = (2I)^2R = 4I^2R$$ **[1]**

$\therefore$ Percentage increase in power dissipation

$$= \frac{P' - P}{P} \times 100$$
$$= \frac{4I^2R - I^2R}{I^2R} \times 100$$
$$= \frac{I^2R(4-1)}{I^2R} \times 100$$
$$= 3 \times 100 = 300\%$$ **[2]**

87. An electrician puts a fuse of rating 5 A in that part of domestic electrical circuit in which an electric heater of rating 1.5 kW, 220 V is operating. What is likely to happen in this case and why? **[2]**

Sol. Given, $P = 1.5\text{ kW} = 1.5 \times 10^3\text{W}$, $V = 220\text{V}$

$\therefore$ The current drawn by heater,

$$I = \frac{P}{V}$$ **[1/2]**

$$= \frac{1.5 \times 10^3 \text{ W}}{220 \text{ V}} = 6.8 \text{ A}$$ **[1/2]**

The above amount of current is greater than the rated value of fuse current. Hence, the fuse will melt and break the circuit. **[1]**

88. The potential difference between two terminals of an electric iron is 220V and the current flowing through its element is 5A. Calculate the resistance and wattage of the electric iron. **[2]**

Sol. The potential difference between two terminals of an electric iron, $V = 220\text{V}$ and current flowing through its element, $I = 5$ A.

Therefore, resistance, $R = \frac{V}{I} = \frac{220}{5}\ \Omega$

$$R = 44\,\Omega$$ **[1]**

We know that, power, $P = V \times I$

$$= 220 \times 5 = 1100\text{ W}$$ **[1]**

89. An electric geyser rated at 1500 W, 250 V is connected to a 250 V line mains. Solve

(i) the electric current drawn by it,
(ii) energy consumed by it in 50 h and
(iii) cost of energy consumed, if each unit costs ₹ 6.

Sol. Given, power, $P = 1500\text{W}$, voltage, $V = 250$ V **[3]**

(i) $\therefore$ Electric current drawn,

$$I = \frac{P}{V} = \frac{1500}{250} = 6\text{A}$$ **[1]**

(ii) $\therefore$ Energy consumed, E = Power $\times$ Time

$= 1500 \times 50$ $(\because t = 50\text{ h})$
$= 75000$ Wh $(\because 1\text{ kW} = 1000\text{ W})$
$= 75$ unit $(\because 1\text{ unit} = 1\text{ kWh})$ **[1]**

(iii) $\therefore$ Cost of energy consumed
$= 75 \times 6 =$ ₹ 450 **[1]**

90. An electric iron consumes energy at a rate of 840 W when heating is at the maximum rate and 360 W when the heating is at the minimum rate. The applied voltage is 220 V. What is the value of current and the resistance in each case? **[3]**

Sol. We know that, the power input is $P = VI$

Thus, current, $I = \frac{P}{V}$ **[1]**

When heating is at the maximum rate,

$$I = \frac{840 \text{ W}}{220 \text{ V}} = 3.82 \text{ A}$$

and the resistance of the electric iron is

$$R = \frac{V}{I} = \frac{220 \text{ V}}{3.82 \text{ A}} = 57.59\,\Omega$$ **[1]**

When heating is at the minimum rate,

$$I = \frac{360 \text{ W}}{220 \text{ V}} = 1.64 \text{ A}$$

and the resistance of the electric iron is

$$R = \frac{V}{I} = \frac{220 \text{ V}}{1.64 \text{ A}} = 134.15\,\Omega$$ **[1]**

91. An electrical bulb is rated 40 W, 220 V. How many bulbs can be connected in parallel with each other across the two wires of 220 V line, if the maximum allowable current is 6 A? **[3]**

Sol. Given, $P = 40$ W, $V = 220$ V, $I = 6$ A

We know that, $R = V^2 / P = (220)^2 / 40$

$$= 48400 / 40 = 1210\Omega$$ **[1]**

Now, $V = IR_{eq} \Rightarrow R_{eq} = V / I = 220 / 6 = 36.66\,\Omega$

Suppose, there are x number of bulb in parallel

$$1/36.66 = x/1210$$

$\therefore \quad x = 1210 / 36.66 = 33.006 \approx 33$ **[2]**

92. B_1, B_2 and B_2 are three identical bulbs and ammeters A_1, A_2 and A_3 are connected as shown in figure. When all the bulbs glow, then the current of 3 A is recorded by ammeter A. **[4]**

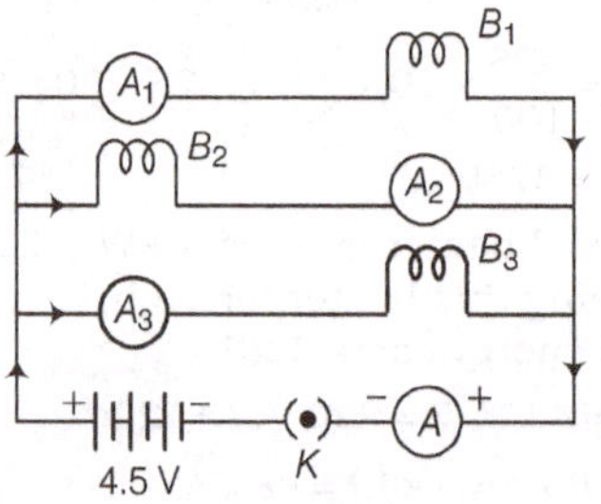

(i) What happens to the glow of the other two bulbs when bulb B_1 gets fused?
(ii) What happens to the reading of A_1, A_2, A_3 and A when the bulb B_2 gets fused?
(iii) How much power is dissipated in the circuit when all the three bulbs glow together?

Sol. Resistance of combination of three bulbs in parallel,

$$R_{eq} = \frac{V}{I} = \frac{4.5}{3} = 1.5\,\Omega$$

If R is the resistance of each bulb, then

$$\frac{1}{R_{eq}} = \frac{1}{R} + \frac{1}{R} + \frac{1}{R} \quad \text{or} \quad \frac{1}{R_{eq}} = \frac{3}{R}$$

or $\quad R = 3R_{eq} = 3 \times 1.5 = 4.5\,\Omega$

Current in each bulb,

$$I = \frac{V}{R} = \frac{4.5 \text{ V}}{4.5\,\Omega} = 1\text{A}$$ **[1]**

(i) When bulb B_1 gets fused, then the currents in B_2 and B_3 remain same $I_2 = I_3 = 1$ A, so their glow remains unaffected. [1]

(ii) When bulb B_2 gets fused, then the current in B_2 becomes zero and currents in B_1 and B_3 remain 1 A.

$\therefore$ Total current, $I = I_1 + I_2 + I_3$

$= 1 + 0 + 1 = 2$ A

Current in ammeter $A_1, I_1 = 1$ A

Current in ammeter $A_2, I_2 = 0$

Current in ammeter $A_3, I_3 = 1$ A

Current in ammeter $A, I = 2$ A [1]

(iii) When all the three bulbs are connected, then power dissipated, $P = \frac{V^2}{R_{eq}} = \frac{(4.5)^2}{1.5} = 13.5$ W [1]

93. (i) An electric bulb is marked 100 W, 250 V. What information does this convey?

(ii) How much current will the bulb draw, if connected to a 250 V supply? [2011]

Sol. (i) It conveys that when the bulb is lighted on 250 V supply, it consumes 100 W electrical power, i.e. 100 J of electrical energy is consumed in 1s. [2]

(ii) Current draw, $I = \frac{P}{V} = \frac{100}{250} = 0.4$ A [1]

94. (i) A fuse is rated 8 A. Can it be used with an electrical appliance rated 5 kW, 200 V? Give reason.

(ii) Name the safety devices which are connected to the live wire of a household electric circuit. [2018]

Sol. (i) Given, power $(P) = 5$ kW $= 5\times 10^3$W

$V = 200$ V

We know that, $I = \frac{P}{V}$

$I = \frac{5\times 10^3}{200} \Rightarrow I = 2.5\times 10$

$\therefore \quad I = 25\text{A} > 8\text{A}$

Thus, it cannot be used as the appliance will get fused. [1½]

(ii) Fuse, MCB [1½]

Structured Questions

95. (i) A copper wire of resistivity 1.63×10^{-8} Ω-m has cross-section area of 16.3×10^{-4} cm^2. Calculate the length of the wire required to make a 20 Ω coil. [3]

(ii) Which resistor arrangement : C or D has the lower resistance?

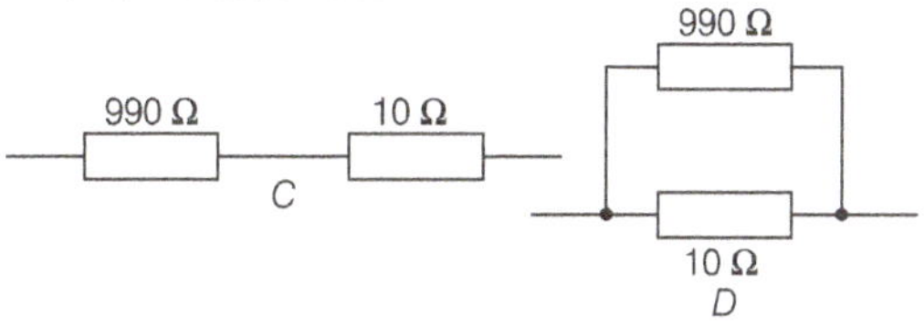

[3]

(iii) (a) A current of 1 A flows in a series circuit having an electric lamp and a conductor of 5 Ω, when connected to a 10 V battery. Calculate the resistance of the electric lamp.

(b) Now, if a resistance of 10 Ω is connected in parallel with this series combination, then what change (if any) in current flowing through 5 Ω conductor and potential difference across the lamp will take place? Give reason. [4]

Sol. (i) Given, resistivity, $\rho = 1.63 \times 10^{-8}$ Ω-m

Area of cross-section, $A = 16.3 \times 10^{-4}$ cm^2

$= 16.3 \times 10^{-8}$ m^2

Resistance of the coil, $R = 20\,\Omega$

Length of the wire (l) = ?

As we know that, $R = \rho\frac{l}{A}$

Thus $\quad l = \frac{R \times A}{\rho}$

$l = \frac{20 \times 16.3 \times 10^{-4} \times 10^{-4}}{1.63 \times 10^{-8}} = 200$ m [3]

(ii) Equivalent resistance in arrangement C,

$R_C = 990 + 10 = 1000\,\Omega = 1\,\text{k}\Omega$

Equivalent resistance in arrangement D,

$\frac{1}{R_D} = \frac{1}{990} + \frac{1}{10}$

$\frac{1}{R_D} = \frac{1+99}{990} = \frac{990}{100}$

$\Rightarrow \quad R_D = 9.9\,\Omega$

Thus, arrangement D has lower resistance. [3]

(iiii) (a) Let the resistance of the lamp be R_1 and resistance of conductor be $R_2 = 5\,\Omega$.

$\therefore$ Total resistance in series, $R_S = R_1 + R_2$

$= R_1 + 5$

Current, $I = 1$ A, voltage, $V = 10$ V

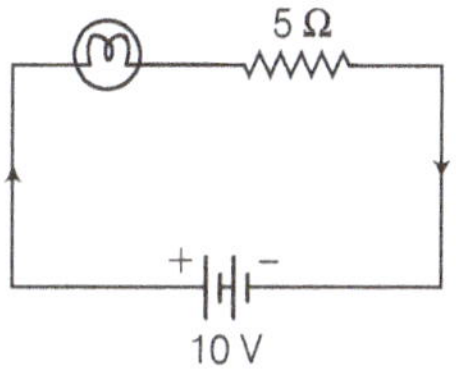

Using Ohm's law, $V = IR_S$

$10 = 1(R_1 + 5)$

$\Rightarrow \quad R_1 = 5\,\Omega$

Thus, the resistance of electric lamp is 5 Ω. [2]

(b) Now, a resistance of 10 Ω is connected in parallel with the series combination. Therefore, the total resistance of the circuit is given by

$\frac{1}{R_P} = \frac{1}{R_1 + 5} + \frac{1}{10}$

$\Rightarrow \quad \frac{1}{R_P} = \frac{1}{5+5} + \frac{1}{10}$

$$\Rightarrow \quad \frac{1}{R_P} = \frac{1}{10} + \frac{1}{10}$$

$$\therefore \quad R_P = 5\,\Omega$$

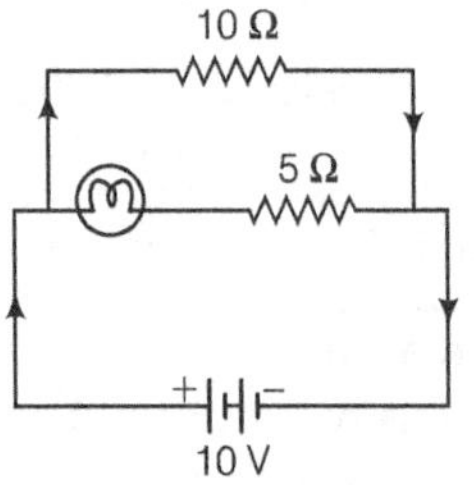

Hence, current flowing in the circuit,

$$I = \frac{V}{R} = \frac{10}{5} = 2\text{ A}$$

Thus, 1 A current will flow through 10 Ω resistor and 1 A will flow through the lamp and conductor of 5 Ω resistance.

Hence, there will be no change in current flowing through 5Ω conductor. Also, there will be no change in potential difference across the lamp. [2]

96. (i) (a) Write one advantage of connecting electrical appliances in parallel combination.

(b) What characteristics should a fuse wire have?

(c) Which wire in a power circuit is connected to the metallic body of the appliance? [3] [2019]

(ii) The figure below shows a dual control switch circuit connected to a bulb.

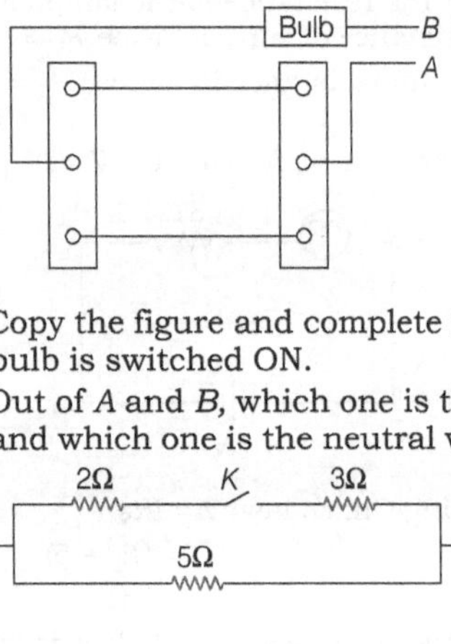

(a) Copy the figure and complete it so that the bulb is switched ON.

(b) Out of *A* and *B*, which one is the live wire and which one is the neutral wire? [3]

(iii)

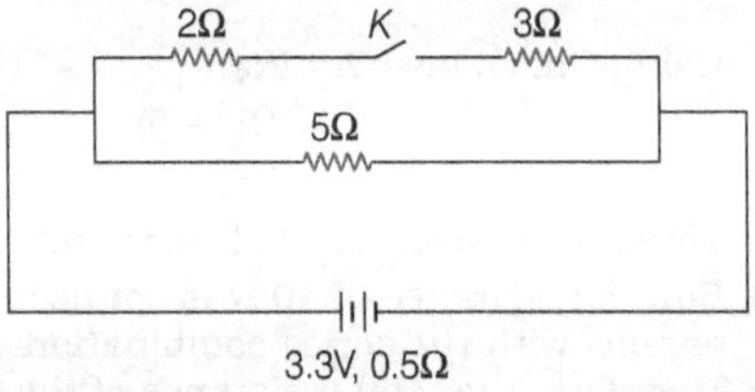

The above figure shows a circuit with the key *K* open. Calculate

(a) the resistance of the circuit when the key *K* is open.

(b) the current drawn from the cell when the key *K* is open.

(c) the resistance of the circuit when the key *K* is closed.

(d) the current drawn from the cell when the key *K* is closed. [4]

Sol. (i) (a) In parallel combination of appliances, if any appliances gets faulty, rest of the circuit gets unaffected by it and no discontinued supply. [1]

(b) I. It should have a low melting point.

II. It should have a high resistance. [1]

(c) Earth wire [1]

(ii) (a)

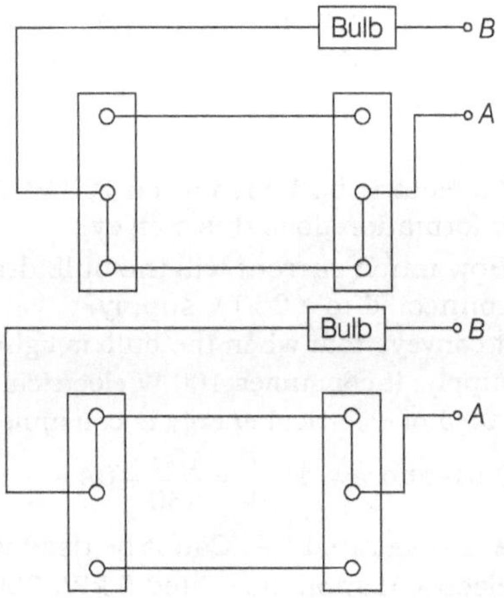

[2]

(b) *A* is live wire and *B* is the neutral wire. [1]

(iii) (a) When key *K* is open, then 2Ω and 3Ω resistance are not in the circuit, i.e. this branch is not accounted in the circuit.

Now, equivalent resistance,

$$R_{eq} = 5 + 0.5 = 5.5\,\Omega$$ [1]

(b) According to the Ohm's law,

$$V = I\,R_{eq}$$

$$I = \frac{V}{R_{eq}}$$

Here, $V = 3.3$ V and $R_{eq} = 5.5\,\Omega$.

So, current, $I = \frac{3.3}{5.5} = 0.6$ A [1]

(c) When the key *K* is closed, then circuit becomes as shown in the figure.

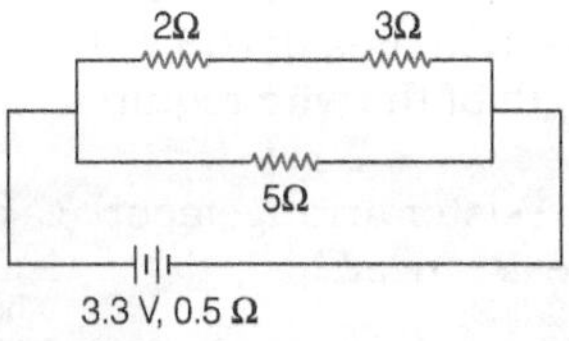

In the circuit, 2Ω and 3Ω resistances are connected in series combination. Hence, equivalent resistance,

$$R' = 2 + 3 = 5\,\Omega$$

Now, circuit becomes

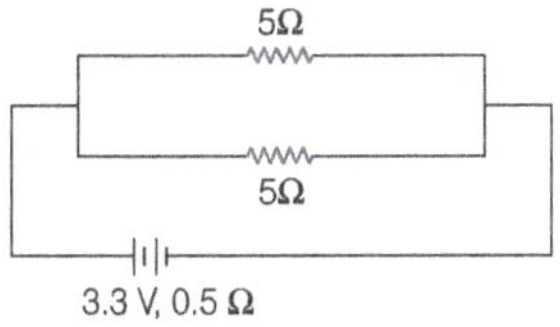

In the circuit, two 5 Ω resistances are connected in the parallel combination.

Hence, equivalent resistance,

$$R_{eq} = 0.5 + \frac{5 \times 5}{5 + 5} = 0.5 + 2.5 = 3.0\,\Omega$$ **[1]**

(d) According to the Ohm's law,

$$V = IR$$

Current, $I = \frac{V}{R_{eq}} = \frac{3.3}{3.0} = 1.1\text{ A}$ **[1]**

97. (i) A heater coil connected to 200 V has a resistance of 80 Ω. If the heater is plugged in for the time t such that 1 kg of water at 20°C attains a temperature of 60°C. Find

(a) the power of heater.

(b) the heat absorbed by water.

(c) the value of t in seconds.

(ii) (a) What are superconductors? **[3]**

(b) Calculate the current drawn by an appliance rated 110 W, 220 V when connected across 220 V supply.

(c) Name a substance whose resistance decreases with the increase in temperature. **[3]**

(iii)

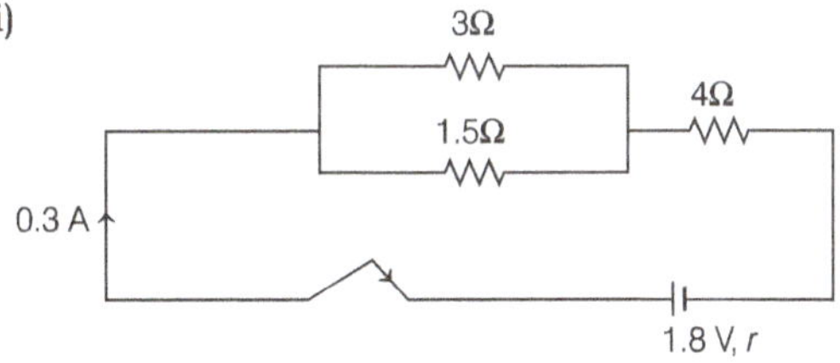

The diagram above shows three resistors connected across a cell of emf 1.8 V and internal resistance r. Calculate **[2020]**

(a) current through 3 Ω resistor and

(b) the internal resistance. **[4]**

Sol. (i) (a) ∴ Power of heater,

$$P = \frac{V^2}{R} = \frac{200 \times 200}{80} = 500\text{ W}$$ **[1]**

(b) ∴ Heat absorbed by water, $H = mC\Delta T$

$= 1 \times 4200 \times 40$

($\because \Delta T = 60° - 20° = 40°$ C, $C = 4200$ J/kg °C)

$= 168000$ J

$= 168$ kJ **[1]**

(c) ∴ Energy consumed by heater, $H = P \times t$

$$168000 = 500 \times t \Rightarrow t = \frac{168000}{500} = 336\text{ s}$$ **[1]**

(ii) (a) The conductors with infinite conductivity or zero resistivity are called superconductors. **[1]**

(b) Given, power of appliance, $P = 110$ W

Supply voltage, $V = 220$ V

We know that, $P = VI$

$$\Rightarrow \quad I = \frac{P}{V} = \frac{110}{220} = 0.5\text{ A}$$ **[1]**

(c) Semiconductor **[1]**

(iii) (a) The given circuit diagram is as shown below

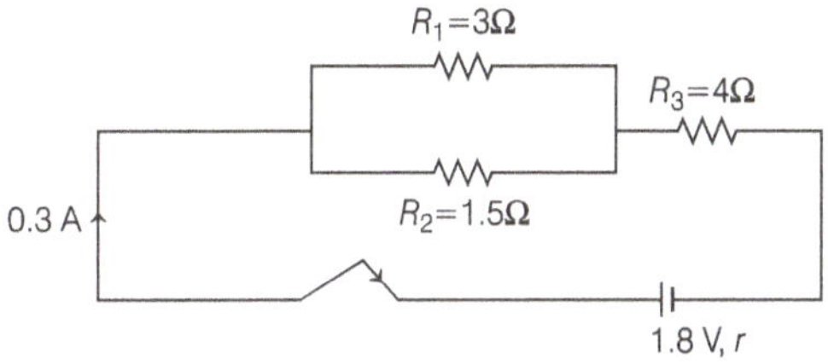

According to current division rule, current through 3 Ω resistance,

$$I' = I \cdot \frac{R_2}{R_1 + R_2} = 0.3 \times \frac{1.5}{3 + 1.5}$$

$$= \frac{0.45}{4.5} = 0.1\text{ A}$$ **[2]**

(b) From circuit diagram, equivalent resistance is given as

$$R = (3 \| 1.5) + 4 + r = \frac{3 \times 1.5}{3 + 1.5} + 4 + r$$

$$= \frac{4.5}{4.5} + 4 + r$$

$$\Rightarrow \quad R = 5 + r$$

∴ Current drawn through battery,

$$I = \frac{V}{R} \Rightarrow 0.3 = \frac{1.8}{5 + r}$$

$$\Rightarrow 5 + r = \frac{1.8}{0.3} \Rightarrow 5 + r = 6$$

$$\Rightarrow \quad r = 6 - 5 = 1\,\Omega$$ **[2]**

98. (i) What is meant by "electrical resistance" of a conductor? State how resistance of a conductor is affected when (a) a low current passes through it for a short duration and (b) a heavy current passes through it for about 30 s. **[3]**

(ii) (a) Write an expression for the electrical energy spent in the flow of current through an electrical appliance in terms of I, R and t.

(b) At what voltage is the alternating current supplied to our houses? **[3]**

(c) How should the electric lamps in a building be connected? **[2012]**

(iii) A battery of emf 12 V and internal resistance 2 Ω is connected with two resistors A and B of resistance 4 Ω and 6 Ω respectively joined in series. **[2016]**

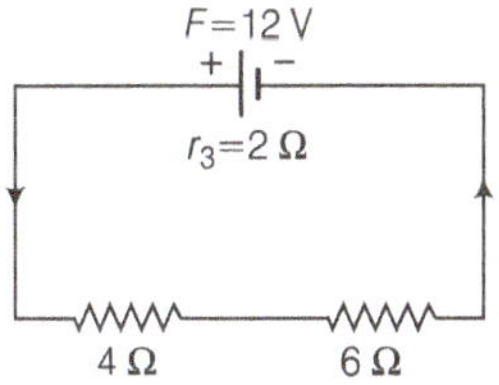

Find
(a) current in the circuit.
(b) the terminal voltage of the cell.
(c) the potential difference across 6 Ω resistor.
(d) electrical energy spent per minute in 4 Ω resistor. [4]

Sol. (i) Electrical resistance of a conductor may be defined as the basis property of any substance due to which it opposes the flow of current through it. Current is inversely proportional to resistance. [1]

(a) The resistance of the conductor will increase when a low current pass through it for a short duration. [1]

(b) The resistance of the conductor will decrease when a heavy current pass through it. [1]

(ii) (a) The expression for the electrical energy, $E = I^2Rt$. [1]

(b) Alternating current supplied to our houses is at voltage 220 V. [1]

(c) The electric lamp in a building should be connected in parallel. [1]

(iii) According to question,

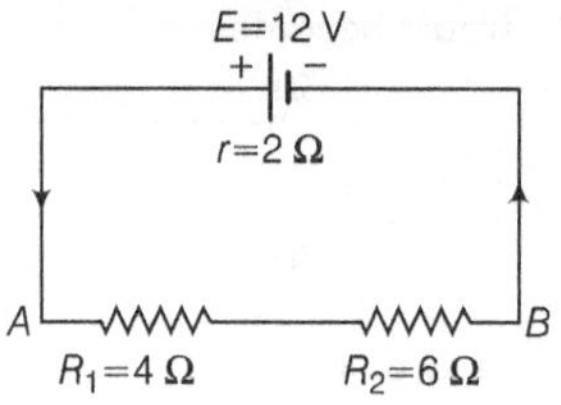

(a) Current in the circuit is given by

$$V = IR_{eq}$$

$$I = \frac{V}{R_{eq}} = \frac{12}{4+6+2} = 1\text{A}$$ [1]

($R_{eq} = R_1 + R_2 + r$, for series combination)

(b) Terminal voltage of cell = $E - Ir$

$$= 12 - 1 \times 2 = 10 \text{ V}$$ [1]

(c) Potential difference across 6 Ω resistance is given by

$$V = IR_2$$
$$= 1 \times 6 = 6 \text{ V}$$ [1]

(d) Electric energy spent per minute is given by

$$I^2Rt = 1^2 \times 4 \times 60 \quad (\because 1 \text{ min} = 60 \text{ s})$$
$$= 240 \text{ J}$$ [1]

Chapter Assessment

1 Mark Questions

1. Which of the following is an ohmic resistance?
   (a) LED
   (b) Junction diode
   (c) Filament of bulb
   (d) Nichrome wire

2. For which of the following substances, resistance decrease with the increase in temperature?
   (a) Copper (b) Mercury
   (c) Carbon (d) Platinum

3. Which of the following is not a characteristic of parallel combination of resistors? **[Latest Specimen Paper, Sem-II]**
   (a) If one resistor is fused, the circuit does not become open.
   (b) The total resistance R is given by the formula $\frac{1}{R} = \frac{1}{R_1} + \frac{1}{R_2} + \frac{1}{R_3}$ ....
   (c) The total resistance becomes less than the least resistor, present in the combination.
   (d) The current through resistor always remains the same.

4. Which of the following combinations have the lowest equivalent resistance between X and Y?

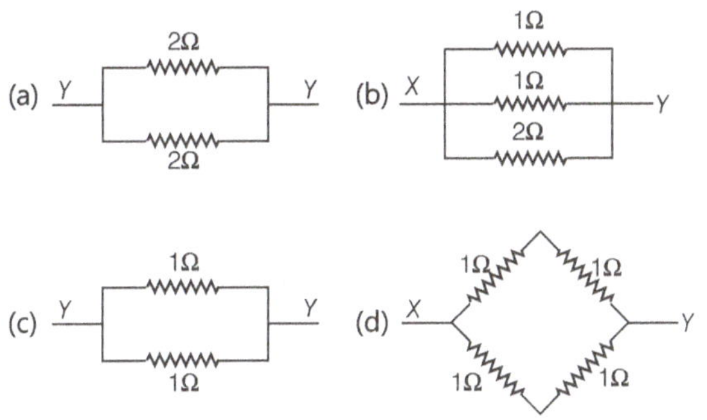

5. The electrical appliance has a rating 100 W, 120 V. The resistance of element of appliance, when in use is
   (a) 1.2 Ω (b) 144 Ω
   (c) 120 Ω (d) 100 Ω

2 Marks Questions

6. Mention special features of the material used as arms element of an electric iron.

7. It is possible to replace resistors joined in series by an equivalent single resistor of resistance. How?

8. Derive the relation between kilowatt hour and joule.

9. What kind of graph is obtained by plotting values of V and I? Why?

10. You are given three bulbs of 40W, 60W and 100W. Which of them has lower resistance?

11. An electrical appliance is rated at 1000 kW, 220 V. If the appliance is operated for 2 h, calculate the energy consumed by the appliance in
    (i) kWh and
    (ii) joule. **[2012]**

12. Two bulbs are marked 100 W, 220 V and 60 W, 110 V. Calculate the ratio of their resistances. **[2011]**

13. An electric heater is rated 1000 W - 200 V. Calculate
    (i) the resistance of the heating element and
    (ii) the current flowing through it. **[2009]**

14. A geyser has a label 2 kW, 240 V. What is the cost of using it for 30 min, if the cost of electricity is ₹ 3 per commercial unit?

15. A family uses a light bulb of 100 W, a fan of 100 W and a heater of 1000 W, each for 8 h a day. If the cost of electricity is ₹ 2 per unit, what is the expenditure for the family per day on electricity? **[2001]**

16. Calculate the electrical energy in SI units consumed by a 100 W bulb and a 60 W fan connected in parallel for 5 min. **[2000]**

Structured Questions

17. (i) (a) Name two devices based on Joule's heating effect.
    (b) Name two safety devices used in domestic circuiting.
    (c) A bulb is rated at 110V, 80W. What does this mean? **[3]**
    (ii) Make a table with the names of three electrical appliances used in your home in one column, their power, voltage rating and approximate time for which each one is used in one day in the other columns. **[3]**
    (iii) A wire is cut into three equal parts and then connected in parallel with the same source.
    How will its
    (a) resistance and resistivity gets affected?
    (b) How would the total current and the current through the parts change? **[4]**

18. (i) (a) How does earthing prevent electrical shock?
    (b) In a 3-pin plug, why is the earth pin made longer and thicker than the other two pins? **[3]**

(ii) Draw a labelled diagram of a 3-pin socket. Also, state the purpose of a fuse in an electric circuit. **[3]**

(iii) Find the equivalent resistance for the following circuit, when

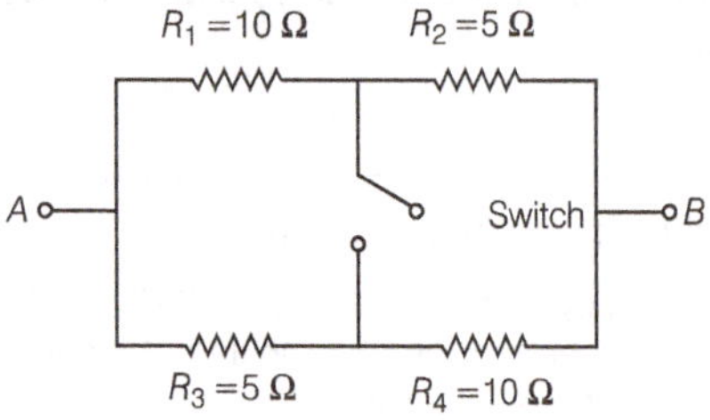

[4]

(a) switch is closed and
(b) switch is open.

19. (i) How does the heat produced in a wire or a conductor depend upon the

(a) current passing through the conductor and
(b) resistance of the conductor with constant supply voltage ? **[3]**

(ii) (a) What is a fuse wire?

(b) The diagrams (a) and (b) given below are of a plug and a socket with arrow marked as 1, 2, 3 and 4, 5, 6 respectively on them. Identify live (L), neutral (N) and the earth (E) wires against the correct number. **[3]**

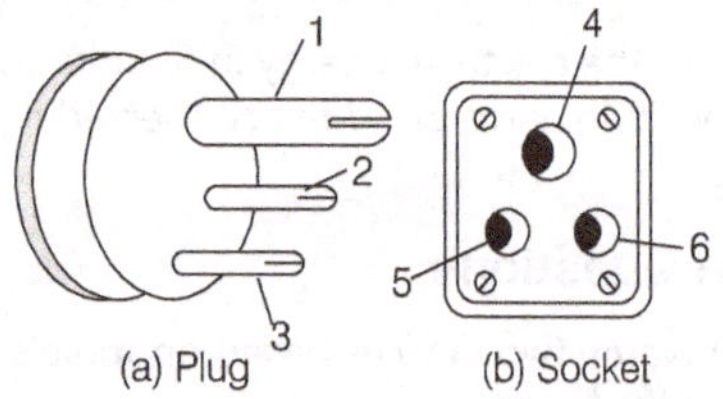

(a) Plug (b) Socket

(iii) Three incandescent bulbs of 100 W each are connected in series in an electric circuit. In another set of three bulbs of the same wattage are connected in parallel to the source. **[4]**

(a) Will the bulb in the two circuits glow with the same brightness? Justify your answer.
(b) Now, let one bulb in both the circuits get fused. Will the rest of the bulbs continue to glow in each circuit? Give reason.

20. (i) State the ohm's law and draw the graph between potential difference (V) and current for metallic conductor. **[3]**

(ii) State the relation between these two works and the work done in moving a unit charge through a cell connected across the resistor. Take the internal resistance of the cell as r. Hence, obtain an expression for the current i in the circuit. **[3]**

(iii) If a wire of resistance 2Ω gets stretched to thrice its original length, **[2022 (Sem-II)]**

(a) calculate the new resistance of the wire.
(b) what happens to the specific resistance of the wire? **[4]**

21. (i) With reference to the diagram given below, calculate

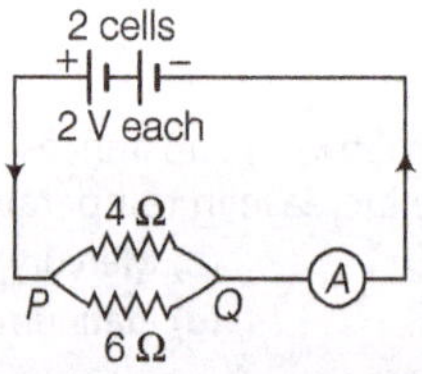

(a) the equivalent resistance between P and Q.
(b) the reading of an ammeter.
(c) the electrical power between P and Q. **[3]**

(ii) Electrical power P is given by an expression $P = \frac{(Q \times V)}{\text{time}}$

(a) What do the symbols Q and V represent?
(b) Express power in terms of current and resistance explaining the symbols used there in. **[3]**

(iii)

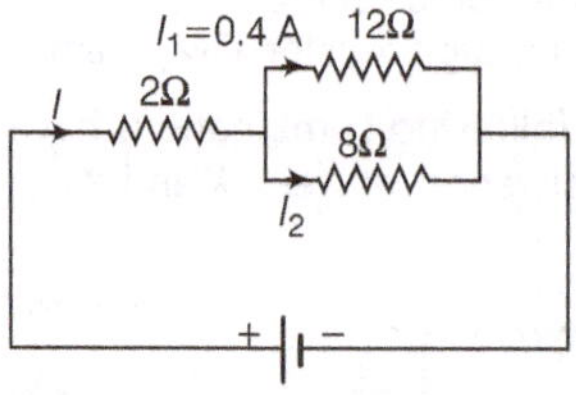

2022 (Sem. II)

In the above circuit diagram, calculate

(a) the external resistance of the circuit
(b) the current I_2
(c) the current I **[4]**

For Solutions Scan the Code

Olympiad Section*

Brain Teasing Questions of Olympiad Pattern

1 The equivalent resistance of network of three 3 Ω resistors cannot be

(a) 1 Ω (b) 9 Ω
(c) 4.5 Ω (d) 6 Ω

2 Determine the equivalent resistance between points X and Y in the following circuit.

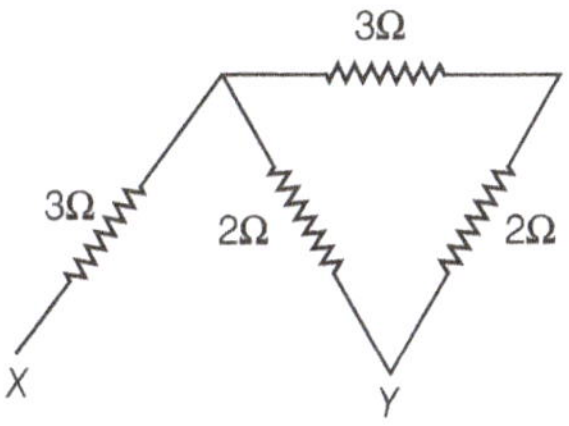

(a) $\frac{31}{5}$ Ω (b) $\frac{21}{5}$ Ω
(c) $\frac{31}{7}$ Ω (d) $\frac{21}{8}$ Ω

3 For the given circuit, name the components which are connected in parallel.

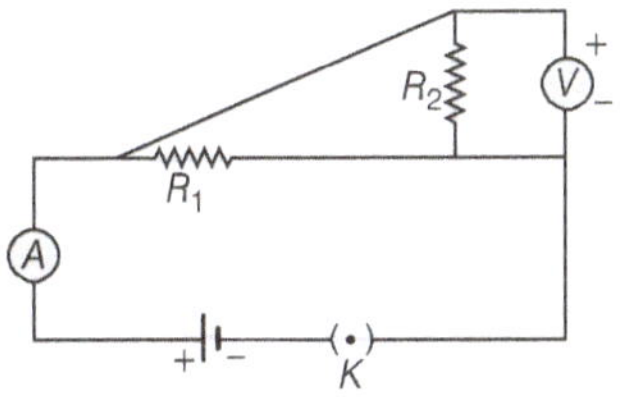

(a) Both R_1 and R_2 (b) R_1, R_2 and V

(c) Both R_2 and V (d) Both R_1 and V

4 The current flowing through a resistor connected in an electric circuit and the potential difference applied across its ends are shown in figure below. The value of the resistance of the resistor is

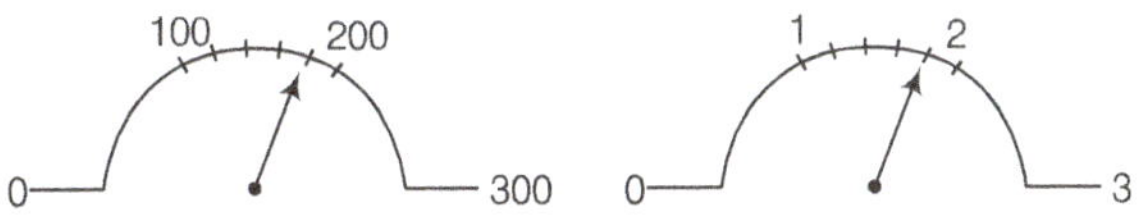

(a) 1 Ω (b) 5 Ω
(c) 8 Ω (d) 10 Ω

5 An electric kettle consumes 1 kW of electric power, when operated at 220 V. A fuse wire of what rating must be used for it?

(a) 4 A (b) 5 A
(c) 2 A (d) 1 A

6 Three filament bulbs made from a metal of low thermal coefficient of resistivity are arranged as shown in the figure. The wattage rating of each bulb is the power output, if it is connected independently across 240 V. The bulb that glows with maximum and minimum brightness respectively, are

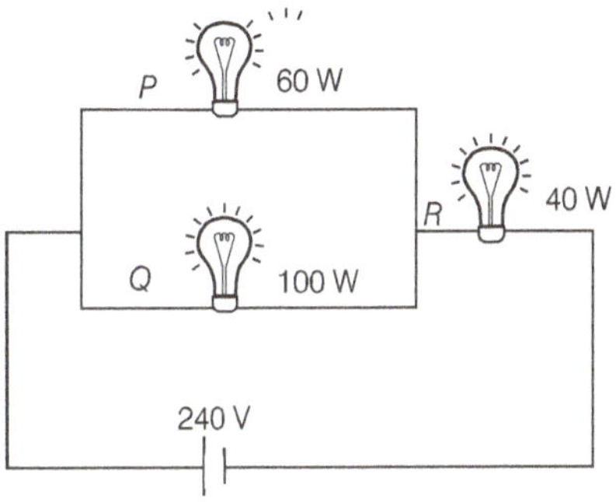

(a) P, Q (b) R, P
(c) Q, R (d) Q, P

7 Three identical electric bulbs are connected parallel to each other. On connecting their combination across a source of emf having stabilised voltage and negligible resistance, all bulbs glow with full brightness. Suddenly a bulb fuses. The other bulbs will glow

(a) brighter
(b) dimmer
(c) with same initial intensity
(d) zero, as those will also fuse

8 The circuit given below is for the operation of an industrial fan. The resistance of the fan is 3Ω. The regulator provided with the fan is a fixed resistor and a variable resistor in parallel.

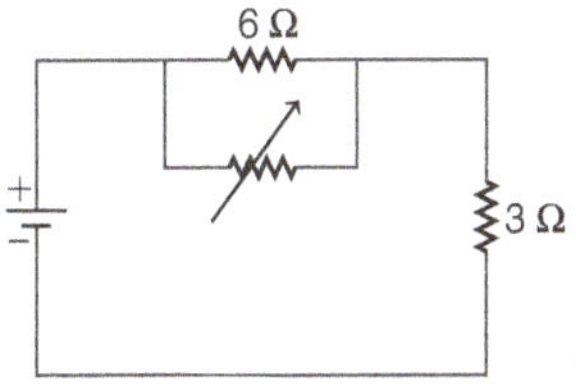

[Olympiad 2012]

Under what value of the variable resistances given below, power transferred to the fan will be maximum? The power source of the fan is a DC source with internal resistance of 6 ohms.

(a) 3 Ω (b) 0 (c) ∞ (d) 6 Ω

9 In the process of electrostatic induction, **[Olympiad 2013]**

(a) a conductor is rubbed with an insulator
(b) a charge is produced by friction
(c) negative and positive charges are separated
(d) electrons are 'sprayed' on the object

10 Three different circuits (I, II and III) are constructed using identical batteries and resistors of R and $2R$ ohm. What can be said about current I in arm AB of each circuit? **[Olympiad 2014]**

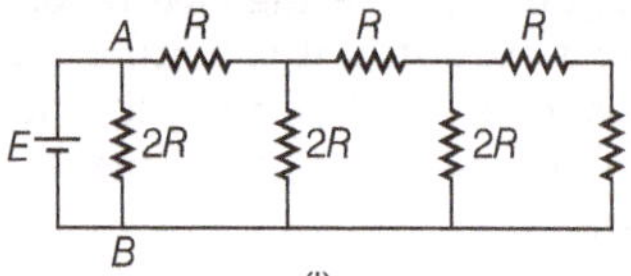

(I)

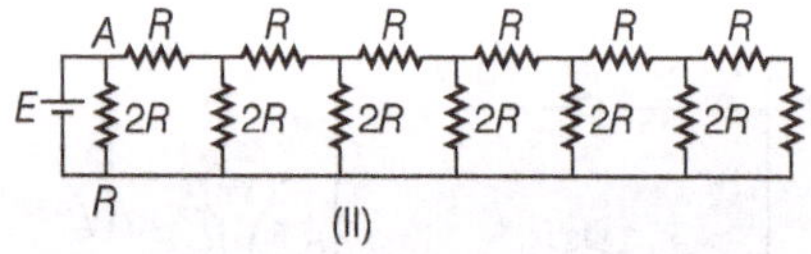

(II)

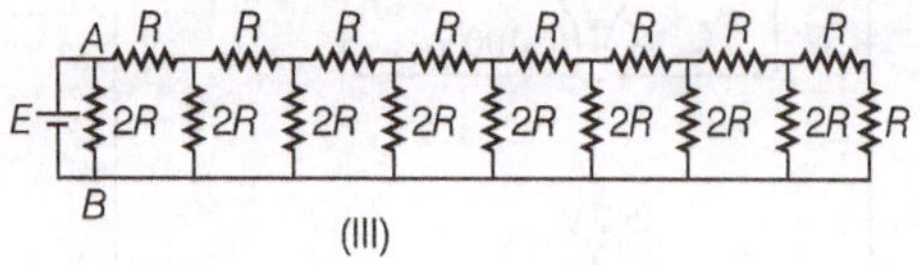

(III)

(a) $I_{\text{I}} > I_{\text{II}} > I_{\text{III}}$
(b) $I_{\text{I}} < I_{\text{II}} < I_{\text{III}}$
(c) $I_{\text{II}} < I_{\text{I}} < I_{\text{III}}$
(d) $I_{\text{I}} = I_{\text{II}} = I_{\text{III}}$

11 In the following circuit, the ammeter is ideal and reads zero. Value of resistance R is

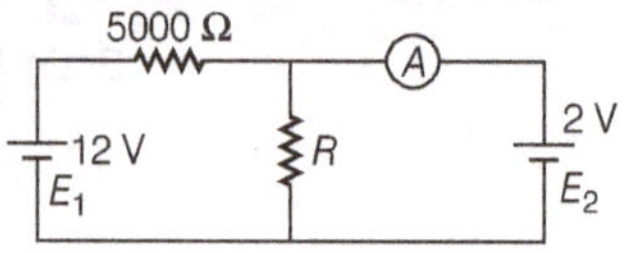

(a) 500 Ω
(b) 1000 Ω
(c) 25000 Ω
(d) 0.5 Ω

12 Bulbs of rating 60 W, 220 V and 250 W, 220 V are connected in series and their combination is connected to 440 V supply. Which bulb will fuse ? **[Olympiad 2014]**

(a) 60 W
(b) 250 W
(c) Both
(d) Neither

13 Consider the arrangements of N identical resistors, one in parallel and the other in series. Each of these arrangements are connected to batteries of the same voltage. The ratio of power dissipated in the parallel arrangement to the series arrangement is

(a) N
(b) $1/N$
(c) N^2
(d) $1/N^2$

ANSWERS

1. (d) **2.** (c) **3.** (b) **4.** (d) **5.** (b) **6.** (b) **7.** (c) **8.** (d) **9.** (c) **10.** (d)
11. (b) **12.** (a) **13.** (c)

* *These questions may or may not be asked in the examination, have been given just for additional practice required for olympiads Scholarship Exams etc. For detailed explanations refer Page No. 269.*

CHAPTER

09

Electromagnetism

SYLLABUS

- Magnetic effect of a current (principles only, laws not required); electromagnetic induction (elementary); transformer.

The branch of Physics which deals with study of electricity and magnetism and the interaction between them is known as electromagnetism. In electrostatics, we have studied that a static charge produces an electric field. Similarly, a moving charge or current flowing through a conductor also produces a magnetic field. This is called the magnetic effect of electric current.

Oersted's Experiment on the Magnetic Effect of Electric Current

In 1820, Hans Oersted observed experimentally that, when an electric current is passed through a conducting wire, a magnetic field is produced around it. **The phenomenon of production of magnetic field around a current carrying conductor is called magnetic effect of current**. The presence of magnetic field at a point around a current carrying wire can be detected with the help of a compass needle, which shows deflection in presence of a magnetic field. This has been depicted in the figure given below

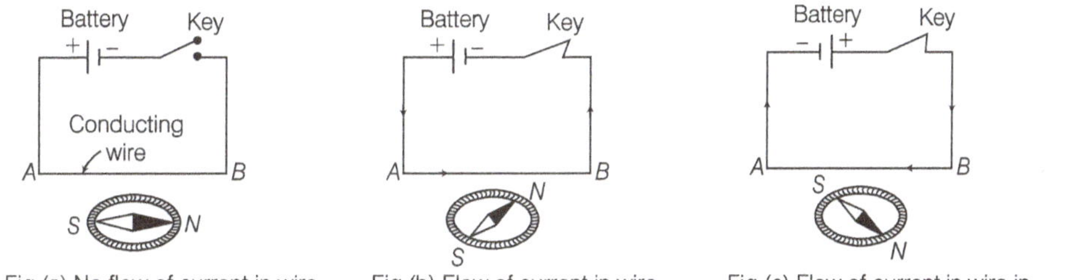

Fig.(a) No flow of current in wire Fig.(b) Flow of current in wire Fig.(c) Flow of current in wire in reverse direction as in Fig.(b)

Phenomenon of magnetic effect of electric current in a conducting wire

When current flows through the conductor, then the compass needle shows deflection. The deflection of the needle indicates that a magnetic field is established around a current carrying wire. If the current is reversed, then the needle is deflected in opposite direction. There is no deflection in compass needle, if no current flows through the conductor.

On increasing the current in the wire and bringing the needle closer to the wire, the deflection of the needle increases.

This experiment shows that, the magnetic field is produced due to electric current or flow of charges.

Magnetic Field

The space around a magnet or a current carrying conductor in which magnetic effect can be experienced i.e., its force can be detected, is called magnetic field.

Magnetic field is a **vector** quantity. Its SI unit is **tesla** (T) named after an American engineer Nikola Tesla.

Its smaller unit is **gauss**.

$$1 \text{ tesla} = \frac{1 \text{ newton}}{1 \text{ ampere - metre}}$$

$$1\,T = 1\,N/A - m = kg\,/A - s^2$$

$$\boxed{1 \text{ tesla} = 10^4 \text{ gauss}}$$

Magnetic Field Lines

The imaginary lines representing magnetic field around a magnet are known as magnetic field lines. When iron filings are kept near a magnet, then they get arranged in a pattern which represent the magnetic field lines.

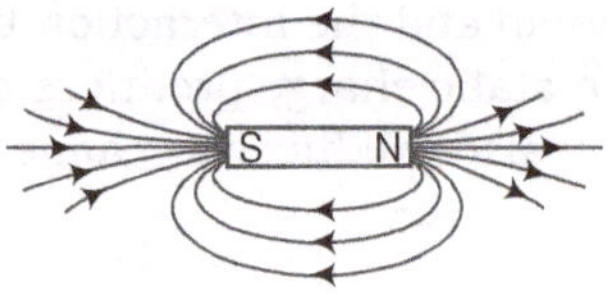

Field lines around a bar magnet

Magnetic field lines can be plotted by using a magnetic compass. The lines are drawn along the direction in which a magnetic North pole of the compass needle would move under the influence of the field produced by the magnet. It is taken by convention that the field lines emerge from North pole and merge at the South pole.

Note A compass needle behave as a small bar magnet whose one end point approximately towards North called North seeking or North pole and other end pointing towards South called South seeking or South pole.

Properties of Magnetic Field Lines

The magnetic field lines have the following properties

(i) The magnetic field lines originate from North pole of a magnet and end at its South pole, by convention.

(ii) The magnetic field lines are closed and continuous curves.

(iii) The magnetic field lines are crowded near the poles, where the magnetic field is strong and separated far from the poles, where the magnetic field is weak.

(iv) The magnetic field lines never intersect each other. If they do so, that would mean there are two directions of the magnetic field at the point of intersection, which is impossible.

(v) When magnetic compass is placed at different points on magnetic field lines, then it comes to rest along the direction of magnetic field at that point.

(vi) The direction of the magnetic field is indicated by the arrow of the lines at any point.

Magnetic Field due to a Current through a Straight Conductor

The magnetic field lines around a current carrying straight conductor are concentric circles whose centres lie on the wire and lying in the plane perpendicular to straight wire.

The strength of magnetic field B produced by a straight current carrying wire at a given point is

(i) Directly proportional to the current I passing through the wire

i.e. $B \propto I$ ...(i)

If current is increased, then the magnetic field produced is stronger and magnetic field lines become closer to each other i.e., become denser. If current is decreased, then weaker magnetic field is produced and magnetic lines of force move away from each other.

(ii) Inversely proportional to the distance r from the wire

i.e. $B \propto \frac{1}{r}$ ...(ii)

The magnetic field is stronger at the point which is nearer to the conductor and goes on decreasing for the far away points.

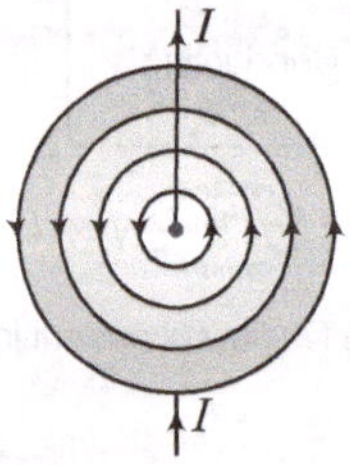

Concentric field lines around a straight conductor

(iii) When direction of current in the wire is reversed, then direction of magnetic field, i.e. direction of magnetic field lines also reverses.

By using Eqs. (i) and (ii), we get

$$B \propto \frac{I}{r}$$

If the direction of current in a straight wire is known, then the direction of magnetic field produced by a straight current carrying conductor is obtained by **Maxwell's right hand thumb rule**.

Maxwell's Right Hand Thumb Rule

It states that, if you hold the current carrying straight wire in the grip of your right hand in such a way that the stretched thumb points in the direction of current, then the direction of the curl of the fingers will give the direction of the magnetic field. This rule is also called Maxwell's corkscrew rule.

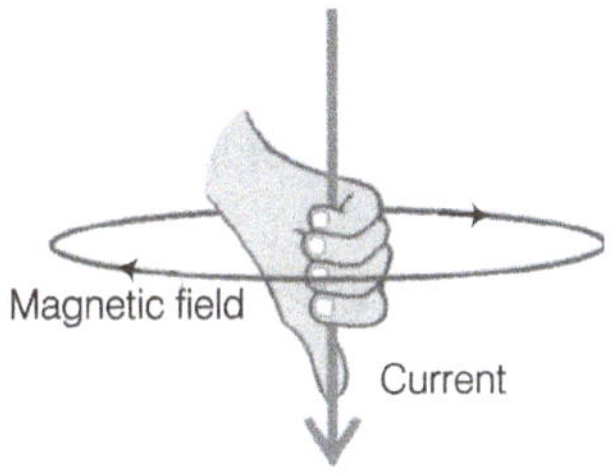

Maxwell's right hand thumb rule

Magnetic Field Due to a Current through a Circular Loop

The magnetic field lines due to a circular coil is shown in given figure. At every point of a current carrying circular loop, the concentric circles represent the magnetic field around it. At the centre of loop, the field appears to be a straight line.

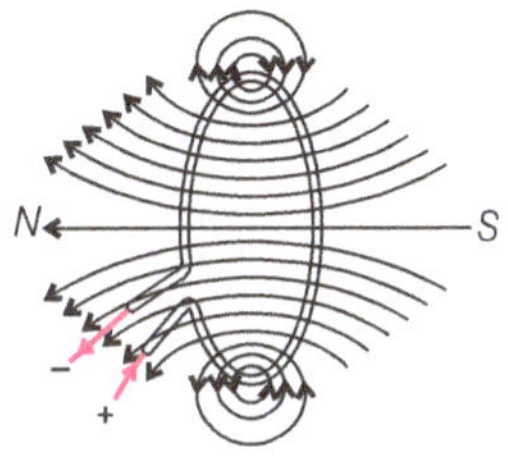

Magnetic field lines due to a current through a circular loop

The magnetic field produced by current carrying circular wire at a given point depends on the following factors

(i) **Amount of Current Flowing through a Wire** The strength of magnetic field (B) due to a current carrying circular wire is directly proportional to the amount of current (I) flowing through it.

i.e. $B \propto I$ ... (i)

(ii) **Number of Turns of the Circular Wire** The strength of the magnetic field due to a current carrying circular wire is directly proportional to the number of turns (N) of the wire.

i.e. $B \propto N$ ... (ii)

Thus, the strength of magnetic field produced by a current carrying circular coil can be increased by

(a) increasing the number of turns of wire in the coil.

(b) increasing the current flowing through the coil.

(c) decreasing the radius of the coil.

By looking at the direction of current in the face of loop, we can identify its polarity i.e., whether it will behave like North pole or South pole. If current around the face in loop is in anti-clockwise direction, then it will behave like North pole while in case of clockwise direction it will behave like South pole.

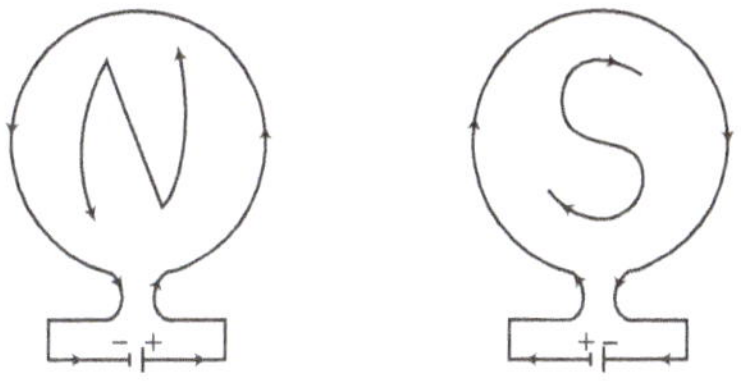

Polarities at the faces of a loop carrying current

Magnetic Field Due to a Current in a Solenoid

A **solenoid** is defined as a coil consisting of a large number of circular turns of insulated copper wire. These turns are wound closely to form a cylinder.

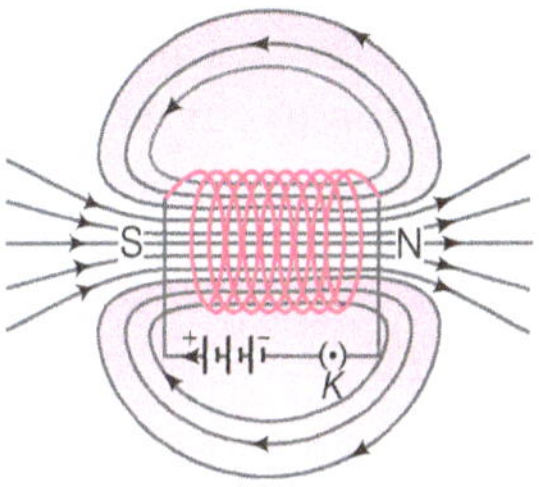

Magnetic field lines of force due to a current carrying solenoid

The field lines around a current carrying solenoid are similar to that produced by a bar magnet. This means that a current carrying solenoid behaves as a bar magnet having North pole and South pole.

The strength of magnetic field produced by a current carrying solenoid depends on the following factors

(i) The number of turns of solenoid ($B \propto N$) i.e., on increasing the number of turns in solenoid, strength of magnetic field produced can be increased.

(ii) The strength of current ($B \propto I$) i.e., by increasing the amount of current flowing in solenoid, strength of magnetic field produced can be increased.

(iii) The nature of core material used to make solenoid.

The field lines inside the solenoid are parallel to each other. Thus, the strength of magnetic field is the same at all points inside a solenoid.

The strong magnetic field produced inside a solenoid can be used to magnetise a piece of magnetic material like soft iron when placed inside the coil.

On reversing the direction of current in the solenoid, the polarities at the ends of solenoid are reversed due to which the direction of magnetic field is reversed. However, strength of magnetic field remains the same.

Comparison of bar magnet and current carrying solenoid

(i) The magnetic field lines of a current carrying solenoid are similar to the magnetic field lines of a bar magnet. Thus, a current carrying solenoid acts like a bar magnet.

(ii) A current carrying solenoid when suspended freely will come at rest in North-South direction similar to the bar magnet.

(iii) Unlike bar magnet, the magnetic field of a solenoid can be varied by changing current.

(iv) The polarity of a magnetic field can also be reversed in a current carrying solenoid by changing direction of current, whereas the polarity of a bar magnet cannot be changed.

Electromagnet

An electromagnet is a solenoid that works like a magnet when current flows through it. It consists of a long insulated copper wire wound around a soft iron core. The magnetic effect remains, till the current is flowing through the solenoid.

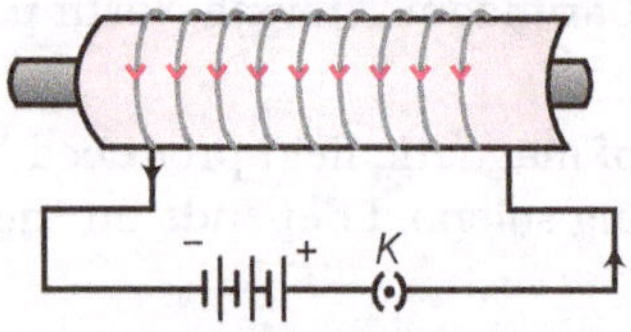

An electromagnet

The strength of an electromagnet increases with

(i) increase in number of turns in the coil

(ii) increase in the amount of current flowing through the coil.

(iii) decrease in the air gap between poles.

Uses of Electromagnet

Following are the uses of electromagnet

(i) It is used for lifting and transporting large masses of iron scrap, girder, plates, etc.

(ii) It is used for loading the furnace with iron.

(iii) It is used for separating the magnetic substances such as iron from debris and raw materials.

(iv) It is used for removing pieces of iron from wounds.

Comparison between Electromagnet and Permanent Magnet

Electromagnet	Permanent Magnet
It is a temporary magnet.	It is a permanent magnet i.e., cannot be demagnetised easily.
It is made up of soft iron.	It is made up of steel.
It produces the magnetic field as long as current flows in its coils i.e., it produces temporary magnetic field.	It produces permanent magnetic field.
The magnetic field strength can be changed.	The magnetic field strength cannot be changed.
It can produce very strong magnetic field.	It produces comparatively weak magnetic field.
Its polarity can be reversed.	Its polarity cannot be reversed.

Check Your LEARNING...

1 How can we predict the strength of a magnetic field in a space?

2 Where is the magnetic field due to a straight current wire (i) stronger (ii) weaker?

3 A circular loop carrying a current is placed on a horizontal surface. If the current is in the clockwise direction, then what is the direction of its magnetic field at the centre? What is the direction of the magnetic field at a point outside the surface of the loop?

4 What is the difference in the pattern of magnetic field due to a circular loop and inside a solenoid?

5 What is electromagnet? State its principle.

6 Mention any two differences between electromagnet and permanent magnet.

Force on a Current Carrying Conductor in a Magnetic Field

When a current carrying conductor is placed in a magnetic field in a direction other than the magnetic field, it experiences a force. The force acting on a current carrying conductor in a magnetic field is due to interaction between magnetic field due to current carrying conductor and external magnetic field in which the conductor is placed.

The direction of force on the conductor depends on

(i) **Direction of Current** The direction of force on the conductor can be reversed by reversing the direction of current.

(ii) **Direction of Magnetic Field** The direction of force on the conductor can be reversed by reversing the direction of magnetic field by interchanging the position of poles.

Force on the current carrying conductor is maximum when the direction of current is at right angles to the direction of magnetic field. If the current carrying conductor is placed parallel to the direction of magnetic field, then no force acts on it.

Fleming's Left Hand Rule

The direction of force which acts on a current carrying conductor placed in a magnetic field is given by Fleming's left hand rule.

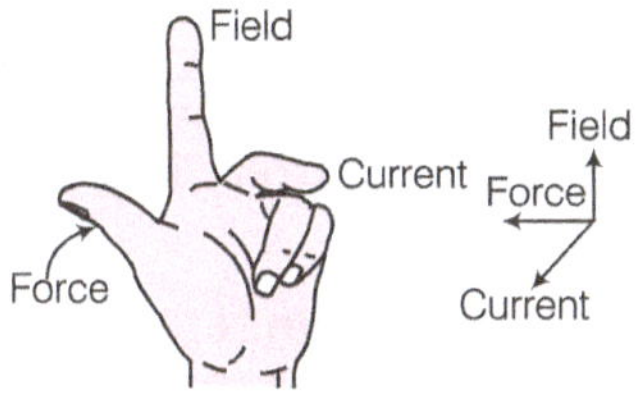

Fleming's left hand rule

It states that, if the forefinger, thumb and middle finger of left hand are stretched mutually perpendicular to each other and the forefinger points along the direction of external magnetic field, middle finger indicates the direction of current, then thumb points in the direction of force acting on the conductor.

Electric Motor

It is a rotating device which is used for converting electrical energy into mechanical energy.

It is based on the principle that when a current carrying rectangular coil is placed in a magnetic field, then torque acts on the coil, which rotates it continuously.

Construction of Electric Motor

The main parts of electric motor are described below

(i) **Armature** It is a rectangular coil wound around a soft iron core which is kept in-between the poles of a permanent magnet. When current flow through armature coil, then magnetic force act on it and it rotates along its axis.

(ii) **Split Rings** These are the parts of a ring, fixed to the coil, these are used to reverse the direction of current flowing through armature coil every time, it passes through the vertical position.

(iii) **Brushes** These are made up of carbon/copper, these are pressed tightly against split rings. Their main function is to connect the coil with the current supply.

(iv) **Magnet** It is a strong horse-shoe magnet either permanent or electromagnet. Its function is to produce magnetic field, so that magnetic force can act on armature coil.

(v) **DC Source** It is battery connected to the brush, to flow the electric current in armature coil, so that magnetic force can act on it.

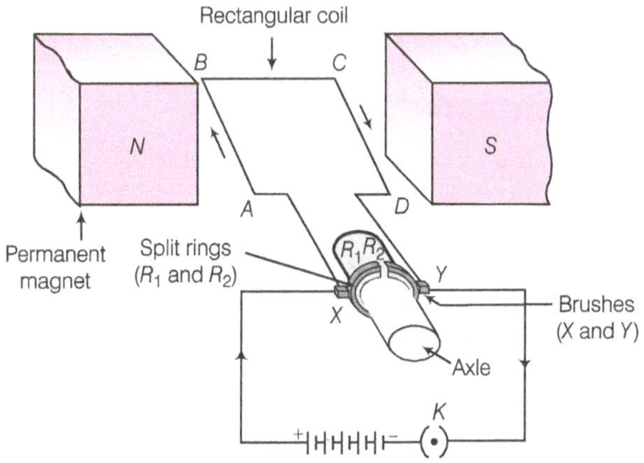

A simple electric motor

Working

Here, working of electric motor is given below in a paper manner.

(i) Let coil *ABCD* be in horizontal position. When the key is switched ON, the current flows in the coil *ABCD* through brush *X* and flows back to the battery through the brush *Y via* ring R_2.

(ii) Applying Fleming's left hand rule, no force acts on arms *BC* and *AD* as they are parallel to magnetic field. Arm *AB* experiences a force in downward direction and arm *CD* experiences an equal force in upward direction. A torque acts on the coil and it rotates in the anti-clockwise direction.

(iii) While rotating, the coil reaches the vertical position, brushes lose contact with the rings and current stops flowing. But the coil does not stop due to inertia of motion.

(iv) When the coil passes through the vertical position, then the rings automatically change their positions and come in contact with opposite brushes. This reverses the direction of current through the coil, but the direction of current on right hand side remains the same.

(v) So, the force on right hand side is always upward and a force on left hand side is always in downward direction. Thus, the coil continues to rotate in anti-clockwise direction.

The speed of rotation of the motor can be increased by

(i) increasing the strength of the current in the coil.

(ii) increasing the number of turns in the coil.

(iii) increasing the area of the coil.

(iv) increasing the strength of magnetic field.

Electromagnetic Induction

The phenomenon of production of emf in a conductor on changing the magnetic field around it, is called electromagnetic induction.

The emf produced here is called **induced emf**, if the circuit is closed, then electric current flows due to this emf, known as **induced current**.

This effect is the reverse effect of magnetic effect of electric current and it was discovered by Michael Faraday.

Ways to Induce the Current in a Circuit

There are different methods by which current can be induced in a circuit as given below

(i) **By Moving a Coil in Magnetic Field** Current can be induced in a coil either by moving it in a magnetic field or by changing the magnetic field around it. In most situations, it is convenient to move coil in a magnetic field.

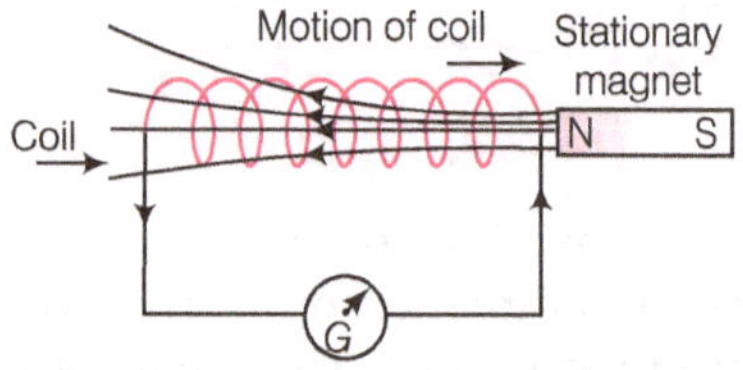

(a) Moving a coil towards a magnet sets up an electric current in the coil circuit as indicated by deflection in galvanometer needle

The induced current is found to be maximum when the direction of motion of the coil is at right angle to the magnetic field. The direction of induced current can be reversed by reversing the direction of magnetic field. If the coil as well as the magnet are stationary, then no current is induced in the coil.

(ii) **In a Stationary Coil** Consider two coils such as coil 1 primary coil and coil 2 as secondary coil. Primary coil is connected with a battery.

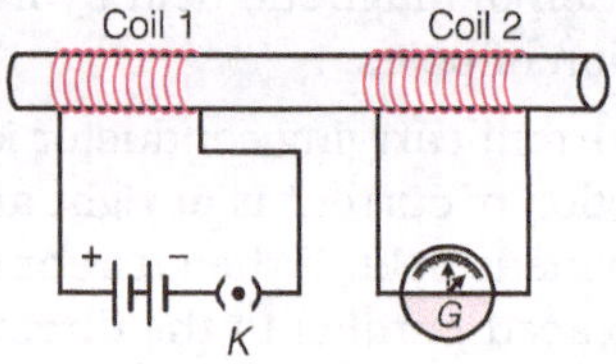

(b) Current is induced in coil 2 when current in coil 1 is changed as indicated by deflection in galvanometer needle

When the current in primary coil is switched on, then it takes a little time to rise from zero to a maximum value, i.e. current in the primary coil changes. This causes a momentary change in the magnetic field around this coil and hence induces a momentary current in the secondary coil. The same happens in the reverse direction when the current in primary coil is switched off.

Galvanometer

It is an instrument that can detect the presence of a current in a circuit. The pointer remains at zero (the centre of the scale) for zero current flowing through it. Depending upon the direction of current, it can be deflected either to the left or to the right of the zero mark.

Fleming's Right Hand Rule

The direction of induced current in a straight conductor is given by Fleming's right hand rule.

It states that, if the forefinger, middle finger and thumb of the right hand are stretched at right angles to each other, with the forefinger in the direction of the magnetic field and the thumb in the direction of the motion of the wire, then the current in the wire is in the direction of the middle finger.

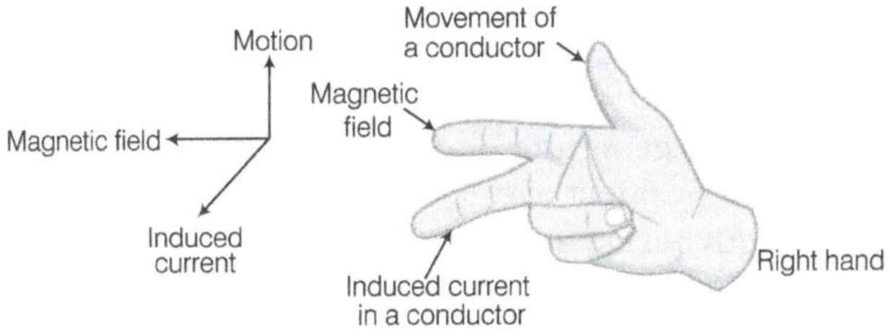

Fleming's right hand rule

Check Your LEARNING...

1. State the function of a split ring in a DC motor.
2. If area of the coil becomes twice, then what is the effect on speed of rotation of the motor?
3. In DC motor, why must the current to the coil be reversed twice during each rotation?
4. Name the phenomenon used for producing current in coil due to relative motion between a magnet and the coil.
5. Explain the meaning of the word 'electromagnetic' and 'induction' in the term electromagnetic induction.

Direct Current and Alternating Current

Direct Current (DC)

An electric current whose magnitude is either constant or variable but the direction of flow in a conductor remains the same is called direct current. It is denoted by DC. Sources of DC are voltaic cell, a dry cell, battery, DC generator, etc.

Alternating Current (AC)

An electric current whose magnitude changes with time and direction reverses periodically is called alternating current. It is denoted by AC. Sources of AC are hydro-electric generators, thermal power generators and nuclear power generators, etc.

The number of cycles completed by the AC in one second is called the **frequency of AC.** The frequency of AC in India is 50 Hz which means that AC changes its polarity after $\frac{1}{100}$ second as it completes one cycle. The major difference between AC and DC is that DC always flows in one direction, while AC reverses its direction periodically.

Advantages of AC over DC

Advantages of AC over DC are as follow

(i) With the help of a transformer, AC at any desired voltage can be obtained.

(ii) AC can be easily converted into DC by using a device called **rectifier**.

(iii) The cost of generation of AC is less than the cost of generation of DC.

(iv) AC can be controlled without much loss of electric power than DC.

(v) AC machines are very durable and do not need much maintenance.

(vi) For long distance transmission, AC is preferred as it causes minimum loss of energy during transmission.

Disadvantages of AC over DC

Disadvantages of AC over DC are as follow

(i) AC is more dangerous than DC as it attracts a person towards it, whereas DC repels.

(ii) AC can give a serious shock to a person as compared to the DC.

(iii) AC cannot be used for electroplating, electrotyping, etc., but DC is used for these processes.

Electric Generator

It is based on the principle of electromagnetic induction. It is used to produce electric current by varying magnetic field through a coil.

Parts of Electric Generator

The different parts of electric generator are explained as below

(i) **Armature** It is a coil having large number of turns of insulated copper wire wound over a soft iron core.

(ii) **Field Magnet** It is a powerful magnet that provides a uniform magnetic field perpendicular to the axis of rotation of coil between the North and South poles.

(iii) **Slip Rings** In an AC generator, we use slip rings (full rings) with which the ends of coil are in contact. DC generator uses split ring type commutator (half rings) with which the ends of the armature coil are in contact.

(iv) **Brushes** There are two stationary metallic carbon brushes which are in contact with external device and rings.

AC Generator

It generates the current which changes its direction after equal intervals of time, i.e. **alternating current**.

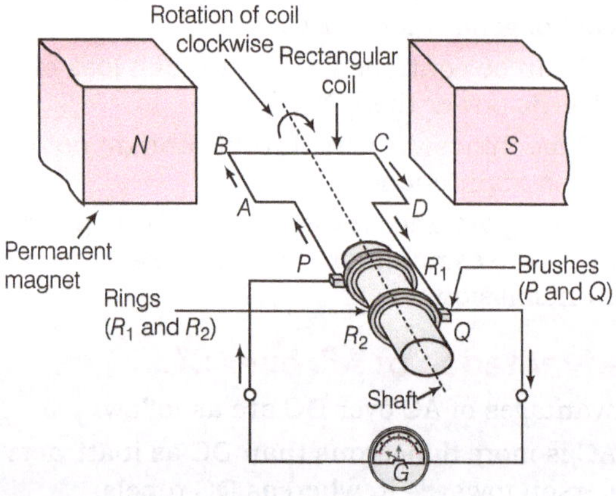

AC generator

Working As the coil rotates, then two rings also rotate with the coil. The brushes *P* and *Q* keep the contact with the rotating ring when the coil starts rotating with arm *AB* moving up and *CD* moving down (clockwise) cutting the magnetic lines. According to Fleming's right hand rule, current is induced in these arms in the direction *ABCD*. After half rotation, arm *CD* moves up and *AB* moves down. As a result, the direction of current in each segment changes giving rise to net induced current in the direction *DCBA*. Thus, after every half rotation, polarity of current in the respective arm changes thereby generating an alternating current.

As the coil rotates, the current induced due to generator is shown by the graph below

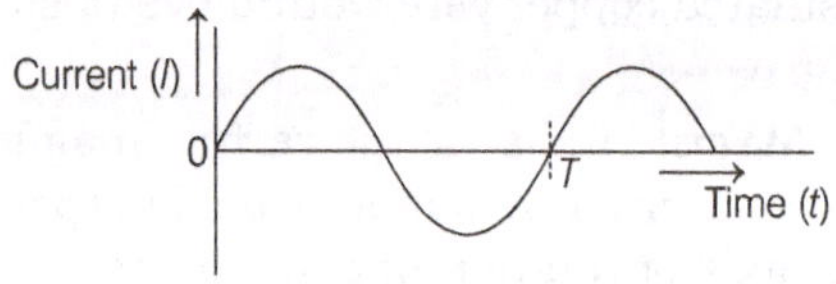

Differences between a DC motor and an AC generator

DC Motor	AC Generator
It converts electrical energy into mechanical energy.	It converts mechanical energy into electrical energy.
It is based on the principle that when a coil carrying current is held in a magnetic field, it experiences a torque which rotates the coil.	It is based on the phenomenon of electromagnetic induction.

Similarities between AC generator and DC motor

The similarities between AC generator and DC motor are as follow

(i) Both AC generator and DC motor work on magnetic effect of electric current.

(ii) In both cases, a coil rotates in a magnetic field between the pole pieces of strong electromagnet.

Transformer

It is a device which is used to increase or decrease the amplitude of an alternating emf without changing the frequency of AC source.

The transformers are of following types

(i) Step-up transformer

(ii) Step-down transformer

Principle of Transformer

It is based on the principle of mutual induction, i.e. producing a momentary current in secondary coil by changing the current in the primary coil.

Construction of Transformer

It consists of two coils primary (*p*) and secondary (*s*), insulated from each other wounded on soft iron core. Oftenly, the primary coil is the input coil and secondary coil is the output coil.

These soft iron cores are laminated to minimise eddy current loss.

Transformer Action

When the primary coil of transformer is connected with an AC supply, then due to the flow of alternating current, a magnetic field of alternating nature is developed in it. i.e., the change in magnetic field takes place.

This varying magnetic field (or magnetic flux) reaches across secondary coil with the help of core. Due to varying magnetic field (or magnetic flux), a momentary current or emf in the secondary coil is induced. In this way without any connection or touch, an electrical energy is transferred between the primary and secondary windings; this action is called the **transformer action.**

Step-up and Step-down Transformer

The transformer which converts low voltage (high current) into high voltage (low current) is called **step-up transformer.** In this transformer, the number of turns in secondary coil (N_S) is more than the number of turns in primary coil (N_p) i.e., $N_s > N_p$. The transformer which converts high voltage (low current) to low voltage (high current) is called **step-down transformer**. In these transformer, the number of turns in secondary coil is less than the number of turns is primary coil. i.e. $N_p > N_s$.

The following figures show step-up and step-down transformer

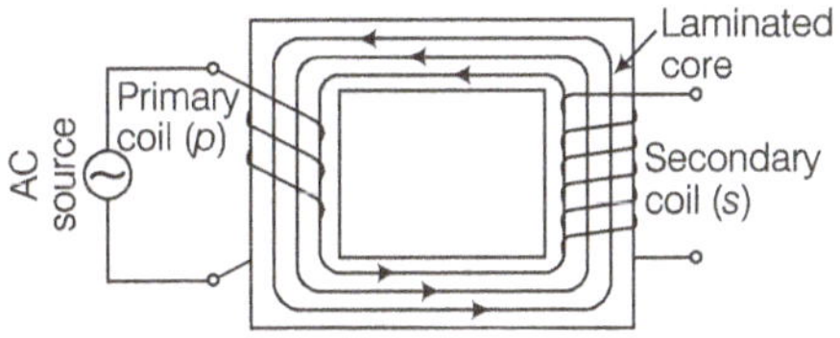

Step-up transformer

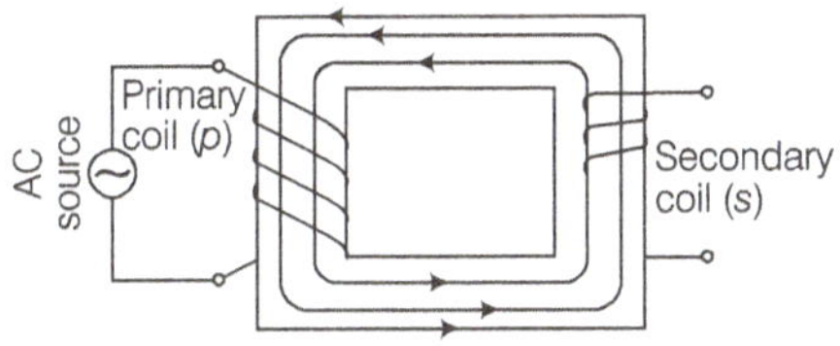

Step-down transformer

Uses of Transformers

Transformers are used in almost all AC operations.

Some of them are given below

(i) It is used in the induction furnaces.

(ii) It is used in the voltage regulators for TV, computer, refrigerator, etc.

(iii) A step-down transformer is used for the purpose of weldings.

(iv) In the transmission of AC over long distances.

Note
- The alternating magnetic flux induces eddy current in the iron core and causes heating. This effect is reduced by having a laminated core.
- The wire used for the winding has some resistance, which causes energy loss due to heating. This can be minimised by using thick wire.
- DC current is not used in transformer, because constant current produces constant magnetic field, which means no change in the magnetic flux. Hence, no emf will be induced.

Check Your LEARNING...

1 The frequency of AC in India is ....

2 The generator is based on which principle?

3 What type of generator is used at power stations?

4 Write one similarity between AC generator and DC motor.

5 In a step-up transformer, what will be the value of $\frac{N_s}{N_p}$?

QUICK Revision

- The region surrounding a magnet or a current carrying conductor in which magnetic effect can be experienced i.e., its force can be detected, is called **magnetic field**.
- Direction of magnetic field is found by **right hand thumb rule**.
- **Electromagnet** is a solenoid that works like a magnet when current flows through it.
- Direction of force on a current carrying conductor in a magnetic field is given by **Fleming's left hand rule**.
- **DC motor** is a rotating device used for converting electrical energy into mechanical energy.
- The phenomenon of generation of an electric current in a closed circuit by changing the magnetic field is called **electromagnetic induction**.
- Current can be induced in a circuit by two methods i.e., **by moving a coil in a magnetic field** or by **changing the magnetic field**.
- **AC generator** generates alternating current. It is based on the phenomenon of electromagnetic induction.
- **Transformer** is used to increase or decrease the amplitude of an alternating emf or current. There are two types of transformer i.e., step-up and step-down transformers.

Chapter Practice

1 Mark Questions

1. By reversing the direction of current in a straight wire, the magnetic field
   (a) will get reversed in direction
   (b) will be increased
   (c) will be decreased
   (d) remains unchanged

Sol. (*a*) By reversing the direction of current in a straight wire, the magnetic field will get reversed in direction.

2. If the strength of the current flowing through a wire is increased, the strength of the magnetic field produced by it **[2023]**
   (a) decreases
   (b) increases
   (c) remains the same
   (d) first increases then decreases

Sol. (*b*) If the strength of the current flowing through a wire is increased, the strength of the magnetic field increases.

3. A coil wound around a piece of soft iron can become an electromagnet only when **[2022 (Sem-II)]**
   (a) the circuit is open
   (b) a magnetic compass is present in the vicinity
   (c) a galvanometer is connected to the circuit
   (d) a current flows in the circuit

Sol. (*d*) A coil wound around a piece of soft iron becomes electromagnet only when a current flows in the circuit.

4. By introduction of soft iron bar inside the current carrying solenoid, the magnetic field
   (a) will become zero
   (b) will increase
   (c) will remain unaffected
   (d) will decrease

Sol. (*b*) The soft iron bar placed inside the current carrying solenoid gets magnetised, therefore the magnetic field will increase.

5. The magnetic field inside a current carrying solenoid
   (a) is circular at end only
   (b) is circular at ends and inside the solenoid
   (c) is along the axis and parallel to each other
   (d) perpendicular to axis and equidistant from each other

Sol. (*c*) The magnetic field inside a current carrying solenoid is uniform inside the solenoid and is along the axis of solenoid. Therefore, option (c) is correct.

6. The diagram shows an electric bell.

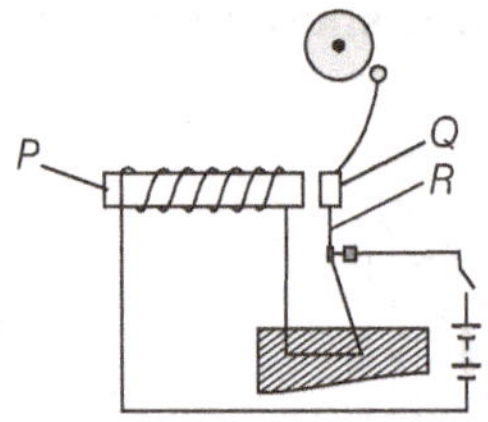

Which materials would be suitable for the parts labelled *P*, *Q* and *R*?

	P	*Q*	*R*
(a)	Soft iron	Brass	Soft iron
(b)	Soft iron	Soft iron	Spring steel
(c)	Soft iron	Brass	Brass
(d)	Spring steel	Soft iron	Spring steel

Sol. (*b*) Material *P* should be made of soft iron, so that it can be magnetised easily.
Material *Q* should be made of soft iron as well, so that it can be attracted by magnetised iron. Material *R* should be made of spring steel, so that it can return to its original position as soon as the current is turned ON/OFF.
Therefore, option (*b*) is correct.

7. The diagram below shows a free conductor *AB* is kept in a magnetic field and is carrying current from *A* to *B* (To avoid confusion complete path of the circuit is not shown). The direction of the force experienced by the conductor will be **[Latest Specimen Sem-II] [1]**

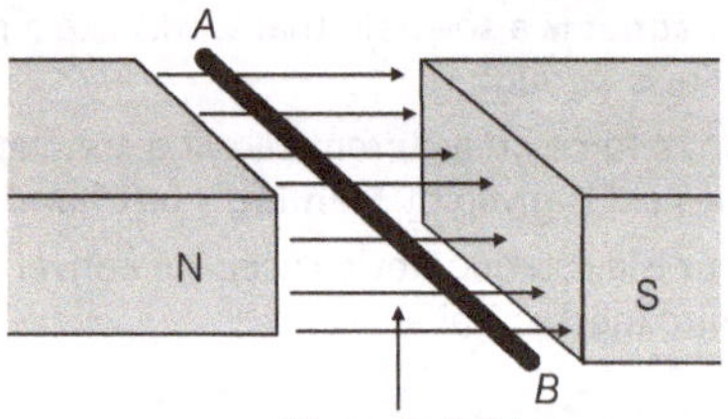

   (a) up
   (b) down
   (c) towards N
   (d) towards S

Sol. (*a*) According to the Fleming's left hand rule, the direction of force experienced by the conductor will be up.

8. A conductor *AB* is kept along North-South direction of the earth above a magnetic needle as shown in figure. When the key *K* is closed, then **[2022 (Sem-II)]**

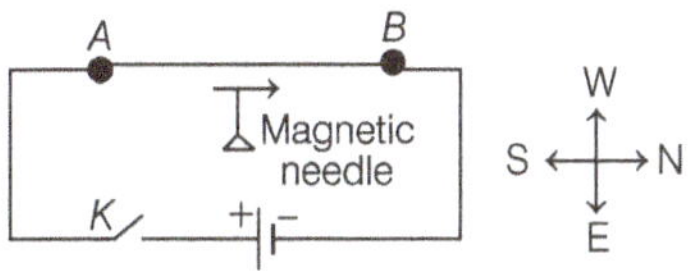

(a) the needle will not show any deflection
(b) the needle will deflect towards East
(c) the needle will turn in the opposite direction i.e. towards South
(d) the needle will deflect towards West

Sol. (*b*) From the figure, we can see that the magnetic needle is kept below the conductor *AB* which is kept an North-South direction. We can see that, the current is in anti-clockwise direction and from the right hand thumb rule, the direction of magnetic field will be from West to East. Hence, according to Fleming's left hand rule, the deflection produced will be towards East.

9. The direction of induced current is obtained by
(a) clock rule
(b) Fleming's left hand rule
(c) Fleming's right hand rule
(d) right hand thumb rule

Sol. (*c*) The direction of induced current is obtained by Fleming's right hand rule.

10. The diagram below shows a magnet moved near a coil along its axis. Which of the diagram shows correct flow of current during this motion? [1]

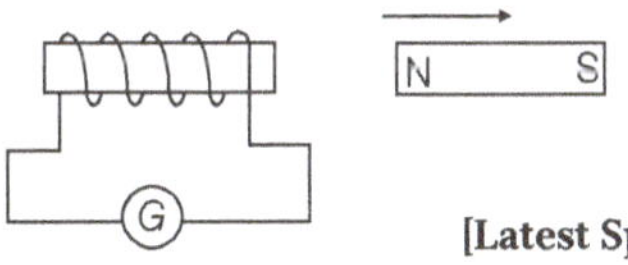

[Latest Specimen Sem-I]

(a)
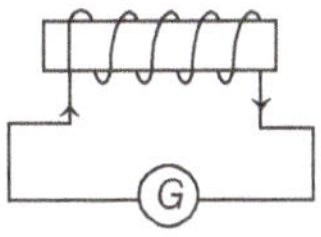

(b)
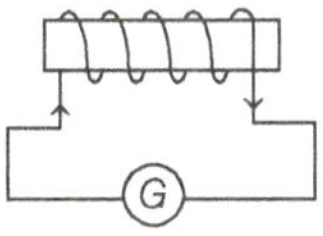

(c)
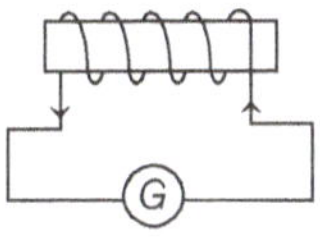

(d)
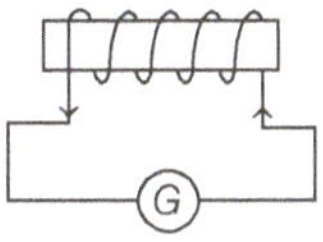

Sol. (c) According to the Fleming's right hand rule, the direction of induced current in the coil near to N-pole will be clockwise. It is shown correctly in option (*c*).

11. Which of the following has its working based on electromagnetic induction?
(a) DC motor (b) AC generator
(c) Transformer (d) Both (b) and (c)

Sol. (*d*) Both AC generator and transformer works on the principle of electromagnetic induction.

2 Marks Questions

12. What will happen to a compass needle when the compass is placed below a wire and a current is made to flow through the wire? Give a reason to justify your answer. [2006]

Sol. The compass needle will shows deflection when the compass is placed below a wire and a current is made to flow through the wire.
It is so because when a current is passed through a conductor, a magnetic field is produced around the conductor due to which, compass needle gets deflected.

13. A magnetic compass needle is placed in the plane of paper near point *A* as shown in figure. In which plane should a straight current carrying conductor be placed, so that it passes through *A* and there is no change in the deflection of the compass?

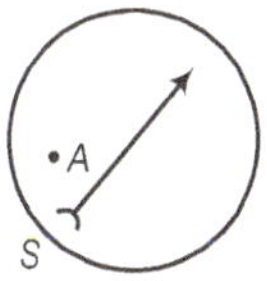

Sol. The straight current carrying conductor should be placed in the plane of paper, so that it passes through *A*. This produces magnetic field in a plane perpendicular to plane of paper. The compass needle remains undeflected due to vertical magnetic field produced by wire, since compass needle is free to rotate only in horizontal plane. [2]

14. It is established that an electric current through a metallic conductor produces a magnetic field around it. Is there a similar magnetic field produced around a thin beam of moving (i) α-particles, (ii) neutrons? Justify your answer.

Sol. In case of movement of a charged particle, the magnetic field is created around the path on which the charged particle moves.
(i) Yes, a thin beam of α-particles (which are positively charged) is like straight conductor carrying current in the direction of motion. [1]
(ii) No, as neutrons carry no charge, so no magnetic field would be created around its path. [1]

15. (i) The diagram shows a bar magnet surrounded by four plotting compasses. Copy the diagram and mark the direction of the compass needle for each of the cases *B*, *C* and *D*.

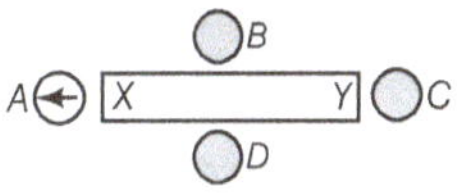

(ii) Which is the North pole : *X* or *Y*?

Sol. (i)
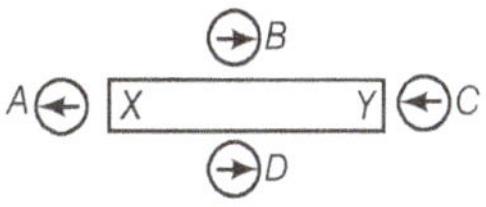

[1]

(ii) *X* is the North pole. [1]

16. How does the strength of magnetic field due to a current carrying conductor depend upon
(i) distance from the conductor
(ii) current flowing through the conductor?

Sol. (i) Strength of magnetic field decreases as the distance from conductor increases. [1]

(ii) Strength of magnetic field increases with an increase in the magnitude of current flowing through the conductor. [1]

17. (i) What is the nature of magnetic field inside a long straight solenoid carrying current?

(ii) Consider a circular loop of wire lying in the plane of table. Let the current pass through the loop clockwise. Apply the right hand rule to find out the direction of the magnetic field inside and outside the loop.

Sol. (i) Magnetic field inside a long straight solenoid carrying current is uniform, i.e. same at all the points. [1]

(ii) Applying right hand rule, the magnetic field inside the loop is in vertically downward direction and outside the loop, it is in vertically upward direction. [1]

18. A plotting compass is placed inside a solenoid and the compass needle is pointing in the direction as shown.

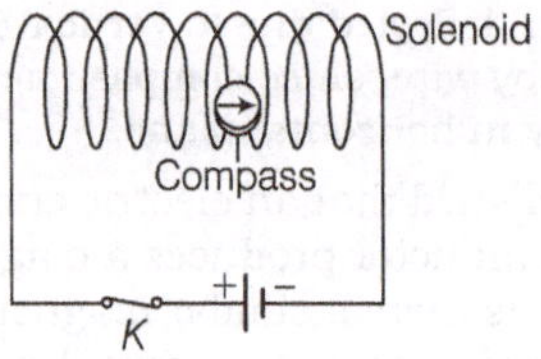

(i) Complete the diagram by drawing arrow heads to indicate the direction of the current flow.

(ii) Describe the direction of the magnetic field inside the solenoid.

Sol. (i)

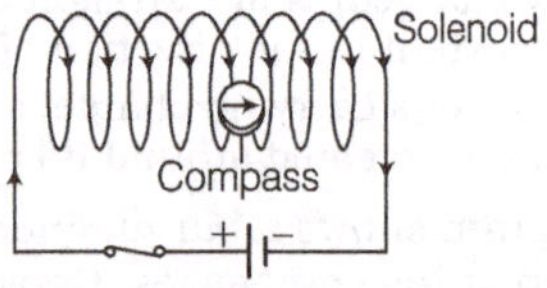

[1]

(ii) The direction of the magnetic field inside the solenoid always points from the induced South pole towards the induced North pole. [1]

19. The figure given below shows an electromagnet.

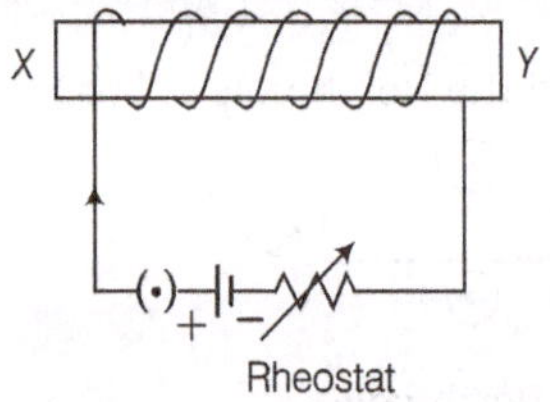

(i) What will be the polarity at the end *X*?

(ii) Suggest a way by which the strength of the electromagnet referred to in the question, may be increased. [2009]

Sol. (i) The polarity at the end *X* is North polarity. [1]

(ii) The strength of the electromagnet can be increased by increasing the strength of the current or by decreasing the resistance in the rheostat. [1]

20. You have been provided with a solenoid *AB*.

(i) What is the polarity at the end *A*?

(ii) Give one advantage of an electromagnet over a permanent magnet. [2013]

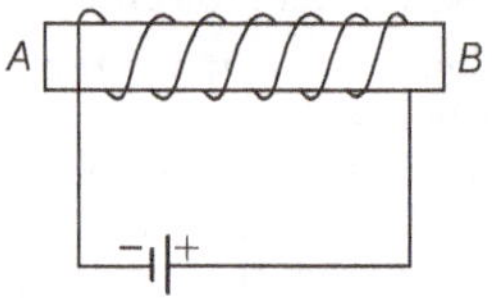

Sol. (i) The polarity at end *A* is South polarity. [1]

(ii) An advantage of an electromagnet over a permanent magnet is that an electromagnet can produce a strong magnetic field. [1]

21. State two advantages of an electromagnet over a permanent magnet. [2018]

Sol. The two advantages of an electromagnet over a permanent magnet are

(i) The polarity of an electromagnet can be changed by reversing the direction of current in the solenoid while polarity of a permanent magnet can never be changed. [1]

(ii) An electromagnet can produce a stronger magnetic field than permanent magnet. [1]

22. The given figure shows a DC motor model used by a student to study electromagnetism.

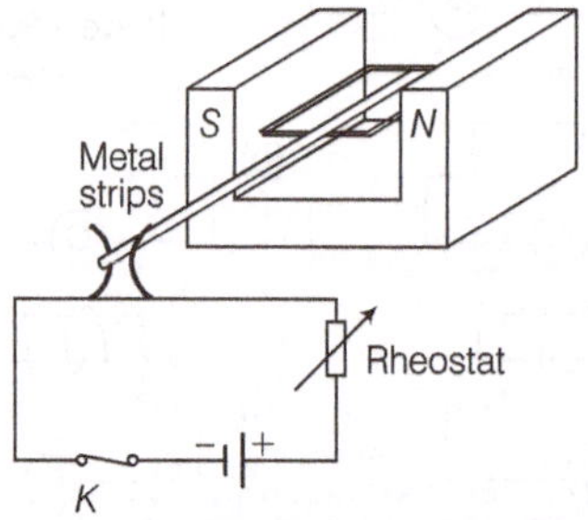

The two ends of the coil are fixed to a pair of curve elastic metal strips. The metal strips are connected to the power supply with a rheostat.

(i) State the direction of rotation of the coil when viewed from the front.

(ii) The student is still testing on the feasibility of using the metal strips in the model. What is he trying to achieve?

Sol. (i) The direction of rotation of the coil when viewed from the front is anti-clockwise. [1]

(ii) He is trying to achieve the rotation of coil in one direction. As the current in the coil reverses for every half turn, the coil rotates in one direction. [1]

23. The figure shows the split ring commutator and the two carbon brushes in their respective positions.

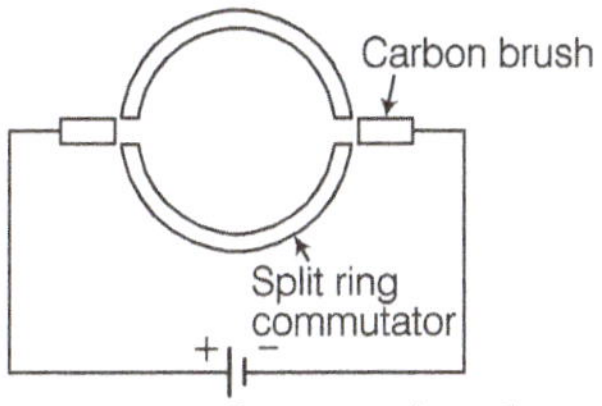

What can you say about carbon brush and split ring commutator?

Sol. When the gaps of the split ring commutator are in alignment with the carbon brushes, then contacts are broken and the current is temporarily cut-off. [1]
However, the coil keeps on rotating in the same direction due to its inertia until the split ring commutator and the carbon brushes are in contact again. [1]

24. State what would happen to the direction of rotation of a motor, if

(i) the current were reversed?

(ii) both current and magnetic field were reversed simultaneously?

Sol. (i) Direction of rotation would be reversed. [1]

(ii) Direction of rotation would remain unchanged. [1]

25. State the energy change which takes place, when a magnet is moved inside a coil having a galvanometer at its ends. Name this phenomenon. [2005]

Sol. When a magnet is moved inside a coil having a galvanometer at its ends, the mechanical energy is converted into electrical energy. This phenomenon is known as electromagnetic induction. [1+1]

26. Two circular coils *A* and *B* are placed close to each other. If the current in the coil *A* is changed, will some current be induced in the coil *B*? Give reason.

Sol. Yes, current will be induced in the coil *B*. When the current in coil *A* is changed, the magnetic field around it changes. So, the changing of magnetic field lines around coil *B* induce a current in it. [2]

27. The wire in the figure below is being moved downwards through the magnetic field so as to produce induced current.

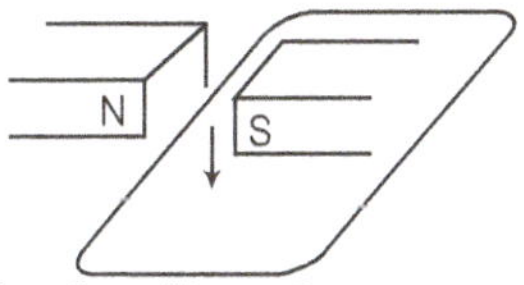

What would be the effect of

(i) moving the wire at a higher speed?

(ii) moving the wire upwards rather than downwards?

(iii) using a stronger magnet?

(iv) holding the wire still in the magnetic field?

Sol. (i) The induced current increases at a higher speed.

(ii) The induced current is reversed.

(iii) The induced current increases.

(iv) The induced current is zero. [1/2 × 4]

28. Explain different ways to induce current in a coil.

Sol. Current is induced in a coil in following ways

(i) When a magnet is moved towards or away from coil or there is a relative motion between coil and magnet, a current is induced in the coil circuit. [1]

(ii) When a current passing through a coil changes, then a current is induced in a coil placed near to it. [1]

29. (i) Which sources produce Alternating Current (AC)?

(ii) Name some sources of direct current.

Sol. (i) Some sources that produce alternating current are AC generators, thermal power stations, car alternators, etc. [1]

(ii) Some sources of direct current are electrochemical dry cells, solar cells, lead acid accumulator batteries, DC generators, etc. [1]

30. Name four appliances wherein an electric motor, a rotating device that converts electrical energy to mechanical energy, is used as an important component. In what respect motors are different from generators?

Sol. The four appliances such as electric fans, mixers grinders, electric drills, tape recorders, etc., use an electric motor as a rotating device that converts electrical energy to mechanical energy.

The motor is a machine which converts the electrical energy into mechanical energy.

The generator is the device which converts mechanical energy into electrical energy. [2]

31. Give two similarities between an AC generator and a DC motor.

Sol. Similarities between an AC generator and a DC motor are

(i) Both AC generator and DC motor work on magnetic effect of electric current. [1]

(ii) In both cases, a coil rotates in a magnetic field between the pole pieces of a strong electromagnet. [1]

32. Give two differences between a DC motor and an AC generator. [2010]

Sol. The two differences between a DC motor and an AC generator are

DC Motor	AC Generator
It converts electrical energy into mechanical energy.	It converts mechanical energy into electrical energy.
It is based on the principle that when a coil carrying current is held in a magnetic field, it experiences a torque which rotates the coil.	It is based on the phenomenon of electromagnetic induction.

[1 × 2]

33. (i) What is an AC generator or dynamo used for?
(ii) Name the principle on which it works. **[2012]**

Sol. (i) An AC generator or dynamo is used to convert mechanical energy into electrical energy. **[1]**
(ii) It works on the principle of electromagnetic induction. **[1]**

34. Draw a simple sketch of a step-down transformer. Label the different parts in the diagram. **[2008]**

Sol. The sketch of step-down transformer is shown as below

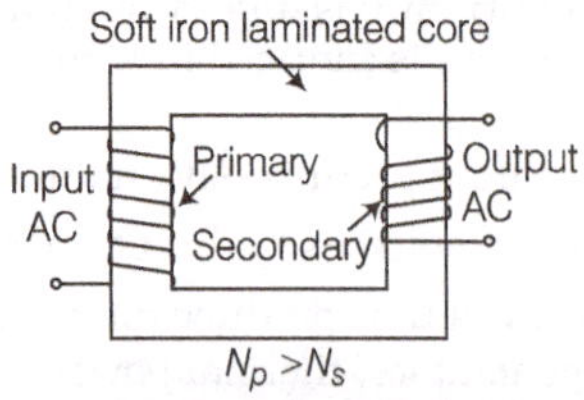

Step-down transfomer **[2]**

35. A device is used to transform 12 V AC to 200 V AC.
(i) What is the name of this device?
(ii) Name the principle on which it works. **[2010]**

Sol. (i) The name of this device is step-up transformer. **[1]**
(ii) It is based on the principle of mutual induction. **[1]**

36. State two causes of energy loss in a transformer. **[2016]**

Sol. The two causes of energy loss in a transformer are as follow
(i) **Eddy Currents** The alternating magnetic flux induces eddy currents in the iron core which causes heating effect. Hence energy loss occur in the iron core due to heating effect. **[1]**
(ii) **Resistance of the Windings** The wire used for the windings has some resistance and so energy is lost due to heat produced in the wire (I^2R). **[1]**

37. In the transmission of power, the voltage of power generated at the generating stations is stepped up from 11kV to 132kV before it is transmitted. Why? **[2017]**

Sol. Step-up transformer increases the amplitude of alternating voltage from 11 kV to 132 kV before it is transmitted to get better efficiency with less loss of energy. **[2]**

38. Which coil of a step-up transformer is made thicker and why?

Sol. Primary coil of a step-up transformer is made thicker, because it carries heavy current at low voltage. **[2]**

3 Marks Questions

39. A horizontal power line carries current in East to West direction. What is the direction of the magnetic field due to the current in the power line at a point above and at a point below the power line?

Sol. According to right hand thumb rule,
(i) the direction of magnetic field at a point above the power line is from South to North. **[1]**
(ii) the direction of magnetic field at a point below the power line is from North to South.

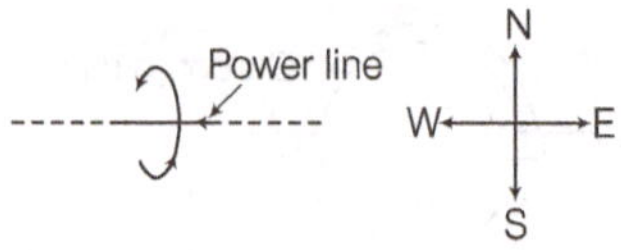

[2]

40. (i) A straight wire conductor passes vertically through a piece of cardboard sprinkled with iron filings as shown in the figure below. Copy the diagram and show the setting of iron filings when a current is passed through the wire in the upward direction and the cardboard is tapped gently. Draw arrows to represent the direction of the magnetic field lines.

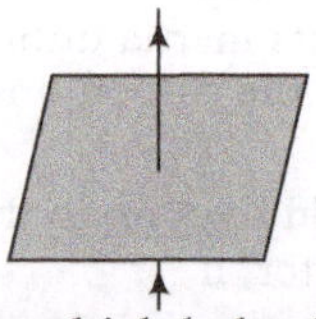

(ii) Name the law which helped you to find the direction of the magnetic field lines. **[2010]**

Sol. (i) The following diagram shows the magnetic field lines.

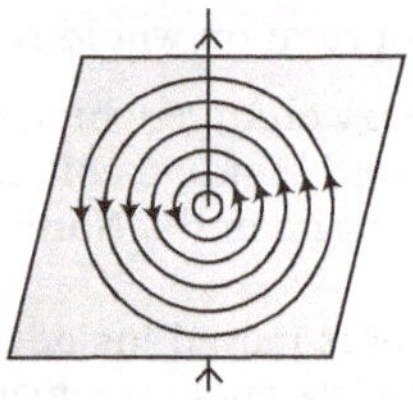
[2]

(ii) The right hand thumb rule helps to find the direction of magnetic field lines. **[1]**

41. (i) Why does a magnetic needle shows a deflection when brought close to a current carrying conductor?
(ii) A wire bent into a circle carries current in an anti-clockwise direction. What polarity does this face of the coil exhibit? **[2008]**

Sol. (i) A magnetic needle shows a deflection when brought close to a current carrying conductor, because the magnet of the current carrying conductor exerts a force on the magnetic needle.

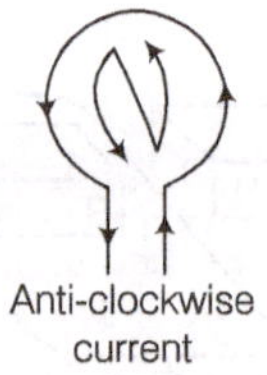

(ii) The face of the coil exhibits North polarity.

42. The flow of current in a circular wire creates a magnetic field at its centre. How can existence of this field be detected? State the rule which helps to predict the direction of magnetic field.

Sol. The existence of this field can be detected by using a magnetic compass needle.

The direction of magnetic field is predicted by using Maxwell's right hand thumb rule. **[1½]**

It states that, if you hold a current carrying conductor in right hand, such that the thumb points in the direction of electric current, then the direction in which fingers encircle, gives the direction of magnetic field. **[1½]**

43. The diagram given shows a current carrying loop or a circular coil passing through a sheet of cardboard at the points M and N. The sheet of cardboard is sprinkled uniformly with iron filings.

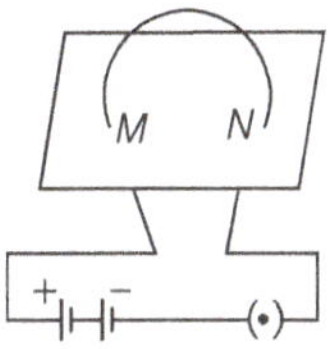

Copy the diagram and draw an arrow on the circular coil to show the direction of current flowing through it. Also draw the pattern of arrangement of the iron filings when current is passed through the loop.

Sol. The direction of current is from M to N as shown below.. **[1]**

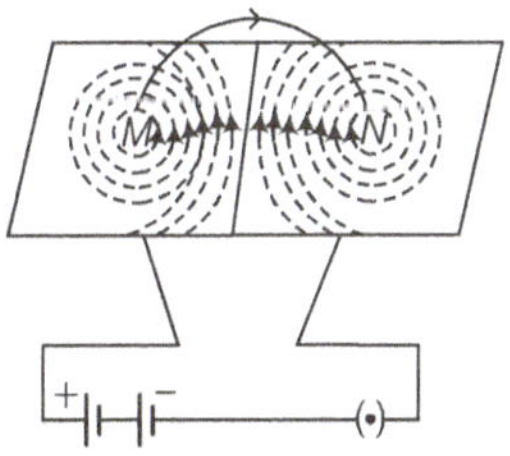

[2]

44. For the current carrying solenoid as shown below, draw magnetic field lines and giving reason explain that out of the three points A, B and C at which point, the field strength is maximum and at which point it is minimum.

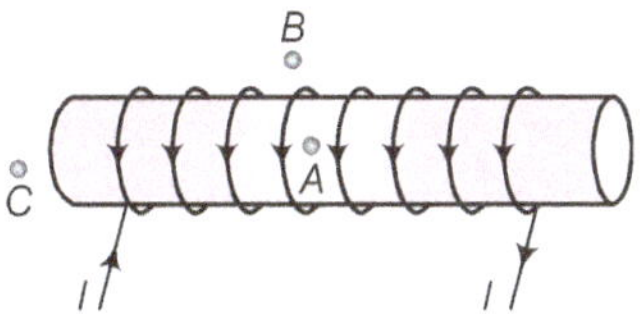

[2015]

Sol. According to the question, we can draw the following diagram.

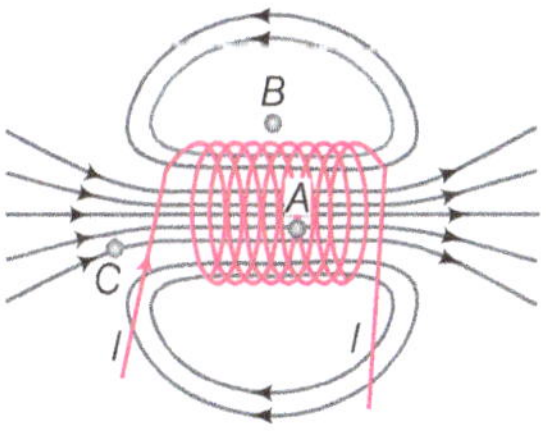

[1]

The magnetic field strength is maximum at point A and is minimum at point B, because magnetic field is strong, where magnetic field lines are crowded and is weak, where magnetic field lines are far apart. **[2]**

45. The diagram shows a coil wound around a U-shape soft iron bar AB.

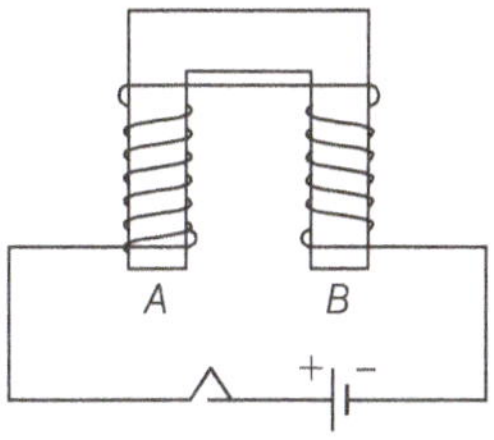

(i) What is the polarity induced at the ends A and B when the switch is pressed?

(ii) Suggest one way to strengthen the magnetic field in the electromagnet.

(iii) What will be the polarities at A and B if the direction of current is reversed in the circuit?

[2018]

Sol. (i) Current enter at point A (clockwise rotation) and leaving from point B (anti-clockwise rotation). Hence, A will be South pole and B will be North pole. **[1]**

(ii) Increasing the number of turns of coils, increases current. **[1]**

(iii) A = North, B = South **[1]**

46. (i) What is the name given to a cylindrical coil, whose diameter is less in comparison to its length?

(ii) A piece of soft iron is placed inside the current carrying coil, what is the name given to the device?

(iii) Give one use of the device named by you in part (*ii*) above.

Sol. (i) A cylindrical coil, whose diameter is less in comparison to its length is also named as solenoid.

(ii) The name of given to the device is electromagnet.

(iii) The electromagnet is used in the electric bell.

47. (i) List three methods of producing magnetic fields.

(ii) Imagine that you are sitting in a chamber with your back to one wall. An electron beam moving horizontally from back wall towards the front wall is deflected by a strong magnetic field to your right side. What is the direction of magnetic field?

Sol. (i) Three methods of producing magnetic field are as given below

(a) Passing electric current through a straight conductor/circuit.

(b) Passing electric current through a circular loop.

(c) Passing electric current through a solenoid. **[2]**

(ii) According to Fleming's left hand rule, the direction of magnetic field is vertically downward. [1]

48. (i) State two factors on which the strength of an induced current depends.

(ii) When a solenoid that is carrying current is freely suspended, it uses to rest along a particular direction. Why does this happen? [2007]

Sol. (i) The two factors on which the strength of an induced current depends are

(a) Rate of change of magnetic flux within the closed coil.

(b) Number of turns in coil. [1½]

(ii) A solenoid carrying a current behaves like a bar magnet. When it is freely suspended, it points in North-South direction. [1½]

49. Explain briefly, how a magnet can be demagnetised using an alternating current?

Sol. To demagnetise a magnet, place it inside a long solenoid with its length in East-West direction.

A 12 V AC supply is connected with a rheostat in series. Switch on the current, when AC is passed, its polarity changes due to which magnetic domains are reversed. [1½]

Thus, it becomes randomly oriented and the bar loses its magnetism to a greater extent.

Gradually, the current is reduced to zero by rheostat which makes the re-alignment of domains most difficult. Thus, the bar of magnet is demagnetised[1½]

50. From the diagram given below

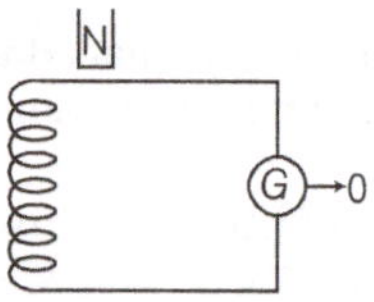

(i) What will you observe, when

(a) the magnet is dropped into the coil?

(b) the number of turns of the coil is increased?

(ii) What will be the direction of current flowing through the coil, when the magnet is dropped in? (Clockwise or anti-clockwise).

(iii) State the phenomenon on which the observation is made.

Sol. (i) (a) When a magnet is dropped into the coil, sudden deflection is observed in the galvanometer due to induced current.

(b) If number of turns of the coil is increased, galvanometer shows large deflection.

It is because, on increasing the number turns, magnetic field associated with coil increases ($\because B \propto N$), hence more current will be induced. [$1/2 \times 2 = 1$]

(ii) The direction of current flowing through the coil, when the magnet is dropped into, will be anti-clockwise. [1]

(iii) The above observation is made on electromagnetic induction. [1]

51. A coil of insulated copper wire is connected to a galvanometer. What will happen, if a bar magnet is

(i) pushed into the coil

(ii) withdrawn from inside the coil and

(iii) held stationary inside the coil?

Sol. (i) The galvanometer shows a deflection which means current is induced in the coil. Current is induced in the coil due to the relative motion between coil and magnet. [1]

(ii) The galvanometer shows a deflection in opposite direction which means current is induced in opposite direction. In this case, the direction of motion is in the opposite directions w.r.t. coil. [1]

(iii) There is no deflection in galvanometer as no current is induced in the coil. There is no relative motion between coil and current, so no current will be induced in the coil. [1]

52. (i) Two circular coils P and Q are kept close to each other, of which coil P carries a current. If coil P is moved towards Q, will some current be induced in coil Q? Give reason for your answer and name the phenomenon involved.

(ii) What happens, if coil P is moved away from Q?

(iii) State few methods of inducing current in a coil.

Sol. (i) When coil P is moved towards Q, current will be induced in coil Q.

This is because on moving P, the magnetic field associated with Q increases and so a current is induced. The phenomenon involved is electromagnetic induction. [1]

(ii) If P is moved away from Q, the magnetic field associated with Q will decrease and a current will be induced but in the opposite direction. [1]

(iii) Some of the methods of inducing current in the coil are

(a) moving a magnet towards or away from the coil.

(b) moving a coil towards or away from a magnet.

(c) rotating a coil within a magnetic field. [1]

53. State the rule to determine the direction of a

(i) magnetic field produced around a straight conductor carrying current.

(ii) force experienced by a current carrying straight conductor placed in a magnetic field.

(iii) current induced in a coil due to its rotation in magnetic field.

Sol. (i) **Maxwell's Right Hand Thumb Rule** It states that, if we hold the current carrying conductor in right hand such that the thumb points in the direction of the current, then the fingers incircle the wire will give the direction of the magnetic field lines.

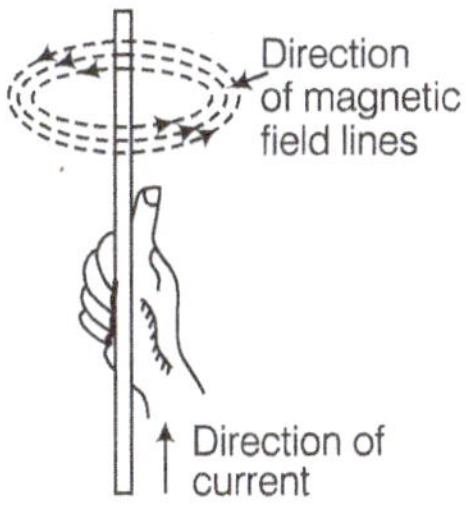

[1]

(ii) **Fleming's Left Hand Rule** This rule provides us the direction of force on a current carrying wire placed in a magnetic field. It states that, if the forefinger, thumb and middle finger of left hand are stretched mutually perpendicular to each other, such that the forefinger points along the direction of external magnetic field, middle finger indicates the direction of current, then the thumb points towards the direction of force acting on the conductor.

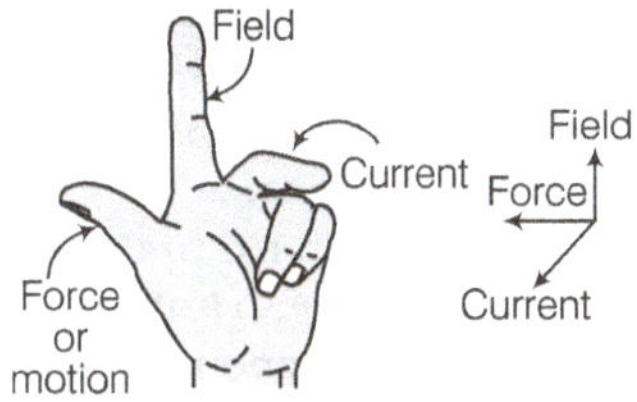

[1]

(iii) **Fleming's Right Hand Rule** Stretch the thumb, middle finger and forefinger of your right hand such that they are mutually perpendicular to each other. If the forefinger indicates the direction of magnetic field and the thumb indicates the direction of motion of conductor, then the middle finger will indicate the direction of induced current.

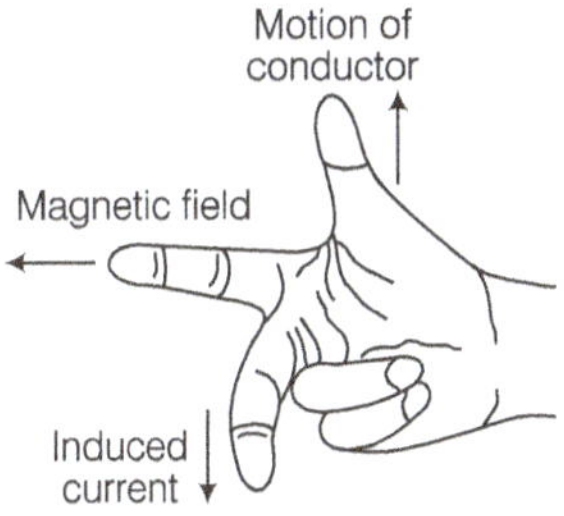

[1]

54. (i) State the Faraday's laws of electromagnetic induction.

(ii) Name one electrical device which works on this principle. **[3] [Latest Specimen Sem-II]**

Sol. (i) According to Faraday's laws of electromagnetic induction, whenever the magnetic field around a conductor changes, an emf is induced in it. **[2]**

(ii) Electrical generator works on the principle of electromagnetic induction. **[1]**

55. (i) Draw a neat and labelled diagram to show the structure of an AC generator.

(ii) State the energy conversion taking place in the AC generator, when it is working. **[2009]**

Sol. (i) The labelled diagram of an AC generator is shown as below

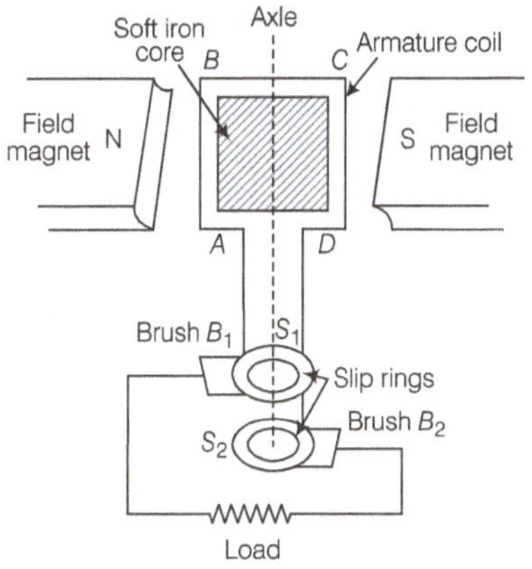

[2]

(ii) In the AC generator, mechanical energy of the rotation of the coil converts into electrical energy. **[1]**

56. State whether the following statements are true or false.

(i) An electric motor converts mechanical energy into electrical energy.

(ii) An electric generator works on the principle of electromagnetic induction.

(iii) The field at the centre of a long circular coil carrying current will be parallel straight lines.

Sol. (i) False, electric motor converts electrical energy into mechanical energy.

(ii) True

(iii) True **[1 × 3 = 3]**

57. What is a commutator? How does it bring direct current?

Sol. A commutator is used in a DC generator and helps to produce direct current. **[1]**

If a commutator is used, one brush is at all times in contact with the wire moving up in the field, while the other is in contact with the wire moving down, as split rings change their position after every half rotation. Thus, a unidirectional current is produced. **[2]**

58. (i) Name the transformer used in the power transmitting station of a power plant.

(ii) What type of current is transmitted from the power station?

(iii) At what voltage is this current available to our household? **[2017]**

Sol. (i) In the power transmission station, step-up transformer is used to minimise the loss of electrical energy in transmission. **[1]**

(ii) Alternating Current (AC) is transmitted from the power station. **[1]**

(iii) At our household, current at 220 V is supplied by the step-down transformer. **[1]**

4 Marks Questions

59. The diagram shows an insulated copper wire wound around a hollow cardboard cylindrical tube. **[Latest Specimen Sem-II]**

Answer the questions that follow.

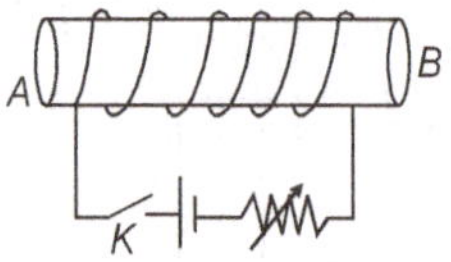

(i) What are the magnetic poles at *A* and *B*, when the key *K* is closed?

(ii) State two ways to increase the strength of the magnetic field in this coil without changing the coil.

(iii) If we place a soft iron bar at the centre of the hollow cardboard and replace the DC source by an AC source, then will it attract small iron pins toward itself when the current is flowing through the coil? **[4]**

Sol. (i) When key *K* is closed, the current starts flowing from end *A* to *B*.
In end *A*, the direction of current is anti-clockwise. So, it has north polarity, i.e. N-pole, while the current at end *B* is clockwise. So, it has south polarity, i.e. S-pole.

(ii) The strength of a magnetic field can be increased by

(a) increasing the amount of current flowing through the coil by decreasing resistance.

(b) decreasing the air-gap between the poles or coils.

(iii) When the DC source is replaced by an AC source, then the soft iron bar gets magnetised or demagnetised periodically as the polarity of current changes. Hence the circuit it sets into vibrations, so it will not attract the small iron pins.

60. (i) What is the function of the split rings in a DC motor? **[2013, 10]**

(ii) State two ways by which the magnetic field of a solenoid can be made stronger.

Sol. (i) In DC motor, when the coil rotates, the split ring rotates with it to make the current flow in the armature coil in such a way that it always keep on rotating in the same manner. **[2]**

(ii) Magnetic field of a solenoid can be made stronger by increasing

(a) the current in the solenoid. **[1]**

(b) the number of turns in the solenoid. **[1]**

61. Draw a representative diagram of a DC motor. Label the following in your diagram.

(i) The field magnet

(ii) The armature

(iii) Commutator

(iv) Wire brushes

What is the energy change in this case? **[2011]**

Sol. The labelled diagram of DC motor is as shown below

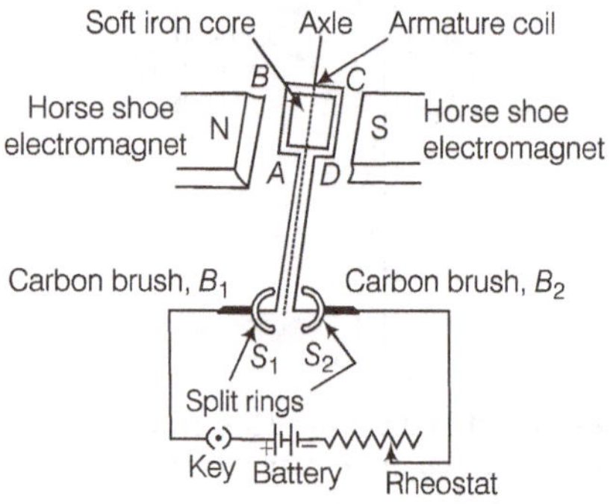

(i) The magnetic field is labelled as *N-S*. It is an electromagnet with concave pole pieces. **[1]**

(ii) The armature coil mounted on an axle is labelled as *ABCD*. **[1]**

(iii) The commutators are labelled as S_1, S_2. **[1]**

(iv) Wire brushes are labelled as B_1, B_2.
In an electric DC motor, the electrical energy is converted into mechanical energy. **[1]**

62. We are able to see the TV channels clearly when we set TV an auto-tuning.

(i) Which phenomenon led to the clear visibility of the channels, due to auto-tuning ?

(ii) Define the above phenomenon mentioned by you.

(iii) Give any one more example of this phenomenon. **[2023]**

Sol. (a) Electromagnetic wave interference **[1]**

(b) Electromagnetic wave interference is a phenomena that occurs when two or more electromagnetic waves interfere with each other as they travel through space. **[2]**

(c) Radiowaves interfering with each other in crowded areas such as airports, cell phones signals. **[1]**

63. The diagram below shows a cardboard on which iron filings are kept. A wire bent in the form of a loop is seen passing through the cardboard. When current flows through it, the iron filings arrange themselves as shown below.

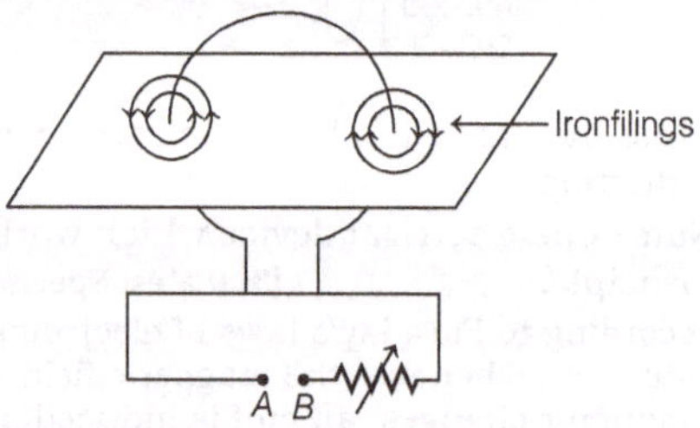

(i) State the polarities of the battery at *A* and *B*.

(ii) State the effect on the magnetic field, if an iron rod is held along the axis of the coil.

(iii) State one way to

(a) Change the polarity of the coil

(b) Decrease the strength of the magnetic field around the coil **[2023]**

Sol. (i) $A \rightarrow$ Positive terminal

$B \rightarrow$ Negative terminal

(ii) Magnetic field will expand in the direction of the held rod.

(iii) (a) Reversing the direction of battery

(b) Reduce the potential difference across the coil.

64. (i) Name two factors on which the magnitude of an induced emf in the secondary coil depends.

(ii) In the given diagram, an arrow shows the motion of the coil towards the bar magnet.

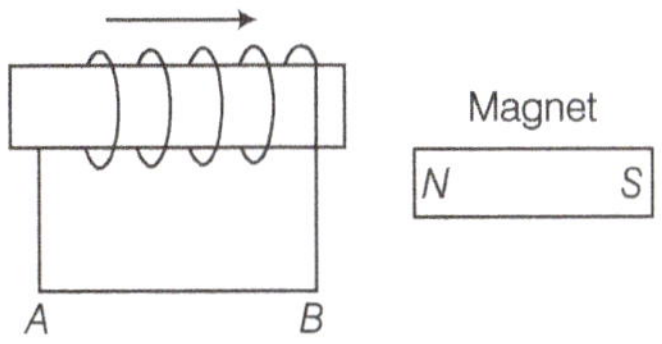

(a) State in which direction the current flows, A to B or B to A?

(b) Name the law used to come in the conclusion. **[2014]**

Sol. (i) The two factors on which the magnitude of an induced emf in the secondary coil depends are

(a) the change in magnetic flux. **[1]**

(b) the time in which magnetic flux changes. **[1]**

(ii) (a) The current flows from B to A. **[1]**

(b) The law used to come to the conclusion is law of electromagnetic induction. **[1]**

65. (i) Draw a labelled diagram to show the various components of a step-up transformer.

(ii) State the main difference between a step-up and step-down transformer.

Sol. (i) The sketch of step-up transformer is shown below

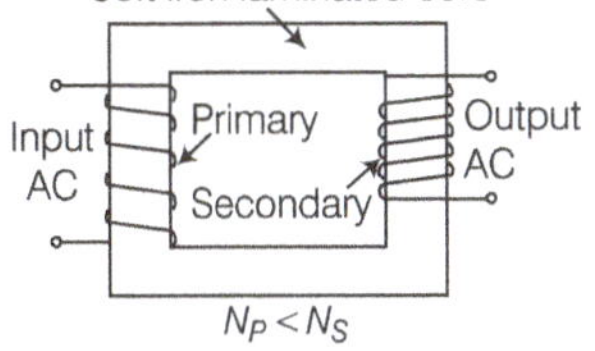

[2]

(ii) The difference between step-up and step-down transformer are as below

Step-up Transformer	Step-down Transformer
It is used to change a low voltage alternating emf to high voltage alternating emf.	It is used to change a high voltage alternating emf to low voltage alternating emf.
The number of turns in primary coil is less than the number of turns in secondary coil.	The number of turns in primary coil is greater than the number of turns in secondary coil.

[1 × 2 = 2]

Structured Questions

66. (i) Draw a neat labelled diagram of AC generator. **[3]**

(ii) Explain **[3]**

(a) Flemings's left hand rule and

(b) Flemings's right hand rule.

(iii) The figure below shows a magnetic needle kept just below the conductor AB which is kept in North-South direction.

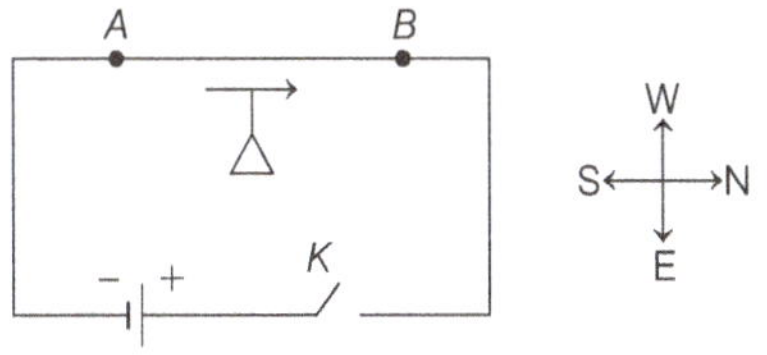

(a) In which direction, will the needle deflect when the key is closed?

(b) Why is the deflection produced?

(c) What will be the change in the deflection, if the magnetic needle is taken just above the conductor AB? **[4]**

(d) Name one device which works on the principle of electromagnetic induction.

Sol. (i)

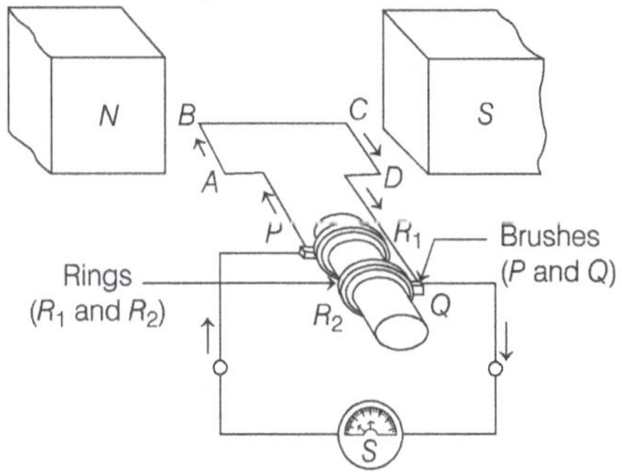

AC Generator

[3]

(ii) (a) **Fleming's Left Hand Rule** The direction of force which acts on a current carrying conductor placed in a magnetic field is given by Fleming's left hand rule.

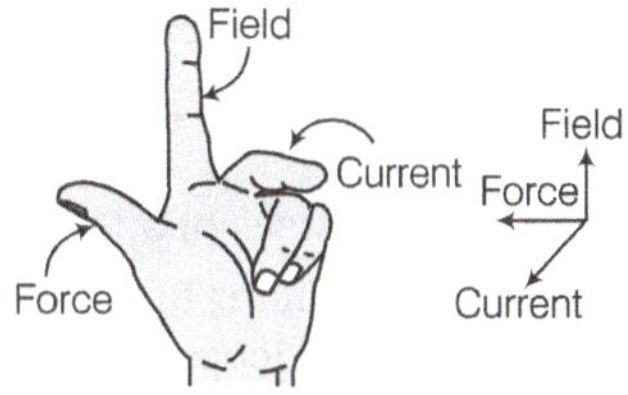

It states that, if the forefinger, thumb and middle finger of left hand are stretched mutually perpendicular to each other and the forefinger points along the direction of external magnetic field, middle finger indicates the direction of current, then thumb points in the direction of force acting on the conductor. [1½]

(b) **Fleming's Right Hand Rule** The direction of induced current in a straight conductor is given by Fleming's right hand rule.

It states that, if the forefinger, middle finger and thumb of the right hand are stretched at right angles to each other, with the forefinger in the direction of the field and the thumb in the direction of the motion of the wire, then the current in the wire is in the direction of the middle finger.

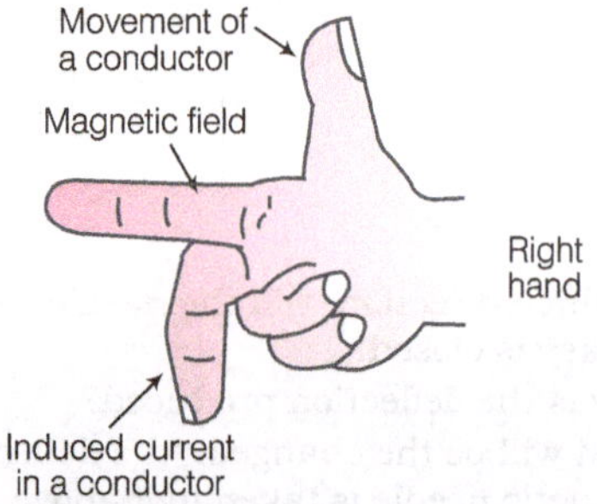

[1½]

(iii) (a) East direction [1]

(b) The needle align itself with the direction of magnetic field lines. Since the lines are perpendicular to the direction of current, the needle will try to align that way also. [1]

(c) The North pole of the compass needle deflects towards West. [1]

(d) Electric generator [1]

67. (i) The diagram below shows the core of a transformer and its input and output connections.

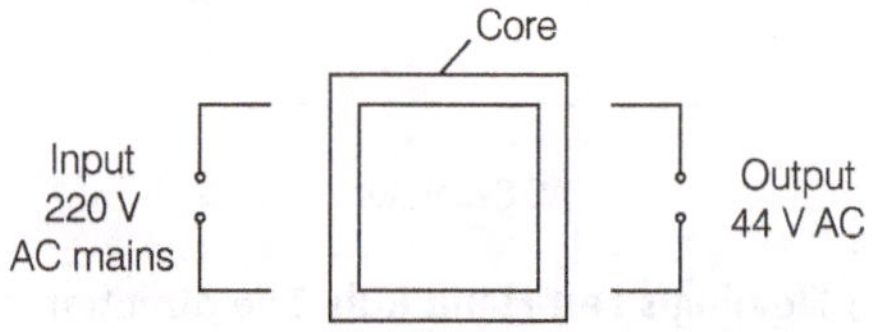

(a) State the material used for the core.

(b) Copy and complete the diagram of the transformer by drawing input and output coils. [3]

(ii) (a) Draw a neat labelled diagram of DC motor. [3]

(b) Write any two uses of a DC motor.

(iii) Describe an experiment to show that a current is set up in a closed loop when an external magnetic field passing through the loop increases or decreases. [4]

Sol. (i) (a) Core of transformer is made of soft iron sheets and these core sheets are laminated to prevent from eddy current. [1½]

(b)

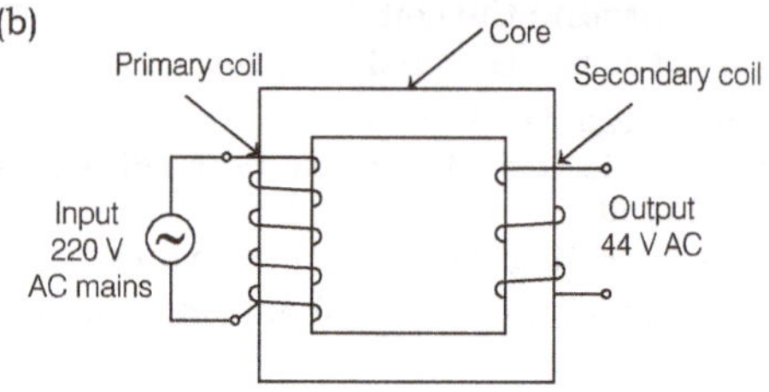

[1½]

(ii) (a) Diagram of DC motor is given below.

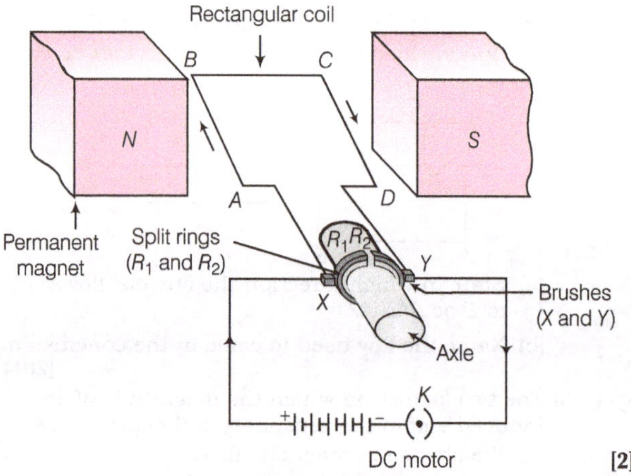

DC motor [2]

(b) DC motor is used in water pump and electric fans. [1]

(iii) Let two different coils of copper wire, namely coil 1 and coil 2, having large number of turns are arranged as per the circuit (as shown in figure).

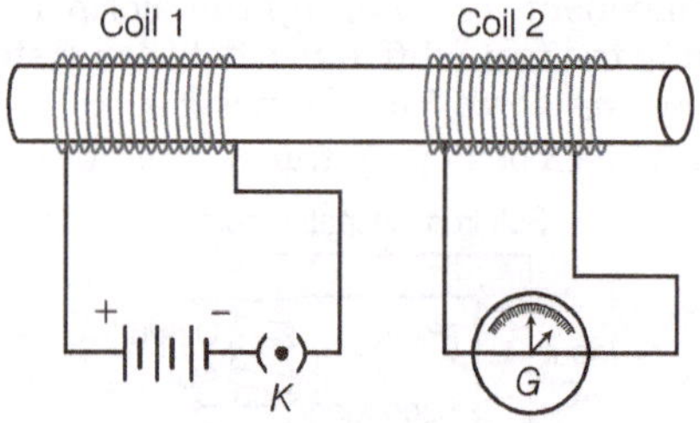

The coil 1, having larger number of turns, is connected in series with a battery and a plug key, whereas the other coil 2 is connected with a galvanometer. [2]

Case I When key K is closed, the galvanometer shows a deflection, its needle instantly jumps to one side and just as quickly returns to zero, indicating a momentary current in coil 2. This happens due to increase of external magnetic field passing through the loop. [1]

Case II When key K is open, the coil 1 is disconnected from the battery. The needle momentarily moves, but to the opposite side. It means that now the current flows in the opposite direction in coil 2. This happens due to decrease of external magnetic field passing through the loop. [1]

Chapter Assessment

1 Mark Questions

1. The presence of a magnetic field at a point can be detected by a
(a) solenoid (b) compass needle
(c) current carrying wire (d) strong magnet

2. The magnetic field due to straight current carrying wire is
(a) same as that of bar magnet
(b) same as that of a solenoid
(c) concentric circles
(d) straight lines

3. A current carrying wire experiences a force, when placed in a magnetic field. The direction of force is given by
(a) Fleming's left hand rule (b) Fleming's right hand rule
(c) Right hand thumb rule (d) All of these

4. An electric motor is
(a) energy converter device
(b) safety device
(c) energy conversion device
(d) All of the above

5. In a step-down transformer,
(a) $N_s = N_p$ (b) $N_s < N_p$
(c) $N_s > N_p$ (d) None of these

6. A transformer
(a) converts electrical energy
(b) stores electrical energy
(c) supplied electric energy
(d) None of the above

7. A simple AC generator produces a voltage that varies with time as shown below

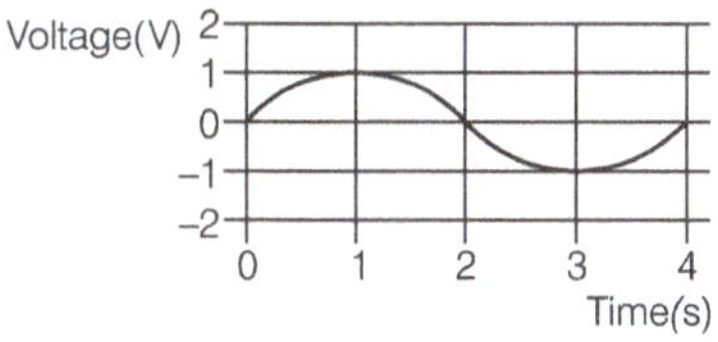

Which graph shows how the voltage varies with time, when the generator rotates at twice the original speed ?

(a)
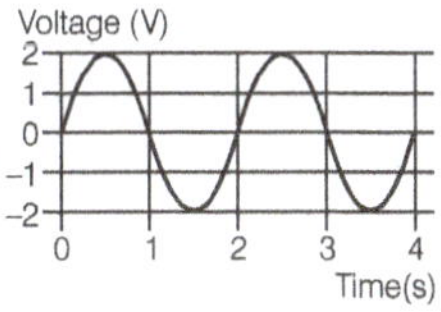

(b)
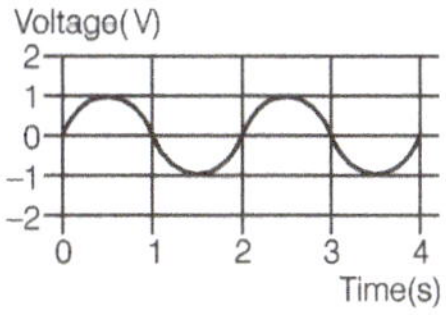

(c)
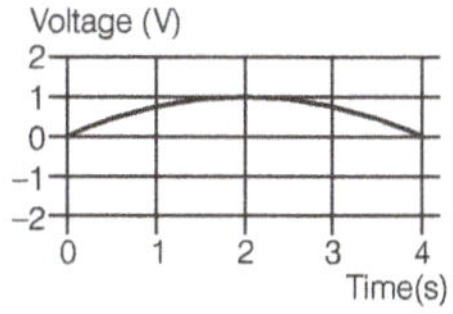

(d)
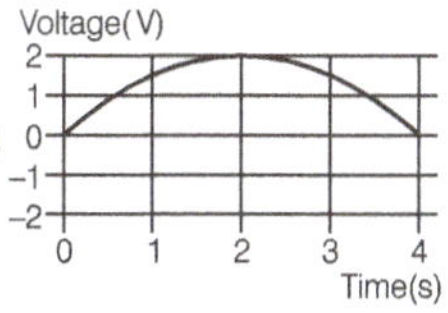

2 Marks Questions

8. The sample of electric motor given below in the following figure, rotates anti-clockwise as seen by the eye from the position X, when current flows in the coil.

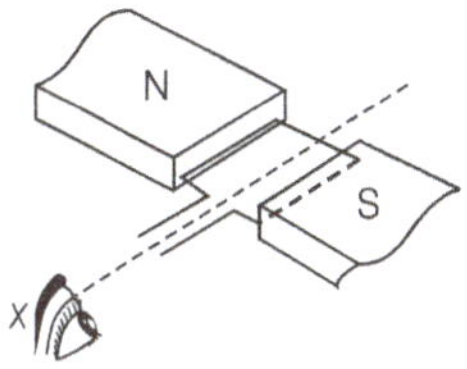

Is the current flowing clockwise or anti-clockwise around the coil, when viewed from above?

9. (i) What is the function of a step-up transformer?
(ii) Can a transformer work, when it is connected to a DC source?

10. When a current carrying conductor is placed in a magnetic field, it experiences a mechanical force. What should be the angle between the magnetic field and the length of the conductor, so that the force experienced is
(i) zero
(ii) and maximum? **[ICSE 2020]**

11. The diagram below shows a loop of wire carrying current I.

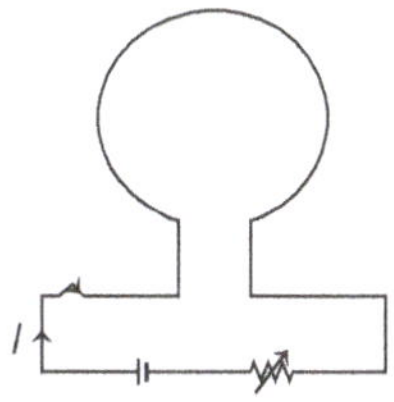

(i) What is the magnetic polarity of the loop that faces us?
(ii) With respect to the diagram, how can we increase the strength of the magnetic field produced by this loop? **[ICSE 2020]**

12. State two ways to increase the speed of rotation of a DC motor. **[ICSE 2019]**

13. A coil is connected to a galvanometer. When the N-pole of a magnet is pushed into the coil, the galvanometer deflected to the right. What deflection, if any is observed, when
(i) the N-pole is removed and
(ii) the S-pole is inserted?

14. A magnet kept at the centre of two coils *A* and *B* is moved to and fro as shown in the figure given below. The two galvanometers show deflection.

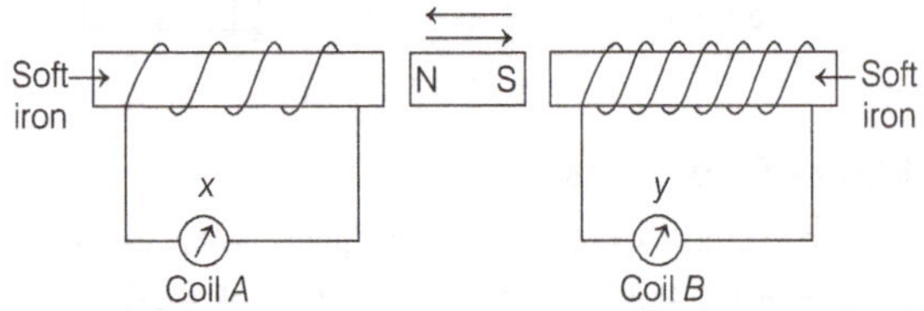

State with a reason whether $x > y$ or $x < y$, where x and y are magnitudes of deflection.

15. How would the strength of magnetic field due to current-carrying loop be affected, if
   (i) radius of the loop is reduced to half of its original value?
   (ii) strength of current through the loop is doubled?

Structured Questions

16. (i) The diagram shows a coil of wire wound on a soft iron core forming an electromagnet. A current is passed through the coil in the direction indicated by the arrows. **[3]**

   Mark the *N* and *S*-poles produced in the iron core.

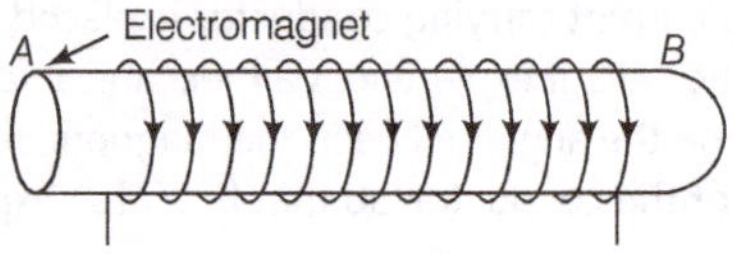

   (ii) What is the purpose of using transformer? Can it be used with both the current sources as alternating and direct? If not, why? What appliance will you use to step-down DC voltage? **[3]**

   (iii) A coil made of insulated copper wire is connected to a galvanometer. What will happen to the deflection of the galvanometer if this coil is moved towards a stationary bar magnet and then moved away from it? Give reason for your answer and name the phenomenon involved. **[4]**

17. (i) (a) Prachi draws magnetic field lines of field close to the axis of a current-carrying circular loop. As she moves away from the centre of the circular loop, she observes that the lines keep on diverging. How will you explain her observation?

   (b) How will you use a solenoid to magnetise a steel bar? **[3]**

   (ii) (a) Name two devices which work on the magnetic effect of current.

   (b) Mention about the essential parts of a DC motor. **[4]**

   (iii) A coil *P* is connected to a torch bulb and placed parallel to another coil *Q* as shown in figure.

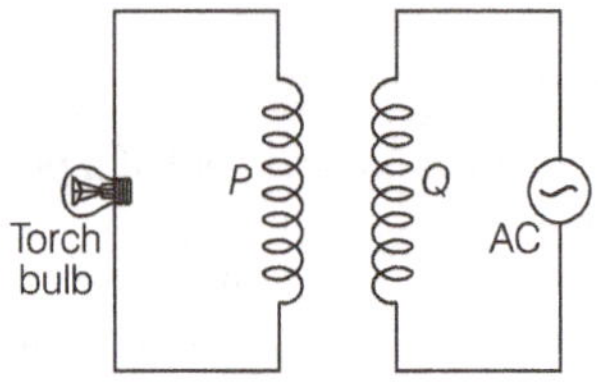

   Explain the following observations.
   (a) Bulb lights
   (b) Bulb gets dimmer, if the coil *P* is moved upwards. **[3]**

18. (i) With proper circuit diagram, draw the magnetic field due to current carrying circular loop. **[3]**

   (ii) (a) Explain the working principle of AC generator.

   (b) Mention one similarity between AC generator and AC motor. **[3]**

   (iii) The diagram shows a coil connected to a galvanometer *G*. The galvanometer shows a deflection to the right when the *N*-pole of a powerful magnet is moved to the right as shown.

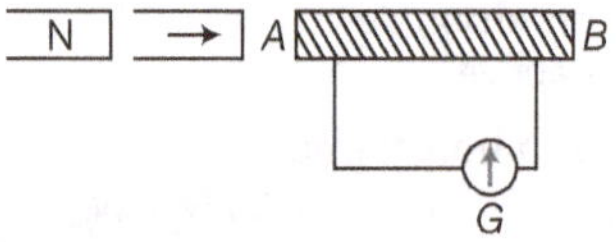

   (a) Explain, why the deflection occur in the galvanometer?
   (bi) Does the direction of the current in the coil appear clockwise or anti-clockwise, when viewed from the end *A*?
   (ci) State the observation in *G* when the coil is moved away from *N*.
   (d) State the observation in *G* when both the coil and the magnet are moved to the right at the same speed. **[4]**

For Solutions Scan the Code

Olympiad Section*

Brain Teasing Questions of Olympiad Pattern

1 A straight wire lying in a horizontal plane carries a current from North to South. Magnetic field at a point directly below the wire is

(a) East (b) West

(c) North (d) South

2 On reversing the direction of current in a wire the magnetic field produced by it

(a) get reversed in direction

(b) increases in strength

(c) decreases in strength

(d) remains unchanged in strength and direction

3 In which of the following cases, emf is not induced?

(a) A current is started in a wire held near a loop of wire

(b) The current is switched off in a wire held near a loop of wire

(c) A magnet is moved through a loop of wire

(d) A loop of wire is held near a magnet

4 Ravi designed the toy shown below using a bar magnet, a spring and an iron ball.

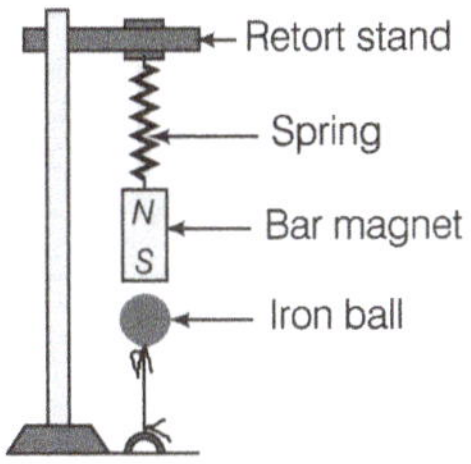

Which of the following correctly shows how the forces are interacting to keep the ball floating?

(a) Magnetic force is equal to gravitational force

(b) Elastic spring force is equal to magnetic force

(c) The sum of elastic spring force and magnetic force is equal to gravitational force

(d) The sum of elastic spring force and gravitational force is equal to frictional force

5 A permanent magnet can be demagnetised by using a solenoid and switching the current ON then OFF.

Which diagram shows the most effective method of producing demagnetisation?

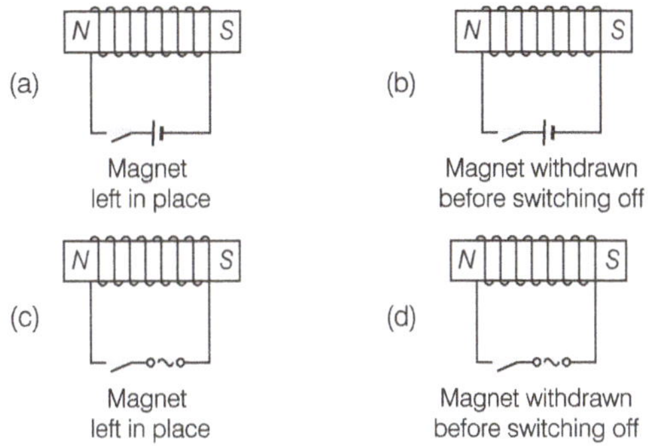

6 The diagram shows a beam of electrons entering a magnetic field,

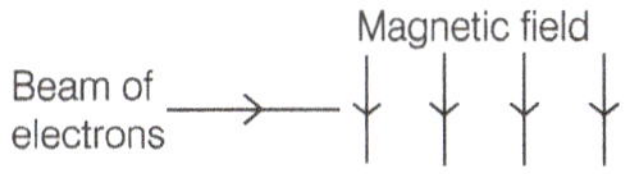

(a) they are deflected along the field

(b) they are deflected opposite to the field

(c) they are deflected towards the bottom of the diagram

(d) they are deflected towards the top of the diagram

7 An electron is travelling horizontally towards East. A magnetic field in vertically downward direction exerts a force on the electorn along

(a) East (b) West

(c) North (d) South

8 A magnet is in the form of a bar. Initially, the axis of the bar magnet is along X-axis. At some distance from the magnet, a coil is kept in the YZ-plane with its centre along X-axis. Which of the following motions of the bar magnet will not induce electric current in the coil ? **[Olympiad 2018]**

(a) Translational vibrations perpendicular to X-axis.

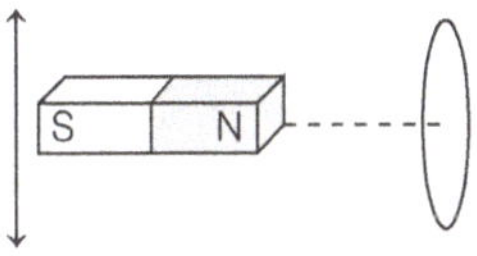

(b) The bar magnet axis is turned to make an acute angle with the X-axis and the magnet is rotated about X-axis with the south pole fixed on X-axis.

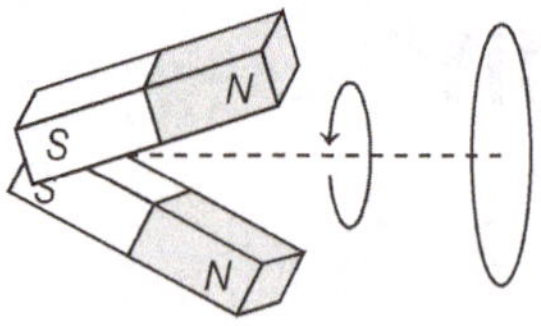

(c) The bar magnet axis is swinging back and forth about the X-axis with the south pole fixed on the X-axis.

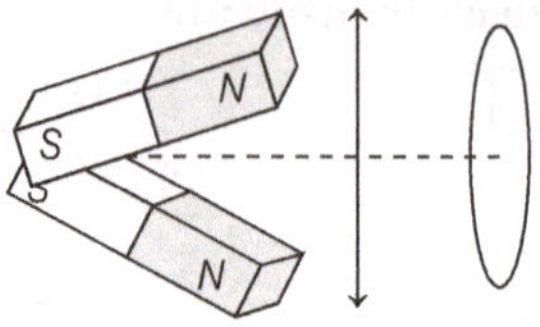

(d) The bar magnet spins about a perpendicular bisector as its axis of rotation, with its center on the X-axis.

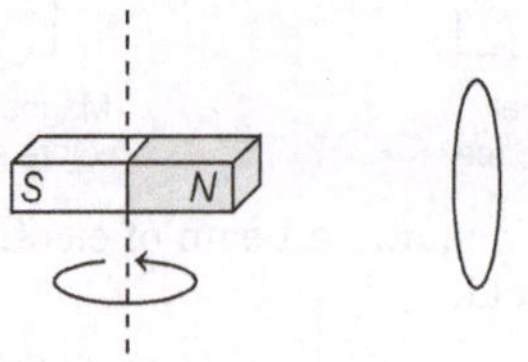

9 In the figure given PQ is a long uniform coil of metal wire, V is a constant voltage source and ASB is a rheostat. Consider the following statements and choose the correct option.

[Olympiad 2017]

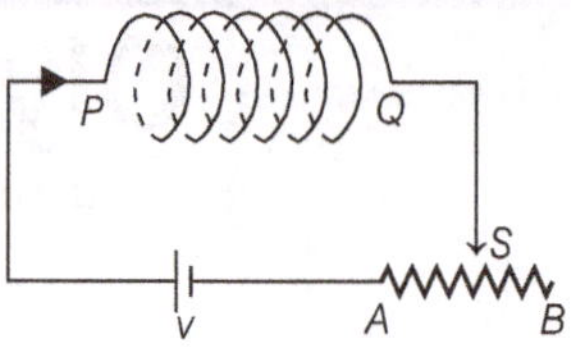

(i) The (equivalent) pole at the end P if slider S of rheostat is moved from A to B is North.
(ii) The (equivalent) pole at the end P if slider S of rheostat is moved from A to B is South.
(iii) The (equivalent) pole at the end P if slider S of rheostat is moved from B to A is North.
(IV) The (equivalent) pole at the end P if slider S of rheostat is moved from B to A is South.

(a) Only III and IV are correct
(b) Only I and II are correct
(c) Only II and IV are correct
(d) Only I and III are correct.

10 Two conducting circular loops F and G are kept in a plane on either side of a straight current-carrying wire as shown in the figure below.

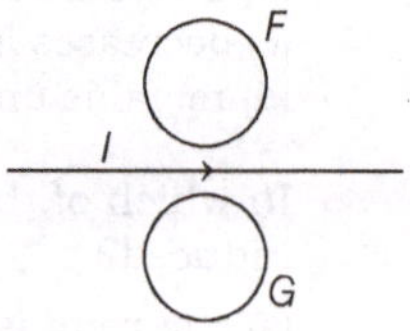

[IJSO, 2013 Pune, India]

If the current in the wire decreases in magnitude, the induced current in the loops will be

(a) clockwise in F and clockwise in G.
(b) anti-clockwise in F and clockwise in G.
(c) clockwise in F and anti-clockwise in G.
(d) anti-clockwise in F and anti-clockwise in G.

ANSWERS									
1. (a)	**2.** (a)	**3.** (d)	**4.** (c)	**5.** (d)	**6.** (d)	**7.** (d)	**8.** (b)	**9.** (c)	**10.** (b)

* *These questions may or may not be asked in the examination, have been given just for additional practice required for olympiads Scholarship Exams etc. For detailed explanations refer Page No. 270.*

CHAPTER

10

Heat

SYLLABUS

(i) Calorimetry : meaning, specific heat capacity; principle of method of mixtures; Numerical Problems on specific heat capacity using heat loss and gain and the method of mixtures..

(ii) Latent heat; loss and gain of heat involving change of state for fusion only.

When heat is introduced to a certain substance, its molecules start moving faster and collide with one another, which produce more heat and increases temperature of the substance. This implies that heat introduced to a substance, changes the temperature of the body. Thus, heat and temperature are interrelated to each other. In this chapter, we will study the concept of heat and its measurement and also the process of transfer of heat during the change of state of a substance, which constitute the concept of latent heat.

Temperature

It is the measure of degree of hotness or coldness of any body. When two bodies are at different temperatures, i.e., T_1 and T_2, where $T_1 > T_2$, then the body with temperature T_1 is called hotter with respect to another body with temperature T_2.

The SI unit of temperature is Kelvin (K). Other units of temperature are Celsius (°C) and Fahrenheit (°F).

Heat

The form of energy which flows from one part to other part of the system due to difference in temperature of two parts is known as heat. It measures the total internal energy possessed by the molecules. It flows from a hot body to a cold body when they are kept in contact. It is represented by Q.

The sum of the potential energy and kinetic energy of a molecule is called its internal energy. The total internal energy of all molecules of a substance is called its heat energy.

Units of Heat

Like other forms of energy, the SI unit of heat is **joule** (J). Apart from this, there are other two commonly used units; **calorie** and **kilocalorie**.

Calorie

The amount of heat energy which is required to raise the temperature of 1 g of water through 1°C is known as a calorie. But, it was found that this definition is not true due to non-uniform thermal expansion of water.

So, the definition of calorie was restated as the amount of heat energy required to raise the temperature of 1 g of water from 14.5°C to 15.5°C is known as one calorie of heat.

Kilocalorie

The amount of heat energy required to raise the temperature of 1 kg of water from 14.5°C to 15.5°C is known as one kilocalorie of heat.

1 kilocalorie = 1000 calories

Kilocalorie is usually used for measuring the energy value of foods.

1 calorie = 4.186 J = 4.2 J (approx)

1 kilocalorie = 4186 J = 4200 J (approx)

Differences between Heat and Temperature

Heat	Temperature
It measures the total internal energy possessed by the molecules of the body.	It measures the degree of hotness or coldness of any body.
Its SI unit is Joule (J).	Its SI unit is Kelvin (K).
By using the principle of calorimetry, this quantity can be measured.	By using thermometer, this quantity can be measured.
It is an additive quantity.	It is not an additive quantity.

Note The quantity of heat which is absorbed by a body to raise its temperature depends upon its mass, rise in temperature and its material.

Thermal (Heat) Capacity

It is defined as the amount of heat needed to raise the temperature of a body by unity, i.e., 1° C or 1 K. It is denoted by C'.

$$\text{Heat capacity, } C' = \frac{\Delta Q}{\Delta T}$$

where, ΔQ = heat absorbed or rejected by body

and ΔT = change in temperature.

Units of Heat Capacity

SI unit of heat capacity is J/K,

Calorie °C^{-1} (or cal K^{-1}) and kilocalorie °C^{-1} (or kilocalorie K^{-1}) are some other units of heat capacity.

$$1 \text{ kilocalorie } °\text{C}^{-1} = 1000 \text{ cal}°\text{C}^{-1}$$

$$1 \text{ cal K}^{-1} = 4.2 \text{ JK}^{-1}$$

Water Equivalent

Mass of water having the same thermal capacity as that of a given body is called **water equivalent** of the body. The SI unit of water equivalent is kilogram (kg).

Example 1. Determine the thermal (heat) capacity of iron ball if it requires 5000 J heat energy to raise its temperature by 10°C.

Sol. Here, Q = 5000 J and ΔT = 10° C

As, the size of a degree is the same on the Celsius and Kelvin scales, so the change in temperature has the same magnitude in °C and K.

Since, heat capacity

$$C' = \frac{\text{Heat energy required } (Q)}{\text{Rise in temperature } (\Delta T)}$$

$$\Rightarrow \quad C' = \frac{5000}{10} = 500 \text{ JK}^{-1}$$

Daily Life Examples of High and Low Thermal Capacity

(i) The calorimeter which is used to measure the heat, is made of thin sheet of copper. It is because the specific heat capacity of copper is low and by making the calorimeter thin, its thermal capacity also becomes low. So, in order to attain its temperature, it takes a negligible amount of heat from its contents.

(ii) In order to increase the thermal capacity of cooking pan, its base is made thick. Due to which, it imparts sufficient heat energy at a low temperature to the food for its proper cooking. It also keeps the food warm for a long time.

(iii) By making the base of an electric iron thick and heavy, the thermal capacity of base of electric iron increases due to which it remains hot for a longer period of time even after switching OFF the current.

Check Your LEARNING...

1 What is the mutual relation between heat and temperature?

2 Which single property decides the direction of the flow of heat?

3 Two bodies at different temperatures are placed in contact. State the direction in which heat will flow.

4 Name the SI unit of heat and how is it related to the unit calorie?

5 Determine the heat capacity of iron ball if it requires 4750 J heat energy to raise its temperature by 10 K.

Ans. 475 JK^{-1}

Specific Heat Capacity

The amount of heat needed to raise the temperature of unit mass of a substance by unity is known as the specific heat capacity or specific heat.
It is denoted by c.

Specific heat capacity, $$c = \frac{1}{m}\frac{\Delta Q}{\Delta T}$$

$$\Rightarrow \quad \Delta Q = m \times c \times \Delta t$$

where, m = mass of given substance.

The substance having low specific heat capacity shows a rapid and high rise in temperature. Thus, it is a better conductor of heat than the substance with high specific heat capacity which shows a slow and small rise in temperature.

Units of Specific Heat Capacity

Joule per kilogram per kelvin ($Jkg^{-1}K^{-1}$) or joule per kilogram per degree celsius ($Jkg^{-1}{}^{\circ}C^{-1}$) is the SI unit of specific heat capacity. $Calg^{-1}{}^{\circ}C^{-1}$ and kilocalorie $kg^{-1}{}^{\circ}C^{-1}$ are some other units of specific heat capacity.

$1\ calg^{-1}{}^{\circ}C^{-1} = 1\ kilocal\ kg^{-1}K^{-1} = 4.2 \times 10^3\ Jkg^{-1}K^{-1}$

Specific Heat Capacity of Some Common Substances

Substance	Specific Heat Capacity	
	In $J\ kg^{-1}\ K^{-1}$	In $cal\ g^{-1}\ {}^{\circ}C^{-1}$
(i) Water	4180	1.0
(ii) Ice	2100	0.50
(iii) Iron	483	0.115
(iv) Copper	399	0.095
(v) Lead	130	0.031

Relationship between Heat Capacity and Specific Heat Capacity

The relationship between the quantities thermal (heat) capacity (C') and specific heat capacity (c) can be given as

$$C' = \text{mass}(m) \times c$$

or $$c = \frac{C'}{m}$$

Differences between Heat Capacity and Specific Heat Capacity

Heat Capacity	Specific Heat Capacity
It is the amount of heat required to raise the temperature of whole body by 1°C.	It is the amount of heat required to raise the temperature of unit mass of the body by 1°C.
Its SI unit is JK^{-1}.	Its SI unit is $Jkg^{-1}K^{-1}$.
It depends on the material and mass of the body.	It is the characteristic of the material of body, so it does not depend on the mass of the body.
It can be calculated as Heat Capacity, $C' = \frac{\Delta Q}{\Delta T}$	It can be calculated as $c = \frac{\text{Heat capacity}(C')}{\text{Mass}(m)} = \frac{1}{m}\frac{\Delta Q}{\Delta T}$

Example 2. Find the specific heat capacity of a body having mass 500 g and requires 2000 J of heat energy to raise its temperature from 35°C to 45°C.

Sol. Given, $m = 500g = 0.5\ kg$

Heat energy required, $\Delta Q = 2000\ J$

Rise in temperature, $\Delta T = (45^{\circ} - 35^{\circ}) = 10^{\circ}C = 10\ K$

$\therefore$ Specific heat capacity,

$$c = \frac{\Delta Q}{m \times \Delta T} = \frac{2000}{0.5 \times 10} = 400\ Jkg^{-1}K^{-1}$$

Example 3. A 10 kW drilling machine is used to drill a bore in a small aluminium block of mass 8.0 kg. How much is the rise in temperature of the block in 2.5 min, assuming 50% of power is used up in heating the machine itself or lost to the surroundings?

(Take, specific heat of aluminium $= 0.91\ Jg^{-1}{}^{\circ}C^{-1}$)

Sol. Given, power, $P = 10\ kW = 10 \times 10^3 W$

Time, $t = 2.5\ min = 2.5 \times 60\ s$

Rise in temperature, $\Delta T = ?$

From $P = \frac{W}{t} \Rightarrow W = Pt$

Total energy used $= Pt$

$$= 10 \times 10^3 \times 2.5 \times 60 = 1.5 \times 10^6\ J$$

Given, energy absorbed by aluminium block,

$\Delta Q = 50\%$ of the total energy

$$\therefore \quad \Delta Q = \frac{1.5 \times 10^6}{2} = 0.75 \times 10^6\ J$$

Applying the formula, $\Delta Q = mc\Delta T \Rightarrow \Delta T = \frac{\Delta Q}{mc}$

Substituting the given values, we get

$$= \frac{0.75 \times 10^6}{8.0 \times 10^3 \times 0.91} = 103.02^{\circ}C$$

Use of Water in Various Natural Phenomena due to its High Specific Heat Capacity

(i) Water is used in cold countries as heat reservoir for wine and juice bottles to prevent their freezing. This is because of its high specific heat capacity. So, it imparts a large amount of heat before reaching to the freezing temperature. Hence due to this, bottles kept in water remains warm and do not get freeze even when there is a considerable decrease in surrounding temperature.

(ii) Almost, all the plants and animals have a high water content in their bodies (i.e., nearly 80% to 90%). It is because of high specific heat capacity of water, the body temperature remains nearly the same in all the seasons.

(iii) For fomentation, the hot water bottles are used. It is because of the high specific heat capacity of water, it does not get cool quickly. So, due to this, a hot water bottle provides the heat energy for fomentation for a longer period of time.

(iv) In car radiators, water is used as coolant. This is because it can absorb a large amount of heat energy from the engine of a car, but itself does not rise to very high temperature.

(v) During a cold winter night, if the atmospheric temperature falls below 0°C, then the chances of destroying of crops becomes high. So, in order to save the crop on such cold nights, farmers fill their fields with water.
It is because of high specific heat capacity of water, it does not permit the temperature in the surrounding area of plant to fall upto 0°C.

(vi) The wet soil does not get heated up so quickly as compared to sandy soil. It is because wet soil requires about five times more heat energy than sandy soil for the same rise in temperature.

Check Your LEARNING...

1. Define the term heat capacity and write its SI unit.
2. Why temperature of a human body is nearly same throughout the year ?
3. Mention any two changes which are possible on heating.
4. If the two substances are mixed at the different temperatures, state whether it is necessary that the temperature of substance at lower temperature increases or not.
5. Give the amount of heat energy required to change the temperature of 1° C of 1 g of water. *Ans.* 1 calorie
6. Mention the name of a liquid which has the highest specific heat capacity.

Calorimetry

The branch of science which deals with the measurement of heat is known as calorimetry. Thus, calorimetry is the process of measuring the amount of heat released or absorbed during a process.

Calorimeter

It is a cylindrical vessel which is used to measure the amount of heat gained (or lost) by a body when it is mixed with the other body.

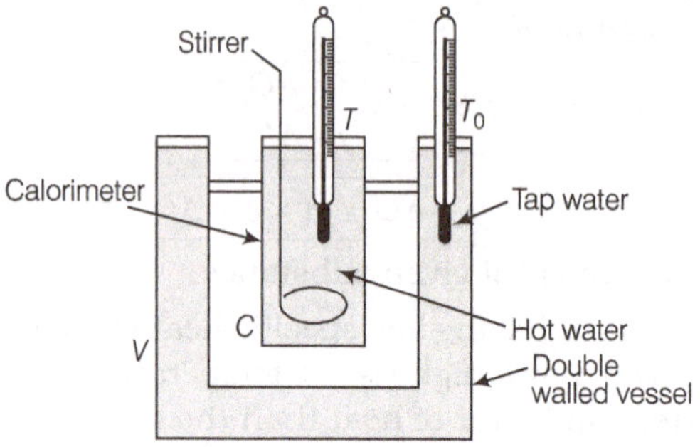

Calorimeter

Principle of Methods of Mixtures (Principle of Calorimetry)

When a body at higher temperature is brought in contact with another body at lower temperature, then the heat flows from the body kept at higher temperature to the body kept at lower temperature.

Thus, the principle of calorimetry states that

"total heat given by a hotter body equals to the total heat received by colder body," i.e.,

Heat lost by hotter body = Heat gained by colder body

If two bodies are kept in contact with each other and if there is no exchange of heat between them, the bodies are then said to be **thermal equilibrium**.

Mathematical Expression

Let a body X of mass m_a, specific heat capacity c_a and at a higher temperature t_a gets mixed with another body Y of mass m_b, specific heat capacity c_b and at a lower temperature t_b. If the final temperature of mixture becomes T, then

Fall in temperature of body, $X = t_a - T$

Rise in temperature of body, $Y = T - t_b$

Heat energy lost by $X = m_a \times c_a \times$ fall in temperature

$$= m_a c_a (t_a - T)$$

Heat energy gained by

$$Y = m_b \times c_b \times \text{rise in temperature} = m_b c_b (T - t_b)$$

If no heat energy is lost to the surroundings, then according to principle of calorimetry,

Heat energy lost by X = Heat energy gained by Y

$$\Rightarrow \quad m_a c_a (t_a - T) = m_b c_b (T - t_b)$$

Example 4. Consider a solid of mass 80 g at 100°C is placed in 200 g of water at 20°C. The final steady temperature recorded is 22°C. What is the specific heat capacity of the solid?

Sol. Given, mass of solid, $m_s = 80$ g

Mass of water, $m_w = 200$ g

Temperature of solid, $T_1 = 100° C$

Temperature of water, $T_2 = 20° C$

Final temperature, $T = 22° C$

Specific heat of water, $c_w = 4.2 J/g/K$

Let, c_s be the specific heat capacity of the solid. As, the heat is being transferred from solid to water, from the principle of calorimetry,

Heat lost by the solid = Heat gained by water

$\Rightarrow \quad m_s \times c_s \times (T_1 - T) = m_w \times c_w \times (T - T_2)$

$\Rightarrow \quad 80 \times c_s \times (100 - 20) = 200 \times 4.2 \times (22 - 20)$

$\Rightarrow \quad 80 \times c_s \times 80 = 200 \times 4.2 \times 2$

$\Rightarrow \quad c_s = \dfrac{400 \times 4.2}{6400} = 0.2625 \text{ J / g°C}^{-1}$

Example 5. A piece of iron of mass 100 g is kept inside a furnace for a long time and then put in a calorimeter of water equivalent 10 g containing 240 g of water at 20°C. The mixture attains an equilibrium temperature of 60°C. Find the temperature of the furnace where specific heat of iron = 470 J/kg-K.

Sol. Let temperature of furnace be T.

Given, $m_i = 100$ g, $m_w = 240$ g

Water equivalent, $m_w = 10$ g

Equilibrium temperature = 60° C

Then, from principle of calorimetry.

Heat given = Heat taken

$$m_i c_i (T - 60) = (m'_w + m_w) c_w (60 - 20)$$

$\Rightarrow \quad 100 \times 470(T - 60) = (10 + 240) \times 4200 \times 40$

$\Rightarrow \quad T - 60 = \dfrac{250 \times 4200 \times 40}{100 \times 470} = 893.6$

$\Rightarrow \quad T = 953.6° C$

Change of Phase (State)

Matter generally exists in three states; solid, liquid and gas. These states can be changed into one another by absorbing or rejecting heat.

The process of converting one state of a substance into another state is known as change of state of a substance or matter.

The common changes of states are

(i) solid to liquid (and *vice-versa*)

(ii) liquid to gas (and *vice-versa*)

The changes can occurr when the exchange of heat takes place between substance and its surroundings.

Interconversion of States of Matter

The states of matter are interconvertible. They can be interchanged by changing temperature or pressure. The phenomenon of change of matter from one state to another and back to the original state by altering the conditions of temperature and pressure is called **interconversion of states of matter.**

Following two factors (or any one of these) make it possible to convert one state of matter into another

(i) Change in temperature

(ii) Change in pressure

Terms Involved in Change of State

Following terms are involved in change of state

(i) **Fusion or Melting and Melting Point** The process of conversion of a matter from its solid state to its liquid state at specific conditions of temperature and pressure, is called **fusion/melting.**

The definite temperature at which a solid starts melting is called the **melting point** of that solid, e.g., Melting point of ice is 0°C or 273.16 K. The melting point is infact, an indication of the strength of the force of attraction between the particles of solid. Higher the melting point of a substance, greater will be the force of attraction between its particles.

(ii) **Boiling and Boiling Point** The process of conversion of a matter from its liquid state to vapours (gaseous state) at specific conditions of temperature and pressure is called **boiling**. It is a bulk phenomenon. And the temperature at which a liquid starts boiling at the atmospheric pressure is known as its **boiling point.**

Particles from the bulk of the liquid gain enough energy to change into the vapour state.

In boiling, all the liquids expands.With the increase in the pressure, boiling point also increases.Due to addition of the impurities, the boiling point increases.

(iii) **Sublimation** The process of change of solid state directly into gaseous state without passing through the liquid state upon heating and *vice-versa* on cooling is known as **sublimation.**

e.g., Naphthalene, camphor, iodine, ammonium chloride, etc., are the solids that undergo sublimation.

(iv) **Vaporisation** The process of conversion of a matter from its liquid state to gaseous state at specific conditions of temperature and pressure is called **vaporisation**.

(v) **Freezing and Freezing Point** The process of conversion of matter from its liquid state to solid state at specific conditions of temperature and pressure, is called **freezing**. It is a reverse process of fusion/melting and the definite temperature at which a liquid changes into solid state by giving out heat energy at 1 atm is called the **freezing point**.

(vi) **Condensation** The process of conversion of matter from its gaseous state to liquid state at specific conditions of temperature and pressure, is called **condensation**. It is a reverse process of vaporisation.

Effect of impurities on the melting point

Melting point of a substance decreases with the increase of the impurities in it. The process of lowering the value of melting point of a substance due to presence of impurities is called depression of melting point. Hence, if we add some salts in ice, then the melting point of ice decreases from 0°C to –22° C.

Effect of impurities on the boiling point

Boiling point of liquid increases with the increase of the impurities in it. The process of the increasing the value of boiling point of a liquid due to presence of impurities is called elevation of boiling point.

Impurities decrease the liquid molecular available for vaporisation during boiling. i.e A greater amount of heat is required to make the some amount of impure solution to vaporise than the heat that is required to make a pure liquid solution to vaporise.

Check Your LEARNING...

1 Why does the water used as an effective coolant?
2 State the principle of calorimetry.
3 Mention the name of the material from which the calorimeter is made of?
4 What is solidification point?
5 Briefly explain how does the increase in pressure affect the melting point of ice?
6 When does the solid and liquid states of a substance co-exists?
7 When 0.2 kg of a body at 100°C is dropped into 0.5 kg of water at 10°C, resulting temperature becomes 16°C. Find specific heat of a body. *Ans.* 0.75×10^3 J/kg/°C
8 What effects occur on the boiling point of water on addition of some amount of salts in it?
9 What do you mean by depression of melting point of a substance?

Latent Heat

When a heat is given to a substance, its temperature increases. However, when heat is supplied to change the physical state of a substance, there is no increase in temperature of a substance.

Thus, the heat energy which has to be supplied to change the state of substance is called its **latent heat**. In actual, the word 'latent' means 'hidden'. Latent heat does not raise (or increase) the temperature. But latent heat is always supplied to change the state of a substance.

Latent heat is of two types

Latent Heat of Fusion (Solid to Liquid Change)

The amount of heat energy that is required to change 1 kg of a solid into liquid at atmospheric pressure at its melting point is known as the **latent heat of fusion**. Particles in water at 0°C (273.16 K) have more energy as compared to particles in ice at the same temperature. It is observed that latent heat of fusion of ice is 3.34×10^5J.

Latent Heat of Vaporisation (Liquid to Gas Change)

The amount of heat energy that is required to convert 1 kg of a liquid into gas (at its boiling point) without any rise in temperature is known as the **latent heat of vaporisation**. Particles in steam, i.e., water vapour at 373 K (100°C) have more energy than water at the same temperature.

Note It has been found that burns caused by the steam are much more severe than those caused by boiling water though both of them are at the same temperature of 100°C.
As particles in steam have absorbed extra energy in the form of latent heat of vaporisation. Thus, when steam falls on our skin and condense to produce water, it gives out 22.5×10^5 J/kg more heat than boiling water at the same temperature.

Units of Specific Latent Heat

(i) Jkg^{-1} is the SI unit of specific latent heat.

(ii) The other common units of specific latent heat are cal g^{-1} and kcal g^{-1}.

Some of the conversions of units are given below

$$1 \text{ kcal g}^{-1} = 1000 \text{ cal g}^{-1}$$
$$1 \text{ cal g}^{-1} = 4.2 \text{ Jg}^{-1}$$
$$1 \text{ cal g}^{-1} = 4.2 \times 10^3 \text{J kg}^{-1}$$

Example 6. A copper block of mass 2.5 kg is heated in a furnace to a temperature of 500° C and then placed on a large ice block. What is the maximum amount of ice that can melt? (Take, specific heat of copper = 0.39 $Jg^{-1}°C^{-1}$ and heat of fusion of water = 335 Jg^{-1}).

Sol. Given, mass of copper block, $m = 2.5 \text{ kg} = 2.5 \times 10^3 \text{ g}$

Specific heat of copper, $c = 0.39 \text{ Jg}^{-1} \text{°C}^{-1}$

Fall in temperature, $\Delta T = 500 - 0 = 500° \text{C}$

Heat lost by copper block $= mc\Delta T$

$$= 2.5 \times 10^3 \times 0.39 \times 500 \text{ J}$$

Let mass of ice melted = mg

Heat gained during fusion of ice = $m \times 335$ J

($\because L = 335 \text{ Jg}^{-1}$)

$\therefore$ Heat gained = Heat lost

$$\therefore \quad m \times 335 = 2.5 \times 10^3 \times 0.39 \times 500$$

or
$$m = \frac{2.5 \times 10^3 \times 0.39 \times 500}{335}$$

$$= 1455.2 \text{ g} = 1.455 \text{ kg}$$

Example 7. A lead bullet penetrates into a solid object and melts. If half of its kinetic energy is used to heat it, calculate the initial velocity of the bullet. The initial temperature of the bullet is 27° C and the melting point of the material of bullet is 327°C. Given that latent heat of fusion of lead is 2.5×10^4 Jkg^{-1} and specific heat capacity of lead is 125 $Jkg^{-1} K^{-1}$.

Sol. Specific heat capacity of lead,

$$c = 125 \text{ Jkg}^{-1} \text{ K}^{-1}$$

Change in temperature,

$$\Delta T = 327 - 27 = 300° \text{C}$$

Latent heat of fusion of lead,

$$L = 2.5 \times 10^4 \text{ J Kg}^{-1}$$

Initial velocity of the bullet, $v = ?$

Heat absorbed by the lead, $\Delta Q_1 = mc\Delta T$

$$\Rightarrow \quad \Delta Q_1 = m \times 125 \times 300$$

$$= m \times 3.75 \times 10^4 \text{ Jkg}^{-1}$$

Heat required to melt the bullet, $\Delta Q_2 = mL$

$$\Rightarrow \quad \Delta Q_2 = m \times 2.5 \times 10^4 \text{ J kg}^{-1}$$

The kinetic energy of bullet $= \frac{1}{2} mv^2$

(where, v is velocity)

Half of kinetic energy $= \frac{1}{2}\left(\frac{1}{2} mv^2\right) = \frac{1}{4} mv^2$

From principle of calorimetry, loss in kinetic energy

$$= \Delta Q_1 + \Delta Q_2$$

$$\therefore \quad (1/4) mv^2 = m (3.75 + 2.5) \times 10^4 \text{ Jkg}^{-1}$$

$$\Rightarrow \quad v = 500 \text{ ms}^{-1}$$

Heating Curve for Water

To evaluate the heating curve for water, the following steps must be followed

(i) First of all, take some water in a flask (at room temperature nearly about 25°C) and suspend a thermometer in it.

(ii) By keeping the flask over a bunsen burner, try to heat it and record its temperature after every half minute till the time, it starts boiling and the flask contains vapours.
Now, by taking the temperature along Y-axis and the time on X-axis, the graph can be plotted. It is called the heating curve for water.

If we see the graph (given below), we will observe that water is at 25°C at C (i.e., room temperature) and the water in a liquid state rises continuously in part CD with the absorption of heat energy.

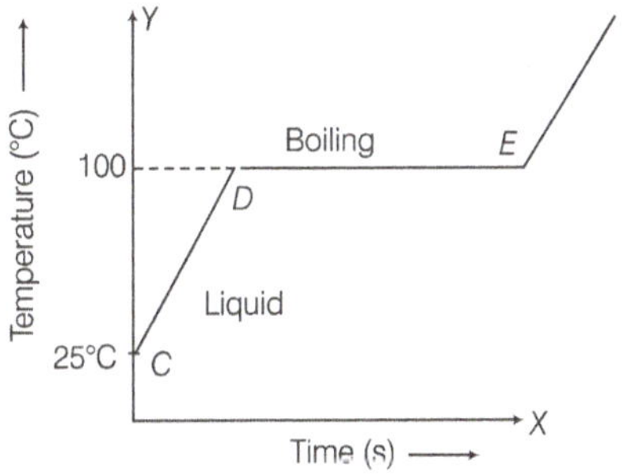

Heating curve of water

At point D, the boiling starts and the temperature does not rise further as shown in part DE. It can be explained as, at point D the water starts to convert into gaseous state from liquid state, so it require latent heat of vapourisation, all the heat being provided here is used in converting the state of water from liquid to gas, so temperature does not rise till all the water converts into vapour.

So, temperature along DE remains constant. Again from point E, temperature starts to increase because the heat being provided now is not used as latent energy (there is no change of state now), so it increases the temperature.

Natural Consequences of High Specific Latent Heat of Fusion of Ice

Natural consequences of high specific latent heat of fusion of ice are as follows

(i) On the mountains in summer, snow melts very slowly. It is because every kilogram of snow requires 336000 J of heat energy, in order to form water at 0°C.

Therefore, there are no flash floods and the rivers contain the water for whole year.

(ii) During the snow storm, the weather becomes mild, it is because a large amount of heat energy is dissipated in the atmosphere due to the freezing of water vapour.

(iii) When the snow starts melting, the environment becomes bitterly cold, it is because every kilogram of ice on melting absorbs 336000 J of heat energy from the atmosphere.

(iv) The icebergs are carried out by ocean currents over very large distances because of high specific latent heat of fusion of ice.

Uses of High Specific Latent Heat of Fusion of Ice

Use of high specific latent heat of fusion of ice are as follows

(i) Ice is used to cool the soft drinks, because every kg of ice will extract out 336000 J of heat energy more than water at 0°C.

(ii) Ice candy feels colder than water at 0°C, because it can extract out more heat from the mouth as compared to water at 0°C.

Check Your LEARNING...

1 How is the volume of water affected when it boils at 100° C?

2 Explain the reason, why is it difficult to cook vegetables on hills and mountains?

3 In what manner does the boiling point of water affect when some salt is added to it?

4 If 1 g of ice at 0°C melts to form 1 g of water at 0° C, then state whether the latent heat is absorbed or given out by ice.

5 Which of the two has more heat 1 g water at 100° C or 1 g of steam at 100° C ? Give reason.

6 Explain the meaning of the given statement, the specific latent heat of fusion of ice is 336 Jg^{-1}.

7 How temperature of the Earth is approximately maintained at 15° C?

QUiCK Revision

- **Temperature** is the property of a state of matter by virtue of which we predict its hotness or coldness, relative to some body. Its SI unit is **Kelvin (K)** other units are **Celsius (°C)** and **Fahrenheit (°F)**.
- **Heat** is a form of energy which determines the change in thermal state of a body. It flows from the body which is at a high temperature to the other at low temperature.
- SI unit of heat is **Joule (J)**. Other units are **calorie** and **kilocalorie**.
- **Heat Capacity** It is the quantity of heat required by the body to raise its temperature by 1°C. It is also known as thermal capacity. Heat capacity = mass (m) × specific heat capacity (c)
- **Water Equivalent** It is the quantity of water whose thermal capacity is same as the heat capacity of the body. It is denoted by W.
  $W = ms =$ Heat capacity of the body
- **Specific Heat** The specific heat (c) of a substance is the quantity of heat in calorie required to raise the temperature of 1g of the substance by 1°C. Its unit is cal g^{-1} $°C^{-1}$.
- **Principle of Methods of Mixtures** Heat lost by hotter body = Heat gained by colder body
  $$m_1c_1\Delta T_1 = m_2c_2\Delta T_2$$
- **Change of state** is the process of converting one state of a substance into another state.
- **Melting** is the change from solid to the liquid state at constant temperature. **Melting point** is the constant temperature at which a solid changes to liquid.
- **Melting point** of a substance decreases with the increase of the impurities in it.
- **Boiling point** of a liquid increase with the increase of the impurities in it.
- **Vaporisation** is the change from liquid to gas (or vapour) phase on heating at a constant temperature.
- **Latent Heat** is the heat required to change the state of a system is proportional to mass of the system. i.e.,
  $$Q \propto m \Rightarrow Q = mL$$
  where, L = latent heat of the material.
- **Specific latent heat of melting** is the amount of heat energy required to convert a unit mass of the substance from solid to liquid state without any change in temperature.
- **Specific latent heat of fusion** is the amount of heat energy released when a unit mass of substance converts from liquid to solid state without any change in temperature.

Chapter Practice

1 Mark Questions

1. If water absorbs 4000 J heat to increase the temperature of 1 kg of water through 1°C, then the specific heat capacity of water is **[2022 (Sem-II)]**

(a) $4\ Jkg^{-1}{}^{\circ}C^{-1}$ (b) $400\ Jg^{-1}{}^{\circ}C^{-1}$

(c) $4\ Jg^{-1}{}^{\circ}C^{-1}$ (d) $4.2\ Jg^{-1}{}^{\circ}C^{-1}$

Sol. (c) Heat gained $= m \cdot c \cdot \Delta T$

$$4000 = 1000\text{g} \times c \times 1^{\circ}\text{C}$$

$$4\ Jg^{-1}{}^{\circ}C^{-1} = c$$

$\Rightarrow$ Specific heat capacity of water $= 4\ Jg^{-1}{}^{\circ}C^{-1}$

2. Water is used in car radiators because **[2022 (Sem-II)]**

(a) it is a good conductor of heat
(b) it conducts heat faster as compared to the other substances and cools the engine quickly
(c) its specific heat capacity is very low
(d) its specific heat capacity is very high, so it can cool the engine without a greater increase in its own temperature

Sol. (d) Water is used in car radiators as coolant because water becomes hot by gaining a large amount of heat due to its high specific heat capacity.

3. Two bodies of specific heats c_1 and c_2 having same heat capacities are combined to form a single composite body. What is the specific heat of the composite body?

(a) $\dfrac{c_1 - c_2}{2c_1 c_2}$ (b) $\dfrac{c_1 + c_2}{2 c_1 c_2}$

(c) $\dfrac{2 c_1 c_2}{c_1 + c_2}$ (d) $\dfrac{2 c_1 c_2}{c_1 - c_2}$

Sol. (c) As the heat capacities are equal, so

$$m_1 c_1 = m_2 c_2 \quad \ldots \text{(i)}$$

where, m_1, m_2 are the masses of two bodies and c_1, c_2 are their specific heats.

Let c be the specific heat of the composite body,

then $(m_1 + m_2)c = m_1 c_1 + m_2 c_2$

$\Rightarrow$ $(m_1 + m_2)c = 2 m_1 c_1$ [from Eq. (i)]

$$\Rightarrow \quad c = \frac{2 m_1 c_1}{m_1 + m_2} = \frac{2 m_1 c_1}{m_1 + m_1 \dfrac{c_1}{c_2}} = \frac{2 c_1 c_2}{c_1 + c_2}$$

4. Which of the following substances A, B and C has the lowest heat capacity, if heat is supplied to all of them at equal rates? The temperature *versus* time graph is shown.

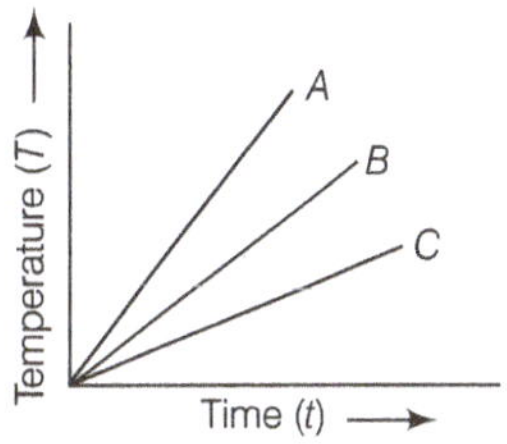

(a) C (b) B
(c) A (d) None of these

Sol. (c) Substances having more heat capacity take longer time to get heated to a higher temperature and longer time to get cooled.

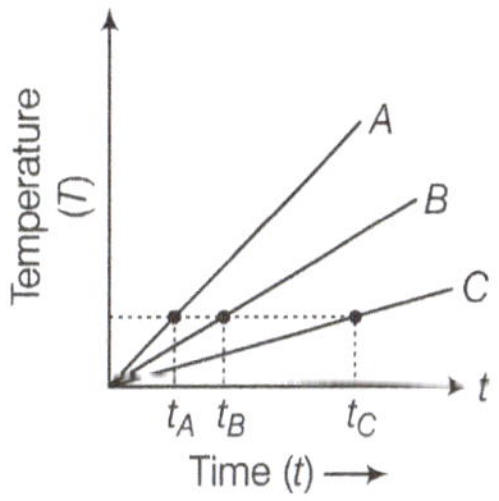

If we draw a line parallel to time axis, then it cuts the given graphs at three different points corresponding points on the time axis, show that $t_C > t_B > t_A$

$$\Rightarrow \quad C_C > C_B > C_A$$

So, option (c) is correct.

5. Heating curve of ice is given below.

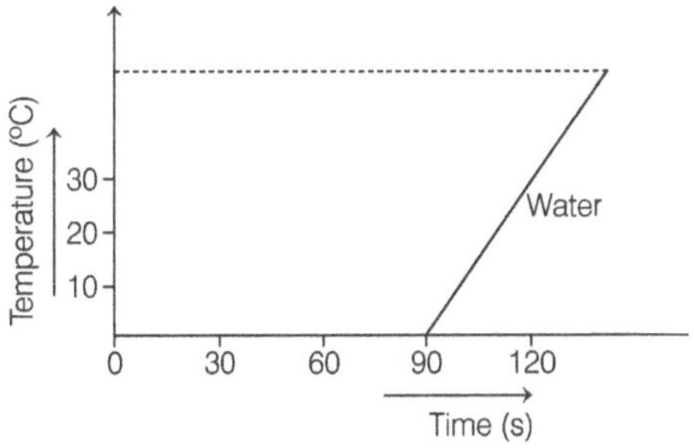

Which of the following statement is correct?
(a) Ice instantly starts melting at $t = 90$ s.
(b) Temperature of ice does not increase initially.
(c) $t = 90$ s is the time taken for phase change.
(d) All of the above

Sol. (*d*) All the statements given are correct.

From the graph, we can see that all, the heat supplied till $t = 90$ s does not increases its temperature. All the heat is utilised to change the phase of ice from solid to liquid, then the temperature of the water starts increasing.

6. Specific latent heat of a substance [2023]
   (a) is directly proportional to the mass
   (b) is directly proportional to the change in the temperature
   (c) depends on the material
   (d) is inversely proportional to the mass

Sol. (*c*) Specific latent heat of a substance depends on the material.

7. Specific heat capacity of a substance X is 1900 $Jkg^{-1}°C^{-1}$ means [2023]
   (a) Substance X absorbs 1900 J for 1°C rise in temperature
   (b) I kg of substance X absorbs 1900 J heat for 1°C rise in temperature
   (c) 1kg of substance X absorbs 1900 J heat to increase the temperature
   (d) 1 kg of substance X absorbs 1900 J heat to cool down by 1°C

Sol. (*b*) 1 kg of substance X absorbs 1900 J heat for 1°C rise in temperature.

8. 200 g of ice at 0°C needs ...... heat to melt. (Take, specific latent heat of ice = 336000 J kg^{-1}) [Latest Specimen Sem-II]
   (a) 6720 J (b) 67200 J
   (c) 672000 J (d) 67.2 J

Sol. (*b*) Given, mass of ice, $m_{ice} = 200$ g

$$= 200 \times 10^{-3} \text{ kg}$$

Specific latent heat of ice, $L = 336000$ Jkg^{-1}

Heat required to melt $= m_{ice} \times L$

$$= 200 \times 10^{-3} \times 336000 = 67200 \text{ J}$$

9. Which of the following substances sublime?
   (a) Sodium carbonate
   (b) Solid carbon dioxide
   (c) Calcium carbonate
   (d) Aluminium carbonate

Sol. (*b*) Solid carbon dioxide is also known as dry ice. It sublimes at very low temperature.

10. The principle of mixture is a direct consequence of
    (a) law of conservation of mass
    (b) law of conservation of momentum
    (c) law of conservation of energy
    (d) All of the above

Sol. (*c*) The principle of mixture is direct consequence of law of conservation of energy.

As, heat gain is equal to heat loss and heat is also a form of energy.

2 Marks Questions

11. Define the term calorie. State its relation with joule.

Sol. 1 calorie of heat is defined as the amount of heat energy required to raise the temperature of 1g of water from 14.5°C to 15.5°C. [1]

1 cal = 4.2 J [1]

12. Differentiate between heat and temperature. [2011]

Sol. Difference between heat and temperature are given below

Heat	Temperature
It is the internal energy of a body.	It is the degree of hotness and coldness of a body.
Its SI unit is joule.	Its SI unit is kelvin.
Other unit of heat is cal or kcal.	Other unit of temperature is °C or °F. [2]

13. Differentiate between heat capacity and specific heat capacity. [2012]

Sol. Specific heat capacity is defined as the amount to heat needed to raise temperature of unit mass of a body, whereas heat capacity is defined as amount of heat needed to raise the temperature for the entire mass of the body.

14. State two factors upon which the heat absorbed by a body depends.

Sol. Heat absorbed by a body depends on
   (i) mass of the body and [1]
   (ii) specific heat of the body. [1]

15. Give two reasons, why copper is preferred over other metals for using calorimeter? [2006]

Sol. The two factors by which copper is preferred over the other metals for using calorimeter are as follows
   (i) It has low specific heat capacity than other metals. [1]
   (ii) It takes least amount of heat from its content to attain its temperature. [1]

16. Why is the base of a cooking pan generally made thick? [2017]

Sol. Thinner base pans definitely transmit heat from the burner to the food, as the base is made up of metal, which is good conductor of heat. But, when it comes to even cooking and maintaining regular heating without hot spots around the pans, it is convenient to use thicker base pans.

Also, it has more thermal mass and it also retain its temperature, i.e. the pan will stay at high temperature above and beyond the amount of heat that can immediately supplied by the heat source. [2]

17. Define calorimetry.

Sol. It is the principle through which we can understand that heat flows from higher temperature to lower temperature and heat lost by a body is equal to the heat gained by another body when kept in contact. [2]

18. Define heat capacity and state its SI unit. **[2017]**

Sol. The quantity of heat given to any substance depends on its mass m, the change in temperature ΔT and the nature of substance which is being heated. To change the temperature of substance, a given quantity of heat is absorbed or rejected by it, which is characterised by a quantity known as heat capacity or thermal capacity.

So, thermal capacity is defined as the total amount of heat required to raise the temperature of a body by 1°C. It is represented by C'. **[1]**

$$\text{Heat capacity } (C') = \frac{\text{Heat supplied to the body } (Q)}{\text{Change in temperature } (\Delta T)}$$

Its SI unit is joule /°C or joule /K. Its older unit is cal/° C or cal/K or kcal/°C. **[1]**

19. What do you understand by the following statements? **[2016]**

(i) The heat capacity of the body is 60 JK^{-1}.

(ii) The specific heat capacity of lead is 130 $Jkg^{-1}K^{-1}$.

Sol. (i) The heat capacity of a body is 60 JK^{-1}. It means that, 60 J of heat is required to raise the temperature of the body by 1° C. **[1]**

(ii) The specific heat capacity of lead is 130 J/kg-K. It means that, 130 J of heat is required to raise the temperature of 1kg of mass by 1° C.

20. (i) How can a temperature in degree celsius be converted into SI unit of temperature?

(ii) A liquid X has the maximum specific heat capacity and is used as a coolant in car radiators. Name the liquid X. **[2018]**

Sol. (i) SI unit of temperature is kelvin. To convert temperature in degree celsius to kelvin, 273.15 is added to celsius.

$$T \text{ (in K)} = T \text{ (°C)} + 273.15$$ **[1]**

(ii) Liquid X will be water, as water has a high value of specific heat capacity. **[1]**

21. Why is water used as a coolant in radiators of a car? **[Latest Specimen Sem-II]**

Sol. Since, water has high specific heat capacity. So, it can absorb a large amount of heat energy from the engine of a car without changing its temperature to a high value.

Due to this reason, it is used as a coolant in radiators of a car. **[2]**

22. What is the reason of spraying of water on the roads in the evening in the hot summer?

Sol. Since, water has the highest specific heat capacity of 4.2 $Jg^{-1}°C^{-1}$. Therefore, water absorbs large amount of heat from the roads, but its own temperature does not rise much. Due to this, the road gets cooled. **[2]**

23. Briefly justify the given statement, "Water is considered as the best liquid for quenching thirst".

Sol. As, water has the highest specific heat capacity of 4.2 $Jg^{-1}°C^{-1}$. Due to which, it absorbs a large amount of heat energy without any rise in temperature. Since, thirst is a natural signal, which means that the body produces more heat energy than required. Therefore, water is ideal for quenching thirst because it absorbs a large amount of heat energy. **[2]**

24. Briefly explain the terms melting and melting point.

Sol. Melting is defined as the change of phase from solid to liquid state on heating at a constant temperature, while the fixed temperature at which this change takes place is known as melting point of given solid. **[2]**

25. What is the effect of pressure on boiling point of a liquid? Give one application of it.

Sol. Boiling point of liquid increases with increase in pressure and decreases with decrease in pressure. **[1]**

Application In pressure cooker boiling point of water increases upto 25%. **[1]**

26. Rishi is surprised, when he sees water boiling at 115°C in a container. Give reasons as to why water can boil at the above temperature. **[2017]**

Sol. The boiling point of water is 100°C at 76 mm of mercury, i.e. atmospheric pressure, but the boiling point increases with increase in pressure. **[1]**

Since, the water is boiling at 115°C, which indicates that the pressure is greater than the atmospheric pressure. **[1]**

27. Explain, why the weather becomes very cold after a hailstorm? **[2011]**

Sol. After the hailstorm, the ice balls begin to melt and require 336 kJ of heat energy per gram to melt which is taken from the atmosphere thereby decreasing the temperature of atmosphere. **[2]**

28. Why are burns caused by steam more severe than those caused by boiling water at the same temperature? **[2007]**

Sol. As the latent heat of vaporisation is more than specific heat of boiling water, so burn caused by steam are more painful than boiling water. **[2]**

29. Explain, why one feels ice cream at 0°C colder than water at 0°C? **[2001]**

Sol. Ice cream at 0°C extracts heat (latent heat of fusion) and freeze to water at 0°C. i.e, ice cream is able to extract more heat, so it produces more cooling effect. **[2]**

30. Why do the surroundings become pleasantly warm when freezing starts in cold countries? **[2000]**

Sol. During the freezing of water in cold countries, it gives out its latent heat of fusion in the surrounding. In this process, cooling upto 0°C takes place. This heat makes the surrounding atmosphere less cool. **[2]**

31. State one example which demonstrates that, when liquid evaporates, it takes heat from the surroundings.

Sol. Let us take an example of surahi in which water gets cooled in summer. It is because of the fact that the surahi is made of clay and has pores through which water seeps out and gets evaporated. The latent heat required for evaporation is taken from the water inside the surahi. Therefore, the temperature of water falls and it gets cooled. [2]

32. Explain, why does the air passing through a desert cooler become cooler?

Sol. Since, in a desert cooler, hot and dry air pass through wet pads of wood-wool. So, water takes heat from the hot air and evaporates. The evaporation of water cool the pads while the water is circulating. So, as a result, the incoming air gets cooled. [2]

33. Explain, why do doctors advise to put strips of wet cloth on the forehead of a person having high temperature?

Sol. When the wet cloth strip is put on the forehead of the person having high temperature, the water being evaporated takes away the necessary heat from the patient's body and lowers his body temperature. [3]

34. In a central heating system, if steam enters a radiator pipe at 100°C and water leaves the radiator pipe at 100°C, state whether this radiator pipe heat the room or not. Give the explanation in support of your answer.

Sol. Yes, this radiator pipe can heat a room. It is because steam at 100°C gives out its latent heat of vaporisation to condense into water at the same temperature of 100°C. [2]

3 Marks Questions

35. Specific heat capacity of substance *A* is 3.8 J/gK, whereas the specific heat capacity of substance *B* is 0.4 J/gK.

(i) Which of the two is good conductor of heat?

(ii) How is one led to the above conclusion?

(iii) If substances *A* and *B* are liquid, then which one would be more useful in car radiators? [2014]

Sol. (i) Since, the specific heat capacity of *B* is less than *A*, so *B* is good conductor of heat. [1]

(ii) As, the specific heat capacity of *B* is much less than *A*, so *B* is good conductor of heat. It is because for the same heat energy and same mass rise in temperature of *B* will be more than that of *A*. [1]

(iii) Since, the specific heat capacity of *A* is higher than that of *B*, so it can absorb more heat therefore, it is useful in car radiator. [1]

36. "Farmers fill their fields with water on a cold winter night." Explain in brief along with a reason.

Sol. In order to protect the crops from frost, farmers fill their fields with water. If on a cold winter night during the absence of water, the atmospheric temperature falls below 0°C, then the water in the fine capillaries of plants will freeze. [1]

So, the veins will burst due to increase in volume of water on freezing. As a result, the plants would die and the crop would be destroyed. [1]

But farmers field their land with water as specific heat capacity of water is large and it imparts a large amount of heat energy while it gets cooled in cold winter night. This heat evolved does not permit the temperatures in the surrounding areas to fall upto 0°C. [1]

37. (i) State the principle of calorimetry.

(ii) Name the material used for making a calorimeter.

(iii) Write one characteristic property of the material chosen for making a calorimeter. [2023]

Sol. (i) Refer to theory (Page 224). [1]

(ii) Calorimeter are made up of copper , which has highly polished surface because they minimised the heat loss due to radiation. [1]

(iii) The material having low specific heat capacity has chosen for making a calorimeter because the amount of heat required is less to increase temperature of calorimeter. [1]

38. (i) Which will absorb more heat : 10 g of ice at 0°C or 10 g of water at 0°C?

(ii) For the same mass of ice and ice-cold water, why does ice produce more cooling than ice-cold water? [3] [Latest Specimen Sem-II]

Sol. (i) Since, heat absorbed ∝ specific heat capacity

The water has high value of specific heat capacity than that of ice at same temperature. So, 10 g of water at 0°C will absorb more heat than 10g of ice at 0°C. [1½]

(ii) The ice has high specific latent heat capacity, which means it takes away more heat from the substance or surroundings. So, ice produces more cooling than ice-cold water. [1½]

39. Some ice is heated at a constant rate and its temperature is recorded after every few seconds, till steam is formed at 100° C. Draw a temperature time graph to represent the change. Label the two phase change in your graph.

Sol. According to question, the heating curve of ice is given below

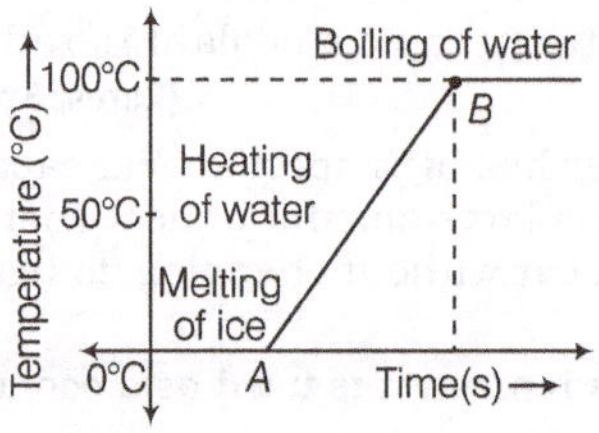

[3]

40. (i) Heat supplied to a solid changes it into liquid. What is this change in phase called?

(ii) During the phase change does the average kinetic energy of the molecules of the substance increase?

(iii) What is the energy absorbed during the phase change called? [2018]

Sol. (i) Heat supplied to solid changes it into liquid. This change in phase is called melting. [1]

(ii) During the phase change, average kinetic energy of the molecules does not change because the temperature remains constant. [1]

(iii) The energy absorbed during the phase change is called latent heat of fusion. [1]

41. (i) Write an expression for the heat energy liberated by a hot body.

(ii) Some heat is provided to a body to raise its temperature by 25°C. What will be the corresponding rise in temperature of the body as shown on the Kelvin scale?

(iii) What happens to the average kinetic energy of the molecules as ice melts at 0°C? [2012]

Sol. (i) The heat energy liberated by a hot body is

$$\Delta Q = mc\Delta T$$

where, m = mass of substance

c = specific heat of substance

and ΔT = change in temperature. [1]

(ii) The temperature rise will be same in both Celsius and Kelvin scale, as it is the change in temperature (ΔT) only. [1]

(iii) The average KE of molecules increases, when ice melts as temperature of body increases. [1]

42. (i) Name the radiation which are absorbed by greenhouse gases in the Earth's atmosphere.

(ii) A radiation X is focused by a particular device on the bulb of thermometer and mercury in the thermometer shows a rapid increase. Name the radiation X.

(iii) Name two factors on which the heat energy liberated by a body depends?

Sol. (i) Infrared radiations are absorbed by greenhouse gases in the Earth's atmosphere. [1]

(ii) Since the thermometer shows a rapid increase, therefore the radiation must be infrared because infrared radiation is responsible for heat. [1]

(iii) The heat energy absorbed is directly proportional to the mass of the body.

The amount of heat absorbed by a body is also directly proportional to the change in the temperature or the rise in the temperature. [1]

4 Marks Questions

43. With reference to climate in coastal areas, briefly describe the role of high specific heat capacity of water.

Sol. Specific heat capacity of water is highest among all the substances. Thus, it can store a large amount of heat energy and retains at an average temperature. [1]

Thus during day time, specially in coastal areas, the temperature of land increases rapidly whereas the temperature of sea water does not vary more. In this way pressure differences occurs, which leads to flow of wind known as sea breeze. [1]

During night, land looses its heat rapidly whereas sea water does not, due to high specific heat capacity. It then leads to land breeze. In this way, the climate of coastal area is not too hot or cold (i.e., moderate). It is due to specific heat capacity of water. [1]

It is important to notice that in solar system only Earth has moderated temperature because it contains 75% of water on it which has very large amount of heat capacity. [1]

44. (i) State two differences between heat capacity and specific heat capacity.

(ii) Give a mathematical relation between heat capacity and specific heat capacity. [2018]

Sol. (i) Differences between heat capacity and specific heat capacity are given below

Heat capacity	Specific heat capacity
It is defined as the total amount of heat required to raise the temperature of a body by 1 °C.	It can be defined as the total amount of heat energy required to raise the temperature of unit mass by 1 °C.
Heat capacity $= \dfrac{\text{Heat supplied to the body}}{\text{Change in temperature}}$	Specific heat capacity $= \dfrac{\text{Heat energy supplied}}{\text{Mass of the body} \times \text{Change in temperature}}$

[2]

(ii) The relation between specific heat capacity and heat capacity is

⇒ heat capacity = mass × specific heat capacity [2]

45. What is the effect of presence of impurity on the melting point of ice? Mention one use of it.

Sol. Due to the presence of impurities, the melting point of ice becomes lowered. The melting point of ice is made lowered to use it in preparing freezing mixture. [1]

It is a mixture of ice and salt which produces a temperature much lower than 0°C.

When ice and salt are mixed, the ice begins to melt. For the melting of each gram of ice, 80 calories of heat are required. The same amount of heat is taken from mixture itself due to which the temperature of the mixture falls below 0°C. Moreover, the salt dissolves in water produced by the melting of ice. [1]

So, the salt also needs the latent heat of fusion to change from solid into the solution. This heat is also taken from the mixture itself, therefore the temperature of the mixture falls still lower.

When one part by weight of salt and three parts of ice are mixed together, a temperature of –22°C is obtained. In the similar manner, freezing mixture of three parts of ice and four parts of calcium chloride by weight can have a very low temperature of –55°C. [2]

46. (i) Define the term specific latent heat of fusion of a substance.

(ii) What energy change would you expect to take place in the molecules of a substance when it undergoes

(a) a change in its temperature?

(b) a change in its state without any change in its temperature? [2010]

Sol. (i) Specific latent heat of fusion is the heat required to change the state of substance from ice to liquid without change in temperature. [2]

(ii) (a) Kinetic energy changes which defines specific heat capacity of the substance. [1]

(b) Intermolecular or space charges defines latent heat of the substance. [1]

47. (i) Water in lakes and ponds does not freeze at once in cold countries. Give a reason in support of your answer.

(ii) What is the principle of calorimetry?

(iii) Name the law on which this principle is based.

(iv) State the effect of an increase of impurities on the melting point of ice. [2015]

Sol. (i) The latent heat of fusion of ice is very high because of which a large amount of heat needs to be withdrawn from water in lakes and ponds to freeze. Hence, water in lakes and ponds do not freeze at once in cold countries. [1]

(ii) The principle of calorimetry states that when two or more bodies at different temperatures are brought into thermal contact, and if no heat is allowed to escape to the surroundings, then the total heat lost by hot bodies must be equal to the total heat gained by cold bodies. [1]

(iii) The principle of calorimetry is based on the law of conservation of energy. [1]

(iv) The melting point of ice decreases from 0° C to – 22° C in presence of impurities. [1]

Numerical Based Questions

48. Determine the specific heat capacity of lead of mass 0.5 kg, if 1300 J of heat is supplied to raise its temperature from 20°C to 40°C. [2]

Sol. Given, mass, $m = 0.5$ kg, heat supplied, $Q = 1300$ J,

Rise in temperature, $\Delta T = 40°\text{ C} - 20°\text{ C} = 20°\text{ C}$

Since, specific heat $= \dfrac{\text{heat supplied}}{\text{mass} \times \text{rise in temperature}}$

$$= \frac{1300}{0.5 \times (40-20)} = \frac{1300}{0.5 \times 20}$$

$$= \frac{1300}{10} = 130 \text{ Jkg}^{-1}\text{K}^{-1}$$ [1]

∴ Specific heat capacity of lead is 130 $\text{Jkg}^{-1}\text{K}^{-1}$. [1]

49. If a liquid A of specific heat capacity 1050 J $\text{kg}^{-1}\text{K}^{-1}$ and at 90°C it is mixed with liquid B of specific heat capacity 2362.5 J $\text{kg}^{-1}\text{K}^{-1}$ and having temperature of 20°C. The final temperature of the mixture is recorded as 50°C. Determine in what proportion of the weights of liquids are mixed ?

Sol. By principle of method of mixture,

Heat lost by A = Heat gained by B

$$m_1 \times 1050 \times (90-50) = m_2 \times 2362.5 \times (50-20)$$ [1]

$$\Rightarrow \frac{m_1}{m_2} = \frac{2362.5 \times 30}{1050 \times 40} = \frac{27}{16}$$ [1]

50. While performing an experiment, it is observed that when 300 g of hot water at 50°C is added to 600 g of cold water, then its temperature rises by 15°C. Find the initial temperature of cold water. [2]

Sol. Consider $t°$ C be the initial temperature of cold water.

∵ Heat gained by the cold water $= mc\Delta t$

(Here, $\Delta T = 15°$ C)

$$\Delta Q = 600 \times 4.2 \times 15$$

Heat lost by hot water $= 300 \times 4.2 \times [50 - (T + 15)]$

∴ According to principle of calorimetry,

Heat lost = Heat gained

$$600 \times 4.2 \times 15 = 300 \times 4.2\ [50 - (T + 15]$$

$$37800 = 1260(35 - T) \Rightarrow T = 5°\text{ C}$$ [2]

51. Calculate the heat energy that will be released, when 5.0 kg of steam at 100°C condenses to form water at 100°C. Express your answer in SI unit. (Take, specific latent heat of vaporisation of steam is 2268 J/kg) [2] [2005]

Sol. As given in question,

Mass, $m = 5$ kg

Latent heat, $L = 2268$ J/kg

As we know that,

$$Q = mL = 5 \times 2268 = 11340 \text{ J}$$

52. 50 g of metal piece at 27°C requires 2400 J of heat energy so as to attain a temperature of 327°C, calculate the specific heat capacity of the metal. [2] [2014]

Sol. Given, mass, $m = 50$ g

$$\Delta t = 327°\text{ C} - 27°\text{ C} = 300°\text{ C}$$

Heat, $Q = 2400$ J

As we know that, $4Q = mc\,\Delta t$

$$\Rightarrow c = \frac{Q}{m\,\Delta t} = \frac{2400}{50 \times 300} = 0.16 \text{ J/g°C}$$

53. A hot solid of mass 60 g at 100°C is placed in 150 g of water at 20°C. The final steady temperature recorded is 25°C. Calculate the specific heat capacity of the solid. (Take, specific heat capacity of water = 4200 J $\text{kg}^{-1}{}°\text{C}^{-1}$). [2] [2012]

Sol. According to principle of calorimetery,

Heat gained = Heat lost

So, that heat gained $= 150 \times 4.2 \times (25-20)$ ...(i)

Heat lost $= 60 \times c \times (100-25)$ ...(ii)

From Eqs. (i) and (ii), we get

$$60 \times c \times 75 = 150 \times 4.2 \times 5$$

$$\Rightarrow c = \frac{150 \times 4.2 \times 5}{60 \times 75} = 0.7 \text{ J/g°C}$$

54. Calculate the total amount of heat energy required to melt 200 g of ice at 0°C to water at 100°C. (Specific latent heat of ice = 336 J g^{-1}, specific heat capacity of water = 4.2 J $\text{g}^{-1}{}°\text{C}^{-1}$) [2023] [3]

Sol. Heat required = Heat required to melt ice at 0°C+ Heat required to raise the temperature of water at 100°C

$$Q = mL + mC\Delta T$$
$$= 200 \times 336 + 200 \times 4.2 \times (100 - 0)$$
$$= 151200\ \text{J}$$
$$Q = 15.12 \times 10^4\ \text{J}$$ [1]

55. Two metals A and B have specific heat capacities in the ratio of 2 : 3. If they are supplied same amount of heat. Answer the questions that follow.

(i) Which metal piece will show greater rise in temperature given their masses are the same?

(ii) Which metal piece will have greater mass, if the rise in temperature is the same for both metals?

(iii) If the mass ratio of metal A and metal B is 3 : 5, then calculate the ratio in which their temperatures rise.

(iv) If specific heat capacity of metal A is $0.26\ \text{Jg}^{-1}\text{°C}^{-1}$, then calculate the specific heat capacity of metal B. **[Latest Specimen Sem-II]**

Sol. Heat rise or fall, $\Delta Q = m \times c \times \Delta T$

Given , $c_A : c_B = 2:3$ and $\Delta Q_A = \Delta Q_B$

(i) If $m_A = m_B = m$,then

$$\frac{\Delta Q_A}{\Delta Q_B} = \frac{m_A \times c_A \times \Delta T_A}{m_B \times c_B \times \Delta T_B}$$
$$1 = \frac{2}{3} \times \frac{\Delta T_A}{\Delta T_B}$$
$$\Rightarrow \frac{\Delta T_A}{\Delta T_B} = \frac{3}{2}$$

So, the rise of temperature is greater in metal A. [1]

(ii) If $\Delta T_A = \Delta T_B$, then

$$\frac{\Delta Q_A}{\Delta Q_B} = \frac{m_A \times c_A \times T_A}{m_B \times c_B \times \Delta T_B}$$
$$\Rightarrow \frac{m_A}{m_B} = \frac{c_B}{c_A} = \frac{3}{2}$$

$\therefore$ Metal A will have greater mass. [1]

(iii) If $m_A : m_B = 3:5$, then

$$\frac{\Delta Q_A}{\Delta Q_B} = \frac{m_A}{m_B} \times \frac{c_A}{c_B} \times \frac{\Delta T_A}{\Delta T_B}$$
$$\Rightarrow 1 = \frac{3}{5} \times \frac{2}{3} \times \frac{\Delta T_A}{\Delta T_B}$$
$$\Rightarrow \frac{\Delta T_A}{\Delta T_B} = \frac{5}{2}$$ [1]

(iv) If $c_A = 0.26\ \text{Jg}^{-1}\ \text{C}^{-1}$, then

$$c_B = \frac{3}{2} \times c_A = \frac{3}{2} \times 0.26$$
$$= 0.39\ \text{Jg}^{-1\circ}\text{C}^{-1}$$ [1]

56. 200 g of hot water at 80°C is added to 300 g of cold water at 10°C. Calculate the final temperature of the mixture of water. Consider the heat by the container to be negligible.
(Take, specific heat capacity of water is $4200\ \text{J kg}^{-1\circ}\text{C}^{-1}$) **[2] [2011]**

Sol. As given in question and from principle of calorimetry,

Heat lost by hot water = Heat gained by cold water

So, $200 \times 4.2 \times (80 - T) = 300 \times 4.2 \times (T - 10)$

where, T is final temperature.

$$\Rightarrow 2(80 - T) = 3(T - 10)$$
$$160 - 2T = 3T - 30$$
$$\Rightarrow 5T = 190$$
$$\Rightarrow T = 38°\text{C}$$ [2]

57. 40 g of water at 60°C is poured into a vessel containing 50 g of water at 20°C. The final temperature recorded is 30°C. Calculate the thermal capacity of the vessel. (Take, specific heat capacity of water is $4.2\ \text{J g}^{-1}\ \text{°C}^{-1}$) **[2] [2009]**

Sol. As from principle of calorimetry,

Heat gained = Heat lost

So, heat lost by hot water = heat gained by cold water + heat gained by vessel

$$\Rightarrow 40 \times 4.2 \times 30 = 50 \times 4.2 \times 10 + (\text{Heat capacity} \times 10)$$

$\Rightarrow$ Heat capacity

$$= \frac{(40 \times 4.2 \times 30) - (50 \times 4.2 \times 10)}{10}$$
$$= 294\ \text{J/°C}$$ [2]

58. Some hot water was added to three times its mass of cold water at 10°C and the resulting temperature was found to be 20°C. What was the temperature of the hot water? **[2] [2007]**

Sol. Let mass of hot water be m kg, so mass of cold water will be = $3m$ kg.

Temperature of hot water is t °C

So, by principle of calorimetry,

Heat taken by cold water = Heat given by hot water

$$mc\,\Delta t = 3mc\,\Delta t$$
$$\Rightarrow m \times c \times (t - 20) = 3m \times c \times (20 - 10)$$
$$\Rightarrow t - 20 = 3 \times 10$$
$$\Rightarrow t = 50°\text{C}$$ [2]

59. In a laboratory experiment to measure specific heat capacity of copper, 0.02 kg of water at 70°C was poured into a copper calorimeter with a stirrer of mass 0.16 kg initially at 15°C. After stirring, the final temperature reached to 45°C. Specific heat of water is taken as 4200 J/kg°C.

(i) What is the quantity of heat released per kg of water per 1°C fall in temperature?

(ii) Calculate the heat energy released by water in the experiment in cooling from 70°C to 45°C.

(iii) Assuming that the heat released by water is entirely used to raise the temperature of calorimeter from 15°C to 45°C, calculate the specific heat capacity of copper. **[3] [2007]**

Sol. (i) Quantity of heat released per kg of water per °C falls in temperature is given by 4200 J/kg°C. [1]

(ii) Quantity of heat released on cooling is given by

$$Q = mc\Delta T$$
$$\Rightarrow Q = 0.02 \times 4200 \times 25 = 2100\ \text{J}$$ [1]

(iii) By assuming that there is no loss of heat, therefore by principle of calorimetry,

Heat gained = Heat taken up by calorimeter

$$2100 = 0.16 \times c \times 30$$

$$\Rightarrow \quad c = \frac{2100}{0.16 \times 30} = 437.5\ \text{J/kg°C}$$ **[1]**

60. The temperature of 170 g of water at 50°C is lowered to 5° C by adding certain amount of ice to it. Find the mass of ice added.
(Take, specific heat capacity of water = 4200 J kg^{-1} °C^{-1} and specific latent heat of ice = 33600 J kg^{-1}) **[2] [2018]**

Sol. Given, $M_w = 170$ g, $s_w = 4200$ J kg^{-1} C^{-1}

ΔT = 5°C, L_f = 80 cal/g = 336000 J/kg

According to the principle of calorimetry, amount of heat given by water = amount of heat absorbed by ice

$$M_w s_w \Delta T = M_{ice} \times L_f$$

$$\Rightarrow \quad 170 \times 1 \times 5 = M_{ice} \times 80$$

$$M_{ice} = \frac{170 \times 1 \times 5}{80} = 10.625\ \text{g}$$ **[2]**

61. The diagram below shows a cooling curve for 200 g of water. The heat is extracted at the rate of 100 Js^{-1}. Answer the questions that follow.

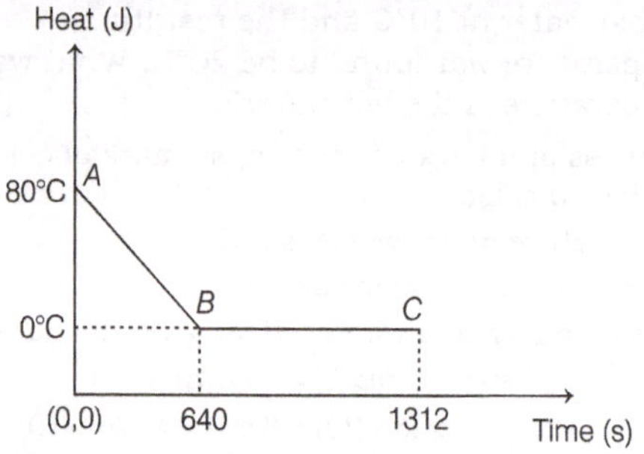

(i) Calculate specific heat capacity of water.
(ii) Heat released in the region *BC*. **[Latest Specimen Sem-II] [3]**

Sol. Given, mass of water, m = 200 g = 0.2 kg

Rate of heat extraction, $\frac{Q}{t} = 100\ \text{Js}^{-1}$

(i) Temperature changes in *AB* region,

$$\Delta T = (80 - 0)°\text{C} = 80°\text{C}$$

Time taken, Δt = 640 s

$$\therefore \quad \frac{Q}{T} = mc\frac{\Delta T}{\Delta t}$$

$$\Rightarrow \quad c = \frac{Q/t}{m \times \Delta T / \Delta t} = \frac{100}{0.2 \times 80} \times 640$$

$$= 4000\ \text{Jkg}^{-1}°\text{C}$$ **[1½]**

(ii) For region *BC*, the water at 0°C changes to ice at 0°C. So, heat released in cooling is given by

$$Q = m \times L = 0.2 \times 336000 \quad (\because L_{ice} = 336000\text{Jkg}^{-1})$$

$$= 67200\ \text{J}$$ **[1½]**

62. (i) If there is no heat loss to the surroundings, the heat released by the condensation of m_1 gram of steam at 100°C into water at 100°C can be used to convert m_2 gram of ice at 0°C into water at 0°C. Find

(a) the heat lost by steam in terms of m_1 and
(b) the heat gained by ice in terms of m_2.

(ii) Form a heat equation to find the ratio of $m_2 : m_1$.
(Take, specific latent heat of vaporisation of steam = 2268 kJ/kg, specific latent heat of fusion of ice = 336 kJ/kg, specific heat capacity of water = 4200 J/kg°C) **[4] [2005]**

Sol. (i) (a) The heat lost by the steam is given by $m_1 L_s$, where L_s = latent heat of steam **[1]**

(b) The heat gained by the ice is given by $m_2 L_i$, where L_i = latent heat of ice. **[1]**

(ii) According to the principle of calorimetry,
Heat taken by ice = Heat given by steam

$$m_2 L_i = m_1 L_s$$

$$\Rightarrow \quad \frac{m_2}{m_1} = \frac{L_s}{L_i} = \frac{2268}{336} = \frac{27}{4}$$

$$\Rightarrow \quad m_2 : m_1 = 27 : 4$$ **[2]**

63. 40 g of ice at 0°C is used to bring down the temperature of a certain mass of water at 60°C to 10°C. Find the mass of water used. (Take, specific heat capacity of water = 4200 J kg^{-1}°C^{-1}, specific latent heat of fusion of ice = 336× 10^3 J kg^{-1}) **[3]**

Sol. Mass of water used, m = 40 g

Temperature of water, t_1 = 0°C

L = 336 J/g, c = 4.2 J/g°C

Mass of the another water = M gram

Change in temperature, Δt = (60 – 10) = 50°C

So, by principle of calorimetry,

Heat gained = Heat lost

$$\Rightarrow M \times 4.2 \times (60 - 10)$$

$$= (40 \times 336) + 40 \times 4.2 \times (10 - 0)$$

$$\Rightarrow \quad M = \frac{13440 + 1680}{42 \times 5} = \frac{15120}{210} = 72\ \text{g}$$ **[3]**

64. 250 g of water at 30°C is present in a copper vessel of mass 50 g. Calculate the mass of ice required to bring down the temperature of the vessel and its contents to 5°C. (Take, specific latent heat of fusion of ice = 336× 10^3 J kg^{-1}, specific heat capacity of copper vessel = 400 J kg^{-1}°C^{-1}, specific heat capacity of water = 4200 J kg^{-1}°C^{-1}) **[3] [2011]**

Sol. According to the principle of calorimetry,

Heat lost = Heat gained by water + Heat gained by copper vessel

$$M \times L_f = m_1 c_w \Delta t + m_2 c_c \Delta t$$

$$\Rightarrow M \times 336 \times 10^3 = \frac{250}{1000} \times 4200 \times (30 - 5) + \frac{50}{1000} \times 400 \times (30 - 5)$$

$$\Rightarrow M \times 336 \times 10^3 = 26250 + 500$$

$$\Rightarrow M = \frac{26750}{336 \times 10^3} = 79.61\ \text{g}$$

$$= 0.07961\ \text{kg}$$ **[3]**

65. Calculate the mass of ice required to lower the temperature of 300 g of water at 40° C to water at 0° C. (Take, specific latent heat of ice = 336 J/g and specific heat capacity of water = 4.2J/g °C) **[2]**

Sol. According to question,

Mass of water, m_w= 300g

Temperature of water, Δt = 40°C

From principle of calorimetry,

Heat loss by the water at 40°C = Heat gain by the ice at 0° C

$$\Rightarrow \quad m_w \times c \times \Delta t = m_i \times L$$

$$\Rightarrow \quad m_i = \frac{m_w \times s \times \Delta t}{L}$$

$$= \frac{300 \times 4.2 \times 40}{336} = 187.5 \text{ g}$$ **[2]**

66. A copper vessel of mass 100 g contains 150 g of water at 50° C. How much ice in needed to cool it to 5°C ?
(Take, specific heat capacity of copper = 0.4 $Jg^{-1}{}^\circ C^{-1}$, specific heat capacity of water = 4.2 $Jg^{-1}{}^\circ C^{-1}$ and specific latent heat of fusion of ice = 336Jg^{-1}) **[2]**

Sol. According to question, mass of Cu vessel = 100g

Initial temperature of water = 50°C

Final temperature of water = 5°C

From principle of calorimetry,

Heat gained by ice = Heat lost by Cu vessel and water **[1]**

$$M \times 336 = (100 \times 0.4) + (150 \times 4.2 \times 45)$$
$$= 40 + 28350$$
$$\Rightarrow \quad M = \frac{40 + 28350}{336} \qquad (\because m = \text{mass of ice})$$
$$= \frac{28390}{336} = 84.49 \text{ g}$$ **[1]**

67. (i) Give an important reason for copper to be used as a material for a calorimeter.
(ii) Calculate the thermal capacity of 40 g of water. [Specific heat capacity of water = 4200 $Jkg^{-1}{}^\circ C^{-1}$] **[2022 (Sem-II)]**

Sol. (i) As copper has low specific heat capacity, so it can be used as a material for a calorimeter.

(ii) Thermal capacity = $m \times c$
$$= 40 \times 4.2 \ Jg^{-1}{}^\circ C^{-1}$$
$$= 168 \ Jg^{-1}{}^\circ C^{-1}$$

68. A refrigerator converts 100 g of water at 20°C to ice at –10°C in 35 min. Calculate the average rate of heat extraction in terms of watts. **[2015]**
(Take, specific heat capacity of ice = 2.1 $Jg^{-1}{}^\circ C^{-1}$, specific heat capacity of water = 4.2 $Jg^{-1}{}^\circ C^{-1}$ and specific latent heat of fusion of ice = 336 Jg^{-1})

Sol. Given, m = 100 g, **[2]**
T_1 = 20 °C,
T_2 = – 10°C

Heat released
$$= mc_w(T_1 - 0) + m\,L_{ice} + mc_{ice}(0 - T_2)$$ **[1]**
$$Q = (100 \times 4.2 \times 20) + (100 \times 336) + (100 \times 2.1 \times 10)$$
$$= 8400 + 33600 + 2100 = 44100 \text{ J}$$ **[1]**
$$\text{Power, } P = \frac{Q}{t} = \frac{44100}{35 \times 60}$$
$$\Rightarrow \quad P = 21 \text{ W}$$

69. A solid metal weighing 150 g melts at its melting point of 800 °C by providing heat at the rate of 100 W. The time taken for it to completely melt at the same temperature is 4 min. What is the specific latent heat of fusion of the metal? **[3] [2018]**

Sol. Given, $m = 150\text{g} = 150 \times 10^{-3} \text{kg} = 0.15$ kg

Power, P = 100 W

Time, t = 4 min = 4 × 60 = 240 s

The amount of heat supplied in 4 min is given as

heat energy = $P \times t = 100 \times 240 = 24000$ J

This heat energy is used in melting.

Let L be the latent specific heat.

$$\therefore \quad mL = 24000$$
$$L = \frac{24000}{0.15} = 16 \times 10^4 \text{ J kg}^{-1}$$ **[3]**

70. While performing an experiment, 17g of ice is used to bring down the temperature of 40 g of water at 34°C to its freezing temperature. The specific heat capacity of water is 4.2 $Jg^{-1}K^{-1}$. Determine the latent heat of ice. **[3]**

Sol. Given, mass of ice, m = 17 g

Mass of water, M = 40 g

Initial temperature of water = 34° C

Final temperature of water = 0° C

Specific heat capacity of water, c = 4.2 $Jg^{-1}K^{-1}$

$\because$ Heat gained by ice = Heat lost by water **[1]**

$$\Rightarrow \quad m \times L = M \times c\,\Delta T$$
$$\Rightarrow \quad 17L = 40 \times 4.2\,(34 - 0)$$
$$\Rightarrow \quad L = \frac{40 \times 4.2 \times 34}{17}$$ **[1]**
$$\Rightarrow \quad L = 336 \text{ Jg}^{-1}$$ **[1]**

71. Heat energy is supplied at a constant rate to 100 g of ice at 0°C. The ice is converted into water at 0°C in 2 min. How much time will be required to raise the temperature of water from 0°C to 20°C? (Take, specific heat capacity of water = 4.2 J $g^{-1}{}^\circ C^{-1}$ and latent heat of ice = 336 J/g) **[4] [2014]**

Sol. Given, mass, m = 100 g,

time, t = 2 min = 2 × 60 = 120 s

Heat energy taken by ice at 0°C to convert it into water at 0°C.

$$Q = mL = 100 \times 336 = 33600 \text{ J}$$ **[1]**

As we know that,

$$\text{Power, } P = \frac{Q(\text{Energy})}{t(\text{Time})} = \frac{33600}{2 \times 60} = 280 \text{ J/s} \quad \ldots(i)$$ **[1]**

Heat energy required to raise the temperature from 0°C to 20°C.

$$Q = mc\Delta T = 100 \times 4.2 \times 20 = 8400 \text{ J} \quad \ldots\text{(ii)}$$

$(\because\ c = 4.2\ \text{Jg}^{-1}{}^\circ\text{C}^{-1})$ [1]

Now, from Eqs. (i) and (ii), we get

$$Q = Pt = 8400 \text{ J}$$

$$t = \frac{8400}{P} = \frac{8400}{280}$$

$$= 30 \text{ s} = \frac{30}{60} \text{ min}$$

$$= 0.5 \text{ min}$$ [1]

72. Calculate the mass of ice needed to cool 150 g of water contained in a calorimeter of mass 50 g at 32° C such that the final temperature is 5°C.

(Take, specific heat capacity of calorimeter = 0.4 J/g°C and latent heat capacity of ice = 330 J/g) **[4] [2017]**

Sol.

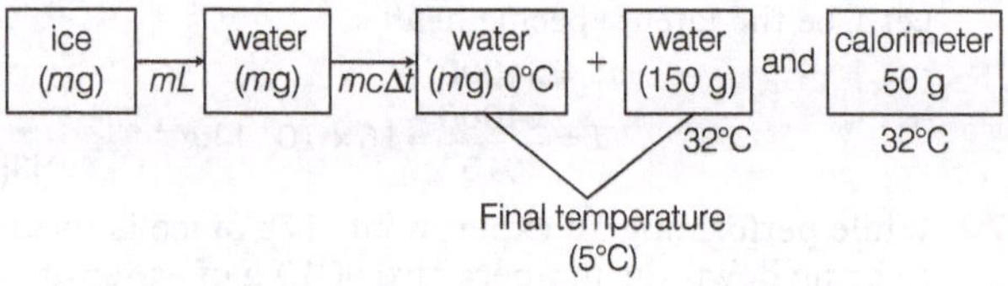

[1]

From the principle of calorimetry,
Heat gained by ice = Heat lost by water + Heat lost by calorimeter

$$mL + mc\Delta t = m_w C_w \Delta t + m_{cal} C_{cal} \Delta t$$ [1]

where, m = mass of ice (suppose),

L = latent heat of ice = 330 J/g,

Δt = change in temperature = 5° C,

C_w = specific heat of water = 4.2 J/g°C,

m_w = mass of water = 150 g,

m_{cal} = mass of calorimeter = 50 g and

c_{cal} = specific heat of calorimeter = 0.4 J/g°C.

Now, heat lost by water and calorimeter will be

$$= 150 \times 4.2 \times (32 - 5) + 150 \times 0.4 \times (32 - 5)$$

$$= 150 \times 4.2 \times 27 + +150 \times 0.4 \times 27$$

$$= 150 \times 27\ (4.2 + 0.4) = 150 \times 27 \times 4.6$$ [1]

Now, according to relation (i), we have

$$m \times 330 + m \times m \times 4.25 \times 5 = 150 \times 27 \times 4.6$$

$$\Rightarrow \quad m(330 + 21) = 150 \times 27 \times 4.6$$

$$\Rightarrow \quad m \times 351 = 150 \times 27 \times 4.6$$

$$\Rightarrow \quad m = \frac{150 \times 27 \times 4.6}{351} = \frac{18630}{351} \text{ g}$$

$$= 53.07 = 53.1 \text{ g}$$ [1]

73. If a block (made of lead) of mass 250 g at 27°C is heated in a furnace till it completely melts. Determine the quantity of heat required

(i) to bring the block to its melting point.

(ii) total heat energy required to melt the block to its melting point.

(iii) total heat energy required.

(Take, melting point of lead = 327° C, specific heat capacity = 0.13 $\text{Jg}^{-1}{}^\circ\text{C}^{-1}$ and specific latent heat of fusion = 26 Jg^{-1}) **[3]**

Sol. (i) The amount of heat required to raise to its melting point (327°C) = $mc\Delta T$

$$= 250 \times 0.13 \times (327 - 27)$$

$$= 250 \times 0.13 \times 300 = 9750 \text{ J}$$ [1]

(ii) So, the heat required to melt the lead at 327°C

$$= 250 \times 26 = 6500 \text{ J}$$ [1]

(iii) Therefore, total heat required completely to melt

$$= 6500 + 9750 = 16250 \text{ J}$$ [1]

Structured Questions

74. (i) (a) A certain amount of heat Q will warm 1 g of material Y by 3°C and 1 g of material X by 4°C. Which material has a highest specific heat capacity? **[2013]**

(b) Water falls from a height of 50 m. Calculate the rise in temperature of water, when it strikes the bottom. (Take, $g = 10\ \text{ms}^{-2}$ and specific heat capacity of water = 4200 J/kg°C) **[3][2005]**

(ii) (a) Name the liquid which has the highest specific heat capacity.

(b) Name two factors on which the heat absorbed or given out by a body depends.

(c) An equal quantity of heat is supplied to two substances A and B. The substance A shows a greater rise in temperature. What can you say about the heat capacity of A as compared to that of B? **[3] [2010]**

(iii) A thermo flask of negligible heat capacity contains 100 g of ice and 30 g of water.

(a) Calculate

I. the mass of steam at 100°C needed to condense in the flask to just melt the ice.

II. the amount of water in the flask after condensation.

(Take, specific latent heat of vaporisation of steam = 2260 J/g, specific latent heat of fusion of ice = 336 J/g and specific heat capacity of water = 4.2 J/g°C)

(b) Is it possible to condense the water formed, back to ice by adding ice at 0°C? Explain, giving a suitable reason to justify your answer. **[4] [2004]**

Sol. (i) (a) As we know that,

$$\text{Specific heat, } c = \frac{Q}{m\,\Delta T} \Rightarrow c \propto \frac{1}{\Delta T}$$

So, material X has a higher specific heat capacity than Y. **[1½]**

(b) From energy conservation,

Heat energy = Potential energy

$$mc\Delta t = mgh$$

$$\Rightarrow \quad c\Delta t = gh$$

$$\Rightarrow \quad \Delta t = \frac{gh}{c} = \frac{10 \times 50}{4200}$$

$= \frac{5}{42} = 0.119° \text{ C}$

$= 0.12° \text{ C (approx)}$ [1½]

(ii) (a) Water has highest specific heat capacity. [1]

(b) Factors on which heat given out or absorbed depends upon

I. Temperature of the body with respect to surrounding.

II. Specific heat capacity of the body. [1]

(c) As substance *A* has greater rise in temperature, so heat capacity of *A* is less than heat capacity of *B*. [1]

(iii) (a) According to the principle of calorimetry,

I. Heat lost by steam = Heat gained by ice

$(M_{steam} \times L_{steam}) + (M_{steam} \times C_{water} \times \Delta\theta) = M_{ice} \times L_{ice}$

$\Rightarrow (M \times 2260) + M \times 4.2 \times 100 = 100 \times 336$

$\Rightarrow M(2260 + 420) = 33600$

$\Rightarrow M = \frac{33600}{2680} = 12.54 \text{ g}$

II. The amount of water present after condensation = 30 + 100 + 12.54

= 142.54 g

[2]

(b) Water will not freeze, only ice added will melt, because water and ice used are at the same temperature i.e 0°C. Therefore no heat transfer will take place. The ice can't remove heat from water. So the water can't freeze. [2]

75. (i) Some ice is heated at a constant rate and its temperature is recorded after every few seconds, till steam is formed at 100°C. Draw a temperature-time graph to represent the change. Label the two phase changes in your graph. [3] [2016]

(ii) A piece of ice is heated at a constant rate. The variation of temperature with heat input is shown in the graph here.

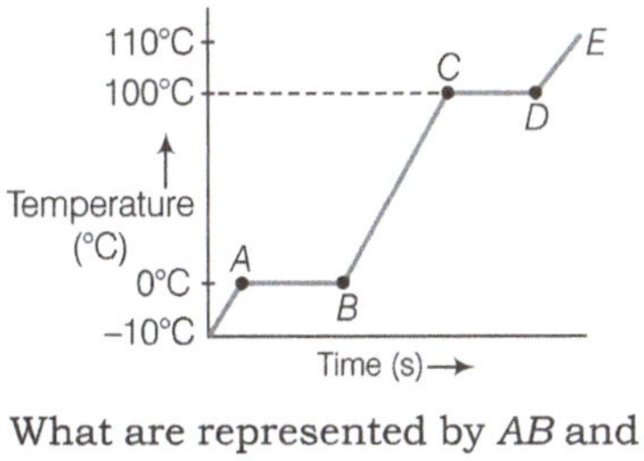

(a) What are represented by *AB* and *CD*?

(b) What conclusion can you draw regarding the nature of ice from the above graph? [3] [2005]

(iii) (a) A calorimeter of mass 50 g and specific heat capacity 0.42 J $g^{-1}°C^{-1}$ contains some mass of water at 20°C. A metal piece of mass 20 g at 100°C is dropped into the calorimeter. After stirring, the final temperature of the mixture is found to be 22°C. Find the mass of water used in the calorimeter.

(Take, specific heat capacity of the metal piece = 0.3 J $g^{-1}°C^{-1}$, specific heat capacity of water = 4.2 J $g^{-1}°C^{-1}$) [2013]

(b) A piece of ice at 0°C is heated at a constant rate and its temperature recorded at regular intervals. Draw a labelled temperature- time graph. [4]

Sol. (i) According to question, the heating curve of ice is given below

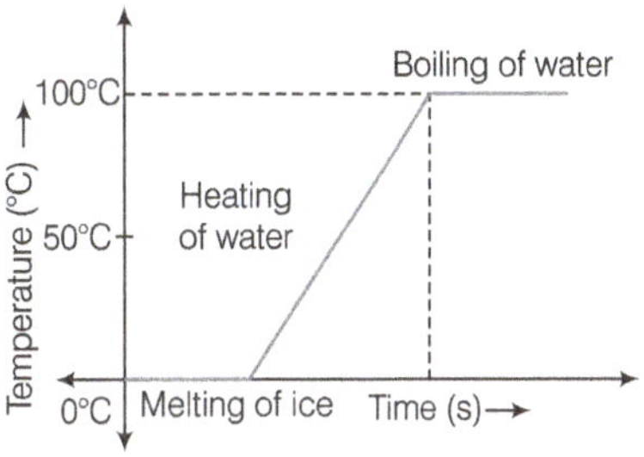

[3]

(ii) (a) As from the graph,

AB represents the time interval in which ice changes into water at 0°C.

CD represents the time in which water converts into vapour at 100°C. [1 ½]

(b) As seen that initial temperature of ice is –10°C, it means there is some salt in water or it is under high pressure. [1½]

(iii) (a) As from the question,

Amount of heat given by metal = $mc\Delta T_1$

$= 20 \times 0.3 \times (100 - 22) = 468 \text{ J}$

Amount of heat gained by water

$= m_w \times c_w \times \Delta t_2$

$= m_w \times 4.2 \times (22 - 20) = 8.4 m_w \text{J}$

According to principle of calorimetry,

$8.4 m_w = 468$

$\Rightarrow m_w = \frac{468}{8.4} = 55.71 \text{ g}$ [2]

(b) The temperature-time graph is shown below

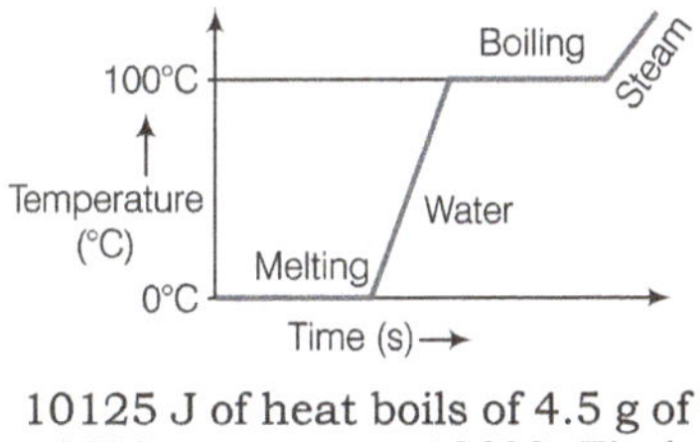

[2]

76. (i) (a) 10125 J of heat boils of 4.5 g of water at 100°C to steam at 100°C. Find the specific latent heat of steam.

(b) State the effect on increase of impurities on the melting point of ice. [3]

(ii) A substance is in the form of a solid at 0°C, the amount of heat added to this substance and the temperature of the substance and the amount of heat energy are ploted on the following graph

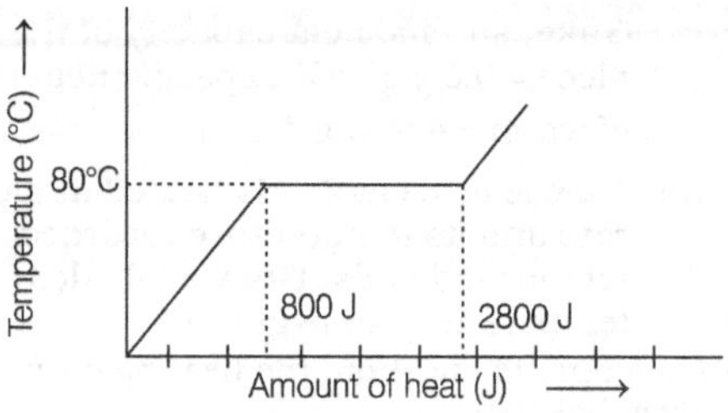

(a) If the specific heat capacity of the solid substance is 500 J/kg°C, then from the above graph, find the mass of the substance.

(b) Find specific latent heat of fusion of the substance. **[4]**

(iii) (a) How is the transference of heat energy by radiation prevented in a calorimeter?

(b) You have a choices of three metals *A*, *B* and *C*, of specific heat capacities 900 J kg^{-1}°C^{-1}, 380 J kg^{-1}°C^{-1} and 460 J kg^{-1}°C^{-1}, respectively. To make a calorimeter, which material will you select? Justify your answer. **[3] [2017]**

Sol. (i) (a) Given, heat supplied $Q = 10125$ J

Mass of water $m = 4.5$ g

Specific latent heat of vaporisation

$$= \frac{Q}{m\Delta T} = \frac{10125}{4.5} \quad (\because \Delta T = 1°C)$$

$= 2250$ J/g **[1½]**

(b) The melting point of ice decreases from 0°C to −22°C in presence of impurities. **[1½]**

(ii) (a) Given, specific heat capacity = 500 J/kg°C

At temperature 80°C, heat = 800 J

$\therefore$ Heat $= m \times c \times \Delta T$

$$\Rightarrow m = \frac{\text{Heat }(Q)}{c \times \Delta T}$$

$$= \frac{800}{500 \times 80} = \frac{1}{50}$$ **[1½]**

$\Rightarrow$ = 0.020 kg or 20 g

(b) Latent heat of fusion $= \frac{\text{Heat supplied}}{\text{Mass}}$

$$= \frac{2800 - 800}{0.020}$$

$$= \frac{2000}{0.020} = 10^6 \text{ J/kg}$$ **[1½]**

(iii) (a) Calorimeter surface (outer) is highly polished, so that to minimise the heat loss due to radiation as polished metallic surfaces are poor absorber and poor emitter of heat. Calorimeters are made up of copper, which has highly polished surface. **[2]**

(b) We shall select *C* whose specific heat capacity is 46 J/kg/°C to make a calorimeter, because of its low specific heat capacity. Specific heat capacity means the total amount of heat required to raise the temperature of unit mass by 1°C. For *C*, the heat required is less to increase temperature of calorimeter. Hence, *C* should be selected. **[2]**

Chapter Assessment

1 Mark Questions

1. Which of the following is more dangerous, when exposed to bare skin?
   (a) Ice
   (b) Steam
   (c) Lake warm water
   (d) Boiling water

2. Which of the following is a unit of temperature?
   (a) C (b) F
   (c) K (d) All of these

3. Which of the following represents the correct expression of specific heat capacity?
   (a) $\frac{\Delta T}{m\Delta Q}$ (b) $\frac{m\Delta T}{\Delta Q}$
   (c) $\frac{\Delta Q}{m\Delta T}$ (d) $\frac{m\Delta Q}{\Delta T}$

4. The meaning of statement specific heat capacity of water is 4200 J $kg^{-1}K^{-1}$ is
   (a) Water needs 4200 J to raise its temperature by 1 K.
   (b) To raise the temperature of water 4200 J of heat is absorbed
   (c) 1 kg water absorbs 4200 J heat to increase its temperature by 1 K
   (d) 1 kg water needs 1 K temperature to absorb 4200 J heat

5. 200 g of ice at 0°C needs ..... heat to melt.
   (Take, specific latent heat of ice = 336000 J kg^{-1})
   (a) 6720 J (b) 67200 J
   (c) 672000 J (d) 67.2 J

6. Temperature-time graph of a substance is given below

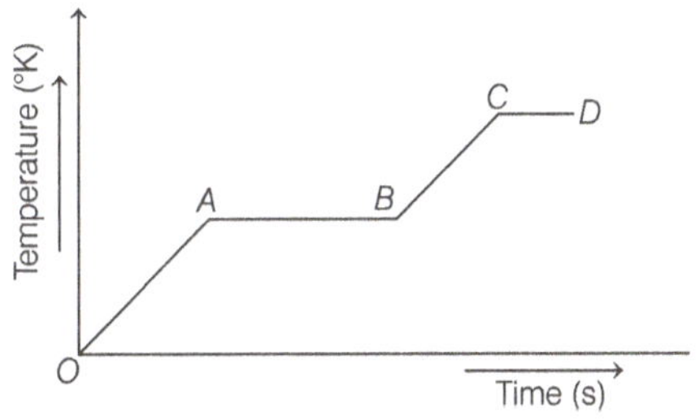

   Which of the following curve represents cooling?
   (a) *OA* (b) *AB*
   (c) *BC* (d) None of these

7. The specific latent heat of fusion of water is
   (a) 80 cal g^{-1} (b) 2260 J g^{-1}
   (c) 80 J g^{-1} (d) 336 J kg^{-1}

8. For the given temperature-time graph, which portion represents phase transition?

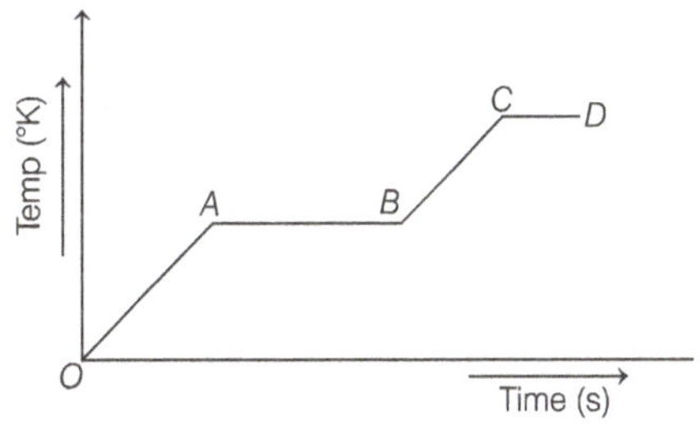

   (a) *OA* and *BC* (b) *AB* and *CD*
   (c) *AB* and *BC* (d) *OA* and *CD*

2 Marks Questions

9. (i) Give an example, where high specific heat capacity of water is used as a heat reservoir.
   (ii) Give an example, where high specific heat capacity of water is used for cooling purposes.

10. If a body had high heat energy, so does it mean that it has high temperature? Justify.

11. We feel relief under a fan when we are perspiring. Explain, why?

12. How is the heat capacity of the body related to its specific heat capacity?

13. Liquids *A* and *B* are at 30°C and 20°C. When mixed in equal masses, the temperature of the mixture is found to be 26°C. Find the ratio of their specific heat capacities.

14. State whether the land cool at a slower or faster rate than water. Give reason in support of you answer.

15. Briefly explain why does a person feel refresh, when his forehead is being sponged with Eau de cologne?

16. Why do pieces of ice added to a drink, cool it much faster than ice cold water added to it?

17. A piece of iron of mass 2.0 kg has a thermal capacity of 996 J/°C.
    (i) How much heat is needed to warm it by 15°C?
    (ii) What is its specific heat capacity in SI unit? **[2006]**

18. Determine the time taken by a 500 W heater to raise the temperature of 50 kg of material of specific heat capacity 920 J kg^{-1} K^{-1}, from 18°C to 38°C. Assume that, all the heat supplied by the heater is given to the material.

Structured Questions

19. (i) (a) Define heat capacity of a substance.
    (b) Write the SI unit of heat capacity.
    (c) What is the relationship between heat capacity and specific heat capacity of a substance?
    [3] [2020]
    (ii) The diagram shows the change of phases of a substance on a temperature *versus* time graph on heating the substance at a constant rate.

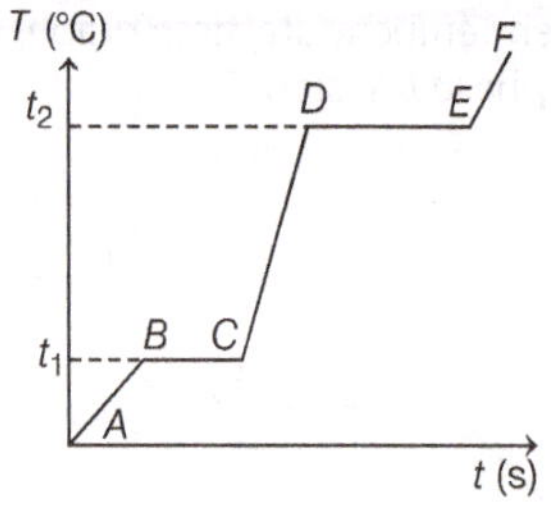

(a) Why is the slope of *CD* is less than slope of *AB*?
(b) What is the boiling and melting points of the substance? **[3]**

(iii) A piece of ice of mass 60 g is dropped into 140 g of water at 50°C. Calculate the final temperature of water when all the ice has melted.
(Assume, no heat is lost to the surrounding)
(Take, specific heat capacity of water = $4.2\ Jg^{-1}K^{-1}$ and specific latent heat of fusion of ice = $336\ Jg^{-1}$) **[4]**

20. (i) (a) Define calorimetry.
(b) Name the material used for making a calorimeter.
(c) Why is a calorimeter made up of thin sheets of the above material answered in part (b)? **[3]**

(ii) The melting point of naphthalene is 80 °C and the room temperature is 30 °C is cooled down to the room temperature. Draw a temperature-time graph to represent this cooling. In this graph, mark the region which corresponds to the freezing process **[3]**

(iii) 104 g of water at 30°C is taken in a calorimeter made of copper of mass 42 g. When a certain mass of ice at 0°C is added to it, the final steady temperature of the mixture after the ice has melted, was found to be 10°C. Find the mass of ice added.
(Take, specific heat capacity of water = $4.2 Jg^{-1}{}^\circ C^{-1}$, specific latent heat of fusion of ice = $336\ Jg^{-1}$ and specific heat capacity of copper = $0.4\ Jg^{-1}{}^\circ C^{-1}$
[4] [2019]

For Solutions Scan the Code

Olympiad Section*

Brain Teasing Questions of Olympiad Pattern

1. If 1 g of steam is mixed with 1 g of ice, then the resultant temperature of the mixture is
   (a) 270°C (b) 230°C
   (c) 100°C (d) 50° C

2. A vessel from which the air is rapidly being pumped out contains 100 g of water at 0° C. The intensive evaporation causes a gradual freezing of the water. What part of the original water can be converted into ice by this method?
   (a) 60 % (b) 86.2 %
   (c) 78 % (d) 56 %

3. Two identical calorimeters *A* and *B* contain equal quantity of water at 20° C. A 5 g piece of metal *X* of specific heat 0.2 cal $g^{-1}\,°C^{-1}$ is dropped into *A* and a 5 g piece of metal *Y* into *B*. The equilibrium temperature in *A* is 22°C and in *B* is 23°C. The initial temperature of both the metals is 40° C. Find the specific heat of metal *Y* in cal $g^{-1}°C^{-1}$.
   (a) $\frac{27}{85}$ cal / g°C (b) 26 cal / g°C
   (c) $\frac{85}{27}$ cal / g° C (d) 27 cal / g°C

4. A child running a temperature of 101°F is given an antipyretic (i.e. a medicine that lowers fever) which causes an increase in the rate of evaporation of sweat from his body. If the fever is brought down to 98°F in 20 min, what is the average rate of extra evaporation caused by the drug?
   Assume the evaporation mechanism to be the only way by which heat is lost. The mass of the child is 30 kg. The specific heat of human body is approximately the same as that of water and latent heat of evaporation of water at that temperature is about 580 cal g^{-1}.
   (a) 4.32 g min^{-1} (b) 3.42 g min^{-1}
   (c) 0.432 g s^{-1} (d) 3.42 g s^{-1}

5. In an industrial process, 10 kg of water per hour is to be heated from 20°C to 80°C. To do this, steam at 150°C is passed from a boiler into a copper coil immersed in water. The steam condenses in the coil and is returned to the boiler as water at 90°C, how many kg of steam is required per hour?
   (Take, specific heat of steam = 1 cal per g°C and latent heat of vaporisation = 540 cal g^{-1})
   (a) 1 g (b) 1 kg (c) 10 g (d) 10 kg

6. How many grams of ice at −14°C are needed to cool 200 g of water from 25°C to 10°C? (Take, specific heat of ice = 0.5 cal $g^{-1}\,°C^{-1}$ and latent heat of ice = 80 cal g^{-1})
   (a) 20 g (b) 27 g (c) 30 g (d) 31 g

7. Some hot water was added to three times its mass of cold water at 10°C and the resulting temperature was found to be 20°C. So, earlier, what was the temperature of hot water?
   (a) 40°C (b) 45°C (c) 50°C (d) 60°C

8. A solid of mass 50 g at 150° C is placed in 100 g water at 11°C when the final temperature recorded is 20°C. The specific heat capacity of the solid is . (Take, specific heat capacity of water = 4.2 J/g°C)
   (a) 0.033 J/g°C (b) 0.2 J/g°C
   (c) 0.1 J/g°C (d) 0.03 J/g°C

9. 250 g of water at 30°C is present in a copper vessel of mass 50 g. The mass of ice required to bring down the temperature of the vessel and its contents to 5°C will be. (Take, specific latent heat of fusion of ice = 336×10^3 J kg^{-1}, specific heat capacity of copper vessel = 400 $Jkg^{-1}°C^{-1}$ and specific heat capacity of water = 4200 $Jkg^{-1}°C^{-1}$)
   (a) 52.6 g (b) 40.5 g (c) 56.8 g (d) 79.6 g

10. 50 g of ice at 0°C is added to 300 g of a liquid at 30°C. What will be the final temperature of the mixture when all the ice gets melted? The specific heat capacity of the liquid is 2.65 $Jg^{-1}°C^{-1}$, while that of water is 4.2 $Jg^{-1}°C^{-1}$. (Take, specific latent heat of fusion of ice = 336 Jg^{-1})
    (a) 7°C (b) 9°C (c) 12°C (d) 15°C

11. 10 g of ice at − 10°C is added to 10 g of water at 85° C. What is the final temperature and amount of ice left in the system? (System is kept inside an ideal insulator).
    (a) 0°C, 0 g (b) 0°C, 2 g
    (c) 37.5°C, 0 g (d) 37.5°C ,5 g

ANSWERS

1. (c)	2. (b)	3. (a)	4. (a)	5. (b)	6. (b)	7. (c)	8. (a)	9. (d)	10. (a)
11. (c)									

* *These questions may or may not be asked in the examination, have been given just for additional practice required for olympiads Scholarship Exams etc. For detailed explanations refer Page No. 271.*

CHAPTER 11

Radioactivity and Nuclei

SYLLABUS

(i) Radioactivity and changes in the nucleus; background radiation and safety precautions.

(ii) Nuclear fission and fusion; basic introduction and equations.

All elements consists of very small indivisible particles which are known as atoms. It consist of three elementary particles, electrons, protons and neutrons. Its central core contains entire positive charge which is known as **nucleus**.

In this chapter, we will study different properties of nucleus and associated phenomena such as radioactivity, nuclear fission and nuclear fusion.

Composition of Nucleus

The nucleus was first discovered in 1911 by **Ernest Rutherford** and his associates by an experiment of scattering of α-particles by atoms. He found that the scattering results could be explained, if atoms consist of a small, central, massive and positive core surrounded by orbiting electrons.The experimental results indicated that the size of the nucleus is of the order of 10^{-14}m and thus it is 10000 times smaller than the size of atom. Further, the study of radioactivity revealed that nucleus is not a composite body, but it is made of nucleons.The positive charge in the nucleus is that of the protons. A proton carries one unit of fundamental charge. (i.e change on electron)

Atomic Number (Z)

The number of protons present inside the nucleus of an atom of the element is known as its atomic number. It is also equal to the number of electrons revolving in various orbits around the nucleus of the neutral atom.

Atomic number, Z = Number of protons = Number of electrons (in neutral atom).

Mass Number (A)

The sum of total number of protons and neutrons inside the atomic nucleus of the element is known as its mass number.

i.e. Mass number,

A = Number of protons + Number of neutrons
= Number of electrons (in neutral atom) + Number of neutrons
= Atomic number + Number of neutrons = $Z + N$

The term **nucleon** is also used for neutron and proton. Thus, the number of nucleons in an atom is its mass number A.

Nuclear species or nuclides are shown by the notation ${}_{Z}^{A}X$, where X is the chemical symbol of the species.

Isotopes, Isobars and Isotones

The atoms of same elements having same number of protons but different number of neutrons are called **isotopes**. e.g., ${}_1H^1, {}_1H^2, {}_1H^3$, etc.

The atoms of different elements having the same mass number (A) but different atomic number (Z) are called **isobars**. e.g., ${}_1H^3$ and ${}_2He^3$, etc.

The atoms of different elements having equal number of neutrons ($A - Z$) but different number of protons are called **isotones**. e.g., ${}_3Li^7$ and ${}_4Be^8$, etc.

Example 1. In a nucleus of ${}_{92}U^{238}$, find the number of proto3eee33e3e33e3ns and the number of neutrons.

Sol. Given, mass number, $A = 238$

Number of protons, $Z = 92$

Number of neutrons, $N = A - Z = 238 - 92 = 146$

Radioactivity

A French Physicist **H Becquerel** discovered radioactivity in 1896. A spontaneous nuclear phenomenon in which an unstable nucleus undergoes a decay with the emission of some particles (α, β) and electromagnetic radiation (γ-rays) is called radioactivity.

Radioactivity is a nuclear phenomenon. It is the process of spontaneous emission of α or β and γ radiations from the nucleus of atoms during their decay.

The elements which show this phenomenon is called radioactive elements.

In nature, three types of radioactive decay occurs which are given below

(i) **α-decay** In this decay, a helium nucleus ${}_2^4He$ is emitted.

(ii) **β-decay** In this decay, electrons or positrons with the same mass as that of electron are emitted.

(iii) **γ-decay** In this decay, high energy $\approx$ 100 keV photons are emitted.

Properties of α-Particles

An α-particle carries $+2e$ charge and mass equal to four times that of proton.

Some important properties of α-particles are as follows

(i) These particles are deflected by electric and magnetic fieldsee3

(ii) The velocity of α-particles varies from 0.01-0.1 times of c (velocity of light).

(iii) These particles have low penetrating power.

(iv) These particles have high ionising power. Their ionising power is 100 times greater than that of β-rays and 10000 times greater than that of γ-rays.

(v) These particles produce fluorescence in substances like zinc sulphide and barium platinocyanide. They produce scintillation on fluorescent screen.

(vi) These particles feebly affect photographic plate. They also produce heating effect, when stopped and cause incurable burns on human body.

Properties of β-Particles

A β-particle (${}_{-1}e^0$) has a charge of electron. Actually, it is a fast moving electron (not the orbital electron of the atom but is emitted from the nucleus).

Some important properties of β-particles are as follows

(i) These particles are also deflected by electric and magnetic fields. Their deflection is much larger than the deflection of α-particles.

(ii) The velocity of β-particles varies from 1% to 99% of the velocity of light.

(iii) As, the velocity of β-particles is of the order of the velocity of light, its mass increases with increase in their velocity.

(iv) These particles have high penetrating power (100 times larger than the penetrating power of α-particles). They can pass through 1 mm thick sheet of aluminium.

(v) These particles have low ionising power i.e., (1/100)th of the ionising power of α-particles.

(vi) These particles produce fluorescence in calcium tungstate, barium platinocyanide and zinc sulphide and they affect photographic plate more than α-particles.

Properties of γ-Rays

γ-rays (${}_0\gamma^0$) are high energy electromagnetic radiation of nuclear origin and short wavelength ($\approx$ 0.01Å). It is about (1/100)th part of the wavelength of X-rays. Radiation of γ-rays is a nuclear property whereas X-rays is atomic property.

Some important properties of γ-rays are as follows

(i) As, the γ-rays do not have any charge, they are not deflected by electric and magnetic fields.

(ii) These rays travel with the speed of light ($3 \times 10^8 ms^{-1}$).

(iii) These rays have highest penetrating power more than that of α and β-particles. They can pass through 30 cm thick iron sheet.

(iv) These rays have least ionisation power as compared to that of α and β-particles.

(v) These rays produce fluorescence. They also affect photographic plate more than β-particles.

(vi) As, the γ-rays have high energy, they can give rise to the phenomenon of pair production. When a photon of γ-rays moves within the vicinity of the nucleus of an atom, its energy is converted into an electron and a positron (positively charged electron).

$$\underset{\text{(photon)}}{\gamma} \longrightarrow \underset{\text{(electron)}}{e^-} + \underset{\text{(positron)}}{e^+}$$

Comparison of the Properties of α, β and γ-radiations

Property	α-particle	β-particle	γ-rays
Nature	Helium nucleus	Fast moving electrons	Electromagnetic waves
Charge	$+2e$	$-e$	zero
Rest mass	6.67×10^{-27} kg	9.1×10^{-31} kg	zero
Speed	1.4×10^7 to 2.2×10^7 ms^{-1}	1 to 99% of c $= 3 \times 10^8$ ms^{-1}	$c = 3 \times 10^8$ ms^{-1}
Ionising power	10^4	10^2	1
Penetrating power	1	10^2	10^4

Check Your LEARNING...

1 What are the elementary particles of an atom?

2 In an atom $_{13}Al^{27}$, find the number of electrons, protons and neutrons.

3 What are the three types of decay occurs in nature?

4 In α, β and γ-particles, which have least ionising power?

5 In α, β and γ-particles, which have most penetrating power?

Radioactive Decay (Changes Within the Nucleus)

A radioactive nucleus (parent nucleus), decays by particle emission into another nucleus (daughter nucleus), this phenomenon is called **radioactive decay**.

Some radioactive decays are as follows

α-Decay

In α-decay, the mass number of the daughter (product) nucleus is four less than that of parent (decaying) nucleus, while the atomic number decreases by two.

The decay can be written as,

$$^A_Z X \longrightarrow {}^{A-4}_{Z-2}Y + {}_2He^4$$

where, X is the parent nucleus and Y is daughter nucleus.

e.g., $\quad {}_{92}U^{238} \longrightarrow {}_{90}Th^{234} + {}_2He^4$

α-decay occurs with nuclei that are very heavy, hence unstable. So, emitting alpha particles, mass number decreases and it moves towards stability.

Example 2. $_{86}Rn^{222}$ is converted into $_{84}Po^{218}$. Name the particle emitted in this case and write down the corresponding equation.

Sol. Let the particle emitted in this case be represented as $_Z X^A$.

Therefore, $\quad {}_{86}Rn^{222} \longrightarrow {}_{84}Po^{218} + {}_Z X^A$.

Using the law of conservation of mass number and charge number , we get

$$222 = 218 + A \quad \text{and} \quad 86 = 84 + Z$$

$\Rightarrow \quad A = 4$ and $Z = 2$

Now, $A = 4$ and $Z = 2$ corresponds to an α-particle i.e ^4_2He. Therefore, emitted particle is an α-particle and the equation is

$$_{86}Rn^{222} \longrightarrow {}_{84}Po^{218} + {}^4_2He$$

β^--Decay

In β-decay, the mass number of the daughter (product) nucleus remains same but atomic number increases by one.

The decay can be written as

$$^A_Z X \longrightarrow {}_{Z+1}X^A + \beta^-({}_{-1}e^0)$$

It is to be noted here that β-particles are nothing but electrons.

Example 3. How many α and β^--particles will be emitted when $_{90}Th^{232}$ changes to $_{83}Bi^{212}$?

Sol. $_{90}Th^{232} \longrightarrow {}_{83}Bi^{212}$

Decrease in mass number e
$= 232 - 212 = 20$

Number of α-particles emitted due to the above decrease in mass number

$$= \frac{20}{4} = 5$$

Expected decrease in atomic number due to emission of 5α-particles $= 5 \times 2 = 10$

Expected atomic number of the nucleus formed

$$= 90 - 10 = 80$$

But the atomic number of nucleus formed = 83

Increase in atomic number

$$= 83 - 80 = 3$$

Number of β^--particles emitted = 3

Thus, 5 α-particles and 3 β^--particles are emitted.

γ-Decay

In γ-decay, there is no change in mass number and atomic number of parent nucleus but energy in form of electromagnetic radiation is released in this decay.

The decay can be written as

$$^{A}_{Z}X \longrightarrow {}^{A}_{Z}X + \gamma \text{ (gamma radiation or energy)}$$

Uses of Radioactivity-Radioisotopes

There are some elements with atomic number $Z < 82$, whose isotopes are also radioactive. These isotopes are called **radioisotopes.**

e.g., Potassium $^{40}_{19}K$ (atomic number = 19, mass number = 40) and Carbon $^{14}_{6}C$ (atomic number = 6, mass number = 14), etc., are the radioisotopes.

Radioisotopes has its applications in different fields, they are discussed as follows

Medical Uses

(i) Diseases like leukemia, cancer, etc., can be cured by radioisotopes.

(ii) γ-rays emitted by $^{60}_{27}Co$ are used to kill the cells in malignant tumour of patient.

(iii) The weak radioactive tracers of isotopes such as radioisotopes of NaCl, I, etc., are used to diagnose the brain tumour, blood clots before they become dangerous.

Industrial Uses

(i) To avoid the accumulation of charge on moving parts of machine due to friction, radioactive isotopes are used. Due to ionisation effect, charges accumulated on moving parts will be neutralised.

(ii) The radioactive isotopes have such an ionisation effect that they can be used in making luminescent signs.

(iii) Radioactive tracers are used to check the underground pipelines.

(iv) Radioisotopes in the form of nuclear fuel are used to produce power.

Scientific Uses

(i) The radioisotopes are used in determining the age of rocks containing carbon, by measuring the percentage of C^{12} and C^{14} in them.

(ii) The age of old objects not containing carbon can be determined by measuring the percentage of isotopes atom in them.

(iii) These are used in α-particle gold foil experiment in order to study the structure of atom.

(iv) Radioactive sources of elements N, P, K are used in agriculture science to study the growth of plants with respect to manure.

Check Your LEARNING...

1 How can we see that radioactive decay is a random phenomena?

2 What is β^- decay?

3 How do atomic number and mass number change during γ-decay?

4 Mention any two medical uses of radioisotopes.

5 How age of rocks can be determined by carbon isotopes?

6 Which elements are used to study the growth of plants?

Sources of Harmful Radiation

Radioactive or nucleus radiation are very harmful for human being, they can cause diseases likes sore throat, loss of hair, cancer, leukemia, etc.

They also have affect on genetics which can appear in later generation.

There are three main sources from where we get the radiations.

Radioactive Fall out from Nuclear Power Plants and Other Resources

It is a fact that now a days, the nuclear power plants are acting as a major source of electricity in the world. In case any accident occured in the reactor of these plants, radioactive radiations will escape into the atmosphere in a large amount. It will not only affect the population around the plant but also affect the life at far off places where they can reach with air currents.

Nuclear Waste

When the activity of the fuel rods used in nuclear power reactor decreases, they get rejected. But still, these rods are quite radioactive in nature. If these are thrown in an open garbage dump, they can contaminate water and soil and can affect the living organisms also.

Cosmic Radiations and X-rays

Cosmic radiations from the sun enter the Earth's atmosphere from outer space. Out of these radiations, substantial amount of uncharged radiations such as γ-ray and X-ray, etc enter the Earth's atmosphere.
These radiations are also very harmful for human beings.

Background Radiations

All the radiations which are present in the atmosphere, even if there is no radioactive source present are called background radiations.

The sources of these radiations are

(i) cosmic radiations.
(ii) natural and artificial radioactive isotopes.
(iii) products after nuclear explosion.
(iv) traces of radioactive substances present in Earth i.e., rocks.

Nuclear Energy

Energy contained in the nucleus of atom is called nuclear energy. It is released during nuclear reaction.
A reaction in which composition of the reacting nuclei changes to form new elements with a simultaneous release of large amount of energy is called a **nuclear reaction**.

Nuclear reactions occur in the following two ways

1. Nuclear Fission

The reaction in which a heavy nucleus splits into two or more smaller nuclei, with the evolution of large amount of energy when it is bombarded with slow moving neutron is called a nuclear fission reaction.

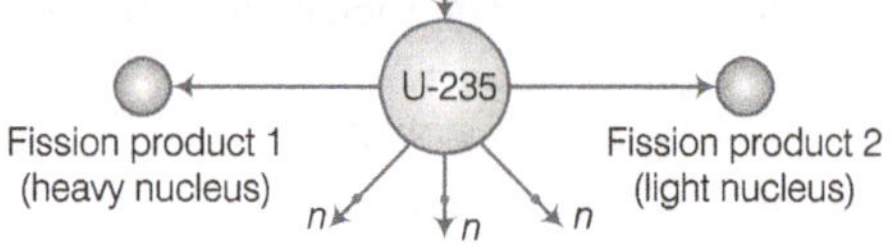

Nuclear fission reaction

Nuclear fission of U-235 as follows

$$\underset{\text{Heavy nucleus}}{{}^{235}_{92}U} + \underset{\text{Thermal neutron}}{{}^{1}_{0}n} \xrightarrow[\text{fission}]{\text{Nuclear}} \underbrace{{}^{139}_{56}Ba + {}^{94}_{36}Kr}_{\text{Fission products}} + \underset{\text{Product neutrons}}{3{}^{1}_{0}n} + \underset{\text{Huge amount of energy (220 MeV)}}{Q}$$

The fission of an atom of uranium, produces 10 million times, the energy produced by the combustion of an atom of carbon from coal. In a nuclear reactor designed for electric power generation, nuclear fuel can be part of a self sustaining fission chain reaction that release energy at a controlled rate.

Energy released in fission reactions In all fission reactions, a small quantity of matter is lost. This lost matter gets converted into energy which is released in any nuclear fission reaction.

The energy (E) obtained due to loss of matter of mass (Δm) is given by the famous Einstein's equation in 1905,

$$E = \Delta mc^2$$

where, c = velocity of light = 3×10^8 m/s

Differences between Nuclear Fission and Radioactive Decay

Nuclear Fission	Radioactive Decay
It is a reaction in which a heavy nucleus splits into two or more smaller nuclei, weith the evolution of large amount of energy when it is bombarded with slow moving neutron.	In this, an unstable nucleus undergoes a decay with the emission of some particles (α, β) and electromagnetic radiations (γ-rays).
It is carried out only when bombarded with neutrons and can be controlled.	It is a spontaneous process and cannot be controlled.

2. Nuclear Fusion

A nuclear reaction in which two or more lighter nuclei fuse to form a heavy nucleus and large amount of energy is released is called nuclear fusion reaction.

Conditions for fusion reaction to take place are as given below

(i) High temperature (~ 4-15 million kelvin)

(ii) High pressure (~ 1 million atmosphere)

Because these reactions require a very high temperature, therefore they are also called **thermonuclear reactions.**

The cause of high heat energy on the Sun is due to fusion of hydrogen nuclei to form helium nuclei.

$$ {}^{2}_{1}H + {}^{2}_{1}H \longrightarrow {}^{3}_{2}He + {}^{1}_{0}n $$

Such nuclear fusion reactions are the source of energy in the Sun and other Stars.

Hydrogen Bomb

The hydrogen bomb is based on **thermonuclear fusion reaction**. A nuclear bomb based on the fission of uranium or plutonium is placed at the core of the hydrogen bomb. This nuclear bomb is embedded in a substance which contains deuterium and lithium. When the nuclear bomb (based on fission) is detonated, then the temperature of this substance is raised to 10^7 K in a few microseconds. The high temperature generates sufficient energy for the light nuclei to fuse and a devastating amount of energy is released.

Differences between Nuclear Fission and Nuclear Fusion

Nuclear Fission	Nuclear Fusion
It involves breaking of a heavy nucleus into lighter nuclei into a heavy two light nuclei.	It involves binding of two nuclei.
It is carried out by the bombardment of two thermal lighter nuclei upto neutrons over a heavy nucleus.	It is carried out by heating at an extreme temperature.
It is a chain reaction.	It is not a chain reaction.
It is a controlled process.	It is an uncontrolled process.
It produces an enormous amount of energy.	It produces more energy than nuclear fission.
Fission products are hazardous.	It does not cause pollution.

Hazards of Nuclear Power Generation

The major hazards of nuclear power generation are as follows

(i) Storage and disposal of spent/used fuels and the uranium continuously decaying into harmful subatomic particles is a big problem.

(ii) Improper nuclear-waste storage and disposal may lead to environmental contamination.

(iii) There is also a risk of nuclear accidents causing due to leakage of nuclear radiation.

Due to all the above factors, large scale use of nuclear energy is prohibited. The nuclear power reactors in India at **Tarapur** (Maharashtra), **Rana Pratap Sagar** (Rajasthan), **Kalpakkam** (Tamil Nadu), **Narora** (Uttar Pradesh), **Kakrapar** (Gujarat) and **Kaiga** (Karnataka) have the installed capacity of less than 3% of total electricity generation capacity of the country.

However, many industrialised countries are producing more than 30% of their electric power needs from nuclear reactors.

Safety Precautions while Using Nuclear Energy

Some of the safety precautions which are required to be undertaken while using nuclear energy are as follows

Safety Measures for Handling the Radioactive Materials

(i) Each type of radiations should have some safety limits and that should be known to each and everyone, so that no one get exposed beyond the safety limit in any case.

(ii) People working with radioactive materials should wear special lead lined aprons and lead gloves.

(iii) In order to stop radiations from spreading all round, the radioactive substances must be kept in thick lead containers with a very narrow opening.

Safety Measures for Establishment of Nuclear Plants

When a nuclear power plant is going to be established to generate the electricity, proper care must be taken, so that the working people in it are not exposed to the nuclear radiations.

Given below are some safety measures which are to be followed during the establishment of nuclear power plants.

(i) The housing of nuclear reactor must be done in an air-tight building of strong concrete structure which can with stand earthquakes, fires and explosion.

(ii) For backup the cooling system must be there for the reactor core, for safety in case of failure.

Safe Disposal of Nuclear Waste

Nuclear wastes are the wastes found after use of radioactive material. It is obtained from different places like laboratories, power plants, hospitals, scientific establishment.

So, it must be first kept them in thick casks and then must be buried in the specially constructed deep under ground stores.

These stores must be far from the populated areas. Even the casks can also be buried in useless mines and these mines must be sealed after storing the casks.

Check Your LEARNING...

1 What is source of cosmic radiations in nature? How these radiations can effect us?
2 Why safe disposal of nuclear waste is needed?
3 What is the unit for background radiations?
4 On what type of reaction does a hydrogen bomb depend?
5 When does nucleus of an atom tend to be radioactive?
6 In between nuclear fission and fusion, which is more hazardous?

QUiCK Revision

- An **atom** consists of electron, proton and neutron.
- A nucleus consist of **proton** and **neutron**.
- **Isotopes** are the atoms belonging to the same elements, having **same atomic number** but **different mass number**, due to difference in neutrons.
- **Isotones** are the atoms with the **same neutron number** but **different atomic number**.
- **Isobars** are the **same mass number** but **different atomic numbers**.
- **Radioactivity** is a spontaneous nuclear phenomenon in which an unstable nucleus undergoes a decay with the emission of some particles and electromagnetic radiation.
- Becquerel rays are of three types: **alpha**, **beta** and **gamma** rays.
- Energy contained in a nucleus of atom is called **nuclear energy**.
- **Nuclear fission** is the reaction in which a heavy nucleus splits into two or more smaller nuclei, with evolution of long amount of energy.
- **Nuclear fusion** is the reaction in which two or more lighter nuclei fuse to form a heavy nucleus and a large amount of energy.

Chapter Practice

1 Mark Questions

1. In β-emission from a radioactive substance, an electron is ejected. This electron comes from the
   (a) outermost orbit of atom
   (b) inner orbits of atom
   (c) surface of substance
   (d) nucleus of atom

Sol. (*d*) In β-emission from a radioactive substance, an electron is ejected. This electron comes from the nucleus of atom.

2. Which of the following radiation suffers most deflection in magnetic field? **[2023]**
   (a) α-particles (b) β-particles
   (c) X-rays (d) γ-radiations

Sol. (*b*) β-particles suffers most deflection in the magnetic field, because charge to mass ratio is higher for β-particles (or electrons).

3. The radiation with maximum penetrating power is **[Latest Specimen Sem-II]**
   (a) γ-rays (b) β-rays
   (c) X-rays (d) α-rays

Sol. (*a*) γ-radiation has maximum penetrating power among given radiations.

4. The nuclear radiation which gets deflected towards negatively charged plate in an electric field is **[Latest Specimen Sem-II]**
   (a) gamma (b) ultraviolet
   (c) beta (d) alpha

Sol. (*d*) Alpha particles carries two units of positive charges. So, when they are placed in an electric field between two charged plates, they are deflected towards negatively charged plate.

5. When a nucleus in an atom undergoes a radioactive decay, then the electronic energy levels of the atom
   (a) do not change for any type of radioactivity
   (b) change for α and β-decay but not for γ-radioactivity
   (c) change for α-decay but not for others
   (d) change for β-decay but not for others

Sol. (*b*) γ-decay occurs due to de-excitation of a nucleus and electronic energy levels involved is essentially in MeV. Electronic energy levels have values only in eV but energy released per nucleon is 26.7 MeV.

6. The particle used in nuclear fission for bombardment is
   (a) α-particle (b) proton
   (c) neutron (d) β-particle

Sol. (*c*) Neutrons are bombarded on heavy nuclei to initiate fission process in unstable nuclei.

7. The required temperature of thermonuclear reaction is
   (a) 10^3 K (b) 10^4 K (c) 10^5 K (d) 10^7 K

Sol. (*d*) Thermonuclear reaction or fusion reaction only takes place under very high pressure and temperature. The approximate temperature required for thermonuclear reaction is 10^7 K.

8. When four hydrogen nuclei combine to form a helium nucleus in the interior of sun, what amount of energy released per nucleon in this process?
   (a) 46.3 MeV (b) 24.5 MeV
   (c) 18.5 MeV (d) 26.7 MeV

Sol. (*d*) When four hydrogen nuclei combine to form a helium nucleus in the interior of the sun, nuclear fusion takes place its a multi-step process in which hydrogen is fused into helium. The proton-proton (*p*, *p*) cycle by which this occurs is represented as

$4{}_1^1\text{H} + 2e^- \longrightarrow {}_2^4\text{He} + 2\nu + 6\nu + 26.7\text{ MeV}$

Hence, energy released per nucleon is 26.7 MeV.

2 Marks Questions

9. How is the radioactivity of a radio isotope affected, if it undergoes a chemical change ? Give a reason for your answer. **[2023]**

Sol. Radioactivity of a radio isotope is not affected by the chemical changes because radioactivity is a nuclear phenomenon and doesn't involve extra-nuclear elecrions. **[2]**

10. (i) What are isobars?
    (ii) Give one example of isobars. **[2018]**

Sol. (i) The atoms of different elements having the same mass number (*A*), but different atomic number (*Z*) are called isobars. **[1]**

(ii) ${}_{11}^{23}\text{Na}$ and ${}_{12}^{23}\text{Mg}$ are isobars having same mass number 23 and different atomic numbers. **[1]**

11. At what condition does the nucleus of an atom become radioactive?

Sol. The nucleus of an atom becomes radioactive when the number of neutrons exceed the number of protons , present inside the nucleus which thereby increases its instability. **[2]**

12. When does the nucleus of an atom, tend to be radioactive? **[2017, 2023]**

Sol. Atoms with unstable nuclei are constantly changing as a result to the imbalance of energy within the nucleus. Instability of an atoms nucleus may result from an excess of either neutrons or protons, since nuclear forces become weak, so to become stable, some amount mass in form of energy is released. This means, when the nucleus loses a neutron, it gives off energy and becomes radioactive. [2]

13. In heavy nuclei, number of neutrons is greater than the number of protons. Why?

Sol. Electrostatic repulsive forces between number of protons is very high in heavy nuclei due to presence of large number of protons. The attraction due to nuclear forces cannot sustain, so much the protons together in the nucleus. Thus, large number of neutrons separate the protons, weakening the repulsion between them. [2]

14. When a radioactive substance is oxidised, will there be any change in the nature of its radioactivity? Give a reason for your answer. [2016]

Sol. There will be no change in the nature of its radioactivity because radioactivity is a nuclear phenomenon and oxidation is a chemical process which does not affects the nucleus of the substance. [2]

15. A mixture of radioactive substances gives off three types of radiations.
(i) Name the radiation which travels with the speed of light.
(ii) Name the radiation which has the highest ionising power. [2011]

Sol. (i) γ-radiation travels with the speed of light. [1]
(ii) α ($^4_2$He) particle has the highest ionising power. [1]

16. Point out the comparison for
(i) the ionising powers and
(ii) penetrating powers of α, β and γ-radiations.

Sol. (i) The ionising power of α-radiations is nearly 100 times that of β-radiations and nearly 10000 times that of γ-radiations. The ionising power for the three particles (α, β, γ respectively) is the order of $10^4 : 10^2 : 1$. [1]
(ii) The penetrating power of α-particle is (1/100)th times that of a β-particle and (1/10000) times that of γ-radiation. [1]

17. "α and β-particles are deflected in an electric field or a magnetic field, while γ-rays are not deflected in such a field". Comment on this statement.

Sol. Since, α and β-particles are the charged particles (i.e. α-particles carry positive charge and β-particles carry negative charge). Due to which, they are deflected in electric or magnetic a field while γ-rays are not deflected in such a field because they are uncharged. [2]

18. What happens to the atomic number of an element, when it emits
(i) an α-particle and
(ii) a β-particle ?

Sol. (i) When an α-particle is emitted, then atomic number decreases by 2 and mass number decreases by 4. [1]
(ii) During β-emission, atomic number increases by 1 as it consists of electron. [1]

19. A certain radioactive nucleus emits a particle that leaves its mass unchanged but increases its atomic number by one. Identity the particle and write its symbol. [2006]

Sol. As β-particle consists of $_{-1}\beta^0$ and after its emission, atomic number increases by 1 and mass number remains as it is. Its symbol is $_{-1}\beta^0$.

20. Which of the radioactive radiations occurs in the following cases:
(i) That can cause severe genetical disorder.
(ii) Are deflected by an electric field? [2013]

Sol. (i) γ- radiation can cause severe genetical disorder. [1]
(ii) Since α, β are charged particles, so they get deflected in the electric field. [1]

21. (i) Which radiation produces maximum biological damage?
(ii) What happens to the atomic number of an element, when the radiation named by you in part (i) above are emitted? [2010]

Sol. (i) γ-radiation produces maximum biological damage as it has maximum penetration power. [1]
(ii) There is no change in atomic and mass number of element formed after γ-radiation or emission. [1]

22. Name the radioactive isotope used to find the age of fossils. Name the radioactive radiation which it emits? [Latest Specimen Sem-II]

Sol. Carbon- 14 is used of find the age of fossils.It is an unstable isotope of carbon that decays into nitrogen-14 through beta decay. [2]

23. What is nuclear fission reaction? Give an example equation to explain it.

Sol. The reaction in which a heavy nucleus splits into two or more smaller nuclei, with the evolution of large amount of energy when it is bombarded with slow moving neutron is called a nuclear fission reaction.

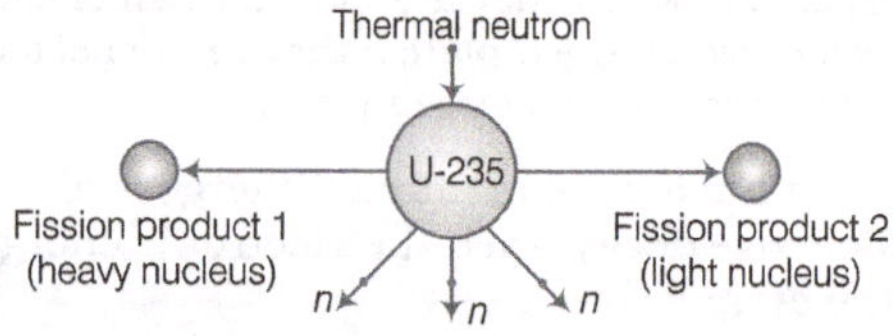

Nuclear fission of U-235 as follows

$$^{235}_{92}U + ^1_0n \xrightarrow{\text{Nuclear fission}} ^{139}_{56}Ba + ^{94}_{36}Kr + 3^1_0n + Q$$

Heavy nucleus; Thermal neutron; Fission products (Ba, Kr); Product neutrons; Huge amount of energy (220 MeV)

[2]

24. (i) What do you understand by the term nuclear fusion?
(ii) Nuclear power plants use nuclear fission reaction to produce electricity. What is the advantage of producing by fusion reaction? [2018]

Sol. (i) In nuclear fusion, two light nuclei are combined to form heavy nucleus with release of energy. **[1]**

(ii) In fusion more energy per unit mass is released than fission, therefore it will be more useful in producing electricity. **[1]**

25. Differentiate between radioactive decay and nuclear fission.

Sol. Differences between Nuclear Fission and Radioactive Decay is given below

Nuclear Fission	Radioactive Decay
It is a reaction in which a heavy nucleus splits into two or more smaller nuclei, with the evolution of large amount of energy when it is bombarded with slow moving neutron.	In this, an unstable nucleus undergoes a decay with the emission of some particles (α, β) and electromagnetic radiations (γ-rays). **[1]**
It is carried out only when bombarded with neutrons and can be controlled.	It is a spontaneous process and cannot be controlled. **[1]**

3 Marks Questions

26. Arrange α, β and γ-rays in ascending order with respect to their

(i) penetrating power (ii) ionising power

(iii) biological effect **[2016]**

Sol. Ascending order arrangement of α, β and γ-particle with respect to their

(i) **penetrating power** : α-particle, β-particle, γ-particle. **[1]**

(ii) **ionising power** : γ-particle, β-particle, α-particle. **[1]**

(iii) **biological effect** : γ-particle, β-particle, α-particle. **[1]**

27. (i) Name the particles given out during radioactive decay.

(ii) Show by equation, the effect on the proton number Z and mass number A of the parent nucleus brought about by the two types of radioactive decay.

(iii) What is carbon-14 dating? **[2007]**

Sol. (i) The particle given out in nuclear reaction are α-particle $({}_2He^4)$, β-particle $({}_{-1}\beta^0)$ and γ-particle $({}_0\gamma^0)$.

(ii) As the parent nucleus be X, so after α-decay is

$$_ZX^A \xrightarrow{-\alpha\,({}_2He^4)} {}_{Z-2}X^{A-4}$$

and β-decay is $_ZP^A \xrightarrow{-\beta\,({}_{-1}\beta^0)} {}_{Z+1}P^A$

(iii) The radioisotopes are used in determining the age of rocks containing carbon, by measuring the percentage of C^{12} and C^{14} in them is called carbon dating.

28. The ore of uranium found in nature contains ${}_{92}U^{238}$ and ${}_{92}U^{235}$.

Although both the isotopes are fissionable, it is found out experimentally that one of the two isotopes is more easily fissionable.

(i) Name the isotope of uranium which is easily fissionable.

(ii) Give a reason for your answer.

(iii) Write a nuclear reaction when uranium 238 emits an alpha particle of form a Thorium (Th) nucleus. **[2018]**

Sol. (i) ${}_{92}U^{235}$ is easily fissionable. **[1]**

(ii) Fission of uranium with mass number of 238 is possible by only fast neutron but the fission of uranium with mass number of 235 is also possible by slow neutron. **[1]**

(iii) ${}^{238}_{92}U \longrightarrow {}^{234}_{90}Th + {}^{4}_{2}He$ (α-particle) **[1]**

29. (i) What is meant by radioactivity?

(ii) What is meant by nuclear waste?

(iii) Suggest one effective process for the safe disposal of nuclear waste.

Sol. (i) Radioactivity is a spontaneous process by which nucleus of an unstable atom decays by emitting radiations such as α, β and γ. **[1]**

(ii) Nuclear waste is the material which remains after the use of radioactive element such as α, β and γ-particles in the form of radiation. **[1]**

(iii) Nuclear waste must be put in a thick casks (dumbell shaped structure), then after buried in the specially constructed deep underground stores reservoirs. **[1]**

30. (i) Complete the following nuclear changes

$${}^{238}_{92}P \rightarrow -\underline{Q} + He^4_2 \rightarrow -\underline{R} + {}^{0}_{-1}e$$

(ii) Name the nuclear radiation which has the highest ionising power. **[2023]**

Sol. (i) ${}^{238}_{92}P \longrightarrow {}^{234}_{90}Q + {}^{4}_{2}He \longrightarrow {}^{234}_{91}R + {}_{-1}e^0$

(ii) Alpha radiation has the highest ionizing power.

31. (i) Define radioactivity.

(ii) What happens inside the nucleus, that causes the emission of β-particle?

(iii) Express the above change in the form of an equation.

Sol. (i) Radioactivity is the sponataneous process by which a nucleus of an unstable atom decay by emitting radiations such as α, β and γ. **[1]**

(ii) Inside the nucleus, to attain stability, neutrons may changes to a proton and emits a β -particle. **[1]**

(iii) $_ZX^A \xrightarrow{{}_{-1}\beta^0} {}_{Z+1}Y^A + {}_{-1}e^0$

where, A = mass number

and Z = atomic number. **[1]**

32. (i) Name the radioactive radiations which have the least penetrating power.

(ii) Give one use of radioisotopes.

(iii) What is meant by background radiation?

Sol. (i) α-particle $({}_2He^4)$ **[1]**

(ii) Radioactive isotopes are used in fuel for atomic energy reactor. **[1]**

(iii) These are the invisible radioactive radiations such as α, β and γ produced during nuclear decay.

33. (i) Mention two important precautions that should be taken while handling radioactive materials.
(ii) Why does the nuclei of increasing mass number fissioned easily?

Sol. (i) Two important precautions of handling radioactive materials are as follows
(a) Put them in a thick lead box.
(b) Wear special protective clothes (lead coated) and gloves on the hand. [2]
(ii) Fission of nuclei is possible because the binding energy per nucleon decreases with mass number. [1]
As, the mass number increases, the binding energy per nucleon gradually decreases and ultimately binding energy per nucleon of heavy nuclei (such as uranium, polonium etc) is comparatively low. Hence, these nuclides are relatively unstable. So, they can be fissioned easily.

4 Marks Questions

34. Explain in brief the given statement: "radioactivity is a nuclear phenomenon."

Sol. The process of spontaneous emission of radiations from the nucleus, is known as radioactivity. The nucleus consists of protons and neutrons. These are bounded inside the nucleus by a strong attractive force called the nuclear force. If in a nucleus, the number of protons is much more than the number of neutron, the nuclear force becomes weak. The nuclei of such element becomes unstable and have a tendency to disintegrate. [2]
This happens in the case of nuclei of elements of atomic number higher than 82. These elements are called natural radioactive elements.
Any physical or chemical condition such as excessive heating, freezing, magnetic fields, etc., cannot alter the rate of disintegration of such elements.
That means the phenomenon cannot be due to the orbital electrons which could be easily affected by such changes. It is the property of the nucleus. Hence, radioactivity is a nuclear phenomenon. [2]

35. Describe briefly, two properties of each of α and β-particles. [2002]

Sol. Two properties of α- particles are
(i) They cannot penetrate skin but is harmful for human body.
(ii) It is an α- particle with least penetration power and highest ionisation power. [2]

Two properties of β-particles are
(i) β-particles are highly energetic electrons.
(ii) β-particles has less ionisation power but it has greater penetration than α-particles. [2]

36. Specify two properties of β-particles and γ-rays.

Sol. Two Properties of β-particles
(i) β-particles are highly energetic electrons, which are released from inside of a nucleus. It is denoted by ${}_{-1}\beta^0$(atomic number – 1 and mass number 0)
(ii) β-particles are negatively charged and they have negligible mass. [2]

Two Properties of γ-rays
(i) The waves from the high frequency end of electromagnetic spectrum which do not have mass are called γ-rays.
(ii) It is neutral in nature and denoted by ${}_0\gamma^0$. They are chargeless and massless. [2]

37. Write a comparison table between α, β and γ-radiations with respect to their nature, speed, rest mass and charge.

Sol. Comparison table between α, β and γ-radiations is given below

Property	α-particle	β-particle	γ-radiation	
Nature	Stream of positively charged particles, i.e. helium nucleus.	Stream of negatively charged particles i.e. energetic electrons.	Highly energetic electromagnetic radiations.	[1]
Speed	Nearly 10^7 ms^{-1}	About 90% of the speed of light or 2.7×10^8 ms^{-1}.	3×10^8 ms^{-1} (in vacuum)	[1]
Rest mass	Four times the mass of proton, i.e. 6.68×10^{-27} kg	Equal to the mass of electron, i.e. 9.1×10^{-31}	No mass (rest mass is zero)	[1]
Charge	Positive charge (two times that of a proton = $+3.2 \times 10^{-19}$C (or + 2e)	Negative charge = -1.6×10^{-19} C (or $-e$)	No charge	[1]

38. Radiations given out from a source when subjected to an electric field in a direction perpendicular to their path are shown below in the diagram. The arrows show the path of the radiation *A*, *B* and *C*. Answer the following questions in terms *A*, *B* and *C*.

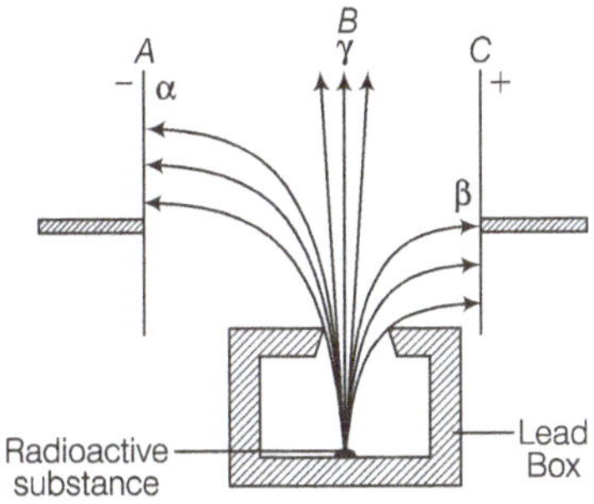

(i) Name the radiation *B* which is unaffected by the electrostatic field.
(ii) Why does the radiation *C* deflect more than *A*?
(iii) Which among the three causes the least biological damage externally?
(iv) Name the radiation which is used in carbon dating. **[2018]**

Sol. (i) Gamma radiations **[1]**
(ii) The radiation *C* deflect more than *A* because the mass of β-particles is less than that of α, hence radiation deflects more than *A*. **[1]**
(iii) γ-rays **[1]**
(iv) β radiation is used in carbon dating. **[1]**

39. (i) What happen to the atomic number of an clement, when it emits
(a) an α-particle and (b) a β-particle?
(ii) Explain, why α-and β-particle are deflected in an electric or a magnetic field but γ-rays are not deflected in such a field? **[2007]**

Sol. (i) (a) When an α-particle is emitted, then atomic number decreases by 2 and mass number decreases by 4.
(b) During β-emission, atomic number increases by 1 as it consists of $_{-1}\beta^0$. **[2]**
(ii) Since, α-particle is a helium nuclei ($_2He^4$) and is positively charged particle and β-particle is ($_{-1}\beta^0$), negatively charged particle.
In an electric field, they experiences some force, so get deflected. **[2]**

40. (i) Represent the change in the nucleus of a radioactive element when a β-particle is emitted from it.
(ii) What is the name given to elements with same mass number and different atomic numbers?
(iii) Under which conditions the nucleus of an atom tend to be radioactive? **[2016]**

Sol. (i) The emission of β-particle by the nuclei of radioactive substance does not change the mass number of the atom but increases its atomic number by one. **[1]**

$$^{A}_{Z}X \longrightarrow \, ^{A}_{Z+1}Y + \, ^{0}_{-1}e$$ **[1]**

(ii) Isobar is the name give to the elements with the same mass number and different atomic numbers. **[1]**
(iii) When a nucleus becomes unstable i.e. number of proton increases for more greater than the neutrons, then a nucleus decays and it is called a radioactive nucleus. **[1]**

41. A certain nucleus *X* has a mass number 14 and atomic number 6. The nucleus *X* changes to $_7Y^{14}$ after the loss of a particle.
(i) Name the particle emitted.
(ii) Represent this change in the form of an equation.
(iii) A radioactive substance is oxidised. What change would you expect to take place in the nature of its radioactivity? Give a reason for your answer. **[2012]**

Sol. (i) β-particle : since during the $_{-1}\beta^0$- emission, there is gain in atomic number. **[1]**
(ii) $_6X^{14} \xrightarrow{-1\beta^0} \, _7Y^{14} + \, _{-1}e^0$ **[1]**
(iii) There is no change in the nature of radioactivity during oxidation. Because oxidation is a phenomena in which involvement of electrons takes place, whereas in radioactivity nucleons takes part in the reaction. **[2]**

42. Briefly explain the term radiation hazards.

Sol. The nuclear radiations such as α, β, γ-rays and neutrons can damage the human body. The radiations produce severe burns on the human body. e.g., When gamma rays pass through a living organism, they knockout the electrons from the organic molecules as a result of which the molecules may breakup. The distortion of the molecules hampers the normal functioning of the living system and may ultimately result in the death of the organism. **[2]**
These radiations causes following two types of damages
(i) **Genetical Damage** Damages of this type are not evident immediately but appear in the subsequent damages. It cause a change in the coding sequence of DNA and the effects may appear in future generations. **[1]**
(ii) **Pathological Damage** If an organism is exposed to high doses of radiation, it might ultimately lead to the death of the organism. Such a damage is known as pathological damage. **[1]**

43. Write any four safety measures to be undertaken during establishement of nuclear power plants.

Sol. Safety measures to be undertaken during establishment of nuclear power plants are given below
(i) Radioactive elements like uranium, barium and krypton used in reactors should be kept in

containers that are made of thick lead walls, so they do not leak out.

(ii) People working in these plants should wear jackets and gloves made of lead linings, so that the radiations do not penetrate into their body.

(iii) A proper arrangement for the safe disposal of the nuclear waste must be carried out.

(iv) The nuclear power plant must be housed in an airtight building of strong concrete structure which can withstand earthquakes, fires and explosions.

Numerical Based Questions

44. A radioactive nucleus undergoes a series of decays according to the sequence.

$$X \xrightarrow{\beta} X_1 \xrightarrow{\alpha} X_2 \xrightarrow{\alpha} X_3$$

If the mass number and atomic number of X_3 are 132 and 69 respectively, what is the mass number and atomic number of X? **[2012]**

Sol. According to the question, ${}_{72}X^{140} \xrightarrow{-1\beta^0} {}_{73}X_1^{140}$

$$\xrightarrow{\alpha\,({}_2He^4)} {}_{71}X_2^{136} \xrightarrow{\alpha\,({}_2He^4)} {}_{69}X_3^{132}$$ **[2]**

45. A nucleus ${}^{194}_{82}X$ emits an alpha particle,

(a) what will be the atomic number of the daughter nucleus Y?

(b) what will be the number of neutrons in the daughter nucleus Y?

(c) write a nuclear reaction showing the emission of this particle. **[4] [Latest Specimen Sem-II]**

Sol. (a) In alpha decay, the mass number A decreases by four while the atomic number Z decreases by two.

∴ Atomic number of

$$Y = Z - 2 = 82 - 2 = 80$$

(b) Here, for Y, $Z = 80$,

$$A = 194 - 4 = 190$$

∴ Number of neutrons,

$$N = A - Z = 190 - 80 = 110$$

(c) The process can be written as

$${}^{194}_{82}X \longrightarrow {}^{190}_{80}Y + {}^{4}_{2}He$$

46. One isotope of uranium has a mass number 235 and atomic number 92.

(i) What is the number of electrons in the neutral atom of this isotope?

(ii) What is the number of protons and number of neutrons in its nucleus?

(iii) Do all isotopes have the same number of neutrons?

(iv) What is the number of protons and neutrons in ${}^{238}_{92}U$? **{4}**

Sol. Given, $A = 235$, $Z = 92$

(i) Atomic number, Z = number of protons

= number of electrons = 92

∴ The neutron atom of ${}^{235}_{92}U$ will have 92 electrons. **[1]**

(ii) The number of protons = Z = 92

The number of neutrons = $A - Z = 235 - 92 = 143$

The nucleus of ${}^{235}_{92}U$ contains 92 protons and 143 neutrons. **[1]**

(iii) No, isotopes of an element have same atomic number, but different mass number, so they have the same number of protons, but different number of neutrons. **[1]**

(iv) In ${}^{238}_{92}U$, number of protons = Z = 92 and number of neutrons = $A - Z = 238 - 92 = 146$. **[1]**

47. The isotope of ${}_{92}U^{238}$ decays by α-emission to an isotope of thorium (Th). The thorium isotopes decays by β- emission to an isotope of protactinium (Pa). Write down the equations to represents these two nuclear charges. **[2] [2003]**

Sol. The equation for α-emission is as follows

$${}_{92}U^{238} \xrightarrow{-\alpha\,({}_2He^4)} {}_{90}Th^{234}$$

The equation for β-emission is as follows

$${}_{90}Th^{234} \xrightarrow{-\beta\,({}_{-1}\beta^0)} \text{(protactinium)}\ {}_{91}Pa^{234}$$ **[2]**

48. An element ${}_ZS^A$ decays to ${}_{85}R^{222}$ after emitting 2α-particles and 1β-particle. Find the atomic number and atomic mass of the element S. **[2] [2016]**

Sol. According to the question,

$${}_{88}S^{230} \longrightarrow {}_{85}R^{222} + 2\alpha + {}^{0}_{+1}e + \nu_e$$

Therefore, atomic number, $Z = 88$

Mass number, $A = 230$ **[2]**

49. A nucleus ${}_{11}Na^{24}$ emits a β-particle to change into magnesium (Mg).

(i) Write the symbolic equation for the process.

(ii) What are numbers 24 and 11 called?

(iii) What is the general name of ${}^{24}_{12}Mg$ with respect to ${}^{24}_{11}Na$? **[3]**

Sol. (i) The symbolic equation of this process is

$${}_{11}Na^{24} \longrightarrow {}_{12}Mg^{24} + {}_{-1}e^0$$ **[1]**

(ii) 24 is the mass number and 11 is the atomic number. **[1]**

(iii) ${}_{11}Na^{24}$ and ${}_{12}Mg^{24}$ are isobars. **[1]**

50. Write nuclear reaction equations for

(i) α-decay of ${}^{226}_{88}Ra$

(ii) α-decay of ${}^{242}_{94}Pu$

(iii) β^--decay of ${}^{32}_{15}P$ **[3]**

Sol. As we know that,

(i) in α-decay, the mass number is reduced by 4 and atomic number is reduced by 2.

(ii) in β-decay, the mass number remains constant and atomic number is increased by 1.

(iii) in a γ-decay, the mass number and atomic number remains same.

The following equations are given

(a) $^{226}_{88}\text{Ra} \xrightarrow{-\alpha} {}^{222}_{88}\text{Rn} + {}^{4}_{2}\text{He}$

(b) $^{242}_{94}\text{Pu} \xrightarrow{-\alpha} {}^{238}_{92}\text{U} + {}^{4}_{2}\text{He}$

(c) $^{32}_{15}\text{P} \xrightarrow{-(\beta)} {}^{32}_{16}\text{S} + {}^{0}_{-1}e + \bar{\nu}$

i.e. β^--decay is accompanied by release of antineutrino. [3]

51. A certain nucleus P has a mass number 15 and atomic number 7.

(i) Find the number of neutrons.

(ii) Write the symbol for the nucleus P.

(iii) The nucleus P losses (a) one proton (b) one β-particle (c) one α-particle.
Write the symbol of the new nucleus in each case and express each charge by a reaction. [4]

Sol. Given, for the nucleus P, $A = 15$, $Z = 7$

(i) Mass number, A = number of protons + number of neutrons Atomic number,
Z = number of protons
∴ Number of neutrons = mass number, A – atomic number, $Z = 15 - 7 = 8$ [1]

(ii) The nucleus P can be written as $^{15}_{7}P$. [1]

(iii) (a) After the loss of proton, the mass number and atomic number of the nucleus $^{15}_{7}P$ will decrease by 1. The new nucleus will be $^{14}_{6}Q$ (say).
The nucleus $^{15}_{7}P$ changes to $^{14}_{6}Q$ (say) as follows

$$^{15}_{7}P \longrightarrow {}^{14}_{6}Q + {}^{1}_{1}P$$

(b) After the loss of one β-particle, the mass number will remain the same but the atomic number will increase by 1.
The nucleus $^{15}_{7}P$ changes to $^{15}_{8}R$ (say) as follows

$$^{15}_{7}P \longrightarrow {}^{15}_{8}R + {}^{0}_{-1}e$$

(c) After the loss of one α-particle, the mass number decreases by 4 and the atomic number decreases by 2.
The nucleus $^{15}_{7}P$ changes to $^{11}_{5}S$ (say) as follows

$$^{15}_{7}P \longrightarrow {}^{11}_{5}S + {}^{4}_{2}\text{He}$$ [2]

52. Complete the following nuclear changes.

(i) $_{11}\text{Na}^{24} \longrightarrow {}_{...}\text{Mg}^{...} + {}_{-1}\beta^{0}$ [2]

(ii) $_{92}\text{U}^{238} \longrightarrow {}_{90}\text{Th}^{234} + \ldots +$ Energy [3] [2010]

Sol. (i) $_{11}\text{Na}^{24} \longrightarrow {}_{12}\text{Mg}^{24} + {}_{-1}\beta^{0}$ [1]

(ii) $_{92}\text{U}^{238} \longrightarrow {}_{90}\text{Th}^{234} + {}_{2}\text{He}^{4}$ (α-particle) + Energy [1]

53. Complete the following nuclear reactions given below:

(i) $^{238}_{92}P \xrightarrow{\alpha} Q \xrightarrow{\beta} R \xrightarrow{\beta} S$

(ii) $^{A}_{Z}X \xrightarrow{\alpha} X_1 \xrightarrow{-\gamma} X_2 \xrightarrow{2\beta} X_3$

Sol. (i) $^{238}_{92}P \longrightarrow {}^{234}_{90}Q + {}^{4}_{2}\text{He}$, $^{234}_{90}Q \longrightarrow {}^{234}_{91}R + {}^{0}_{-1}\beta$

$^{234}_{91}R \longrightarrow {}^{234}_{92}S + {}^{0}_{-1}\beta$

Therefore, the complete radiation series can be represented as [1½]

$$^{238}_{98}P \xrightarrow{\alpha} {}^{234}_{90}Q \xrightarrow{\beta} {}^{234}_{91}R \xrightarrow{\beta} {}^{234}_{92}S$$

(ii) $^{A}_{Z}X \longrightarrow {}^{A-4}_{Z-2}X_1 + {}^{4}_{2}\text{He}$

$^{A-4}_{Z-2}X_1 \longrightarrow {}^{A-4}_{Z-2}X_2 + \gamma$

$^{A-4}_{Z-2}X_2 \longrightarrow {}^{A-4}_{Z}X_3 + 2\,{}^{0}_{-1}\beta$

Therefore, complete radioactive series can be given as

$$^{A}_{Z}X \xrightarrow{\alpha} {}^{A-4}_{Z-2}X_1 \xrightarrow{\gamma} {}^{A-4}_{Z-2}X_2 \xrightarrow{2\beta} {}^{A-4}_{Z}X_3$$

54. In fusion of a nuclei, the loss in mass is 0.25 amu. Find the energy released. [1½]

Sol. Given, mass loss $\Delta m = 0.25$ amu

Energy released $= \Delta m \times 931$ MeV
$= 0.25 \times 931 \text{ MeV} = 232.75$ MeV

Structured Questions

55. (i) (a) State the statement "nuclear force is a short range force."

(b) Write two industrial use of radioisotopes. [3]

(ii) (a) Define nuclear fission.

(b) Rewrite and complete the following nuclear reaction by filling in the atomic number of Ba and mass number of Kr.

$$^{235}_{92}\text{U} + {}^{1}_{0}n \longrightarrow {}^{144}_{\cdots\cdots}\text{Ba} + {}^{\cdots\cdots}_{36}\text{Kr} + 3{}^{1}_{0}n + \text{Energy}.$$ [3] [2019]

(iii) (a) Is it possible for a hydrogen ($^{1}_{1}$H) nucleus to emit an alpha particle? Give a reason for your answer.

(b) Why is a nuclear fusion reaction called a thermonuclear reaction?
Complete the reaction.
$^{3}\text{He}_2 + {}^{2}\text{H}_1 \longrightarrow {}^{4}\text{He}_2 + \ldots + $ Energy

Sol. (i) (a) Nuclear force are short range force. It does not depend on the charges of nucleons. Nuclear forces are strongest forces in nature. [1]

(b) Uses of radioisotopes in industrial purpose are

(I) To avoid accumulation of charges or moving charges of machine due to friction, radioactive isotopes are used.

(II) Radioactive tracers are used to check the underground pipelines. [2]

(ii) (a) Nuclear fission is the phenomenon of spliting of a heavy nucleus (usually $A > 230$) into two or more lighter nuclei. [1]

(b) $Z_{\text{LHS}} = Z_{\text{RHS}}$
$92 = 36 + x + 0$
$92 - 36 = x \Rightarrow x = 56$
$A_{\text{LHS}} = Z_{\text{RHS}}$

$235 + 1 = 144 + y + 3$
$y = 236 - 147 = 89$

Now, the complete reaction is

$^{235}_{92}U + ^{1}_{0}n \rightarrow ^{144}_{56}Ba + ^{89}_{36}Kr + 3^{1}_{0}n + \text{Energy}$ [2]

(iii) (a) No, it is not possible because it is alpha particle consists of two protons and two neutrons. However none of the isotopes of hydrogen has the same number or more of protons and neutrons in its nuclei. Thus, they cannot emit an alpha particle. [2]

(b) Nuclear fusion is also called thermonuclear reaction because it takes place at extremely high temperature and hence enormous amount of energy, e.g. reactions in the sun.

$^{3}He_2 + ^{2}H_1 \longrightarrow ^{4}He_2 + ^{1}H_1 + \text{Energy}$ [2]

56. (i) (a) When does the nucleus of an atom become radioactive?

(b) How is the radioactivity of an element affected, when it undergoes a chemical change to form a chemical compound?

(c) Mention one use and one harmful effect of radioactivity. [3]

(ii) (a) Differentiate between nuclear fusion and nuclear fission.

(b) State one safety precaution in the disposal of nuclear waste. [3] [2020]

(iii) An atomic nucleus A is composed of 84 protons and 128 neutrons. The nucleus A emits an α-particle and is transformed into a nucleus B. [4]

(a) What is the composition of B?

(b) The nucleus B emits a β-particle and is transformed into a nucleus C. What is the composition of C ?

(c) What is mass number of the nucleus A?

(d) Does the composition of C change, if it emits γ-radiations?

Sol. (i) (a) If the atomic number of an element is more than 82, then after it becomes radioactive. Atomic number between 82 to 92 are good radioactive element. [1]

(b) There is no change in the radioactivity during the chemical reaction, because chemical reaction involves electrons of shell, whereas radioactivity involves nucleons (i.e. neutron and protons). [1]

(c) Uses of radioactivity is in production of electricity in nuclear reactor and in carbon dating by (C^{14}) and in harmful effect, it can cause skin cancer and eye diseases. [1]

(ii) (a) Differences between Nuclear Fission and Nuclear Fusion

Nuclear Fission	Nuclear Fusion
It involves breaking of a heavy nucleus into lighter nuclei into a heavy two light nuclei.	It involves binding of two nucleus.
It is carried out by the bombardment of two thermal lighter nuclei upto neutrons over a heavy nucleus.	It is carried out by heating at an extreme temperature.
It is a chain reaction.	It is not a chain reaction.
It is a controlled process.	It is an uncontrolled process.

[3]

(b) Disposal of nuclear waste should be grounded in deep mines because there is a risk of nuclear accidents causing due to leakage of nuclear radiation.

(iii) (a) Number of proton in atomic nucleus $A = 84$

$\therefore$ Atomic number of A, $Z = 84$

Number of neutron, $N = 128$

$\therefore$ Mass number of A,

$$M = Z + N$$
$$= 84 + 128 = 212$$

$\therefore$ When an α-particle is emitted from a nucleus, then its mass number is decreased by 4 units and atomic number is decreased by 2 units.

$\therefore \quad {}_{84}A^{212} \xrightarrow{\alpha} {}_{82}B^{208}$ [1]

(b) When a β-particle is emitted from a nucleus, then atomic number is increased by one unit and mass number is unaffected.

$\therefore \quad {}_{82}B^{208} \xrightarrow{\beta} {}_{83}C^{208}$ [1]

(c) Mass number of nucleus $A = Z + N$

$= 84 + 128 = 212$ [1]

(d) There is no change in the composition of C by the emission of γ-radiations. [1]

Chapter Assessment

1 Mark Questions

1. The heaviest nuclear radiation is **[2022 (Sem-II)]**
   (a) X-radiation (b) α-radiation
   (c) γ-radiation (d) β-radiation
2. Which of the following species represent isotonic pair?
   (a) ${}_1^1H$ and ${}_1^2H$ (b) ${}_1^3H$ and ${}_2^3He$
   (c) ${}_3^7Li$ and ${}_4^8Be$ (d) None of these
3. The radiation with maximum penetrating power is
   (a) γ-ray (b) β-ray
   (c) X-ray (d) α-ray
4. The nuclear radiation which gets deflected towards negatively charged plate in an electric field is
   (a) gamma (b) ultraviolet
   (c) beta (d) alpha
5. Which of the following rays can give rise to pair production?
   (a) γ-rays (b) X-rays
   (c) β-rays (d) α-rays
6. A nuclear fission is given below
   $${}_{92}^{235}U + {}_0^1n \xrightarrow[\text{Fission}]{\text{Nuclear}} {}_{56}^{139}Ba + {}_{36}^{94}Kr + Q + X$$
   where, X represents number of neutrons produced in the nuclear fission.
   The value of X is
   (a) 2 (b) 3
   (c) 4 (d) 1

2 Marks Questions

7. How can you define the term isobar? Give its one example.
8. The nucleus ${}_{84}X^{202}$ emits an α-particle and forms the nucleus Y. Represent this change in the form of an equation.
9. In order to form an element C, an element D disintegrates by α-emission and the new element suffers two further disintegrations, both by β-emission. Explain the fact that the new elements P and Q are isobars.
10. "We usually use isotopes emitting γ-radiations as radioactive tracers in medical science". Justify the statement with the help of a reason.
11. An element X changes to another element Y with the emission of β-particles. Write down the equation showing changes in the nucleus. Take, the proton number and mass nuclear of X as Z and A, respectively. **[2002]**

Structured Questions

12. (i) The diagram given below is showing a radioactive source R in a thick walled container having a narrow opening. The radiations pass through an electric field between the plates C and D.

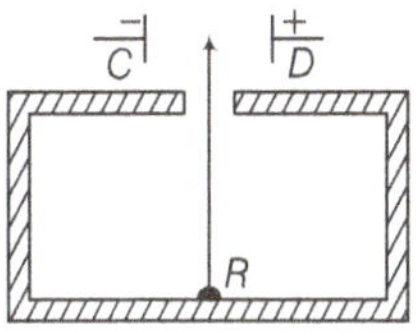

   (a) Consider the above diagram and complete it in order to show the paths of α, β and γ-radiations.
   (b) What is the reason of keeping the source R in a thick lead walled container with narrow opening? **[3]**

   (ii) Briefly mention any three precautions while handling the source of γ-radiation? **[3]**

   (iii) Uranium nucleus ${}_{92}^{238}U$ undergoes several disintegrations and ultimately decays to lead nucleus ${}_{82}^{206}Pb$. How many α and β-particles are emitted? **[4]**
13. (i) State any two safety measures that should be taken while establishing a nuclear power plant. **[3]**

   (ii) Write the thermonuclear reaction occurring in the sun. **[3]**

   (iii) (a) Explain two sources of harmful radiations.
   (b) How background radiations are produced? **[4]**
14. (i) Write the three scientific use of radioisotopes. **[3]**

   (ii) What do you mean by background radiation? Write the name of four sources of background radiation.

   (iii) (a) What is nuclear energy? **[2022 (Sem-II)]**
   (b) After emission of a nuclear radiation, the atomic number of the daughter nucleus increases by 1. Identify the nuclear radiation.
   (c) Write a nuclear reaction indicating the nuclear change mentioned in (b).
   (d) What is the special name given to the parent and daughter nucleus when this radiation is emitted?

For Solutions Scan the Code

Olympiad Section*

Brain Teasing Questions of Olympiad Pattern

1. In fission of one U-235 nucleus, the loss in mass is 0.2 amu. Calculate the energy released.
   (a) 186.2 MeV
   (b) 182.6 MeV
   (c) 156.4 MeV
   (d) 189.1 MeV

2. Heavy stable nuclei have more neutrons than protons. This is because of the fact that
   (a) neutrons are heavier than protons
   (b) electrostatic force between protons are repulsive
   (c) neutrons decay into protons through beta decay
   (d) nuclear forces between neutrons are weaker than that between protons

3. M_x and M_y denote the atomic masses of the parent and the daughter nuclei respectively, in radioactive decay. The Q-value for a β^--decay is Q_1 and that for a β^+-decay is Q_2.

   If m_e denotes the mass of an electron, then which of the following statements is correct?
   (a) $Q_1 = (M_x - M_y)c^2$ and $Q_2 = (M_x - M_y - 2m_e)c^2$
   (b) $Q_1 = (M_x - M_y)c^2$ and $Q_2 = (M_x - M_y)c^2$
   (c) $Q_1 = (M_x - M_y - 2m_e)c^2$ and $Q_2 = (M_x - M_y + 2c_e)c^2$
   (d) $Q_1 = (M_x - M_y + 2m_e)c^2$ and $Q_2 = (M_x - m_y + 2m_e)c^2$

4. The gravitational force between a H-atom and another particle of mass m will be given by Newton's law $F = G\dfrac{M \cdot m}{r^2}$, where r is in metre and
   (a) $M = m_{\text{proton}} + m_{\text{electron}}$
   (b) $M = m_{\text{proton}} + m_{\text{electron}} - \dfrac{B}{c^2}$ $(B = 13.6 \text{ eV})$
   (c) M is not relate to the mass of the hydrogen atom
   (d) $M = m_{\text{proton}} + m_{\text{electron}} - \dfrac{|V|}{c^2}$ ($|V|$ = magnitude of the potential energy of electron in the H-atom)

5. A stationary radioactive nucleus of mass 210 units disintegrates into an α-particle of mass 4 units and residual nucleus of mass 206 units. If the kinetic energy of the α-particle is E, then the kinetic energy of the residual nucleus is
   (a) $\left(\dfrac{2}{105}\right)E$ (b) $\left(\dfrac{2}{103}\right)E$
   (c) $\left(\dfrac{103}{105}\right)E$ (d) $\left(\dfrac{103}{2}\right)E$

6. The Sun radiates energy in all directions. The average radiation received on the earth surface from the Sun 1.4 kW/m^2. The average Earth-Sun distance 1.5×10^{11} m. The mass lost by the Sun per day is (1 day = 86400 s)
   (a) 4.4×10^9 kg (b) 7.6×10^{14} kg
   (c) 3.8×10^{12} kg (d) 3.8×10^{14} kg

7. In a nuclear reactor, 48 kJ of energy is produced per minute. If the energy released per fission is 3.2×10^{-11}J, then the number of fission which would betaking place in a reactor per second will be
   (a) 2.5×10^{13} (b) 4.5×10^{12}
   (c) 2.56×10^{11} (d) 3.25×10^{15}

8. The mass number of four different elements A, B, C and D are 2, 35, 135 and 239, respectively. Which of them would provide the most suitable for nuclear fission?
   (a) A (b) C (c) D (d) B

9. The amount of energy released in the fission reaction of a single $_{92}U^{235}$ nuclear is about 100 MeV. If $_{92}U^{235}$ reactor operating at power of 16 W, then rate of fission is
   (a) 10^{11} s^{-1} (b) 10^{12} s^{-1}
   (c) 10^{13} s^{-1} (d) 10^{10} s^{-1}

10. The ratio of the size of the atom to the size of the nucleus is typically **[2001]**
    (a) 10 (b) 10^2 (c) 10^4 (d) 10^8

ANSWERS

1. (a)	2. (b)	3. (a)	4. (b)	5. (b)	6. (d)	7 (a)	8 (c)	9 (b)	10 (c)

* *These questions may or may not be asked in the examination, have been given just for additional practice required for olympiads Scholarship Exams etc. For detailed explanations refer Page No. 272.*

Explanations to Olympiad

Chapter 1. Force

1. (a) Mass of the particle = m

As, the particle is executing a uniform circular motion,

it will be accelerated with $\frac{v^2}{r}$ directed towards the centre as it is moving with a circle of radius r and moving with uniform speed v.

According to Newton's second law of motion,

centripetal force, $F_c = \frac{mv^2}{r}$.

Rearranging, it can be written as

$$F_c = \frac{mv^2}{r} \cdot \frac{m}{m} = \frac{(mv)^2}{mr} = \frac{p^2}{mr}$$

Hence, option (a) is correct.

2. (d) When a car of mass M passes through a convex bridge of radius r with velocity v, it exerts a force on it, in following ways

(i) The weight mg of the car acting vertically downwards.

(ii) Normal reaction R of the road on the car, acting vertically downwards. As the radius of the bridge is r, hence the centripetal force is along the surface of the road, towards the centre of turn.

Hence, the magnitude of force = $Mg - \frac{Mv^2}{r}$.

3. (c) As the vehicle is moving in forward direction, but wheels are revolving, i.e. executing circular motion. Hence, a vehicle and its wheels execute translatory and rotatory motions.

4. (c) A nut cracker is an example of second class of lever, where fulcrum is one side and load (nut) is between fulcrum and effort.

According to the question,

Moment of force = $F \times d$

$$= 120 \times \frac{50}{100} = 60 \text{ N-m}$$

As the same moment of force acts on the nut cracker by applying a force of 40N, then

Moment of force = $F \times d$

$$60 = 40 \times d$$

$$\Rightarrow \quad d = \frac{60}{40} = \frac{3}{2} = 1.5 \text{ m}$$

5. (b) Force in linear motion has its analogue with torque in rotational motion, because moment of force = force × the perpendicular distance of the line of action of the force moving towards the point.

6. (b) Essential characteristics of equilibrium is the total force, i.e. the vector sum of all forces acting on the rigid body is r.

i.e. $\quad \sum_{i=1}^{n} F_i = 0 = F_1 + F_2 + \ldots + F_n$

As, mass cannot be 0, hence acceleration equals to zero.

7. (b) Length of seconds hand of a clock = 10 cm.

$\therefore$ Angular speed, $\omega = \frac{\theta}{t}$

But $\quad \theta = 2\pi, t = 60$ s

$$\therefore \quad \omega = \frac{2\pi}{60} = \frac{\pi}{30} \text{ rads}^{-1}$$

8. (a) We know that, centripetal force,

$$F_C = \frac{mv^2}{r}$$

Hence, $\quad F_1 = \frac{m_1 v_1^2}{r_1^2}$ for mass m_1 ...(i)

and $\quad F_2 = \frac{m_2 v_2^2}{r_2^2}$ for mass m_2 ...(ii)

Hence, the ratio of their centripetal force is obtained dividing Eqs. (i) and (ii).

i.e. $$\frac{F_1}{F_2} = \frac{\frac{m_1 v_1^2}{r_1}}{\frac{m_2 v_2^2}{r_2}}$$

But as the masses of both the particles are same, i.e. $m_1 = m_2 = m$ and speeds are also same. i.e. $v_1 = v_2 = v$.

Then, $$\frac{F_1}{F_2} = \frac{mv^2}{r_1} \times \frac{r_2}{mv^2} = \frac{r_2}{r_1}$$

9. (c) From the given figure in questions,

(i) **At point *P*** Two torques τ_1 and τ_2 acting from distances 0.05 m and (0.2 – 0.05 = 0.15) 0.15 m.

Hence, torque, τ_1 = force × distance

= 25 × 0.05 = 1.25 N, clockwise

and torque, τ_2 = 25 × 0.15

= 3.75 N, clockwise

Hence, (net) total torque = $\tau_1 + \tau_2$ = 1.25 + 3.75

= 5 N-m, clockwise

(ii) **At point *Q*** Two torques τ_1 and τ_2 will be

$$\tau_1 = F_1 \times 0 = 0$$

$$\tau_2 = 25 \times 0.2 = 25 \times \frac{2}{10} = 5 \text{ N, clockwise}$$

Hence, net torque = $\tau_1 + \tau_2$ = 0 + 5 = 5 N-m, clockwise

10. (b) To open the gate with least force, it should be applied at the maximum distance from the axis of rotation or hinges.

Distance of point of application of force,

$$d = 3 \text{ m}$$

Moment of force, $\tau = F \times r$ ... (i)

As, the gate is opened by a force of 200 N initially. So,

$\therefore \quad F_1 = 200$ N

and $\quad r_1 = \frac{1}{2} \times 3 = 1.5$ m

$\therefore$ Torque needed to open the gate, $\tau = F_1 \times r_1$

$= 200 \times 1.5 = 300$ N-m

From Eq. (i), $\quad 300 = F \times 3 \Rightarrow F = 100$ N

Hence, least force required is 100 N.

11. (*b*) The given situation is shown below.

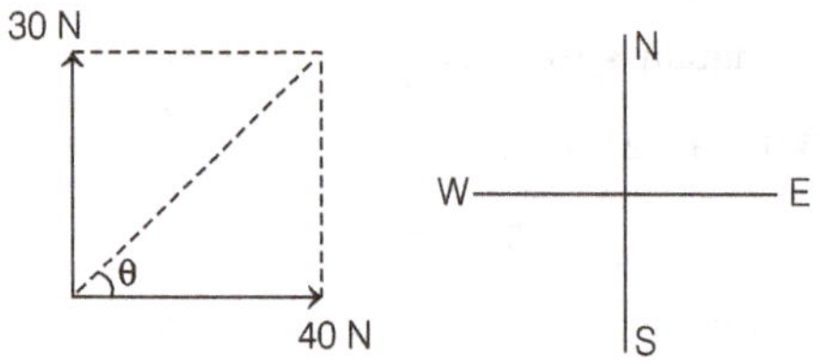

Magnitude of resultant force,

$$F = \sqrt{30^2 + 40^2} = 50 \text{ N}$$

If resultant force makes an angle of θ, then

$$\theta = \tan^{-1}\left(\frac{30}{40}\right) = \tan^{-1}(0.75) = 37°$$

$$\therefore \text{Acceleration, } a = \frac{F}{m} = \frac{50}{15} = 3.33 \text{ ms}^{-2}$$

12. (*a*) Time taken by particle *Q* to make one revolution around *P* = Time taken by particle *Q* to complete one revolution – Time taken by *P* to complete one revolution.

= 5 min – 2 min

= 3 min

Chapter 2. Work, Power and Energy

1. (*c*) The graph given below gives the force-distance variation.

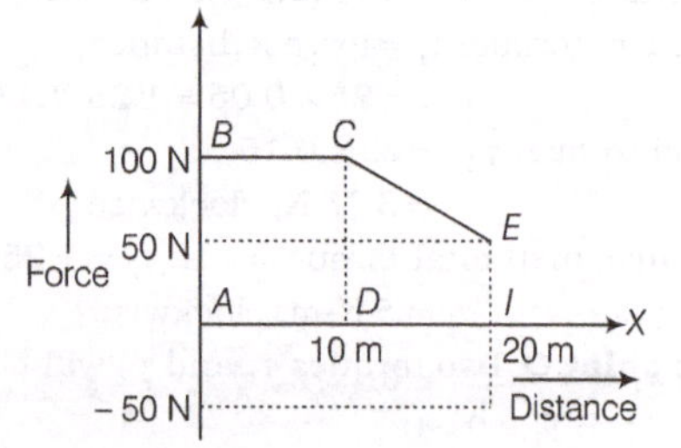

Given, frictional force = 50 N

As, it opposes motions, acts in opposite direction.

Work done by the woman = W_F = Area of rectangle *ABCD* + Area of trapezium *CEID*

$= 100 \times 10 + \frac{1}{2} \times (100 + 50) \times 10$

$= 1000 + 750 = 1750$ N

Work done by the frictional force is – 1000 N.

Hence, net work done = 1750 – 1000

= 750 J

Hence, option (c) is correct.

2. (*c*) Given, $m = 0.5$ kg, $v = ax^{\frac{3}{2}}$

where, $\quad a = 5 \text{ ms}^{-2}$

As we know from work-energy theorem, work done by net force acting on a body is equal to its change in KE. If velocity of the body corresponds to $x = 0$ and $x = 2$ m and represented as u and v, then

$$W = \frac{1}{2}mv^2 - \frac{1}{2}mu^2 = \frac{1}{2}m(v^2 - u^2)$$

$$u = a \cdot (0)^{3/2} = 0 \quad (\because v = u + at)$$

$$= a \cdot (2)^{3/2} = a\,2^{3/2}$$

$$W = \frac{1}{2} \times 0.5\,[\{a(2)^{3/2}\}^2 - 0]$$

$$= \frac{1}{2} \times 0.5 \times a^2 \times (2)^3$$

$$= \frac{1}{2} \times 0.5 \times (5)^2 \times 8 = 50 \text{ J}$$

3. (*b*) For *P*, $m = 20$ kg, $v = 5$ m/s

For *Q*, $m = 5$ kg, $v = 20$ m/s

$$\therefore \quad \frac{\text{Momentum of } P}{\text{Momentum of } Q} = \frac{20 \times 5}{5 \times 20} = \frac{1}{1}$$

4. (*c*) Given, mass of boy = 40 kg

Vertical distance, $h = 12$ m

Time interval = 40 s

$$\text{Hence, power} = \frac{\text{work done}}{\text{time}}$$

$$= \frac{mgh}{t} = \frac{40 \times 10 \times 12}{40} = 120 \text{ W}$$

5. (*c*) Given, kinetic energy of electron = 10 keV

Kinetic energy of proton = 100 keV

Mass of electron, $m_e = 9.11 \times 10^{-31}$ kg

Mass of proton, $m_p = 1.67 \times 10^{-27}$ kg

As, $\quad K = \frac{1}{2}mv^2 \text{ or } v = \sqrt{\frac{2K}{m}}$

$$\text{Hence, } \frac{v_e}{v_p} = \sqrt{\frac{K_e}{K_p} \times \frac{m_p}{m_e}}$$

$$= \sqrt{\frac{10 \times 1.67 \times 10^{-27}}{100 \times 9.11 \times 10^{-31}}}$$

$$= \sqrt{\frac{167}{911} \times 10^3} = 13.54$$

$$\Rightarrow \quad v_e = 13.54\,v_p$$

Hence, electron is travelling faster.

6. (*c*) As, the body is moving along a straight line, delivering constant power, distance moved by the body,

$$s = ut + \frac{1}{2}at^2 \Rightarrow s = \frac{1}{2}at^2 \quad (\because u = 0)$$

$$\Rightarrow \quad s^2 = \frac{1}{4}a^2t^4 \quad \text{...(i)}$$

$$\text{But we know, power} = \frac{\text{work}}{\text{time}}$$

$$= \frac{F \times s}{t} = F \times v \quad \left(\because v = \frac{s}{t}\right)$$

$$P = F \times v \quad (\because v = u + at, \text{ for } u = 0, v = at)$$

$= ma \times at \Rightarrow P = ma^2t$

$\Rightarrow \quad a^2t = \frac{P}{m}$ ...(ii)

Substituting $a^2t = \frac{P}{m}$ in Eq. (i), we get

$$s^2 = \frac{1}{2}a^2t \cdot t^3$$

Now, $a^2t = \frac{P}{m}$, substituting above equation,

$$s^2 = \left(\frac{1}{2} \cdot \frac{P}{m}\right)t^3 \Rightarrow s = \text{constant } t^{3/2}$$

Hence, $s \propto t^{3/2}$

7. (*b*) Given, power of the pump = 200 W

Mass of water = 2 kg

Depth, $h = 10$ m

$\therefore$ Power = Force × Velocity

$$\text{Velocity} = \frac{\text{Power}}{\text{Force}} = \frac{200}{mg} = \frac{200}{2 \times 9.8}$$

$$= \frac{1000}{98} \text{ m/s} = 10.2 \text{ m/s}$$

8. (*c*) $\because$ Power = Force × Velocity

Velocity has to be increased by twice mass of water flowing from same pipe, hence

$$\frac{\text{mass}}{\text{time}} = \frac{\text{volume} \times \text{density}}{\text{time}} = \frac{v \times d}{t}$$

$$= \frac{\text{area} \times \text{length} \times \text{density}}{\text{time}}$$

$$= a \times \rho \times \text{velocity}$$

$$\text{Rate of increase of KE} = \frac{mv^2}{2 \times \text{time}}$$

$$= \frac{A \times \rho \times \text{velocity} \times v^2}{2} = \frac{A \times \rho \times v^2}{2}$$

Mass m flowing out per second can be increased to m_1, by increases v to v_1, then power increases for P to P_1.

$$\therefore \quad \frac{P_1}{P} = \frac{A \times \rho \times v_1^3}{A \times \rho \times v^3} = \frac{v_1^3}{v^3}$$

But given, $m_1 = 2m$, $v_1 = 2v$, then

$$\frac{P_1}{P} = 2^3 = 8$$

$$P_1 = 8P$$

9. (*c*) From law of conservation of momentum,

$$0 = m \times 16 + 2m \times v$$

$$v = -\ 8 \text{ ms}^{-1}$$

$$\text{Total kinetic energy} = \frac{1}{2}m_1v_1^2 + \frac{1}{2}m_2v_2^2$$

$$= \frac{1}{2} \times m \times (16)^2 + \frac{1}{2} \times 2m \times (8)^2$$

$$= \frac{1}{2}(256 + 128) \times m = 192 \text{ mJ}$$

10. (*d*) Given, $\frac{\text{kinetic energy (KE)}}{\text{potential energy (PE)}} = \frac{3}{4}$

$$\Rightarrow \quad \text{KE} = \frac{3}{4}\text{PE}$$

As, from the law of conservation of energy,

$$\text{KE} + \text{PE} = mgh$$

$$\Rightarrow \quad \frac{7}{4}\text{PE} = mgh$$

So, for height (h') from the ground, PE = mgh'

$$\Rightarrow \quad \frac{7}{4}mgh' = mgh \quad \text{or} \quad h' = \frac{4}{7}h$$

11. (*c*) Total load $w = mg = 60 \times 10 = 600$ N

Load arm = 70 cm = 0.7 m

Effort arm = 70 + 50 = 120 cm = 1.2 m

Now,

Load × Load arm = Effort × Effort arm

600 × 0.7 = Effort × 1.2

$$\Rightarrow \text{Effort} = \frac{600 \times 0.7}{1.2} = \frac{420}{1.2} = 350 \text{ N}$$

Work done = 350 × 0.5 = 175 J

12. (*d*) Given, net force on the car

$$F \propto t^2$$

$$\Rightarrow \quad \frac{m(v-u)}{t} \propto t^2 \qquad \left[\because F = \frac{\Delta p}{t} = \frac{m(v-u)}{t}\right]$$

$$\Rightarrow \quad \frac{mv}{t} \propto t^2 \qquad [\because u = 0]$$

$$\Rightarrow \quad v \propto t^3 \qquad [m = \text{constant}]$$

$$\Rightarrow \quad v = kt^3 \qquad \text{... (i) } [k = \text{constant}]$$

$\therefore$ kinetic energy of car

$$\text{KE} = \frac{1}{2}mv^2$$

$$\Rightarrow \quad \text{KE} = \frac{1}{2} \times m \times (kt^3)^2$$

$$\Rightarrow \quad \text{KE} = \frac{1}{2}mk^2t^6$$

$$\Rightarrow \quad \text{KE} \propto t^6$$

Chapter 3. Machines

1. (*b*) The mechanical advantage of a fixed pulley

$$= \frac{\text{Load } (L)}{\text{Effort } (E)}$$

Effort (force applied), $E = 70$ N

Weight of the bucket = mg

$$= 6 \times 10 = 60 \text{ N}$$

$$\text{Hence, mechanical advantage} = \frac{60}{70}$$

Hence, mechanical advantage = 0.86

2. (*c*) Mechanical Advantage (MA) given as

$$\text{MA} = \frac{\text{Load } (L)}{\text{Effort } (E)}$$

Hence, MA and efforts are inversely proportional to each other.

The MA of single fixed pulley = 1

For single movable pulley, MA = 2

Load on both the pulleys = 50 kgf

$\therefore$ Effort for single fixed pulley

$$= \frac{\text{Load}}{\text{MA}} = \frac{50}{1} = 50 \text{ kgf} \qquad \text{...(i)}$$

$$\text{Effort for single movable pulley} = \frac{\text{Load}}{\text{MA}} = \frac{50}{2}$$

$= 2.5$ kgf ...(ii)

On dividing Eq. (i) by Eq. (ii), we get

$$\frac{\text{Effort single fixed pulley}}{\text{Effort single movable pulley}} = \frac{50}{25} = \frac{2}{1}$$

Hence, $\frac{\text{effort for single movable pulley}}{\text{effort for single fixed pulley}} = \frac{1}{2}$

3. (*b*) As, velocity ratio $= \frac{\text{distance travelled by effort}}{\text{distance travelled by load}}$

Efficiency $= \frac{MA}{VR} = \frac{\text{Mechanical advantage}}{\text{Velocity ratio}}$

Given, VR = 5, efficiency = 75%

$$\Rightarrow \frac{75}{100} = \frac{MA}{5}$$

$$MA = 5 \times \frac{75}{100}$$

But, $MA = \frac{\text{load}}{\text{effort}} = \frac{L}{150 \text{ kgf}}$

$$L = 5 \times \frac{75}{100} \times 150 = \frac{1125}{2} = 562.5 \text{ kgf}$$

4. (*d*) Given, VR = 5, efficiency = 80%

$$\therefore \frac{MA}{VR} = \text{Efficiency}$$

$$80 = \frac{MA}{5}$$

$$\Rightarrow MA = \frac{80}{100} \times 5 = 4$$

5. (*d*) Given, MA = 4, load = 10 kgf

$= 10 \times 9.8$ N

Distance = 2 m, time = 10 s

$$\therefore \text{Power} = \frac{\text{Work done}}{\text{Time taken}}$$

$$MA = 4 = \frac{\text{Load}}{\text{Effort}} = \frac{10 \times 9.8}{E}$$

$$\text{Effort} = \frac{10 \times 9.8}{4}$$

Now, power $= \frac{\text{Work}}{\text{Time}} = \frac{F \times s}{t}$

$$= \frac{10 \times 9.8}{4} \times \frac{2}{10} = \frac{49}{10} = 4.9 \text{ W}$$

6. (*b*) Resistance due to movable parts of the machine and friction,

$$R = E(VR - AMA)$$

where, E = effort

and AMA = Actual Mechanical Advantage.

Given, $w = 400$ N, $d_L = 50$ cm $= 0.5$ m

$E = 100$ N, $\eta = 80\% = 0.8$

$$\Rightarrow AMA = \frac{L}{E} = \frac{w}{E} = \frac{400}{100} = 4$$

$$VR = \frac{AMA}{\eta} = \frac{4}{0.8} = 5$$

$$\therefore R = 100(5 - 4) = 100 \text{ N}$$

7. (*c*) Given, $E = 0.06$ N

Effort arm = 10 cm = 01 m

Load arm = 3 cm = 0.03 m

From principle of simple machine,

$L \times$ Load arm $= E \times$ Effort arm

$$\Rightarrow L = \frac{0.06 \times 0.1}{0.03} = 0.2 \text{ N}$$

So, the resistance offered by lemon is 0.2 N.

8. (*a*) Given, $L = 10 \times 10 = 100$ N

$E = 120$ N

$d_E = d_L = 5$ m

$$\therefore MA = \frac{L}{E} = \frac{100}{120} = 0.83$$

$$VR = \frac{d_E}{d_L} = \frac{5}{5} = 1$$

Efficiency, $\eta = \frac{MA}{VR} \times 100$

$= 0.83 \times 100$

$= 83\%$

9. (*d*) Given, number of pulley, $n = 8$

Load, $L = 1000$ kgf

Effort, $E = 250$ kgf

$$MA = \frac{\text{Load } (L)}{\text{Effort } (E)} = \frac{1000}{250} = 4$$

$$VR = \frac{d_E}{d_L} = \frac{s}{s/n} = n = 8$$

$$\therefore \frac{MA}{VR} = \frac{4}{8} = 0.5$$

10. (*a*) Given, load, $L = 10000$ N

Height, $h = 0.25$ m

Length of rod, $l = 0.3$ m

Work done on the load is equal to the work done by the effort.

$\Rightarrow L \times h = E \times$ Distance moved by rod

$= E \times 2\pi l$

$$\Rightarrow E = \frac{L \times h}{2\pi l} = \frac{10000 \times 0.25}{2\pi \times 0.3}$$

$= 1326.30 \text{ N} \approx 1326$ N

Chapter 4. Refraction of Light

1. (*b*) As we know, whenever incident light falls on the interface of glass slab for different values of i, the ratio $\frac{\sin i}{\sin r}$ = constant = refractive index. Thus, refractive index measures the light bending capacity or it measures ability of bending of light when light ray travels from one transparent medium to another medium.

If the light enters obliquely and angle of incidence is more, then angle of refraction will also increase, Hence, bending is directly proportional to the angle of incidence.

2. (*c*) As glass is an optically denser medium, it bends the light rays towards the normal. After refraction, when light emerge out of the denser medium like glass to the rarer medium like air, it bends away from the normal which is not shown in figure (c). Hence, it is not following rules of refraction.

3. (*d*) As the ray of light is entering a semi-circular glass block normal to curved surface, part of the light will be reflected following laws of reflections, $\angle i = \angle r$.

Part of the light will be refracted following laws of refraction at the glass-air interface.

4. (*a*) According to the definition of refractive index, $\mu = \frac{\sin i}{\sin r}$. As we know, when $\angle i$ increases, $\angle r$ also increases to keep the value of μ constant. Hence, it will show a linear increase, so graph (b), (c) are showing decrease, hence cannot be the possibilities. Graph (d) is not justified as value of $\sin i$ can be between 0 and 1.

5. (*c*) According to Snell's law,

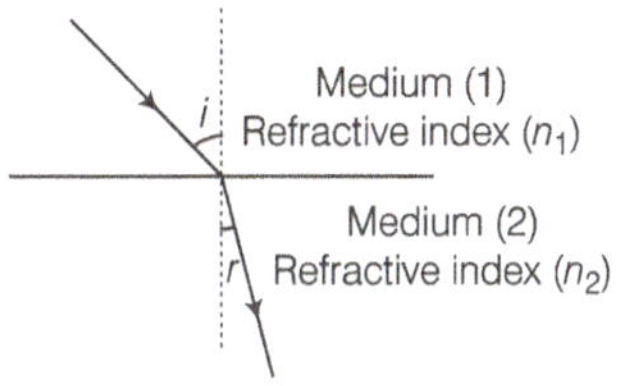

$n_1 \times \sin i = n_2 \times \sin r$

$$\therefore \quad \frac{\sin i}{\sin r} = \frac{n_2}{n_1}$$

6. (*d*) Velocity of light waves in material, $v = \nu\lambda$ ...(i)

Refractive index of material, $\mu = \frac{c}{v}$ ...(ii)

where, c is speed of light in vacuum or air

$$\Rightarrow \quad \mu = \frac{c}{\nu\lambda} \quad \text{...(iii)}$$

Given, $\nu = 2 \times 10^{-14}$ Hz, $\lambda = 5000$ Å $= 5000 \times 10^{-10}$ m

and $c = 3 \times 10^8$ ms^{-1}

From Eq. (iii), $\mu = \frac{3 \times 10^8}{2 \times 10^{14} \times 5000 \times 10^{-10}} = 3$

7. (*b*) Here, angle of incidence, $i = 45°$

$$\frac{\text{Lateral shift } (d)}{\text{Thickness of glass slab } (t)} = \frac{1}{\sqrt{3}}$$

Lateral shift, $d = \frac{t \sin \delta}{\cos r} = \frac{t \sin(i - r)}{\cos r}$

$$\Rightarrow \quad \frac{d}{t} = \frac{\sin(i - r)}{\cos r}$$

$$\Rightarrow \quad \frac{d}{t} = \frac{\sin i \cos r - \cos i \sin r}{\cos r}$$

$$\Rightarrow \quad \frac{d}{t} = \frac{\sin 45° \cos r - \cos 45° \sin r}{\cos r}$$

$$\Rightarrow \quad = \frac{\cos r - \sin r}{\sqrt{2} \cos r}$$

$$\Rightarrow \quad \frac{d}{t} = \frac{1}{\sqrt{2}}(1 - \tan r)$$

$$\Rightarrow \quad \frac{1}{\sqrt{3}} = \frac{1}{\sqrt{2}}(1 - \tan r)$$

$$\Rightarrow \quad \tan r = 1 - \frac{\sqrt{2}}{\sqrt{3}}$$

$$\therefore \quad r = \tan^{-1}\left(1 - \frac{\sqrt{2}}{\sqrt{3}}\right)$$

8. (*a*) Refractive index $= \frac{\text{Real depth}}{\text{Apparent depth}}$

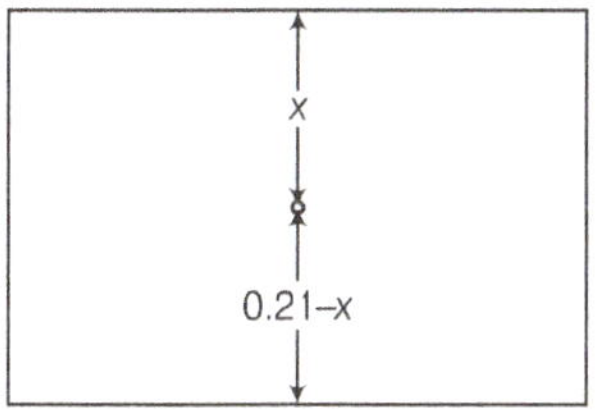

$$\therefore \quad \frac{x}{0.04} = \frac{0.21 - x}{0.10}$$

$$\Rightarrow \quad 0.21 \times 0.04 - x \times 0.04 = 0.10\,x$$

$$\Rightarrow \quad x = \frac{0.21 \times 0.04}{0.14} = 0.06 \text{ m}$$

9. (*a*) The given situation is shown in the figure.

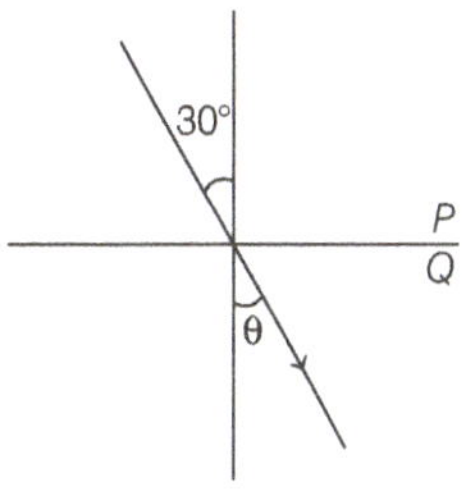

Given, $\mu_P = 1.5$

$$\Rightarrow \quad \mu_P = \frac{c}{v_P}$$

$$\Rightarrow \quad v_P = \frac{c}{\mu_P} \quad (v_P \rightarrow \text{speed of light in medium } P)$$

$$= \frac{3 \times 10^8}{1.5} = 2 \times 10^8 \text{ m/s}$$

Again, we know that,

$$\frac{\sin i}{\sin r} = {}_P\mu_Q = \frac{v_P}{v_Q}$$

$$\Rightarrow \quad \frac{\sin 30°}{\sin \theta} = \frac{v_P}{v_Q}$$

$$\Rightarrow v_Q = \frac{v_P \sin \theta}{\sin 30°} = \frac{2 \times 10^8 \times 7}{\frac{1}{2} \times 20}$$

$$= 14 \times 10^7 = 1.4 \times 10^8 \text{ m/s}$$

10. (*b*) When white light is incident on one of the refracting faces of a prism, then at normal and oblique incidence, the blue light slows down more than red light inside the prism because wavelength of blue light is less than that of the red light. Hence Statement I and IV are correct.

For oblique incidence, blue light bends more than red light because its wavelength is less than that of red light. Hence, Statement III is correct.

Chapter 5. Lenses

1. (a) For rays coming from infinity to a lens having different refractive indices μ_1 and μ_2 will form two images at two different foci.

2. (a) Using the lens formula,

$$\frac{1}{v}-\frac{1}{u}=\frac{1}{f}$$

$$\Rightarrow \quad \frac{u}{v}-1=\frac{u}{f} \quad \text{...(i)}$$

As, $$m=\frac{v}{u}=n \text{ (given)}$$

$$\Rightarrow \quad \frac{u}{v}=\frac{1}{n}$$

Substituting the above values in Eq. (i), we get

$$\Rightarrow \quad \left(\frac{1}{n}-1\right)=\frac{u}{f} \Rightarrow u=\left(\frac{1-n}{n}\right)f$$

3. (d) When an object is at infinity, the nature of image formed by concave lens is virtual, erect and highly diminished.

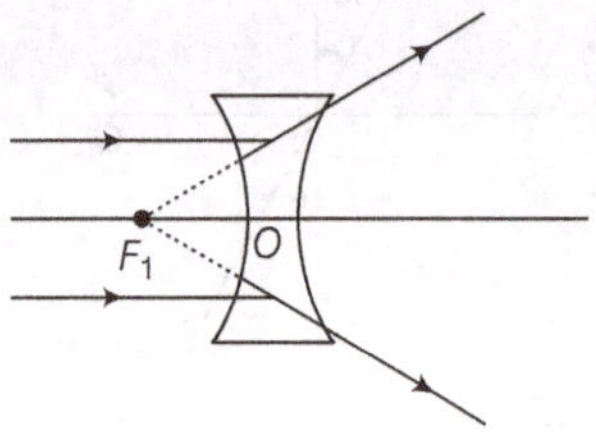

4. (a) All the distances are measured from the optical centre of the lens according to the sign convention of lens.

5. (c) Image distance, $v = 36$ cm

Focal length, $f = 12$ cm

Using lens formula,

$$\frac{1}{v}-\frac{1}{u}=\frac{1}{f}$$

$$\Rightarrow \quad \frac{1}{u}=\frac{1}{v}-\frac{1}{f}$$

$$=\frac{1}{36}-\frac{1}{12}$$

$$\Rightarrow \quad \frac{1}{u}=\frac{1-3}{36}=\frac{-2}{36}$$

$$\Rightarrow \quad \frac{1}{u}=\frac{-1}{18} \Rightarrow u=-18 \text{ cm}$$

Here, position of object will be between 12 cm to 24 cm from the lens as image is formed beyond $2F$.

6. (b) If two convex lenses are in contact with each other, the equivalent focal length (f) and power of the combination (P) can be calculated as

$$\frac{1}{f}=\frac{1}{f_1}+\frac{1}{f_2} \text{ and } P=P_1+P_2$$

It increases the sharpness of image and converging power.

7. (d) As $\mu_2 > \mu_1$, hence in the interface of material of refractive index μ_1 and convex lens, i.e. from denser to rarer medium, parallel ray will bend away from normal and for $\mu_1 > \mu_3$, i.e. interface of material of refractive index μ_1 and μ_3, ray will become convergent, towards the normal, hence a convergent and a divergent beam is produced.

8. (c) Given, focal length, $f = -20$ cm

Object distance, $u = -25$ cm

Object height, $h_o = 10$ cm

Using lens formula,

$$\frac{1}{v}-\frac{1}{u}=\frac{1}{f}$$

$$\frac{1}{v}=\frac{1}{f}+\frac{1}{u}$$

$$=\frac{1}{-20}+\frac{1}{(-25)}$$

$$=\frac{-5-4}{100}=\frac{-9}{100}$$

$$v=\frac{-100}{9}\text{cm}=-11.11 \text{ cm}$$

Magnification, $m=\frac{h_i}{h_o}=\frac{v}{u}$

Image height, $h_i=\frac{v}{u}\cdot h_o$

$$=\frac{-11.11}{-25}\times 10$$

$$h_i = 4.4$$

As, magnification is positive. So, nature of image is virtual, erect and diminshed. Due to this, it is not possible to capture its image.

9. (d) Given, $P_1 = -3.5$ D, $P_2 = +1.0$ D

As, both the lenses are in contact, combination of lenses will have power

$$=P_1+P_2=-3.5+1.0$$

$$=-2.5 \text{ D}$$

Hence, focal length,

$$f=\frac{1}{P_{comb}}=-\frac{1}{2.5}\text{ D}$$

$$=-\frac{1000}{25}=-40 \text{ cm}$$

10. (d) Given, f_1 of convex lens = 40 cm

f_2 of first concave lens = – 40 cm

f_3 of second concave lens = – 15 cm

Hence, total focal lengths of the combination

$$=f_1+f_2+f_3$$

$$=40-40-15$$

$$=-15 \text{ cm}$$

As, $$P=\frac{1}{f}=-\frac{1}{15}$$

$$=-\frac{100}{15}$$

$$=-6.67 \text{ D}$$

11. (c) According to the given diagram, focal length of the lens = 6 cm.
As, the object is between optical centre and focus, the image formed will be virtual, erect (upright) and magnified.

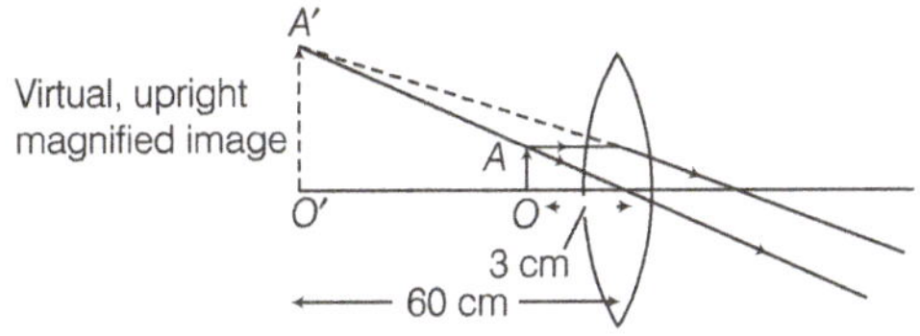

12. (a) This lens behaves as a convex lens and is used to correct hypermetropia or long-sightedness.

13. (c) Given, $u = -45$ cm

Applying lens formula, $\frac{1}{v} - \frac{1}{u} = \frac{1}{f}$

$$\frac{1}{v} - \frac{1}{u} = \frac{1}{f} \Rightarrow \frac{1}{90} - \frac{1}{(-45)} = \frac{1}{f}$$

$$\frac{1}{90} + \frac{1}{45} = \frac{1}{f} \Rightarrow \frac{1+2}{90} = \frac{1}{f}$$

$$\therefore \quad f = \frac{90}{3} = 30 \text{ cm}$$

$$\therefore \text{ Power, } P = \frac{1}{f} = \frac{100}{30} \text{ D} = 3.33 \text{ D}$$

14. (d) Green filter will allow green colour while red filter will allow red colour, so image will contain both the colours. Hence, image will be yellow.

Chapter 6. Spectrum of Light

1. (b) Yes, a passenger in an aeroplane may see a rainbow as concentric circles. Sometimes many people confuse this phenomena of rainbow with glory which is caused by interference effects between particles in a cloud, not reflection and refraction in raindrops from a storm.

2. (a) As, $\lambda_{red} > \lambda_{blue}$
and $v = \nu\lambda$ (ν is same for red and blue)
Then, $v_{red} > v_{blue}$, so red light is slowed down less and refracted less.

3. (c) When white light comprises of seven colours refract through glass prism, then a band of seven colours is obtained in which red bends the least, has maximum velocity and violet colour of light bends maximum, has minimum velocity.

4. (d) All the statements given are correct because sky appears blue due to scattering of light due to atmosphere. Smoke and dust particles in the atmosphere cause greyish appearance of sky.
Red has the maximum wavelength in the visible spectrum, hence velocity of red is more than other primary colour, according to Rayleigh's scattering, amount of scattering $\propto \frac{1}{\lambda^4}$, hence red scatters the least.

5. (b) To get white light from recombination of prism, both the prism should be placed apex to base.

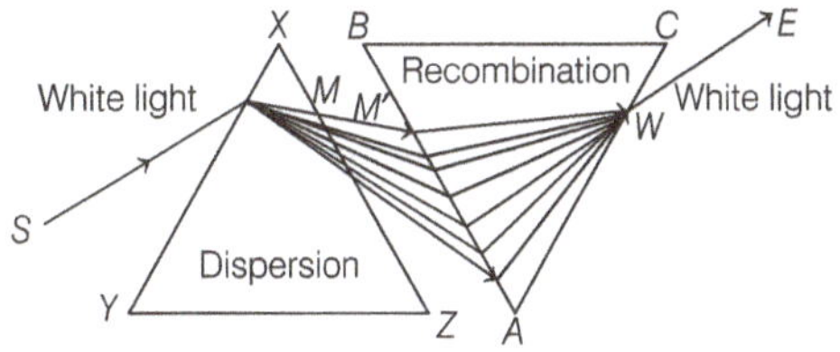

Statement I is incorrect (false).
Statement II is correct as dispersive power,

$$\omega = \frac{\mu_V - \mu_R}{(\mu - 1)}$$

It depends on (a) angle of prism, (b) nature of material used.
Hence, water's refractive index is more than air, so dispersive power decreases.
Statement III Tyndall effect is scattering, of light when it passes through colloidal solution, where size of the particles is relatively larger.
Sunlight comes down through the clouds, showing Tyndall effect because earth's atmosphere is a heterogeneous, mixture of minute particles of smoke.
Statement IV is also correct as yellow light scatters comparatively less and has comparatively low wavelength, visibility also more.

6. (c) Though violet has the smallest wavelength, but colour of sky is blue because our eyes are more sensitive to blue colour and less sensitive to violet colour. Most of the violet rays are absorbed by the atmosphere.

7. (d) According to the Snell's law,

$$\text{Refractive index, } \mu = \frac{\text{Speed of light in air}}{\text{Speed of light in medium}}$$

$$1.5 = \frac{3 \times 10^8}{v}$$

$$\Rightarrow \quad v = \frac{3 \times 10^8}{1.5} = 2 \times 10^8 \text{ m/s}$$

8. (b) One of the condition for formation of rainbow is to looking at the sky through water with sun (source) behind observer, total internal reflection can take place in rainbow formation.

Chapter 7. Sound

1. (d) The sound level in dB is expressed as

$$\beta = 10 \log_{10}\left(\frac{I}{I_0}\right)$$

If β_1 and β_2 are the sound levels and I_1 and I_2 are the intensities in the two cases.

$$\beta_2 - \beta_1 = 10\left[\log_{10}\left(\frac{I_2}{I_0}\right) - \log_{10}\left(\frac{I_1}{I_0}\right)\right]$$

or $$30 = 10 \log_{10}\left(\frac{I_2}{I_1}\right) \text{ or } \frac{I_2}{I_1} = 10^3$$

As, the intensity is proportional to the square of the pressure amplitude, we have

$$\frac{p_2}{p_1} = \sqrt{\frac{I_2}{I_1}}$$

$$= \sqrt{1000} \approx 32$$

Relation between intensity and pressure amplitude of sound waves $I \propto p_0^2$

where, p_0 = pressure amplitude.

2. (*d*) Statements I, III and IV are incorrect about note with high pitch. Pitch is the characteristics of sound by which we can distinguish between different sounds of the same loudness. High pitch sound corresponds to more number of compressions and rarefactions, *i.e.* higher the pitch, higher is the frequency. As $v = \nu\lambda$, hence higher is the frequency lower will be the wavelength.

3. (*d*) Percussion instruments produce sound when its membrane is struck, sound will be louder when struck with greater force. When vibrating surface is touched, then the sound will stop. Faint sound can also be produced by striking the membrane gently.

4. (*c*) Initially, sound wave has wavelength = λ.

Now, speed, $v = \nu\lambda$ ...(i)

where, ν is the frequency of sound wave.

Now, in another medium, let the speed = $2v$

Then, $v_1 = 2v = \nu\lambda_1$ ...(ii)

On dividing Eq. (ii) by Eq. (i), we get

$$\frac{v_1}{v} = \frac{2v}{v} = \frac{\nu\lambda_1}{\nu\lambda}$$

$$\lambda_1 = 2\lambda$$

5. (*b*) The source of sound creates a disturbance in the medium which travels through the medium. The particles of the medium do not move forward but the disturbance is carried forward. Hence, statement I is false.

Progressive wave or travelling wave moves away from the source

Statement II is true.

In compression, density of particles is more in a longitudinal wave. Hence, statement III is true. During tsunami, shock waves propagate.

Statement IV is false.

In water waves, ripples are created by the oscillatory movement of particles.

6. (*b*) As, $I = \frac{p^2}{2\rho v}$

where, p = pressure amplitude, I = intensity, ρ = density

and v = velocity.

i.e. $I \propto p^2$

$$\Rightarrow \quad \frac{I_1}{I_2} = \frac{p_1^2}{p_2^2}$$

$$\Rightarrow \quad I_2 = \frac{p_2^2}{p_1^2} \cdot I_1 = \frac{2.5\times10^{-2}\times2.5\times10^{-2}\times5\times10^{-7}}{2\times10^{-2}\times2\times10^{-2}\times100}$$

$$= \frac{25\times25}{80}\times10^{-7}$$

$$= \frac{625}{80}\times10^{-7}$$

$$= 7.8\times10^{-7}\ \text{W/m}^2$$

7. (*b*) Given, time, $t = 4$ s

Speed of sound, $(v) = 330\ \text{ms}^{-1}$

Sound has to travel twice the distance $(2d)$. From the cracker to the cliff and from cliff to the cracker.

Therefore, distance $(2d) = v \times t$

$$2d = 330\times4 \Rightarrow d = 660\ \text{m}$$

8. (*c*) Given, length of the corridor = 86 m

Time taken from the blast of fifth echo = 2.5 s

For five echoes, the sound wave must travel to and from 5 times.

Therefore, total distance $(d) = 86\times10 = 860$ m

Speed of the sound $= \frac{\text{Distance}}{\text{Time}} = \frac{860}{2.5} = 344\ \text{ms}^{-1}$

9. (*d*) Given, frequency, $\nu = 5$ Hz

Time period $= \frac{1}{5}$ s

Time period for 8 vibrations $= \frac{8}{5}$ s

Velocity of the wave = $340\ \text{ms}^{-1}$

Distance travelled by the wave

$$= 340\times\frac{8}{5} = 68\times8$$

$$= 544\ \text{m}$$

Thus, the distance between the pendulum and cliff

$$= \frac{544}{2} = 272\ \text{m}$$

10. (*b*) The natural voices of men, women and children are different and can be distinguished due their different frequency (or pitch). The frequency of the voice depends upon the length of the vocal cord. The vocal cord of a man is about 20 mm long and that for woman is 5 mm long whereas the length of vocal cord of a child is very small.

11. (*a*) Distance travelled by sound in first echo

$s_1 = 30 + 30 = 60$ m

$\therefore$ Time taken, $t_1 = \frac{s_1}{u} = \frac{60}{360} = \frac{1}{6}$ s

In second echo, distance travelled by sound

$s_2 = 45 + 45 = 90$ cm

$\therefore$ Time taken, $t_2 = \frac{90}{360} = \frac{1}{4}$ s

In third echo, disfance travelled by found

$s_3 = 30 + 75 + 45 = 150$ m

$\therefore$ Time taken, $t_3 = \frac{s_3}{v} = \frac{150}{360} = \frac{5}{12}$ s

In fourth echo, disfance travelled by found

$s_4 = 45 + 75 + 30 = 150$ m

$\therefore$ Time taken, $t_4 = \frac{s_4}{v} = \frac{150}{360} = \frac{5}{12}$ s

Chapter 8. Electricity

1. (*d*) Possible combination and their R_{eq} is given as

$\Rightarrow R_{eq} = 9\ \Omega$

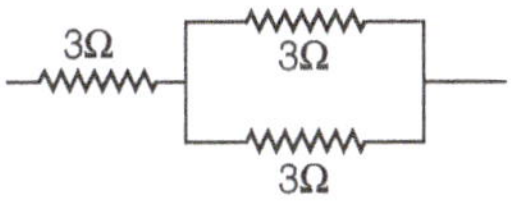

$\Rightarrow R_{eq} = 4.5\ \Omega$

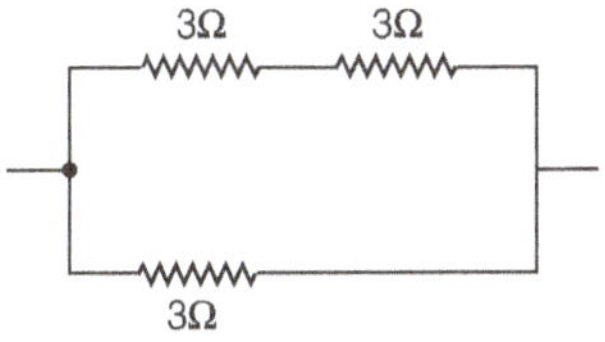

$\Rightarrow R_{eq} = 2\ \Omega$

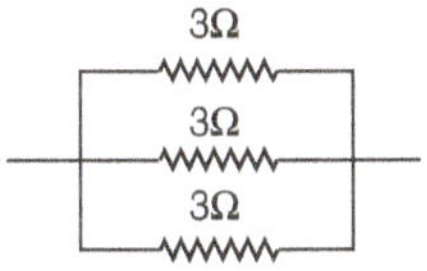

$\Rightarrow R_{eq} = 1\ \Omega$

2. (*c*) The given circuit can be redrawn as

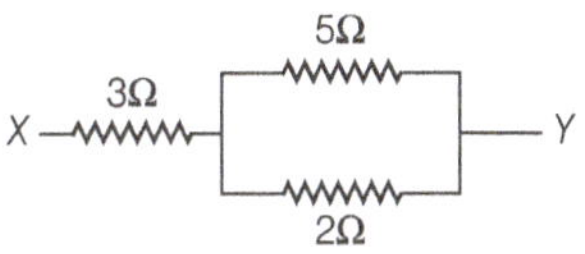

The resistance in parallel, $\frac{1}{R_p} = \frac{1}{5} + \frac{1}{2} \Rightarrow R_p = \frac{10}{7}$

The equivalent resistance $= \frac{10}{7} + 3 = \frac{31}{7}\ \Omega$

3. (*b*) For the given circuit diagram, the components R_1, R_2 and V are connected in parallel combination because terminals of the resistance and voltmeter are connected together.

4. (*d*) Reading of ammeter,

$$I = 180 \text{ mA} = 0.18 \text{ A}$$

Reading of voltmeter, $V = 1.8$ V

$\therefore$ Resistance of the resistor, $R = \frac{V}{I}$

$$= \frac{1.8}{0.18} = \frac{180}{18} = 10\ \Omega$$

5. (*b*) As, power, $P = VI$

$$\Rightarrow \quad I = \frac{P}{V} = \frac{1000}{220} = 4.66 \text{ A}$$

Therefore, fuse rating should be 5A, it is safe upto 4.6 A current.

6. (*b*) Resistance of bulb *Q*,

$$R_Q - \frac{(240)^2}{100} \qquad \left[\because R = \frac{V^2}{P}\right]$$

$$= 576\Omega$$

Similarly, resistance of bulbs, *P* and *R*,

$$R_P = \frac{(240)^2}{60} = 960\ \Omega$$

and $\quad R_R = \frac{(240)^2}{40} = 1440\ \Omega$

Since, bulbs *P* and *Q* are connected in parallel, hence their equivalent resistance,

$$R_{PQ} = \frac{960 \times 576}{960 + 576} = 360\ \Omega$$

Current in the circuit,

$$I = \frac{V}{R_{PQ} + R_R}$$

$$= \frac{240}{360 + 1440} = 0.133 \text{ A}$$

Since, $I_P + I_Q = I_R$ ...(i)

$$I_P = I \cdot \frac{R_Q}{R_P + R_Q} = 0.133 \times \frac{576}{576 + 960} = 0.05$$

$\therefore$ From Eq. (i)

$$I_Q = I_R - I_P = 0.133 - 0.05 = 0.08 \text{ A}$$

$\therefore \quad P = I^2 R$

Since, $I_P < I_Q$, hence brightness of bulb *Q* will be more than that of bulb *P*.

Since, resistance of bulb *R* is maximum and also having maximum current of 0.133 A. Hence, it will consumed maximum power, therefore brightness of bulb *R* will be maximum whereas brightness of bulb *P* will be minimum.

7. (*c*) In parallel combination, all the three bulbs can be operated independently of each other. Hence, if a bulb is fused, then it will not result in the disconnection of the other bulbs. Hence, when suddenly any one bulb fuses, then other bulbs will glow with the same initial intensity.

8. (*d*) The given circuit diagram is redrawn as :

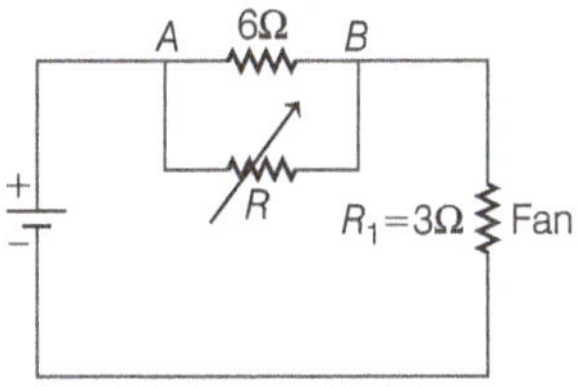

A source can transfer maximum power to the load (fan) if load resistance is equal to internal resistance of source.

i.e. $\quad R_{AB} = R_1$

$$\Rightarrow \quad \frac{6 \times R}{6 + R} = 3$$

$$\Rightarrow \quad 6R = 18 + 3R$$

$$\Rightarrow \quad 3R = 18$$

$$\Rightarrow \quad R = 6\ \Omega$$

9. (*c*) The process of electrostatic induction is the physical phenomena in which a mateiral can be charged without any actual contact with a charged body. In the presence of a charged body, an insulated conductor develops a positive charge on one end and negative charge on the other end.

10. (d) Resistance between points A and B for each circuit diagram is same and equal to R. Hence,

$$I_I = I_{II} = I_{III}$$

11. (b) According to given condition, the reading of ammeter is zero. Thus, potential difference across resistance R is equal to 2 V.

If I be the current flowing through resistance R, then

$$2 = IR$$

$$\Rightarrow \quad I = \frac{2}{R} \quad \text{...(i)}$$

Current flowing through the battery $E_1 = 12$ V will be also I.

$$\therefore \quad I = \frac{12}{5000 + R}$$

$$\Rightarrow \quad \frac{2}{R} = \frac{12}{5000 + R}$$

$$\Rightarrow \quad 6R = 5000 + R$$

$$\Rightarrow \quad R = 1000\ \Omega$$

12. (a) Resistance of bulb of rating 60 W, 220 V is given as,

$$R_1 = \frac{V_1^2}{P_1} = \frac{220 \times 220}{60} = 806.6\ \Omega$$

$$\because \quad I_1 = \frac{V_1}{R_1} = \frac{220}{806.6} = 0.28\ \text{A}$$

Resistance of bulb of rating 250 W, 220 V.

$$R_2 = \frac{V_2^2}{P_2} = \frac{220 \times 220}{250} = 193.6\ \Omega$$

$$\therefore \quad I_2 = \frac{V_2}{R_2} = \frac{220}{193.6} = 1.14\text{A}$$

When both bulbs are connected in series, then equivalent resistance,

$$R_{eq} = R_1 + R_2 = 806.6 + 193.6 = 1000.2\ \Omega$$

When these bulbs are connected with supply of 440 V, then current flowing through the circuit,

$$I_3 = \frac{V_3}{R_{eq}} = \frac{440}{1000.2} = 0.44\text{A}$$

Since, $I_3 > I_1$, hence bulbs of power 60 W will be fused.

13. (c) When N identical resistors of resistance R each are connected in parallel, then equivalent resistance,

$$\frac{1}{R_P} = \frac{1}{R} + \frac{1}{R} + \frac{1}{R} + \dots N \text{ times}$$

$$\Rightarrow \quad \frac{1}{R_P} = \frac{N}{R}$$

$$\Rightarrow \quad R_P = \frac{R}{N}$$

Similarly way, for series combination.

$$R_S = R + R + R + \dots N \text{ times}$$

$$\Rightarrow \quad R_S = NR$$

$$\therefore \text{ Power dissipated, } P = \frac{V^2}{R}$$

$$\Rightarrow \quad P \propto \frac{1}{R}$$

$$\therefore \quad \frac{P_{\text{parallel}}}{P_{\text{series}}} = \frac{R_S}{R_P} = \frac{NR}{R/N} = N^2$$

Chapter 9. Electromagnetism

1. (a) A straight wire lying in a horizontal plane carries a current from North to South. Magnetic field at a point directly below the wire is towards East according to Ampere's swimming rule or SNOW rule. If current flows from south to North, magnetic field will be towards West but if current flows from North to South, magnetic field will be towards East.

2. (a) According to Ampere's swimming rule, on reversing the direction of current in a wire, the magnetic field produced by it get reversed in direction.

3. (d) As the loop of the wire is held near the magnet but no relative motion occurs between the coil and magnet, hence no emf is induced.

4. (c) The spring is being pulled downwards by the magnet, hence elastic spring force is acting upwards. The magnetic force is acting upwards to attract the ball to the magnet. But gravitational force is pulling the ball downwards. Since, the ball is kept floating, the sum of elastic spring force and magnetic force must be equal to gravitational force.

5. (d) AC current in Figs. (c) and (d) are applied, AC current is applied to demagnetise a magnet and DC current is applied to magnetise a magnetic material. If magnet is withdrawn before switching off the DC power supply, then dipoles will remain aligned and magnetisation will be retained by the magnet.

6. (d) As the beam of electrons are entering a magnetic field, horizontally and perpendicular to magnetic field, according to Fleming's left hand rule, electrons are deflected towards the top of the diagram.

7. (d)

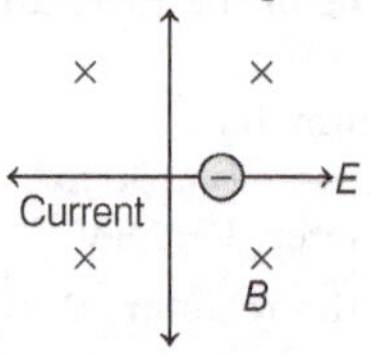

If an electron is travelling horizontally towards East and magnetic field in vertically downward, then according to left hand rule, force on electron is towards South.

8. (b) When the axis of bar magnet is turned to make acute angle with the X-axis and the magnet is rotated about X-axis with the south pole fixed on X-axis, then there is no change in magnetic field due to the bar magnet and hence no change in magnetic flux. Hence, no current is induced in the coil in case (b).

9. (c) According to given diagram direction of current in the coil is from P to Q. According to law of electromagnetic induction, when slider S of rheostat is moved from A to B or from B to A, the equivalent pole at the end P will become south. Therefore, statements II and IV, both are correct.

10. (b) The magnetic field produced due to current carrying wire is out of the plane. If the current in the wire decreases in magnitude, then magnetic flux decreases and is compensated by the current in loop F. Therefore, the current in loop F will be anti-clockwise and for the loop G, the situation is opposite.

Chapter 10. Heat

1. (c) Heat required by 1g ice at 0°C to mix with 1 g water at 0°C,

$$Q_1 = mL = 1 \times 80 = 80 \text{ cal}$$

(latent heat of fusion of ice, $L = 80$ cal/g)

Heat required by 1 g of water at 0°C to boil at 100°C,

$$Q_2 = mc\,\Delta T = 1 \times 1 \times (100 - 0)$$

(specific heat of water, $c = 1$ cal/g°C)

$$= 100 \text{ cal}$$

Thus, total heat required by 1 g of ice to reach a temperature of 100°C,

$$Q = Q_1 + Q_2 = 80 + 100 = 180 \text{ cal}$$

Heat available with 1 g of steam to condense into 1g of water at 100°C,

$$Q' = mL' = 1 \times 536$$

(latent heat of vaporisation, $L' = 536$ cal/g)

$$= 536 \text{ cal}$$

Obviously, the whole steam will not be condensed and ice will attain temperature of 100°C. Out of 536 cal, 80 cal used in fusion of ice, while remaining 456 cal will raise the temperature of mixture upto 100°C.

2. (b) As latent heat of vaporisation of water at 0°C,

$$L_1 = 2.10 \times 10^6 \text{ J/kg}$$

$$= 2.10 \times 10^3 \text{ J/g}$$

Latent heat of fusion of ice,

$$L_2 = 3.36 \times 10^5 \text{ J/kg} = 3.36 \times 10^2 \text{ J/g}$$

Let mass of ice formed $= m$ g

Then, mass of water evaporated $= (100 - m)$ g

As, no water is left in the vessel.

Heat gained by water in evaporation = Heat lost by water in freezing

$$(100 - m)L_1 = m\,L_2$$

$$(100 - m) \times 2.10 \times 10^3 = m \times 3.36 \times 10^2$$

$$\Rightarrow \quad m = 86.2 \text{ g}$$

If we write in terms of %, it will be 86.2%.

3. (a) Given, calorimeters A and B are identical in size.

Quantity of water is same in both the calorimeters $= x$

Temperature of water = 20°C

For metal X Mass = 5 g

Specific heat, $c_1 = 0.2$ cal $g^{-1}°C^{-1}$

Initial temperature = 40°C

Final temperature = 22° C

For metal Y Mass = 5 g

Specific heat, $c_2 = c$ cal $g^{-1}°C^{-1}$

Initial temperature = 40° C

Final temperature = 23° C

Now, for metal X,

Heat lost by X = Heat gained by water

$$\Rightarrow \quad 5 \times 0.2 \times (40 - 22) = x \times 1 \times (22 - 20)$$

$$\Rightarrow \quad 5 \times 0.2 \times 18 = x \times 2$$

$$\Rightarrow \quad x = \frac{5 \times 0.2 \times 18}{2} = 9 \text{ g}$$

As, calorimeter B also contain equal of water, i.e. 9 g.

Heat lost by metal Y = Heat gained by water

$$5 \times c \times (40 - 23) = 9 \times 1 \times (23 - 20)$$

$$5 \times c \times 17 = 9 \times 3$$

$$\Rightarrow \quad c = \frac{9 \times 3}{5 \times 17} = \frac{27}{85} \text{ cal/g°C}$$

4. (a) Given, mass of child

$m = 30\text{kg} = 30 \times 10^3 \text{g}$

Fall in temperature from fever,

$$\Delta\theta = 101° - 98° = 3° \text{ F}$$

$$= 3 \times \frac{5}{9} = \frac{5}{3} °\text{C}$$

Specific heat of human

= Specific heat of water = 1 cal g^{-1} $°C^{-1}$

Heat lost by child in the form of evaporation (sweat),

$$Q = mc\,\Delta\theta = 30 \times 10^3 \times 1 \times \frac{5}{3} = 50000 \text{ cal}$$

If m'g of sweat evaporates from the body of the child, heat gained by sweat $= m'L = m' \times 580$

(given, $L_{vap} = 580$ cal/g)

∴ Heat gained by sweat = Heat lost by child

$$m' \times 580 = 50000$$

$$m' = \frac{50000}{580} = 86.2 \text{ g}$$

Time taken by sweat to evaporate = 20 min

∴ Rate of evaporation of sweat $= \frac{86.2}{20} = 4.32 \text{ g min}^{-1}$

5. (b) Let steam required per hour $= m$ kg

Heat released by steam in following three steps

(i) When steam at 150°C $\xrightarrow{Q_1}$ Steam at 100°C

$$Q_1 = mc_s\,\Delta t = m \times 1(150 - 100) = 50\,m \text{ cal}$$

(ii) When steam at 100° C $\xrightarrow{Q_2}$ Water at 100°C

$$Q_2 = m\,L_v = m \times 540 = 540\,m \text{ cal}$$

(iii) When water at 100° C → Water at 90°C

$$Q_3 = m\,c_w\,\Delta t = m \times 1 \times (100 - 90) = 10\,m \text{ cal}$$

Hence, total heat lost by the steam,

$$Q = Q_1 + Q_2 + Q_3 = 600\,m \text{ cal}$$

Heat absorbed by 10 kg water,

$$Q' = mc_w\Delta t = 10 \times 10^3 \times 1 \times (80 - 20)$$

$$= 600 \times 10^3 \text{ cal}$$

Hence, $\quad Q = Q'$

$$\Rightarrow \quad 600\,m = 600 \times 10^3 \Rightarrow m = 10^3 \text{g} = 1 \text{ kg}$$

6. (b) Heat gained by ice = Heat lost by water

Let $\quad m$ = mass of ice

$$L_{ice} = 80 \text{ cal/g}$$

$$c_{ice} = 0.5 \text{ cal/g/°C}$$

Temperature of ice = – 14°C

Heat gained by ice

$= mL + mc_{ice}\,\Delta t + mc_{water}\,\Delta t$

$= m(L + c_{ice}\,\Delta t + c_{water}\,\Delta t)$

$= m[80 + 0.5(0+14) + 1\times(0+25)]$

$= m(80 + 7 + 25)$

$= m \times 112$ ...(i)

Heat lost by water

$= 200 \times 1 \times (25-10)$

$= 200 \times 15$ ...(ii)

From Eqs. (i) and (ii), we get

$m \times 112 = 200 \times 15$

$\Rightarrow \quad m = \frac{200\times 15}{112} = 26.7 = 27\text{ g}$

7. (c) Let mass of cold water be m_c and mass of hot water be m_h.

Temperature of cold water = 10 °C

Temperature of mixture = 20 °C

According to calorimetry,

Heat gain = Heat loss

$m_c c\,(20-10) = m_h c\,(T-20)$

Since, $3\times m_h = m_c$

Therefore, $3m_h \times 10 = m_h(T-20)$

$30 = T - 20$

$\Rightarrow \quad T = 50\text{ °C}$

8. (a) According to the question,

Mass of solid = 50 g,

Temperature of solid = 150°C,

Mass of water = 100 g

Temperature of water = 11°C,

Final temperature of mixture = 20°C

Specific heat of water = 1 cal/g/°C

Let specific heat capacity of solid = x

According to the principle of thermal equilibrium,

Q_L (heal lost) = Q_C (heat gained)

$\Rightarrow \quad 50 \times x \times (150-20) = 100\times 1 \times (20-11)$

$\Rightarrow \quad x = \frac{100\times 9}{50\times 130}$

$\therefore$ Specific heat $= \frac{9}{65} = 0.13$ cal/g/°C

Capacity of solid $= \frac{0.13}{4.2\text{ J/g°C}} = 0.033$ J/g°C

9. (d) Given, mass of copper vessel = 50 g = 0.050 kg

Mass of water = 250 g = 0.25 kg

Specific heat capacity of copper = 400 J kg^{-1}°C^{-1}

Specific heat capacity of water = 4200 J kg^{-1}°C^{-1}

Latent heat of fusion of ice, $L = 336\times 10^3$ J kg^{-1}

Final temperature = 5° C

Change in temperature, ΔT = 30°–5° = 25° C

Heat lost by water $= m\times c\times \Delta T$

$= 0.25 \times 4200 \times 25$

$= 26250$ J

Heat lost by copper $= m\times c\times \Delta T$

$= 0.05\times 400\times 25 = 500$ J

Total heat lost = 26750 J

Heat gained by ice = 26750 J

$m\times L = 26750$

$m = \frac{26750}{336\times 10^3}$ $(\because L = 336\times 10^3\text{J kg}^{-1})$

$= 79.6\times 10^{-3}$ kg

$\simeq 79.6$ g

10. (a) Given, mass of ice = 50 g

Mass of liquid = 300 g

Temperature, t_1 = 0°C

Temperature, t_2 = 30°C

Temperature of mixture, T = ?

Specific heat of liquid = 2.65 Jg^{-1}°C^{-1}

Heat energy given by liquid = Heat taken by water + Heat used to melt ice

$\therefore$ Heat used to melt ice $= m\times L$

$= 50\times 336$ $(\because L = 336\text{ J/g})$

$= 16800$ J

$\therefore$ Heat energy given by liquid $= m\times c\times \Delta T$

$= 300\times 2.65\times(30-T)$

By principle of calorimetry,

$300\times 2.65\times(30-T) = 16800 + 50\times(T-0)\times 4.2$

$\Rightarrow 795\times(30-T) = 16800 + 210T$

$\Rightarrow \quad T = 7.014°\text{C} \simeq 7°\text{ C}$

11. (c) Mass of ice, $m_i = 10$ g

Temperature of ice, $T_i = -10°$ C

That of water are, $M_w = 10g$, $T_w = 85°$ C

Let T be the final temperature.

According to principle of calorimetry.

Heat gained by ice = Heat lost by water

$m_i\, C_i\, \Delta T_i = m_w C_w \Delta T_w$

$\Rightarrow m_i\, \Delta T_i = m_w \Delta T_w$ $[\because C_i = C_w]$

$\Rightarrow \Delta T_i = \Delta T_w$ $[\because m_i = m_w = 10g]$

$T - (-10) = 85 - T$

$\Rightarrow \quad T + 10 = 85 - T$

$\Rightarrow \quad T = 37.5°$ C

Since, whole ice will melt and convert into water.

Hence, mass of ice left in the system = 0 g

Chapter 11. Radioactivity and Nuclei

1. (a) In fission of U-235 nucleus, the loss of mass, $\Delta m = 0.2$ amu.

Energy released, $\Delta E = \Delta m \times 931$ MeV

$= 0.2\times 931.5$ MeV = 186.2 MeV

2. (b) Heavy stable nuclei have more neutrons than protons because protons are positively charged and repel each other. This repulsion force is more, so that an excess of neutrons are required to reduce this repulsion. Nuclear forces are strongest attractive forces between nucleons, whereas electrostatic force between protons is repulsive.

3. (a) For a β^--decay, ${}^A_ZX \longrightarrow {}^A_{Z+1}Y_1 + {}^0_{-1}e + \bar{\nu}$

$\therefore$ Q_1-value of decay

$= [(M_X - ZM_e) - \{M_Y - (Z+1)M_e\} - M_e]c^2$

$= (M_X - M_Y)c^2$

For β^+-decay, ${}^A_ZX \longrightarrow {}^A_{Z-1}Y_2 + {}^0_1e + \nu$

∴ Q_2-value of decay

$$= [(M_X - ZM_e) - \{M_Y - (Z-1)M_e\} - M_e]c^2$$
$$= (M_X - M_Y - 2M_e)c^2$$

4. (b) Given, $F = \frac{GMm}{r^2}$

M = effective mass of hydrogen atom

$= \text{mass of electron} + \text{mass of proton} - \frac{B}{c^2}$

where, B = binding energy of hydrogen atom

$= 13.6$ eV.

5. (b) Momentum remains constant, $K = \frac{p^2}{2m}$

$$K \propto \frac{1}{m}$$

Now, for α-particle, KE = K_n

Mass = $m_\alpha = 4$

For residual nucleus, KE = K_α

Mass = $m_n = 210 - 4 = 206$

$$\frac{K_n}{K_\alpha} = \frac{m_\alpha}{m_n} = \frac{4}{206} = \frac{2}{103}$$

$$K_n = \left(\frac{2}{103}\right)K_\alpha$$

Given, energy of α-particle is E.

Hence, $K_n = \left(\frac{2}{103}\right)E$.

6. (d) Energy radiated by Sun = 1.4 kW/m^2

$= 1.4$ kJ/sm^2 $\left(\because \text{power} = \frac{\text{energy}}{\text{time}}\right)$

$$= \frac{\frac{1.4}{1}}{86400}\ \frac{\text{kJ}}{\text{day-m}^2}$$

$$= \frac{1.4 \times 864000}{\text{day m}^2}\ \text{kJ}$$

Total energy radiated per day

$$E = \frac{4\pi \times (1.5 \times 10^{11})^2 \times 1.4 \times 86400}{1}\ \frac{\text{kJ}}{\text{day}}$$

∴ We have, $E = mc^2$

$$\Rightarrow \quad m = \frac{E}{c^2} = \frac{4\pi \times (1.5 \times 10^{11})^2 \times 1.4 \times 86400 \times 10^3}{(3 \times 10^8)^2}$$

$= 3.8 \times 10^{14}$ kg

7. (a) Given, power $= \frac{\text{energy}}{\text{time}} = \frac{48\text{kJ}}{60\text{ s}} \Rightarrow \frac{4}{5}$ kJ/s

Energy released per fission = 3.2×10^{-11}J

∴ Number of fission per second $= \frac{\frac{4}{5} \times 10^3 \text{ J}}{3.2 \times 10^{-11}}$

$$= \frac{0.8}{3.2} \times 10^{14}$$
$$= 0.25 \times 10^{14}$$
$= 2.5 \times 10^{13}$ fission per second

8. (c) Element D would be most suitable for nuclear fission. As, it has greater mass which therefore will be converted into energy by producing lighter nuclei.

9. (b) Energy released in the fission of single $_{92}U^{235}$ nucleus = 100 MeV

$$= 100 \times 10^6 \times 1.6 \times 10^{-19} = 1.6 \times 10^{-11}\text{ J}$$

Total power of the reactor, $P = 16$ W

∴ Fission rate $= \frac{\text{total power}}{\text{energy relsed fission}}$

$$= \frac{16}{1.6 \times 10^{-11}} = 10^{12}\text{s}^{-1}$$

10. (c) We know that, size of nucleus of an atom 10^{-14} m and size of atom is about 10^{-10}m

$$\therefore \frac{\text{size of atom}}{\text{size of nucleus}} = \frac{10^{-10}}{10^{-14}} = 10^4$$

Internal Assessment of Practical Work

Experiment 1-A

Aim

To determine the mass of a meter scale using it as a lever.

Apparatus Required

A wooden wedge, thin thread of negligible mass, a set of weights (10 gf and 20 gf), a meter scale of uniform thickness and a half meter ruler.

Theory/Principle Used

In order to achieve the aim of this experiment, the **law of lever** will be followed. According to which, **in equilibrium condition, the clockwise moment of the load about the fulcrum is equal to the anti-clockwise moment of the effort about the fulcrum.** It then behaves like a lever of first kind.

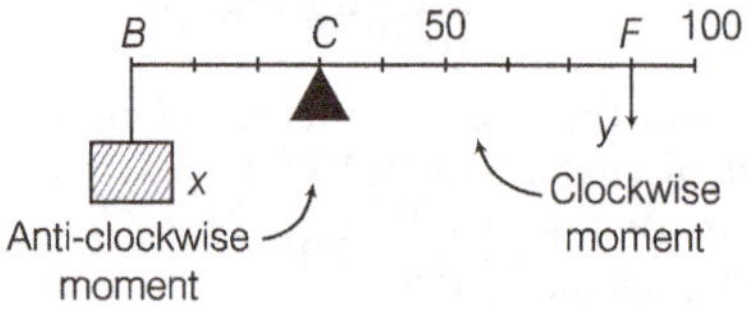

Load × Load arm = Effort × Effort arm

Or $x \times BC = y \times FC$

Important Terms

Mechanical advantage It is defined as the ratio of length of effort arm to the length of load arm.

i.e., Mechanical advantage

$$(\text{MA}) = \frac{\text{Load}(x)}{\text{Effort }(y)} = \frac{\text{Effort arm}(FC)}{\text{Load arm }(BC)} \text{ or MA} = \frac{FC}{BC}$$

Velocity ratio It is defined as the ratio of velocity of effort to the velocity of the load.

i.e., Velocity ratio (VR)

$$= \frac{\text{Velocity of effort }(v_y)}{\text{Velocity of load }(v_x)}$$

$$= \frac{\text{Displacement of effort}}{\text{Displacement of load}}$$

$$= \frac{\text{Effort arm }(FC)}{\text{Load arm }(BC)} \text{ or VR} = \frac{FC}{BC}$$

Procedure

1. First of all, make a loose loop of thread.
2. Tie the slotted weight at the other end of loop of thread.
3. Now, put the meter scale on the wooden wedge and try to adjust the position of scale on the wedge such that it gets balanced horizontally.
4. Record the position of wedge on the scale as centre of gravity (CG) of meter scale. It should lie nearly about 50 cm mark on the scale.
5. Choose a weight of 20 gf and suspend it on the one side of centre of gravity.

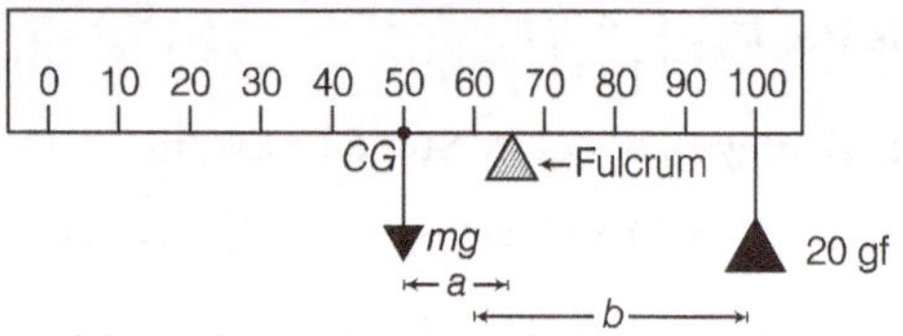

6. By taking the reference from the figure (given above), place the wedge between centre of gravity and weight hanged.
7. After holding the meter scale, adjust it on wedge by shifting it either left or right.
8. The moment, the scale gets balanced in a horizontal position, record the position of wedge and weight hanged on scale. (it will be the distance between CG and wedge i.e. a cm and the distance between wedge and weight hanged i.e. b cm in observation table)
9. By changing the position of hanged weight on meter scale, repeat the experiment.
10. After this, note down the position of wedge.

Observations

Least count of the meter scale = ... cm.

Observation table to determine the mass of a meter scale

Weight suspended on the scale w (in gf)	Distance of a (in cm)	Distance of b (in cm)	Mass of meter scale, $m' = \frac{wb}{a}$ (in gf)
20			$m_1' =$
30			$m_2' =$
40			$m_3' =$

Calculations

The mass of a meter scale can be calculated by using,

$$m' = \frac{b}{a} w$$

where, m' = mass of meter scale,

w = mass of suspended weight,

a = distance between centre of gravity (CG) and fulcrum and

b = distance of known weight from fulcrum.

Mean mass of meter scale,

$$m' = \frac{m_1' + m_2' + m_3'}{3} = \text{.........} \text{ gf.}$$

Result

The mass of a given meter scale = ... g.

Precautions

1. Meter scale should be in a horizontal equilibrium position while taking observations.
2. It should be ensured that while shifting the position of weight, the position of fulcrum should be same.
3. Scale of uniform thickness should be used.
4. Scale should be balanced horizontally.

Experiment 1-B

Aim

To find out the mass of the given meter scale by using spring balance.

Apparatus Required

A thin thread of negligible mass, meter scale of uniform thickness, a wooden wedge and a set of weights (10 gf, 20 gf, etc.) and spring balance.

Theory/Principle Used

In the case of a spring balance, extension in the spring is always directly proportional to the force applied on it.

i.e., $F \propto x \Rightarrow F = kx$

where, k is the proportionality constant.

On the basis of above equation, it can be said that in spring balance, length of spring increases on increasing the weight suspended on it. Here, the meter scale whose mass is to be determined with the help of a spring balance is suspended on the hook of the spring balance. Due to the weight of the meter scale, it stretches the spring of spring balance. Ultimately, the pointer of the spring balance reads the weight (or gravitational mass) of the meter scale either in the terms of newton or gf (gram force).

If mass of scale $= m$. This can be calculated by the formula,

$$\text{Mass of the body} = \frac{\text{Gravitational mass}}{\text{Acceleration due to gravity}}$$

Or $$m = \frac{m_g'}{g}$$

Procedure

1. Firstly, suspend the spring balance to a rigid support like retort stand.
2. Record the least count of the spring balance.
3. Now, note down the zero error of spring balance.
4. Suspend the scale horizontally at 50 cm mark on meter scale with the help of loop of thread as shown in figure.

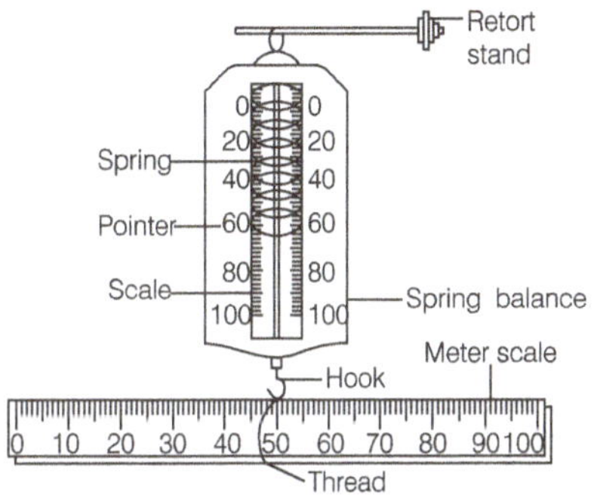

5. Now, note down the reading of spring balance.
6. After noting down the reading of spring balance, repeat the above steps for atleast two times.
7. At last, take the mean of the observations.

Observations

Least count of spring balance = ... gf.

Error in the spring balance = ±......... gf.

Correction to be applied in reading = ∓ .... gf.

Observed gravitational mass,

(i) m_1 = ... gf. (ii) m_2 =......... gf.

(iii) m_3 = ... gf. (iv) m_4 = ... gf.

Calculations

Mean observed gravitational mass,

$$m' = \frac{m_1 + m_2 + m_3 + m_4}{4} = \text{... gf.}$$

Corrected gravitational mass, m'' = ... gf

Therefore, mass of meter scale $= \frac{m_g''}{g}$

Result

Mass of meter scale = ... g.

Precautions

1. The position of scale, i.e. up or down should be properly adjusted, so as to bring the pointer at zero mark of scale.
2. The value of acceleration due to gravity varies from place to place. Since, the spring balance depends on the value of *g*, so in order to determine the inertial mass at a given place, the standard value of *g* must be used.
3. To get the final reading, displace the suspended weights slightly upward or downward.

Experiment 1-C

Aim

To prove that MA< VR, MA= VR and MA> VR using meter scale as a lever where, MA is mechanical advantage and VR is velocity ratio of the lever.

Apparatus Required

Wooden wedge, known weight, a meter scale and thin thread.

Theory/Principle Used

According to the law of lever/principle of moments, **in equilibrium position, the clockwise moment of the load about the fulcrum is equal to the anti-clockwise moment of the effort about the fulcrum.**

i.e. Load × load arm = Effort × Effort arm

Procedure

1. Put the meter scale on a wooden wedge at 40 cm mark.
2. Suspend a known weight w_1 gf at 10 cm mark at LHS of fulcrum and another known weight w_2 gf at 60 cm mark on RHS of fulcrum, such that the meter scale balance in horizontal equilibrium.
3. Now, shift the fulcrum at 50 cm mark and then adjust the weights by moving to and fro such that the meter scale is balanced in horizontal equilibrium.
4. Again, repeat step 3 but now shift the fulcrum at 60 cm mark.
5. In each case calculate MA and VR using the relation,

$$\text{MA} = \frac{\text{Load } (L)}{\text{Effort } (E)} = \frac{\text{Effort arm } (QF)}{\text{Load arm } (PF)}$$

$$\text{VR} = \frac{\text{Distance of effort from fulcrum (QF)}}{\text{Distance of load from fulcrum (PF)}}$$

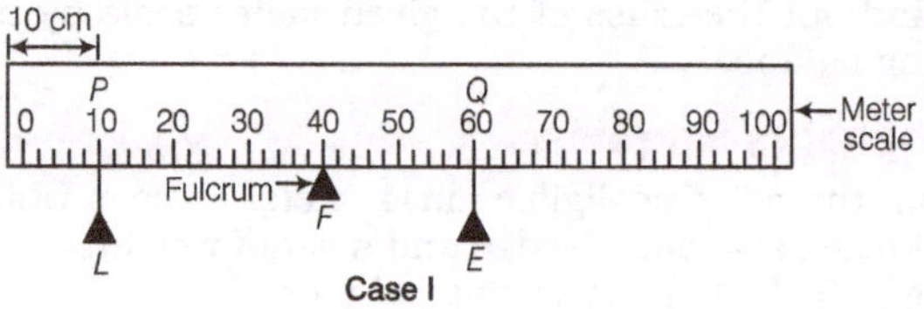

Case I

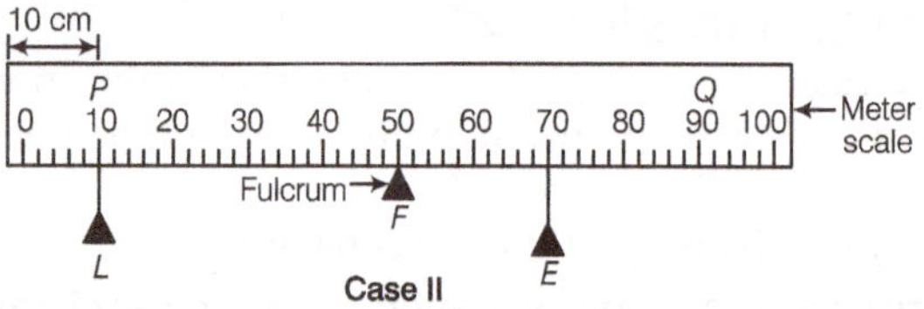

Case II

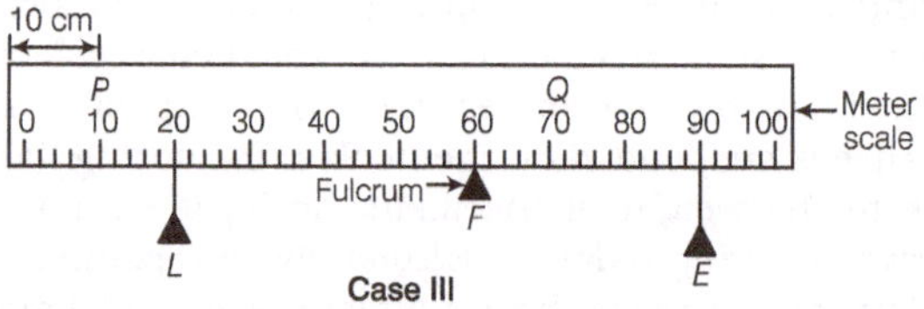

Case III

Observations

Mass of meter scale, m = ... gf.

Observation table to prove MA < VR, MA = VR and MR > VR

S.No.	Load, *L* (gf)	Effort, *E* (gf)	Position of fulcrum, *F* (cm)	Position of Load, *P* (cm)	Position of Effort, *Q* (cm)	Load arm *PF* (cm)	Effort arm *QF* (cm)	MA = $\frac{L}{E}$	VR = $\frac{QF}{PF}$
1.		40							
2.		50							
3.		60							

Result

Case I When $F = 40$ cm, then MA > VR

$\therefore$ In equilibrium position,

Load × load arm = Mass of meter scale × 10 + effort × effort arm

$\Rightarrow L \times PF = m \times 10 + E \times QF$

Case II When $F = 50$ cm, then MA = VR

$\therefore L \times PF = E \times QF$

Case III When $F = 60$ cm, then MA < VR

$\Rightarrow L \times PF + m \times 10 = E \times QF$

Precautions

1. The scale of uniform thickness should be used.
2. The position of fulcrum should not be changed while shifting the position of known weight.
3. Balancing of scale on the wedge should be done properly.
4. Meter scale should be balanced in horizontal equilibrium.

Viva-Voce

1. How can you define the term centre of gravity?

Ans. The point at which the whole weight of the body is supposed to be concentrated, is known as centre of gravity.

2. Define the term lever.

Ans. A simple machine which turns about a fixed point (called the turning point) due to a load and efforts applied on it, is known as lever. So, it is a simple machine having three points, fulcrum, effort and load.

3. State principle of moments.

Ans. According to the principle of moments, when a body is in equilibrium under the action of number of forces, then sum of the clockwise moments is equal to sum of the anti-clockwise moments.

4. What is least count of an instrument?

Ans. Least count of an instrument can be defined as the minimum reading which that instrument can record accurately.

5. State the difference between mass and weight.

Ans. The quantity of matter contained in a body defines its mass, while the weight of the body is the force with which it is attracted towards the centre of Earth.

6. What is the weight of the body at the centre of Earth?

Ans. The weight of the body is always zero at the centre of the Earth because the value of g is zero at the centre of Earth.

7. Mention the class of lever which is used as force multiplier.

Ans. IInd class of lever is used as a force multiplier.

8. State whether the mechanical advantage of the experiment can be changed or not? If yes, then explain how?

Ans. Yes, the mechanical advantage (MA) of the experiment can be changed by changing the position of fulcrum between the load and effort point.

9. Mention whether the weight of a body is a constant quantity.

Ans. No, the weight of a body is not a constant quantity as it varies from place to place due to the varying value of acceleration due to gravity (g).

10. Distinguish between effort and effort arm.

Ans. The force applied on the lever to overcome the resistance due to load is known as effort.

While the distance of the effort point from fulcrum is known as effort arm.

11. Give the name of SI unit of weight.

Ans. The SI unit of weight is newton (N).

12. Mention the least count of a meter scale.

Ans. The least count of a meter scale is 1 mm or 0.1 cm.

13. What does the weight gf imply?

Ans. It means the force exerted by body towards the centre of Earth on an object of 1 g due to force of gravity.

14. Define the term velocity ratio of a machine.

Ans. The velocity ratio of a machine can be defined as the ratio of velocity or displacement of effort point to load point.

Experiment 2

Aim

To determine the velocity ratio (VR) and mechanical advantage (MA) of a given pulley system.

Apparatus Required

Block and tackle, scalepan, threads, weights, pulley, spring balance and rigid stand.

Theory/Principle Used

A simple machine which can change the direction of force or can multiply the force is known as pulley. In appearance, it is a flat circular disc having a groove in its edge and capable of rotation about a fixed axis which passes through its centre called the axle as shown in Fig. (a).

A single fixed pulley has mechanical advantage (MA) of 1, due to which it does not multiply force. But it helps to change the direction of applied force.

In a system of two pullies one is fixed and the other is movable, having a mechanical advantage (MA) of 2.

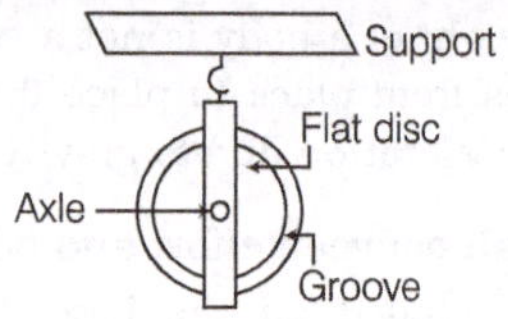

Fig.(a)

In order to achieve a large mechanical advantage, we usually use a block and tackle system of pulleys. This system consists of two blocks carrying the pulleys. In this, the lower block is movable and upper block is fixed. Moreover, the number of pulleys in the upper block is either equal to or is more than the number of pulleys in the lower block. A massless and a single inextensible rope passes over all the pulleys and the load which is to be lifted, is attached to lower movable pulley. The mechanical advantage or velocity ratio of an ideal pulley and tackle is equal to the total number of pulleys in the two blocks. Mechanical advantage (MA) is slightly less than velocity ratio (VR) in actual system of block and tackle, it is due to the weight of the lower block and the friction in pulley.

Efficiency of pulley block and tackle system of pulleys is $= \frac{\text{MA}}{\text{VR}} \times 100$

If n be the number of pulleys which is used in block and tackle arrangement and effort (E) is applied in the downward direction then,

Load (L) $= nT$

Effort E = Tension in string (T) as shown in Fig. (b).

$\therefore$ Mechanical Advantage $= \frac{\text{Load}}{\text{Effort}}$

Or $\quad \text{MA} = \frac{L}{E} = \frac{nT}{T} = n \quad$ ...(i)

On applying effort (E), if load moves a distance d, then effort will move by nd.

$\therefore$ Velocity Ratio $= \frac{\text{Distance travelled by effort}}{\text{Distance travelled by load}}$

Or $\quad \text{VR} = \frac{nd}{d} = n \quad$ ...(ii)

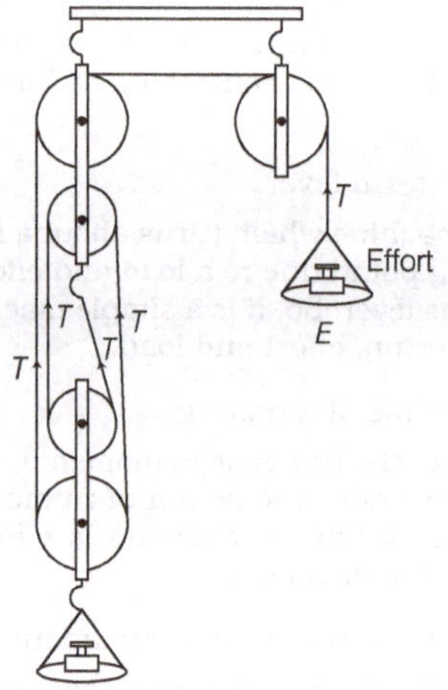

Fig. (b)

In an ideal pulley system, $\quad \text{VR} = \text{MA} \quad$ ...(iii)

If total weight of pulleys in the lower block be W, then

$L + W = nT$

and $\quad E = T$

$\therefore \quad \text{MA} = \frac{L}{E} = \frac{nT - W}{T} = n - \frac{W}{T} \quad$ ...(iv)

$\therefore \quad \text{VR} > \text{MA}$

From Eqs. (ii) and (iv), we get

$\therefore$ Efficiency, $\eta = \frac{\text{MA}}{\text{VR}}$

$$= \frac{\left(n - \frac{W}{T}\right)}{n} = \left(1 - \frac{W}{nE}\right) \quad \text{...(v)}$$

(As, $E = T$)

Procedure

1. Firstly, take a pulley block and tackle in which the number of pulley can be adjusted.
2. It should be ensured that there is no friction at the pulleys axle.

3. If required, oil the pulleys.
4. Now, try to support a weight of 500 g from the lower block to serve as load x.

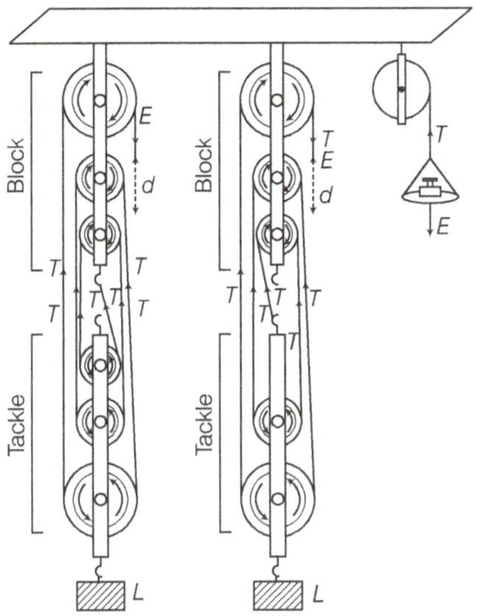

Fig. (c)

5. Attach one end of a string of suitable length to a hook in the lower block and pass it around the pulleys in such a way that free end of the string passes around the pulley in the upper block.
6. Determine the weight of the scale pan with the help of a spring balance.
7. Suspend the pan with string and at upmost pulley as shown in Fig. (c).
8. Place the suitable weights in the scale pan in such a way that the load x from the lower block is supported.
9. Carefully observe that the scale pan does not touch the pulley or the block.
10. Record the weights in the pan.
11. Repeat the experiment with the same load.
12. To have sets of different readings, repeat the experiment with atleast three different loads.

Observations

Least count of spring balance = ...gf.

Zero error in the spring balance = ±.........gf.

Correction to be applied to the weight in observed reading = ∓.....gf.

Corrected weight of the pan as measured with the spring balance, y = ∓ .... gf.

Observation table to obtain mechanical advantage and velocity ratio of a given pulley system

S.No.	Load, x	Weights in the pan in equilibrium m position F_1 (gf)	F_2 (gf)	Mean $F(gf)$	Effort $E = F + y(gf)$	MA	VR	$\eta = \frac{MA}{VR} \times 100$
1.								
2.								
3.								

Calculations

Mean MA = ...

Mean VR = ...

It should be noted that the above experiments can be performed by taking different number of pulleys.

Mean efficiency = ...

Result

MA of given system of pulleys = ...

VR of given system of pulleys = ...

Efficiency of given system of pulleys = ...

Precautions

1. Carefully measure the displacement of effort and load point with the help of meter scale.
2. The scale pan should not touch any part of the apparatus.
3. It should be ensured that the friction in the pulleys is minimum.
4. If required, then only the correction of the spring balance must be used properly.

Viva-Voce

1. What do you mean by the term pulley?

Ans. A grooved wheel that can turn readily on an axle is known as pulley.

2. State the factors on which the weight of the string lifted depends.

Ans. The weight of string lifted depends on the distance between the pulley and blocks, but the weight of the lower block remains constant.

3. Is it possible that mechanical advantage can be less than 1?

Ans. Yes, the mechanical advantage can be less than one in class III lever.

4. State the principle of a machine.

Ans. The principle of a machine states that, "work done by a machine is always equal to the work done on the machine".

5. What is single movable pulley and its mechanical advantage?

Ans. A pulley whose axis of rotation can change is known as single movable pulley. Its mechanical advantage is 2, i.e., it can multiply force.

6. Define efficiency of a machine.

Ans. The ratio of the work done by the machine to the work done on the machine is known as efficiency of a machine.

7. Mention the relation between mechanical advantage (MA), velocity ratio (VR) and efficiency (η).

Ans. The relation between MA, VR and η can be given as, $MA = (\eta \times VR)/100$

8. Give a reason, why the efficiency of an actual machine can never be equal to one?

Ans. Since, frictional forces acts within the parts of a machine which decreases the output of work. As, we know that,

$$\eta = \frac{\text{Output work}}{\text{Input work}}$$

So, if input work is larger than the output work, then η for the actual machine will always be less than one.

9. Give a relation between mechanical advantage (MA) and velocity ratio (VR) in the case of

(i) ideal machine (ii) real machine

Ans. (i) In an ideal machine, $VR = MA$

(ii) In a real machine, $MA < VR$

10. Define a single fixed pulley.

Ans. A pulley whose axis of rotation is fixed is known as a single fixed pulley.

11. What is the mechanical advantage of a single fixed pulley?

Ans. The mechanical advantage of a single fixed pulley is 1.

12. What does the term useless load means?

Ans. The useless load is the combination of the weight or force of lower block, string and friction in the string and bearing in axle and pulleys.

Experiment 3

Aim

To trace the course of different rays of light through a rectangular glass prism at different angles of incidence and measure angles of incidence, refraction and emergence. Also, measure the lateral displacement.

Apparatus Required

A rectangular glass slab, a drawing board, sharp alpins, a sharp pencil, eraser, protractor, drawing thumb pins, white drawing sheets and 15 m scale.

Description of Apparatus

Figure given below is representing a rectangular glass slab *ABCD*. When a ray of light *OI* is incident at an angle of incidence *i* with the normal *NON'* at the point of incidence *O*. After suffering the refraction from the surface *AB* of the rectangular glass slab, this ray gets refracted along *OO'* and bent towards the normal. It is because it is travelling from air (rarer) to the glass (denser medium). This refracted ray again suffers the refraction at surface *CD* of glass slab and it gets bent away from the normal *MOM'* and emerges along *O'E* (i.e., emergent ray).

The emergent ray becomes parallel to the incident ray (which is laterally displaced). The distance between the emergent ray and extended incident ray is known as lateral displacement.

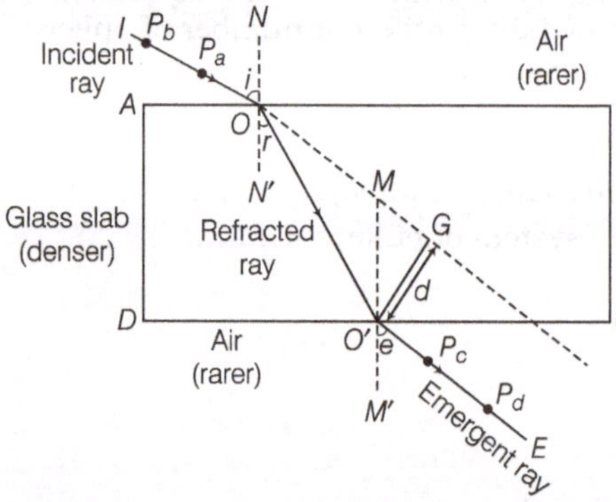

Theory/Principle Used

The phenomenon of bending of light when the ray of light passes from an optical medium to another medium at oblique incidence is known as refraction. There are following observations which are usually noticed when a ray of light passes through rectangular glass slab.

(i) Incident and emergent rays are parallel to each other but laterally shifted.

(ii) Angle of incidence and angle of emergence are always equal.

(iii) When angle of incidence is zero i.e. at normal incidence, then no lateral shift of emergent ray takes place.

Procedure

1. Take a sheet of white paper and fix it on the drawing board with the help of drawing pins at the four corners of the sheet.
2. Put a glass slab at the centre of paper and with the help of a pencil, draw its boundary *ABCD*.
3. Now, remove the glass slab and draw a line *OI* by making an angle of 30° with the normal at the point *O*.
4. After putting the glass slab back on its boundary line, fix the two pins P_a and P_b vertically on the line *OI* atleast 10 cm apart and one pin close to the slab.
5. Now, try to look for the images of these pins in the slab from the opposite side *CD*.
6. Again, fix two more pins P_c and P_d in such a way that they should be in line with the images of P_a and P_b as observed through the slab and atleast 10 cm apart.
7. After this, join the point of P_c to the point P_d in order to obtain the emergent ray.
8. Draw a normal to *CD* at point *O′* and join *OO′* in order to get refracted ray.
9. Take the measurement of angle of incidence, angle of refraction and angle of emergence.
10. Extend the ray *OI* forward and draw a perpendicular from *O′* on *OI* to meet it at *G*. So, the lateral displacement is given by *O′G*.
11. Repeat the same experiment with different angles of incidence (i.e., 45°, 60°).

Observations

Least count of scale = ... cm.

Least count of protractor = ... degree.

Observation table for measuring the angle of incidence (*i*), angle of refraction (*r*) angle of emergence (*e*) and lateral displacement (*d*)

S. No.	Angle of incidence (*i*)	Angle of refraction (*r*)	Angle of emergence (*e*)	Lateral displacement (*d*)
1.				
2.				
3.				

Result

There are following conclusions that are drawn within the experimental error limit, they are as follows

1. The incident rays and emergent rays are parallel to each other but laterally displaced.
2. Angle of incidence is equal to the angle of emergence.
3. Lateral displacement increases on increasing the thickness of glass slab for refracted ray and on increasing the angle of incidence.
4. If a ray of light passes from air to glass, the refracted ray bend towards the normal.

Precautions

1. The angles should be measured carefully.
2. The tips of the pins should be in a straight line.
3. In order to draw the rays, sharp pencils should be used.
4. The marking of arrow heads should be done gently in order to show the direction of light.

Viva-Voce

1. In what manner do the frequency of light gets affected when it passes
(i) from the rarer to denser medium?
(ii) from denser to the rarer medium?

Ans. In both cases, the frequency of light remains constant.

2. What do you understand by the term refraction?

Ans. The phenomenon of bending of ray of light when it passes from one optical medium to another is known as refraction of light.

3. State law of refraction.

Ans. According to the law of refraction,
(i) the "incident ray, the refracted ray and the normal, all lie in the same plane at the point of incidence".
(ii) the ratio of sine of angle of incidence to the sine of angle of refraction for a given pair of media is always constant.
This constant is known as refractive index (μ) of the medium in which the refraction takes place.
This law is also known as Snell's law of refraction
i.e. $^1\mu_2 = \dfrac{\sin i}{\sin r}$
where, $^1\mu_2$ is the refractive index of medium 2 w.r.t 1.

4. Mention the cause of refraction of light.

Ans. Due to different optical densities of the medium, there is change in speed of light in the different medium, which causes the refraction of light.

5. State whether a parallel sided glass slab produce any deviation in the incident light.

Ans. No, a parallel sided glass slab does not produce any deviation in the incident light. Emergent ray is always parallel to the incident ray but laterally displaced.

6. Define the term optical density.

Ans. The ratio of velocity of light in vacuum to the velocity of light in medium is known as the optical density of a medium.

7. State the factors on which the lateral displacement produced by a glass slab depends.

Ans. The lateral displacement depends upon
(i) angle of incidence
(ii) refractive index of the medium
(iii) thickness of the glass slab

8. Is it possible for angle of incidence to be lesser than the angle of refraction?

Ans. Yes, it is possible in the condition when the ray of light suffers refraction from optically denser to optically rarer medium.

9. Mention the factors on which the refractive index of a medium depends?

Ans. The refractive index of a medium depends upon
(i) nature of medium (ii) colour of incident ray

10. What is the angle of refraction, if the angle of incidence is zero?

Ans. If the angle of incidence is zero, then the angle of refraction will be zero.
It is because when the incident ray falls normally on the surface no refraction takes place.

11. State whether the refractive index of water with respect to glass is more than one or less than one?

Ans. Since, refractive index of water with respect to glass, $^g\mu_w = \dfrac{v_g}{v_w}$

As it is known that, $v_g < v_w \Rightarrow {}^g\mu_w < 1$

∴ Refractive index of water with respect to the glass is less than 1.

12. If a ray falls on glass and water at some angle of incidence, then state whether the angle of refraction will be larger or smaller in glass?

Ans. As, we know that, bending of light increases on increasing refractive index, ${}^a\mu_w < {}^a\mu_g$. So, bending of a ray of light for same angle of incidence will be larger in glass. So, angle of refraction in glass will be smaller than in water for same angle of incidence.

Experiment 4-A

Aim

To determine the focal length of a convex lens by the distant object method.

Apparatus Required

Lens holder (optical bench), a small screen fixed on a stand, thin convex lens and a meter scale.

Theory/Principle Used

When the parallel rays of light coming from the distant object falls on a convex lens, then after refraction they form real, inverted and very small image on screen at the principal focus.

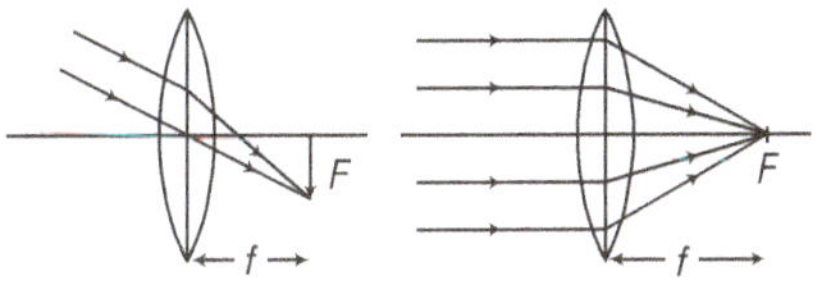

Procedure

1. First of all, take a convex lens and with the help of holder, put it on a table between a window of laboratory and screen on the table.

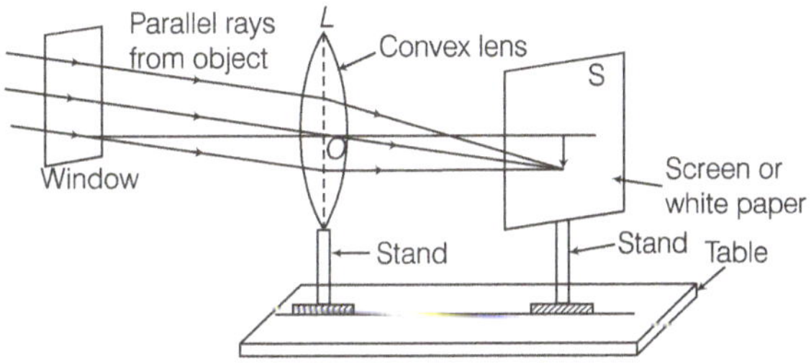

2. Now, try to focus the sharp image of the object on the sheet of paper or a wall as a screen.
3. With the help of a meter scale, measure the distance between the lens and the screen as the image is formed at focus.
4. Repeat this experiment for atleast two more times by obtaining the images of two different distant objects and measure the distance between the convex lens and the screen. Then, record them in observation table.
5. At last, take the mean distance to obtain focal length.

Observations

Least count of meter scale = ... cm.

Observation table to obtain the distance between lens and screen

S. No.	Position of lens x (cm)	Position of screen y (cm)	Distance between lens and screen f' (cm)
1.			f_a = ...
2.			f_b = ...
3.			f_c = ...
4.			f_d = ...

Calculations

Mean focal length, $f' = \frac{f_a + f_b + f_c + f_d}{4}$ = ... cm.

Result

Focal length of convex lens by distant object method,

f' = ... cm.

Precautions

1. The lens should be cleaned before using it.
2. The image of the object should be properly focused on the screen.
3. There should be no obstacle in the path of rays of light from the distant object incident on the convex lens.

Experiment 4-B

Aim

To determine the focal length of a convex lens by using a needle and plane mirror.

Apparatus Required

There is no use of optical bench in the experiment. A convex lens, an iron stand with a clamp, a plane mirror, plumb line, a half meter scale, an optical pin.

Theory/Principle Used

When incident rays of light from an object placed on focus of convex lens, passes through the lens, then they become parallel to the principal axis after refraction and falls perpendicularly on a plane mirror placed behind it.

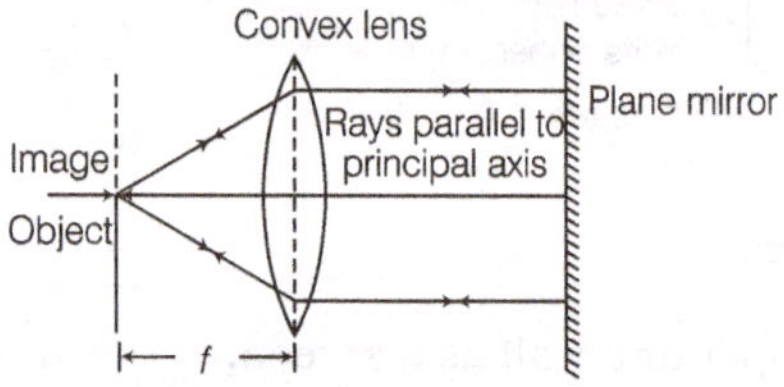

So, these rays covers the same path after reflecting back from the mirror and then after suffering the refraction again from convex lens form an inverted image at the focus itself.

Focal length of convex lens is the distance between the object and optical centre of the lens.

Procedure

1. Determine the rough focal length of convex lens, which forms the image of an object.
2. Then, put the convex lens over a plane mirror on the base of the stand.
3. With the help of clamp of stand, mount the object optical pin near the focal length of lens in such a way that the tip of pin comes over the centre of lens as shown in figure given below.

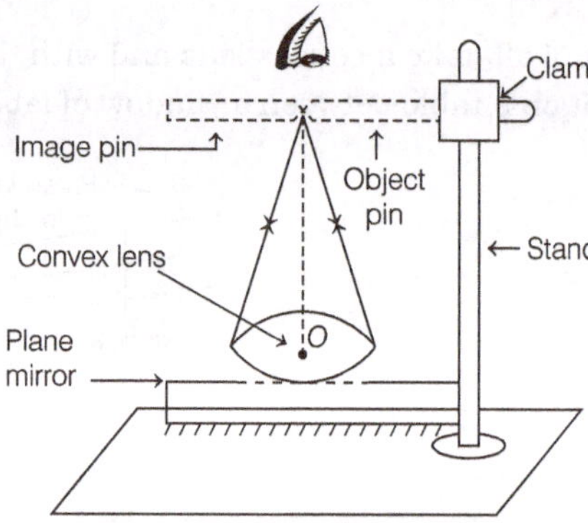

4. Try to look from the top and adjust the pin at height when the tip of the pin coincide with object pin.
5. After removing the parallax, tight the clamp of stand at this position.
6. Record the height between pin and lens and plane mirror.
7. The mean of above two heights gives the focal length of lens.
8. Repeat the experiment for atleast three to four times.

Observations

Least count of meter scale = ... cm.

Observations table to obtain mean focal length of the convex lens

S. No.	Height between object pin and		Focal length of convex lens, $f' = \frac{a+b}{2}$ (cm)
	plane mirror a (cm)	convex lens b (cm)	
1.			f_a = ...
2.			f_b = ...
3.			f_c = ...
4.			f_d = ...

Calculation

Mean focal length, $f' = \dfrac{f_a + f_b + f_c + f_d}{4} = $ ……… cm.

Result

The focal length of the convex lens, $f' = $ ……… cm.

Precautions

1. While taking observations, eye should be exactly focused over the tip of pin.
2. Carefully, measure the height of pin from mirror and lens.
3. The parallax should be removed between the tip of pin and its image.

Experiment 5

Aim

To find the focal length of a convex lens using u-v method and the formula, $f = \dfrac{uv}{u + v}$.

Apparatus Required

A thin convex lens, optical bench, white screen and an illuminated object (say candle or a needle).

Theory/Principle Used

If an object is placed between F and $2F$ in the case of convex lens, then a real, inverted and enlarged image of the object is formed beyond $2F$.

So, focal length f can be calculated by measuring the image distance v and object distance u.

$\therefore$ By applying lens formula, $\dfrac{1}{f} = \dfrac{1}{v} - \dfrac{1}{u}$

$\Rightarrow$ According to sign convention u is taken as negative, so

$\dfrac{1}{f} = \dfrac{1}{v} - \dfrac{1}{(-u)} \Rightarrow \dfrac{1}{f} = \dfrac{1}{v} + \dfrac{1}{u} \Rightarrow$ focal length, $f = \dfrac{uv}{u + v}$

Procedure

1. On the optical bench, arrange the lens, screen and object (say candle) in such a way that the lens gets positioned between the screen and the candle.
2. Now, try to adjust the height of the candle, lens and screen in such a way that the candle flame, centre of the lens and the screen are on the same level.
3. Make the illuminated object to get focused on the screen.
4. By to and fro movement of screen along the optical bench a clear image of the object should be formed on it.
5. Now, take the measurement of distance between the screen, i.e., image and the lens v.
6. Also, measure the distance between the object and lens u.
7. For obtaining the corresponding values of u and v, repeat the same experiment for the different positions of the object.

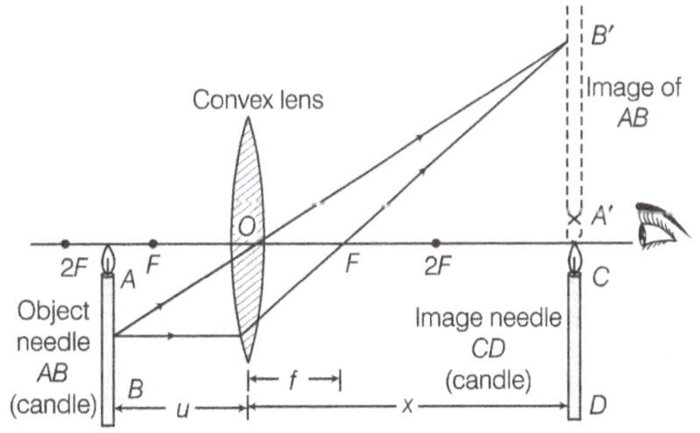

8. Determine the focal length f of the convex lens using the lens formula for each case. Also, position of screen will also change in each observation.

Observations

Least count of meter scale = …… cm.

Observations table to obtain the focal length of convex lens

S. No.	Distance of the object, u (cm)	Distance of the image, v(cm)	Focal length, $f = \dfrac{uv}{u+v}$ (cm)
1.			f_a = ………
2.			f_b = ………
3.			f_c = ………
4.			f_d = ………

Calculations

Mean focal length, $f = \dfrac{f_a + f_b + f_c + f_d}{4}$ =...... cm.

Result

The focal length of a convex lens, f' = ... cm.

Precautions

1. Sign conventions must be applied properly.
2. In order to the get a bright image on the screen, the experiment should be performed in the dark room.
3. The candle should not be disturbed by the air currents.
4. The centre of screen, the optical centre of lens and the candle flame should not be at the same height.

Viva-Voce

1. Define the term magnification.

Ans. The ratio of the size of an image to the size of an object is known as magnification.

$$\text{Magnification, } m = \frac{\text{Size of the image}}{\text{Size of the object}}$$

2. Is the virtual image ever inverted?

Ans. No, virtual image is always erected in lens and mirrors.

3. In which manner, do the parallax can be removed?

Ans. When the apparent shift in the position of tips of object and image does not take place, when observer's eye is moved side ways, then it is said that parallax is removed.

4. Is it possible to obtain a real image with a concave lens?

Ans. No, concave lens always forms virtual image of the real object.

5. What is the position of the object when a convex lens is used as a magnifying glass?

Ans. When a convex lens is used as a magnifying glass, then the position of the object will be in between the focus and optical centre of the convex lens.

6. What type of lens is the eye lens?

Ans. An eye lens is a double convex lens.

7. Is it possible to determine the rough focal length of a concave lens?

Ans. No, it is not possible to calculate the rough focal length of a concave lens because concave lens always forms a virtual image.

8. Which formula is used to find the focal length of the convex lens?

Ans. The formula used to find the focal length of convex lens is given by

$$\frac{1}{f} = \frac{1}{v} - \frac{1}{u}$$

where, u = object distance,

v = image distance

and f = focal length.

9. Between the convex and concave lens, which one has virtual focus?

Ans. In concave lens, parallel incident rays diverges after refraction, so forms virtual focus.

10. State whether the focal length of a lens depends on the position of object in front of lens.

Ans. No, the focal length of a lens does not change on changing the position of an object. It is because on changing the position of object, position of image also changes accordingly, so that the focal length stays the same by formula,

$$f = \frac{uv}{u + v}$$

11. What does the negative power of lens indicates?

Ans. As, it is known that, $P = \dfrac{1}{f}$

So, if f will be negative, then P will also be negative. So, negative power, indicates that the lens will be a concave lens.

12. Define the term parallax.

Ans. Parallax is defined as the apparent shift in position of two things, object and image, when the observer's eye move side ways.

Experiment 6

Aim

To trace the path of a ray of light through a prism and to show that $i_1 + i_2 = A + \delta$ and $A = r_1 + r_2$.

Apparatus Required

Pins, board pins, sheet of paper, drawing board, a triangular equilateral prism, a protractor.

Theory/Principle Used

Whenever a ray of light suffers the refraction at the two faces of prism, then it gets deviated.

This is shown in the figure given below.

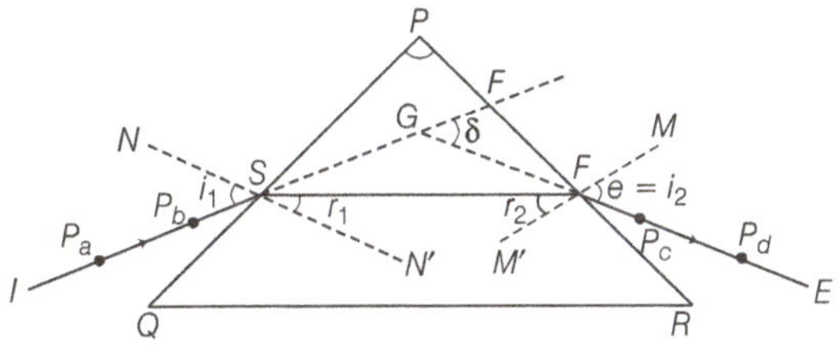

The angle between the incident and the emergent ray is called the angle of deviation.

There are following factors on which the value of angle of deviation depends, they are as follows

(i) The angle of incidence, i

(ii) The material of the prism

(iii) The colour or wavelength of the light

(iv) The angle of prism

The value of angle of deviation for a certain angle of incidence is minimum. This position is known as the position of minimum deviation of the prism with respect to the incident ray.

Therefore, angle of minimum deviation is given by the relation,

$$i_1 + i_2 = A + \delta$$

where, i_1 = angle of incidence,

i_2 = angle of emergence,

A = angle of prism

and δ = angle of deviation.

Procedure

1. Firstly, take a sheet of white paper and fix it on the drawing board with drawing pins.
2. Put the prism in the middle of paper and draw its outline as PQR.
3. Measure angles of ΔPQR, i.e. angle P, Q and R.
4. After taking the mean of all the angles of ΔPQR, the calculated value of the angle P, will be the angle of prism.
5. Now, take a point S on PQ and draw the normal SN.
6. With the help of a sharp pencil, draw a line SI making any angle preferably angle between 30° and 60°.
7. Put the prism again on its original position PQR.
8. Now, fix two pins P_a and P_b around 10 cm apart.
9. Try to observe from the side PR and erect two more pins P_c and P_d in such a way that all four pins (i.e. images of P_a and P_b and pins of P_c and P_d) form a straight line.
10. Encircle the points clearly.
11. After removing the prism, join P_a and P_b and extend it to meet PQ at S.
12. In the similar manner, join P_c and P_d and extend it to meet PR at F.
13. Now, join S and F.
14. Extend P_a, P_b and P_c, P_d to meet at G. This angle δ is known as angle of deviation.
15. Take the measurement of angle e which is equal to i_2 and also measure r_1 and r_2.
16. For the different values of angle of incidence, repeat the same experiment and measure i_2 in each case.
17. Calculate the value of angle of prism for each case by formula,

$$i_1 + i_2 = \delta + A$$

Observations

Least count of protractor = ... degree.

Angle of prism, A = ... degree.

Observation table to verify the relation, $i_1 + i_2 = \delta + A$

S. No.	Angle of incidence (i_1)	Angle of refraction		Angle of emergence = i_2	Angle of deviation, δ	$i_1 + i_2$	$A+\delta$	$r_1 + r_2$
		r_1	r_2					
1.								
2.								
3.								

Result

From the observation table, it is verified that within the limit of experimental error,

$$i_1 + i_2 = A + \delta \quad \text{and} \quad A = r_1 + r_2$$

Precautions

1. During the course of experiment, the prism should not be disturbed.
2. In order to show the direction of rays of light, arrow heads should be marked.
3. Encircle the marked position of pins.
4. The bases of pins must be in a straight line.

Experiment 7

Aim

To trace the course of a ray of light incident normally ($i = 0°$) on different types of prisms and also to measure the angle of deviation, δ.

Apparatus Required

Drawing board, drawing sheet, alpins, scale, protractor, thumb pins, three types of prisms.

1. Right angled (45°, 90°, 45°) prism
2. Equilateral (60°, 60°, 60°) prism
3. Triangular (30°, 90°, 60°) prism

Theory/Principle Used

As, shown in the figure given below that whenever a ray of light passes from denser to rarer medium, i.e. from glass to air, then the refracted ray bends away from normal. So, $i < r$.

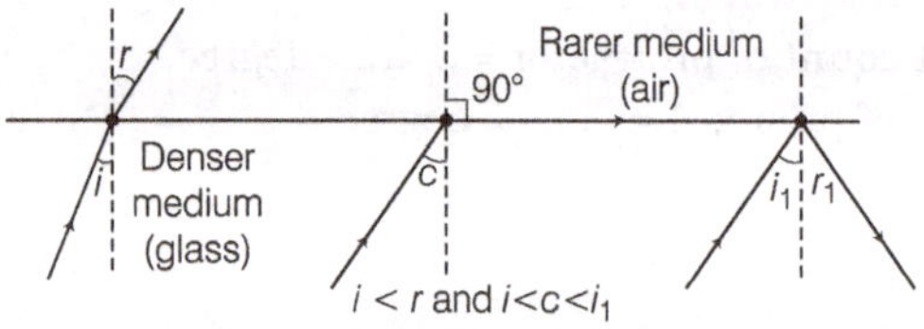

So, in case, if angle of incidence is increased in such a manner that the refracted angle becomes 90°, then such angle of incidence is known as critical angle.

The phenomenon in which, if angle of incidence in denser medium is increased beyond the critical angle, then the refraction does not take place in rarer medium and the ray get reflected back in same medium obeying law of reflection without any valuable loss of intensity of light, is known as total internal reflection.

Procedure

1. Take a sheet of white paper and with the help of thumb pins, fix it on the drawing board.
2. With the help of a sharp pencil, draw a straight line $X'X$ near the middle of paper and parallel to its length.

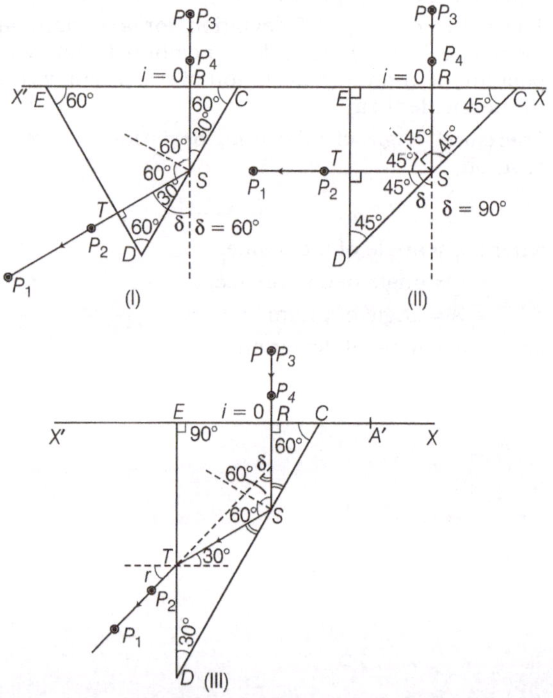

3. Now, mark the point of incidence R at 3 places on $X'X$ line equidistant each other.
4. At the point of incidence R on line $X'X$, draw a normal PR.
5. Atleast 10 cm apart, fix two points P_3 P_4 vertically on PR.
6. Put a triangular face prism CDE on $X'X$ near R in such a manner that the desired angle is towards the right side and side CE on XX'.
7. Construct the boundaries of prism.
8. Try to observe the images of P_3P_4 pins through the face DE.
9. Prism can be shifted along XX' to observe the images P'_3 P'_4.
10. Now, try to fix up the pins P_1P_2 in the line of images P'_3 and P'_4.
11. After removing the pins, encircled the pins position.
12. Geometrically, measure the various angles with the help of protractor.
13. Repeat the same procedure for other two prisms.

Observations

Least count of protractor = ... degree.

Since, for equilateral prism, $\angle C = \angle D = \angle E = 60°$

For right angled isosceles prism, $\angle C = 45°$, $\angle D = 45°$, $\angle E = 90°$

For right angle prism, $\angle C = 60°$, $\angle D = 30°$, $\angle E = 90°$.

Observation table to obtain angle of deviation for different prisms

S.No.	Type of prism	Angle of prism	Angle of incidence on face		Angle of refractions on face		$\angle PST$	Angle of deviation, $\angle\delta$
			CE	CD	CE	CD		
1.								
2.								
3.								

Result

When a ray of light falls normally on face CE of prism, then angle of deviation suffered by

1. equilateral prism (60°, 60°, 60°) is .... degree.
2. right angled isosceles prism (45°, 90°, 45°) is .... degree.
3. right angled prism (30°, 90°, 60°) is .... degree.

Precautions

1. During the course of experiment, prism should not be displaced.
2. The sharp and vertical pins must be used.
3. Each ray should be marked by an arrow head.
4. After removing the drawing board, position of all pins should be encircled.

Viva-Voce

1. Define the term prism.

Ans. A transparent, homogeneous medium bounded by three rectangular triangular plane surfaces is known as a prism.

2. In what manner do the angle of deviation changes with the angle of incidence?

Ans. The angle of deviation increases with increase in angle of incidence till it reaches a certain minimum angle (δ_m). So, on further increasing the angle of incidence, angle of deviation also increases.

3. What do you understand by the term angle of deviation?

Ans. The angle made by the incident ray and the emergent ray is called angle of deviation.

4. State the relation between refractive index and the angle of minimum deviation produced by a prism.

Ans. The relation between refractive index and the angle of minimum deviation produced by a prism is given by

$$\mu = \frac{\sin\left(\frac{A+\delta_m}{2}\right)}{\sin\left(\frac{A}{2}\right)}$$

5. Mention the factors on which the angle of deviation depends?

Ans. The angle of deviation depends on
(i) angle of incidence
(ii) angle of prism
(iii) material of the prism
(iv) wavelength of light ray

6. How does a ray of light bends after refraction in prism?

Ans. After suffering refraction through prism, ray of light bends towards the base of the prism.

7. When the prism is set in the position of minimum deviation, how does the refracted ray passes through prism?

Ans. When the prism is set in the position of minimum deviation, the refracted ray passes parallel to the base of the prism.

8. Name the colour which deviates the most and which deviates the least?

Ans. Violet colour deviates the most while red colour deviates the least.

9. Define critical angle.

Ans. When a ray of light passes from denser to the rarer medium, the angle of incidence in denser medium for which angle of refraction in rarer medium becomes 90° is known as critical angle.

10. Mention the difference that you detect between the direction of emergent ray in a glass slab and prism?

Ans. In the case of glass slab, the emergent ray is laterally displaced but it is parallel to the incident ray. In the case of prism, the emergent ray is deviated. It is because in a glass slab, the two refracting faces are parallel to each other, while in a prism, they are inclined at an angle *A*.

11. What do you understand by refracting edge or angle of prism in prism?

Ans. The angle at which the two refracting surfaces of prism meet is called refracting edge or angle of prism.

Experiment 8

Aim

To calculate the specific heat of the material of given calorimeter, from the temperature readings and masses of cold water, warm water and its mixture taken in the calorimeter.

Apparatus Required

Weight box, physical balance, two half degree thermometers and a calorimeter with outer jacket.

Theory/Principle Used

By the method of mixtures, the specific heat of the material (or copper) can be determined. Consider that a mass m_a of hot water at temperature t_a is added to cold water of mass m_b at temperature t_b in a calorimeter of mass m.

Since, according to the principle of calorimetry,

heat lost by hot water = heat gained by cold water and calorimeter ...(i)

The final temperature becomes T.

$\because$ Heat lost by hot water $= m_a(t_a - T)$

Heat gained by cold water and calorimeter

$$= m_b(T - t_b) + mc(T - t_b) = (T - t_b)(m_b + mc)$$

where, c is specific heat of material of calorimeter.

$\therefore$ From Eq. (i), we get

$$(T - t_b)(m_b + mc) = m_a(t_a - T)$$

$$\Rightarrow \quad c = \frac{m_a(t_a - T)}{m(T - t_b)} - \frac{m_b}{m}$$

Procedure

1. Firstly, measure the room temperature with the two thermometers *B* and *D*.
2. Determine the mass of empty and dry calorimeter along with the stirrer.

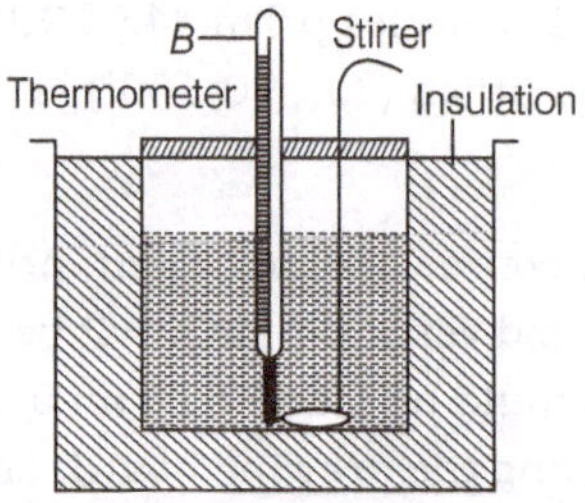

Copper calorimeter

3. Fill the calorimeter with some cold water and find its mass again.
4. Now, put this calorimeter in the outer jacket.
5. Record the temperature of this cold water.
6. Observe that thermometer does not touch the sides or bottom of this calorimeter.
7. After determining the temperature of some hot water, check that its temperature should be in between 70°C–80°C.
8. Mix this water into the cold water already taken in calorimeter.
9. Gently, stir it with the help of stirrer and record the final temperature.

10. Determine the mass of calorimeter along with the mixture of cold water, hot water and stirrer using a physical balance.

Observations and Calculations

Reading of thermometer, $B = t_1$ °C

Reading of thermometer, $D = t_2$ °C

Correction to be applied to $B = (t_1 - t_2)$°C

Mass of calorimeter + stirrer (m) = ... g.

Mass of calorimeter + stirrer + cold water

(W_a) = ... g.

Corrected initial temperature of cold water

(t_b) = ... °C.

Corrected initial temperature of hot water

(t_a) = ... °C.

Final temperature of mixture (T) = ... °C.

Mass of calorimeter + stirrer + cold water + hot water

= .... g.

Mass of cold water

$(m_b) = (W_a - m)$ = ... g.

Mass of hot water

$(m_a) = (W_b - W_a)$ = ... g.

Specific heat of material of copper

$$c = \frac{m_a(t_a - T)}{m(T - t_b)} - \frac{m_b}{m}$$

= .... cal g^{-1}°C^{-1}

or .... J $kg^{-1}K^{-1}$

Actual value of specific heat of copper from standard table = ... J $kg^{-1}K^{-1}$.

Result

The specific heat capacity of material of calorimeter is .... cal g^{-1}° C^{-1} or .... J $kg^{-1}K^{-1}$.

Precautions

1. The quantity of water in the calorimeter must not be more than about three-fourth.
2. Gently, stir the contents of calorimeter, so that water does not splash out from calorimeter.
3. The correction of temperature should be applied.
4. Physical balance should be in proper working condition.

Experiment 9

Aim

To determine the specific heat of a metal by the method of mixtures.

Apparatus Required

Two half degree thermometers, fractional weights, weight box, burner, physical balance, a calorimeter with non conducting jacket, the given metal in the form of powder and hypsometer apparatus.

Theory/Principle Used

Specific heat of metal can be determined by the method of mixture. It is done when some hot metal is put into the water taken in the calorimeter, then the heat is lost by the metal and it is gained by water and calorimeter due to which its temperature rises.

So in case, if the heat is not allowed to radiate from the surface of calorimeter, then

heat lost by metal = heat gained by water and calorimeter

Procedure

1. Determine the room temperature with the help of thermometer B and D.

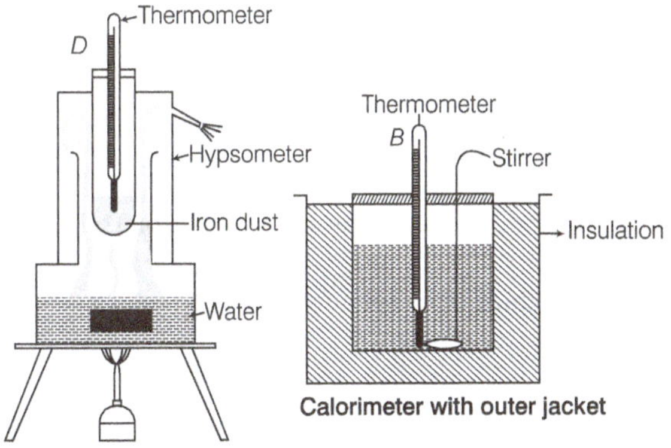

Calorimeter with outer jacket

2. Now, determine the mass of some metal powder by using the physical balance and fractional weights.
3. After putting the iron dust (metal powder) in the copper calorimeter, heat it till its temperature becomes constant as recorded by thermometer D. Record its temperature.
4. Now, find the mass of empty and dry calorimeter.

5. Fill the calorimeter with some cold water and again determine its mass.
6. Calculate the mass of water from the two readings calculated in step (4) and (5).
7. Record the initial temperature of water.
8. Now, place the calorimeter in the insulating jacket.
9. Immediately, transfer the hot iron dust into the calorimeter without any loss of time and stir it gently.
10. After this, note down the final maximum temperature of mixture of water and iron dust.
11. At last, note down the specific heat of copper from the standard table.

Observations and Calculations

Room temperature with thermometer, $B = T_a$

Room temperature with thermometer, $D = T_b$

Correction to be applied to thermometer,

$B = T_a - T_b$

Mass of iron dust (m) = ... g.

Corrected initial temperature of iron dust

(t') = ... °C.

Mass of empty calorimeter + stirrer

(W_a) = ... g.

Mass of calorimeter + water + stirrer

(W_b) = ... g.

Mass of water, $(m_a) = W_b - W_a$ = ... g.

Initial temperature of water

(t'') = ... °C.

Final temperature of mixture

(T) = ... °C.

Specific heat of copper (from standard table)

(c) = ... cal $g^{-1\circ}C^{-1}$.

Water equivalent of calorimeter

$(W) = W_a \times c$ = ... g.

Fall in temperature of iron dust

$(t' - T)$ = ... °C.

Rise in temperature of water and calorimeter

$(T - t'')$ = ... °C.

Let specific heat of iron dust = c

Let specific heat of water = S

Heat lost by iron dust = $mc(t' - T)$

Heat gained by water and calorimeter

$$= (m_a s + W)(T - t'')$$

According to principle of calorimetry,

heat lost = heat gained

$$mc(t' - T) = (m_a s + W)(T - t'')$$

$$c = \frac{(m_a s + W)(T - t'')}{m(t' - T)} \text{ cal g}^{-1\circ}\text{C}^{-1} = ..\text{J kg}^{-1}\text{K}^{-1}$$

Actual value from standard tables

= .... cal $g^{-1\circ}C^{-1}$.

Percentage error

$$= \frac{\text{Difference between the calculated and actual value}}{\text{Actual value}} \times 100$$

= .... %

Result

The specific heat capacity of given metal piece by experiment is .... cal $g^{-1\circ}C^{-1}$.

Precautions

1. Metal dust must be preferred in the place of metal piece.
2. The correction of temperature must be applied in both the readings of thermometer.
3. Calorimeter jacket must be in good condition.
4. During heating, stir the water, so that the temperature of water and metal must be same.

Experiment 10

Aim

To determine the specific latent heat of ice.

Apparatus Required

Fractional weights, weight box, a small piece of ice, calorimeter with non-conducting jacket, half degree thermometer, blotting papers and physical balance.

Theory/Principle Used

The amount of heat required to melt unit mass of ice at 0°C without any rise of temperature, is known as latent heat of fusion of ice. It is denoted by L.

Consider if mass m_a of ice is dipped into the water of mass m_b at temperature t_a, contained in a calorimeter of water equivalent W, the ice takes the heat from water for its melting. Assume T be the final temperature. So, if no heat is lost by the radiation, then according to the principle of calorimetry,

heat gained = heat lost ...(i)

Let specific heat of water = c

Heat gained by ice $= m_a L + m_a c(T - 0)$

$= m_a L + m_a cT$ ...(ii)

Heat lost by water and calorimeter

$= (m_b c + W)(t_a - T)$ ...(iii)

From Eqs. (i), (ii) and (iii), we get

$$m_a cL + m_a cT = (m_b c + W)(t_a - T)$$

$$\Rightarrow \quad L = \frac{(m_b c + W)(t_a - T) - m_a cT}{m_a c}$$

By the above formula, the value of L can be calculated.

Procedure

1. Firstly, determine the mass of empty and dry calorimeter along with the stirrer.
2. Try to fill about half of calorimeter with water and determine its mass again with the help of a physical balance.

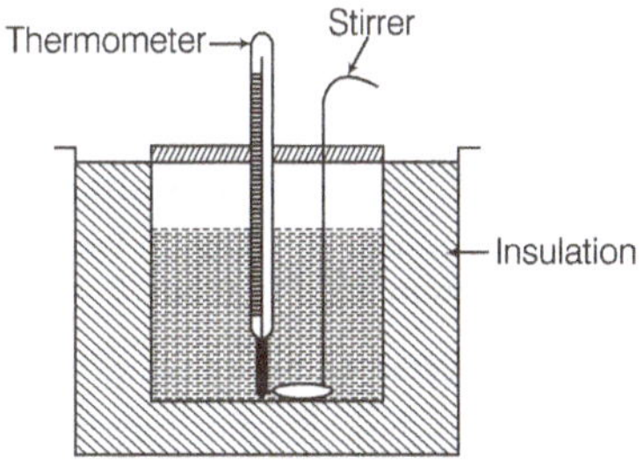

Calorimeter with outer jacket

3. Now, put this calorimeter in the insulating jacket.
4. By using a thermometer, determine the final temperature of water.
5. Dry the small piece of ice by placing it between the layers of blotting papers.
6. Immediately use the forces to put this ice into the calorimeter.
7. Gently, stir the water and keep on doing it till the whole of the ice melts.
8. Observe whether the temperature starts falling or not.
9. If it starts, then note down the final and minimum temperature of water when the whole of ice melts.
10. At last, determine the mass of calorimeter including the original water and melted ice using a physical balance.

Observations and Calculations

Mass of calorimeter (m) = ... g

Mass of calorimeter + water (W_a) = ... g

Mass of water, $m_b = (W_a - m)$ = ... g

Initial temperature of water (t_a) = ... °C

Final temperature when whole ice melts

(T) = ... °C

Mass of calorimeter + water + ice (W_b) = ... g

Mass of ice $(m_a) = (W_b - W_a)$ = ... g

Specific heat of copper from standard table

(c) = ... cal $g^{-1}\,{}^\circ C^{-1}$

Water equivalent $(W) = m \times c$ = ... g

where, m = mass of copper (calorimeter)

Let latent heat of ice = L

$$\Rightarrow \quad L = \frac{(m_b c + W)(t_a - T) - m_a cT}{m_a c} \text{ cal } g^{-1}$$

= .... J kg^{-1}

Actual value from standard tables = ... J kg^{-1}

Percentage error

$$= \frac{\text{Difference between the actual and calculated values}}{\text{Actual value}} \times 100$$

= .... %

Result

The specific latent heat of ice = ... cal $g^{-1}\,{}^\circ C^{-1}$ or .... J $kg^{-1}K^{-1}$.

Precautions

1. It should be ensured that during transferring of water, droplets of water in calorimeter should get left.
2. During measurement of temperature, correction of thermometer must be applied.
3. In order to minimise the radiations of heat, calorimeter must be cleaned.
4. Final temperature must be recorded when it becomes steady.

Viva-Voce

1. Define calorimetry.

Ans. The branch of Physics which deals with the measurement of heat energy, specific heat, latent heat, etc., of material is known as calorimetry.

2. State the relation between the units J $kg^{-1}K^{-1}$ and cal $g^{-1}\,{}^\circ C^{-1}$.

Ans. $\because$ 1 cal $g^{-1}\,{}^\circ C^{-1} = \dfrac{4.186 \text{ J}}{1 \text{ g}^\circ\text{C}}$

$$= \frac{4.186 \text{ J}}{\frac{1}{1000} \text{ kg K}}$$

$\therefore$ 1 cal $g^{-1}\,{}^\circ C^{-1}$ = 4186 J $kg^{-1}K^{-1}$

3. Give reason of stirring water during the measurement of temperature.

Ans. Since, water is a bad conductor of heat. It is stirred by stirrer continuously, so that the temperature of whole water remains the same.

4. Mention the latent heat of ice.

Ans. The latent heat of ice is 80 cal g^{-1}.

5. State the principle of calorimetry.

Ans. According to the principle of calorimetry, heat gained by one substance is always equal to the heat lost by the other substance, when they are mixed together provided that the heat is not lost to the surroundings by any other way.

6. Give the SI unit of latent heat.

Ans. The SI unit of latent heat is $J\,kg^{-1}$.

7. Define latent heat of fusion.

Ans. The amount of heat required to melt the unit mass of the substance at its melting point, is known as latent heat of fusion of that substance.

8. Define the term specific heat capacity.

Ans. The amount of heat required to raise the temperature of 1g of the body through 1°C, is known as specific heat capacity of the body.

9. State whether the specific heat capacity is a constant quantity or not?

Ans. No, specific heat capacity is not a constant quantity because it varies from substance to substance and is constant for the given substance.

10. Define the term water equivalent of a body.

Ans. It is equal to the quantity of water which has the same thermal capacity as that of body. In practical, it is equal to the product of mass and specific heat.

11. Name the liquid which has highest specific heat capacity.

Ans. Water has the highest specific heat capacity.

12. When heat is transferred between substance, a final temperature is attained by the substance. What is the name of this final temperature?

Ans. The name of this final temperature is equilibrium temperature.

13. Ice cream at 0°C is colder than water at 0°C, Why?

Ans. It is because ice cream can extract 80 cal/g more heat from mouth as compared to that of water at 0°C.

14. Which metal is used to make a calorimeter?

Ans. Copper is used to make a calorimeter.

15. Why is calorimeter made of copper?

Ans. Because copper is a very good conductor of heat.

Experiment 11

Aim

To verify Ohm's law and hence find the value of unknown resistance.

Apparatus Required

A resistance wire, dry cells, key, voltmeter of range 0-15 V, ammeter of range 0-1.5 A, rheostat, connecting wires and sand paper.

Theory/Principle Used

As, per the Ohm's law, if the physical conditions like length, breadth, temperature, etc., of a conductor are constant, then the current flowing through the conductor in a closed circuit is directly proportional to the potential difference across its two ends.

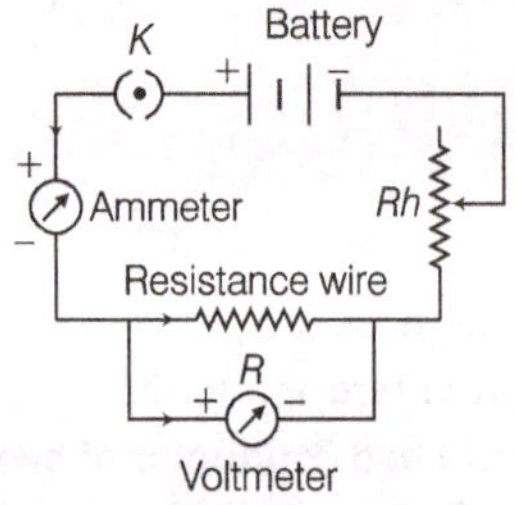

Circuit diagram

$$\therefore \quad I \propto V \Rightarrow \frac{V}{I} = \text{constant} = R \text{ (say)} \Rightarrow R = \frac{V}{I}$$

where, R is a constant for the conductor and is known as resistance of conductor.

The property of a conductor which opposes the flow of current (I) in the conductor or increases the potential difference (V) across its ends, is known as resistance of conductor. The SI unit of resistance is ohm (Ω).

Since, $\frac{V}{I} = R$

where, R is a constant.

Therefore, the I *versus* V graph will be a straight line, also the components that conducts the current in accordance with Ohm's law are said to be Ohmic.

Procedure

1. Firstly, arrange the apparatus on the table and make the circuit connections as shown in the above circuit diagram.
2. With the help of connecting wires, connect the ammeter in series and voltmeter in parallel with the resistance.
3. Record the least count and zero errors of voltmeter and ammeter.
4. After inserting the plug key, adjust the rheostat in order to register a small current in the resistance wire.
5. Now, note down the corresponding ammeter and voltmeter readings.
6. In order to increase the current in the regular steps, move the variable terminal of the rheostat and note down the ammeter and voltmeter readings.

7. To have the different sets of observations, take more readings.
8. Lastly, draw the graph between voltage (V) and current (I), find its slope.

Observations

1. Range of ammeter = ... A
2. Least count of ammeter = ... A
3. Zero error of ammeter = ... A
4. Range of voltmeter = ... V
5. Least count of voltmeter = ... V
6. Zero error of voltmeter = ... V
7. Correction applied to the ammeter = ... A
8. Correction applied to the voltmeter = ... V

Observation table for calculating the resistance

S. No.	Reading of Ammeter (I)		Reading of Voltmeter (V)		Resistance, $R = V/I$ (ohm)
	Observed	Corrected (A)	Observed	Corrected (A)	
(i)					$R_a = \ldots$
(ii)					$R_b = \ldots$
(iii)					$R_c = \ldots$
(iv)					$R_d = \ldots$

Calculations

Mean value of resistance,

$$R = \frac{R_a + R_b + R_c + R_d}{4} = \ldots\ldots\ldots\ \Omega$$

Graph

Plot a graph between the voltage (V) and the current (I) by taking V along Y-axis and I along X-axis.

Here, we will find that

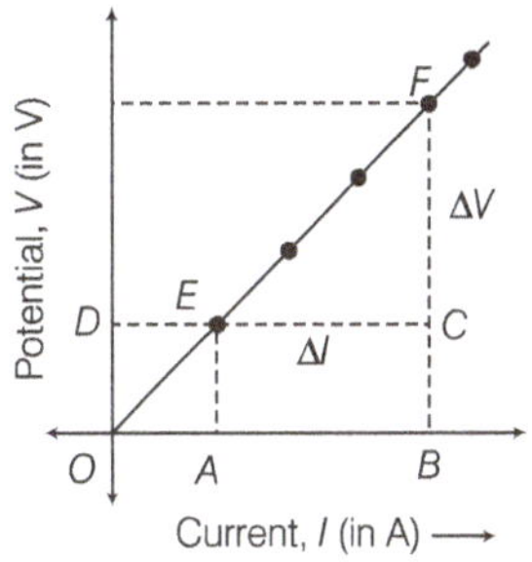

$$\text{Slope} = \frac{FC}{EC} \Rightarrow R = \frac{FC}{EC} = \frac{\Delta V}{\Delta I} \Rightarrow R = \frac{\Delta V}{\Delta I} = \ldots\ldots\ \Omega$$

Result

The graph of V *versus* I is a straight line. It shows that $V \propto I$ which proves Ohm's law.

From observation table, resistance of a conductor = ... Ω

From graph, resistance of a conductor = ... Ω

Precautions

1. The end of the connecting wires should be rubbed with the sand paper.
2. The emf of the cell should be less than the range of the voltmeter.
3. In order to avoid heating of conductor, fan should be used.
4. The key should be removed for sometime and then reconnect while taking the reading so that the resistance wire becomes cold.
5. While making the connections, join the positive ends of ammeter and voltmeter with the positive terminal of the battery.
6. A rheostat of low resistance should be used.

Viva-Voce

1. Define the term current.

Ans. Current can be defined as rate of flow of charge.

2. Why thick connecting wires are used?

Ans. Since, thin wires have higher resistance while the thick wires have low resistance which will not affect the result. Hence, they are used as connecting wires.

3. What is meant by the term resistance of a conductor?

Ans. The property of a conductor which opposes the flow of current through it, is known as the resistance of a conductor.

4. State the function of rheostat.

Ans. Rheostat is a device which is used to provide variable resistance in a circuit.

5. What is meant by one ohm?

Ans. If current passing through the resistance is one ampere and potential difference between the ends of a conductor is one volt, then the resistance of conductor is said to be one ohm.

6. Is it possible to have a negative resistance?

Ans. Resistance can be negative if on increasing the potential, its current decreases. It may be in semiconductor devices like transistors, etc.

7. State how resistance of a conductor can be increased?

Ans. Resistance of a conductor increases on

(i) increasing the length of conductor.
(ii) decreasing area of cross-section.
(iii) increasing the temperature of conductor.

8. What is the meaning of cell or a battery?

Ans. Cell or a battery is a device in which potential difference between the two points or terminals is maintained by either chemical reaction or generator.

9. State any one limitation of Ohm's law.

Ans. It is not applicable for diode, triode or where temperature resistance is high like bulbs.

10. If a wire of resistance 2 Ω is stretched to double its length, what will be its new resistance?

Ans. If a wire of resistance 2 Ω is stretched to double its length, then its new resistance will be 8 Ω.

11. Do the resistance of a conductor vary with temperature?

Ans. Yes, resistance of a conductor varies with temperature. It increases with rise of temperature.

Experiment 12

Aim

To set up a model of household wiring circuit including main wiring circuit and to study the functions of switches and fuse.

Apparatus Required

Plugs, bulb, bulb holder switch (30 A, 20 A, 15 A, 5 A, 5 A), three core electric wire, brown colour, black colour, green colour wire with yellow strip, five fuses (25 A, 15 A, 10 A, 5 A, 5 A), plugs, wall socket, tester and tools, etc.

Theory/Principle Used

A ring system of wiring is followed in the household circuiting. In this system, the three wires, live, neutral and Earth as separate wires runs from the main switch to different rooms or parts of a house and ends again at main switch from where it starts.

A separate fuse wire (MCB) is connected to a room or a part of house for the power supply to all appliances of a room or part. Also, all connections of room are in parallel and all switches and fuses are in series.

The responsibility of electric power supply to the consumer is undertaken by the state electricity board. It provides the power supply upto the input and output of electric meter with two fuses in series to live wire or phase wire. The cable from pole to electric meter and wires in the house wiring has following codes of colour.

Type of Wire	Colour of Insulation	
	Old Convention	International Colour Coding
Live	Red	Brown
Neutral	Black	Light blue
Earth	Green	Green with yellow strip or *vice-versa*

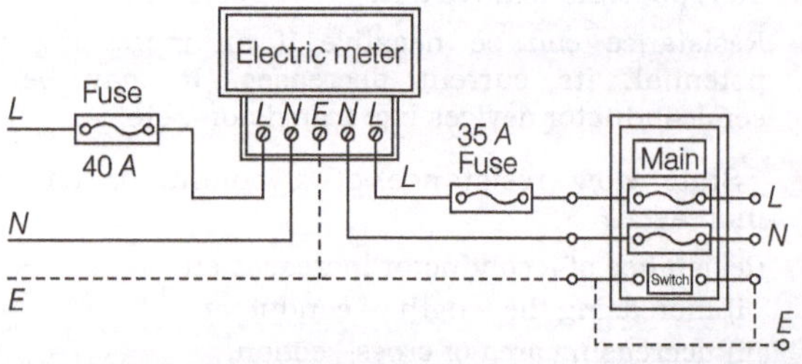

Main switch wiring

Procedure

1. By taking a panel board, spread the red coloured wire in a form of a ring *PQRS*. Its terminal will be used as live wire.
2. Now, use black coloured wire and spread it in the form of another ring *XYWZ*. Then, connect a wire at any point on the ring and the other terminal to the main fuse as shown in the figure given below. This black wire will be used as neutral wire.
3. Next, take a yellow coloured wire and spread in the form of ring *ABCD* connect a wire to the main fuse as shown in the figure. This yellow wire will be used as Earth wire.
4. Take some copper wire with proper insulation with the PVC as covers red, black and yellow.
5. Using red wires, make a connection with one terminal of fuse F_1 and its another terminal to one terminal of switch S_1 as shown in the figure.

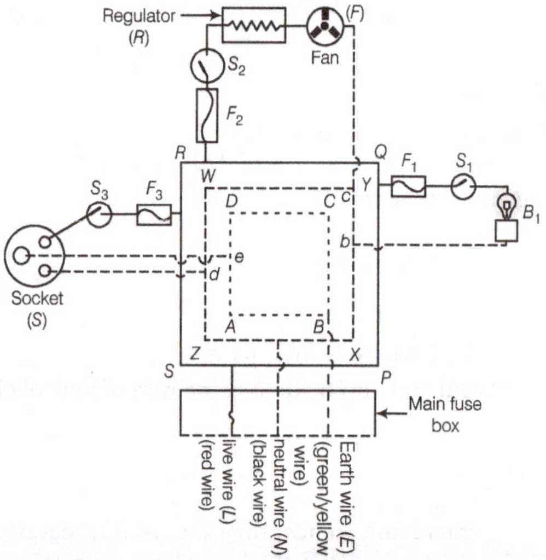

6. Then, connect the second terminal by switch S_1 to one terminal of bulb B_1 and another terminal of this bulb to any point on the ring *XYWZ* using black wire.
7. Similarly make other connections of regulator, fan, socket and switches as given in the figure.
8. Connect the terminals *L*, *N* and *E* to the source of alternating current i.e. AC mains.

Observations

Function of Switches

S.No.	Switch	ON/OFF	Bulb, B_1	Fan, F	Appliance connected to the socket, S
(i)	S_1	ON	ON	OFF	OFF
(ii)	S_2	ON	OFF	ON	OFF
(iii)	S_3	ON	OFF	OFF	ON
(iv)	S_1 and S_2	ON	ON	ON	OFF
(v)	S_2 and S_3	ON	OFF	ON	ON
(vi)	S_1 and S_3	ON	ON	OFF	ON
(vii)	S_1, S_2 and S_3	ON	ON	ON	ON

Function of Fuse

When switches S_1, S_2 and S_3 are ON.

S.No.	Fuse blown	Bulb, B_1	Fan, F	Appliance connected with socket, S
(i)	F_1	OFF	ON	ON
(ii)	F_2	ON	OFF	ON
(iii)	F_3	ON	ON	OFF
(iv)	F_1 and F_2	OFF	OFF	ON
(v)	F_2 and F_3	ON	OFF	OFF
(vi)	F_1 and F_3	OFF	ON	OFF
(vii)	F_1, F_2 and F_3	OFF	OFF	OFF

Result

All the electrical appliances example fans, bulbs, etc., when connected in parallel combination can operate at the same voltage. Also, they can be operated independently.

Precautions

1. All the connection should be made light.
2. Use sand paper to clean the ends of the wires for proper connections.
3. Use fuse of proper rating.
4. Always covers the connections with an electric insulation tape.

Viva-Voce

1. What is the potential difference between live wire and neutral wire in domestic power supply?

Ans. In India, the potential difference between the live wire and the neutral wire is 220 V.

2. How are lamps or bulbs or fans connected in a house?

Ans. All the electrical appliances in a house are connected in parallel combination.

3. Name the device which is used to protect the electric circuits from overloading and short circuits.

Ans. Electric fuse is used to protect overloading and short circuits.

4. State the feature why tungsten filament is used in bulbs?

Ans. As, tungsten has high resistivity and very high melting point.

5. Name the wire (live or neutral) through which electric fuse is connected in a circuits?

Ans. Live wire is used to connect fuse in a circuits.

6. What is the unit of electrical energy?

Ans. The unit of electrical energy is kWh (Kilowatt-hour).

7. What is an electric meter?

Ans. It is a device used in houses to measure the electrical energy used.

ICSE
SAMPLE PAPER 1

(Fully Solved)

Physics-X

Time : 2 hrs

Max Marks : 80

General Instructions

1. Answer to this paper must to be written on the paper provided separately.
2. You will not be allowed to write during the first 15 minutes. This time is to be spent in reading the question paper.
3. The time given at the head of this paper is the time allowed for writing the answers.
4. **Section A** is compulsory. Attempt any four questions from **Section B**.
5. The intended marks for questions or parts of questions are given in brackets [ ].

Section-A

[40 Marks]

(Attempt all questions from this section)

1. Choose the correct answers to the questions from the given options. [15]

(i) The mechanical advantage in class III types of lever is less than one. Which of the following is the correct reason for this? *• Understanding*

(a) Effort arm length < load arm length

(b) Effort arm length > load arm length

(c) Effort arm length = load arm length

(d) None of the above

(ii) How does the medium affect the amplitude of free vibrations ?

(a) It decreases due to force of friction between vibrating body and medium particles.

(b) It increases due to force of friction between vibrating body and medium particles.

(c) It remains unaffected by medium.

(d) Either (b) or (c). *• Recall*

(iii) An electrician puts a fuse of rating 5 A in that part of domestic electrical circuit in which an electric heater of rating 1.5 kW, 220 V is operating. What is likely to happen in this case?

(a) The heater will burn and break the circuit.

(b) The fuse will melt and break the circuit.

(c) Both the heater and fuse will burn.

(d) Nothing happens to the circuit. *• Application*

(iv) If both current and magnetic field are reversed simultaneously, then the direction of rotation of a motor

(a) reverses once (b) reverses periodically

(c) remains unchanged (d) Cannot be said

• Recall

(v) **Assertion** (A) The refractive index of a medium decreases with increase in wavelength of incident light.

Reason (R) The speed of light remains same in all media. *• Understanding & Recall*

(a) Both A and R are true and R is the correct explanation of A.

(b) Both A and R are true but R is not the correct explanation of A.

(c) A is false but R is true.

(d) A is true but R is false.

(vi) Which of the following ray diagrams is correct for the ray of light incident on a lens shown in figure?

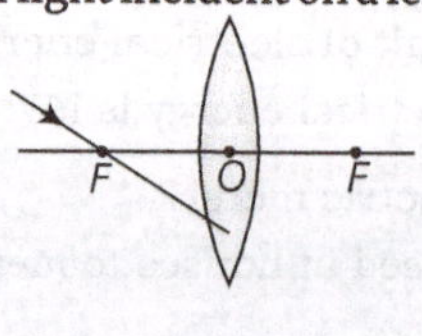

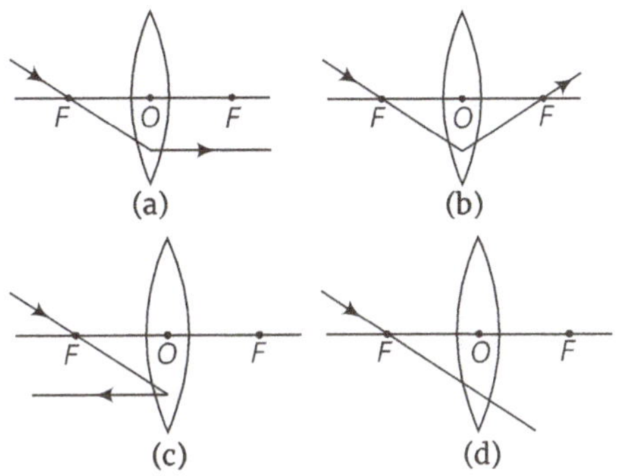

• *Recall & Application*

(vii) A body of mass 1 kg moves with a velocity 5 ms^{-1}. A force is applied on it for 1 ms, such that its velocity is increased to 7 ms^{-1}. The force applied on the body is • *Understanding*

(a) 2000 N (b) 200 N
(c) 400 N (d) 20 N

(viii) Work done on a body depends on • *Recall*

(a) the magnitude of external force applied on the body only
(b) the displacement of the body only
(c) Both the displacement of body and the component of external force acting in the direction of its displacement
(d) None of the above

(ix) The diagram below shows the balanced position of a meter scale. • *Understanding & Recall*

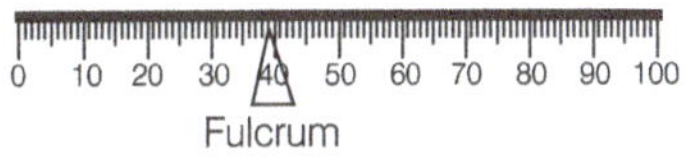

Which one of the following diagrams shows the correct position of the scale, when it is supported at the centre?

(a)
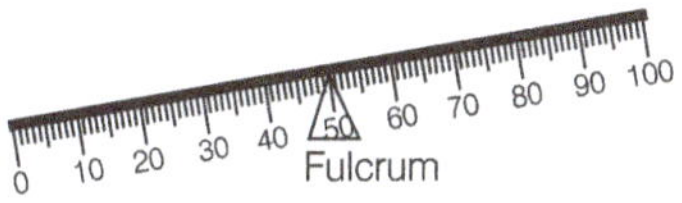

(b)
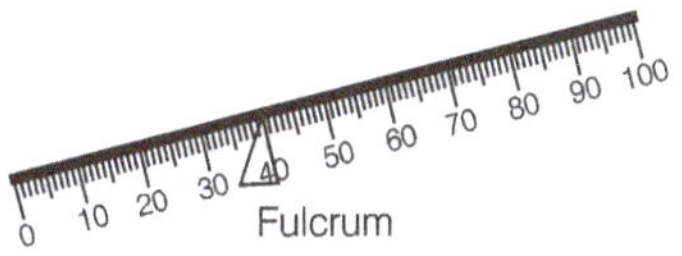

(c)
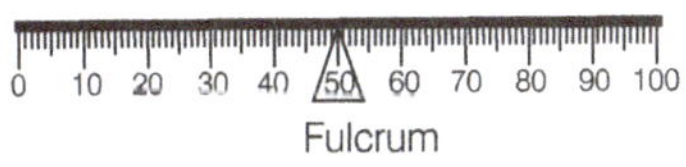

(d)
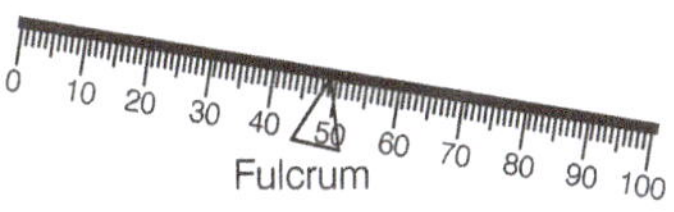

(x) In the diagram shown below • *Recall & Application*

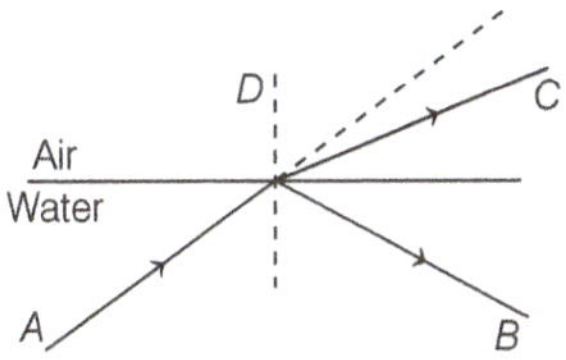

(a) *B* is incident ray and *C* is refracted ray
(b) *A* is incident ray and *B* is refracted ray
(c) *C* is incident ray and *B* is refracted ray
(d) *A* is incident ray and *C* is refracted ray

(xi) The wavelength of red light is 800 nm. If speed of light is 3×10^8 ms^{-1}, then its frequency is • *Recall*

(a) 3×10^{14} Hz (b) 3.75×10^{14} Hz
(c) 4.25×10^{14} Hz (d) 4.8×10^{14} Hz

(xii) A small air bubble in a glass block, when seen from above appears to be raised because of • *Recall*

(a) refraction of light
(b) reflection of light
(c) reflection and refraction of light
(d) None of the above

(xiii) Two bodies of specific heats c_1 and c_2 having same heat capacities are combined to form a single composite body. What is the specific heat of the composite body? • *Understanding*

(a) $\frac{c_1 - c_2}{2c_1 c_2}$ (b) $\frac{c_1 + c_2}{2 c_1 c_2}$
(c) $\frac{2 c_1 c_2}{c_1 + c_2}$ (d) $\frac{2 c_1 c_2}{c_1 - c_2}$

(xiv) To determine the equivalent resistance of two resistors when connected in series, a student arranged the circuit components as shown in the figure. But he did not succeed to achieve the objective. • *Analysis & Application*

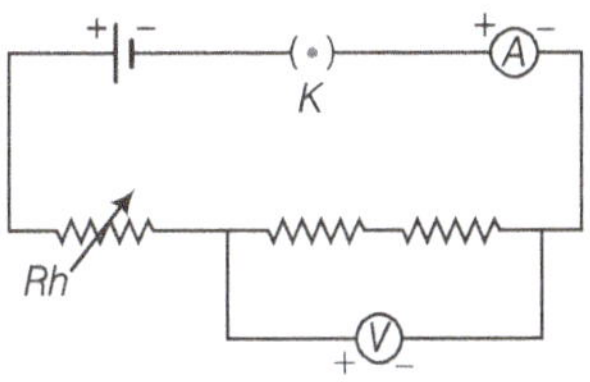

Which of the following mistakes has been committed by him in setting up the circuit?

(a) Position of ammeter is incorrect
(b) Position of voltmeter is incorrect
(c) Terminals of ammeter are wrongly connected
(d) Terminals of voltmeter are wrongly connected

(xv) Water is used in car radiators because
(a) it is a good conductor of heat
(b) it conducts heat faster as compared to the other substances and cools the engine quickly
(c) its specific heat capacity is very low
(d) its specific heat capacity is very high, so it can cool the engine without a greater increase in its own temperature
• *Application*

2. (i) Complete the following by choosing the correct answers from the bracket. [6]
(a) Bat emit high frequency or high pitched ......(ultrasonic waves/Infrasonic waves)
(b) The sound of frequencies higher than ...... (20000 Hz/30000 Hz) are called as ultrasonic sound.
(c) The direction of force on a current-carrying conductor in a magnetic field is given by...... (Fleming's left hand rule/Fleming's right hand rule/Right hand thumb rule).
(d) Boiling point of a liquid ...... (increases/decreases) with increase of the impurities in it.
(e) Echocardiogram is based on ...... (reflection/refraction of sound using .... (ultrasound/infrasonic).
• *Recall & understanding*

(ii) (a) Give one example of pure rotational motion. [1]
(b) Comment on the movement of particles on the axis of rotation in pure rotational motion. [1]

(iii) A lens forms an erect, magnified and virtual image of an object. Name the lens used and draw a labelled ray diagram to show the image formation.
• *Understanding*

3. (i) (a) If the lens is placed in water instead of air, how does its focal length change? [1]
• *Recall*
(b) Which lens, thick or thin has greater focal length? [1]
• *Recall*

(ii) (a) State Ohm's law. [1]
• *Recall*
(b) Diagrammatically illustrate how you would connect a key, a battery, a voltmeter, an ammeter, an unknown resistance R and a rheostat, so that it can be used to verify the above law? [1]
• *Understanding*

(iii) It is established that an electric current through a metallic conductor produces a magnetic field around it. Is there a similar magnetic field produced around a thin beam of moving (a) α-particles, (b) neutrons? Justify your answer. [2]
• *Understanding*

(iv) Find the specific heat capacity of a body having mass 500 g and requires 2000 J of heat energy to raise its temperature from 35°C to 45°C. [2]
• *Understanding & Evaluate*

(v) A body of mass 50 kg has a momentum of 3000 kg-ms^{-1}. Calculate • *Understanding*
(a) the kinetic energy of the body and [1]
(b) the velocity of the body. [1]

(vi) (a) The diagram shows a bar magnet surrounded by four plotting compasses. Copy the diagram and mark the direction of the compass needle for each of the cases B, C and D. [1]

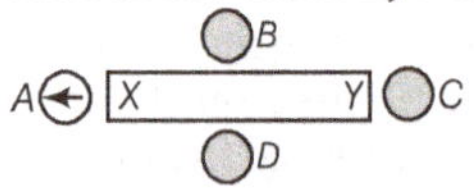

• *Application*
(b) Which is the North pole : X or Y? [1]

(vii) A stretched wire 0.5 m long is made to vibrate in two different nodes as shown in diagrams (A) and (B) given below. [3]

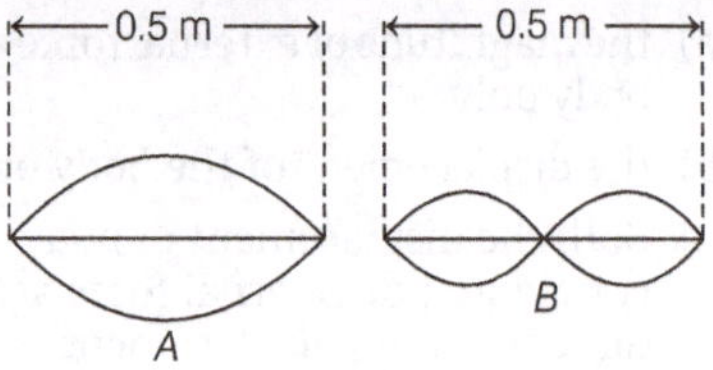

(a) If the wavelength of the wave produced in node A is 1 m then, what is the wavelength of the wave produced in node B?
(b) In which case is the note produced louder?
(c) In which case is the pitch of the note produced higher?
• *Application*

Section-B [40 Marks]

(Attempt any four questions from this section)

4. (i) When a ray of monochromatic green light enters a liquid from air as shown in the figure given below.

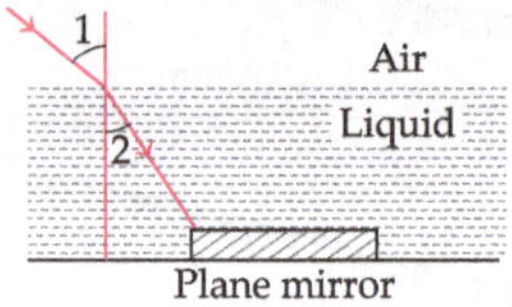

The first angle is 45° and second angle is 30°.
(a) Determine the refractive index of the liquid. [1]
• *Understanding & Recall*
(b) I. Represent in the diagram showing the path of the ray after it strikes the mirror and re-enters air. Mark in the diagram whenever necessary.
II. Draw the diagram again, if plane mirror becomes normal to the refracted ray inside the liquid. Name the principle used. [2]
• *Application*

(ii) A block and tackle system has the velocity ratio 4.

(a) Draw a labelled diagram showing point of application and direction of load and effort. *• Recall*

(b) A man can exert a pull of 500N. What is the maximum load he can raise with the pulley system, if its efficiency is 80%? [3] *• Understanding & Evaluate*

(iii) The diagram below shows the displacement-time graph for a vibrating body.

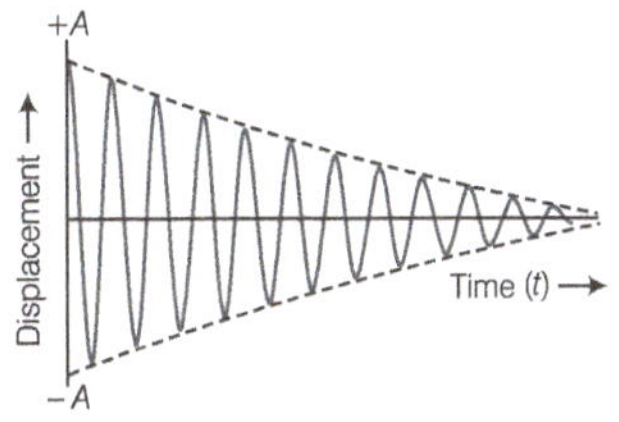

(a) Name the type of vibrations produced by the vibrating body. *• Recall*

(b) Mention one example of a body producing such vibrations. *• Recall*

(c) Why is the amplitude of the wave gradually decreasing? *• Recall*

(d) What will happen to the vibrations of the body after sometime? [4] *• Understanding*

5. (i) A lens forms an erect, magnified and virtual image of an object. *• Understanding & Evaluate*

(a) Name the lens.

(b) Draw a labelled ray diagram to show the image formation. [3]

(ii) A ray of light *XY* passes through a right angled isosceles prism as shown below.

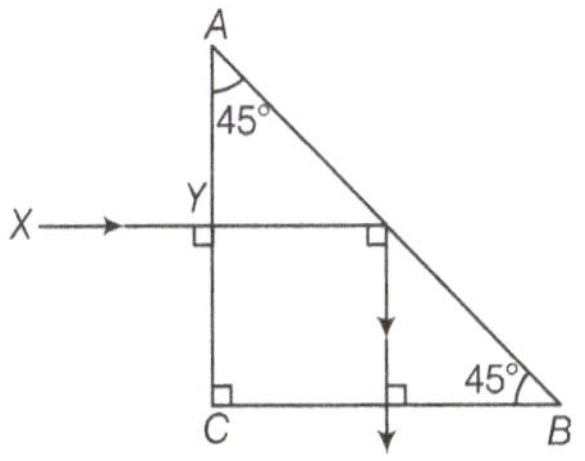

(a) What is the angle through which the incident ray deviates and emerges out of the prism? *• Application & Evaluate*

(b) Name the instrument, where this action of prism is put into use. *• Recall*

(c) Which prism surface will behave as a mirror? *• Recall* [4]

(iii) Calorimeter is used to measure the amount of heat gained (or lost) by a body when it is mixed with the other body. A calorimeter is shown in the figure given below.

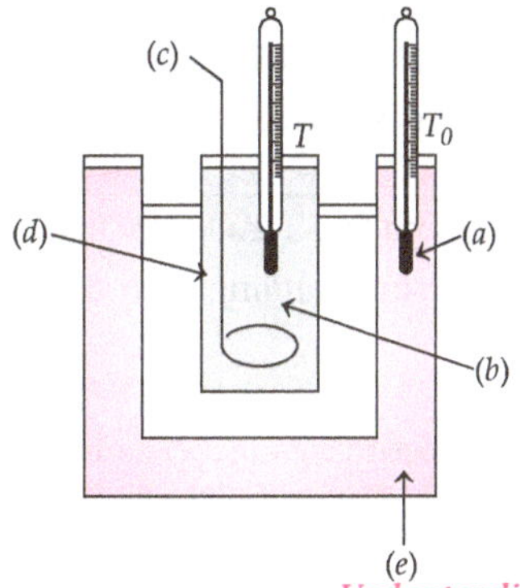

• Understanding & Application

Complete the table using the labels from the figure. The first label is done for you.

S. No.	Description	Label
1.	Stirrer	*c*
2.	Tap water	
3.	Hot water	
4.	Calorimeter	
5.	Double walled vessel	

[3]

6. (i) Specific heat capacity of substance *A* is 3.8 J/gK, whereas the specific heat capacity of substance *B* is 0.4 J/gK. *• Understanding & Recall*

(a) Which of the two is good conductor of heat?

(b) How is one led to the above conclusion?

(c) If substances *A* and *B* are liquid, then which one would be more useful in car radiators? [3]

(ii) The figure given below shows a thin beam of white light from a source *S* striking on one face of prism. *• Understanding & Application*

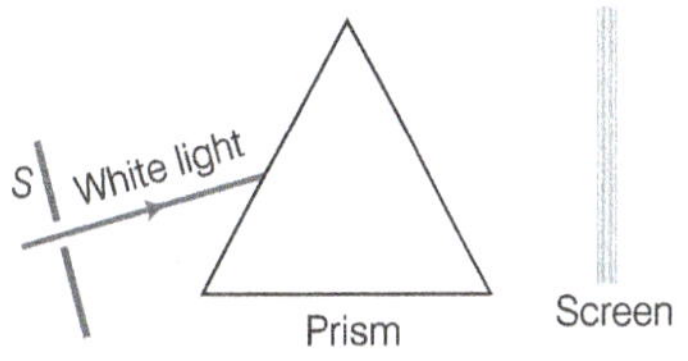

(a) In order to show the effect of the prism on the beam, complete the diagram, so that it can represent what is seen on the screen.

(b) Assume if a slit is placed between the prism and the screen to pass only the light of green colour, then what observation will you get on the screen?

(c) State the conclusion that you draw from the observation in part (b) above. [3]

(iii) Given below are a few situations, study them and state in which of the given cases work is said to be done. Give reason for your answer.
• Understanding & Evaluate

(a) A person pushing a hard huge rock but the rock does not move.

(b) A bullock pulling a cart up to 1 km on road.

(c) A girl pulling a trolley for about 2 m distance.

(d) A person standing with a heavy bag on his head. **[4]**
• Understanding & Evaluate

7. (i) (a) An electrical gadget can give an electric shock to its user under certain circumstance. Mention any two of these circumstances.
• Understanding

(b) What preventive measure provided in a gadget can protect a person from an electric shock? **[3]**
• Recall

(ii) Arrange α, β and γ-rays in ascending order with respect to their
• Recall

(a) penetrating power (b) ionising power

(c) biological effect **[3]**

(iii) Radiations given out from a source when subjected to an electric field in a direction perpendicular to their path are shown below in the diagram. The arrows show the path of the radiation *A*, *B* and *C*. Answer the following questions in terms *A*, *B* and *C*.
• Understanding & Application

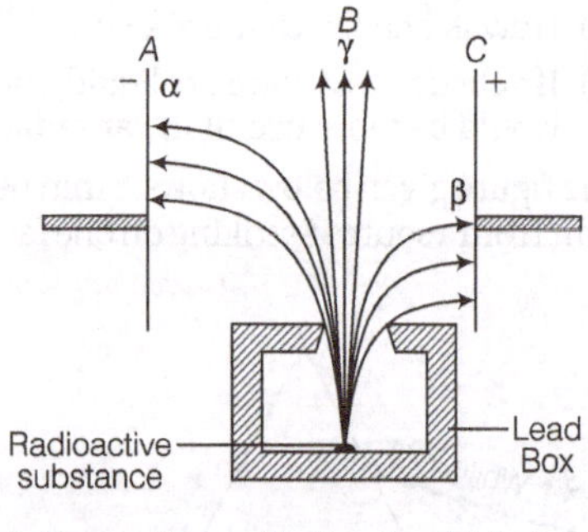

(a) Name the radiation *B* which is unaffected by the electrostatic field.

(b) Why does the radiation *C* deflect more than *A*?

(c) Which among the three causes the least biological damage externally?

(d) Name the radiation which is used in carbon dating. **[4]**

8. (i) Hema uses two appliances in her home. One appliance is rated at 100 W and operates at 220 V, while the other appliance is rated at 60 W and also operates at 220 V. These appliances are connected to the electrical main supply in both series and parallel configurations as shown in the figures a and b.
• Application

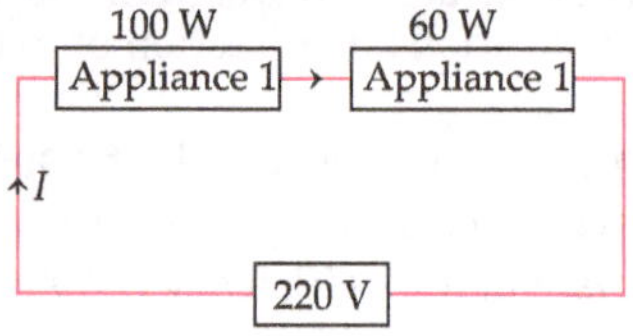

(a)

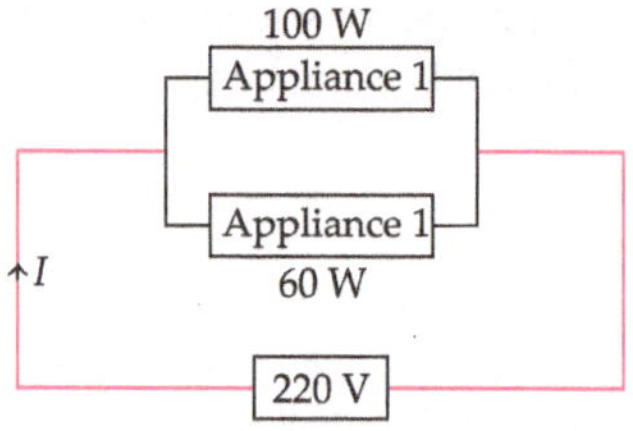

(b)

(a) Calculate the total power consumption when the two appliances are connected in series. **[1]**

(b) Calculate the total power consumption when the two appliances are connected in parallel. **[1]**

(c) Which configuration results in higher total power consumption, series or parallel? **[1]**

(ii) The ore of uranium found in nature contains $_{92}U^{238}$ and $_{92}U^{235}$.

Although both the isotopes are fissionable, it is found out experimentally that one of the two isotopes is more easily fissionable.
• Understanding & Recall

(a) Name the isotope of uranium which is easily fissionable.

(b) Give a reason for your answer.

(c) Write a nuclear reaction when uranium 238 emits an alpha particle to form a thorium (Th) nucleus. **[3]**

(iii) A circuit diagram is given as shown below
• Understanding & Evaluate

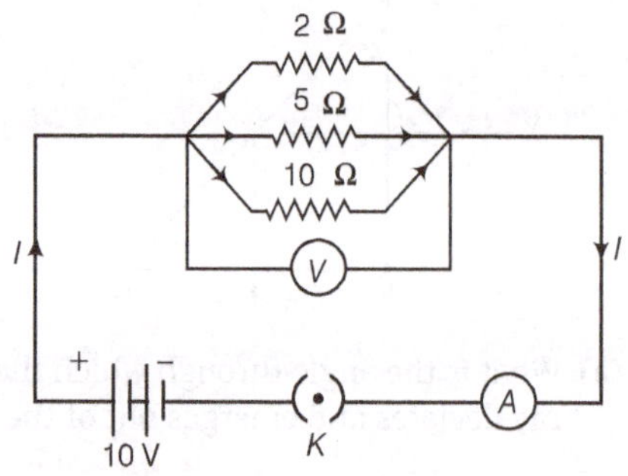

Calculate

(a) the total effective resistance of the circuit,

(b) the current through each resistor and

(c) the total current in the circuit. **[4]**

9. (i) Assume that a pair of scissors and a pair of pliers belong to the same class of levers.
• *Understanding & Recall*

(a) Which one has mechanical advantage less than one?

(b) What is the advantage of a machine whose mechanical advantage is less than one? [3]

(ii) "Farmers fill their fields with water on a cold winter night." Explain in brief along with a reason.
• *Understanding & Evaluate* [3]

(iii) The figure below shows a magnetic needle kept just below the conductor *AB* which is kept in North-South direction.

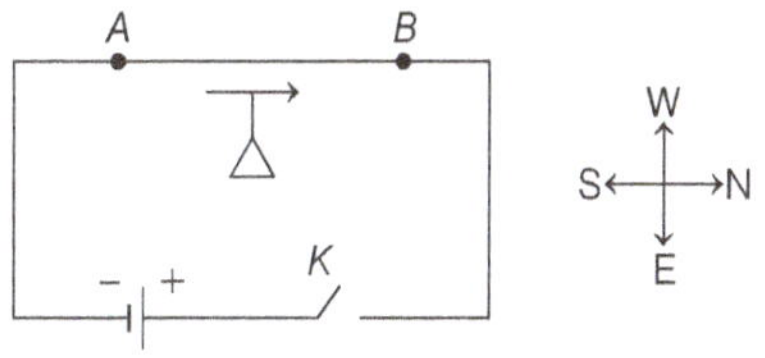

(a) In which direction, will the needle deflect when the key is closed?
• *Understanding & Application*

(b) Why is the deflection produced?

(c) What will be the change in the deflection, if the magnetic needle is taken just above the conductor *AB*?

(d) Name one device which works on the principle of electromagnetic induction. [4]
• *Understanding & Recall*

Answers

1. (i) (*a*) Mechanical advantage,

$$\text{MA} = \frac{\textit{Effort arm length}}{\textit{Load arm length}}$$

In class III order of lever,

effort arm length < load arm length

$\therefore \quad \text{MA} < 1$

(ii) (*a*) Amplitude of free vibration decreases due to the force of friction between vibrating body and medium particles.

(iii) (*b*) Given, $P = 1.5\,\text{kW} = 1.5 \times 10^3\ \text{W}$

$V = 220\ \text{V}$

∴ The current drawn by heater,

$$I = \frac{P}{V} = \frac{1.5 \times 10^3}{220} = 6.8\ \text{A}$$

The above amount of current is greater than the rated value of fuse current. Hence, the fuse will melt and break the circuit.

(iv) (*c*) Direction of rotation would remain unchanged.

(v) (*d*) The speed of light is different for different media. The speed of light varies depending on the medium.

It is fastest in a vacuum and slower in any other medium, such as air, water or glass.

(vi) (*a*) A ray of light passing through the principal focus of a convex lens after refraction will emerge parallel to the principal axis.

(vii) (*a*) Given, mass of body, $m = 1\,\text{kg}$

Initial velocity, $u = 5\,\text{ms}^{-1}$

Final velocity, $v = 7\,\text{ms}^{-1}$

Time taken, $t = 1\,\text{ms} = 1 \times 10^{-3}\,\text{s}$

Force, $\quad F = ma = m\left(\frac{v-u}{t}\right) = 1\frac{(7-5)}{1 \times 10^{-3}} = 2000\ \text{N}$

(viii) (*c*) The work done on a body is given by

$W = F \times d$

So, it depends on both the displacement (*d*) of the body and the component of external force acting in the direction of its displacement.

(ix) (*a*) According to principle of moments,

$$40 \times m_1 = 60 \times m_2$$
$$\frac{m_1}{m_2} = \frac{3}{2}$$

Hence, $m_1 > m_2$.

Thus, the meter scale will tilt towards m_1 (left) side when supported at the centre.

Hence, option (a) is correct.

(x) (*d*) When a ray falls obliquely on a surface of air-water interface, then its is partially reflected and partially refracted. Here *A* is incident ray, *B* is reflected ray and *C* is refracted ray.

(xi) (*b*) Given, $\lambda = 800\ \text{nm} = 800 \times 10^{-9}\ \text{m}$

$c = 3 \times 10^8\ \text{ms}^{-1}$

Since, frequency,

$$\nu = \frac{c}{\lambda} = \frac{3 \times 10^8}{800 \times 10^{-9}}$$
$$= 3.75 \times 10^{14}\ \text{Hz}$$

(xii) (*a*) The apparent shift in the position of an object in a denser medium is due to the refraction of light.

Hence, due to refraction of light, the air bubble in the glass block appears to be raised when viewed from above.

(xiii) (*c*) As the heat capacities are equal, so

$$m_1 c_1 = m_2 c_2 \qquad \text{...(i)}$$

where, m_1, m_2 are the masses of two bodies and c_1, c_2 are their specific heats.

Let *c* be the specific heat of the composite body,

then $\quad (m_1 + m_2)c = m_1 c_1 + m_2 c_2$

$\Rightarrow \quad (m_1 + m_2)c = 2 m_1 c_1 \quad$ [from Eq. (i)]

$$\Rightarrow \quad c = \frac{2 m_1 c_1}{m_1 + m_2}$$
$$= \frac{2 m_1 c_1}{m_1 + m_1 \frac{c_1}{c_2}}$$
$$= \frac{2 c_1 c_2}{c_1 + c_2}$$

(xiv) (c) According to the figure, student has connected the apparatus, but terminals of the ammeter are wrongly connected because ammeter is in series. Hence, positive terminal of ammeters should be connected with positive terminal of cell.

(xv) (d) Water is used in car radiators as coolant because water becomes hot by gaining a large amount of heat due to its high specific heat capacity.

2. (i) (a) Ultrasonic waves

(b) 20000 Hz (c) Fleming's left hand rule

(d) increases (e) Ultrasound

(ii) (a) Rotation of a potter's wheel.

(b) The particles on the axis of rotation are stationary in pure rotational motion.

(iii) A convex lens form this type of image of an object.

The ray diagram showing the formation of image is shown below

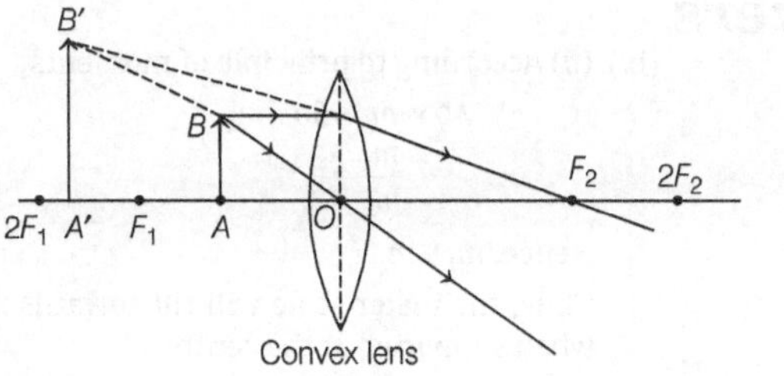

In this case, object is between optical centre O and focus F_1 of lens.

3. (i) (a) The refractive index of water is more than air.

When lens is placed in water, its focal length increases.

(b) A thin lens has greater focal length.

(ii) (a) According to Ohm's law, the electric current flowing through a conductor is directly proportional to the potential difference applied across its ends, providing the physical conditions (such as temperature, dimensions etc.) remain unchanged.

(b) To illustrate the Ohm's law, we draw the following circuit as

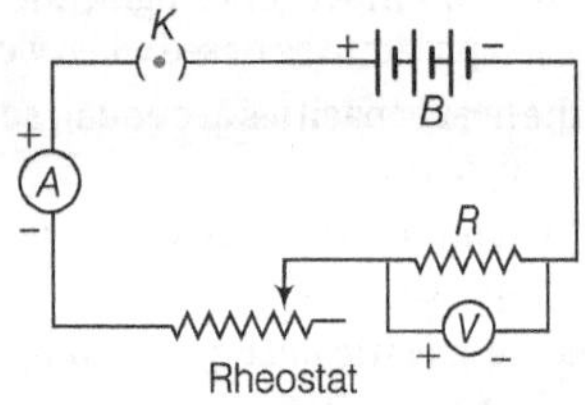

where, B is battery, V is voltmeter and A is ammeter.

(iii) In case of movement of a charged particle, the magnetic field is created around the path on which the charged particle moves.

(a) Yes, a thin beam of α-particles (which are positively charged) is like straight conductor carrying current in the direction of motion.

(b) No, as neutrons carry no charge, so no magnetic field would be created around its path.

(iv) Given, $m = 500\text{g} = 0.5\text{ kg}$

Heat energy required, $\Delta Q = 2000\text{ J}$

Rise in temperature, $\Delta T = (45° - 35°)$

$= 10°\text{C} = 10\text{ K}$

∴ Specific heat capacity,

$$c = \frac{\Delta Q}{m \times \Delta T} = \frac{2000}{0.5 \times 10} = 400\text{ Jkg}^{-1}\text{K}^{-1}$$

(v) (a) $\text{KE} = \frac{p^2}{2m} = \frac{3000 \times 3000}{2 \times 50} = 90000\text{ J}$

(b) $p = mv$

where, p = momentum and m = mass of the body.

Here, $m = 50\text{ kg}$ and $p = 3000\text{ kg-ms}^{-1}$

∴ $3000 = 50 \times v$

⇒ $\frac{3000}{50} = v$

⇒ $v = 60\text{ m/s}$

(vi) (a)

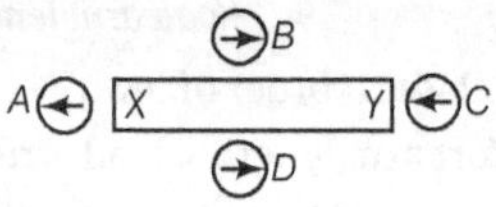

(b) X is the north pole.

(vii) (a) The wavelength of the wave produced in node B is half of that in node A.

The wavelength of the wave produced in node A, $\lambda_A = 1\text{ m}$.

The wavelength of the wave produced in node B, $\lambda_B = \frac{\lambda_A}{2} = \frac{1}{2} = 0.5\text{ m}$

(b) The note produced in node A is louder. Because the amplitude of node A is more than that of node B.

(c) The pitch of the note produced in node B is higher.

4. (i) (a) Refractive index of liquid $= \frac{\sin 45°}{\sin 30°} = \frac{0.7}{0.5} = 1.4$

(b) I. The path of the reflected and refracted ray is shown below

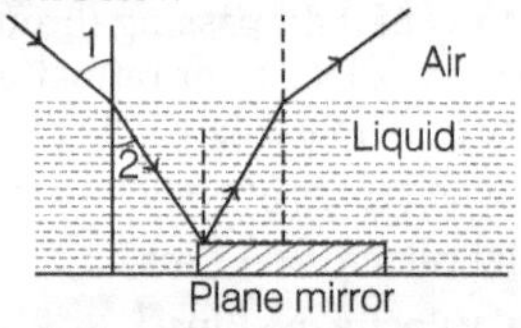

II. The principle used is reversibility of path of light.

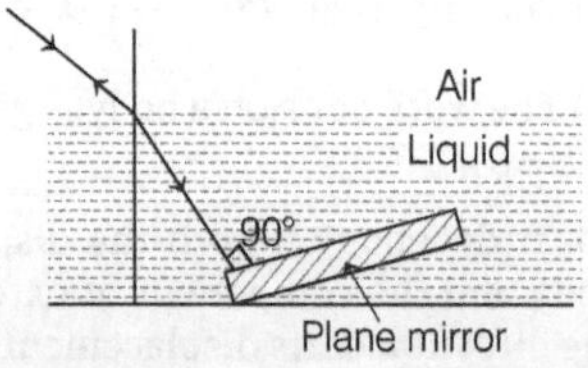

(ii) (a)

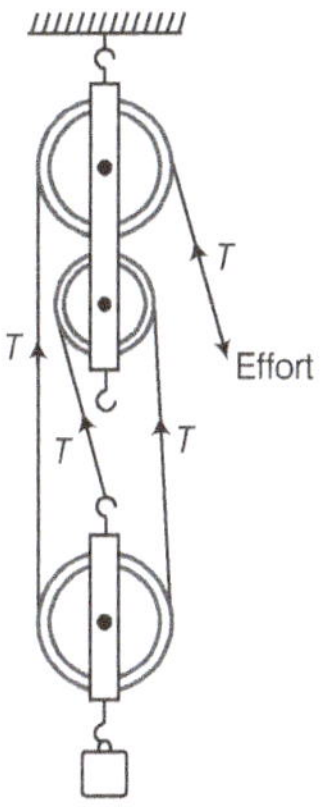

(b) Given, VR = 4

Efficiency, $\eta = 80\% = \frac{4}{5}$

$\therefore$ MA = VR $\times \eta$

$\Rightarrow$ MA $= 4 \times \frac{4}{5} = \frac{16}{5} = 3.2$

But MA $= \frac{L}{E}$

$\Rightarrow 3.2 = \frac{L}{500} \Rightarrow L = 500 \times 3.2 \Rightarrow L = 1600$ N

The maximum load can be raised is 1600 N.

(iii) (a) Damped vibrations are produced by the vibrating body.

(b) A simple pendulum oscillating in air, tuning fork vibrating in air are examples of a body producing such vibrations.

(c) The amplitude of the wave gradually decreasing, because of friction due to which energy is decreased continuously.

(d) As its amplitude decreases, so the vibrations of the body finally stops.

5. (i) (a) A convex lens forms an erect, magnified and virtual image of an object when the object is placed between the focus and optical centre.

(b) The ray diagram showing the formation of image is shown below

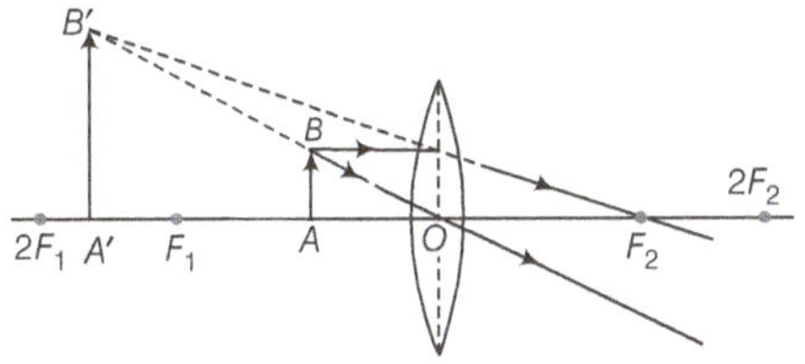

(ii) (a) 90°

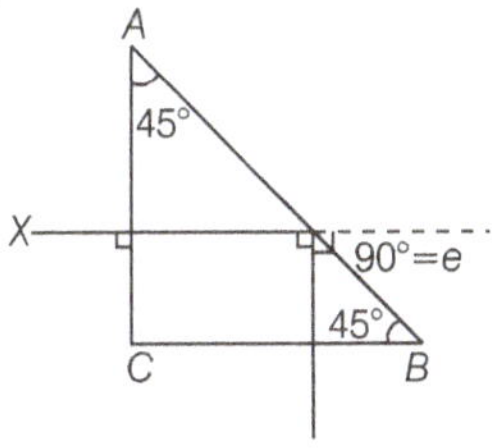

(b) Periscope

(c) Surface *AB* behaves like a mirror. Because on this surface, total internal reflection occurs.

(iii)

S. No.	Description	Label
1.	Stirrer	*c*
2.	Tap water	*a*
3.	Hot water	*b*
4.	Calorimeter	*d*
5.	Double walled vessel	*e*

6. (i) (a) Since, the specific heat capacity of *B* is less than *A*, so *B* is good conductor of heat.

(b) As, the specific heat capacity of *B* is much less than *A*, so *B* is good conductor of heat. It is because for the same heat energy and same mass rise in temperature of *B* will be more than that of *A*.

(c) Since, the specific heat capacity of *A* is higher than that of *B*, so it can absorb more heat therefore, it is useful in car radiator.

(ii) (a) As we can see in the figure, a pattern of seven colours is formed on the screen with red on the top and violet at the bottom.

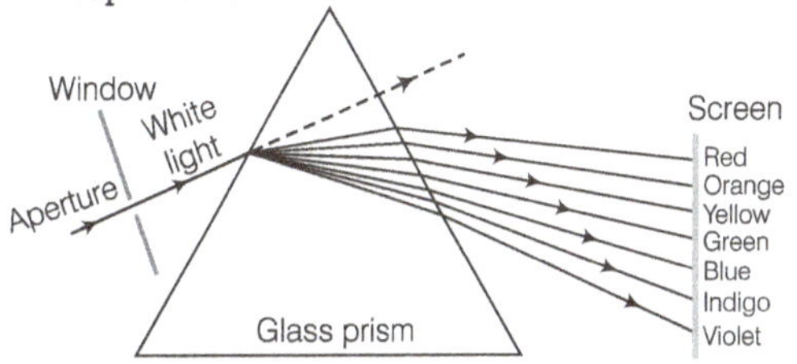

(b) Since, a green filter transmits only green light. Therefore, it is placed between the prism and the screen, the spectrum on the screen will appear dark except for the region near the green part in the original spectrum.

(c) It proves that the prism by itself produces no colour.

(iii) (a) As the displacement is zero in this case, so work done = zero.

(b) The work done in pulling a cart by the bullock will be positive. As, *F* and *s* are in same direction.

(c) Work done in case of pulling a trolley by the girl will be positive. As, force and displacement are in same direction.

(d) As there is no displacement, so work done by a person standing with a heavy bag on his head is zero.

7. (i) (a) The two circumstances, which give electric shock are as

I. An electric shock may be caused due to poor insulation of wires.

II. When wires of electric appliances are touched with wet hands.

(b) To prevent from electric shocks, the insulation of wires must be of good quality and it should be checked from time to time particularly when they become old.

(ii) Ascending order arrangement of α, β and γ-particles with respect to their

(a) **penetrating power** α-particle, β-particle, γ-particle.

(b) **ionising power** γ-particle, β-particle, α-particle.

(c) **biological effect** γ-particle, β-particle, α-particle.

(iii) (a) Gamma radiations

(b) The radiation C deflect more than A because the mass of β-particles is less than that of α, hence radiation deflects more than A.

(c) γ-rays

(d) β radiation is used in carbon dating.

8. (i) (a) To calculate the total power consumption when the appliances are connected in series, we need to determine the equivalent resistance and then use the formula $P = \frac{V^2}{R}$

where, V = voltage,

R = resistance

and P = power

Given, $P_1 = 100$ W, $P_2 = 60$ W at $V = 220$ V

For appliance 1,

$$R_1 = \frac{V_1^2}{P_1} = \frac{(220)^2}{100} = \frac{48400}{100} = 484\ \Omega$$

For appliance 2,

$$R_2 = \frac{V_2^2}{P_2} = \frac{(220)^2}{60} = \frac{48400}{60} = 806.6\ \Omega$$

Therefore, total resistance in the series circuit,

$$R_{total} = R_1 + R_2$$

$$R_{total} = 484 + 806.6 = 1290.6\ \Omega$$

Hence, total power consumption in the series circuit,

$$P_{total} = \frac{V^2}{R_{total}} = \frac{(220)^2}{(1290.6)} = 37.5\ \text{W}$$

(b) $P_{total} = P_1 + P_2 = 100\ \text{W} + 60\ \text{W} = 160\ \text{W}$

Therefore, the total power consumption when the two appliances are connected in parallel is 160 W.

(c) The parallel configuration results in higher total power consumption compared to the series configuration.

(ii) (a) ${}_{92}U^{235}$ is easily fissionable.

(b) Fission of uranium with mass number of 238 is possible by only fast neutron but the fission of uranium with mass number of 235 is also possible by slow neutron.

(c) ${}^{238}_{92}U \longrightarrow {}^{234}_{90}Th + {}^{4}_{2}He$ (α-particle)

(iii) Given, $R_1 = 2\ \Omega$, $R_2 = 5\ \Omega$, $R_3 = 10\ \Omega$, $V = 10$ V

(a) Total effective resistance as the combination is in parallel,

$$\frac{1}{R_{eff}} = \frac{1}{R_1} + \frac{1}{R_2} + \frac{1}{R_3} = \frac{1}{2} + \frac{1}{5} + \frac{1}{10} = \frac{5+2+1}{10} = \frac{8}{10}$$

$$\Rightarrow R_{eff} = \frac{10}{8} = 1.25\ \Omega$$

(b) Current through each resistor, $I_1 = \frac{V}{R_1} = \frac{10}{2} = 5\ \text{A}$,

$$I_2 = \frac{V}{R_2} = \frac{10}{5} = 2\ \text{A} \text{ and } I_3 = \frac{V}{R_3} = \frac{10}{10} = 1\ \text{A}$$

(c) Total current, $I = I_1 + I_2 + I_3 = 5 + 2 + 1 = 8$ A

9. (i) (a) A pair of scissors and a pair of pliers both belong to class I levers.

For class I levers, MA >1 or MA $=1$ or MA <1

As, we know that

$$\text{Mechanical advantage} = \frac{\text{Load}\,(L)}{\text{Effort}\,(E)} = \frac{\text{Effort arm}}{\text{Load arm}}$$

In a pair of scissors, effort arm is less than the load arm.

$\therefore$ Mechanical advantage of a pair of scissors is less than one.

(b) The machines with MA <1 can help us to apply the effort at a more convenient point or to gain in speed.

(ii) In order to protect the crops from frost, farmers fill their fields with water. If on a cold winter night during the absence of water, the atmospheric temperature falls below 0°C, then the water in the fine capillaries of plants will freeze.

So, the veins will burst due to increase in volume of water on freezing. As a result, the plants would die and the crop would be destroyed.

But farmers field their land with water as specific heat capacity of water is large and it imparts a large amount of heat energy while it gets cooled in cold winter night. This heat evolved does not permit the temperatures in the surrounding areas to fall upto 0°C.

(iii) (a) East direction

(b) The needle align itself with the direction of magnetic field lines. Since the lines are perpendicular to the direction of current, the needle will try to align that way also.

(c) The North pole of the compass needle deflects towards West.

(d) Electric generator

ICSE
SAMPLE PAPER 2
(Unsolved)

Physics-X

Time : 2 hrs | Max Marks : 80

General Instructions

1. Answer to this paper must to be written on the paper provided separately.
2. You will not be allowed to write during the first 15 minutes. This time is to be spent in reading the question paper.
3. The time given at the head of this paper is the time allowed for writing the answers.
4. **Section A** is compulsory. Attempt any four questions from **Section B**.
5. The intended marks for questions or parts of questions are given in brackets [ ].

Section-A [40 Marks]

(Attempt all questions from this section)

1. Choose the correct answers to the questions from the given options. **[15]**

(i) The refractive index of glass with respect to air is 1.5.The value of the refractive index of air with respect to glass is *• Understanding*

(a) 1.5
(b) 0.67
(c) 0.5
(d) 2.67

(ii) A planet moving around the sun is in a state of .... equilibrium. *• Recall*

(a) stable
(b) unstable
(c) neutral
(d) None of these

(iii) It is easier to open a door by applying the force at the free end of it. Which of the following is the correct reason for it? *• Recall*

(a) The torque on longer arm is more
(b) The torque on longer arm is less
(c) The torque on every point is same
(d) The torque on shorter arm is more.

(iv) **Assertion** (A) The centrifugal force is in the opposite direction to the direction of centripetal force .

Reason (R) Centrifugal force is not the force of reaction of centripetal force. *• Understanding & Recall*

(a) Both A and R are true and R is the correct explanation of A.
(b) Both A and R are true but R is not the correct explanation of A.
(c) A is fasle but R is true.
(d) A is true but R is false.

(v) The diagram shows a small car of mass 500 kg approaching a hill. It moves up the hill with uniform speed. *• Analysis & Application*

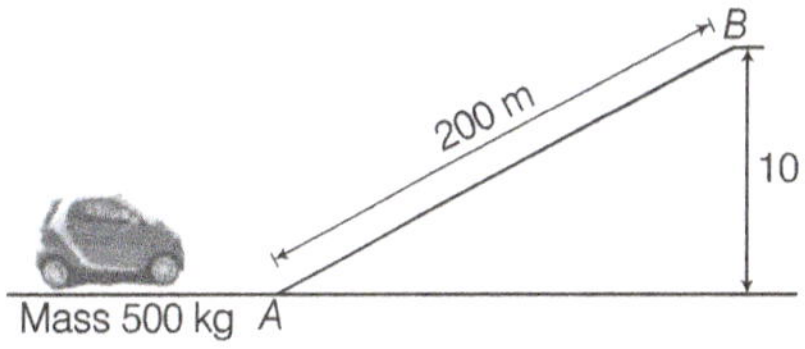

Ignore friction and take the value of g to be 10 N/kg. Which of the following statement(s) is/are correct for given information?

(a) The work done is equal to gain in gravitational potential energy
(b) The work done is equal to 50 kJ
(c) The work done is equal to 5 kJ
(d) Both (a) and (b)

(vi) The diagram shows how the emf of a simple generator varies with time.

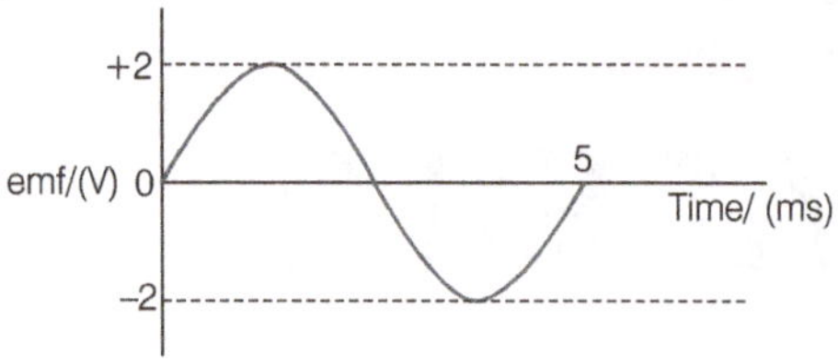

Which of the following statement(s) is/are correct for the graph ? • *Application*

(a) The maximum value of emf is 16V
(b) The maximum value of emf is 8V
(c) The frequency of emf variation is 200 Hz
(d) Both (a) and (c)

(vii) The value of VR for a class II lever is • *Recall*

(a) equal to one (b) less than one
(c) greater than one (d) equal to zero

(viii) The terminals of a battery are joined by a length of resistance wire. Which change, on its own, will increase the current through the battery? • *Understanding*

(a) By reducing length
(b) By increasing thickness
(c) By decreasing thickness
(d) Both (a) and (b)

(ix) Which of the following graphs shows correct relation of kinetic energy (*E*), potential energy (*U*) and height (*h*) from the ground of a particle ? • *Understanding & Recall*

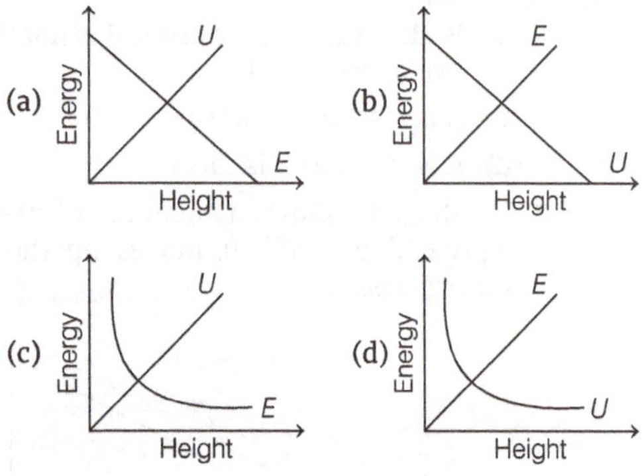

(x) A beam of monochromatic light undergoes minimum deviation through an equilateral prism. With respect to its base, the beam will pass through the prism • *Recall & Application*

(a) parallel to the base
(b) perpendicular to the base
(c) at 45° with the base
(d) at 60° with the base

(xi) A current carrying wire experiences a force, when placed in a magnetic field. The direction of force is given by • *Application*

(a) Fleming's left hand rule
(b) Fleming's right hand rule
(c) Right hand thumb rule
(d) All of the above

(xii) The specific latent heat of fusion of water is • *Recall*

(a) 80 cal g^{-1} (b) 2260 J g^{-1}
(c) 80 J g^{-1} (d) 336 J kg^{-1}

(xiii) An object of height 8 cm is placed at a distance of 40 cm in front of a convex lens of focal length 20 cm. The size of image is • *Understanding*

(a) 12 cm (b) 4 cm (c) −8 cm (d) 16 cm

(xiv) The frequency of a source is 20 kHz. The frequency of sound wave produced by it in water and air will be • *Recall*

(a) same as that of source (b) > 20 kHz
(c) < 20 kHz (d) depend upon velocity

(xv) 200 g of ice at 0°C needs ..... heat to melt. (Take, specific latent heat of ice = 336000 J kg^{-1}) • *Recall*

(a) 6720 J (b) 67200 J
(c) 672000 J (d) 67.2 J

2. (i) Complete the following by choosing the correct answers from the bracket. **[6]**

• *Recall and understanding*

(a) A concave lens produces only.....(virtual/real/ same size) image. **[1]**
(b) The size of the nucleus is of the order of ..... (10^{-14} / 10^{-18}) **[1]**
(c) Clockwise moment produced by a force about a fulcrum is considered to be....(negative/positive). **[1]**
(d) The ratio of real depth and apparent depth is equal to ....(refractive index/reflection/critical angle). **[1]**
(e) When we throw a ball.....(muscular/chemical) energy which is stored in our body, gets converted into.......(potential/kinetic) energy of the ball. **[2]**

(ii) If the speed of light in air is 3×10^8 ms^{-1}, determine the speed of light in glass. The refractive index of glass is 1.5. • *Recall* **[2]**

(iii) Figure shows a trace of a sound wave which is produced by a particular tuning fork. • *Understanding*

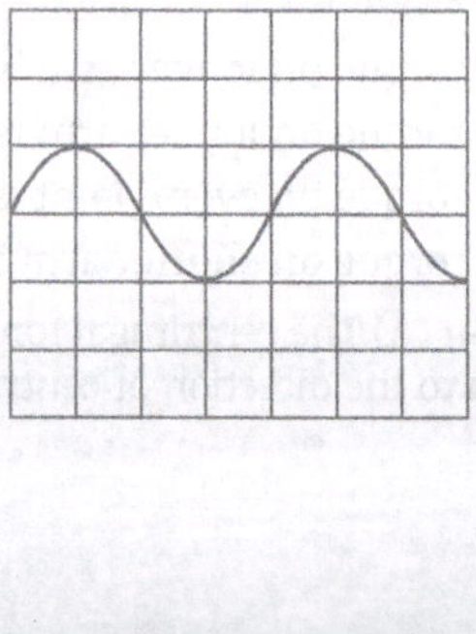

(a) Draw a trace of the sound wave which, has a higher pitch than that shown in figure. [1]

(b) Draw a trace of the sound wave which is louder than that shown in figure. [1]

3. (i) The diagram shows a point source of light *S*, a convex lens *L* and a plane mirror *M*. These are placed such that rays of light from *S* return to it after reflection from *M*. • *Application*

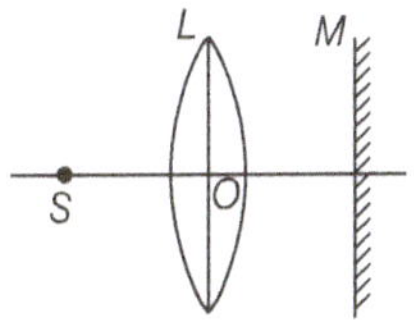

(a) What is the distance *OS* called? [1]

(b) To which point (left of *S* or right of *S*) will the rays return, if *M* is moved to the left and brought in contact with *L*? [1]

(ii) An electrical appliance is rated at 1000 kW, 220 V. If the appliance is operated for 2 h, calculate the energy consumed by the appliance in • *Understanding*

(a) kWh and (b) joule. [2]

(iii) A coil is connected to a galvanometer. When the *N*-pole of a magnet is pushed into the coil, the galvanometer deflected to the right. What deflection, if any is observed, when • *Understanding & Evaluate*

(a) the *N*-pole is removed and [1]

(b) the *S*-pole is inserted? [1]

(iv) A piece of iron of mass 2.0 kg has a thermal capacity of 996 J/°C. • *Understanding & Recall*

(a) How much heat is needed to warm it by 15°C? [1]

(b) What is its specific heat capacity in SI unit? [1]

(v) What happens to the atomic number of an element, when it emits • *Recall*

(a) an α-particle and [1]

(b) a β-particle ? [1]

(vi) A meter scale is balanced in horizontal positions as shown in figure below. Find the value of *W*. • *Understanding*

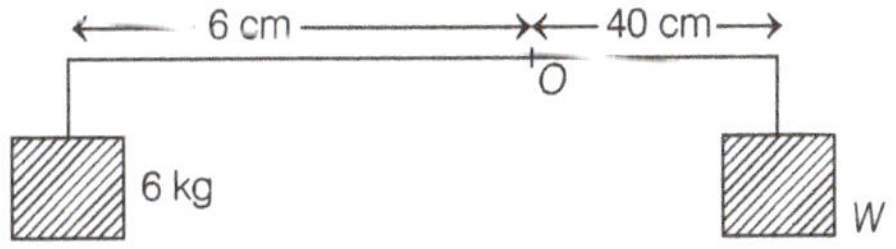

(vii) Monika has drawn the electric circuit to study Ohm's law as shown in figure.

Her teacher told that the circuit diagram require correction.

• *Application* [3]

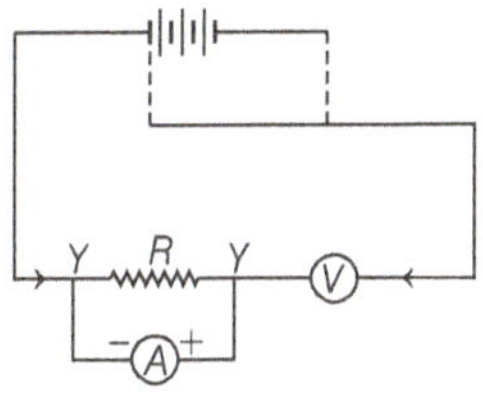

(a) What corrections Monika should do in above circuit to be correct?

(b) Redraw the correct circuit.

(c) Can you explain the function of voltmeter?

Section-B [40 Marks]

(Attempt any four questions from this section)

4. (i) (a) Which colour of white light is deviated • *Recall*

I. least? II. most?

(b) Draw a diagram to illustrate the use of a total reflecting prism to turn the ray of light through 180°. Name an instrument in which the device is used. • *Understanding & Recall* [3]

(ii) (a) State two factors on which the strength of an induced current depends. • *Recall*

(b) When a solenoid that is carrying current is freely suspended, it uses to rest along a particular direction. Why does this happen? • *Understanding* [3]

(iii) The figure given below shows a thin beam of white light from a source *S* striking on one face of prism. [4]

• *Understanding & Application*

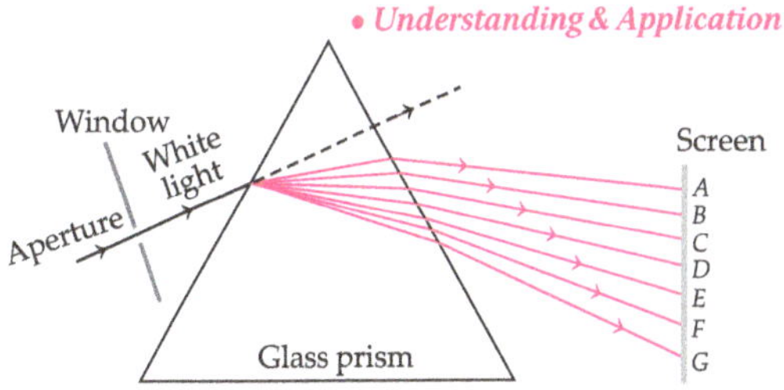

Complete the table using the label from the figure. The first label is done for you.

S.No.	Description	Label
(a)	Indigo	*F*
(b)	Yellow	
(c)	Blue	
(d)	Green	
(e)	Orange	

5. (i) An object is placed in front of a lens between its optical centre and the focus and forms a virtual, erect and diminished image.

(a) Name the lens which formed this image. *• Recall*

(b) Draw a ray diagram to show the formation of the image with the above stated characteristics. *• Understanding & Evaluate* **[3]**

(ii) Given below is a diagram showing the section of a semi-circular glass block having centre at *O*, *D*, *E*, *F* are the monochromatic rays of light of the same colour.

(a) I. Mark the critical angle by i_c.

II. Draw the path of rays *F* and *D* after they strike the edge *GH*. *• Understanding & Recall*

(b) Name the phenomenon which the rays *F* and *D* exhibit. **[3]**

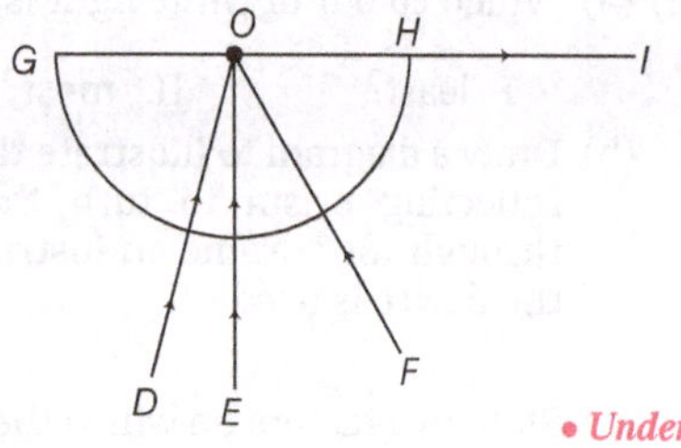

• Understanding

(iii) If a ray of light is incident normally on one face of the equilateral glass prism, answer the following questions.

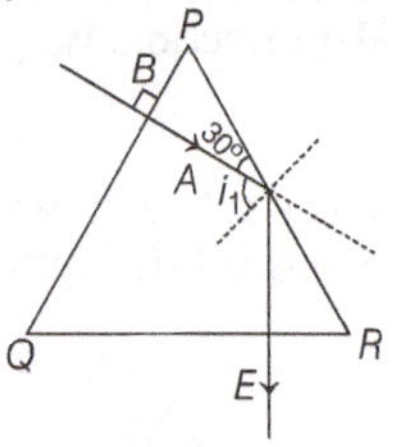

(a) Determine the angle of incidence on first face of prism. *• Application*

(b) Calculate the angle of refraction from first face of the prism. *• Recall*

(c) Find the angle of incidence (i_1) at the second face of the prism. *• Recall*

(d) Will the ray of light suffers minimum deviation by the prism? *• Recall* **[4]**

6. (i) State in brief, the meaning of each of the following. *• Understanding & Evaluate*

(a) The specific latent heat of fusion of ice is 336000 J kg^{-1}.

(b) The specific heat capacity of copper is 0.4 Jg $^{-1}$°C.

(c) What is the principle of method of mixtures? **[3]**

(ii) In the diagram shown below, a ray of light *PQ* is incident normally on one face *AB* of an equilateral glass prism. The critical angle of the glass is 42°. **[3]**

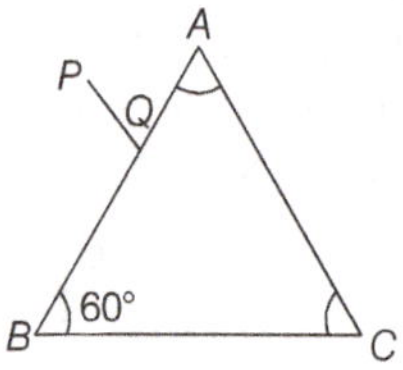

Complete the ray diagram showing its emergence into air after passing through the prism. *• Understanding & Application*

(iii) In a dam, water falls at a rate of 1000 kg s^{-1} from a height of 100 m. *• Understanding & Evaluate*

(a) Calculate the initial potential energy of the water.

(b) Assuming that 60% of the energy of the falling water is converted to electrical energy, calculate the power generated.
(Take, $g = 9.8$ ms^{-2}) **[4]**

7. (i) (a) Name two systems of wiring used in a household electricity. *• Understanding & Recall*

(b) What is an AC generator or dynamo used for?

(c) Name the principle on which it works. **[3]**

(ii) The diagram below shows the core of a transformer and its input and output connections.

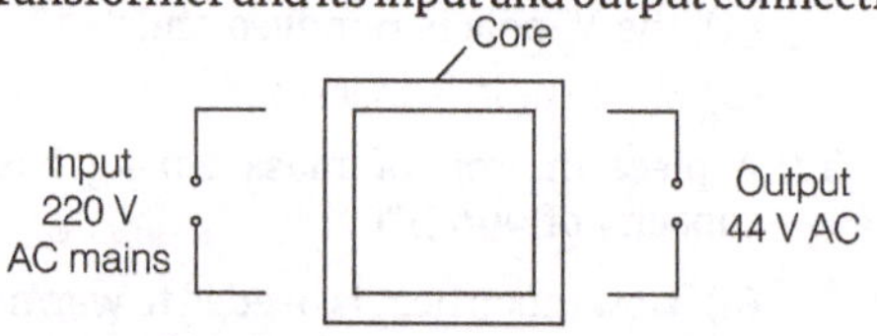

(a) State the material used for the core. *• Recall*

(b) Copy and complete the diagram of the transformer by drawing input and output coils. *• Understanding* **[3]**

(iii) The figure below shows a simple pendulum of mass 200 g. It is displaced from the mean position *A* to the extreme position *B*. The potential energy at the position *A* is zero. At the position *B*, the pendulum bob is raised by 5 m.

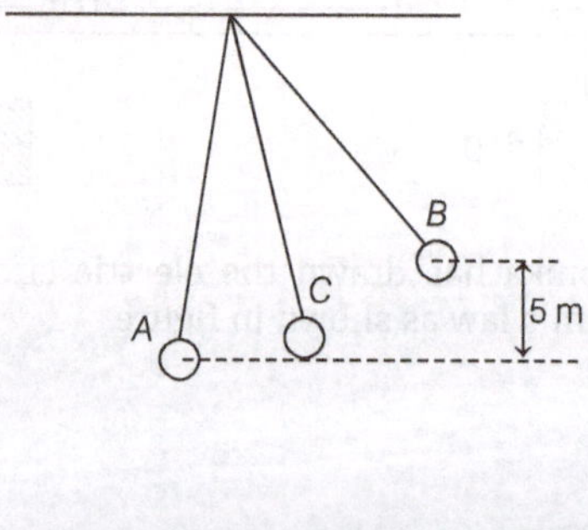

(a) What is the potential energy of the pendulum at the position *B*? • *Recall*

(b) What is the total mechanical energy at point *C* ? • *Recall*

(c) What is the speed of the bob at the position *A*, when released from *B*? • *Application & Evaluate*

(Take, $g = 10\ \text{ms}^{-2}$ and there is no loss of energy)

(d) At which point, potential energy is maximum? Explain. • *Recall* *[4]*

8. (i) (a) State three properties common to all types of electromagnetic radiations.

(b) Name the radiations, which are absorbed by green house gases in earth's atmosphere • *Understanding & Recall* **[3]**

(ii) Two parallel rays of red and violet light travelling through air, meet the air glass boundary as shown in the given figure. • *Understanding & Application*

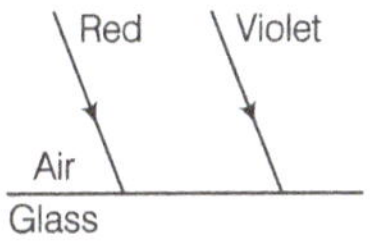

(a) Will their paths inside the glass be parallel? Give a reason for your answer.

(b) Compare the speeds of the two rays inside the glass. **[3]**

(iii) The diagram shows two lamps in parallel in a circuit.

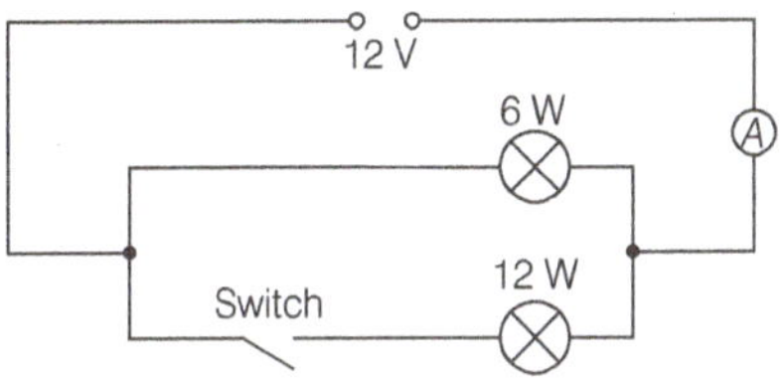

When the switch is open, the ammeter reads 0.5 A. • *Understanding & Evaluate*

(a) What is the reading, when the switch is closed?

(b) Find potential difference across 12 W lamp. **[4]**

9. (i) A 10 kW drilling machine is used to drill a bore in a small aluminium block of mass 8.0 kg. How much is the rise in temperature of the block in 2.5 min, assuming 50% of power is used up in heating the machine itself or lost to the surroundings? • *Understanding & Evaluate*

(Take, specific heat of aluminium $= 0.91\ \text{Jg}^{-1}\,{}^\circ\text{C}^{-1}$) **[3]**

(ii) (a) Explain, why the weather becomes very cold, after a hailstorm?

(b) Write an expression for the heat liberated by a hot body.

(c) Same amount of heat is supplied to two liquids *A* and *B*. The liquid *A* shows a greater rise in temperature.s What can you say about the heat capacity of *A* as compared to that of *B*? • *Understanding & Recall* **[3]**

(iii) The diagram shows a coil connected to a centre zero galvanometer G. The galvanometer shows a deflection to the right, when the *N*-pole of a powerful magnet is moved to the right as shown in below figure.

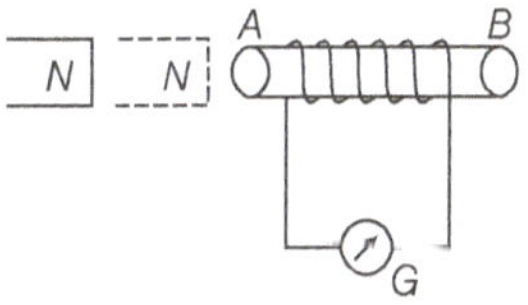

(a) Explain, why the deflection occurs in the galvanometer?

(b) Does the direction of the current on the coil appear clockwise or anti-clockwise, when viewed from the end *A*? • *Understanding & Application*

(c) State the observation in G, when the coil is moved away from *N*.

(d) State the observation in G, when both the coil and the magnet are moved to the right at the same speed. • *Understanding & Recall* **[4]**

ANSWERS

1. (i) (b) (ii) (b) (iii) (a) (iv) (a) (v) (d)
(vi) (c) (vii) (c) (viii) (d) (ix) (a) (x) (a)
(xi) (a) (xii) (a) (xiii) (c) (xiv) (a) (xv) (b)

2. (i) (a) Virtual (b) 10^{-14} (c) negative
(d) refractive index (e) muscular, kinetic
(ii) 2×10^8 m/s

3. (ii) (a) 2000 kWh (b) 7.2×10^9 J
(iv) (a) 14490 J (b) 483 J $\text{kg}^{-1}\ \text{K}^{-1}$
(vi) 9 kg

6. (iii) (a) 980000 J (b) 5.88×10^5 W

8. (iii) (a) 1.5 A (b) 12 V

9. (i) 103°C

ICSE
SAMPLE PAPER 3
(Unsolved)
Physics-X

Time : 2 hrs | Max Marks : 80

General Instructions

1. Answer to this paper must to be written on the paper provided separately.
2. You will not be allowed to write during the first 15 minutes. This time is to be spent in reading the question paper.
3. The time given at the head of this paper is the time allowed for writing the answers.
4. **Section A** is compulsory. Attempt any four questions from **Section B**.
5. The intended marks for questions or parts of questions are given in brackets [ ].

Section-A [40 Marks]

(Attempt all questions from this section)

1. Choose the correct answers to the questions from the given options. **[15]**

(i) A body is acted upon by two unequal forces in opposite directions, but not in the same line. The effect is that *• Recall*

(a) the body will only have rotational motion

(b) the body will only have translational motion

(c) the body will have neither rotational nor translational motion

(d) the body will have rotational as well as translational motion

(ii) The line joining the centre of gravity of a cuboid and the centre of the earth will fall within the base of the body even after being disturbed by an external force, then the body is said to be in *• Recall*

(a) neutral equilibrium

(b) stable equilibrium

(c) unstable equilibrium

(d) dynamic equilibrium

(iii) The correct relationship betweem Mechanical Advantage (MA), Velocity Ratio (VR) and efficiency (η) is *• Understanding*

(a) $MA = \eta \times VR$

(b) $VR = \eta \times MA$

(c) $\eta = MA \times VR$

(d) None of these

(iv) The stone of hand floar grinder is provided with a handle near its rim. Which of the following gives the true reason for this? *• Recall*

(a) The moment of force gets reduced

(b) The moment of force gets increased

(c) The force required increases

(d) None of the above

(v) **Assertion** (A) The amount of heat energy which is required to raise the temperature of 1 g of water through 1°C is known as calorie.

Reason (R) The SI unit of heat is calorie. *• Understanding & Recall*

(a) Both A and R are true and R is the correct explanation of A.

(b) Both A and R are true but R is not the correct explanation of A.

(c) A is false but R is true.

(d) A is true but R is false.

(vi) A horse does 5000 J of work in 100 s. What is its power? *• Recall*

(a) 50 W (b) 50 J (c) 10 W (d) 10 J

(vii) A swimming pool is lit by a lamp in the bottom of the pool. The directions of three rays from the lamp are shown in figure bottom. *• Analysis & Application*

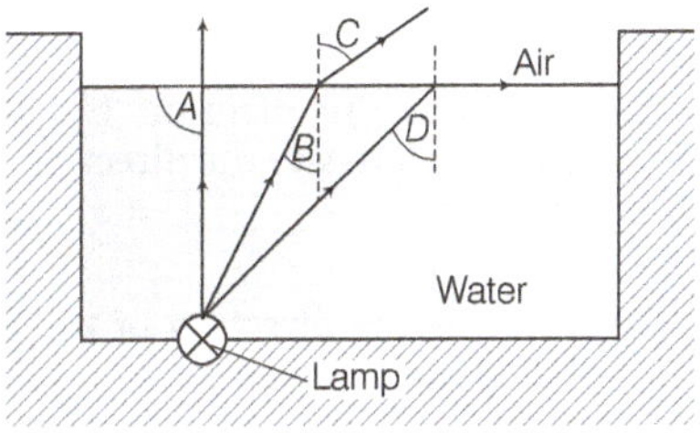

Which of the marked angles is the critical angle for the light?

(a) A (b) B

(c) C (d) D

(viii) A permanent magnet can be demagnetised by using a solenoid and switching the current ON then OFF.

Which diagram shows the most effective method of producing demagnetisation? *• Application*

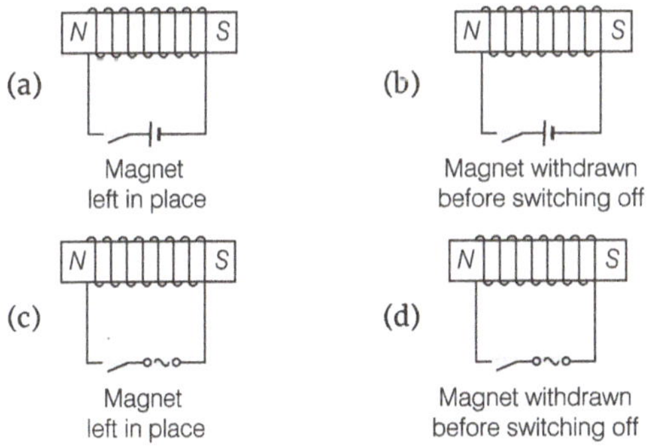

(ix) A small coil is connected to a meter as shown.

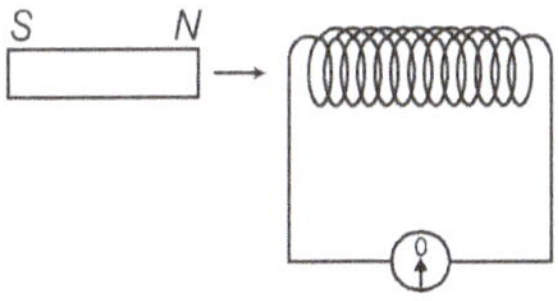

When a magnet is pushed into the coil, the pointer of the meter kicks to the right of zero.

When the magnet is pulled back from the coil, then the pointer will kicks to the *• Understanding*

(a) right of zero

(b) left of zero

(c) remains stationary

(d) Nothing can be said

(x) The equivalent resistance of the following combination of resistors R_1, R_2, R_3 and R_4 between A and B is *• Understanding*

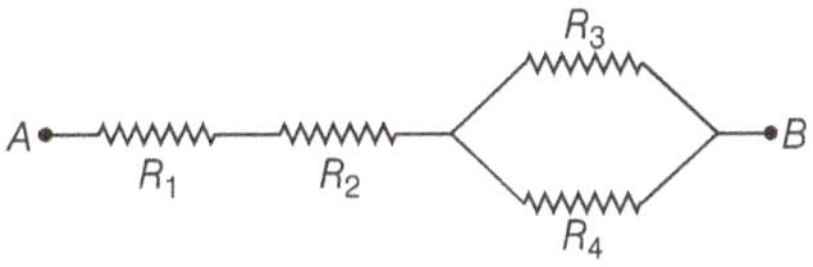

(a) $R_1 + R_2 + R_3R_4$

(b) $\dfrac{R_3 + R_4}{R_1R_2}$

(c) $R_1 + R_2 + \dfrac{R_3R_4}{R_3 + R_4}$

(d) $\dfrac{R_1R_2}{R_1 + R_2} + R_3R_4$

(xi) Which of the following statement(s) is /are the necessary condition for a conductor to obey Ohm's law? *• Application*

(a) The conductor should be an ohmic conductor.

(b) The physical conditions of the conductor should remains constant.

(c) The temperature of the conductor should remains constant.

(d) All of the above

(xii) The specific latent heat of fusion of ice is 336 Jg^{-1}. Which of the following statements is true about this? *• Recall & Application*

(a) 1 g of ice at 0°C absorbs 336 J of heat energy to convert into water at 0°C.

(b) 1 g of ice at 0 K absorbs 336 J of heat energy to convert into water at 0°C.

(c) 1 g of ice at 0°C releases 336 J of heat energy in converting into water at 0°C.

(d) 1 g of ice at 0 K releases 336 J of heat energy in converting into water at 0 K.

(xiii) To an astrounaut in a spaceship, the earth appears *• Recall*

(a) white (b) red

(c) blue (d) black

(xiv) Which of the following substances A, B and C has the lowest heat capacity, if heat is supplied to all of them at equal rates? The temperature *versus* time graph is shown *• Understanding & Recall*

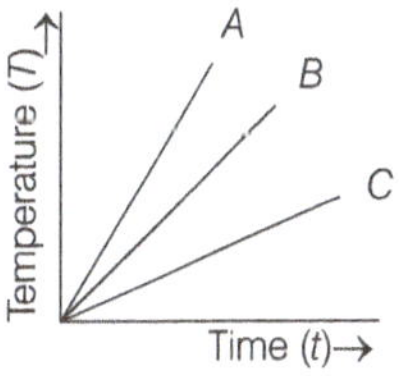

(a) C (b) B

(c) A (d) None of these

(xv) The particle used in nuclear fission for bombardment is • *Recall*

(a) α-particle (b) proton
(c) neutron (d) β-particle

2. (i) Complete the following by choosing the correct answer from the bracket. [6]

• *Recall and understanding*

(a) In camera.....(convex/concave) lens is used which forms a real and inverted image of an object. [1]

(b) In the spectrum of white light by a prism, the colour at the extreme end opposite to the base of prism is....(red/blue/violet). [1]

(c) A wire stretched between two fixed supports, is plucked exactly in the middle then released, it executes .... (natural/damped/forced) vibration. [1]

(d) In an electric bulb, the electrical energy is converted into......(heat/chemical) energy and ....(kinetic/light) energy. [2]

(e) The sum of total number of protons and neutrons inside the atomic nucleus of the element is known as its......(atomic/mass) number. [1]

(ii) (a) Is it possible a body possesses energy without having momentum? • *Recall* [1]

(b) It is possible a body possesses momentum without having energy? • *Recall* [1]

(iii) When a 20 N force acts in two different ways to displace a trolley in the same displacement. Find the ratio of the work done as determined in both the cases. • *Understanding* [2]

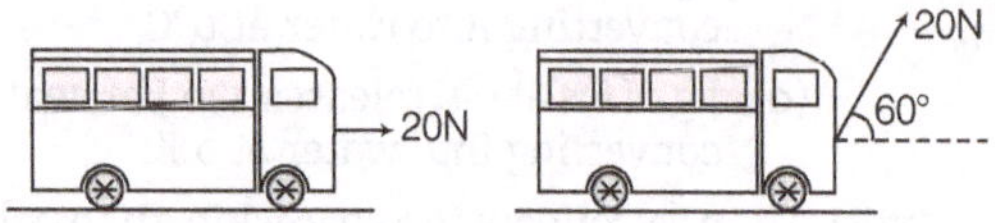

3. (i) (a) Copy and complete the diagram to show the formation of the image of an object *AB*. [1]

(b) What is the name given to *X*? • *Application*

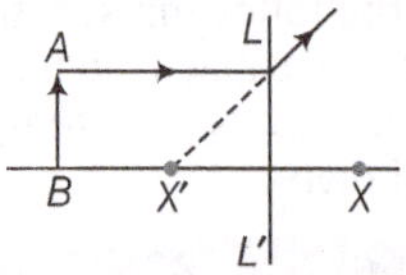

[1]

(ii) (a) What is an ohmic resistor? • *Recall* [1]

(b) Two coper wires are of the same length, but one is thicker than the other. • *Understanding*

I. Which wire will have more resistance?

II. Which wire will have more specific resistance? [1]

(iii) A plotting compass is placed inside a solenoid and the compass needle is pointing in the direction as shown.

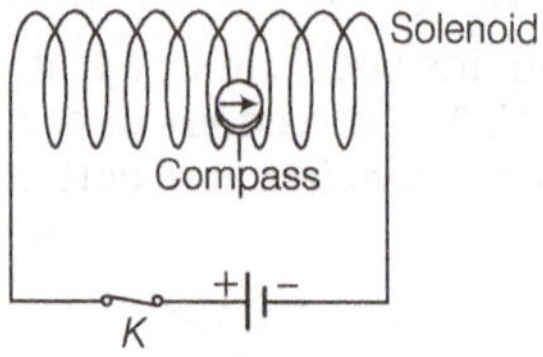

(a) Complete the diagram by drawing arrow heads to indicate the direction of the current flow. • *Understanding* [1]

(b) Describe the direction of the magnetic field inside the solenoid. • *Recall* [1]

(iv) (a) Give an example, where high specific heat capacity of water is used as a heat reservoir. • *Recall* [1]

(b) Give an example, where high specific heat capacity of water is used for cooling purposes. • *Recall* [1]

(v) "α and β-particles are deflected in an electric field or a magnetic field, while γ-rays are not deflected in such a field". Comment on this statement. [2]

• *Understanding & Evaluate*

(vi) The diagram below shows a lever in use.

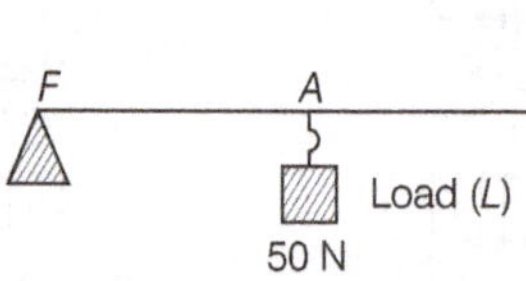

If $FA = 40$ cm, $AB = 60$ cm, then find the mechanical advantage of the lever. [2]

• *Understanding*

(vii) The diagram below shows a point source *P* inside a water container. Four rays *A*, *B*, *C* and *D* starting from the source *P* are shown upto the water surface. • *Application*

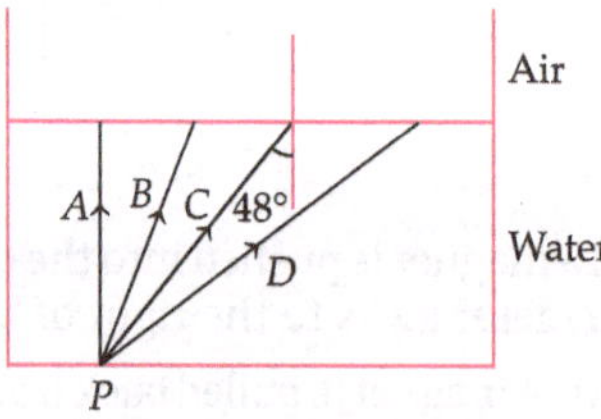

(a) Show in the diagram, the path of these rays after striking the water surface. The critical angle for water-air surface is 48°. [1]

• *Understanding & Recall*

(b) Name the phenomenon which the rays *B* and *D* exhibit. [1]

(c) Can total internal refraction occur when rays travel from rarer medium to denser medium? [1]

• *Application*

Section-B [40 Marks]

(Attempt any four questions from this section)

4. (i) A convex lens has focal length of 20 cm. At what distance from the lens should the object be placed, so that the image is formed at 40 cm on the other side of the lens? Also, state the nature of the image formed. [4]

(ii) (a) Define the term dispersion and spectrum of light. • *Recall*

(b) Which colour is dispersed with maximum deviation? • *Recall*

[3]

(iii) A diver in water looks obliquely at an object *AB* in air.

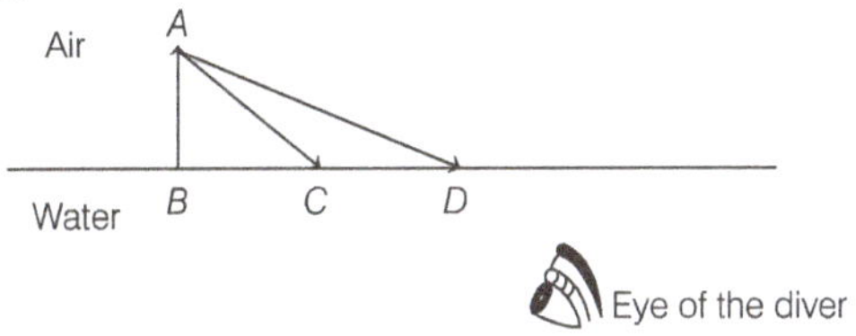

(a) Does the object appear taller, shorter or of the same size to the diver? • *Recall*

(b) Show the path of two rays *AC* and *AD* starting from the tip of the object as it travels towards the diver in water and hence obtain the image of the object. • *Understanding & Application*

[3]

5. (i) A schematic diagram of main circuit is given below.

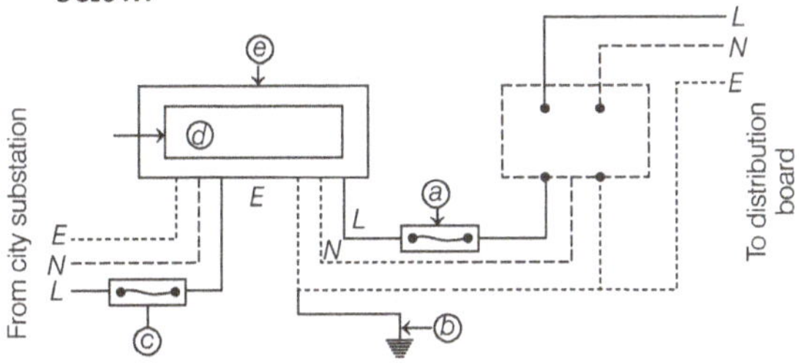

Complete the table using the labels from the figure. The first label is done for you.

S.No	Description	Lebel
(a)	Main fuse	a
(b)	KWh meter	
(c)	Local earthing	
(d)	pole fuse	
(e)	Main switch	

[4]

• *Understanding & Application*

(ii) (a) Name the electrical appliance shown in the diagram below. • *Recall*

(b) A fuse wire consists of an alloy of copper and gold. State true or false. • *Recall*

(c) Name two important characteristics of fuse wire. [3]

• *Recall*

(iii) When a ray of monochromatic green light enters a liquid from air as shown in the figure given below.

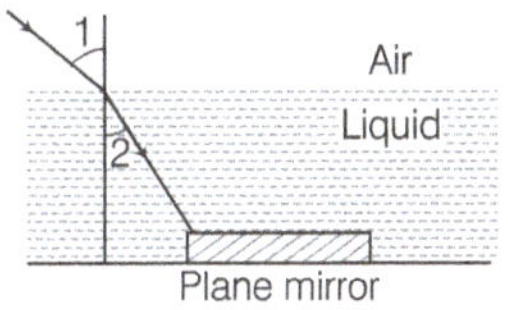

• *Understanding & Evaluate*

The angle 1 is $45°$ and angle 2 is $30°$.

(a) Determine the refractive index of the liquid.

(b) Represent in the diagram showing the path of the ray after it strikes the mirror and re-enters air. Mark in the diagram wherever necessary.

(c) Draw the diagram again, if plane mirror becomes normal to the refracted ray inside the liquid. Name the principle used.

[3]

6. (i) (a) Define work. State its SI unit. • *Recall*

(b) State the energy changes in the following cases while in use • *Understanding & Evaluate*

I. An electric iron.

II. A ceiling fan. [3]

(ii) Two men were going to market, then suddenly they see two boxes which are on the ground. If a man raises a box of 50 kg mass to a height of 2m in 2 min, while the other man raises the same box to a same height in 5 min. [4]

(a) Find the work done by them. • *Recall*

(b) Calculate the power developed by them.

• *Application & Evaluate*

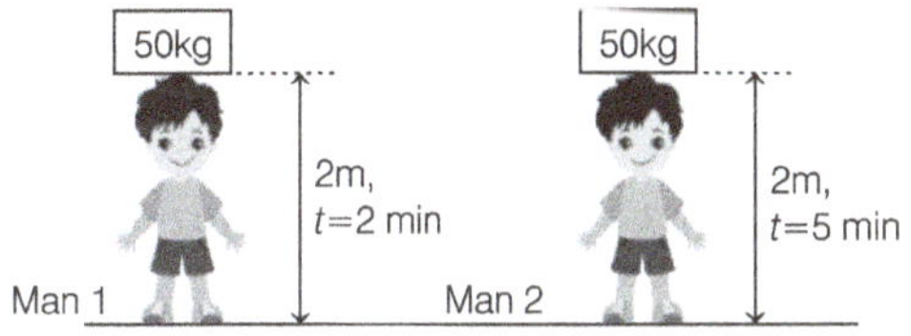

(iii) (a) State the class of levers and the relative positions of load (L), effort (E) and fulcrum (F) in each of the following cases:
• *Understanding & Recall*

I. A bottle opener II. Sugar tongs

(b) Why is less effort needed to lift a load over an inclined plane as compared to lifting the load directly?
• *Understanding*
[3]

7. (i) (a) Which one of the following graphs A or B shows free vibrations in vacuum and which one shows free vibrations in a medium?

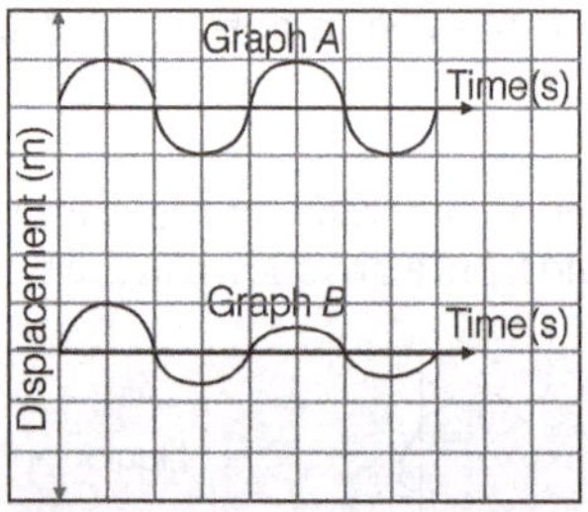

• *Application*

(b) How did you come to this conclusion? [4]

(ii) Write nuclear reaction equations for • *Understanding*

(a) α-decay of $^{226}_{88}Ra$

(b) α-decay of $^{242}_{94}Pu$

(c) β^--decay of $^{32}_{15}P$ [3]

(iii) From the diagram given below

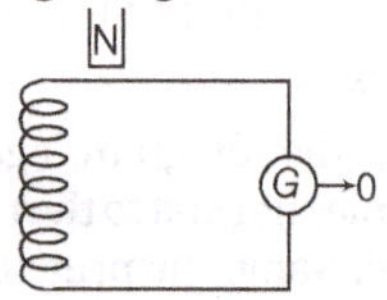

(a) What will you observe, when
• *Understanding & Evaluate*

I. the magnet is dropped into the coil?

II. the number of turns of the coil is increased?

(b) What will be the direction of current flowing through the coil, when the magnet is dropped in? (Clockwise or anti-clockwise).

(c) State the phenomenon on which the observation is made. [3]
• *Understanding & Recall*

8. (i)

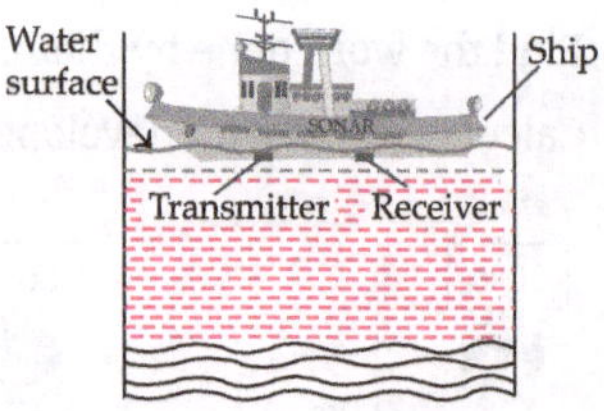

SONAR is an apparatus used to find the depth of sea or to locate the under water things. It consists of transmitter and receiver shown in the figure. [3]

(a) Name the waves which are used in SONAR.

(b) What is the significance of transmitter and receiver in SONAR?
• *Application*

(ii) (a) Observe the diagram given below and state whether the bulb will glow or not, when we switch ON.
• *Understanding & Evaluate*

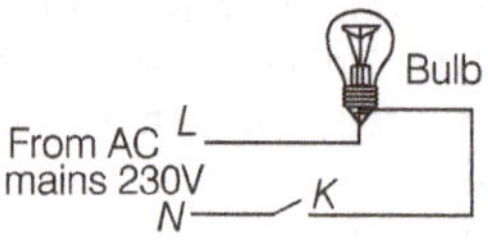

(b) Is it safe to handle the bulb, when the switch is OFF?

(c) Give a reason for your answer in (b). [3]

(iii) A cell of emf 1.5 V and internal resistance 1.0 Ω are connected to two resistors of 4.0 Ω and 20.0 Ω in series as shown in the figure.

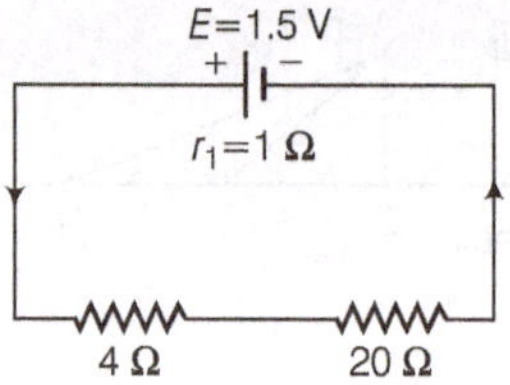

Calculate the
• *Understanding & Recall*

(a) current in the circuit.

(b) potential difference across the 4.0Ω resistor.

(c) voltage drop across internal resistance when the current is flowing.

(d) potential difference across the cell. [4]

9. (i) 250 g of water at 30°C is present in a copper vessel of mass 50 g. Calculate the mass of ice required to bring down the temperature of the vessel and its contents to 5°C.

(Take, specific latent heat of fusion of ice $= 336 \times 10^3$ J kg^{-1}, specific heat capacity of copper vessel = 400 J kg^{-1}°C^{-1}, specific heat capacity of water = 4200 J kg^{-1}°C^{-1})
• *Understanding & Evaluate*
[3]

(ii) (a) Write a relation expressing the mechanical advantage of a lever.
• *Understanding & Recall*

(b) Write an expression for the mechanical advantage of an inclined plane.

(c) Give two reasons as to why the efficiency of a single movable pulley system is always less than 100%? [3]

(iii) The diagram shows a coil connected to a galvanometer G. The galvanometer shows a deflection to the right when the N-pole of a powerful magnet is moved to the right as shown.

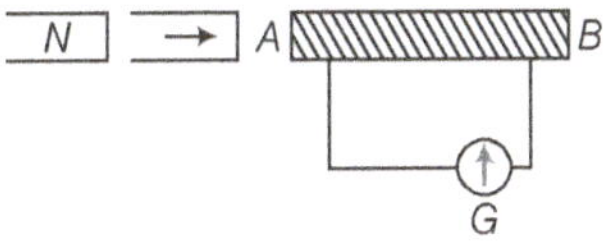

(a) Explain, why the deflection occur in the galvanometer?

(b) Does the direction of the current in the coil appear clockwise or anti-clockwise, when viewed from the end A?

• Understanding & Application

(c) State the observation in G when the coil is moved away from N.

(d) State the observation in G when both the coil and the magnet are moved to the right at the same speed.

• Understanding & Recall

[4]

ANSWERS

1. (i) (a) (ii) (b) (iii) (a) (iv) (b) (v) (d)
(vi) (b) (vii) (d) (viii) (d) (ix) (b) (x) (c)
(xi) (d) (xii) (a) (xiii) (c) (xiv) (c) (xv) (c)

2. (v) 1

3. (vi) – 2.5

4. (i) –40 cm, real inverted and same size

5. (iii) (a) 1.414

6. (ii) (a) 1000 J (b) 5 : 2

8. (iii) (a) 0.06 A (b) 0.24 volt
(c) 0.06 volt (d) 1.44 volt

9. (i) 74.93 g

ICSE

LATEST SPECIMEN QUESTION PAPER

Time 2 hrs **Max. Marks 80**

GENERAL INSTRUCTIONS

1. Answer to this paper must be written on the paper provided separately.
2. You will not be allowed to write during first 15 minutes. This time is to be spent in reading the question paper.
3. The time given at the head of this paper is the time allowed for writing the answers.
4. **Section A** is compulsory. Attempt any four questions from **Section B**.
5. The intended marks for questions or parts of questions are given in brackets [].

Section-A

(Attempt all questions from this section)

1. Choose the correct answers to the questions from the given options. **[15]**

(*i*) A moment of couple has a tendency to rotate the body in an anti-clockwise direction. Then, the moment of couple is taken as • *Recall*

(a) positive (b) negative (c) maximum (d) zero

(*ii*) The kinetic energy of a given body depends on the • *Understanding*

(a) position (b) centre of gravity of the body

(c) momentum (d) displacement

(*iii*) For burning of coal in a thermoelectric station, the energy conversion taking place is • *Recall*

(a) chemical to heat to mechanical (b) chemical to heat to mechanical to electrical

(c) chemical to heat to light (d) heat to chemical to mechanical

(*iv*) The adjacent diagram shows the movable block of a block and tackle system with effort in a convenient direction. From the diagram, we can conclude that the number of pulleys used in the fixed block are……… • *Analysis & Application*

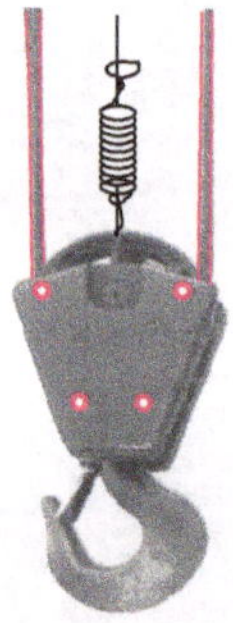

(a) 1 (b) 3 (c) 2 (d) 4

(*v*) White light is dispersed by a prism. Inside the prism, compared to the blue light, the red light • *Analysis & Application*

(a) slows down less and refracts more (b) slows down more and refracts less

(c) slows down more and refracts more (d) slows down less and refracts less

(*vi*) An endoscope uses optic fiber to transmit high resolution images of internal organs without loss of information. The principle of light that is used by the optic fiber is based on • *Recall*

(a) refraction (b) reflection

(c) scattering (d) total internal reflection

(*vii*) A convex lens has focal length 12 cm with an object at a distance of 20 cm in front of the lens. He obtains a blurred image on the screen placed at a distance of 23 cm in front of the lens. In order to obtain the clear image, he has to move the screen • *Application*

(a) towards the lens (b) away from the lens

(c) to a position very far away from the lens (d) either towards or away from the lens

(*viii*) **Assertion** (A) Infrared radiations travel long distances through a dense fog and mist.

Reason (R) Infrared radiations undergo minimal scattering in the earth's atmosphere. • *Understanding & Recall*

(a) Both A and R are true and R is the correct explanation of A.

(b) Both A and R are true and R is not the correct explanation of A.

(c) A is false but R is true.

(d) A is true but R is false.

(*ix*) Two sound waves X and Y have the same amplitude and the same wave pattern but their frequencies are 60 Hz and 120 Hz respectively, then • *Understanding*

(a) X will be shriller and Y will be grave (b) X will be grave and Y will be shriller

(c) X will differ in quality than Y (d) X is louder than Y

(*x*) The graph of voltage *versus* current for four different materials is shown below.

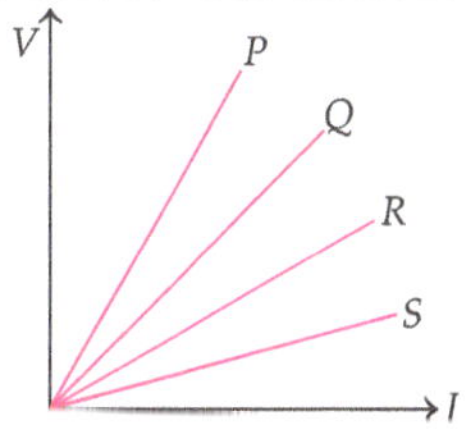

Which of these four materials would be used for making filament of a bulb? • *Understanding & Recall*

(a) Q (b) S (c) P (d) R

(*xi*) According to the old convention, the colour of the earth wire is • *Recall*

(a) black (b) green (c) yellow (d) red

(*xii*) Current is flowing through a coil as shown in the figure. Which one of the given figures will correctly depict the magnetic polarity and the direction of the lines of force along the axis of the coil. • *Application*

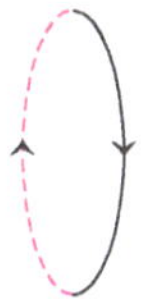

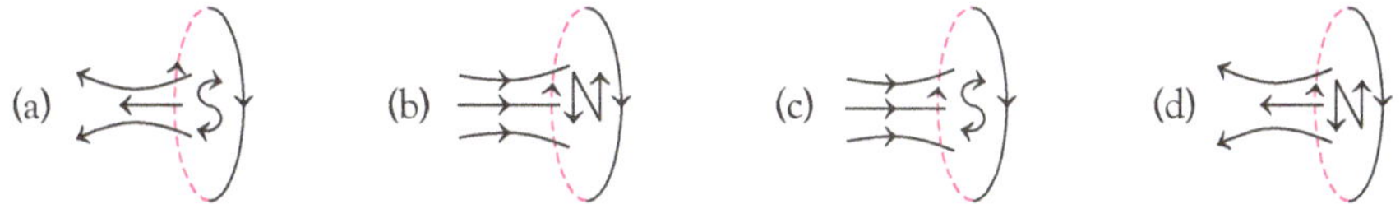

(*xiii*) Heat capacity of a body is the • *Recall*

(a) energy needed to melt a body without change in its temperature.

(b) energy needed to raise the temperature of a body by 1°C.

(c) increase in volume of the body when its temperature increases by 1°C.

(d) total amount of internal energy that is constant.

(*xiv*) The amount of heat energy required to melt a given mass of a substance at its melting point without any rise in its temperature is called as the • *Recall*

(a) specific heat capacity (b) specific latent heat of fusion

(c) latent heat of fusion (d) specific latent heat of freezing

(*xv*) A nucleus of an atom consists of 146 neutrons and 95 protons. It decays after emitting an alpha particle. How many protons and neutrons are left in the nucleus after an alpha emission? • *Understanding*

(a) Protons = 93, neutrons = 142
(b) Protons = 95, neutrons = 144
(c) Protons = 93, neutrons = 144
(d) Protons = 95, neutrons = 42

2. (i) Complete the following by choosing the correct answers from the bracket. **[6]**

(a) A .... [class I/class II/class III] lever will always have MA > 1.

(b) In a block and tackle system, increase in the weight of the movable block .... [decreases/does not affect/increases] the efficiency of the pulley system.

(c) If the mass as well as the velocity of a body is doubled, then the kinetic energy of the body .... [is doubled/becomes eight times/becomes four times] the initial kinetic energy.

(d) Unit of power used in mechanical engineering is .... [watt/horse power/erg per second].

(e) Two copper wires can have the different .... [resistivity/resistance] but will have same .... [resistance / resistivity].

• *Recall & Understanding*

(*ii*) Draw a graph of potential energy *versus* height for a body thrown vertically upwards. [Assume no friction is present]. • *Understanding* [2]

(*iii*) (a) Name the waves used for echo depth sounding.

(b) Give one reason for their use in the above purpose. • *Recall* [2]

3. (*i*) (a) Refer to the diagram given below. A lens with two different refractive indices is shown. If the rays are coming from a distant object, then how many images will be seen ? • *Understanding*

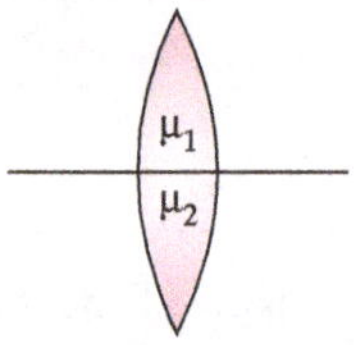

(b) A glass lens always forms a virtual, erect and diminished image of an object kept in front of it. Identify the lens. • *Recall* [2]

(*ii*) If live wire makes an accidental contact with the metal case, which circuit (A or B) in the diagram, illustrating an electric iron, is considered to be safe for the user (assuming the fuse is present in the live wire in both circuits)? Justify your answer. **[2]**

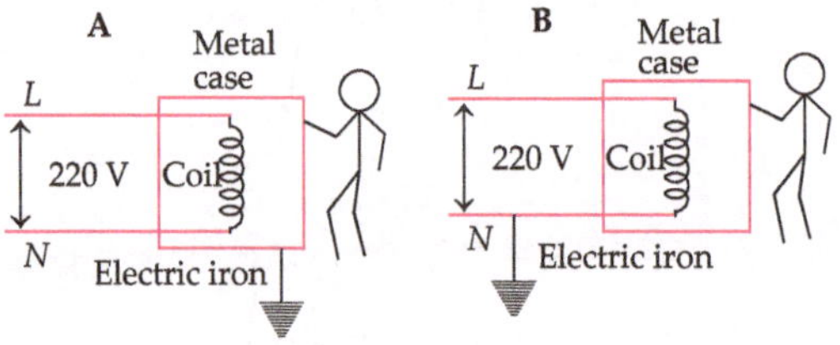

• *Application*

(*iii*) A transformer is used to change a high alternating emf to a low alternating emf of the same frequency.

(a) Identify the type of transformer used for the above purpose. • *Understanding*

(b) State whether the turns ratio of the above transformer is = 1 or > 1 or < 1. • *Recall* [2]

(*iv*) A solid of mass 60 g at 100°C is placed in 150 g of water at 20°C. The final steady temperature is 25°C. Calculate the heat capacity of solid. [Specific heat capacity of water = $4.2\ Jg^{-1}K^{-1}$] • *Understanding & Evaluate* [2]

(*v*) (a) Name the principle of AC generator.

(b) State its one use. • *Recall* [2]

(*vi*) (a) Name the radiations that are emitted during the decay of a nucleus, which have the highest penetrating power? • *Recall*

(b) Does the emission of the above-mentioned radiation result in a change in the mass number? • *Understanding* [2]

(*vii*) The graph (Fig. A) illustrates the correlation between the number of protons (X-axis) and the number of neutrons (Y-axis) for elements *A*, *B*, *C*, *D* and *E* in the periodic table. These elements are denoted by the letters rather than their conventional symbols. When the element C, depicted in the graph, undergoes radioactive decay, it releases radioactive rays. When these rays are directed into the plane of the paper in the presence of a magnetic field, as indicated in the (Fig. B), they experience deflection, causing them to move upwards.

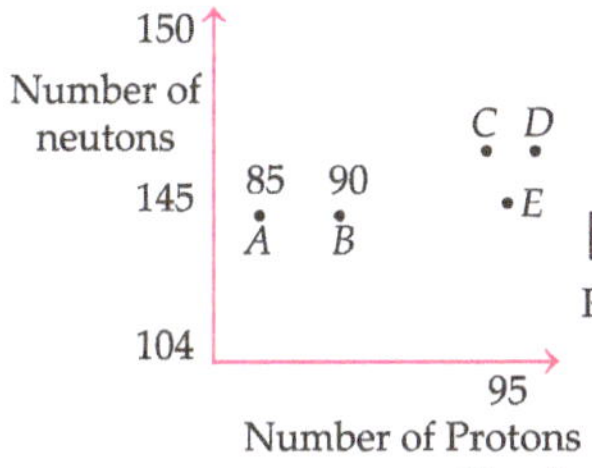

Fig. A

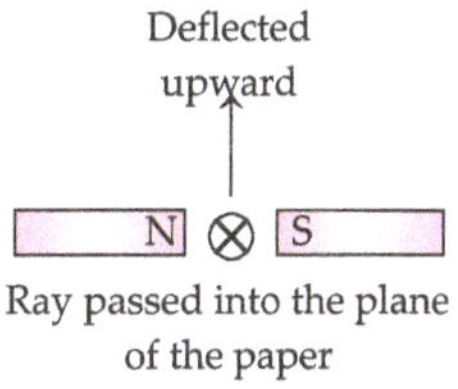

Fig. B

(a) Name the radioactive radiations emitted by the element C.

(b) Identify the daughter element from the graph.

(c) Name the law used to identify the radioactive radiations emitted by the element. • *Application* [3]

Section-B

(Attempt any four questions from this section)

4. (i) The diagram given below shows a fish in the tank and its image is seen on the surface of water. [3]

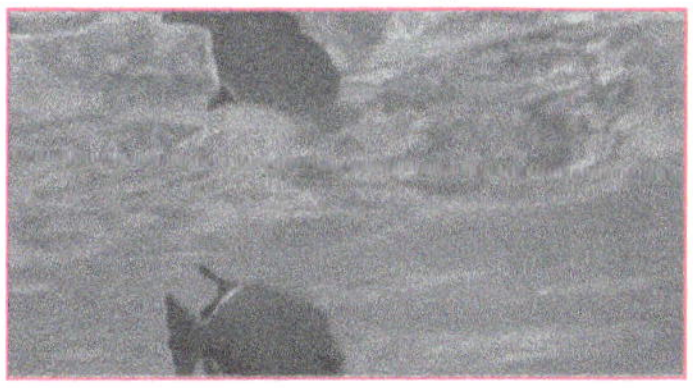

(a) Name the phenomenon responsible for the formation of this image. • *Understanding & Recall*

(b) A double convex lens with refractive index μ_1 inside two liquids of refractive indices μ_2 and μ_3 are shown in the diagrams below. The refractive indices are such that $\mu_2 > \mu_1$ and $\mu_1 > \mu_3$.

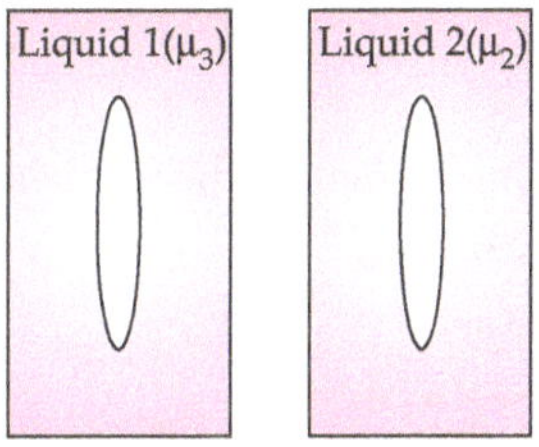

Fig. A Fig. B

How would a parallel incident beam of light refract when it comes out of the lens in each of the cases shown above? • *Application*

1. In Fig. A. 2. In Fig. B.

(ii) The refractive index of water is 1.33 at a certain temperature. When the temperature of water is increased by 10 °C, the refractive index changes to *x*. [3]

(a) State whether $x < 1.33$ or $x > 1.33$. • *Understanding*

(b) State two differences between normal reflection and total internal reflection. • *Recall*

(iii) (a) Mixture of red+blue+green colours is passed through a convex lens as shown in the diagram below. State whether the ray passes through a single point or through different points on the principal axis after refraction. • *Understanding*

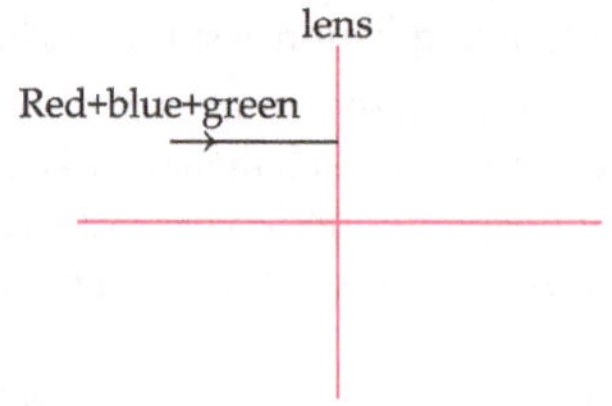

(b) Name the invisible radiations which are studied using the quartz prism. • *Recall*

(c) State one use of these radiations. • *Recall*

(d) Name one radiation having the wavelength longer than the wavelength of these radiations. • *Recall* [4]

5. (i) An object is placed at a distance 24 cm in front of a convex lens of focal length 8 cm.

(a) What is the nature of the image so formed?

(b) Calculate the distance of the image from the lens. • *Understanding & Evaluate* [3]

(ii) When sunlight passes through water droplets in the atmosphere, it gets dispersed into its constituent colours forming a rainbow. A similar phenomenon is observed when white light passes through a prism. **[3]**

(a) Which colour will show the maximum angle of deviation and which colour will show the minimum angle of deviation? • *Recall*

(b) If instead of sunlight, a green-coloured ray is passed through a glass prism. What will be the colour of the emergent ray? • *Understanding*

(*iii*) O is a luminescent particle trapped inside a glass block. A student traces the path of rays coming out of it and reflecting over a plane mirror as shown in the figure below.

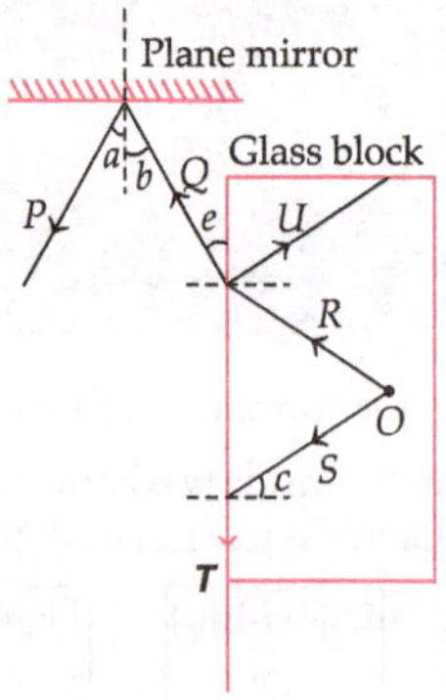

Complete the table using the labels from the figure. The first label is done for you.

Sr. No.	Description	Label
a.	an angle of reflection on the mirror	*a*
b.	a partially reflected ray in the glass slab	
c.	a critical angle	
d.	refracted rays	
e.	an angle of refraction of the ray *R*	

• *Understanding & Application* [4]

6. (*i*) A metal rod *AB* of length 80 cm is balanced at 45 cm from the end A with 100 gf weights suspended from the two ends.

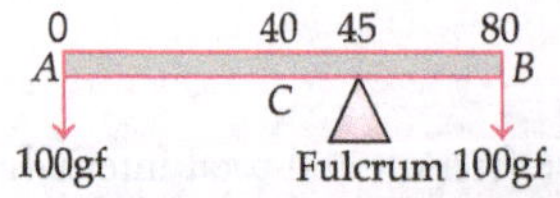

[3]

(a) If this rod is cut at the centre C, then compare the weight of AC to the weight of BC. • *Understanding & Application*

(b) Give a reason for your answer in (a).

(*ii*) For each of the following scenarios, state whether the work done by gravity is positive, negative or zero. **[3]**

(a) A person walks on a levelled road.

(b) A person climbs a ladder.

(c) A car in neutral gear is coming down the slope. • *Understanding & Recall*

(*iii*) The figure below shows a simple pendulum of mass 200 g. It is displaced from the mean position A to the extreme position B. The potential energy at the position A is zero. At the position B, the pendulum bob is raised by 5 m. **[4]**

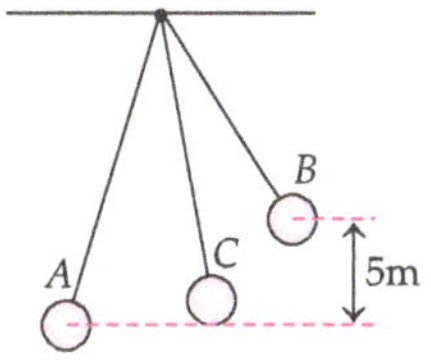

(a) What is the potential energy of the pendulum at the position B? • *Recall*

(b) What is the total mechanical energy at point C? • *Recall*

(c) What is the speed of the bob at the position A when released from B? • *Application & Evaluate*
(Take, $g = 10 \text{ ms}^{-2}$ and given that there is no loss of energy).

7. (*i*) A block and tackle system of pulleys has velocity ratio 4. **[3]**

(a) Draw a labelled diagram of the system indicating clearly the direction of the load and effort. • *Recall*

(b) Calculate the potential energy of the load 100 kgf lifted by this pulley to a height 5 m. (Take, $g = 10 \text{ ms}^{-2}$) • *Understanding & Evaluate*

(*ii*) A person standing in front of a cliff fires a gun and hears its echo after 3 s. If the speed of sound in air is 336 ms^{-1}, **[3]**

(a) calculate the distance of the person from the cliff.

(b) After moving a certain distance from the cliff, he fires the gun again and this time the echo is heard 1.5 s later than the first. Calculate the distance that the person moved. • *Understanding & Evaluate*

(iii) The above picture shows a mother pushing her daughter sitting on a swing. The swing is going through the positions A, B, C where A and C are extreme positions and B is the mean position. **[4]**

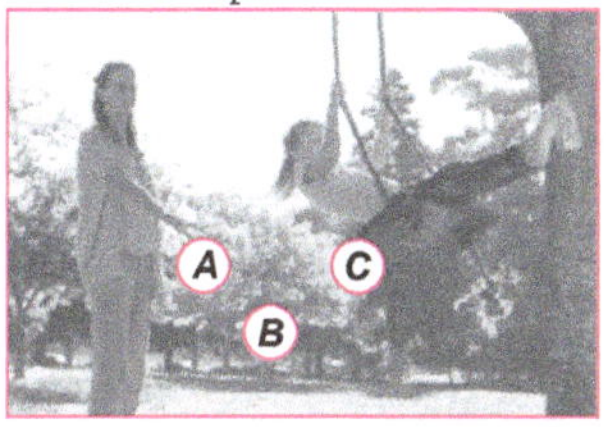

(a) Which is the right position, i.e. at A, B or C, for the mother to give a constant periodic push to the swing every time in the forward direction to increase the amplitude of the swing?

(b) Name the phenomenon involved in this.

(c) Explain with this example, how this phenomenon helps to increase the amplitude of the swing. • *Application*

8. (*i*) The circuit depicted in the figure is employed for studying Ohm's Law. Instead of using a standard resistor, a student opts for a glass tube filled with mercury (tube 1), connected to the circuit through two electrodes E_1 and E_2. He records the readings of the ammeter and voltmeter, thereby calculates the resistance. The student repeats the experiment by substituting tube 1 with tube 2, where the same amount of mercury fills the tube 2.

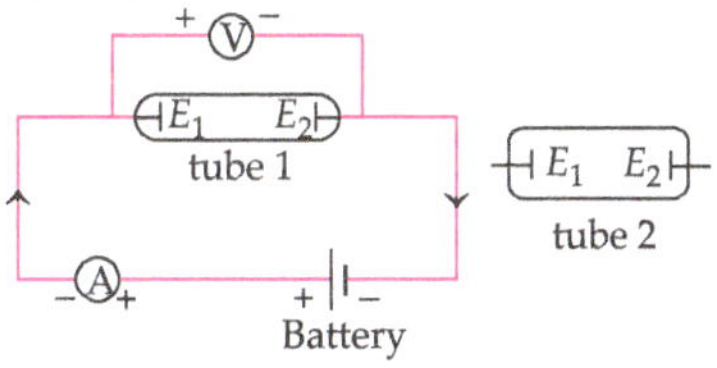

Neglecting internal resistance of the cell use (> or < or =) to compare

(a) the resistance in both the cases.

(b) the voltmeter readings in both the cases.

(c) the specific resistance in both the cases. • *Understanding & Application* [3]

(ii) A radioactive nucleus X emits an alpha particle followed by two beta particles to form nucleus Y.

(a) With respect to the element X, where would you position the element Y in the periodic table?

(b) What is the general name of the elements X and Y?

(c) If the atomic number of Y is 80, then what is the atomic number of X? • *Understanding & Recall* [3]

(iii) Observe the given circuit diagram and answer the questions that follow.

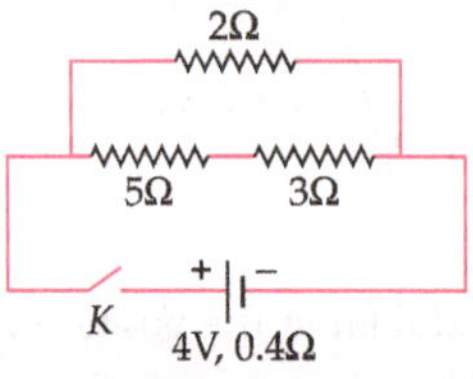

(a) Calculate the resistance of the circuit when the key K completes the circuit.

(b) Calculate the current through 3Ω resistance when the circuit is complete. • *Understanding & Evaluate* [4]

9. (i) What mass of ice at 0°C added to 2.1 kg water, will cool it down from 75°C to 25°C? [Given, specific heat capacity of water = $4.2\ Jg^{-1}\ °C^{-1}$, specific latent heat of ice = $336\ Jg^{-1}$]. • *Understanding & Evaluate* [3]

(ii) The diagram below shows a cooling curve for a substance. [3]

(a) State the temperature at which the substance condenses.

(b) The temperature range in which the substance is in liquid state.

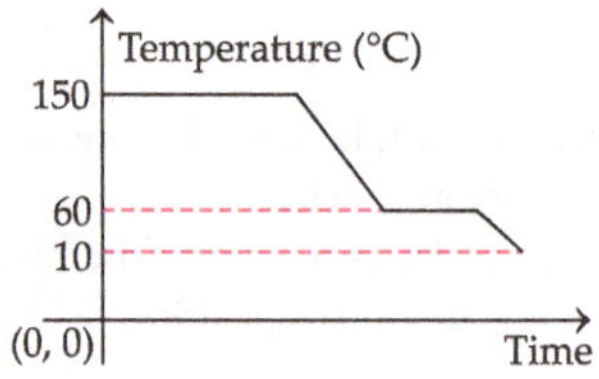

(c) Why do we prefer ice to ice-cold water for cooling a drink? • *Understanding & Recall*

(iii) The diagram below shows a cardboard on which iron filings are kept. A wire bent in the form of a loop is seen passing through the cardboard. When current flows through it, the iron filings arrange themselves as shown below with the direction of magnetic field. [4]

(a) State the polarities of the battery at A and B.

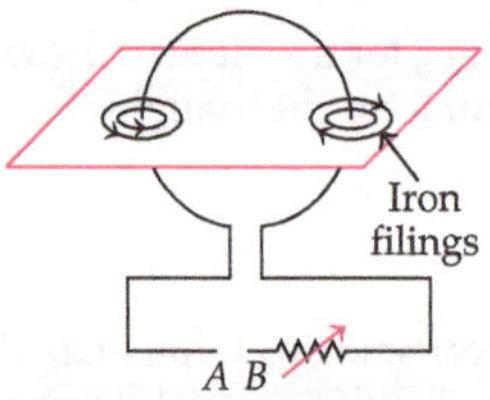

(b) State the effect on the magnetic field, if an iron rod is held along the axis of the coil. • *Understanding & Application*

(c) State one way to

1. change the polarity of the coil.
2. decrease the strength of the magnetic field around the coil.

• *Understanding & Recall*

Solutions

1. (i) (a) The anti-clockwise couple is taken as positive and clockwise couple is taken as negative.

(ii) (c) The kinetic energy of a body is

$$KE = \frac{p^2}{2m}$$

$$KE \propto (\text{momentum})^2$$

(iii) (b) In thermoelectric station, the energy conversion taking place is chemical to heat to mechanical to electrical.

(iv) (c) From the diagram, we can conclude that the number of pulleys used in the fixed block are 2.

(v) (d) Inside the prism, compared to the blue light, the red light slows down less and refracts less because the wavelength of red colour is maximum.

(vi) (d) The phenomenon of light governing in optical fibre is based on total internal reflection.

(vii) (b) By lens formula,

For convex lens, $f = +12$ cm

$u = -20$ cm

$$\frac{1}{f} = \frac{1}{v} - \frac{1}{u}$$

$$\Rightarrow \quad \frac{1}{12} = \frac{1}{v} - \frac{1}{(-20)} \quad \Rightarrow \quad \frac{1}{12} = \frac{1}{v} + \frac{1}{20}$$

$$\Rightarrow \quad \frac{1}{v} = \frac{1}{12} - \frac{1}{20} \quad \Rightarrow \quad \frac{1}{v} = \frac{5-3}{60} = \frac{2}{60}$$

$$\Rightarrow \quad \frac{1}{v} = \frac{1}{30} \quad \Rightarrow \quad v = 30 \text{ cm}$$

Image will be formed at a distance 30 cm. So, in order to obtain a clear image, he has to move the screen away from the lens.

(viii) (a) Both A and R are true and R is the correct explanation of A.

The infrared radiations have long wavelengths, so they undergo minimal scattering in earth's atmosphere and travel long distances in dense fog and mist.

(ix) (b) The pitch or shrillness of a sound is directly proportional to its frequency.

$\therefore$ X will be grave and Y will be shriller.

(x) (c) Resistance, R = Slope of V-I graph = $\tan\theta$

As, $\quad \theta_P > \theta_Q > \theta_R < \theta_S$

$\Rightarrow \quad R_P > R_Q > R_R > R_S$

The filament of a bulb is made up of high resistance material. So, material P is used to make its filament.

(xi) (b) According to old convention, the colour of live, neutral and earth wires are red, black and green respectively.

(xii) (c) According to Maxwell's right hand thumb rule, the figure given in option (c) will be correct.

(xiii) (b) Heat capacity of a body is the heat or energy required to raise its temperature by 1°C.

(xiv) (c) The amount of heat energy required to melt a given amount of substance at its melting point is called as the latent heat of fusion.

(xv) $p = 95$, $n = 146$

$A = p + n = 95 + 146 = 241$

Now, $\; _{95}X^{241} \longrightarrow \, _{93}X^{237} + \, _2He^4$

Number of neutrons $= A - Z = 237 - 93 = 144$

Number of protons, $Z = 93$

Hence, option (c) is correct.

2. (i) (a) class II (b) decreases

(c) becomes eight times (d) horse power

(e) resistance, resistivity

(ii) The potential energy of a body at height h,

$$U = mgh$$

$$U \propto h$$

$\therefore$ The graph of U *versus* h is given below

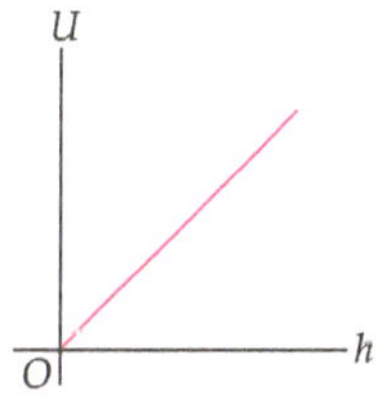

(iii) (a) The waves used for echo depth sounding are ultrasonic waves.

(b) Ultrasonic waves are used in echo depth sounding because these waves have very high frequency and short wavelength. So, these waves can penetrate undeviated through long distances in sea water.

3. (i) (a) As, the lens is made of two different refractive indices material so number of images formed will be two.

(b) In a concave lens, the image formed is always virtual, erect and diminished.

(ii) In circuit A, metal case is earthed. So, the person would not get electric shock but in circuit B, metal case is not earthed. So, the circuit will be completed through the body of the person giving him a shock. Therefore, circuit A is safe for the user.

(iii) (a) The transformer used to change a high alternating emf to a low alternating emf of same frequency is called step-down transformer.

(b) As, turns ratio, $r = \frac{N_s}{N_p} = \frac{E_s}{E_p}$

For step-down transformer,

$$E_s < E_p \Rightarrow \frac{E_s}{E_p} < 1$$

$\therefore \quad r < 1$ (less than 1)

(iv) Given, $s_w = 4.2\ Jg^{-1}\ K^{-1}$

For solid, $m_s = 60$ g, $T_s = 100°C$

For water, $m_w = 150$ g, $T_w = 20°C$

Final temperature, $T_f = 25°C$

By principle of calorimetry,

Heat lost by solid = Heat gained by water

$$\Rightarrow \quad m_s \cdot s_s (T_s - T_f) = m_w s_w (T_f - T_w)$$

$\therefore$ Heat capacity of solid, $m_s s$

$$= \frac{m_w c_w (T_f - T_w)}{(T_s - T_f)}$$

$$= \frac{150 \times 4.2 \times (25 - 20)}{(100 - 25)} = 42\ JK^{-1}$$

(v) (a) Faraday's first law or principle of electromagnetic induction.

(b) AC generator is used as a power source in major power stations like wind turbines.

(vi) (a) Gamma radiations (b) No

(vii) (a) Beta (b) Daughter element E

(c) Fleming's left hand rule

4. (i) (a) The image formed of fish on the water surface is based on the phenomenon of total internal reflection.

(b) 1. Converge 2. Diverge

(ii) (a) As, refractive index $\propto \dfrac{1}{\text{temperature}}$

$$\therefore \quad x < 1.33$$

(b) Two differences between normal reflection and total internal reflection :

Normal reflection	Total internal reflection
In this reflection, light rays can be incident at any angle.	In this reflection, light rays must be incident at an angle greater than critical angle.
The energy of reflected rays is less than that of incident rays, i.e. there is loss of energy.	The energy of reflected rays is same as that of incident rays, i.e. there is no loss of energy.

(iii) (a) When mixture of red + blue + green colours is passed through a convex lens, each ray passes through a different points on the principal axis after refraction.

(b) Ultraviolet radiations are obtained by a quartz prism, as they are not absorbed by it.

(c) These radiations are used for killing bacteria.

(d) Visible radiation or infrared or microwaves or radiowaves.

5. (i) For convex lens, $f = 8$ cm, $u = -24$ cm

(a) As $u > 2f$, so the image formed is real, inverted and smaller size than object.

(b) By lens formula,

$$\frac{1}{f} = \frac{1}{v} - \frac{1}{u}$$

$$\Rightarrow \quad \frac{1}{8} = \frac{1}{v} - \frac{1}{(-24)}$$

$$\Rightarrow \quad \frac{1}{v} = \frac{1}{8} - \frac{1}{24} = \frac{1}{12}$$

$$\therefore \quad v = 12 \text{ cm}$$

(ii) (a) As, deviation $\propto \dfrac{1}{\text{wavelength}}$

$\therefore$ Violet colour will show maximum deviation and red colour will show minimum deviation because wavelength of violet colour is minimum and wavelength of red colour is maximum.

(b) When green-coloured ray is passed through a glass prism, then the colour of emergent ray will be also green because green light has not any component of light.

(iii)

Sr. No.	Description	Label
a.	an angle of reflection on the mirror	a
b.	a partially reflected ray in glass slab	U
c.	a critical angle	c
d.	refracted rays	Q, T
e.	an angle of refraction of the ray R	$90 - e$

6. (i)(a) Weight of $AC <$ Weight of BC

(b) Since, the rod is balanced at F (fulcrum)

$$\therefore \quad w_{AF} = w_{BF}$$

Now, $\quad w_{AF} - w_{CF} < w_{CF} \propto w_{BF} + w_{CF}$

[subtracting weight of CF from left and adding to right]

$$\Rightarrow \quad w_{AC} < w_{BC}$$

(ii) (a) No work is done.

(b) Negative work is done.

(c) Positive work is done

(iii) (a) The potential energy of the pendulum at point B

$$(PE)_B = mgh = 0.2 \times 10 \times 5 = 10\ J$$

(b) Applying conservation of mechanical energy,

$$E_A = E_B = E_C$$

$\therefore$ Total mechanical energy at point C,

$$E_C = E_B = (KE)_B + (PE)_B = 0 + 10 = 10\ J$$

(c) Applying conservation of mechanical energy at points A and B,

$$\frac{1}{2} mv^2 = mgh$$

$$\therefore \quad v = \sqrt{2gh}$$

$$= \sqrt{2 \times 10 \times 5} = 10 \text{ m/s}$$

7. (i) (a) A block and tackle system of pulley,

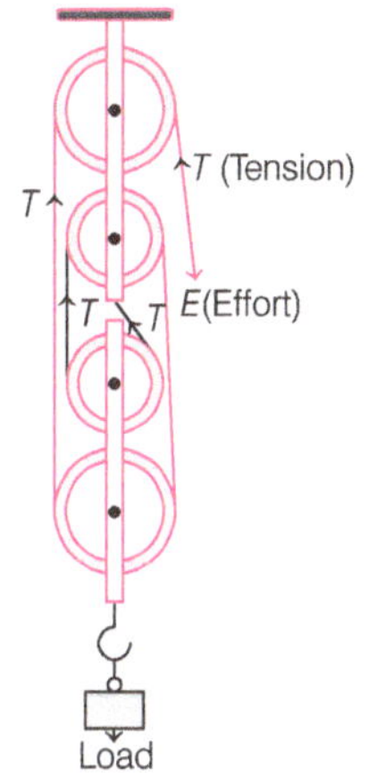

(b) Potential energy,

$$U = mgh = 100 \times 10 \times 5$$
$$U = 5000 \text{ J}$$

(ii) (a) Given, $t = 3$ s,

speed of sound, $v = 336$ m/s

Let d = distance of person from cliff.

$\therefore\ 2d = v \times t \Rightarrow 2d = 336 \times 3 \Rightarrow d = 504$ m

(b) Let the extra distance moved by person from the cliff $= x$

$$t = 3 + 1.5 = 4.5 \text{ s}$$
$$\therefore\ 2(d + x) = v \times t$$
$$\Rightarrow\ 2(504 + x) = 336 \times 4.5$$
$$\therefore\ x = 252 \text{ m}$$

(iii) (a) At point A

(b) Resonance

(c) The natural frequency of the swing will equal the frequency of the force applied by mother. Due to which the amplitude of swing will increase.

8. (i) (a) $R_1 < R_2$ (b) $V_1 = V_2$ (c) $S_1 = S_2$

(ii) Atomic number Z and mass number A

$$^{A}_{Z}X \xrightarrow{\alpha} {}^{A-4}_{Z-2}X \quad \text{and} \quad ^{A}_{Z}Y \xrightarrow{2\beta} {}^{A-4}_{Z-2}Y$$

(a) As, the atomic number of both the elements X and Y are same, so they are placed at the same position in the periodic table.

(b) X and Y are isotopes.

(c) Atomic number of X = Atomic number of Y = 80

(iii) (a) When key K is closed, then the circuit diagram is as shown below.

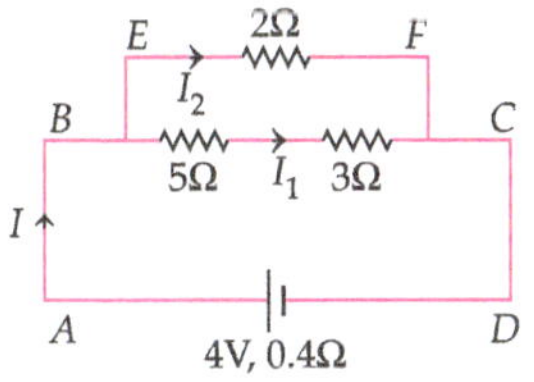

The resistance of the circuit is given by

$$R = \frac{2 \times (5 + 3)}{2 + (5 + 3)} + 0.4 = 2\ \Omega$$

(b) Current, $I = \dfrac{\varepsilon}{R + r} = \dfrac{4}{2 + 0.4} = 2$ A

Current in 3 Ω, $I_{3\,\Omega} = \dfrac{IR_1}{R_1 + R_2} = \dfrac{5}{3} \times \dfrac{2}{[2 + (5 + 3)]}$

$$I_{3\,\Omega} = \frac{1}{3} \text{ A}$$

9. (i) Given, $m_w = 2.1$ kg,

$(\Delta T)_{w,\text{ Heat lost}} = (75 - 25) = 50°$C

$s_w = 4.2$ Jg^{-1}° C^{-1}, $L_{ice} = 336$ Jg^{-1}

Let m = mass of ice added at 0°C.

$\therefore$ By principle of calorimetry,

Heat lost by water from 75° to 25° C = Heat gained by ice at 0°C to water at 0° C + Heat gained by water at 0°C to water at 25°C

$$\Rightarrow\ m_w s_w (\Delta T)_{w,\text{ Heat lost}} = mL_i + ms_w(\Delta T)_{w,\text{ Heat gain}}$$
$$\Rightarrow\ 2.1 \times 10^3 \times 4.2 \times 50 = m\,[336 + 4.2 \times 25]$$
$$\therefore\ \text{Mass of ice, } m = 1000 \text{ g} = 1 \text{ kg}$$

(ii) The cooling curve for the substance is shown below.

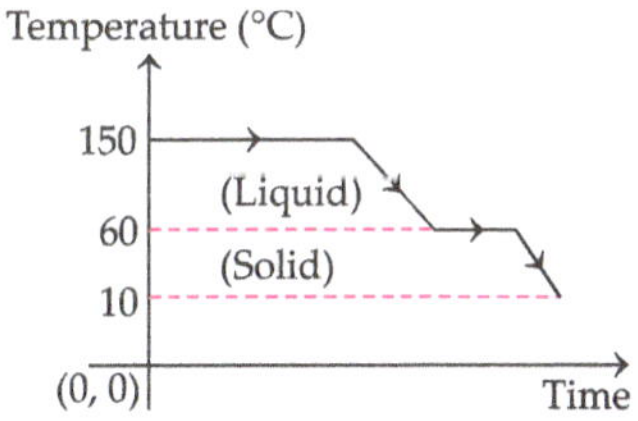

(a) The substance is condensed at the temperature of 150°C.

(b) The temperature range for which the substance is in liquid state is 60°C to 150°C.

(c) When ice melts to water at 0°C, it absorbs heat equal to latent heat of melting of ice and gets converted into water. This is the reason why drinks get even more colder when kept in ice as ice absorbs heat from the drink.

(iii) (a) $A \rightarrow$ Positive terminal

$B \rightarrow$ Negative terminal

(b) Magnetic field will expand in the direction of the held rod.

(c) 1. Reversing the direction of the current.

Or

Reversing the direction of the battery.

2. Reduce the potential difference across the coil.

Or Decreasing the strength of the current through the coil.

ICSE

EXAMINATION PAPER 2025

GENERAL INSTRUCTIONS

1. You will not be allowed to write during the first 15 minutes. This time is to be spent in reading the question paper.
2. The time given at the head of this paper is the time allowed for writing the answers.
3. **Section A** is compulsory. Attempt any four questions from **Section B**.
4. The intended marks for questions or parts of questions are given in brackets [ ].

Section A [40 Marks]

(Attempt all questions from this section)

1. Choose the correct answers to the questions from the given options. **[15]**

(i) A body is acted upon by two equal and opposite forces, that are not along the same straight line. The body will
(a) remain stationary
(b) have only rotational motion
(c) have only rectilinear motion
(d) have both rectilinear and rotational motion

(ii) Which among the following is a vector quantity?
(a) Work
(b) Power
(c) Energy
(d) Moment of couple

(iii) What is the correct energy transformation during burning of a candle?
(a) Heat $\rightarrow$ Kinetic + Potential
(b) Heat $\rightarrow$ Chemical + Light
(c) Chemical $\rightarrow$ Heat + Light
(d) Mechanical $\rightarrow$ Chemical + Heat

(iv) When a ray of light passes from one optical medium to another, which of the following physical quantities does not change?
(a) Amplitude of the wave
(b) Frequency of the wave
(c) Wavelength of the wave
(d) Speed of the wave

(v) Which one of the following combinations is the correct ascending order of electromagnetic waves in terms of wavelength?
(a) Gamma-rays, visible light, microwaves
(b) Microwaves, visible light, gamma-rays
(c) Gamma-rays, microwaves, visible light
(d) Microwaves, gamma-rays, visible light

(vi) For a lever, a graph is plotted with load on Y-axis and effort on X-axis. Which of the following represents the slope of the graph?
(a) Mechanical advantage
(b) Velocity ratio
(c) 1/ Velocity ratio
(d) 1 Mechanical advantage

(vii) For a real image formed by a convex lens, the ratio of $I : O = 2 : 5$, then the object is I is the height of the image and O is the height of the object)
(a) between O and F
(b) beyond $2F$
(c) at F
(d) between F and $2F$

(viii) A ray of light is incident normally on a face of an equilateral prism. The ray gets totally reflected at the second refracting surface. The total deviation produced in the path of the ray is
(a) 30° (b) 60°
(c) 90° (d) 120°

(ix) In a closed circuit containing a bulb and a cell, the electromotive force (ε) and the terminal voltage (V) is related as
(Given, I is current and r is internal resistance)
(a) $V = \varepsilon + Ir$ (b) $V = \varepsilon - Ir$
(c) $V = \varepsilon \div Ir$ (d) $V = \varepsilon \times Ir$

(x) A metal piece of mass 5 g has thermal capacity $2.5\ JK^{-1}$. If the mass of the metal is tripled, then its specific heat capacity will be
(a) $7.5\ JK^{-1}$ (b) $2.5\ JK^{-1}$
(c) $1.5\ Jg^{-1}K^{-1}$ (d) $0.5\ Jg^{-1}K^{-1}$

(xi) **Assertion (A)** As the level of water in a tall measuring cylinder kept under running tap rises, the pitch of sound gradually increases.

Reason (R) Frequency of sound is inversely proportional to the length of the water column.

(a) Both A and R are true and R is correct explanation of A.
(b) Both A and R are true but R is not the correct explanation of A.
(c) A is true but R is false.
(d) A is false but R is true.

(xii) In the given circuits Y and Z, the resistors R_1 and R_2, are connected in

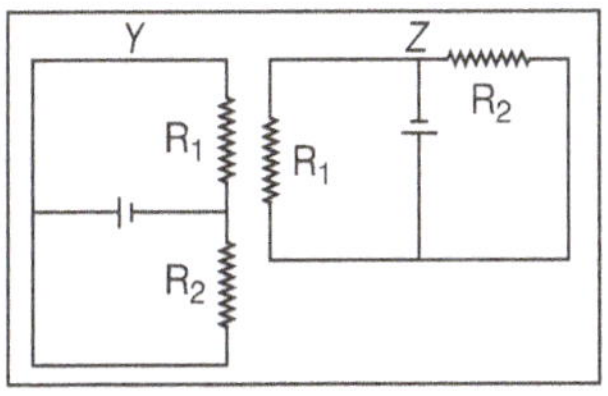

(a) series in both the circuits
(b) parallel in both the circuits
(c) parallel in Y and series in Z
(d) series in Y and parallel in Z

(xiii) A radioactive element P emits one α-particle and transforms to a new element Q. What will be the position of the element Q in the periodic table?
(a) One group to the left of P
(b) One group to the right of P
(c) Two groups to the right of P
(d) Two groups to the left of P

(xiv) Each of the substances given below is supplied with same amount of heat.
Which one will attain the highest temperature?

Substance	Lead	Aluminium	Copper	Iron
Specific heat capacity (cal/g°C)	0.031	0.21	0.095	0.115

(a) Aluminium (b) Copper
(c) Iron (d) Lead

(xv) The following figure shows a small bar magnet falling freely through a copper ring. For the observer at A, the direction of the induced current will be

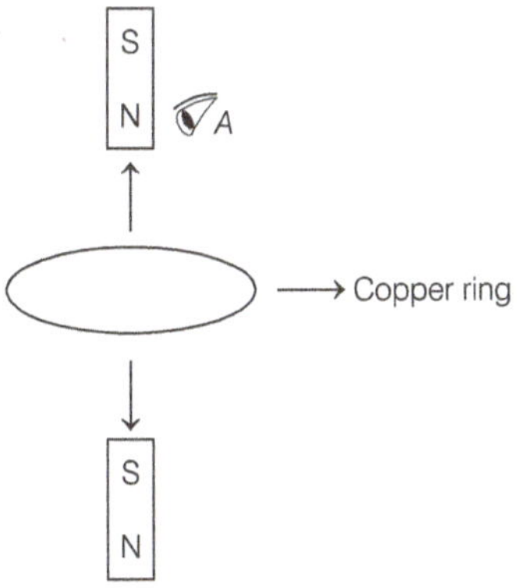

(a) clockwise when magnet is above and below the ring
(b) anti-clockwise when magnet is above and below the ring
(c) anti-clockwise when magnet is above the ring and clockwise when the magnet is below the ring
(d) clockwise when magnet is above the ring and anti-clockwise when the magnet is below the ring

2. (i) Complete the following by choosing the correct answers from the bracket **[6]**
(a) In uniform circular motion the centrifugal force acts .... (towards the centre/away from the centre/along the tangential direction).
(b) Refractive index of a medium is independent of .... (temperature/angle of incidence/wavelength of light).
(c) Heat absorbed during change of phase depends on .... (mass/change in temperature/specific heat capacity) of the substance.
(d) Emf of a cell is .... (greater than / less than / equal to) the terminal voltage when the cell is in open circuit.
(e) In a step-up transformer the turns ratio is .... (more than 1/less than 1/equal to 1)
(f) The nuclear radiation with lowest ionising power is .... (α / β / γ).

(ii) A non-uniform kite is hanging freely from the branch of a tree as shown. Study the figure and answer the following **[2]**

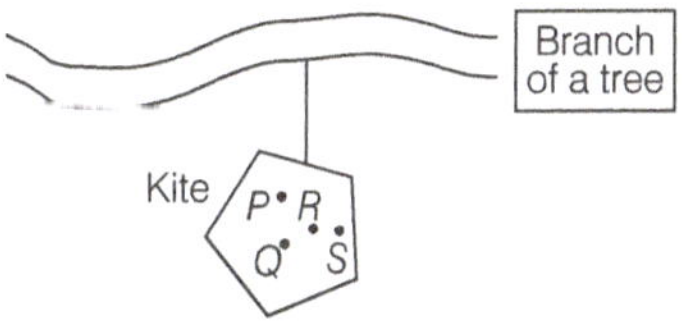

(a) Fill in the blank.
.... (P, Q, R or S) is the most probable position of its centre of gravity.
(b) Support your answer to (a) with a reason.

(iii) The displacement-time graph of a sound wave produced by a vibrating wire is shown below. **[2]**

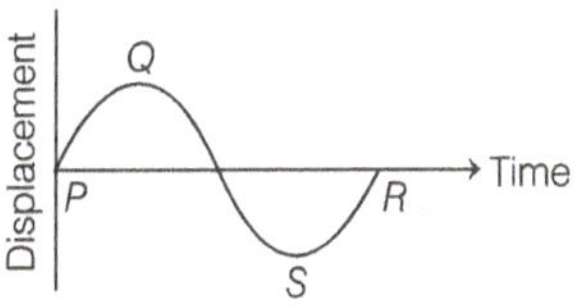

(a) How will you adjust the tension in the wire, to reduce the length of PR?
(b) Which characteristic of sound is affected by the reduction in the length of PR?

3. (i) A ray of light enters a rectangular glass slab submerged in water at an angle of incidence 55°. Does this ray undergo total internal reflection when it moves from water to glass? Justify your answer. (The critical angle for glass-water interface is 54°.) **[2]**

(ii) According to the new colour convention which colour of wire is connected to **[2]**

(a) the metal body of the appliance

(b) the switch of the appliance?

(iii) (a) Which of the two, alternating current or direct current, produces a varying magnetic field when it flows through a conductor? **[2]**

(b) State the frequency of the alternating current supply in India

(iv) Calculate the amount of heat absorbed by 200 g of paraffin wax to melt completely at its melting point [Specific latent heat of fusion of paraffin wax $= 146\, \text{Jg}^{-1}$] **[2]**

(v) Copper wire is wound around a steel bar *FT*. Current is allowed to pass through the coil for some time and then the bar is removed. **[2]**

(a) Draw only the magnetised bar *FT* and mark its poles.

(b) Trace two magnetic lines of force around *FT* clearly indicating the direction.

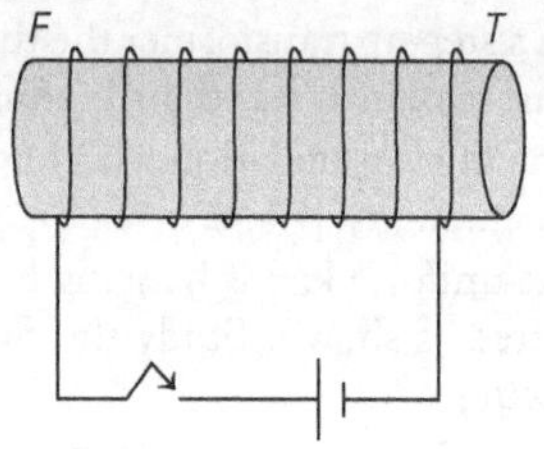

(vi) A current flows through a metallic conductor for a long period of time. State the change you would expect in its **[2]**

(a) Resistance (b) Resistivity

(vii) Curium is a radioactive element with the symbol $^{247}_{96}\text{Cm}$ named in honour of Madam Curie. The graph of number of protons *versus* number of neutrons for some elements are shown below

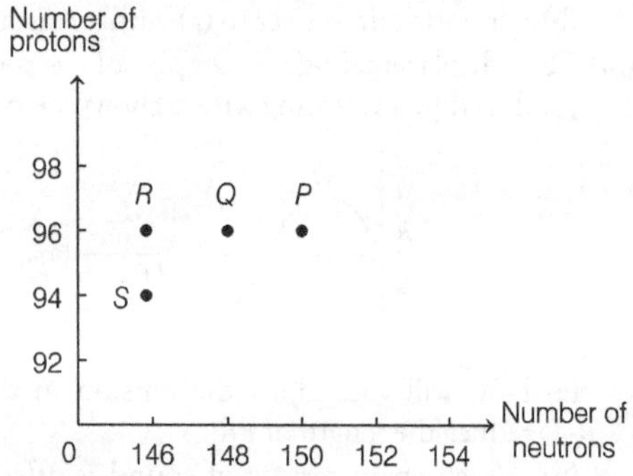

(a) Which point on the graph indicates the element Cm? **[1]**

(b) Which point on the graph indicates daughter nucleus after Cm undergoes radioactive decay of 1α followed by 2β? **[1]**

(c) State the mass number of the daughter nucleus. **[1]**

Section B

(Attempt any four questions from this section)

4. (i)

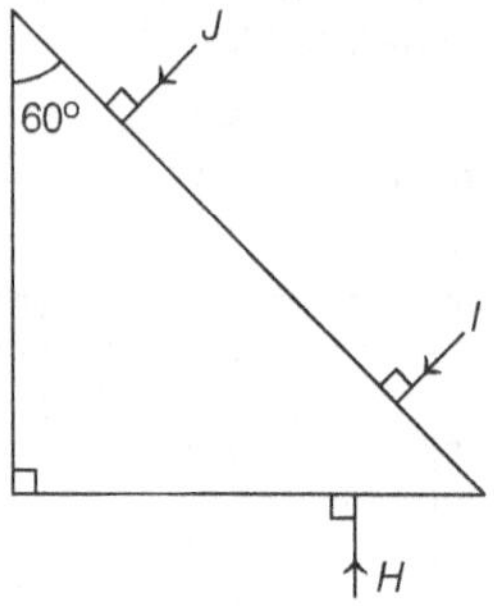

[3]

(a) Out of the three rays (*I*, *J*, *H*) shown in the diagram, which ray will suffer total internal reflection, while inside the prism? (Critical angle of the prism is 42°.)

(b) Copy the diagram to complete the path of the ray which you have named in (a) till it comes out of the prism

(ii) A rectangular glass block of refractive index 1.5 has an air bubble trapped inside it as shown in the diagram. When seen from the surface *AB*, it appears to be 4 cm deep. **[3]**

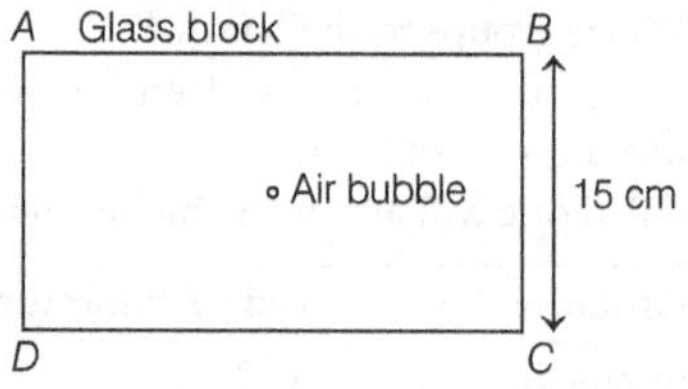

(a) Calculate the actual depth of the air bubble from the surface *AB*.

(b) For which colour of light, blue or yellow, the apparent depth will be greater?

(c) Turning the glass block upside down, does not change the apparent depth of the air bubble. State true or false.

(iii) (a) An object is placed at 2*F* position of a convex lens. Draw a ray diagram showing the formation of the image.

(b) How will the size of the image change if we, only replace the lens in the above arrangement with another lens of a greater focal length? **[4]**

5. (i) An object is placed in front of a concave lens at a distance of 45 cm from it. If its image is formed at a distance of 30 cm from the lens, calculate the focal length of the lens? **[3]**

(ii) Two rays *PQ* and *RS* are incident on a rectangular glass block as shown in the diagram. Observe the diagram and answer the questions that follow. **[3]**

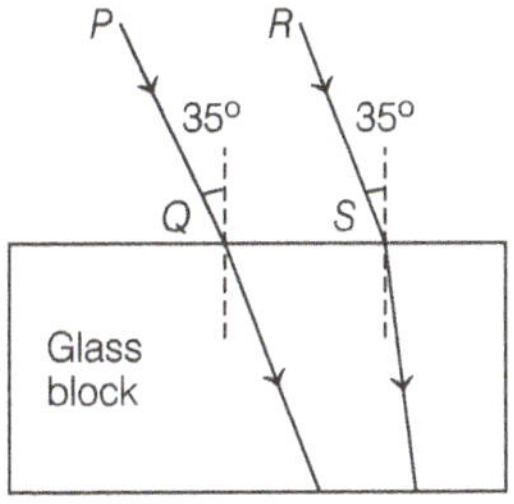

Which of these two rays will

(a) have greater lateral displacement on emerging out of the block?

(b) travel with greater speed in the block?

(c) scatter more in the atmosphere?

(iii) (a) Name the radiations **[4]**

1. for which a quartz prism is used to study the spectrum.
2. which are used in remote sensing devices.
3. which are used in traffic signals m India.

(b) Name one property common to all electromagnetic radiations.

6. (i) Akash takes a uniform meter scale and suspends a weight of 2 N at one end 'X' and a weight of 5 N on the other end 'Y'. He then balances the ruler horizontally on a knife edge placed at 70 cm from X. Draw a diagram of the arrangement and calculate the weight of the ruler. **[3]**

(ii) Three levers X, Y, Z of equal lengths are shown in the diagram.

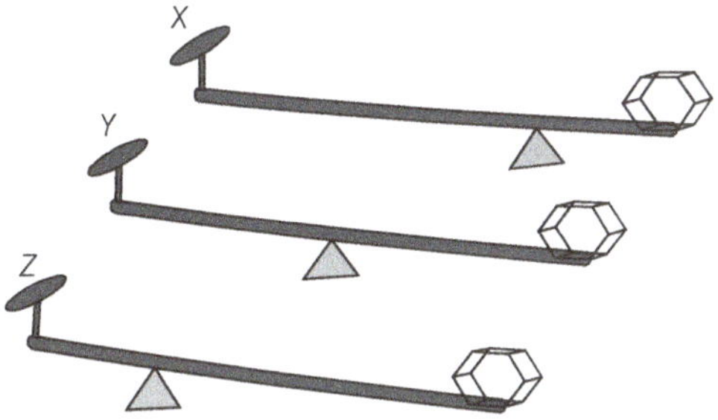

(a) Which class of lever do these belong to?

(b) Among these (X, Y or Z) which one will give the maximum mechanical advantage? Justify your answer.

(iii)

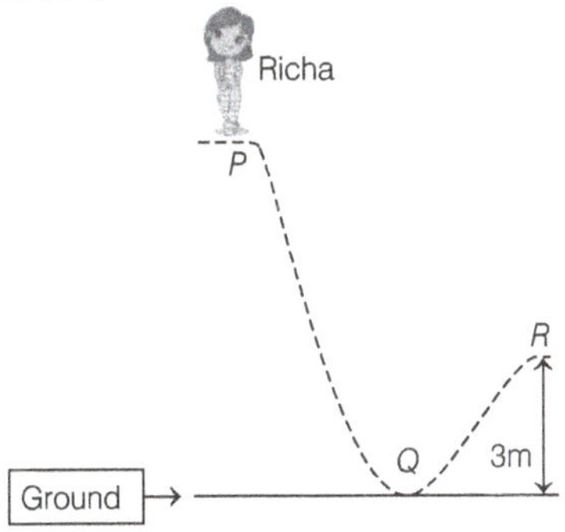

Richa weighing 40 kgf leaves point P on her skateboard and reaches point Q on the ground with velocity 10 ms^{-1}. Calculate **[4]**

(a) the kinetic energy of Richa at point Q.

(b) the vertical height of point P above the ground. (Use g as 10 m/s^2 and neglect friction

(c) the kinetic energy of Richa at point R. (While moving from Q to R, she loses 500 J of energy against friction)

7. (i) Draw a block and tackle system of pulleys with velocity ratio equal to 3. **[3]**

(ii) A submarine in the sea, sends ultrasonic ping and a stopwatch is started simultaneously. The stopwatch stops on receiving the reflected wave from an obstacle and reads 1 minute 40 seconds. Calculate the distance of the obstacle from the submarine. (Speed of sound in water 1500 ms^{-1}) **[3]**

(iii) The diagrams given below show two sound boxes A and B with wires of same length (l) and tension (10 kgf) but different cross-sectional areas. Simultaneously, vibrating tuning forks of frequency 300 Hz are placed on the boxes A and B. The paper rider falls off in case of B but not in case of A. **[4]**

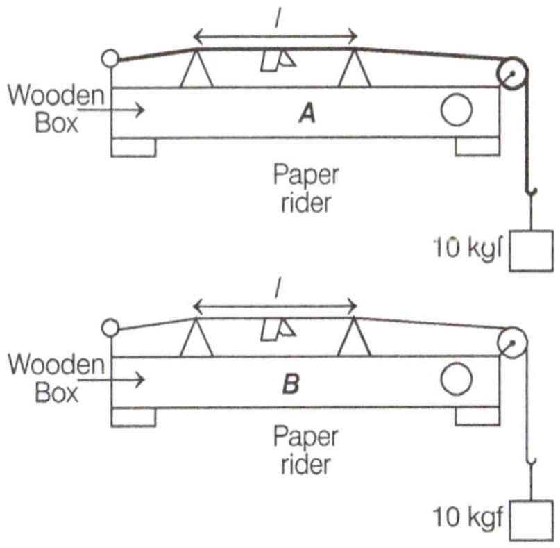

(a) Name and explain the phenomenon responsible for the falling off of the paper rider in B.

(b) The wire A resonates with a tuning fork of frequency f. Is f greater than, less than or equal to 300 Hz? Justify your answer.

8. (i) The diagram shows wiring in a meter room of a building. **[3]**

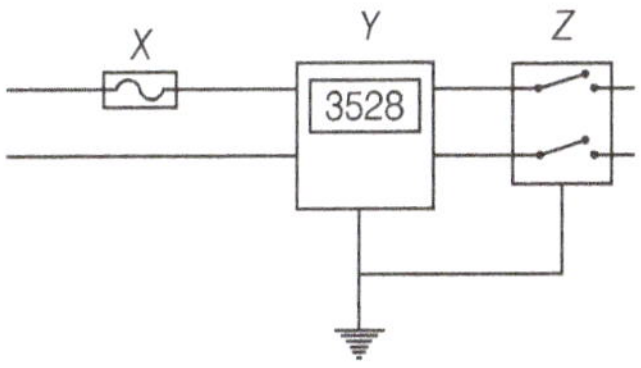

(a) What is the current rating of device X?

(b) What is the difference between the switch Z shown in the diagram and the switches you use to operate different appliances at home?

(c) What is the unit of the physical quantity displayed in Y?

(ii) Study the diagram given below and answer the questions that follow:

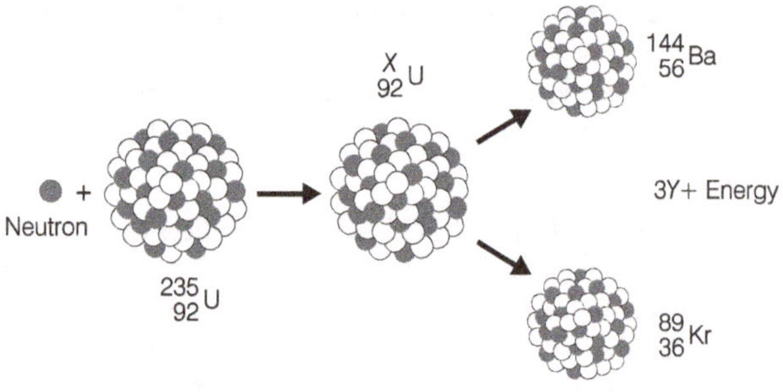

(a) Name the process depicted in the diagram.

(b) What is the value of X?

(c) Identify Y. the missing product of the reaction.

(iii)

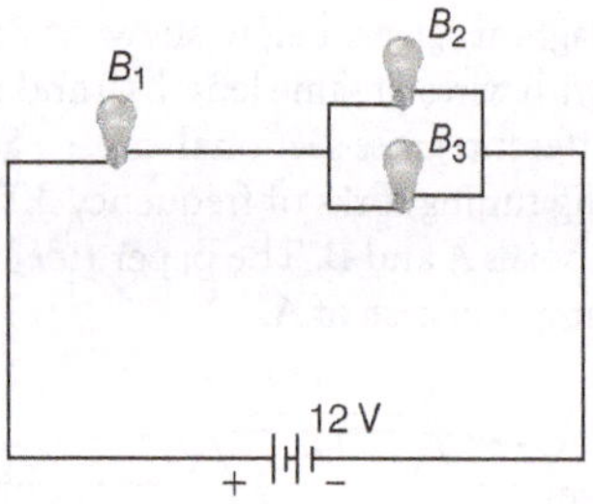

Three identical bulbs B_1, B_2, and B_3 each of power rating 18 W, 12 V are connected to a battery of 12 V. **[4]**

(a) Calculate:

1. the resistance of each bulb
2. the current drawn from the cell

(b) If the bulb B_3 is removed from the circuit, then will the brightness of the bulb B_1 increase, decrease or remain the same?

9. (i) 30 g of ice at 0°C is used to bring down the temperature of a certain mass of water at 70 °C to 20 °C. Find the mass of water (Specific heat capacity of water = 4.2 Jg^{-1} $°C^{-1}$ and specific latent heat of ice = 336 Jg^{-1}) **[3]**

(ii) (a) A certain amount of heat will warm 1 g of material X by 10 °C and 1 g of material Y by 40°C. Which material has higher specific heat capacity? **[3]**

(b) Which material, X or Y, would you select to make a calorimeter?

(c) The specific heat capacity of a substance remains the same when it changes its state from solid to liquid. State true or false.

(iii) A copper rod PQ carrying-current is kept in a magnetic field as shown in the diagram.

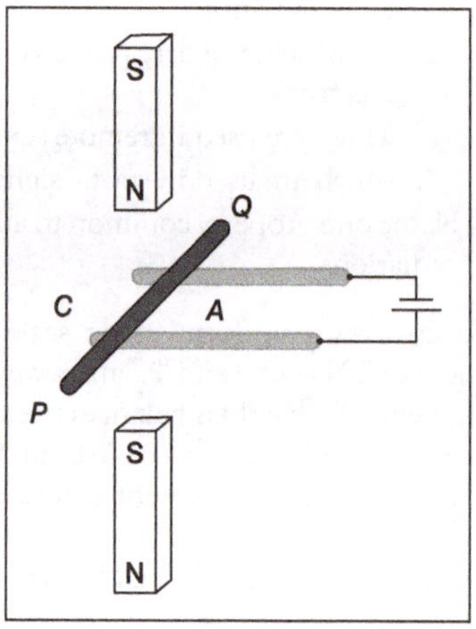

(a) The copper rod PQ will move towards C. State true or false.

(b) Name the law used to determine the direction of motion of PQ.

(c) What will be the effect on the force experienced, if the rod PQ is replaced by another copper rod of same length but of greater cross-sectional area?

(d) Justify your answer in (c).

Solutions

1. (i) (b) When two equal and opposite forces not acting along the same line acts on a body, it forms a couple.
A couple is always needed to produce rotation in a body.
(ii) (d)
(iii) (c) When a candle burns, a chemical reaction occurs where wax reacts with oxygen which converts the chemical potential energy into heat and light.
(iv) (b)
(v) (a)
(vi) (a)
$$\text{Mechanical advantage} = \frac{\text{Load}}{\text{Effort}}$$
$$\text{and slope of a graph} = \frac{\Delta Y}{\Delta X}$$
(vii) (b) Here the image formed is real and diminished which depicts that the object is kept beyond $2F$.
(viii) (d)

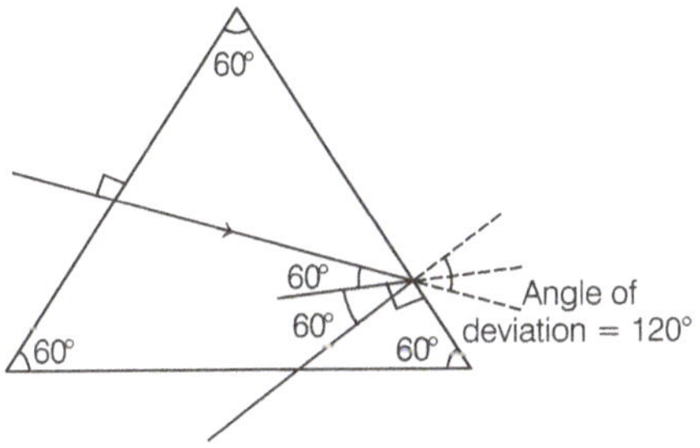

(ix) (b)
(x) (d) Specific heat capacity of the metal piece is
$$\frac{\text{thermal capacity}}{\text{mass}} = \frac{2.5}{5} JK^{-1}g^{-1}.$$
$$= 0.5\, JK^{-1}g^{-1}.$$
When the mass of the metal is tripled, the specific heat capacity remains unchanged as it is independent of the mass of the body.
(xi) (a) Both A and R are true and R is the correct explanation of A because as the water level rises, the air column decreases which increases the frequency of vibration of the air column thereby increasing the pitch of the sound.
(xii) (b)
(xiii) (d)
(xiv) (d) Since, lead has the lowest specific heat capacity, so the rise in temperature in case of lead will be the highest.
(xv) (c)

2. (i) (a) away from the centre
(b) angle of incidence
(c) specific heat capacity
(d) equal to
(e) more than 1
(f) γ
(ii) (a) Q.
(b) For a stable equilibrium of a body, the centre of gravity should be as low as possible and also near the geometric centre of the body and in the above case Q is the most appropriate point for the centre of gravity of the kite.
(iii) (a) The frequency of note produced by a stretched string is related to the tension in the string as $f \propto \sqrt{T}$.
When the length PR is reduced, the wavelength of the wave is reduced thereby increasing the frequency of the wave.
So, the tension must be increased in case if PR has to be reduced.
(b) The pitch of the vibration of sound increases when the length PR is reduced.

3. (i) Yes, the ray will undergo total internal reflection as the critical angle of the glass-water interface is less than the angle of incidence of the ray of light.
(ii) (a) Green or Yellow (Earth).
(b) Brown (Live).
(iii) (a) Alternating current would produce a varying magnetic field when it flows through a conductor.
(b) Frequency of alternating current supply in India is 50 Hz.
(iv) Specific latent heat of fusion of paraffin wax $= 146\, Jg^{-1}$.
$\therefore$ Amount of heat absorbed by 200 g of paraffin wax to meet completely is $= (146 \times 200)\, J = 29200\, J$.
(v) (a)

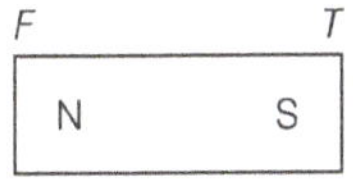

(b)

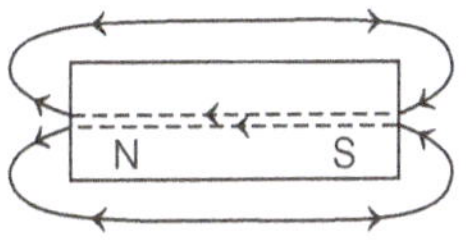

(vi) (a) Since the current flows for a long period of time so the resistance will increase due to the heating effect of current.
(b) Since, resistivity is also dependent on temperature and it increases with the increase in temperature so the resistivity is also affected in the above case.
(vii) (a) Point P
(b) Point R
(c) Mass number of the daughter nucleus is 243.

4. (i) (a) Ray J

(b)

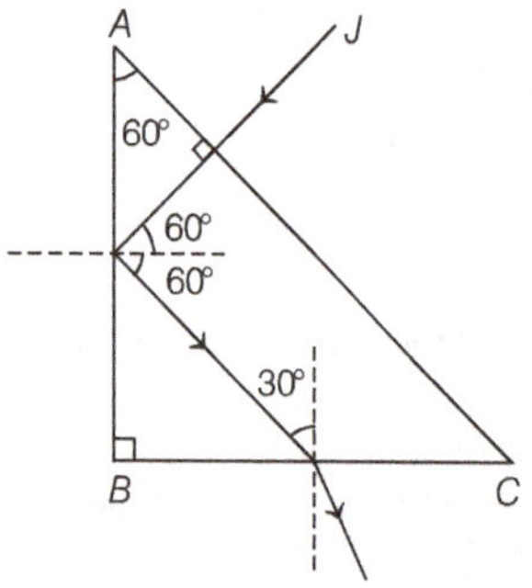

(ii) (a) Refractive index of a medium with respect to air,

$$\mu = \frac{\text{Real depth or actual depth}}{\text{Apparent depth}}$$

$$\therefore \quad 1.5 = \frac{\text{Actual depth}}{4}$$

$\Rightarrow$ Actual depth $= (1.5 \times 4) = 6$ cm

(b) Apparent depth $\propto \frac{1}{\text{RI}}$

$\therefore$ The apparent depth will be greater for yellow light, since its refractive index for yellow light is lower.

(c) When the glass block is turned upside down, the real depth of the air bubble becomes 9 cm.

$\therefore$ Apparent depth $= \frac{9}{1.5} = 6$ cm.

$\therefore$ The statement is false.

(iii) (a)

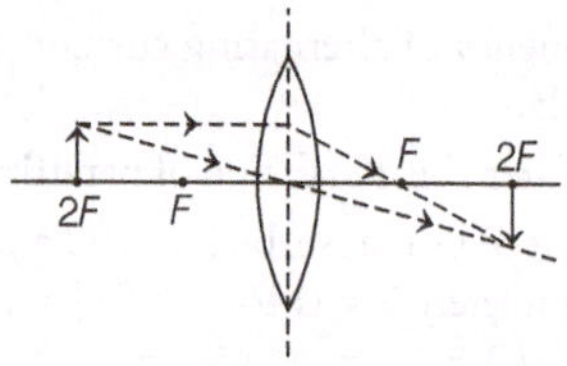

(b) Since the size of the image in the above case is same as that of the object so it will remain same even if the lens is replaced with a lens of a different focal length.

5. (i) From lens formula, we know that

$$\frac{1}{v} - \frac{1}{u} = \frac{1}{f}$$

where v is the image distance, u is the object distance and f is the focal length of the lens.

Here, $v = -30$ cm, $u = -45$ cm.

$$\therefore \quad \frac{1}{f} = \frac{1}{(-30)} - \frac{1}{(-45)} = \frac{-1}{30} + \frac{1}{45} = \frac{-1}{90}$$

$$\therefore \quad f = -90 \text{ cm}$$

$\therefore$ The focal length of the concave lens is 90 cm.

(ii) (a) Ray RS

Since, it bends more inside the glass block.

(b) Ray PQ.

Since, it bends less inside the glass block and hence has a lower refractive index as compared to ray RS.

(c) The light ray having greater refractive index will suffer less deviation as compared to the light having lower refractive index.

Therefore, PQ having lower refractive index will scatter more.

(iii) (a) 1. Ultraviolet radiation

2. Infrared radiation

3. Visible light

(b) All electromagnetic waves travel with the same speed in vacuum that is 3×10^8 m/s.

6. (i)

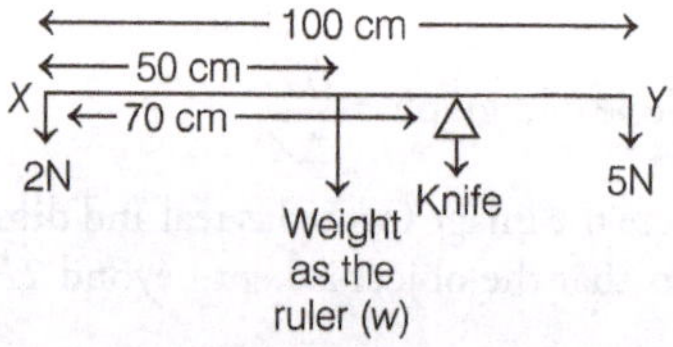

From the principle of moment, we know that sum of anti-clockwise moment = sum of clockwise moment.

$$\therefore \quad (2 \times 70) + w \times 20 = 5 \times 30$$

$$\Rightarrow \quad 140 + 20w = 150$$

$$\Rightarrow \quad w = \frac{150 - 140}{20} = 0.5 \text{ N}$$

$\therefore$ The weight of the ruler is 0.5 N.

(ii) (a) Class I lever.

(b) Mechanical advantage $= \frac{\text{Effort arm}}{\text{Load arm}}$

Since the effort arm is greatest and the load arm is the least for Z, so Z will have the maximum mechanical advantage.

(iii) (a) Weight of Richa = 40 kgf

$= 40 \times 10$ N

$= 400$ N

$\therefore$ Mass of Richa $= \frac{400}{10} = 40$ kg

$\therefore$ Kinetic energy of Richa when she reaches point Q

$= \left(\frac{1}{2} \times 40 \times 10^2\right)$ J.

$= 2000$ J.

(b) From conservation of energy,

we know PE = KE

$$\Rightarrow \quad mgh = \frac{1}{2} mv^2 = 2000 \text{ J}$$

where, h = length of PQ.

$$\therefore \quad h = \frac{2000}{400} = 5 \text{ m}$$

(c) PE of Richa at point $R = (400 \times 3)\,J = 1200\,J$

Loss of energy $= 500\,J$

$\therefore$ KE $+ 500 = 1200$, by law of conservation of energy

$\therefore$ KE $= 700$ J, at point R.

7. (i)

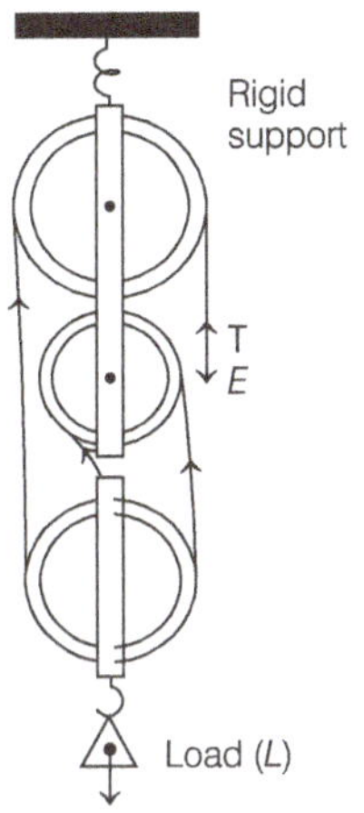

(ii) Let the total distance travelled by the ultrasonic wave from sending to receiving the signal be $2d$ m

Total time taken $= 1$ m 40 s $= 100$ s.

Speed of the ultrasonic wave in water $= 1500\ \text{ms}^{-1}$.

$\therefore \quad 2d = (1500 \times 100)$ m

$\Rightarrow \quad d = 75000$ m $= 75$ km.

$\therefore$ The distance of the obstacle from the submarine – 75 km.

(iii) (a) The wire B undergoes resonance which is responsible for the falling off of the paper rider in B.

Refer to theory on page 139 (Resonance).

(b) f will be less than 300 Hz. because frequency of a stretched string is inversely proportional to the radius of the string. Since, the string in A has a greater radius, so it will have smaller resonant frequency as compared to the resonant frequency of B.

8. (i) (a) 5 ampere.

(b) Switch Z is the main switch which is a double pole switch which helps in breaking the connection with both neutral and live wires simultaneously from the main supply which is not present in switches used for operating household appliances.

(c) Kilowatt hour (KWh).

(ii) (a) Nuclear fission

(b) 236

(c) ${}_{0}^{1}n$ (neutron)

(iii) (a) 1. Power rating of each bulb $= 18$ W.

Since, all the bulbs have the same resistance so let each have a resistance of $R\,\Omega$.

The maximum voltage that the bulbs can draw are 12 V.

$$\therefore R = \frac{V^2}{P} = \frac{12 \times 12}{18} = 8\,\Omega$$

2. The effective resistance in the circuit,

$$R_{EF} = R + \frac{R \times R}{R + R}$$

$$= R + \frac{R}{2} = \frac{3R}{2}$$

$$\therefore R_{EF} = 3 \times \frac{8}{2} = 12\,\Omega$$

$$\therefore \text{Current drawn} = \frac{\text{Supplied voltage}}{R_{EF}}$$

$$= \frac{12}{12} = 1\,\text{A}$$

(b) If the bulb B_3 is removed from the circuit, then R_{EF} becomes $2R = 2 \times 12\,\Omega$

$= 24\,\Omega$

$$\therefore \text{Current drawn} = \frac{12}{24} = 0.5\,\text{A}$$

So, the brightness of bulb B_1 will decrease.

9. (i) Let the mass of the water required be m grams.

Heat released by water = Heat absorbed by ice

$\therefore \quad m \times 4.2 \times (70 - 20) = 30 \times 336$

$$\Rightarrow \quad m = \frac{30 \times 336}{4.2 \times 50}$$

$$= \frac{10080}{210} = 48\,\text{g}$$

$\therefore$ The mass of water required $= 48$ g

(ii) (a) Material X has a higher specific heat capacity.

(b) Material Y

(c) False

(iii) (a) True

(b) Fleming's left hand rule

(c) Remains same

(d) Since $F \propto l$, where l is the length of the rod so it will not be affected due to the increase in cross - sectional area since the length remains same.